EU LAW IN THE DIGITAL AGE

In this book expert lawyers from across the full spectrum of EU law explore the impact of the digital age on the Union's legal framework.

The fifth industrial revolution is impacting on all aspects of society. This open access collection looks at how the European Union and its legal framework is reacting, responding, and evolving to best accommodate the reality of this new environment. Drawn from the insightful and thought-provoking views of acknowledged experts in the field, it examines the questions from all aspects of EU law. This is a thoughtful and timely collection on a question that will continue to dominate EU law in the coming years.

EU Law in the Digital Age

Swedish Studies in European Law

Volume 19

Edited by
Maria Bergström
and
Valsamis Mitsilegas

•HART•
OXFORD • LONDON • NEW YORK • NEW DELHI • SYDNEY

HART PUBLISHING

Bloomsbury Publishing Plc

Kemp House, Chawley Park, Cumnor Hill, Oxford, OX2 9PH, UK

1385 Broadway, New York, NY 10018, USA

Bloomsbury Publishing Ireland Limited, 29 Earlsfort Terrace, Dublin 2, D02 AY28, Ireland

HART PUBLISHING, the Hart/Stag logo, BLOOMSBURY and the Diana logo are trademarks of Bloomsbury Publishing Plc

First published in Great Britain 2025

A catalogue record for this book is available from the British Library.

A catalogue record for this book is available from the Library of Congress.

Library of Congress Control Number: 2024950020

ISBN: HB: 978-1-50998-118-2
ePDF: 978-1-50998-120-5
ePub: 978-1-50998-119-9

Typeset by Compuscript Ltd, Shannon

For product safety related questions contact productsafety@bloomsbury.com

To find out more about our authors and books visit www.hartpublishing.co.uk. Here you will find extracts, author information, details of forthcoming events and the option to sign up for our newsletters.

Foreword: Key Developments in EU Law and the Role of the EU Court of Justice

MACIEJ SZPUNAR*

TECHNOLOGY HAS, TIME and time again, transformed society and, by extension, in order to accommodate new technology, the law. It is the task of lawyers of all times to reflect technical changes in the law. In the industrial revolution, new phenomena like electricity had to be legally assessed. In the digital revolution, law faces new challenges, such as dealing with the infinite space of the Internet or the use of artificial intelligence (AI). The legislature and the judiciary in particular have been adapting the law to the new realities of the Internet for years – still, many questions are open and new questions will arise. Yet, with the legal assessment of AI we are entering *terra incognita*. Questions will arise that we are not even dreaming of today.

The legislator as well as the Court of Justice have to face the fact that – as the Internet did many years ago – AI systems are increasingly becoming part of our everyday lives. Nowadays, people mainly think of AI as a phenomenon of the digital world, for example, when chatbots answer their questions. Or to give a negative example: Many will also link AI with the generation of fake news or even deepfakes – which can have serious political consequences and violate the personal rights of individuals. Yet, AI systems will also find their way into our analogue daily lives – from robots used in healthcare to AI being used for border and security controls. For companies, AI systems can introduce a new era of production – processes can be automated and AI can evaluate vast amounts of data in a fraction of the time it would take humans to do so. Furthermore, AI will be used increasingly in law enforcement and take on the role of 'judge' – as is already the case on platforms where upload filters are the first instance to decide on the legality of user-generated content. It is even possible to use AI in criminal proceedings to generate evidence. All this can be summarised as follows: There are areas in which one computer will replace many humans and areas in which an efficient use of AI can support humans.

* Advocat General of the Court of Justice of the European Union.

The use of AI systems holds many opportunities – but it also has its limits. Not everything can be translated into variables. Not everything can be algorithmised. Algorithms must be free of bias and must not violate fundamental rights. It is therefore of utmost importance to recognise the limits of AI and to create a legal framework in which it can be used for the common good. The Union legislator is aware of this and has therefore drafted an AI regulation (Regulation (EU) 2024/1689)[1] which will provide for a risk classification for AI systems with regard to fundamental rights, privacy and security. In addition to this legislative project, the EU institutions are also examining the extent to which existing law must be adapted to the use of AI systems. Besides the legislator, the legal containment of AI is the task of the courts. They have to interpret the law in such a way that it can be applied to AI systems. Old legal concepts may need to be reconsidered and adapted and opened up to AI technologies.

If AI itself becomes the judge, the algorithmic decisions made must meet the requirements of the rule of law. Decision-making must be predictable as well as transparent and, above all, the fundamental rights of the individuals concerned must not be violated. In this respect, it should be remembered that law can be algorithmised to different degrees. An examination of a violation of fundamental rights, which always includes a case-by-case proportionality test, demands more of an algorithm than checking whether passengers in clearly defined constellations have claims for compensation against airlines due to delays.

AI can only have a place in our lives if the general public has faith in it. And this trust depends on its regulation. The legal containment of AI will therefore be one of the major tasks of our times. This book not only highlights the legal challenges that the Union legislator and the Court of Justice will face with regard to the use of AI technology. It also provides answers to fundamental legal questions in dealing with AI systems and raises new questions. It thus makes a very important contribution to the legal assessment of AI systems, which will become part of our everyday lives just as the Internet did. The legal assessment of situations that take place on the Internet have shown how long it takes to contain legally new phenomena – we must therefore address the legal assessment of AI now, otherwise the law will not be able to keep up with technological progress.

[1] Regulation (EU) 2024/1689 of the European Parliament and the Council of 13 June 2024 laying down harmonised rules on artificial intelligence and amending Regulations (EC) No 300/2008, (EU) No 167/2013, (EU) No 168/2013, (EU) 2018/858, (EU) 2018/1139 and (EU) 2019/2144 and Directives 2014/90/EU, (EU) 2016/797 and (EU) 2020/1828 [2024] OJ L2024/1689.

Contents

PART III
ARTIFICIAL INTELLIGENCE AND CRIMINAL JUSTICE

PART IV
AI AND EVIDENCE

PART V
AI AND MIGRATION, DATABASES AND MOBILITY

1

Introduction

MARIA BERGSTRÖM AND VALSAMIS MITSILEGAS

FOLLOWING THE INDUSTRIAL revolution and the introduction of the Internet, little has changed our lives as much as the ongoing digitalisation of our societies and what could be called the artificial intelligence (AI) revolution. The increased usage of AI technology not only provides opportunities and challenges for society in general, this enormously fast and overarching development gives rise to a wide variety of legal issues that need to be addressed on different levels. Within the European Union (EU), the adaption to digitalisation in general and AI in particular are high on the political agenda, and general as well as more specific legislative instruments are being negotiated and adopted continuously.

This publication aims to critically evaluate the transformation of EU law in the digital age. Contributions from a multi-disciplinary perspective address the challenges digitalisation poses to well-established legal principles, fundamental rights and the rule of law. The book brings together leading experts on a wide range of areas of EU law, from internal market and data protection law, to criminal justice and immigration law. After the Foreword by Advocate General Maciej Szpunar from the Court of Justice of the European Union (CJEU) reflecting on the key developments in EU law and the role of the CJEU, and this introductory chapter, the chapters of the volume are grouped together under five different themes. First, in Part I, three chapters set out what the challenges and initiatives of AI are. In Part II, four chapters deal more specifically with digital data, trust and fundamental rights mainly in the internal market context. Part III brings together five chapters all concerned with AI and criminal justice from a variety of different perspectives, and in Part IV the focus of attention is narrowed down to AI and evidence in three different chapters on this theme. Finally, Part V consists of four chapters analysing the role and challenges of AI in relation to migration, databases and mobility. As a result, this volume provides a multifaceted legal analysis and a variety of different viewpoints on EU law providing an in-depth analysis of the ongoing shift and status of digital justice in the EU.

Although not representing the official viewpoint of these institutions, Part I brings together three chapters on the challenges of AI and initiatives to address those challenges from the viewpoint of public officials both from the European Commission and the Council of Europe, on the one hand, and a more theoretical analysis and mapping exercise of the challenges posed by AI, on the other. In chapter two, Gösta Petri of the European Commission underlines the importance of the safe use of AI in the justice field given the underlying tension between the efficiency of justice on the one hand and impartiality and the respect of fundamental rights with fair and foreseeable outcomes on the other. He thereby reflects on the existing and upcoming regulatory environment to see what boundaries it will set for the justice area, and how to navigate safely within these boundaries to make efficient use of AI. He further assesses how the use of AI technology fits within the overall Commission policy on the digitalisation of justice referring to some specific examples.

In chapter three, Peter Kimpian of the Council of Europe focuses on Council of Europe AI initiatives and in particular on those relating to the right to privacy and data protection. Concerned about unlawful harm and damage to individuals and the negative impact on the human rights system, democratic institutions and processes, as well as the resilience of the rule of law frameworks, the Council of Europe has initiated, from 2015 onwards, several normative activities that are being presented. The most important of these is the initiation of the drafting of a new international convention on the development, design and application of AI, based on the Council of Europe's standards on human rights, democracy and the rule of law, still conducive to innovation. The chapter ends by explaining how the previous initiatives and the Convention on Artificial Intelligence, Human Rights, Democracy and the Rule of Law will interact in the field of privacy and data protection, and how this Convention will relate to a recent initiative modernising the existing rules on the free flow of data globally, including to and from the EU, and that the respect for human dignity in the digital age has legal guarantees.

Finally, in chapter four of this section, Karine Caunes at the Center for AI and Digital Policy (CAIDP) takes on a theoretical mapping exercise setting out and analysing the challenges of AI. According to her analysis, if unregulated, AI as the embodiment of power in the twenty-first century, is a threat to what we consider as legitimate governance in a democratic context. In this respect, she argues that the rule of law can hardly be confused with rule by code or rule of the non-digitalised few, and therefore constitutes an interesting benchmark for assessing the challenges posed by AI. She further argues that the triangular relationship between the rule of law, democracy and human rights highlights that ultimately AI challenges represent challenges to legitimate governance as conceived in democratic societies. She then concludes that only if meaningful political deliberation is preserved is it possible to avoid the transfer of power to the new AI sovereign, which is the digital manifesto of citizenship as self-determination. To preserve it is the *raison d'être* of democratically legitimate governance and the rule of law in the digital age.

In the subsequent Part II on digital data, trust and fundamental rights, four chapters focus on different issues mainly in the broad internal market context. In chapter five, Annegret Engel and Xavier Groussot analyse the EU's Digital Package from a fundamental rights perspective. Regardless of the increasing focus of the EU on fundamental rights protection, and the prominent role of the EU Charter of Fundamental Rights, digital transparency and digital sovereignty, these principles need to be balanced against other fundamental rights. According to the authors' analysis, striking the right balance between different fundamental rights, is still work in progress for the EU.

In chapter six, Béatrice Schütte examines how product liability will be positioned in the future framework on AI regulation. Given that AI and other digital technologies have a significant impact on fundamental concepts, she analyses such concepts in the latest EU initiatives to regulate AI and other new technologies, and provides suggestions on how to make them fit for AI. Her analysis includes the new rules to tackle non-contractual liability for damage caused by AI, and revised Product Liability Directive (PLD). She provides suggestions on making the main concepts of the PLD fit for AI, thereby arguing that understandable concepts and a clear division of labour will contribute to legal certainty in the field.

The problems connected to uncertainties are at the core of chapter seven, in which Johanna Chamberlain and Andreas Kotsios critically analyse the legal concepts of risk and trust in the broader context of defining risk, and promoting trust in AI systems. Despite not necessarily being legal concepts, also requiring delimitation, these concepts have become predominant in the AI discourse and legislative processes concerning AI, in particular the proposed EU general regulation on AI. Their analysis focuses upon the risk discourse in law set against the rapid technical developments on the one hand, and the concept of trust, the connection between risk and trust in an AI setting, and the meaning of trust in relation to new technologies, on the other. The authors thereby argue that the central role of these concepts as emerging legal notions can be rather problematic given the uncertainties involved in this new way of looking at regulatory goals and techniques.

Regulating risk and uncertainty has for many years been predominant in the area of anti-money laundering, and chapter eight by Eleni Kosta takes on an analysis of the proposed legislative package on Anti-Money Laundering and Countering the Financing of Terrorism from July 2021, and in particular the central regulation on the Anti-Money Laundering Authority (AMLA) and Financial Intelligence Unit (FIU) collaboration in Europe. Due to the fact that the work of the central EU authority AMLA, in collaboration with and between the Member State FIUs, will build upon the enhanced sharing of personal data, this chapter aims to identify and analyse the potential clashes between the AMLA regulation and the existing EU data protection framework. The focus of the analysis thereby lies with potential problems in the sharing of data between FIUs, and possible ways to address these problems.

In Part III, on AI and criminal justice, five authors provide detailed analyses of AI and digital justice in the field of criminal law. While the first chapter in this part focuses on a more theoretical perspective of algorithmic justice and its shortcomings, the following four chapters analyse the potential benefits and challenges of AI technology for procedural and fair-trial rights against the requirements of upholding the rule of law within the EU.

In chapter nine, Yulia Razmetaeva analyses algorithmic justice and the new meaning of human rights and privacy under the influence of algorithms. Despite the seemingly more predictable outcome of algorithms and smart machines and their apparent conformity to reasonable and fair standards, the author argues that algorithmic justice in its current form can be called into question, and that algorithms are not compatible with the requirement of justice. In particular, the understanding and application of human rights is changing under the influence of algorithms, making it incredibly important to save the human understanding of law and justice in the digital age.

Likewise, in chapter 10, Emmanouil Billis, in his chapter on AI in criminal justice and whether it strengthens or challenges the rule of law, first states that the design and implementation of effective and transparent policy plans and regulations require both a better understanding of the AI applications from a theoretical and practice perspective, and that AI developers need to be better informed of the ideas behind key legal concepts, and their different meaning in different legal traditions. In this respect, the author argues that the primary focus needs to be on the requirements of the rule of law, including the principles of legality, equality and proportionality, as well as the respect for fundamental rights and procedural guarantees.

In chapter 11, Michele Caianiello provides an account of the CrossJustice Project on legal certainty and the protection of suspects' and defendants' rights in criminal proceedings, and of its outcome. The focus of attention of the project was to verify whether and to what extent the use of AI can allow the effective protection of individual rights of suspects and defendants to be strengthened, in a complex and multilevel system such as the EU.

Not strictly concerned with criminal justice, the focus in chapter 12 by Clementina Salvi, then shifts to another, albeit important aspect of AI technology, and more specifically to the role of digital media generated by AI techniques, in particular deep learning and neural networks, commonly referred to as deepfakes. Developing fast, this type of technology is not only able to create or manipulate digital information and to create digital individuals and scenarios, but it can also create systems in which existing individuals seem to do things they have never actually done. The risks connected with this type of technology are emphasised, rising to new dimensions when deepfakes are used for disinformation in the digital media landscape of social networks, video-sharing platforms and search engines, and political disinformation in the EU. After contextualising deepfakes and explaining the specific challenges connected to such techniques, the author then turns to an analysis of the main challenges related to deepfakes regulation, and finally analyses the EU Digital Services Act and the EU AI Act.

Last in this part of the publication, Rudi Fortson in chapter 13, provides us with an analysis of the United Kingdom's (UK) strategy on AI and its implication for English criminal law, including policing, legal practice and procedure, the presentation of evidence, as well as a tool for carrying out legal research, the triaging of cases and influencing judicial decisions and certain administrative outcomes. While AI poses challenges to ensure that its use is subject to meaningful procedural safeguards, the UK vows to work with international partners whilst ensuring that UK ethical values and principles such as those proposed in the withdrawn UK Bill of Rights are imbedded in international agreements.

Part IV brings together three additional chapters on AI and criminal justice, where the focus is more specifically on AI and evidence. In chapter 14, Katalin Ligeti evaluates how fair trial rights can be upheld in the digital world focusing on AI evidence. While the usage of AI evidence could improve both the accuracy and objectivity of fact-finding, there are related problems when it comes to using such evidence in criminal procedures. Issues arise both in relation to the probative value of such evidence, if it is admissible at all, and in relation to its reliability, the degree to which a result can be expected to occur again under equal circumstances. These uncertainties might indeed, as the author argues, undermine procedural and fair-trial rights and violate the rule of law. She therefore explores whether existing rules on criminal procedure are sufficient to address the specific nature and the associated pitfalls of EU evidence, focusing on evidence law and procedural guarantees. In this respect, she examines whether existing rules elaborated for the analogue world might suffice, or whether new rights specifically tailored for the scrutiny of AI evidence need to be introduced with the aim of providing solutions for supranational and national policy choices.

Continuing this theme, Eftychia Bampasika focuses in chapter 15 on AI-based means of evidence and the defendant's rights in the EU. In this respect, AI-based means of evidence include AI applications that either produce or process existing evidentiary material. As in the previous chapters, the author underlines that AI-based means of evidence might be helpful for criminal justice officials, but could also lead to imbalances in the system, thereby challenging the effective participation of the defendant. This is an essential element in guaranteeing the fairness of criminal proceedings with implications for the rule of law. The author thereby argues that EU legislation must provide procedural rights that safeguard the participatory role of defendants and counterbalance the intrusiveness of AI technology.

In chapter 16, Teresa Quintel and Mark D Cole analyse transborder access to e-Evidence. In particular, they address concerns regarding the role of private companies as the 'extended arm' of law enforcement authorities and discuss the impact of the updated framework on access to e-Evidence with regard to

EU data protection standards. Besides the EU e-Evidence Regulation, they also touch upon the developments within the Council of Europe and the United States, including the Clarifying Lawful Overseas Use of Data Act. Although the e-Evidence Regulation touches upon additional fundamental rights, the main analysis of this chapter lies on data protection concerns, bridging over to the next part.

The final part of the book on AI and migration, databases and mobility brings together four chapters on these themes. The objective of chapter 17 by Elspeth Guild is to understand the data-privacy relationship of the border and the traveller and to apply international legal standards to that intersection. To that end, she examines the privacy rights of travellers from the perspective of the international human rights legal framework. This is a particularly well-chosen area since the crossing of international borders of individuals interacts with the Member States' desire to control the identity and intention of travellers, which may infringe privacy and human rights. On the basis of personal data, admission or rejection takes place, and personal data is included in sophisticated databases including visa information, travel authorisation data, advanced passenger information and passenger name records. Searches based on AI techniques allow for extensive searches of data and by using databases to determine who might be a security risk, the privacy of travellers is at stake, where searches based on nationality, place of birth, age, etc are potentially discriminatory.

Likewise, in chapter 18, Niovi Vavoula argues that AI has the potential to revolutionise the way states manage mobility, decision-making and community integration. She provides an overview of the use of AI in the area mapping inherent fundamental rights challenges concerning non-discrimination, privacy and data protection in the related developments. First, she analyses the regulation of AI systems in migration, asylum and border management following the adoption of the EU act. Thereafter, the focus is on the implementation of AI tools in the operationalisation of interoperable large-scale IT systems, and lastly, the role of EU agencies in developing and promoting the use of AI in this field is analysed. Hence, the evolution of EU immigration policy has been marked by a growing reliance on the digitalisation of border controls. The EU digital border consists primarily of a growing number of EU immigration databases.

In chapter 19, Valsamis Mitsilegas focuses on the impact of the digitalisation of EU border controls on the rule of law, by analysing the evolution, design and consequences of the establishment of the European Travel Information and Authorisation System (ETIAS). ETIAS thereby constitutes a prime example of the new paradigm of a securitised, pre-emptive, algorithmic digital border in EU law, and the chapter concludes with an analysis of the rule of law implications of interoperability, which lies at the heart of the ETIAS design and operation.

Last but not least, Didier Bigo in chapter 20 critically reflects upon digital controls, mobility and surveillance within the social universe of reasonable suspicion and its different guilds. While digitisation has made it possible to check travellers before they land, this possibility has been used to justify a philosophy of preventive security introduced after the declaration of the war on terror and the ideology of counter-terrorism that has followed. The chapter critically examines how mobility and border controls have been affected by this change and the following practice of exchanging data of travellers for security reasons. The author thereby argues that the mixture of these two logics need to be separated and challenged by lawyers and courts alike.

As a result, this publication with its 20 different chapters provides an interesting read with qualified analyses of the status of EU law in the digital age, where stakeholders such as the EU institutions, recent legislative proposals and already adopted directives and regulations, with their respective challenges, make the EU at least partly prepared for the remaining challenges. Upholding a strong perspective on the rule of law and clear human rights protection remains central to a sound development that can be respected and enhanced.

Instrumental in this development, is the central role of the CJEU that plays an imperative role in upholding the rule of law and constantly refining and developing human rights in close collaboration with national courts of the Member States, in particular in preliminary rulings cases. Illustrative are three long-awaited judgments that all concerned digital communication, access to and usage of electronic data, and the balancing of different fundamental rights, thereby focusing not only on the correct balancing between the needs of criminal investigations and the protection of the fundamental rights to private life and to the protection of personal data, but also on the sovereignty of the Member States.

In Case C-670/22 *Staatsanwaltschaft Berlin v MN* (*EncroChat*),[1] and Case C-178/22 *Procura della Repubblica presso il Tribunale di Bolzano* (*Bolzano*),[2] the Grand Chamber ruled on the transmission and use of digital evidence in criminal cases, and on the limits on access to telephone records, respectively. And on the same day, the even more prestigious Full Court delivered its ruling in Case C-470/21 *La Quadrature du Net a.o. c. Premier Ministre and Ministre de la Culture* (*La Quadrature du Net II*),[3] on limits on access to data retained, thereby underlining the incredible importance and relevance of the theme of this volume, EU Law in the Digital Age.

[1] Case C-670/22 *Staatsanwaltschaft Berlin v MN* Judgment of 30 April 2024, EU:C:2023:817 (*EncroChat*).

[2] Case C-178/22 *Procura della Repubblica presso il Tribunale di Bolzano*, Judgment of 30 April 2024, EU:C:2024:371 (*Bolzano*).

[3] Case C-470/21 *La Quadrature du Net a.o. c. Premier Ministre and Ministre de la Culture*, Judgment of 30 April 2024, EU:C:2024:370 (*La Quadrature du Net II*).

Part I

What are the Challenges and Initiatives of Artificial Intelligence?

2

Artificial Intelligence and Justice – From Policy to Practice

GÖSTA PETRI*

I. INTRODUCTION

IN RECENT YEARS, artificial intelligence (AI) has become ubiquitous. Everyone wants to be part of the game, launching AI tools for all kinds of uses, or trying to 'rock' traditional automation technologies into 'AI powered' ones. It is therefore only natural for the European Union's (EU) institutions to want to keep up with the times. Witness the recently published AI Act,[1] which tries to square the circle by regulating 'high risk' AI without stifling innovation or pushing Europe's IT sector even further behind its US and Chinese competitors.

The justice domain is certainly not immune to the AI fever. AI tools for lawyers and judges have appeared, such as, for instance, certain (in)famous 'predictive justice' tools, allowing the user to feed facts into the tool and getting a legal analysis of them as output. There is also the Estonian robot-judge project, announced with some fanfare by *Wired Magazine* in 2019,[2] which turned out to be not so much about R2-D2[3] delivering high-minded justice at the bench,

* Team leader e-Justice in the Unit 'Digital transition and judicial training' at the Directorate-General for Justice and Consumers of the European Commission. The information and views set out in this chapter are those of the author and do not necessarily reflect the official opinion of the European Commission. For most of the content of this chapter, I am indebted to present and former colleagues in the e-Justice team: Nicolas Breczewski, Jolanta Brozyna, Katerina Entcheva, Sara Hjeltnes, Alexander Ivantchev, Yoana Nikolova, Matthias Tomaszewski, Maria Rosaria Coduti and Sabina Valek Derganc. Special thanks also to my former Head of Unit Cristian Nicolau and to Eike Gräf, DG CONNECT, European Commission, and to the former trainees Chiara Andreoli and Tim D Stehle.

[1] Regulation (EU) 2024/1689 of the European Parliament and the Council of 13 June 2024 laying down harmonised rules on artificial intelligence and amending Regulations (EC) No 300/2008, (EU) No 167/2013, (EU) No 168/2013, (EU) 2018/858, (EU) 2018/1139 and (EU) 2019/2144 and Directives 2014/90/EU, (EU) 2016/797 and (EU) 2020/1828 (Artificial Intelligence Act or AI Act) [2024] OJ L2024/1689, 1–144.

[2] E Nitler, 'Can AI Be a Fair Judge in Court? Estonia Thinks So' (Wired, 25 March 2019), available at www.wired.com/story/can-ai-be-fair-judge-court-estonia-thinks-so/.

[3] A Star Wars character.

but rather about automatising certain steps in the order for payment procedure, with no use of AI in the stricter sense of machine learning technology.[4]

There is nevertheless a need to reflect on the safe use of AI in the justice field – increased use of such technologies is after all inevitable. The starting point for any such reflection should be the tension between the efficiency of justice – which is a challenge as demonstrated by the EU Justice Scoreboard[5] – and the need for justice to be rendered impartially, in respect of fundamental rights, with fair and foreseeable outcomes. AI tools, which fit within this paradigm, should in principle be welcome. While black box judges, without human oversight and involvement, could be dangerous, it would be an unfortunate overreach to ban all AI technology in the justice field. It should be possible to harness AI technologies for safe use in justice. The efficiency gains that technology can bring should be exploited, since 'justice delayed is justice denied'.

This chapter looks at the existing and upcoming regulatory environment to see what boundaries it will set for the justice area, and how to navigate safely within these boundaries to make efficient use of AI. It will then assess how the use of AI technology fits within the overall Commission policy on the digitalisation of justice, and present some fact-finding carried out in the Commission's Directorate-General for Justice and Consumers (DG JUST). The chapter concludes by presenting some use cases that DG JUST has studied more closely in the context of a series of webinars.

Fig 1 'A robot judge presiding at a court hearing', illustration by FLUX.1 (open-source AI image generating model developed by Black Forest Labs)

[4] Republic of Estonia Ministry of Justice, 'Estonia Does Not Develop AI Judge' (16 February 2022), available at www.just.ee/en/news/estonia-does-not-develop-ai-judge.

[5] See https://ec.europa.eu/info/sites/default/files/eu_justice_scoreboard_2022.pdf.

II. REGULATORY INITIATIVES

A. Regulation on a European Approach for AI – The AI Act

i. The Objectives of the AI Act

In April 2021, the Commission presented a proposal for a Regulation on a European Approach for Artificial Intelligence.[6] The objective of the Regulation is the protection of fundamental rights and safety where AI is used and enhancing the effective enforcement of EU rules.

The Regulation follows a risk-based approach. The risks that can arise from AI use can be quite different in nature. One possible risk is that new tools make existing practices – such as surveillance – more effective and therefore more invasive. This leads to a need to pay attention to the proportionality of their use. In other situations – for example, where automated systems are used to take or support decisions that affect people – it is important to make sure that this use is lawful and reasonable.

It is no secret that automated decision-making can often be discriminatory. For example, gender or other biases that exist in training datasets reflect the biases in our societies. In other cases, the use of automation might fall short of procedural safeguards such as the individual examination of, for instance, loan applications. Well-known examples include the Dutch child benefit scandal where fraud-detection software used by the State flagged innocent people as fraudsters in a discriminatory way.[7] Another example is consumer credits decision-making in Finland based on algorithmic credit-scoring that did not respect the procedural requirements.[8] These examples show that the use of automation can affect many fundamental rights of individuals – including non-discrimination, privacy and data protection.

Where complex AI systems are used in any process, they can make that process more opaque. This can be a challenge in situations where people's procedural rights need to be safeguarded, or where authorities or companies are obliged to give reasons for their actions. Therefore, the AI Act has identified high risks in areas such as safety components of products, education, employment, essential private and public services such as access to credits or public assistance benefits, law enforcement, migration and asylum, as well as the justice systems. Remote biometrics systems like facial recognition applications have also been classified as high risk.

[6] Proposal for a Regulation of the European Parliament and of the Council of 21.04.2021 laying down harmonised rules on Artificial Intelligence (AI Act), COM(2021) 206 final.

[7] G Geiger, 'How a Discriminatory Algorithm Wrongly Accused Thousands of Families of Fraud' (*Vice*, 1 March 2021), available at www.vice.com/en/article/jgq35d/how-a-discriminatory-algorithm-wrongly-accused-thousands-of-families-of-fraud.

[8] Equinest, 'Algorithmns in Credit Scoring: Discrimination Based on Use of Statistical Data in Finland' (8 July 2021), available at https://ai.equineteurope.org/library/algorithms-credit-scoring-discrimination-based-use-statistical-data-finland.

We already have rules protecting fundamental rights in those areas. But certain 'black box' AI applications pose a challenge to those who must respect or enforce these rights when they are very complex and opaque. So the AI Act will help ensure that high risk AI systems are designed in a fundamental rights compliant way, and that possible breaches of fundamental rights obligations can be investigated and addressed by national authorities and courts.

The AI Act defines four levels of risk for AI systems: unacceptable risk, high risk, limited risk and minimal risk (not regulated). Certain particularly harmful practices which carry unacceptable risk are banned outright (this includes AI systems or applications that manipulate human behaviour to circumvent users' free will – for example, toys using voice assistance encouraging dangerous behaviour in minors – and systems that allow 'social scoring' by governments). High risk systems have to comply with a number of strict requirements before they can be put on the market (see Chapter 2 of the AI Act). There are also transparency obligations for a limited number of systems:

- AI systems intended to interact with natural persons;
- Emotion recognition systems and biometric categorisation systems;
- AI systems that generate or manipulate image, audio or video content: https://this-person-does-not-exist.com/en.

ii. The Definition of AI in the AI Act

The AI Act contains the following definition of an AI system:

> [An] 'AI system' means a machine-based system that is designed to operate with varying levels of autonomy and that may exhibit adaptiveness after deployment, and that, for explicit or implicit objectives, infers, from the input it receives, how to generate outputs such as predictions, content, recommendations, or decisions that can influence physical or virtual environments.

This definition of an AI system aims to be as technology neutral and future-proof as possible, taking into account the fast technological and market developments related to AI.[9]

The Commission proposal's definition was relatively broad, which was met with some criticism. For instance, the European Parliament's Committee on Legal Affairs (JURI) wanted to restrict the definition to machine learning only while the Committees on the Internal Market and Consumer Protection

[9] The report by the European Parliament's joint LIBE/IMCO committee, voted on 11 May 2023, proposed to align the definition of AI with that of the Organisation for Economic Co-operation and Development (OECD): '"Artificial intelligence system" (AI system) means a machine-based system designed to operate with varying levels of autonomy and that can, for explicit or implicit objectives, generate outputs such as predictions, recommendations, or decisions, that influence physical or virtual environments'.

(IMCO) and on Civil Liberties, Justice and Home Affairs (LIBE) wanted to keep it broad. See further section II.A.iii on the Parliament's position.

A number of Member States had criticised the AI definition proposed by the Commission as too broad and applicable to many types of software, even less complex ones.[10] However, the Commission did not exclude systems from the technical scope for not being complicated enough. Rather, the approach is based on the risk that a system could pose if used in certain contexts. A broad definition would seem preferable to ensure that the Regulation remains future-proof and relevant in the face of rapid technological change.[11] In the end, the proponents of a wide definition prevailed.

iii. Regulating High Risk Systems

Chapter 2 of the AI Act sets out the legal requirements for high risk AI systems in relation to, among other things, risk management, data and data governance, logging of activity, documentation and record keeping, transparency and the provision of information to deployers/users, human oversight, robustness, accuracy and security. The minimum requirements in the Act are the result of two years of preparatory work within the Commission's High Level Expert Group (HLEG) on AI, including the Ethics Guidelines issued by HLEG in 2019. The rules are already state-of-the-art for many diligent operators and are also largely consistent with other international recommendations and principles, which ensures that the AI framework is compatible with those adopted by the EU's international trade partners. The exact technical solutions to achieve compliance with those requirements may be provided by standards or by other technical specifications or otherwise be developed in accordance with general engineering or scientific knowledge at the discretion of the provider of the AI system. This flexibility is particularly important, because it allows providers of AI systems to choose the way they wish to meet these requirements, taking into account the state-of-the-art and technological and scientific progress in this field.

It is the deployers of AI systems who need to respect fundamental rights, so they need information from the providers to ensure a suitable use of their applications. This aspect is therefore regulated in the Act, and deployers must have an appropriate understanding of the tools they put into operation. Especially where the deployer is a public authority, which already has accountability and transparency obligations under existing legislation, there is a need to fulfil these

[10] The General Approach adopted by the Council on 6 December 2022 confirmed the narrowing down of the definition to systems developed through machine learning approaches and logic and knowledge-based approaches.

[11] A possibility is, however, foreseen in Article 4 for the Commission to adopt delegated acts to update the list in Annex I to market and technological developments.

legal obligations when AI tools are used. It is important to remember here that compliance with the AI Act does not mean that the use of a given AI system would be automatically lawful. There are sometimes more rules that govern the behaviour of a potential AI user in the public sector than in the private sector. Nevertheless, all other rules that would apply to the use of AI continue to do so, such as data protection rules.

Deployers need to perform a fundamental rights impact assessment prior to deploying a high risk AI system in accordance with Article 27 of the AI Act. This assessment must in particular describe the implementation of human oversight measures in the system. This requirement was added by the European Parliament during the negotiations of the Act.

Furthermore, the Act does not govern all types of practices or behaviours. In most contexts, there are already targeted rules applying specifically to different practices and in different contexts. Rather, the main focus of the AI Act is on AI systems that would present a high risk once put to use.

Article 6, paragraph 2 and Annex III to the AI Act set out the high risk AI systems that are covered by the mandatory requirements. A number of AI systems in the area of law enforcement are considered high risk – for example, predictive policing systems or systems for evaluation of the reliability of evidence.[12] The Council proposed, however, to adjust this provision in its General Approach adopted on 6 December 2022, by adding an additional horizontal layer on top of the high risk classification made in Annex III in order to ensure that AI systems that are not likely to cause serious fundamental rights violations or other significant risks are not captured. New provisions were proposed according to which the significance of the output of the AI system in respect of the relevant action or decision to be taken should also be considered when classifying AI systems as high risk. The significance of the output of an AI system would be assessed based on whether it is purely accessory in respect of the relevant action or decision to be taken.[13] These provisions were accepted in the final agreement on the Act and can be found in Article 6, paragraph 3.

In the European Parliament, a joint report by the IMCO Committee (rapporteur: Brando Benifei, S&D, Italy) and the LIBE Committee (rapporteur: Dragos Tudorache, Renew, Romania) was presented in April 2022[14] and

[12] The General Approach adopted by the Council on 6 December 2022 has deleted crime analytics and deepfake detection, together with some other systems, from the list of high risk systems in Annex III.

[13] European Council, 'Artificial Intelligence Act: Council Calls for Promoting Safe AI that Respects Fundamental Rights' (6 December 2022), available at www.consilium.europa.eu/en/press/press-releases/2022/12/06/artificial-intelligence-act-council-calls-for-promoting-safe-ai-that-respects-fundamental-rights/.

[14] European Parliament, Committee on the Internal Market and Consumer Proteection Committee on Civil Liberties, Justice and Home Affairs, Draft Report 2021/0106(COD), available at www.europarl.europa.eu/doceo/document/CJ40-PR-731563_EN.pdf.

adopted by the committees on 11 May 2023,[15] The report proposes to expand the classification of high risk areas to include harm to people's health, safety, fundamental rights or the environment. The high risk classification also applies to AI systems that aim to influence voters in political campaigns and to recommender systems used by social media platforms. Another important novelty is the adaptation of the Act to recent development of general purpose AI such as foundation models and generative AI like ChatGPT. Foundation models would have to guarantee robust protection of fundamental rights, health and safety and the environment, democracy and rule of law, while generative models have to comply with additional transparency requirements, like disclosing that the content was generated by AI, designing the model to prevent it from generating illegal content and publishing summaries of copyrighted data used for training the model.In the area of 'administration of justice and democratic processes' the following AI systems are considered high risk:

> AI systems intended to be used by or on their behalf to assist a judicial authority in researching and interpreting facts and the law and in applying the law to a concrete set of facts or to be used in a similar way in alternative dispute resolution.[16]

A typical example are predictive justice systems, which at this point in time are more used by law firms than by judicial authorities. These systems are further analysed in section III.B.iii.

AI systems used in justice may not always be high risk. According to Article 6, paragraph 3, systems which do not pose a significant risk of harm to the health, safety or fundamental rights of natural persons, including by not materially influencing the outcome of decision-making, are not considered high risk. The provisions provides four concrete examples:

- the AI system is intended to perform a narrow procedural task;
- the AI system is intended to improve the result of a previously completed human activity;
- the AI system is intended to detect decision-making patterns or deviations from prior decision-making patterns and is not meant to replace or influence the previously completed human assessment, without proper human review; or
- the AI system is intended to perform a preparatory task to an assessment relevant for the purposes of the use cases.

When it comes to the use of AI in justice specifically, recital 61 clarifies that the classification of AI systems as high risk should not extend to AI systems

[15] European Parliament, 'AI Act: A Step Closer to the First Rules on Artificial Intelligence' (11 May 2023), available at www.europarl.europa.eu/news/en/press-room/20230505IPR84904/ai-act-a-step-closer-to-the-first-rules-on-artificial-intelligence.

[16] AI Act (n 1) Annex III, point 8(a).

intended for purely ancillary administrative activities that do not affect the actual administration of justice in individual cases, such as anonymisation or pseudonymisation of judicial decisions, documents or data, communication between personnel, administrative tasks.

There are a number of tasks and processes in courts and other judicial authorities that could fall within these exceptions and thus not be considered high risk. This could be the case for instance for the automation of tasks related to the processing of mass claims, such as filling in templates, or transferring information from documents and evidence to the template. Such systems could also be used for the management of cases, eg allocation of cases to judges. Other examples could include administrative tasks such as managing timetables and schedules for court staff or allocation of court rooms.

iv. Governance of AI Systems

The new rules are envisaged to apply to high risk systems without distinction concerning the public or private entity that would develop or use the system (with some exceptions in the area of law enforcement, notably to protect the secrecy of investigations).

One key objective is to help users with information about the system to assess the legality of the practice they envisage and to adapt or avoid it where necessary. The AI Act also seeks to empower supervisory authorities that are in charge of fundamental rights enforcement. Where an AI system falls within their mandate, they should have access to all documentation about that system and could team up with competent market surveillance authorities to test it. The European Parliament's report reinforces the enforcement architecture by adding a stronger role for the Commission, giving it the task of settling disputes among national authorities on dangerous AI systems. In addition, an EU-level AI Office has been proposed by the Parliament, with the role of providing guidance and coordinating joint investigations. In May 2024, the Commission established the AI Office, which will play a key role in the implementation of the AI Act.

These requirements to test, document and share information about high risk AI systems is one side of the coin. The otherside of the coin is that AI users and public authorities must be able to make use of that information. This will require capacity building in all Member States. For this reason, the Commission worked with the Member States on aspects like investments, coordination of research and fostering skills under the 'Coordinated Plan on AI'.[17] An update of this plan was presented jointly with the AI Act proposal. Furthermore, in

[17] European Commission, 'Coordinated Plan on Artificial Intelligence', available at https://digital-strategy.ec.europa.eu/en/policies/plan-ai.

January 2024, the Commission launched an AI innovation package to support European startups and SMEs in the development of trustworthy AI.[18]

In conclusion, the AI Act will help users, including those from the public sector, to use AI systems in full compliance with fundamental rights.

B. The AI Liability Proposal

In September 2022, the Commission adopted a proposal for a Directive on adapting non-contractual civil liability rules to AI, or the AI Liability Directive.[19] This proposal aims to achieve two main goals:

- to allow courts to order the disclosure of evidence on high risk AI systems to enable a claimant to substantiate a non-contractual fault-based civil law claim for damages, and
- to regulate the burden of proof in the case of non-contractual fault-based civil law claims brought before national courts for damages caused by an AI system.

The obligation to disclose evidence[20] would apply to both providers and users of high risk AI systems. The national courts must be empowered to order the disclosure at the request of claimants or potential claimants. The disclosure rule is combined with a rebuttable presumption that, in case of failure to comply with a court order to disclose or to preserve evidence, the defendant is not in compliance with a relevant duty of care. Such non-compliance with a duty of care is one of the conditions for the rule on a rebuttable presumption of a causal link in case of fault to apply.[21]

The main provision of the proposal for a Directive[22] aims to provide a legal basis for claiming compensation for damages caused by an AI system, where the fault consists of a lack of compliance with a duty of care under Union or national law. It can be challenging for claimants to establish a causal link between such non-compliance giving rise to damage and the output produced by the AI system, or the failure of the AI system to produce an output. The proposal therefore introduces a targeted rebuttable presumption of such a causal link, subject to certain conditions. Such a presumption is considered to be the least burdensome measure to address the need for fair compensation for the victim.

[18] European Commission, 'Commission Launches AI Innovation Package to Support Artificial Intelligence Startups and SMEs' (24 January 2024), available at https://ec.europa.eu/commission/presscorner/detail/en/ip_24_383.

[19] Proposal for a Directive of the European Parliament and the Council on adapting non-contractual civil liability rules to artificial intelligence (AI Liability Directive) COM(2022) 496 final.

[20] ibid Art 3.

[21] ibid Art 4(1)(a).

[22] ibid Art 4.

The AI Liability proposal is presented together with proposed adaptations to the producer's liability for defective products under the Product Liability Directive (PLD).[23] The two initiatives are closely linked, as claims falling within their scope deal with different types of liability. The PLD covers the producer's no-fault liability for defective products, leading to compensation for certain types of damages, mainly suffered by individuals. The AI Liability proposal covers national liability claims mainly based on the *fault* of any person with a view to compensating any type of damage and any type of victim.

There are some similarities between the structure of the burden of proof rules in the two proposals, but there are also differences. While the PLD has rebuttable presumptions on both the defectiveness of the product and the causal link between the defectiveness and the damage, the AI Liability proposal only has a presumption on the causal link,[24] in the latter case between the fault of the defendant and the output produced by the AI system or the failure of the AI system to produce an output. The causal link presumption in the PLD appears simpler to prove, since it is sufficient to establish that the product is defective and the damage caused is of a kind typically consistent with the defect in question. Under the AI Liability proposal, however, three cumulative conditions need to be met:[25]

1. Fault consisting in the non-compliance with a duty of care laid down in Union or national law directly intended to protect against the damage that occurred can be demonstrated or presumed.
2. It can be considered reasonably likely, based on the circumstances of the case, that the fault has influenced the output produced by the AI system or the failure of the AI system to produce an output.
3. The claimant has demonstrated that the output produced by the AI system or the failure of the AI system to produce an output gave rise to the damage.

The AI Liability proposal has special rules on the presumption of a causal link for providers of high-risk AI systems,[26] which are linked with the requirements in the AI Act on the quality criteria for the training of models, transparency, human oversight, level of accuracy, robustness and cybersecurity, or the need for corrective action. The fault consisting of non-compliance with a duty of care shall be considered to have been demonstrated if the claimant instead demonstrates a failure to comply with any of these requirements in the AI Act. For users, there is a similar rule linking the presumption of a causal link to

[23] Proposal for a directive of the European Parliament and of the Council on liability for defective products COM(2022) 495 final. At the time of writing, the revised Product Liability Directive has been agreed by the co-legislators and voted by the European Parliament, but not yet formally adopted by the Council.

[24] Rather naturally since it is fault-based liability.

[25] AI Liability Directive Proposal (n 19) Art 4, para 1.

[26] ibid Art 4, paras 2 and 3.

non-compliance with instructions or irrelevant input data to the AI system. For non-high risk AI systems, it is further specified that the presumption only applies where 'the national court considers it excessively difficult for the claimant to prove the causal link'.

To illustrate the interplay between the PLD and the AI Liability proposal, consider the following example. If an AI operated mobile robot hits a baby stroller and the child is injured, the child's parents can claim compensation under the PLD against the manufacturer of the robot for physical injury to the child by claiming that the robot was defective. If the same robot hits a car owned by an SME that is only used for professional purposes, the damage would not be recoverable on the basis of the PLD, as this only covers damage suffered by natural persons. The AI Liability proposal could come into play instead. Moreover, if the damage is not due to a defect but rather to the operator's fault in supervision, or because it was used under conditions prohibited by the instructions, this kind of claim for damage will be covered by the AI Liability Directive. In addition, the latter Directive proposal covers harm done by AI used not only in products, but also in services or any other activity.

III. AI AND DIGITALISATION OF JUSTICE

The Covid 19 pandemic contributed to bringing digitalisation to the top of the agenda, with face-to-face meetings having to be replaced by online ones, including in the area of justice. The considerable impact of the pandemic on the functioning of national justice systems also adversely affected EU cross-border judicial cooperation, leading in many cases to delays and obstacles to access to justice for individuals and businesses alike. In the midst of the pandemic, the Commission therefore presented a Communication on the digitalisation of justice in the EU,[27] with the aim of setting up a 'toolbox' of measures to foster digitalisation of justice, both at the EU and national levels.

The toolbox includes tools within four main categories: i) financial support to Member States; ii) legislative initiatives; iii) IT tools; and iv) promotion of national coordination and monitoring instruments. The Communication also addresses certain AI aspects, stressing the need to balance the opportunities that the use of AI tools in justice could bring against the risks of bias or discrimination. Concluding on the need for the involvement of a human judge in judicial decision-making, the Communication suggests two actions going forward: firstly, to explore ways to increase the availability of relevant machine-readable data produced by the judiciary for purposes of machine learning, and secondly, to exchange best practices and lessons learned on the

[27] Communication from the Commission of 2.12.2020, 'Digitalisation of Justice in the European Union – A Toolbox of Opportunities' COM(2020) 710 final.

use of innovative technologies in justice between EU Member States, institutions and stakeholders.

A. Commission Study on the Use of Innovative Technologies in the Justice Field

In 2020, the Commission published a study on the use of innovative technologies in the field of justice. This study takes stock of the AI and blockchain technology solutions that are currently being developed, implemented or are already deployed in the justice area. Thanks to the wide support of Member States, legal professional organisations and private companies, the study identified 93 national projects, eight projects of legal professionals and 29 off-the-shelf solutions available on the market.

The study identified eight specific domains of relevance to the justice field where AI and blockchain technologies could bring value:

- **Anonymisation and pseudonymisation** – Using AI technology to automate the manual identification and removal of personal data (and/or other sensitive data). Such solutions are typically used to ensure compliance with the data protection legislation.
- **Data authenticity and traceability** – Using blockchain/Distributed Ledger Technology (DLT)[28] for digital signatures, smart contracts, registers, etc, to perform data validation and enhance traceability and integrity.
- **Digital assistance** – Using AI technology, such as chatbots, to improve citizens' access to information and navigate them through administrative processes.
- **Facial and/or object recognition** – Using AI technology to detect, identify and verify a person or an object from a digital image or video footage based on specific facial or other features. Such solutions, for example, are used in criminal justice to improve victim identification from pictorial material or to detect abnormal behaviour in inmates in prisons.
- **Predictive analytics** – Using AI technology to analyse current and historical facts to make predictions about the future or and/or identify risks and opportunities. In the justice field, such solutions are typically referred to as 'predictive justice' and are used to help law firms in the decision-making process.
- **Process automation** – Using AI technology and robot process automation, to automate processes, such as organisation, planning and facilities management, prioritisation, categorisation and the allocation of documents and

[28] Distributed Ledger Technology – the technology behind blockchains.

tasks. In the justice field, process automation is usually used to improve efficiency by automating manual and repetitive tasks such as analysing case-related information (for example, data collected from house searches), payment of fines by citizens, etc.

- **Search optimisation** – Using AI technology to expedite and facilitate searches in the relevant case law, registers and digital libraries, usually creating semantic links and possibilities for document annotation.
- **Speech-to-text / text-to-speech solutions** – Using AI technology, such as voice recognition and machine translation. In the justice field, such a solution is typically used to facilitate court hearings by replacing the manual typing of court minutes and other documents or for translations from foreign languages.

Of the AI projects covered by the study, 18 per cent focus on using AI technologies for automatic data pseudonymisation and anonymisation, 13 per cent have objectives striving towards automating document management, and 13 per cent towards the optimisation of search engines and data management.

Other projects explore the use of AI for transcription tools (11 per cent), process automation (11 per cent), visual data processing (10 per cent) and the processing of high volume data (eight per cent), chatbots (five per cent), automatic machine translation (five per cent) and predictive justice (six per cent).

Fig. 2 AI projects by category identified in the study on the use of innovative technologies in the justice field

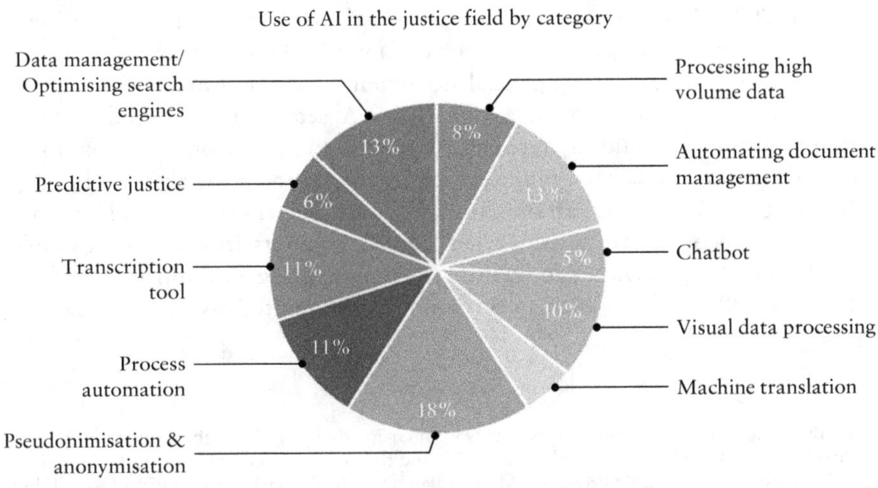

It is indeed pleasing to see that AI-based solutions are not only considered, but are actually already used in the justice field. Nonetheless, the study also identified the need for further collaboration and coordination with regard to the development and deployment of innovative solutions in this area.

B. AI Webinars Organised by the Commission's DG JUST

As a follow-up to the AI actions set out in the Communication of December 2020, and in particular with regard to the objective of coordinating exchanges of best practices, DG JUST has organised a series of webinars with the participation of Member State representatives, legal professionals, academia and suppliers of IT solutions. Five such webinars were held between December 2020 to December 2022 – on anonymisation of court decisions, on speech-to-text and text-to-speech solutions, on predictive justice, on forensic AI in e-evidence and on AI-powered chatbots and access to information. The four first webinars are covered in the following sections.

i. Anonymisation of Court Decisions

It is important to ensure the widest possible online publication of court decisions, for the sake of transparency and public confidence in the justice system. Efficient access to case law is of course also crucial for legal professionals to be able to do their work properly. However, in order not to fall foul of data protection rules, court decisions need to be anonymised (or more precisely pseudonymised) before they can be published online. AI technology is a prime candidate to help in this arduous work, as it can automatically recognise and pseudonymise names and other identifiers of natural persons in the texts of judicial decisions or their metadata.

DG JUST organised a webinar on the anonymisation of court decisions in March 2021.[29] At the webinar, a number of projects on anonymisation / pseudonymisation were presented.[30] For example, in Finland there is a project involving publishing and using legal documents such as Linked Open Data on the Semantic Web for legal applications. A series of tools and systems related to content pseudonymisation, knowledge extraction, data exploration, and data analysis are being created in collaboration with the Ministry of Justice of Finland, the Parliament of Finland, universities, and IT companies. The main objective is to provide legal documents in machine-readable format. Linked Open Data can be used to create intelligent applications, such as the ANOPPI tool,[31] which performs semi-automated pseudonymisation.

[29] I would like to thank the presenters at this webinar for their most valuable contributions and insights: Professor Eero Hyvönen (Aalto University and the Helsinki Centre for Digital Humanities at the University of Helsinki); Professor Monica Palmirani (Bologna University); Professor Edita Gruodytė (Vytautas Magnus University, Kaunas); Louis Béziaud (University of Rennes 1 and University of Quebec at Montreal).

[30] National projects on anonymisation / pseudonymisation were presented by Finland, Germany, Estonia, Romania, Latvia, Poland, Spain, France, Austria and Italy.

[31] Automatic Anonymization and Annotation of Legal Documents, for more information, see https://seco.cs.aalto.fi/projects/anoppi/en/.

The tool identifies and classifies names mentioned in documents and replaces them with pseudonyms. A user can then verify the result and make corrections if necessary. Case law has been available online since 1997 but only for decisions made by higher and special courts. Once pseudonymisation is automated, it will be possible to publish more decisions, even those made by district courts.

Other projects include a solution developed by the Belgium-based company Consono, first tested successfully through a pilot project with the Dutch Police and then used for the purposes of the Court of Appeal of Antwerp. The company's Dynamic Access Architecture is intended to tackle the main challenges courts face, such as having to handle large amounts of information, needing to recognise patterns in that information, and being able to analyse and compare data. Their anonymisation solution focuses on data on who, what, where and when. Another project by TanaCorp has implemented an anonymisation solution for the French Conseil d'Etat. Anonymisation is provided for patronymic names, rare first names, addresses of private persons, names of legal entities where a private person's name appears elsewhere in the document with its real name. Anonymisation is not provided for the members of the judgment panel, the clerk or secretary of the section, the lawyers, the other agents of the parties, and legal entities and their addresses.

ii. Speech-to-Text and Text-to-Speech

Speech-to-text tools could be very important to improve the efficiency of courts. The automatic transcription of hearings and the taking of evidence could alleviate the burden of court staff to a large extent. Of course, commercial tools are available for this on the market. The second webinar was aimed at addressing the use of such tools in the justice area, to identify particular challenges.[32]

The Commission itself has developed a tool for machine translation (eTranslation)[33] but has also been working on speech-to-text applications. While widely spoken languages such as English, French, German and Spanish are well served by commercial tools available on the market, other less used languages are often not covered. The Commission is therefore continuing to develop this service to ultimately ensure coverage for all the official languages of the EU.

[32] I would like to thank the speakers at this webinar: Markus Foti (Head of Sector for Machine Translation, DG Translation, European Commission); Frank Callewaert (Regional Technology Officer, Microsoft); Célia Santos (judge, Portugal); John Lagström (lawyer and IT strategist, Swedish National Courts Administration); Antonio Pernía (Head of Area of DG for Digital Transformation of the Justice Administration, Spain); Silvije Šeremet and Marina Jurić (Croatia).

[33] Public authorities, universities and enterprises can use this Commission service following registration and authentication: https://webgate.ec.europa.eu/etranslation/public/welcome.html.

There is a limited number of customised solutions for the justice field, but this may not necessarily be a problem, since commercial products from large companies like Microsoft could be adapted for use in the judiciary for example. Many existing tools are modular, and dictionaries and data sets developed in one context can be reused in other areas.

The webinar discussed different ongoing projects at Member State level. In Portugal, the GAVTA project[34] is aimed at developing audio and video automatic transcription. Similarly, in Spain, the justice administration has observed major benefits from the adoption of speech-to-text technologies in the justice field and is committed to expanding the use of such technologies further in the next few years. In Croatia, the 'Newton dictate' software[35] is used to transcribe spoken language into text in real time. The tool also provides several other options, such as text-to-speech for reading texts on the web adapted for visually impaired individuals.

A particular challenge in the justice area relates to the quality of transcriptions when multiple, overlapping voices at a hearing need to be identified and transcribed.

iii. Predictive Justice

Predictive justice tools are AI powered tools that can be fed with the facts of a case and can then deliver a prediction of the outcome and the likely court decision. Such tools can provide valuable help to, for example, law firms when advising clients about the likelihood of a law suit succeeding. There are of course risks involved, in particular due to the fact that predictive justice tools will be trained on the basis of the data sets of previous cases, and may therefore reinforce existing biases or reproduce errors in that data. The use of predictive justice tools – classified as high risk in the AI Act as we have seen above – in the judiciary, is probably going to be highly circumscribed in the foreseeable future.

At the webinar on predictive justice, we looked at a couple of examples of projects in the field, and discussed the possibilities and risks involved. One of the projects presented uses of AI in legal analytics aimed at building a platform which makes legal grounds, outcomes and proxy claims easily identifiable for legal professionals through the extraction of relevant data from important legal documents with the help of a semantic model.[36]

[34] For more information, see https://igfej.justica.gov.pt/Instrumentos-de-gestao/Projetos-Cofinanciados/T-GAVTA-Tribunal-Gestao-de-Audio-Video-e-Transcricao-Automatica.

[35] For more information, see www.newtontech.net/en/newton-dictate/.

[36] Presentation by Hans Suijkerbuijk, VP Global Product Development of Wolters Kluwer Legal & Regulatory Division responsible for accelerating and managing digital innovation and product development.

Some predictive justice tools use mathematical modelling of the judicial decision-making process to visualise all possible outcomes of a case based on more than just statistical data. In this way, the user can obtain information not only on potential outcomes, but also on what data is taken into account and how important that data is for the given case. This modelling can be implemented in any area of law for which a sufficiently large body of case law is available, and for which there is substantial uncertainty about the outcome.[37]

In terms of risk, the webinar also looked at how to 'open the black box of AI' and to address bias in AI tools used in the justice area. Eticas Consulting presented their work on algorithmic auditing to promote the ethical use of AI. Two examples of algorithmic auditing in Spain were presented. First, an algorithm used to assign a risk to women who report being victims of domestic violence and which determines the level of police and judicial protection they receive and second, a system used to predict the risk of recidivism among inmates.[38]

One presentation looked at strategies for responsible use of outcomes of predictive AI models. The element of uncertainty must always be taken into account, with two possible strategies that can be deployed. The first strategy consists of searching for evidence that weakens the hypothesis (self-denying prophecy), which would reduce false positives with the risk of a true hypothesis being marked as false. The second strategy consists of searching for evidence that strengthens the hypothesis (self-fulfilling prophecy), which reduces false negatives but increases the risk of a false hypothesis being marked as true. A cost-benefit analysis of the impact of false positives or negatives could be used to determine which strategy to use.[39]

The risks associated with predictive justice should be carefully considered in particular in criminal justice. There are several examples where criminal justice data was used to create, train and operate AI and automated decision-making systems that reflected systemic, institutional and societal biases, resulting in disproportionately negative effects for minority groups. Several such systems use AI in pre-trial detention and prosecution contexts as well as in the contexts of sentencing and probation. The risks involved include discriminatory practices, violation of the right to a fair trial, the presumption of innocence, technological barriers that prevent effective and meaningful scrutiny, transparency and accountability, as well as underlying automation bias.[40]

[37] Presentation by Jacques Lévy Véhel, co-founder of Case Law Analytics.

[38] Presentation by Gemma Galdon Clavell, founder and CEO of Eticas Research & Consulting.

[39] Presentation by Mortaza S Bargh and Mr Sunil Choenni from the Research and Documentation Centre of the Ministry of Justice and Security of the Netherlands.

[40] Presentation by Griff Ferris, Legal and Policy Officer at FairTrials.

iv. Forensic AI in e-Evidence

There are various applications of forensic AI available for use by law enforcement authorities. Among the best known to the general public are those used for the detection of deepfakes. The fourth webinar focused on such tools and the risks and opportunities related to the use of forensic AI for the purpose of analysing electronic evidence.

AI-powered tools could be used to check the coherence of witness statements, perform background checks of witnesses to test whether they may have incentives not to tell the truth and remind judges of the need to consider contextual information, such as light conditions and factors related to assessing whether the witness is under the influence of substances. AI could also be used to analyse human behaviour and body language in courtrooms. AI analysis of expert electronic evidence might be used with the aim of increasing efficiency, yet the results of such e-evidence naturally focus on the past and are therefore not necessarily reliable: past decisions may have been judged wrongly and AI data sets may be biased towards such potential flaws. Moreover, since body language may fail to reveal deception, AI analysis of witnesses may not always be reliable. Therefore, it is more important to check the content of the testimonies than the behaviour of the witness while expressing the testimony. Ultimately, despite potential flaws in AI data sets for expert evidence, tools could be useful to evaluate methods, and to ensure scientific acceptance.[41]

Machine learning can also be used to find relevant documents in very large data sets. With iterative human intervention from lawyers, the accuracy of the data set can be gradually improved. Such methods are mostly accepted by courts in the United States, and there is also a trend towards the use of AI solutions to this end in international arbitration.[42] Searches of large and different files are useful, but there are challenges here as well, with respect to text recognition, for example from scanned files. Spelling errors and abbreviations may cause information to be misrepresented. There are, however, software products used, for example, in the context of investigating economic crime cases in Austria, to address these challenges with pattern recognition, classification and content 'unification' features. This allows the structuring of data, the building of ontologies, and making connections between people, places, and dates. These tools are mostly rule-based recognition systems, but there are also machine learning approaches. Future tools might be used to evaluate the quality of evidence, match information to relevant offences and even generate suggestions. Nevertheless, there is currently a lack of suitable training data.[43]

[41] Presentation by Professor Jordi Nieva-Fenoll from Universitat de Barcelona.

[42] Presentation by Spandana Tammineedi and Raphael Kiess from the German Forensic Technology practice, A&M GmbH Wirtschaftsprüfungsgesellschaft.

[43] Presentation by Professor Mark Engelhart from Goethe-Universität Frankfurt a. M.

A particular type of forensic AI is deepfake detection algorithms. Deepfakes can be relevant in criminal proceedings as the object of the proceeding, for example, in the case of harassment or defamation, or as fake evidence in relation to other crimes, for example, a fake video of an armed robbery. In the United Kingdom, a deepfake audio was used in a custody case to portray the father as violent and as a threat to his children. If not detected, deepfakes can lead to wrong decisions and could be tantamount to a risk of eroding trust in audio-visual evidence.[44] Detection algorithms have therefore an important role to play, yet in many cases constitute opaque black boxes that lead to results that cannot be used as legal evidence. This could be solved by letting a tool that does not provide explanations carry out initial detection and thereafter humans can look for justifications based on human understanding. One example of detection algorithms uses the unique shapes of ears to spot deepfakes or to justify an assertion that a video is fake. Another issue that may be exploited is the fact that the iris in GAN generated images[45] is sometimes not perfectly round, and reflections are sometimes not similar in both eyes. Of course, in the future, deepfake generation tools will probably evolve further and improve on these aspects.[46]

IV. CONCLUSION

The EU has come a long way towards establishing a comprehensive legal framework for the development and use of AI systems, which would also cover AI in justice. With this, respect for fundamental rights should be sufficiently catered for in the development phase of AI systems. The risk-based approach means that the regulatory safeguards focus on high risk use cases, such as predictive justice tools for use by judicial authorities. The transparency requirements regarding the testing and documentation of such systems should help in reducing the inherent risks of bias and discrimination. At the same time, if an AI system which has passed this scrutiny still causes damage, the proposed rules on liability will ensure, on the one hand, that the victim has access to relevant evidence, and on the other, that the burden of proof is alleviated, eventually leading to compensation for the damage caused.

The positive side of the risk-based approach is that a number of non-high risk AI-based tools should be made available for use in the field of justice without additional hurdles.

[44] Presentation by Francesca Palmiotto, PhD researcher at the European University Institute.

[45] Generative adversarial networks (GANs) are algorithmic architectures that use two neural networks, pitting one against the other (thus the 'adversarial') in order to generate new, synthetic instances of data that can pass for real data. They are used widely in image generation, video generation and voice generation.

[46] Presentation by Professor Siwei Lyu, founding co-Director of the multi-disciplinary Center of Information Integrity at the University at Buffalo, State University of New York.

The webinars organised by DG JUST have highlighted practical tools, for example, for the pseudonymisation of court decisions or transcription purposes, which should greatly facilitate routine tasks in the judiciary, freeing resources for more complex legal tasks. At the same time, systems with higher risk, such as predictive justice tools and tools for analysis of e-evidence,[47] will also be available provided that the requirements of the AI Act have been complied with.

[47] Note that the Council's General Approach of 6 December 2022 has removed crime analytics systems from the list of high risk systems in the AI Act.

3

Council of Europe Initiatives on Artificial Intelligence with Special Focus on the Right to Privacy and Data Protection

PETER KIMPIAN*

I. THE COUNCIL OF EUROPE

THE COUNCIL OF Europe, as a leading, international human rights organisation, has demonstrated a keen interest in artificial intelligence (AI) related regulation since a very early stage through an increased policy-making and standard-setting activity. For an international organisation which was created after the Second World War to uphold human rights, democracy and the rule of law initially on the continent, but which sees its standards based on open conventions (on corruption, data protection, cybercrime, money-laundering, etc) being adhered to and implemented by countries outside Europe as well, this came as a natural choice after having realised that AI '(…) will have an impact on our societies that we hardly imagine'.[1]

Concerned about unlawful harm and damage to individuals as well as the negative impact, if not frictions, such technology could cause to the human rights system, to democratic institutions and processes as well as to the resilience of the rule of law frameworks if used unregulated as cases[2] have shown, several normative activities started within the Council of Europe as early as 2015. These concerned mainly the areas of privacy and data protection, justice and public administration, action against crime, healthcare and biomedicine, children's rights, and freedom of expression.[3] In parallel, major transversal documents

* Council of Europe.

[1] Quote from Director, Information Society – Action against Crime, J Kleijssen, 'How to Regulate the Development of Artificial Intelligence?' (Council of Europe and Artificial Intelligence).

[2] Early scandals include the Cambridge Analytica case, Dutch tax authority case, etc.

[3] Full list of past and ongoing activities: Council of Europe's Work in Progress – Artificial Intelligence, available at www.coe.int.

have emerged as a way of setting acceptable international standards with regard to the use of this technology which over time has already become part of our everyday lives: Recommendation 2102(2017) of the Parliamentary Assembly of the Council of Europe on Technological Convergence, Artificial Intelligence and Human Rights;[4] Declaration (13/02/2019)1 of the Committee of Ministers on the Manipulative Capabilities of Algorithmic Processes;[5] Recommendation of the Commissioner for Human Rights, 'Unboxing AI: 10 Steps to Protect Human Rights';[6] Recommendation CM/Rec(2020)1 of the Committee of Ministers to Member States on the Human Rights Impacts of Algorithmic Systems.[7]

In addition to all these initiatives, the most important endeavour was to initiate the drafting of a new international convention on AI. Based on decisions made at the 131st Session of the Committee of Ministers (Hamburg, 21 May 2021), a Committee on Artificial Intelligence (CAI) was created and tasked with establishing, and starting from 1 January 2022,

> an international negotiation process and conduct work to elaborate an appropriate legal framework on the development, design, and application of artificial intelligence, based on the Council of Europe's standards on human rights, democracy and the rule of law, and conducive to innovation (…).

This decision was preceded by an extensive coordination and stakeholder involvement process under the Ad hoc Committee on Artificial Intelligence (CAHAI), which examined the feasibility and potential elements, based on broad multi-stakeholder consultations, of a legal framework for the development, design and application of AI. The ultimate goal was to identify the main components of an AI Treaty based on the Council of Europe's standards on human rights, democracy and the rule of law. The CAHAI fulfilled its mandate in 2021 and has been succeeded by the CAI which delivered the draft Framework Convention on Artificial Intelligence and Human Rights, Democracy and the Rule of Law (Framework Convention on Artificial Intelligence) in May 2024.[8]

II. THE RIGHT TO PRIVACY AND TO THE PROTECTION OF PERSONAL DATA IN AN EARLY AI CONTEXT

When various bodies within the Council of Europe started to reflect on these matters there was a general understanding that AI had a great deal to do with

[4] Recommendation of the Parliamentary Assembly of the Council of Europe about Technological Convergence, Artificial Intelligence and Human Rights.

[5] Declaration of the Committee of Ministers on the Manipulative Capabilities of Algorithmic Processes – Decl(13/02/2019)1.

[6] 'Unboxing AI: 10 Steps to Protect Human Rights' – Recommendation of the Commissioner for Human Rights, May 2019.

[7] Recommendation of the Committee of Ministers to Member States on the Human Rights Impacts of Algorithmic Systems – CM/Rec(2020)1.

[8] Council of Europe Framework Convention on Artificial Intelligence and Human Rights, Democracy and the Rule of Law, Council of European Treaty Series – No 225.

the processing of personal data and/or the private life of individuals. Available studies and research[9] pointed out that behind the phenomenon that the general public called AI, there was a large data set mostly composed of personal data and an algorithm or an algorithmic system that was capable of processing those. These, by today's standards basic processes, were very often combined with the technique of data mining, machine learning, profiling and big data analysis. It also became obvious at a very early stage that even if the whole processing phase does not involve personal data, or rather it does involve personal data but in an anonymised form (to which data protection regulations are not applicable in principle), the result, the end product or service often has an impact on individuals' privacy. It was also obvious at the beginning, although it has not been assessed in any depth if at all, that all these processes imply the massive use of cloud computing technologies or at least some sort of international data transfer, very often through multiple jurisdictions, especially when put in a communication device (through which the daily use of AI started for most of us).

Against this background, which came as no surprise to anyone, the call came in the Recommendation 2102(2017) from the Parliamentary Assembly on the Committee of Ministers to

> finalise without further delay the modernisation of the Convention for the Protection of Individuals with regard to Automatic Processing of Personal Data (ETS No. 108) in order to have new provisions making it possible to put rapidly in place more appropriate protection'.

Being the first, high-level, principle-based international data protection regulation drafted well before the digital age, also with a bearing on the facilitation of international data flows, many thought it could solve some of the major problems that came up early, namely giving control (back) to data subjects over their personal data in order to ensure that human rights and fundamental freedoms can be enjoyed at their fullest while removing all privacy related barriers before an innovation and transborder flow of data. Although several others have raised doubts whether the negotiation of a modernised Convention will ever be finalised and bearing in mind what everyone seemed to agree on already back then, there seems to be a dire need for strong privacy protection to gain and retain trust and confidence in the use of this new technology in the private and public sectors.

[9] A Rouvroy, Most importantly: '"Of Data and Men" Fundamental Rights and Freedoms in a World of Big Data', (Council of Europe, 2016), available at https://rm.coe.int/CoERMPublicCommonSearchServices/DisplayDCTMContent?documentId=09000016806a6020; and A Mantelero, 'Artificial Intelligence and Data Protection: Challenges and Possible Remedies' (Council of Europe, 2019), available at https://rm.coe.int/artificial-intelligence-and-data-protection-challenges-and-possible-re/168091f8a6.

III. CONVENTION 108, THE INTERNATIONAL CONVENTION ON PRIVACY AND DATA PROTECTION

As the European Court of Human Rights has pointed out in several decisions, the right to private life as enshrined in Article 12 of the Universal Declaration of Human Rights, Article 17 of the International Covenant on Civil and Political Rights and in Article 8 of the European Convention of Human Rights, is and will increasingly be 'an enabling right' which, in simple terms, enables the free exercise and full enjoyment of other human rights and fundamental freedoms. It will also remain a core factor in preserving human dignity and individuals' right to informational self-determination.

For this reason, the Convention for the Protection of Individuals with regard to the Automatic Processing of Personal Data ('Convention 108'), as the only legally binding multilateral instrument on the protection of privacy and data protection open for any country in the world and operational since 1981 with the aim of reconciling '(…) the respect for privacy and the free flow of information between peoples', seemed to be an important instrument for the Council of Europe to support and promote and also to be a response to concerns that emerged with the widespread use of new processing technologies.

As a result, Convention 108 managed to welcome 55 parties and 36 observers and its Conventional Committee gathered representatives and experts from all continents. From the inside, it is largely regarded as a principle-based and thus flexible framework for the protection of individuals' privacy and personal data and a viable forum for cooperation to supervisory authorities. The Conventional Committee with its growing membership and active observer institutions and organisations continues to offer a unique forum for discussions and deliberations concerning the rights to privacy and data protection, contributing greatly to the convergence towards a high set of standards globally.

The Convention has recently been modernised through the amending Protocol CETS No 223 ('Convention 108+') which will ensure, upon its entry into force, hopefully in 2024, early 2025, that the free flow of data is facilitated globally, including to and from the European Union (EU) and that the respect for human dignity in the digital age has legal guarantees.

Based on its territorial and material scope, its new concepts (such as accountability, privacy by design, privacy by default, privacy impact assessment, etc) and commonly acceptable provisions also in the field of public security, there is an understanding within State Parties that it can easily be applicable to all data processing involving personal data, even if carried out by new data processing techniques and technologies (such as big data analytics, AI, machine learning, profiling, facial recognition, etc). Convention 108+ is not very detailed at every level – this is on purpose to ensure flexibility and to ensure that it can be transposed easily into different legal systems and jurisdictions. While being flexible, it is believed that its provisions could certainly give enough reassurance to a country and to individuals covered by its jurisdiction to address personal data/privacy related concerns in relation to the use of new data processing techniques and technologies in both the public and private sectors.

Building on the effective and efficient implementation of its provisions underpinned by new powers and functions of its Conventional Committee (Article 4, paragraph 3 and in Article 23, litterae e, f and h) and on the prospect that an increasing number of UN Member States wish to accede to it, Convention 108+ has the promise of becoming a global benchmark in the area. This is also due to the fact that from an EU perspective, Convention 108 has always been seen as a bridge between the EU and other parts of the world.

The EU is leading the way in regard to 'digital regulation' and it has the most detailed and fully harmonised regional binding legal framework for data protection which foresees that the protection afforded to personal data in the bloc flies with it when it leaves the EU. In addition, it has 27 very active privacy regulators, a central coordinating body (EDPB), and a supreme court in Luxembourg which is not shy to point out legal shortcomings and gaps even outside the bloc. This means that data protection and the international transfer of personal data with adequate protection will remain high on the agenda. Therefore, the provisions in the Convention on the transfer of data and cooperation between authorities were among the most appreciated provisions next to the same fundamental principles and fully comparable rules in the EU.

Besides the EU context and more from a global standard-setting perspective, more than 20 recommendations, one additional protocol and one amending protocol have been developed on the basis of the provision of the Convention, the latter already having an impact far beyond the European continent. This implies that in order to deliver on this, many international negotiations have been conducted which have all ended in a consensus in what has often been very difficult areas, such as profiling, the use of algorithms, health-related data, etc. Soft law measures developed by the Committee of Convention 108 and cooperation programmes carried out by the Council of Europe are having a considerable impact on regional and national legislation as well as the jurisprudence of various judicial institutions.

Furthermore, there is an unprecedented potential offered by the Convention in at least two areas that have just recently been explored: the possibility for inter-governmental organisations to accede to it (there already being a strong connection with and active participation from Interpol, Organisation for Economic Co-operation and Development, EU, International Committee of the Red Cross, Organization of American States, etc) and to potentially become a form of cooperation and exchange in public security related data protection matters such as the external oversight of national security agencies (as emphasised by the fifth International Intelligence Oversight Forum[10]).

[10] 'Intelligence Oversight in the Brave New World of Proportionality' – 5th International Intelligence Oversight Forum (IIOF) Data Protection, available at www.coe.int.

There are also examples where Convention 108 has been used in domestic debates to ensure, for example, the independence of the supervisory authority (such as in Tunisia), thus contributing to the democratic development of a country, while its standard-setting work has had a positive impact on public policy, on the legislative and judicial work of a country (such as in relation to the Argentinian national AI strategy).

Furthermore, on the one hand and given the present geo-political situation, there is currently no alternative to Convention 108+ and in the near future it is highly unlikely that a similar convention based on the voluntary acceptance of reciprocal obligations could be drafted, adopted and ratified by 55 parties within the UN or any other international organisation. Convention 108+, on the other hand, enables its State Parties to offer to anyone in their jurisdiction a level of protection of personal data that meets the highest standards that are accepted and recognised both by countries and regional organisations. As discussed above, in order to gain or maintain the confidence of individuals, it is becoming increasingly important to governments and economic actors that an appropriate level of protection is defined and if possible, at a global level. In recent cases, where courts have invalidated transfer agreements and mechanisms because of a lack of protection for individuals, Convention 108+ can effectively help any country that is a State Party to use the Convention as a framework in its endeavour to converge towards high data protection standards globally.

Since one of the main objectives of Convention 108+ is to ensure the free flow of data between its State Parties, it can trigger inclusive growth and greatly contribute to businesses being able to operate and interact more freely without constraints on data export and in general, in the digital and highly integrated global economy. In such an environment, a country can ensure, by acceding to Convention 108+ and through cooperation, that it is part of an ideal legal framework and where there is a business and trade-friendly environment which is at the same time respectful of universally recognised human rights.

As an additional benefit, State Parties to Convention 108+ commit to mutual co-operation in order to ensure the highest level of data protection as well as a high level of compliance with international standards. Belonging to the 'Convention 108+ club' does not only mean demonstrating a high level of data protection, but it also means being able to rely on a strong network of peer states able to provide assistance, advice and support. In an era of increasing digitalisation and identical global challenges, it also means allowing competent authorities to work together. Accession to Convention 108+ also means a recognition of international best practice which opens opportunities for further and enhanced cooperation, including via joint investigations and joint regulatory actions.

Any country joining Convention 108+ participates at the highest possible multilateral level in shaping the future right to data protection while contributing to maintaining the free flow of data globally.

International cooperation often supposes a mutually agreeable regime on transborder data transfers. In areas such as law enforcement, financial surveillance, tax matters, humanitarian actions, security, etc, the authorities of a State Party to Convention 108+ can interact more readily with authorities of another or multiple State Parties, thus increasing the efficiency of their cooperation. International organisations will very likely join Convention 108+ in the future which will also mean that the data transfer regime within the organisation and its Member States will also be aligned with Convention 108+. For instance, the long debated second additional Protocol to the Budapest Convention also recognises the potential of better cooperation between law enforcement authorities, including those responsible for cybercrime and cyber security if both are based in a State Party to Convention 108+.

As the implementation of Convention 108+ is key to its success, the Council of Europe provides expertise to State Parties and candidate countries through technical assistance programmes on the drafting of national legislation, capacity building, empowering institutions, training staff, etc. This could also represent an opportunity to harmonise national practices and to shape internationally recognised 'best practices'. For non-EU countries, it can certainly play an important role in obtaining and/or maintaining adequacy decisions from the EU (which entails the free flow of data to the EU market).

These characteristics and features are the result of a common endeavour by the State Parties and the Secretariat of the Council of Europe which have long perceived it as 'a common response to collective challenges in the digital age' and which were particularly attentive to its very special relationship with the EU data protection instruments, which are recognised as golden standards. These were the main factors that supported the negotiations on the amending Protocol CETS No 223 and most recently when elaborating guidelines in the area of data protection and new processing techniques and technologies.

IV. CONVENTION 108 AND THE EU

As regards data protection today, even at the international level, it is not possible to have a discussion without mentioning the EU and its instruments. And rightly so, as the EU General Data Protection Regulation[11] and the Law Enforcement Directive[12] have created a legal framework where the protection

[11] Regulation (EU) 2016/679 of the European Parliament and of the Council of 27 April 2016 on the protection of natural persons with regard to the processing of personal data and on the free movement of such data, and repealing Directive 95/46/EC (General Data Protection Regulation or GDPR) [2016] OJ L119/1.

[12] Directive (EU) 2016/680 of the European Parliament and of the Council of 27 April 2016 on the protection of natural persons with regard to the processing of personal data by competent authorities for the purposes of the prevention, investigation, detection or prosecution of criminal offences or the execution of criminal penalties, and on the free movement of such data, and

of personal data has been elevated to an unprecedented level to ultimately avoid any harm, negative impact or unlawful interference to individuals' private lives. Statistics indicate that this regulatory package, which has mostly had a direct effect, has resulted in enhancing confidence in the digital economy, goods and services within the European Single Market, which has provided considerable support to the economic growth and further economic and political integration of the bloc. At the same time, it has brought to light some important questions: how can we send personal data across jurisdictions without the risk of lowering the protection of personal data or of unlawful interference by another country's public authorities concerning the privacy of an individual. Another question is how to enforce those rules with respect to tech and internet giants and how to harmonise data protection regimes all around the world as fast as possible.

Some say that Convention 108+ has a great deal of potential to offer viable solutions to all these questions, and for a very good reason: the EU and its Member States have always considered the Convention as a bridge between the bloc and the outside world. While others are of the opinion, something which this chapter will not be able to discuss in detail, that, on the contrary, this bridge has never existed, or even if it has existed, it was never operational. However, the fact of the matter is that Recital 11 of EU Directive 95/46[13] stipulates that 'Whereas the principles of the protection of the rights and freedoms of individuals, notably the right to privacy, which are contained in this Directive, give substance to and amplify those contained in the Council of Europe Convention'. The GDPR does not refer to any direct link with the Convention but states in Recital 105 that 'the Commission should take account of obligations arising from the third country's […] participation in multilateral or regional systems […]. In particular, the third country's accession to Convention 108 should be taken into account'. So, the recognition of the synergy between the principles of Convention 108 and those enshrined in the new EU data protection rules is evident. The potential of Convention 108+ to contribute to the convergence to a set of high data protection standards was repeated and amplified via several communications from the European Commission, such as in the 'Communication from the Commission to the European Parliament and the Council on "Exchanging and Protecting Personal Data in a Globalised World"', Section 3.3.1 (page 11), second paragraph:

> In particular, the Commission encourages accession by third countries to Council of Europe Convention 108 and its additional Protocol. […] It is currently in the process of being revised and the Commission will actively promote the swift adoption of the modernised text with a view to the EU becoming a Party standards.

repealing Council Framework Decision 2008/977/JHA (Law Enforcement Directive or LED) [2016] OJ L119/89.

[13] Directive 95/46/EC of the European Parliament and of the Council of 24 October 1995 on the protection of individuals with regard to the processing of personal data and on the free movement of such data [1995] OJ L281/31.

This was also one of the messages conveyed by Didier Reynders, Commissioner for Justice at the European Commission, in his video message[14] delivered on the occasion of the 41st international data protection day on 28 January 2022 emphasising the Convention's importance in the process of EU adequacy decisions and its role in achieving a higher degree of regulatory convergence and a stronger cooperation of supervisory authorities in the field.

It is also worth noting when considering the role of Convention 108+ and its potential that the former UN Special Rapporteur on the Right to Privacy has called upon all UN member countries to accede to the Convention seeing no alternative to it, first in its Annual Report (Report A/73/45712) presented to the UN General Assembly (2018): 'As an interim minimum response to agreeing to detailed privacy rules harmonised at the global level, ALL UN Member States have been encouraged to ratify data protection Convention108+ […].' And thereafter also in his Annual Report (Report A/HRC/40/63) presented to the UN Human Rights Council (2019).

All these helped to make Convention 108 the convention of the Council of Europe with the second highest number of members, whose organisation and State Parties see the strategic potential of the Convention in the digital age.

V. AI AND DATA PROTECTION AT THE COUNCIL OF EUROPE

As discussed earlier, the Council of Europe's work in the field of AI has long been aiming at preventing unlawful harm and damage caused by algorithmic systems and processes. It was meant to contribute to the creation of a legal space for the use of such systems that promote and support innovation while guaranteeing an effective protection of human rights, democracy, and the rule of law. The Recommendation of the Council of Europe Committee of Ministers on the impact on human rights of algorithm systems (2020/21) to which the Committee of Convention 108 had also contributed, addresses the impact on human rights of AI technologies with guidance on the obligations of states and responsibilities of companies. The Recommendation also provides advice for the private sector in view of determining each actor's role with respect to human rights and fundamental freedoms in the context of algorithmic systems. At the same time, it warns of significant challenges to human rights related to the use of algorithmic systems, mostly concerning the right to a fair trial; privacy and data protection; freedom of thought, conscience, and religion; the freedoms of expression and assembly; the right to equal treatment; and economic and social rights. The Recommendation particularly reiterates the need to comply with applicable data protection rules when using algorithmic systems as provided for by Convention 108+ while emphasising that the impact on human rights of

[14] Conference on Convention 108+ as the global privacy standard, building a free data transfer area while preserving human dignity – Data Protection (Council of Europe, 28 January 2022).

algorithmic systems is broader and call for additional protections. It furthermore calls on states 'to endow their relevant national supervisory, oversight, risk assessment and enforcement institutions with the necessary resources and authority to investigate, oversee and co-ordinate compliance with their relevant legislative and regulatory framework, in line with this recommendation'.

Another important hard law instrument was adopted by the Committee of Ministers of the Council of Europe (on 3 November 2021) in a form of a recommendation on the protection of individuals with regard to the automatic processing of personal data in the context of profiling.[15] The text, prepared by the Committee of Convention 108, updates a previous recommendation on the same topic adopted in 2010 and aims to align its provisions with Convention 108+. It highlights that profiling techniques can impact individuals by placing them in predetermined categories, very often without their knowledge. This lack of transparency can pose significant risks to human rights, particularly for vulnerable persons, including children. The Recommendation therefore calls on states to promote and make the use of a 'privacy by design' approach during the whole duration of the processing legally binding, notably through the use of privacy-enhancing technologies. It provides that processing for the purpose of detecting or predicting racial or ethnic origin, political opinions, trade union membership, religious or other beliefs, health or sexual life should only be allowed where appropriate safeguards are enshrined in law and the data are strictly necessary for the lawful and specific purposes of processing. The instrument emphasises the necessity for the

> respect for fundamental rights and freedoms, notably the rights to human dignity and to privacy but also the freedom of expression and the principle of non-discrimination, but also the imperatives of social justice, cultural diversity and democracy, should be guaranteed during the processing of personal data, in both the public and private sectors.

When it comes to the Committee of Convention 108, guidelines have been developed in relation to the use of new data processing technologies from as early as 2015. In the 'Guidelines on the Protection of Individuals with Regard to the Processing of Personal Data in a World of Big Data',[16] it is acknowledged that the 'nature of Big Data may impact the application of traditional principles of personal data protection, such as purpose limitation or data minimisation'. The Committee nevertheless set the goal and ambition of delivering that guidance to ensure that a similar protection to the one already existing for individuals

[15] Recommendation CM/Rec(2021)8 of the Committee of Ministers to member States on the protection of individuals with regard to automatic processing of personal data in the context of profiling.

[16] See 'Guidelines on the Protection of Individuals with Regard to the Processing of Personal Data in a World of Big Data' T-PD(2017)01 (Council of Europe, 23 January 2017), available at https://rm.coe.int/t-pd-2017-1-bigdataguidelines-en/16806f06d0.

is attainable while their data are processed by these new processing technologies. When it comes to data protection and new technologies, one of the main premises of the Committee of Convention 108 can already be found in this early document: It is '(...)crucial to ensure that personal autonomy and the right to control personal data are guaranteed and can be exercised by individuals in a Big Data context'.

The Guidelines recommend that data is used in an ethical and socially aware way, and if relevant, also with the involvement of the Ethics Committee. Furthermore, data controllers, as a general guidance, are to integrate a precautionary approach and implement preventive policies. Quite uniquely at this stage, a methodology for an impact assessment is provided which aims at examining the likely impact of the intended data processing on the rights and fundamental freedoms of data subjects. It consists of:

a) identifying and evaluating the risks of each processing activity involving big data and its potential negative outcome on individuals' rights and fundamental freedoms, in particular the right to the protection of personal data and the right to non-discrimination, taking into account the social and ethical impacts;
b) developing and providing appropriate measures, such as 'by-design' and 'by-default' solutions, to mitigate these risks; and
c) monitoring the adoption and the effectiveness of the solutions provided. Other novelties in these Guidelines include a warning against the use of big data analytics merely on de-contextualised information or data processing.

The Guidelines underline the need to preserve the autonomy of human intervention in the decision-making process also when big data analytics are used. The risks-based approach is favoured which requires the avoidance of all possible harm, and not only direct harm, caused by the use of this technology. Finally, they foresee for data subjects the right to obtain the reasoning underlying the processing, a right that was also included later on in the amending Protocol CETS No 223.

The next instrument relates to the Council of Europe Recommendation (87)15 regulating the use of personal data in the police sector which provides a general set of principles as of the late 1980s to be applied to ensure the respect for the right to private life and data protection as provided for by Article 8 of the European Convention on Human rights and by Convention 108. While it was found[17] that the principles of the Recommendation continued to provide a sound basis for the elaboration of regulations on this issue at a domestic level,

[17] Recommendation (87)15 has undergone several evaluations (in 1993, 1998 and 2002) which assessed application and relevance. In 2010, the Committee of Convention 108 decided to carry out a survey on the use of personal data by the police across Europe: JA Cannataci, 'Twenty–Five Years Down the Line' (Council of Europe Report, 2013).

the 'Practical Guide on the Use of Personal Data in the Police Sector'[18] was prepared to highlight the most important issues that may arise concerning the use of personal data within the police sector, including the use of new data processing technologies by the police. The Guide recommends that when new data processing technologies are introduced, a data protection impact assessment is carried out as the introduction of new data processing technologies *per se* bears a potential risk to cause unlawful harm or damage. It also recommends that the assessment of risk is not static, but considers specific cases of use, is repeated at reasonable intervals, touches upon relevant phases of the data processing activity and takes accountability considerations into account. On data security and safety of communications it suggests that the highest standard is taken into account when introducing such technologies. Regarding the use of the 'internet of things' within the police, it is required that measures such as data authentication, access control and strong end-to-end encryption are appropriately put in place to ensure data security and resilience to (cyber) attacks. The Guide also refers to the Big Data Guidelines and calls, quite uniquely, on authorities to ensure human intervention and the combination of new analytical methods with traditional ones.

The main instrument with respect to privacy, data protection and AI developed by the Committee of Convention 108 is and remains to date the 'Guidelines on Artificial Intelligence and Data Protection'[19] which were published on 25 January 2019. Those Guidelines, building largely on the outcome of the discussions held and agreements reached within the framework of the 'Big Data Guidelines', lay down – still at a quite early stage – the main building blocks for an appropriate protection of individuals in the digital age while maintaining the idea of the facilitation of international data flows irrespective of national regimes when using AI systems. The Guidelines start by recognising that AI may be a useful tool for decision-making in particular for supporting evidence-based and inclusive policies. They state once more the main position of the Committee that AI development and use shall respect the rights to privacy and data protection in order that AI applications do not undermine the human dignity and the human rights and fundamental freedoms of individuals, in particular with regard to the right to data protection.

As a general guidance, the Guidelines suggest that the protection of human dignity and the safeguarding of human rights and fundamental freedoms, in particular the right to the protection of personal data, is especially important when AI applications are used in decision-making processes. They emphasise that AI development relying on the processing of personal data should be based

[18] 'Practical Guide on the Use of Personal Data in the Police Sector' T-PD(2018)01 (Council of Europe, 16 February 2018).

[19] 'Guidelines on Artificial Intelligence and Data Protection' T-PD(2019)01 (Council of Europe, 25 January 2019), available at https://rm.coe.int/guidelines-on-artificial-intelligence-and-data-protection/168091f9d8.

on the principles of Convention 108+ such as: lawfulness, fairness, purpose specification, proportionality of data processing, privacy-by-design and by default, responsibility and demonstration of compliance (accountability), transparency, data security and risk management. The Guidelines underline that for the processing of personal data through AI, a risk-based approach which aims at avoiding and mitigating the potential risks seems to be preferable (as opposed to the harm-based approaches), where a wider view which considers not only human rights and fundamental freedoms but also the functioning of democracies and social and ethical values of the possible outcomes of data processing should be adopted.

Data subject rights as spelled out in Article 9 of Convention 108+ are crucial: new generation rights (the right not to be subject to a decision significantly affecting the data subject based solely on an automated processing of data without having his or her views taken into consideration, the right to obtain, on request, knowledge of the reasoning underlying data processing where the results of such processing are applied to him or her and the right to object) are fully applicable in an AI context. Some of these rights were, not surprisingly, designed and drafted during the Protocol negotiations, which already had AI-type data processing in mind. But still, you might ask yourself whether these descriptions, including those in the Explanatory Report to the amending Protocol, are detailed enough. Do these Guidelines contain any specific suggestion or recommendation regarding how to make them work in practice? No, as such a detailed description would require describing a specific technology as well as full openness from data controllers on how the algorithm works which was deemed to be counterproductive.

As most of the processing is happening via deep learning and machine learning or similar methods which were simply not meant for full transparency and human control, the choice of the Committee in this area in order not to disrupt innovation was to indicate the goal a data controller is required to achieve: give meaningful control to data subjects over the data processing and their related effects on them and, if relevant, on society as a whole. In this way, the Guidelines remained technologically neutral and offered a solution that can be used for other instruments and for other technology as well. Furthermore, the Guidelines also suggest tools and instruments for developers, manufacturers and service providers to achieve this goal. The first suggestion is to adopt a values-oriented approach in the design of their products and services. It is suggested that they regularly question themselves about the values the end-product is creating. It was considered that the high risks this processing may entail by potentially producing errors (due to the collection of large data sets for the algorithm to learn, the biases in the programming of the algorithm, which is very difficult to completely exclude, the impossibility to control what is happening in the 'black boxes', the constant need for human validation which is more and more challenging and costly as the model develops, etc) would only be acceptable even at a very low level if the purpose of such new processing is to create value and to serve a general public good and the development of society.

The other main feature of the Guidelines is that they recommend an initial and a repeated assessment to identify possible adverse consequences of AI applications on human rights and fundamental freedoms. Considering the outcome of this assessment, a precautionary approach in the design of the products and services is required to be followed which involves that appropriate measures are to be put in place in order to mitigate the risks identified. While creating and setting up the whole processing environment or designing the end-product or service, a human rights by-design approach should be adopted and any potential biases, including unintentional or hidden, should be removed while the risk of discrimination or other adverse impacts on the human rights and fundamental freedoms of data subjects should be mitigated appropriately.

In order to offer a way to comply with data protection principles such as purpose limitation, the Guidelines suggest that unnecessary, redundant or marginal data during the development and training phases should be reduced and that the model's accuracy as it is fed with new data should be constantly monitored. The use of synthetic data may be considered just as well as any risk of adverse effects on individuals and society due to de-contextualised data and de-contextualised algorithmic models. As presented above, the desire to not only assess the direct consequences and the impact of a given data processing activity, carried out through or empowered with new data processing technologies, and to have a wider impact for the data processing also assessed before the start of the processing, has always been at the forefront of reflections within the Committee of Convention 108. These particular guidelines now offer some innovative solutions on how to ensure it is carried out appropriately: they suggest the consultation of external bodies (committees of experts, academic institutions); they recommend the introduction of a new form of assessment: participatory forms of risk assessment which they offer as the norm. Participatory forms of risk assessment, based on the active involvement of the individuals and groups potentially affected by AI applications are essential to give voice to citizens and to assess the consequences of AI applications more accurately. Finally, co-design solutions for developing AI applications, actively involving the groups potentially affected by them could also help in the wider acceptance and use of these new processing technologies.

One more, rather new definition is offered by the Guidelines for AI developers, manufacturers, and service providers which is: algorithm vigilance. It is meant

> to promote the accountability of all relevant stakeholders throughout the entire life cycle of these applications, to ensure compliance with data protection and human rights law and principles. This could lead supervisory authorities and data controllers to adopt forms of algorithm vigilance analogous to pharmacovigilance to react quickly in the event of unexpected and dangerous outcomes.

When it comes to specific guidance for developers, manufacturers, and service providers, one of the most important areas is to provide data subjects information if they interact with an AI application and ensure them the right to obtain information on the reasoning underlying AI data processing operations applied to them. This should include the consequences of such reasoning. Furthermore, it is suggested that feasible alternatives to AI applications is provided should data subjects object to the use of AI on their data. It is also required that forms of algorithm vigilance (specific duties on transparency and the prior assessment of the impact of data processing on human rights and fundamental freedoms) that promote accountability are adopted. Finally, the right to object is recommended to also ensure that processing is based on technologies that influence the opinions and personal development of individuals.

The Guidelines also encourage legislators, regulators and policymakers to follow the principle of accountability closely, to consider the adoption of risk assessment procedures and the application of other suitable measures, such as codes of conduct and certification mechanisms. To ensure transparency and human rights compliance, algorithm vigilance should be applied during public procurement procedures, whereas supervisory authorities must be sufficiently empowered to support and monitor the algorithm vigilance programmes.

Legislators and policymakers are, moreover, advised to embrace the principle of accountability to consider the mandatory adoption of risk assessment procedures and the development of codes of conduct and certification mechanisms. They are called upon to ensure that the possibility of human intervention is preserved in every circumstance. They are also advised to promote the national supervisory authority and support it if it is consulted when AI applications have the potential to significantly impact the human rights and fundamental freedoms of data subjects and that cooperation among regulatory authorities such as consumer protection; competition; anti-discrimination; sector regulators and media regulatory authorities is ensured. As such authorities can have an enormous impact on the implementation of public policies and national laws it is recommended that their independence, as described in Chapter IV of Convention 108, is guaranteed. Furthermore, there is a general call for supporting public debate on AI and to ensure that all stakeholders are included in the shaping of social dynamics, and in the decision-making processes affecting them.

The Guidelines end with an important policy consideration: they stress the need to raise digital literacy, public awareness, ensure the provision of high-quality education and training, and allow and promote scientific research and international cooperation in those fields to achieve the best results.

Following this horizontal document, several other instruments have been elaborated either following a sectoral approach or on a specific topic or technology. It is worth noting that the 'Children's Data Protection in an Education

Setting' Guidelines (2020)[20] were one of the first documents of this kind and also one of the first in this area as well. They also include a chapter on the use of new technologies, in which the Guidelines suggest that the profiling of children should be prohibited by law and this restriction can only be lifted in exceptional circumstances and when it is in the best interests of the child or if there is an overriding public interest, on the condition that appropriate safeguards are provided for by law. The Guidelines do not recognise measuring the performance of schools or teachers as an overriding public interest; therefore, they recommend that children's attainments and achievements should not be routinely profiled.

The 'Guidelines on Facial Recognition' (2021),[21] which are included in the series of more specific guidelines, start by emphasising that facial recognition presupposes a type of processing of biometric data which shall only be allowed with an appropriate legal basis and additional guarantees provided for by law in line with Article 6 of the modernised Convention 108. The Guidelines stress that certain uses of facial recognition technologies should be banned to avoid any risk of discrimination. It is also suggested that the use of facial recognition for the sole purpose of determining a person's skin colour, religious or other beliefs, sex, racial or ethnic origin, age, health or social condition, is banned unless appropriate safeguards are provided by law. This ban should also be applied to affect recognition technologies, which can identify emotions and be used to detect personality traits, inner feelings, mental health or workers' commitment, since they pose important risks in fields such as employment, access to insurance or education. Developers, manufacturers, and service providers are required to ensure the quality of data and algorithms, the reliability of the tools used, data security and should educate users. Entities using facial recognition technologies are subject to compliance with the principles and provisions applicable in terms of data protection (legitimacy of the processing, transparency, fairness, accuracy, accountability, minimisation, limited retention period, data security, impact analysis, etc). Finally, the Guidelines underscore that the rights of individuals as set forth in Article 9 of Convention 108+ must be guaranteed including via requests of rectification in case of false matches.

VI. PRIVACY AND DATA PROTECTION AND THE NEW COUNCIL OF EUROPE FRAMEWORK CONVENTION ON AI

Article 8 of the European Convention on Human Rights guarantees the right to respect for private and family life – to privacy – and to the human dignity

[20] 'Children's Data Protection in an Education Setting' Guidelines (Council of Europe, 2020), available at https://rm.coe.int/prems-001721-gbr-2051-convention-108-txt-a5-web-web-9-/1680a9c562.

[21] 'Guidelines on Facial Recognition' (Council of Europe, 2021), available at https://rm.coe.int/guidelines-facial-recognition-web-a5-2750-3427-6868-1/1680a31751.

that depends on. It is therefore important to highlight that today one of the main priorities of the Council of Europe and its Member States, reinforced by the Reykjavik declaration[22] and during the celebration of the 75th anniversary of the Organisation,[23] is to secure human dignity, personal autonomy, and the right of individuals to remain in control of their personal life in the digital age. To do this an integrated approach across relevant instruments, committees, and institutions would be preferred that would contribute to such objectives through the protection of personal data, the protection of cyberspace and the regulation of the use of AI. This approach appears to be even more needed today as we face unprecedented challenges: war, extremism, democratic back-sliding are occurring in many countries and there is now an unimaginable computing capability, which according to some experts will be able soon to research, innovate, re-create itself and, perhaps, even to make autonomous decisions without human intervention. Privacy in this current context is perceived not only as an individual universal human right and an indicator of democracy as many studies show, but becomes a national security and even military interest that often requires the same multi-stakeholder protection as the ones of the critical infrastructures.

In summary the Council of Europe stands ready for all countries that are committed to adjusting their legal framework and ensuring compliance to join and fully implement, if possible, all relevant existing open conventions, notably on data protection, cybercrime and AI, actively participate in their integrated evaluation and follow-up mechanisms, and to request its readily available and modular cooperation 'packages' on digital matters available to all types of stake-holders. One of the key successes of such approach could be witnessed during the opening for signature of the Framework Convention on Artificial Intelligence where 10 signatures[24] made a strong political commitment to uphold the stand-ards of the Framework Convention and to create a legal basis for cooperation among the state parties related to this new technology.

Finally, it remains to explain how all this interaction will be carried out in the field of privacy and data protection and how the new Framework Convention on AI will relate to Convention 108+. First and foremost, there always was a general understanding that when it comes to the processing of personal data and the right to privacy the applicable Council of Europe convention is and will remain Convention 108 and Convention 108+ (upon its entry into force) which is widely believed to have a growing global potential.[25] This view was also

[22] United around our values – Reykjavík declaration, available at www.coe.int.

[23] 75th anniversary year for the Council of Europe – Portal, available at www.coe.int.

[24] Signatories on 5 September 2024 in Vilnius: Andorra, Georgia, Iceland, Norway, the Republic of Moldova, San Marino, the UK as well as Israel, the USA and the EU.

[25] See G Greenleaf, 'Default Whitelists: Networking Trust to Reduce Personal Data Export Problems' [PPT Presentation] (3 May 2022). Panel: 'Regulation of Global Data Flows: A Story of the Impossible' (Computers Privacy & Data Protection (CPDP) Conference, Brussels May 2022), available at https://ssrn.com/abstract=4119391.

shared by important stakeholders[26] and by negotiating delegations, such as the European Commission.[27]

The CAI's work took account of the provisions of Convention 108+ notably on automated data processing, on transparency, on data security, on accountability for data processing, on privacy – even human rights-centred impact assessments, on the right to request human intervention, on a new generation of data subjects' rights, and the specific inputs from the Committee of Convention 108 throughout the process. As a result, the specific section of the new Framework Convention on AI on privacy and personal data protection (Article 11) is not a detailed one and the new instrument refers to 'applicable domestic and international laws, standards and frameworks'. One would note that the new instrument makes reference to Convention 108+ in its Preamble[28] and in its Explanatory Report[29] to give further guidance for its ratifying parties and beyond.

When it comes to the ratification of Convention 108+ the highly appreciated efforts of 31 countries which already ratified it is truly commendable.[30] It is nevertheless also worthwhile noting that many would have hoped that by now Convention 108+ will be partially in force by 2024 in order to ensure the next phase of the modernisation process. In the current geopolitical context, the fear that without appropriate protection of individuals and a free flow of data between like-minded countries, we could have even higher risks and challenges to our democratic systems, but also the rule of law and human rights regime seems to be more and more real. The main fear is regards to the lowering of standards by the adoption of other governance models that require less safeguards and considerations but result in a concentration of power based on the processing of easily available data, leading to an even more fragmented world which should instead continue to be safely increasingly inter-connected. Instruments that favour a rights-based approach, such as Convention 108+ and the Framework Convention on AI, are also to be used to guard against the technology-driven, all-time easiest and most affordable mass surveillance capabilities that have and can now be implemented for the perceived short-term benefit by autocratic regimes and undemocratic tendencies. The idea of the establishment of a free data transfer area, where individuals benefit from an

[26] See final Recommendation 14, available at https://rm.coe.int/report-of-the-high-level-reflection-group-of-the-council-of-europe-/1680a85cf1.

[27] See European Commission, 'Annex to the Recommendation for a Council Decision authorising the opening of negotiations on behalf of the European Union for a Council of Europe convention on artificial intelligence, human rights, democracy and the rule of law' COM(2022) 414 final, para 9.

[28] Framework Convention on AI (n 8) recital 17: 'Mindful also of the privacy rights of individuals and the protection of personal data, as applicable and conferred, for example, by the 1981 Convention for the Protection of Individuals with regard to Automatic Processing of Personal Data (ETS No. 108) and its protocols'.

[29] ibid para 83.

[30] Full list – Treaty Office, available at www.coe.int.

appropriate protection against any unwanted interference with their private life caused by traditional or new data processing techniques or technologies, can only grow with more signatures and ratifications as the whole mechanism is believed to also gain in effectiveness and usefulness. In such a way more synergies and cohesion could be ensured between like-minded countries.

In this spirit an important preparatory work has already started within the secretariat and ratifying countries based on this integrated approach. This would facilitate in the area of data protection notably the transition from a consultative committee to a conventional committee, facilitation of free flow of data, rise and hopefully levelling up of the level of protection of individuals underpinned by an evaluation and follow up mechanism (in line with Article 4). The latter is set to encompass the evaluation of every party's level of protection they afford to personal data and an assessment on how they live up to their commitment of enabling, even ensuring a free flow of data between parties. Such evaluation can be highly beneficial for facilitating the free flow of data outside of parties too. Such evaluation will surely imply the assessment of how parties are giving effect to the new generation of data subjects' rights (Article 9) also regarding new processing technologies.

The expertise on data protection regarding a new impact assessment methodology and model for AI will be also another area where the new committee under Convention 108+ could play an important role in cooperation with the new committee established under the Framework Convention on AI based on the above described work, experience and interconnections. An integrated methodology for impact assessment encompassing all privacy and AI considerations for parties but also for individual data controllers could be highly beneficial. In this way, the Council of Europe's inventory for modern, human rights-based multilateral instruments that can promote and support an effective rights protection also in evolving circumstances, the functioning of our democratic institutions and processes as well as a strong rule of law framework will become even more complete and fit for an inclusive and sustainable digital development.

4

The Challenges of AI: A Mapping Exercise

KARINE CAUNES*

I. INTRODUCTION: A THEORETICAL MAPPING OF THE CHALLENGES POSED BY AI

THE TRIANGULAR RELATIONSHIP between the rule of law, democracy (collective self-determination) and human rights (individual self-determination) highlights that ultimately concrete challenges posed by artificial intelligence (AI) represent challenges to legitimate governance as conceived in democratic societies.

The rule of law has been the beating heart of democracies during the period of relative peace since the Second World War, and the beating drum of democracies facing authoritarian threats.[1] The rule of law presupposes democracy understood as providing an equal opportunity for individuals in a society to participate in policy-making regarding rules that will impact them.[2] Ultimately, they are entitled to an *equal right to determine* the outcomes of the policy-making process. Mechanisms are also created in order to safeguard this right. Individuals can, for example, contest, directly or through their representatives, the validity of the outcome of the policy-making process when it results in binding rules. Individuals are also entitled to a right to an effective remedy when the non- or misapplication of such rules results in violations of their fundamental rights. In sum, the rule of law enables freedom[3] through rights under the condition of equality of opportunity.[4] This egalitarian underpinning also

* Executive Director, Centre for AI and Digital Humanism (Digihumanism.eu).

[1] See European Law Journal (ELJ) Special issue on the rule of law 'Between Ought and Is: European Integration through the Rule of Law' (2021) 27 *European Law Journal* 1–3. See also (2024) *European Law Journal* 3.

[2] See K Caunes, 'Editorial: #IAmPetra; Prologue: The Paradoxes of the Rule of Law in EU Context – with Special Emphasis on the Polish RRP and EAW Sagas' (2021) 27 *European Law Journal* 1–3.

[3] See F Hayek, *The Road to Serfdom* (Chicago, University of Chicago Press, 1944) 90; J Locke, *Second Treatise of Government* (1690) section 137, 73; BZ Tamanaha, *The Dark Side of the Relationship Between the Rule of Law and Liberalism* (2008) 3 *New York University Journal of Law & Liberty*.

[4] See S Sadurski, *Equality and Legitimacy* (Oxford, Oxford University Press, 2008) and his exploration of three kinds of equality: political, legal and social.

demonstrates that the rule of law necessarily limits freedom.[5] If you consider Martin Krygier's definition of the rule of law as a tempering power,[6] power can be tempered, on the one hand, through an institutional system of checks and balances. While on the other, power can be tempered through the equal granting of rights. Yet, what if it is not tempered? What if freedom is unbridled? The conditions for equality of opportunity disappears, rights and democracy are threatened and ultimately so is freedom, except for a happy few.

This is exactly the core challenge posed by AI to our democratic societies. AI as the embodiment of power in the twenty-first century, if unregulated, threatens what we consider as legitimate governance in a democratic context. This is also exactly the reason why the rule of law constitutes an interesting benchmark for assessing the challenges posed by AI. The rule of law can hardly be confused with rule by code or rule of the non-digitalised few, contrary to the fashionable 'digital constitutionalism' which might on the contrary legitimise them.[7] We will thus be mapping out these very concrete challenges as challenges to legitimate governance that the rule of law is supposed to ensure in order to identify potential remedies (section II). However, the specificity of these challenges is that they are the concrete instantiation of a greater challenge: the sovereignty claim of the non-digitalised few. It is thus of the utmost importance to deconstruct the narratives that support such a claim in order to devise a sustainable and comprehensive response from a rule of law perspective (section III).

II. TACKLING AI CHALLENGES TO LEGITIMATE GOVERNANCE: A MAPPING EXERCISE

The interconnectedness between the rule of law and democracy highlights the different legitimacy mechanisms that it crystallises and which compound legitimate governance: input (political) legitimacy, which focuses on political

[5] See BZ Tamanaha, *On the Rule of Law: History, Politics, Theory* (Cambridge, Cambridge University Press, 2004); BZ Tamanaha, 'Functions of the Rule of Law' in M Loughlin and J Meierhenrich (eds), *The Cambridge Companion to the Rule of Law* (Cambridge, Cambridge University Press, 2018). For an emphasis on the limiting aspect in the digital context, see N Suzor, 'Digital Constitutionalism: Using the Rule of Law to Evaluate the Legitimacy of Governance by Platforms' (2018) *Social Media + Society*; G De Gregorio, 'The Rise of Digital Constitutionalism in the European Union' (2021) 19 *International Journal of Constitutional Law* 2.

[6] M Krygier, 'The Rule of Law: Pasts, Presents, and Two Possible Futures' (2016) 12 *Annual Review of Law and Social Science*, 216.

[7] From a methodological standpoint, we do not intend to 'surf' on the 'digital constitutionalism' wave currently present in scholarship. As much as constitutionalism can be used normatively to assess what power beyond the State is still lacking in terms of upholding fundamental rights, democracy and the rule of law, it also participates in legitimating forms of power beyond the State. A strand of contemporary 'digital constitutionalism' scholarship thus results in validating rather than questioning the transfer of sovereignty to digital private actors. However, when the State is totally removed from the equation, this becomes particularly problematic from a democratic standpoint and constitutionalism does not seem to be the most appropriate tool in order to assess the challenges posed by AI without the risk of complacency.

participation and government responsiveness; output (performance) legitimacy, which encompasses both policy effectiveness and outcomes, thus potentially fostering trust and in turn reinforcing input legitimacy; and throughput (procedural) legitimacy, which is concerned with the quality of governance processes, based on the accountability of the policy-makers and the transparency, openness and inclusiveness of governance processes.[8] Although these legitimacy frameworks are usually operationalised to assess governance in its objective dimension, you can perfectly well imagine that they could serve as a tool to evaluate governance in its subjective dimension as well. Input legitimacy corresponds with political rights such as the right to vote, whereas output legitimacy corresponds with judicial rights[9] such as the right to an effective remedy and throughput legitimacy with legal rights such as the right to transparency or non-discrimination.

As conceptualised, the rule of law in both its subjective and objective dimensions is the source of what could be termed *human determinism*. It embodies the right to self-determination, both in its individual and collective dimensions.

The right to self-determination in a democracy can be digitally threatened by two opposite phenomena: not enough or too much public intervention. The former can lead to horizontal AI challenges (section II.A). They consist of threats to the rule of law by some of its subjects, the source of sovereignty, who are acting in breach of equality before the law. The latter can lead to vertical AI challenges (section II.B). They consist of threats to the rule of law by the custodian of sovereignty (eg, the 'State'), the object of the rule of law, acting in breach of liberty.

A. Horizontal AI Challenges

As famously argued by Frank Pasquale, major digital firms have transmuted from 'market participants' into

> market makers, able to exert regulatory control over the terms on which others can sell goods and services. Moreover, they aspire to displace more government roles over time, replacing the logic of territorial sovereignty with functional sovereignty. In functional arenas from room-letting to transportation to commerce, persons will be increasingly subject to corporate, rather than democratic, control.[10]

[8] See, eg, V Schmidt and M Wood, 'Conceptualizing throughput Legitimacy: Procedural Mechanisms of Accountability, Transparency, Inclusiveness and Openness in EU Governance' (2019) 97 *Public Administration*.

[9] See in this regard, JH Ely, *Democracy and Distrust: A Theory of Judicial Review* (Cambridge, Harvard University Press, 1981); SK Katyal, 'Democracy & Distrust in an Era of Artificial Intelligence' (2022) 151 *Daedalus*.

[10] F Pasquale, 'From Territorial to Functional Sovereignty: The Case of Amazon' (*LPE Project*, 2017), available at https://lpeproject.org/blog/from-territorial-to-functional-sovereignty-the-case-of-amazon/; Suzor (n 5).

Even more so, digital firms have transformed human experience into the main asset traded in the global digital market they are shaping and in which human data are the raw material and predictions of human behaviour are the product.[11] This definitively confirms that digital firms have the potential to disrupt traditional input, output and throughput mechanisms of legitimate democratic governance. In sum, they have acquired the power to disrupt the rule of law, if not replace it outright.

As for input legitimacy, AI poses a double challenge to collective and individual self-determination. On the one hand, it is almost trite to say that individuals do not have a say in the business model of digital firms and the policies they implement despite their control over ever-broader realms of individuals' lives.[12] The right to consent to terms of services is a far cry from democratic participation. On the other hand, digital firms have the power to impact the results of elections and referendums by influencing voters' behaviour, as exemplified by the Cambridge Analytica scandal with regard to Donald Trump's 2016 presidential election in the United States (US) or Brexit in the United Kingdom (UK).[13] This highlights, by way of example, the necessity of having legal rules ensuring accountability of online platforms regarding illegal and harmful content.[14] In the meantime, collective and individual self-determination, which finds a concrete expression in the right to vote, is at risk of being both constricted and manipulated.

Regarding output legitimacy, one of the main challenges of AI reflects the traditional dilemma between democracy and its perversion through *panem et circences*. Does the end justify the means? For example, does access to digital platforms, services and products justify citizens surrendering their privacy and data? First, the question is somewhat biased. It assumes an inevitable trade-off

[11] See S Zuboff, *The Age of Surveillance Capitalism: The Fight for a Human Future at the New Frontier of Power* (London, Profile Books, 2019).

[12] This is part of the digital divide between digital natives and those in the know, which calls into question the very essence of democracy. See S Zuboff in J Naughton, 'The Goal is to Automate Us: Welcome to the Age of Surveillance Capitalism' *The Guardian* (20 January 2019), available at www.theguardian.com/technology/2019/jan/20/shoshana-zuboff-age-of-surveillance-capitalism-google-facebook.

[13] See A Acquisti, L Brandimarte and G Loewenstein, 'Secrets and Likes: The Drive for Privacy and the Difficulty of Achieving it in the Digital Age' (2020) *Journal of Consumer Psychology* 736; M Rosenberg, N Confessore and C Cadwalladr, 'How Trump Consultants Exploited the Facebook Data of Millions' *New York Times* (2018); UK Information Commissioner's Office, 'Investigation into Data Analytics for Political Purposes' (2022) Actions we've taken so far – until February 2022: see, among others Information Commissioner's Office, 'Investigation into the Use of Data Analytics in Political Campaigns, A Report to Parliament' (6 November 2018); Information Commissioner's Office, 'Democracy Disrupted? Personal Information and Political Influence?' (11 July 2018); J Bartlett, J Smith and R Acton, 'The Future of Political Campaigning' (Demos Report, 2018).

[14] See at EU level, Regulation (EU) 2022/2065 of the European Parliament and of the Council of 19 October 2022 on a Single Market For Digital Services (Digital Services Act). See Thierry Breton's comments in European Commission, 'Digital Services Act: Commission Welcomes Political Agreement on Rules Ensuring a Safe and Accountable Online Environment' (Press release, 2022). See also, for China 'Internet Information Service Algorithmic Recommendation Management Provisions' which entered into effect on 1 March 2022.

between access to commodities and commodification whereas it is precisely a regulatory approach that could prevent such a trade-off by rebalancing the current power asymmetry between digital firms and consumers. Second, studies have shown that individuals actually do care about their privacy.[15] The question is rather one of education[16] and access to knowledge as well as the means to secure them.[17] This is, for example, the reason why ensuring the correct functioning of law-making as well as the existence of effective remedies through administrative and judicial review are essential. There is thus a clear link between the collective and individual dimensions of the right to self-determination which reinforce each other.[18] Needless to say, the rights to privacy and data protection[19] also constitute key assets for remedying wrongdoings by digital firms by limiting their hold on what they consider a mere commodity, and even more so, a free commodity waiting to be seized from digital natives.[20]

With regard to throughput legitimacy, one of the main issues concerns the collective impact of 'filter bubbles'[21] and 'echo chambers' which individuals are confined to, more often than not without their knowledge, via their online profiling by digital firms whose business model is based on the harvesting and selling of personal data for advertising purposes.[22] These digital fora play a similar role to, if not replacing entirely, public agora in the eyes of citizens whose

[15] See Acquisti et al (n 13).

[16] It is rather telling that in the UNESCO report, UNESCO, 'Here, There and Everywhere, AI in Education, State of the Education Report for India 2022', (2022), available at https://unesdoc.unesco.org/ark:/48223/pf0000382661.locale=en, 'ethics of artificial intelligence in education' are mainly discussed with regard to the challenges in the current use of AI in education but not concerning ethics of AI as a compulsory part of curricula. The theme is promoting AI in education rather than education as it pertains to AI.

[17] See in this regard, P Nemitz, 'Democracy through Law – The Transatlantic Reflection Group and its Manifesto in Defence of Democracy and the Rule of Law in the Age of "Artificial Intelligence"' (2021) *European Law Journal*.

[18] See European Commission, 'Proposal for a Directive on Adapting Non Contractual Civil Liability Rules to Artificial Intelligence (AI Liability Directive)' COM(2022) 496 final, Brussels.

[19] See in the EU context, Articles 7 and 8 of the Charter of Fundamental Rights as well the (other) rights enshrined in Regulation (EU) 2016/679 of the European Parliament and of the Council of 27 April 2016 on the protection of natural persons with regard to the processing of personal data and on the free movement of such data, and repealing Directive 95/46/EC (General Data Protection Regulation) [2016] OJ L119/1 (hereinafter 'GDPR'), such as the right to rectification or the right to be forgotten.

[20] Although some have argued that the adoption of the 'data' narrative is already playing the Big Tech game. See, eg, Zuboff in Naughton (n 12). See C D'Cunha, '"A State in the Disguise of a Merchant": Tech Leviathans and the Rule of Law' (2021) 27 *European Law Journal* 109.

[21] See E Pariser, *The Filter Bubble: What the Internet Is Hiding from You* (New York, The Penguin Press, 2011). See also the French Data Protection Authority-CNIL, 'How can Humans Keep the Upper Hand? The Ethical Matters Raised by Algorithms and Artificial Intelligence' (Report on the public debate led by the French Data Protection Authority (CNIL) as part of the ethical discussion assignment set by the Digital Republic Bill, December 2017).

[22] Personalisation techniques may take various forms. For a systematisation, see J Ørmen, 'Testing the Myth of Enclaves: A Discussion of Research Designs for Assessing Algorithmic Curation' in S Eldridge and B Franklin (eds), *The Routledge Handbook of Developments in Digital Journalism Studies* (New York, Routledge, 2018) 132.

trust and involvement in traditional politics is fading by the day. Without proper regulation ensuring respect for democratic values, the pursuit of economic profit maximisation might lead to online extremisation and partyism.[23] From a democratic standpoint, some of the key questions these practices raise are:

> What are the social preconditions for a well-functioning system of democratic deliberation or individual liberty itself? Might serendipity be important, even if people do not want it? Might a perfectly controlled communications universe – a personalized feed – be its own kind of dystopia? How might social media, the explosion of communications options, machine learning, and artificial intelligence alter the capacity of citizens to govern themselves?.[24]

Here again the link between collective and individual self-determination plays an important role. As far as individual self-determination is concerned, the black box of AI is a crucial issue even more so when (biased) automated decision-making has a detrimental impact on people's lives. This points to the importance of rights such as the right to transparency and explainability[25] or the right to non-discrimination,[26] adapted to the new, technological reality.[27] Such rights, if properly enforced, could trigger changes in the design of machine learning systems or the circumscription of their use.[28]

[23] See on the importance of considering 'information systems (such as social media recommender systems (…) that may manipulate one's mental traits [as] high-risk systems and must be regulated as such' in the framework of the EU AI Act proposal and in line with the right to mental integrity enshrined in the EU Charter of Fundamental Rights, S Russel, 'Remarks to the Joint LIBE-IMCO meeting of the European Parliament' (2022), available at caidp.org. See also on the risk of extremisation and partyism, CR Sunstein, *#Republic: Divided Democracy in the Age of Social Media*, (Princeton, Princeton University Press, 2017) 10. For another perspective focusing on fragmentation and polarisation of the public sphere, see B Stark, D Stegmann, M Magin and P Jürgens, 'Are Algorithms a Threat to Democracy? The Rise of Intermediaries: A Challenge for Public Discourse, Governing Plaftorms' (2020) *AlgorithmWatch* 15.

[24] Sustein, ibid 5.

[25] See for a discussion on whether transparency also includes a 'right to explanation' in the EU context based on recital 71 of the GDPR (n 19), De Gregorio (n 5) 25. For a positive answer, see Art 29 of the Data Protection Working Party, 'Guidelines on Automated Individual Decision-Making and Profiling for the Purposes of Regulation 2016/679' (2018) and 'Guidelines on Transparency under Regulation 2016/679' (2018). This interpretation seems to be confirmed if the GDPR is interpreted in the light of the 2021 UNESCO Recommendation on the Ethics of Artificial Intelligence, SHS/BIO/REC-AIETHICS/2021, signed by all EU Member States.

[26] See The White House Office of Science and Technology Policy, 'Blueprint for an AI Bill of Rights': 'Algorithmic Discrimination Protections' (2022).

[27] The fact that the right to non-discrimination typically includes qualifiers such as gender, sexual orientation, religion, however, does not always make it adapted to encompass differentiations made by machine learning systems. See, eg, M Hildebrandt, 'Discrimination, Data-Driven AI Systems and Practical Reason' (2021) 7 *European Data Protection Law Review* 358; R Xenidis and L Senden, 'EU Non-Discrimination Law in the Era of Artificial Intelligence: Mapping the Challenges of Algorithmic Discrimination' in U Bernitz et al (eds), *General Principles of EU law and the EU Digital Order* (Zuidpoolsingel, Kluwer Law International, 2020) 151; P Hacker, 'Teaching Fairness to Artificial Intelligence: Existing and Novel Strategies against Algorithmic Discrimination under EU Law' (2018) 55 *CMLR* 1146.

[28] See Case C-817/19 *Ligue des droits humains*, Judgment of the Court (Grand Chamber) of 21 June 2022, as well M Rotenberg, 'CJEU PNR Decision Unplugs the "Black Box"' (2022) 8 *European Data Protection Law Review*.

These horizontal AI challenges are further strengthened by their global scale, in terms of speed, pervasiveness in all fields of everyday life and geographical scope. The territorial extraneity of digital firms, shielded from the consumers they target, often allows them to evade State control or regulation. The extraterritorial scope of the relevant legislation, such as the General Data Protection Regulation (GDPR) or the EU AI Act,[29] is likely to be part of the solution in order to close the impunity gap digital firms take advantage of. International cooperation and regulation are also necessary to match the global reach of digital firms. Collective redress mechanisms might also be part of the solution.

B. Vertical AI Challenges

If digital firms, under a 'surveillance capitalism'[30] paradigm, are in competition with States for societal control over individuals and can thus constitute a threat to both collective and individual self-determination, so can State-Big Tech collaborations[31] or States themselves. These State practices not only put democracy, fundamental rights and the rule of law at risk, but they also call into question the legitimacy of democratic governance in the three dimensions previously identified. It suffices here to take a few examples of the threats to collective and individual self-determination AI systems may pose when used by States.

As for input legitimacy and the perversion of the democratic model, a straightforward example is that of election tampering through the use of AI.[32] Election tampering refers to various practices that can broadly be covered by the umbrella term 'information manipulation'.[33] This can range from voter-targeting through advertising[34] to disinformation through bot(net)s during

[29] Regulation (EU) 2024/1689 of the European Parliament and of the Council of 13 June 2024 laying down harmonised rules on artificial intelligence and amending Regulations (EC) No 300/2008, (EU) No 167/2013, (EU) No 168/2013, (EU) 2018/858, (EU) 2018/1139 and (EU) 2019/2144 and Directives 2014/90/EU, (EU) 2016/797 and (EU) 2020/1828 (Artificial Intelligence Act or AI Act) [2024] OJ L2024/1689.

[30] See Zuboff (n 11).

[31] See the use of Clearview AI by law enforcement authorities in Europe, Canada or the US as mentioned in K Caunes (ed), *2022 AI and Democratic Values Index* (Washington, CAIDP, 2023).

[32] See the Venice Commission, 'Joint Report of the Venice Commission and of the Directorate of Information Society and Action against Crime of the Directorate General of Human Rights and Rule of Law (DGI), on Digital Technologies and Elections' adopted by the Council of Democratic Elections at its 65th meeting and by the Venice Commission at its 119th Plenary Session CDL-AD(2019)016-e (2019).

[33] See J-B Jeangène Vilmer, A Escorcia, M Guillaume and J Herrera, 'Information Manipulation: A Challenge for Our Democracies' (Report by the Policy Planning Staff (CAPS) of the Ministry for Europe and Foreign Affairs and the Institute for Strategic Research (IRSEM) of the Ministry for the Armed Forces, 2018).

[34] See E Schrage, 'Hard Questions: Russian Ads Delivered to Congress' (*Meta Newsroom*, 2017); SSCI Research Summary, 'An Assessment of the Internet Research Agency's US-Directed Activities in 2015–2017 Based on Platform-Provided Data' (Yonder Report, 2016 Disinformation Report, 2018).

electoral campaigns.[35] Disinformation more particularly involves the use of fake automated social media accounts with the aim of amplifying divisive and polarising content. Their nefarious impact could also be accentuated by the combined use of generative AI such as ChatGPT. Information warfare is used by autocracies against democracies which they view as a destabilising threat.[36] The objective is to undermine trust in democracy in return or as a preventive measure. International cooperation among intelligence services, transparency and accountability of providers of online intermediary services and citizens' digital literacy are part of the remedies in this digital equation.[37]

With regard to output legitimacy, AI could facilitate the advent of Bentham's panopticon,[38] as revisited by Foucault.[39] It indeed potentially allows for mass surveillance at such a scale and with such velocity as was previously unimaginable. Such practices do not only take place within authoritarian regimes.[40] They are exported to democratic countries or are used by democratic countries.[41] On the one hand, it is very telling that EU Member States have pushed for the exclusion of national security from the scope of the EU AI Act[42] and a similar exemption has been sought for the Council of Europe Convention on AI.[43]

[35] See, eg, the 2016 US presidential campaign, the 2017 French presidential campaign or the 2017 German federal elections. See Report of the Select Committee on Intelligence United States Senate on Russian Active Measures Campaigns and Interference in the 2016 US Election (2020), Vol I–V, Vol 2 Russia's Use of Social Media with Additional Views, Senate Report 116–290; PN Howard, B Ganesh and D Liotsiou, 'The IRA, Social Media and Political Polarization in the United States, 2012–2018' (Computational Propaganda Research Project, 2019); M Aaltola, 'Democracy's Eleventh Hour. Safeguarding Democratic Elections against Cyber-Enabled Autocratic Meddling (FIIA Briefing Paper 226, 2017).

[36] ibid.

[37] For some suggestions, see Jeangène Vilmer et al (n 33).

[38] J Bentham, *The Panopticon Writings* (Brooklyn, Verso Books, 1995).

[39] M Foucault, *Discipline and Punish: The Birth of the Prison* (New York, The Penguin Press, 2019).

[40] See, eg, about China, R Andersen 'The Panopticon is Already Here' (*The Atlantic*, 2020), available at www.theatlantic.com/magazine/archive/2020/09/china-ai-surveillance/614197/.

[41] See, eg, banfacialrecognition.com interactive map; the reclaimyourface.eu campaign. See also the European Parliament, 'Resolution on Artificial Intelligence in Criminal Law and its Use by the Police and Judicial Authorities in Criminal Matters' (2021); European Data Protection Board, 'Guidelines 05/2022 on the Use of Facial Recognition Technology in the Area of Law Enforcement' (2022).

For various country examples with regard to the use of facial recognition by law enforcement authorities, such as Clearview AI, see Caunes (n 31), eg, Sweden. See recently the UK Information Commissioner's Office, 'ICO Fines Facial Recognition Database Company Clearview AI Inc More than £7.5m and Orders UK Data to be Deleted' (23 May 2022).

[42] EU AI Act, Article 2 (n 29).

[43] Council of Europe Framework Convention on Artificial Intelligence and Human Rights, Democracy and the Rule of Law, Council of Europe Treaty Series – No 225, Vilnius, 5 September 2024. Regarding the lack of consensus on a ban on lethal autonomous weapons through a revision of the UN Convention on Certain Conventional Weapons. See CAIDP, 'UN Fails to Act on "Slaughter Bots"' (CAIDP Update 2.44, 23 December 2021); CAIDP, 'Statement on Russia's Unjustified and Unprovoked Attack on Ukraine' (11 March 2022).

On the other, this also explains the necessity to prohibit the use of AI for mass surveillance and social scoring as called for in the UNESCO recommendation on the ethics of AI, signed by no less than 193 States. The recently adopted EU AI Act contains similar red lines, but marred with significant exceptions.[44] These examples highlight the potential risks for collective and individual self-determination emerging from the use of AI.[45] The transformation of democratic States into totalitarian regimes through digital mass surveillance is nevertheless not the only risk.

With regard to throughput legitimacy and the quality of public decisions, the spread of automated decision-making in public institutions,[46] from school grading systems[47] to childcare allowances[48] or judicial decisions,[49] also gives cause for concern in view of its potential adverse effects on individuals' lives and their trust in democratic institutions.[50] Fully automated decision-making constitutes a fundamental encroachment on the right to self-determination. This explains why it is prohibited as a matter of principle in the EU GDPR.[51] The use of predictive AI is different from human determination in the sense that, apart from 'hallucinations' as well as potential biases of various forms and origins[52] – which raise issues of discrimination and, more broadly speaking, fairness and equity

[44] Note that the Court of Justice of the European Union has so far developed a human-centric case law based on the higher (constitutionally) ranked EU Charter of Fundamental Rights. See for an example regarding Directive (EU) 2016/681 of the European Parliament and of the Council of 27 April 2016 on the use of passenger name record (PNR) data for the prevention, detection, investigation and prosecution of terrorist offences and serious crime [2016] OJ L119/132, *Ligue des droits humains* (n 28), paras 193–213. Perhaps more puzzling is the adoption in the Council of Europe Convention on AI of a risk-based approach and not a human rights-based approach. See for a nuanced analysis, A Mantelero, *Beyond Data. Human Rights, Ethical and Social Impact Assessment in AI* (The Hague, Springer-Asser, 2022) 140 et seq.

[45] See the reference in the UNESCO Recommendation on the ethics of AI to the principles of 'human oversight and determination' in both their collective and individual dimensions.

[46] See for various examples in different countries, Caunes (n 31).

[47] See, eg, D Kolkman, '"F**k the Algorithm"?: What the World Can Learn from the UK's A-Level Grading Fiasco' (*LSE Impact Blog*, 26 August 2020), available at https://blogs.lse.ac.uk/impactofsocialsciences/2020/08/26/fk-the-algorithm-what-the-world-can-learn-from-the-uks-a-level-grading-fiasco/.

[48] M Heikkila, 'Dutch Scandal Serves as a Warning for Europe Over Risks of Using Algorithms' (*Politico*, 2022), available at www.politico.eu/article/dutch-scandal-serves-as-a-warning-for-europe-over-risks-of-using-algorithms/.

[49] See, eg, the Ultima Ratio system in Poland mentioned in Caunes (n 31) 335.

[50] See, eg, S Kumlin, I Stadelmann-Steffen and I Haugsgjerd, 'Trust and the Welfare State' in EM Uslaner (ed), *The Oxford Handbook of Social and Political Trust* (Oxford, Oxford University Press, 2017) 385.

[51] GDPR (n 19) Art 22. See Data Protection Working Party (n 25), Art 29.

[52] For the different possible origins of biases see, eg, N Geslevich Packin and Y Lev-Aretz, 'Learning Algorithms and Discrimination' in U Pagallo and W Barfi (eds), *Research Handbook on the Law of Artificial Intelligence* (Cheltenham, Edward Elgar Publishing, 2018) 88. There may also be biased algorithms due to human choices, see ML Rich, 'Machine Learning, Automated Suspicion Algorithms, and the Fourth Amendment' (2016) 164 *University of Pennsylvania Law Review* 883.

that are particularly puzzling in a democratic context[53] – its 'logic' is not only based on correlation (as opposed to causation) but also on the reproduction of past patterns. However, to only take the example of judicial decisions, the rule of law does not require that judicial decisions follow earlier judgments; it simply requires judicial decisions to be justified on the basis of the law currently in force. Aspects of morality, and its evolution through time, fairness or specific or potential circumstances might lead a judge to depart from existing case law. This also illustrates the difference between code and language: the open texture of the latter[54] renders the future unpredictable yet allows for 'automatic' human adaptability.[55] This is also the difference between computation and thinking: understanding, ie the question of 'why'[56] that guides the 'how'[57] and the meaningful selection of relevant factors.

Whether through societal control or decision automation, the untempered digitisation of the State through the un(der-)regulated use of AI might be a source of fundamental rights violations, distrust in democracy and destruction of the rule of law. This calls for a Charter of digital rights, bringing together both rights specific to the digital context as well as classical rights adapted to it, such as those mentioned above.[58] The primacy of fundamental rights protection also entails the full or partial prohibition of, as well as limitations to, the use of AI under conditions of proportionality. The promotion of human-centric AI by design and the introduction of human rights impact assessments as enshrined in the UNESCO Recommendation on the Ethics of AI or the EU AI Act[59] could also constitute assets in fostering accountability, on top of responsibility translated into redress mechanisms.[60] In this regard, independent monitoring would

[53] See, eg, The White House Office of Science and Technology Policy (n 26); see also Hildebrandt (n 27); F Zuiderveen Borgesius, 'Discrimination, Artificial Intelligence and Algorithmic Decision-Making' (Strasbourg, Council of Europe, Directorate General of Democracy, 2018).

[54] See in this regard, Nemitz (n 17); see also BS Jackson, *Semiotics and Legal Theory* (London, Routledge and Paul Kegan, 1985); N McCormick, *Rhetoric and The Rule of Law: A Theory of Legal Reasoning* (Oxford, Oxford University Press, 2005).

[55] On the conception of human identity as the product of inherent characteristics and the environment, see P Ricoeur, *From Text to Action: Essays in Hermeneutics, II* (Evanston, Northwestern University Press, 2007). This defers from AI which needs regular upgrades. See Nemitz (n 17).

[56] See J Pearl and D Mackenzie, *The Book of Why, The New Science of Cause and Effect* (New York, The Penguin Press, 2018).

[57] See Y Katz, 'N. Chomsky on Where Artificial Intelligence Went Wrong' (*The Atlantic*, 2012), available at www.theatlantic.com/technology/archive/2012/11/noam-chomsky-on-where-artificial-intelligence-went-wrong/261637/.

[58] For some attempts, see for Portugal, Law No 27/2021, of 17 May 2021, approving the Portuguese Charter of Human Rights in the Digital Era; for Spain, Charter of Digital Rights, 14 July 2021; The White House Office of Science and Technology Policy (n 26).

[59] See Articles 9, 27 and 56 of the EU AI Act (n 29). See also Article 16 of the Council of Europe Convention on AI (n 43).

[60] See also in the literature, eg, D Reisman, J Schultz, K Crawford and M Whittaker, 'Algorithmic Impact Assessments: A Practical Framework for Public Agency Accountability' (*AINow*, 2018). More recently, see Mantelero (n 44).

play a key role.[61] In the meantime, international convergence around shared democratic values[62] translated into key AI principles such as those crafted in the Council of Europe Convention on AI or the Universal Guidelines for AI[63] would allow States to pledge and renew their commitment to protecting these values with the aim of maximising 'the benefits of AI, to minimize the risk, and to ensure the protection of human rights'.[64]

A rule of law perspective on the concrete challenges posed by AI for collective and individual self-determination permits a more effective delineation of them. Ultimately, they all relate to the way AI systems are designed[65] and used. However, a deeper understanding of these challenges necessitates putting them into context as well as analysing and assessing the narratives that actually aim to legitimise them to the detriment of the rule of law. Only then will a sustainable human-centric AI uphold its promises.

III. TACKLING THE ULTIMATE AI CHALLENGE TO LEGITIMATE GOVERNANCE: ON THE IMPORTANCE OF NARRATIVES

Regulation is the 'mouth' of the rule of law. If you believe that the *raison d'être* of regulation is to ensure the pacification of societal relationships, the ordering of human conduct, the quest for happiness or a good life, regulation translates essentially into the mitigation of risks, the prevention of harmful conduct and its redress. In so doing, regulation reflects and enforces the core values of a society.[66] Words and narratives do matter. They lie at the heart of the collective identity of a society or individuals' collective understanding. Narratives often guide collective and individual self-determination. This is one of the main reasons why it is of the utmost importance to decipher AI challenges, including those related to regulating AI, in context. In this regard, three types of digital narratives can be identified as alternatives to the rule of law: the 'artificial intelligence' narrative characterising artificial input legitimacy (section III.A), the 'AI opportunities'

[61] See in this regard, Caunes (n 31).

[62] Note that the US Office of Science and Technology Policy Blueprint for an AI Bill of Rights could serve as a catalyst for such convergence with the EU among others through negotiations in the framework of the EU-US Trade and Technology Council. It remains to be seen whether the Council of Europe Convention of AI, which will be open for signature and ratification to any countries in the world, will play a similar role at the international level.

[63] The Public Voice, Universal Guidelines for Artificial Intelligence, October 2018, https://archive.epic.org/international/AIGuidleinesDRAFT20180910.pdf.

[64] The Public Voice, 'Universal Guidelines for Artificial Intelligence' (2018), Preamble.

[65] See famously, L Lessig, 'Code is Law – On Liberty in Cyberspace' (*Harvard Magazine*, 2000).

[66] See, eg, the reference to socialist core values in the 2022 Chinese 'Regulations on the Administration of Algorithm Recommendation of Internet Information Services' (Art 1); to not only human but also peoples' rights as well as 'African norms, ethics, values, such as Ubuntu, communitarian ethos, freedom from domination of one people by another in Africa' in the African Commission on Human and Peoples' Rights (2021), '473 Resolution on the need to undertake a Study on human and peoples' rights and artificial intelligence (AI), robotics and other new and emerging technologies in Africa' ACHPR/Res. 473, EXT.OS/XXXI (Preamble), to 'Union values of respect for human dignity, freedom, equality, democracy and the rule of law and Union fundamental rights' in the AI Act (n 29) (Preamble).

narrative by way of artificial output legitimacy (section III.B) and neoliberal narratives as a form of artificial throughput legitimacy (section III.C). Together they promote a competing artificial governance framework.

A. Artificial Input Legitimacy: The 'Artificial Intelligence' Narrative

Let there be AI! The challenge posed by AI to democratic governance in terms of input legitimacy relies on its very depiction as 'artificial intelligence'. A key question is indeed why we use the term 'artificial intelligence' in the first place.[67] Do the practices mentioned in the previous section fit with the definition of intelligence if characterised by understanding? Serious doubts are permissible. Therefore, what is the performative function of this expression?

From a psychoanalytic perspective, you may see in this expression the threat of what Freud called the 'omnipotence of thought', whereby the structural conditions of the mind are projected onto the external world. More worryingly perhaps, Freud identifies three stages:

> If we accept the evolution of man's conceptions of the universe mentioned above, according to which the *animistic* phase is *succeeded* by the religious, and this in turn by the scientific, we have no difficulty in following the fortunes of the 'omnipotence of thought' through all these phases. In the animistic stage man ascribes omnipotence to himself; in the religious he has ceded it to the gods, but without seriously giving it up, for he reserves to himself the right to control the gods by influencing them in some way or other in the interest of his wishes. In the scientific attitude towards life there is no longer any room for man's omnipotence; he has acknowledged his smallness and has submitted to death as to all other natural necessities in a spirit of resignation.

Depending on the constitutive myths of societies and individuals, the use of the term 'artificial intelligence' may lead to the legitimation of the AI black box, through magic thinking, sacralisation or pseudo-scientific techno-determinism or absolutism. AI indeed epitomises or is deemed to represent in its promise the ultimate stage of 'scientific' evolution. The answer to the question, 'why permit some specific design or use of AI systems despite their adverse impact on individuals' lives?' is an unquestionable 'because'. This delegitimises attempts to create the conditions of possibility of a human-centric approach to AI by design. Rights such as the right to transparency and principles such as accountability lose their *raison d'être*. The counterpart of the omnipotence of thought attributed to 'AI' is the negation of human self-determination. Nevertheless, the use of the term AI is spreading, be it in policy and legal documents such as national AI strategies,[68] international instruments such as the OECD AI Principles or the UNESCO Recommendation on the Ethics of AI, the Council of Europe Convention on AI or the EU AI Act.

[67] For a definition see, eg, AEPD-EDPS Joint Paper, '10 Misunderstandings about Machine Learning' (Joint paper, 2022). See also, AI Act (n 29) Art 3(1).
[68] For examples, see Caunes (n 31).

In this context, if AI has become the commonly accepted expression in science, politics, law and everyday life, its meaning should not be left unquestioned. On the contrary, AI should be defined and understood from a human-centric perspective since it is manmade. The key word in the expression 'artificial intelligence' is thus not 'intelligence' but 'artificial'. 'Artificial' qualifies 'intelligence', which essentially means that 'intelligence' does not have a meaning per se, separate from its artificial substrate. An artificially intelligent system is a system which is characterised by its inherent 'Canada Dry effect': at best it mimics human intelligence.

The answer to Alan Turing's question,[69] 'can a machine think?' with regard to precise tasks and so in terms of inferences from collected data to achieve a certain goal, is probably yes. However, Turing himself acknowledged that the question does not make much sense in abstract terms. The abstract Cartesian *cogito ergo sum* is what sets humans apart from AI systems.[70] The omnipotence of thought, apart from being a very human projection, is the perverted version of the primacy of thinking which in turn points to the primacy of human self-determination and to the limits of AI. A narrative which would emphasise the fantasised inherent superiority of AI over human beings as a justification for a transfer of sovereignty, in terms of power, to the new AI sovereign, as a source of power,[71] is a definite threat to democracy, fundamental rights and the rule of law. In order to prevent such a threat, humans should refrain from artificially conferring input legitimacy to AI. This points to the importance of civic education in digital matters, including the deconstruction of the AI narrative and the discussion of the democratic narrative.

B. Artificial Output Legitimacy: The 'AI Opportunities' Narrative

Another challenge in tackling the risks posed by AI efficiently is 'the big data imperative' driven by an economic rationale. Although you could call into question the use of the term 'big data', which somehow presupposes what it wants to achieve, the main threat comes from the associated narrative which consists of affirming that the full potential of AI can only be unleashed through the harvesting of the maximum amount of data.[72]

This is in sum an output legitimacy narrative. The extraordinary opportunities AI has to offer come at the expense of human self-determination through

[69] AM Turing, 'Computing Machinery and Intelligence' (1950) 49 *Mind* 433.

[70] On the link between Turing and Descartes see D Abramson, 'Descartes' Influence on Turing' (2011) 42 *Studies in History and Philosophy of Science*.

[71] On the different meanings of sovereignty, see M Troper, *Pour une théorie juridique de l'État*, (Paris, P.U.F., 2014).

[72] See, eg, K Fu-Lee, 'How AI Will Completely Change the Way We Live in the Next 20 *Years*' (*Time 2030*, 2021). For a discussion on the big data mythology, see also, K Crawford, K Milner and ML Gray, (2014) 'Critiquing Big Data: Politics, Ethics, Epistemology Special Section Introduction' (2014) 8 *International Journal of Communication* 1666.

the datafication of the 'digital natives'. However, if self-determination is what defines human beings, can something that destroys it be considered as an 'opportunity'? The only possible answer from a democratic standpoint seems to be in the negative. In the same vein, there is no balance to be achieved between respect for fundamental rights, democracy and the rule of law and AI opportunities branded as innovation. On the contrary, human-centric innovation, whereby AI is at the service of citizens and not the other way around, shall guide the definition of what constitutes AI opportunities in the design and use of AI systems. This is the reason why the design and use of AI ought to be framed by law as the expression of collective self-determination in democratic societies.[73]

'AI opportunities' as a rhetorical statement is often used as an output legitimacy discourse justifying the business model of digital firms and preventing its questioning or public regulation conceived as an economic burden to be avoided. However, the 'big data imperative' is artificial at best. More important is the quality of the data and their representativeness.[74] The EU legislator for his part did not follow such economic logic, favouring instead a rights-based approach relying on the right to privacy and data protection as enshrined in Articles 7 and 8 of the Charter of Fundamental Rights. Article 5(1) of the GDPR for its part provides for principles that limit the processing of personal data, such as lawfulness, fairness and transparency, purpose limitation, data minimisation, storage limitation, integrity and confidentiality. This suggests that, contrary to the ideas driven by the 'AI opportunities' narrative, AI opportunities can and ought to be interpreted from a human-centric perspective.

C. Artificial Throughput Legitimacy: Neoliberal Narratives and Castoriadis' Critique of Marxism

The absence of public regulation on AI has fuelled the digital privatisation of power. This phenomenon has also been supported and legitimated by alternative governance narratives. Some of the most influential of these have been moulded as a web of neoliberal narratives whose common mantra could be described as freedom from government, in lieu of individual self-determination, and self-regulating markets, in lieu of collective self-determination.[75] The reason is twofold. First, and albeit a simplification, in neoliberalism as a political theory, the combination of the primacy of economic freedom and the rule of free markets 'naturally' leads to and justifies market determinism under conditions of free competition. Second, neoliberalism as a political doctrine, has

[73] See Nemitz (n 17).

[74] See, eg, AEPD-EDPS Joint Paper (n 67).

[75] For some interesting accounts tying together informationism and neoliberalism, see, eg, R Neubauer, 'Neoliberalism in the Information Age, or Vice Versa? Global Citizenship, Technology, and Hegemonic Ideology' (2011) 9 *triple* C 195. For a US perspective, see P Starr, 'How Neoliberal Policy Shaped the Internet – and What to Do About It Now' (2019) *The American Prospect. Ideas, Politics and Power*. For an EU perspective on 'digital liberalism', see De Gregorio (n 5) 3 et seq.

proved very influential in real-life politics.[76] In terms of a narrative adapted to the digital context, the neoliberal tenets have been translated into the freedom of our digital self from government (artificial input legitimacy)[77] and the rule of the free digital market as the highest public good to be achieved (artificial output legitimacy). This essentially means that a combination of artificial input legitimacy and artificial output legitimacy has conveniently diminished the importance of the question of throughput legitimacy. However, a mechanistic approach cannot replace processes (in a democratic setting). One of the key flaws to this approach applied to real-life politics lies in the absence of consideration for the adverse effects of market determinism on individual freedom due to a conflation, within the notion of public good, of what is good for the individual and what is good for the market. Applied neoliberalism has this in common with applied communism,[78] in that it ultimately suppresses individual and collective self-determination. This explains why the democratic question becomes at best secondary, and at worst obsolete. In the meantime, the rule of law is slowly but surely being replaced by the rule by code or the rule of the non-digitalised few.[79]

This probably also explains why a counter-narrative which would restore the centrality of throughput legitimacy, thus exposing the shortcomings of its artificial version, can actually be found in Castoriadis' critique of Marxism. A theory of history such as the one Marxism aims at is a 'closed theoretical system [which] must of necessity posit people as passive objects of its theoretical truth'.

> This is due to the fact that, on the one hand, it remains almost unavoidably the development and the condensation of experience already acquired, and that, even if it foresees something 'new', this is always in every respect a repetition on some other level, the 'linear transformation' of what has already occurred.[80]

This static world imbued with its own rules leading to the de-individualisation of human beings is a perfect metaphor for the world according to AI.[81] (Heteronomous) determinism[82] legitimates the transformation of throughput processes ensuring continuing political participation into digital participation, which some may describe as colonialisation. The democratic throughput legitimacy question becomes superfluous or redundant. In this sense, the heteronomous 'artificial' is the opposite of the autonomous social-historical 'imaginary' which dynamically articulates both 'the union and the tension of instituting society and of instituted society, of history made and of history in

[76] See, eg, D Harvey, *A Brief History of Neoliberalism* (Oxford, Oxford University Press, 2005); D Stedman Jones, *Masters of the Universe: Hayek, Friedman, and the Birth of Neoliberal Politics* (Princeton, Princeton University Press, 2012).

[77] See John Perry Barlow's Declaration of the Independence of Cyberspace' (Davos, 8 February 1996).

[78] 'Applied' is here used to signify the discrepancy between political theory and political doctrine.

[79] See, eg, C Castoriadis, *The Imaginary Institution of Society* (Hoboken, Blackwell Publishers, 1987) 109.

[80] ibid at 69.

[81] With the caveat that causation would have to be replaced by correlation.

[82] See on determinism, Castoriadis (n 79) 29, 42 *et seq*.

the making'[83] and which is key in avoiding the alienation of individuals and absolutism of power, in other words, totalitarianism.[84] It is through the constant exercise of individual and collective self-determination that the democratic question emerges and democratic regimes flourish. This is what makes throughput legitimacy an essential component of a theory of democratic governance. It is what needs to be reinvented for the rule of law, democracy and fundamental rights to survive in a digital environment.

The deconstruction of some key AI narratives and the examination of some concrete AI challenges from a rule of law perspective, summarised in the Table below, show that only if the space for meaningful political deliberation is preserved, can the transfer of sovereignty, in terms of power, to the new AI sovereign, as a source of power, be avoided. This is the digital manifesto of citizenship as self-determination. To preserve it is the *raison d'être* of democratically legitimate governance and the rule of law in the digital age.

Table 4.1 Map of the challenges posed by AI and possible remedies

THE MATRIX	HORIZONTAL AI CHALLENGES (Big Techs)	VERTICAL AI CHALLENGES (States)	ARTIFICIAL NARRATIVES
INPUT LEGITIMACY	• Right to vote: (elections & referendums) – Constricted (big techs' functional sovereignty) – Manipulated (influence on voters' behaviour) • *Accountability of online platforms*	• Election tampering through information manipulation (bot(net)s disinformation/ voter-targeting through advertising) Information warfare to destabilise democracy • *Intelligence S. international cooperation* – *Transparency & accountability of providers of online intermediary services* – *Citizens' digital literacy*	• Let there be AI! Self-determination v. omnipotence of thought • '*Artificial intelligence*'

(continued)

[83] ibid 108.

[84] See ibid 108 et seq. See also, interestingly, H Arendt, *Totalitarianism: Part Three of The Origins of Totalitarianism* (San Diego, Harvest-Harcourt, 1979).

Table 4.1 ***(Continued)***

THE MATRIX	HORIZONTAL AI CHALLENGES (Big Techs)	VERTICAL AI CHALLENGES (States)	ARTIFICIAL NARRATIVES
OUTPUT LEGITIMACY	• Democracy perversion through panem & circenses • Trade off between access to commodities & commodification • *Correct power asymetry:* – *Education* – *Well functioning law-making process* – *Effective remedies* – *Rights to privacy & data protection*	• Digital panopticon through mass surveillance & risk of transformation of democratic States into authoritarian States (e.g.: security & defence exemptions in EU Al Act) • *Prohibition of use of Al for mass surveillance (e.g. facial recognition) & social scoring*	• 'AI opportunities' The big data imperative • *Rights-based approach*
THROUGHPUT LEGITIMACY	• Digital fora 'as' public fora (filter bubbles & echo chambers) through online profiling/harvesting & selling of personal data for advertising purposes. Risk of online extremisation and partyism • *Address design & use of Al systems:* – *Right to transparency and explainability (black box)* – *Non-qualified right to non-discrimination*	• Quality of public decisions & spread of automated decision-making in public institutions > potential adverse effects on individuals' lives and trust in democratic institutions • *Ban on fully automated decision-making*	• Neoliberal narratives • *Castoriadis' critique of Marxism Constant exercise of individual & collective self-determination*

Part II

Digital Data, Trust and Fundamental Rights in the Internal Market Context

5

The EU's Digital Package: Striking a Balance for Fundamental Rights in the DSA and DMA Regulations

ANNEGRET ENGEL* AND XAVIER GROUSSOT**

'La justice sans la force est impuissante,
la force sans la justice est tyrannique.'

—Blaise Pascal (1623–1662)

I. INTRODUCTION

According to the Treaty on European Union (TEU), Article 2, the EU is 'founded on the values of respect for human dignity, freedom, democracy, equality, the rule of law and respect for human rights'. In combination with the EU Charter on Fundamental Rights, the EU constitutes a role model in upholding human rights and other European values worldwide. However, while the EU Charter became fully effective with the entering into force of the Lisbon Treaty in 2009, its original drafting dates back much further to the year 2000. As such, it does not take full account of the more recent technological developments in the digital sphere. Indeed, its application is mainly bound to the non-digital sphere, while for the most part and until recently, internet services remained largely unregulated and heavily driven by economic

* Associate Professor in EU Law at Lund University, Sweden. Email: Annegret.engel@jur.lu.se.
** Professor of EU Law at Lund University, Sweden. Email: Xavier.groussot@jur.lu.se. This chapter is part of a wider research project, entitled 'The Application and Impact of the EU Charter of Fundamental Rights in Competition Law, the Digital Single Market and Sweden', funded by the Swedish Competition Authority.

considerations. The result of this being the creation of a human-rights-free space, a 'Wild West' internet.[1]

Hence, it was suggested that the creation of a Digital Single Market should not only be informed by economic considerations, but also take into account fundamental rights.[2] At the other end of the spectrum, however, looms the danger of over-regulation once the EU takes on a particular field, a claim which may sound all too familiar for some Member States[3] or even third countries to whom the EU has given a rather protectionist impression at times.[4] Neither extreme can be said to be ideal as was observed already centuries ago by Blaise Pascal. The truth lies somewhere in between after carefully balancing the different interests and rights at stake.

However, with regard to the digital sphere, this poses certain problems unknown to the offline world.[5] The following will, therefore, provide a brief overview of those challenges peculiar to the digital sphere as regards the enforcement of fundamental rights. After that, the recently introduced Digital Services Act (DSA)[6] and Digital Markets Act (DMA)[7] regulations will be analysed as key examples of the EU's legislation in digitalisation heralding the new digital era, with a particular focus on the constitutional principles of digital transparency and digital sovereignty. The EU's ambitions as a driving force in this field and a defender of fundamental rights will come under scrutiny – individually for each legislative act and collectively as a package – and will be evaluated according to whether the right balance has been struck or not. Additionally, as will be argued,

[1] See T Berg, 'www.wildwest.gov: The Impact of the Internet on State Power to Enforce the Law' (2000) *Brigham Young University Law Review* (4), 1305–62; and S Shipchandler, 'The Wild Wild Web: Non-Regulation as the Answer to the Regulatory Question' (2000) *Cornell International Law Journal* 33(2), 435–63.

[2] X Groussot et al, 'Towards General Principles 2.0: the Application of General Principles of EU Law in the Digital Society' in U Bernitz et al (eds), *General Principles of EU Law and the Digital Legal Order* (Kluwer, 2020) 425–51. See also K Karppinen and O Puukko, 'Four Discourses of Digital Rights: Promises and Problems of Rights-Based Politics' (2020) *Journal of Information Policy* 10(1), 304–28.

[3] See, eg, concerning the EU's over-regulation in the field of climate policy, C Böhringer et al, 'Good Things Do Not Always Come in Threes: On the Excess Cost of Overlapping Regulation in EU Climate Policy' (2016) *Energy Policy* 94(July), 502–508.

[4] See, eg, R Wodak and S Boukala, 'Talking about Solidarity and Security in the Age of Crisis: The Revival of Nationalism and Protectionism in the European Union – A Discourse-Historical Approach' in C Carta and J-F Morin (eds), *EU Foreign Policy through the Lens of Discourse Analysis: Making Sense of Diversity* (London, Routledge, 2014).

[5] See, eg, Report from the Commission to the European Parliament, the Council, the European Economic and Social Committee and the Committee of the Regions, 'Protecting Fundamental Rights in the Digital Age – 2021 Annual Report on the Application of the EU Charter of Fundamental Rights' (2021).

[6] Regulation (EU) 2022/2065 of the European Parliament and of the Council of 19 October 2022 on a Single Market for Digital Services and amending Directive 2000/31/EC (Digital Services Act) [2022] OJ L277/1.

[7] Regulation (EU) 2022/1925 of the European Parliament and of the Council of 14 September 2022 on contestable and fair markets in the digital sector and amending Directives (EU) 2019/1937 and (EU) 2020/1828 (Digital Markets Act or DMA) [2022] OJ L265/1.

the package serves not only to uphold European values internally on the EU internal market, but also accomplishes to export them to other third countries, thus placing the EU at the forefront of international regulatory control over the digital sphere.

II. THE FUNDAMENTAL RIGHTS CHALLENGE FOR THE DIGITAL SPHERE

While other areas of EU law have received ample attention from the EU legislator over the course of recent decades, the Internet has long been neglected and exempt from being regulated at EU level. In particular, this concerns the application of fundamental rights. The specific challenges for the digital sphere are numerous: worldwide scope; easy access; interoperability; rapid technological change; fluctuating market conditions; anonymity; disinformation; lack of traceability and thus enforcement, to name but a few. Fundamental EU values, in particular including democracy and the respect for human rights, have suffered as a direct result of these growing problems in the digital sphere. The EU has thus changed its approach more recently and has started to regulate the new technologies more actively in order to avoid European values such as data protection being undermined without taking away any of the benefits offered by the openness of the Internet.[8]

As was already established in the 2020 Commission Communication on 'A European Strategy for Data', the 'Commission's vision stems from European values and fundamental rights and the conviction that the human being is and should remain at the centre'.[9] More recently, in its Declaration on European Digital Rights and Principles[10] as well as the Declaration for the Future of the Internet,[11] the EU's goal is the creation of a level playing field which envisages the same rules and principles to govern the digital sphere as they also do in the offline world.[12] This does not, however, necessarily require as its ultimate goal an interaction of both offline and online services with each other on the same market as was suggested by Andrej Savin.[13] Rather, this means a one-to-one

[8] See also the speech by EVP Margrethe Vestager at the Council's High-level Presidency Conference: 'A Europe of Rights and Values in the Digital Decade' (8 December 2020).

[9] European Commission, 'A European Strategy for Data' COM(2020) 66 final, available at https://ec.europa.eu/info/sites/info/files/communication-european-strategy-data-19feb2020_en.pdf.

[10] European Declaration on Digital Rights and Principles for the Digital Decade, proposed by the European Commission, published on 26 January 2022.

[11] Signed by the EU, the US and more than 60 other international partners, published on 28 April 2022.

[12] See also Communication from the Commission to the European Parliament, the Council, the European Economic and Social Committee and the Committee of the Regions, '2030 Digital Compass: the European Way for the Digital Decade' COM/2021/118 final.

[13] A Savin, 'The EU Digital Services Act: Towards a More Responsible Internet' (Copenhagen Business School, Law Research Paper Series No 21-04, 2021).

application of Charter rights online in order for the Internet to become a fair and secure place for businesses and end users alike, in a similar manner to the offline world.[14]

This then begs the question as to which ingredients make up a fair and secure Internet and more specifically which fundamental rights are currently underrepresented in the digital sphere. As already mentioned, the protection of personal data is of significance in the context of digitalisation. This is one of the freedoms enshrined under Article 8 of the EU Charter,[15] which stipulates in paragraph two that any such data 'must be processed fairly for specified purposes and on the basis of the consent of the person concerned or some other legitimate basis'.[16] In addition, it provides that everyone 'has the right of access to data which has been collected concerning him or her, and the right to have it rectified'. This also relates to Article 7 of the EU Charter on the respect for private and family life. Another important fundamental right worth mentioning in this context is the freedom to conduct a business as protected by Article 16 of the EU Charter. Hence, regulating the digital sphere requires acquiring a balance between the benefits of free data flow[17] and the different personal and business interests, in due consideration of other institutional and procedural rights prescribed in the Charter.[18]

In addition, the transfer of data to third countries plays a major role in a worldwide operating digital sphere and places additional constraints on the enforceability of laws in a traditional legislative framework restricted to national boundaries. While the General Data Protection Regulation (GDPR)[19] provides for such transfers to be made only under the condition of an adequate level of data protection in the third country concerned, and despite international agreements in place aimed at the alignment of different standards of protection,

[14] Others have argued even further and actively advocate a new Charter of Fundamental Rights in order to accommodate the societal and technological changes that have taken place since its original drafting more than 20 years ago, particularly in the digital sphere, see F von Schirach, 'Jeder Mensch' (*Luchterhand Verlag; YouMoveEurope initiative*, 2021), available at https://you.wemove.eu/campaigns/fur-neue-grundrechte-in-europa.

[15] See also Treaty on the Functioning of the European Union (TFEU), Art 16.

[16] As regards the concept of processing of personal data, see, eg, case C-101/01 *Lindqvist* EU:C:2003:596; case C-131/12 *Google Spain and Google* EU:C:2014:317. As regards consent by a user of a particular website for storage of or access to personal data, see, eg, case C-673/17 *Planet49* EU:C:2019:801.

[17] Some have even argued that this should be added to the four freedoms of movement in the internal market, see Swedish National Board of Trade (*Kommerskollegium*) 2016 Report on 'Data Flows: A Fifth Freedom for the Internal Market?', available at www.kommerskollegium.se/en/publications/reports/2016/data-flows---a-fifth-freedom-for-the-internal-market/.

[18] See also D Redeker, 'Towards a European Constitution for the Internet? Comparative Institutionalization and Mobilization in European and Transnational Digital Constitutionalism' (GigaNet Annual Symposium, 2019), available at www.giga-net.org/2019symposiumPapers/22_Redeker_Towards-a-European_Constitution.pdf.

[19] Regulation (EU) 2016/679 of the European Parliament and of the Council of 27 April 2016 on the protection of natural persons with regard to the processing of personal data and on the free movement of such data, and repealing Directive 95/46/EC (General Data Protection Regulation) (GDPR) [2016] OJ L119/1.

equivalence of rights may still not be achieved as is evidenced by the *Schrems* saga concerning the transfer of personal data to the United States.[20] Additional safeguards are now being put in place under the new EU–US Trans-Atlantic Data Privacy Framework as announced in the joint statement by the European Commission and the United States on 25 March 2022,[21] bearing in mind that this would not have materialised without such high profile litigation and the thus forced review of previous legislation.[22]

The main issue regarding an insufficient protection of fundamental rights in a particular field and the reliance on private litigation in order to bring about certain legislative change concerns the antithetic lapse of time with lengthy court proceedings as opposed to a fast-paced digital development. Therefore, as can be argued, the legal maxim of 'justice delayed is justice denied' applies even more so in the digital sphere, which also correlates with Article 41 of the EU Charter and the right to good administration in a timely manner. As has been argued by Andrea Renda, the current legislative framework at the EU level is still 'too sparse and uncoordinated' to achieve the Union's objectives.[23] The following section will analyse the DMA and DSA regulations regarding their compliance with fundamental rights enshrined in the EU Charter and whether they are able to deliver on the promise of a fairer and safer online environment.[24]

III. THE DMA AND THE PRINCIPLE OF DIGITAL SOVEREIGNTY

In the specific field of competition law, the development of new technologies has created many challenges and raised questions for the legislator on how to regulate major market players: their cross-border nature, vicissitudes, and enormous market powers allow some of them to be able to escape legal scrutiny under the current set of rules. This can lead to severe imbalances in market power.[25] The problems surrounding the traditional *ex-post* enforcement in competition laws can be seen in the *Google Shopping* case.[26] While the General Court in its judgment delivered on 10 November 2021 held that Google was indeed liable for

[20] See cases C-362/14 *Schrems I* EU:C:2015:650; and C-311/18 *Facebook Ireland and Schrems (Schrems II)* EU:C:2020:559.

[21] See European Commission, 'European Commission and United States Joint Statement on Trans-Atlantic Data Privacy Framework' (2022) Available at https://ec.europa.eu/commission/presscorner/detail/es/ip_22_2087.

[22] See also M Zalnieriute, 'Data Transfers after Schrems II: The EU-US Disagreements over Data Privacy and National Security' (2022) *Vanderbilt Journal of Transnational Law* 55(1), 1–48.

[23] A Renda, 'Making the Digital Economy "Fit for Europe"' (2020) *European Law Journal* 26(5–6) 345–54.

[24] For a more detailed analysis of the different issues involved with the new legislative package, see A Engel et al, *New Directions in Digitalisation: Perspectives from EU Competition Law and the Charter of Fundamental Rights* (Springer Nature International, 2024).

[25] European Commission (n 9).

[26] T-612/17 *Google and Alphabet v Commission (Google Shopping)* EU:T:2021:763.

abuse of dominant position by means of the self-preferencing of its comparison shopping services, the decision is currently under appeal before the Court of Justice of the European Union,[27] which further delays meaningful and timely enforcement[28] in a fast-paced digital space and potentially causes fragmentation of the market between Member States. The DMA seeks to close this gap[29] by laying down *ex-ante*[30] 'harmonised rules ensuring contestable and fair markets in the digital sector across the Union where gatekeepers are present'.[31]

On 1 November 2022, the highly anticipated DMA entered into force and became applicable, for the most part, on 2 May 2023. The new legal instrument in the shape of a regulation claims to be aligned with the procedural and institutional rights granted in the Charter, in particular Article 16 thereof.[32] However, the freedom to conduct a business is restricted by the DMA for so-called gatekeepers, ie a provider of core platform services, as defined in Article 3 of the DMA. Chapter III of the DMA identifies *per se* practices of gatekeepers which are perceived as limiting contestability or as being unfair and therefore places them under specific obligations according to Articles 5 and 6 of the DMA, aimed at limiting gatekeepers' powers. Crucially, the above-mentioned *Google Shopping* case would be captured by Article 6(5) of the DMA, which seeks to prevent exactly that under the *ex-ante* approach.[33]

The obligations for gatekeepers listed in the DMA may only be suspended under exceptional circumstances (Article 9 DMA) or for overriding reasons of public interest (Article 10 DMA), with close scrutiny of potential cases of misuse.[34] As such, it can be argued that the provisions in the DMA limiting the behaviour of large tech giants operating as gatekeepers are narrowly construed and defensive, with the aim of imposing some element of control over them in order to ensure the protection of other democratic values, most notably security

[27] Case C-48/22 P *Google and Alphabet v Commission (Google Shopping)*.

[28] In accordance with the procedural requirements under TEU, Art 19 in conjunction with the EU Charter, Art 41.

[29] P van Cleynenbreugel, 'The Commission's Digital Services and Markets Act Proposals: First Step Towards Tougher and More Directly Enforced EU Rules?' (2021) *Maastricht Journal of European and Comparative Law* 28(5), 667–86.

[30] Z Georgieva, 'The Digital Markets Act Proposal of the European Commission: Ex-ante Regulation, infused with Competition Principles' (2021) *European Papers* (6), 25–28.

[31] DMA (n 7) Art 1. Gatekeepers are defined as providers of core platform services if they have: (a) a significant impact on the internal market; (b) serve as an important gateway for business users to reach end users; and (c) enjoy or are likely to enjoy a durable position (Art 3).

[32] ibid recital 109 of the Preamble.

[33] See also Op-ed by M Botta, 'The Ruling of the EU General Court in Google Shopping: An Endorsement of the EU Commission Antitrust Enforcement Policy in Digital Markets' (*EU Law Live*, 25 November 2021), available at https://eulawlive.com/op-ed-the-ruling-of-the-eu-general-court-in-google-shopping-an-endorsement-of-the-eu-commission-antitrust-enforcement-policy-in-digital-markets-by-marco-botta/.

[34] According to the DMA, Art 13, a gatekeeper must comply with its obligations and their implementation shall not be undermined by any behaviour of the undertaking to which the gatekeeper belongs, 'regardless of whether that behaviour is of a contractual, commercial, technical or any other nature'.

and transparency for the end user. This has been referred to as the principle of digital sovereignty,[35] which was declared as the 'leitmotiv of European digital policy' by the German Council Presidency.[36] References to the fundamental rights of the actual service providers as the target of this regulation remain scarce in the new legislative act. Article 34 of the DMA gives service providers the right to be heard and access to their files, and, in addition, an obligation of professional secrecy according to Article 36 DMA for the information obtained from service providers in the course of enforcement of the DMA.

While thus appearing much stricter from an enforcement perspective than the traditional *ex-post* competition law framework, the *ex-ante* rules under the DMA provide for a dialogue between the Commission and the addressee of the obligations.[37] This dialogue on whether or not compliance with the imposed obligations has been achieved allows for the necessary margin of discretion on the part of the Commission to adjust if necessary to the individual circumstances and behaviour of the gatekeeper in question. As such, this introduces a new level to the traditional competition law framework, which is, however, inherently broad and subject to further interpretation. It was suggested that this constitutes 'opacity by design', purposefully 'shifting the bargaining power in interpreting the obligations to the enforcers',[38] ie the European Commission.

IV. THE DSA AND THE PRINCIPLE OF DIGITAL TRANSPARENCY

From the perspective of having taken the DMA as a starting point for this analysis, the DSA subsequently broadens the spectrum to all digital service providers and imposes certain obligations on all of them – including gatekeepers addressed by the DMA – in an incremental format of five main categories.[39] Here, the principle of digital sovereignty in the DMA is complemented with an additional layer of transparency requirements provided for under the DSA. Crucially, under the principle of digital transparency, online service providers are not only obliged to

[35] See, eg, E Celeste, 'Digital Sovereignty in the EU: Challenges and Future Perspectives' in Fabbrini et al (eds), 'Data Protection beyond Borders: Transatlantic Perspectives on Extraterritoriality and Sovereignty" (Hart Publishing, 2021); and H Roberts et al, 'Safeguarding European Values with Digital Sovereignty: An Analysis of Statements and Policies' (2021) *Internet Policy Review* 10(3).

[36] Programme for Germany's Presidency of the Council of the European Union (1 July to 31 December 2020), 'Together for Europe's Recovery', available at www.eu2020.de/eu2020-en/programme#:~:text=The%20Presidency%20Programme%20describes%20the,this%20site%20in%20eight%20languages.

[37] DMA (n 7) Arts 8 and Chapter V.

[38] O Andriychuk, 'Shaping the New Modality of the Digital Markets: The Impact of the DSA/DMA Proposals on Inter-Platform Competition' (2021) *World Competition* 44(3), 273.

[39] These are dependent on average monthly active recipients of digital services, ranging from micro to very large online platforms. Gatekeepers addressed by the DMA would qualify as the latter category, which, however, also includes other service providers which do not qualify as gatekeepers themselves.

report to the respective authorities, but are also required to make certain information available to the public, including their competitors.[40]

The DSA and its increased transparency obligations imposed on service providers in the digital sphere have received mixed responses from academic scholarship. While applauding transparency mechanisms in general and the more burdensome requirements for bigger market players, Oles Andriychuk makes a point in arguing that it is typically the established service providers which are capable of adapting more quickly to new market conditions and utilising them to their advantage, which would again work to the disadvantage of new and less agile market entrants.[41] The main factor determining the success of the intended level playing field will thus be whether or not the new rules on transparency can actually benefit new competitors entering the market in order to ultimately increase competition between online service providers.

Another point of criticism is that the principle of transparency as a fundamental right enshrined and derived from the Charter cannot be viewed in isolation as it interplays and may even conflict with other fundamental rights at the same level, such as privacy and data protection, freedom of expression, freedom to conduct a business, or the protection of intellectual property rights, amongst others.[42] As can be understood from the incremental categorisation set up by the DSA, online service providers growing in size will see their transparency obligations increase which directly impacts on their fundamental rights protection in other areas. Ultimately, the question that arises here is whether the established system of categorisation by the DSA will stand the test of proportionality according to Article 5(4) TEU and Protocol No 2 on the application of the principles of subsidiarity and proportionality in order to justify the decline in fundamental rights protection for larger online service providers and therefore achieve the overarching objectives of safety and fairness in the digital market.

In order to satisfy the requirement of proportionality, the Court held *in Poland v Parliament and Council*, with regard to Directive 2019/790 on copyright and related rights,[43] that

> the legislation which entails an interference with fundamental rights must lay down clear and precise rules governing the scope and application of the measure in question and imposing minimum safeguards, so that the persons whose exercise of those rights is limited have sufficient guarantees to protect them effectively against the risk of abuse.[44]

[40] See, eg, DSA (n 6) Arts 13(1), 15(4), 23(2), 27(2) and 33.

[41] Andriychuk (n 38) 261–86.

[42] See G Frosio and C Geiger, 'Taking Fundamental Rights Seriously in the Digital Service Act's Platform Liability Regime' (2021) *European Law Journal*. In line with DSA, Art 26, very large online platforms are required to carry out risk assessments in order to avoid adverse effects for the exercise of fundamental rights.

[43] Directive (EU) 2019/790 of the European Parliament and of the Council of 17 April 2019 on copyright and related rights in the Digital Single Market and amending Directives 96/9/EC and 2001/29/EC [2019] OJ L130/92.

[44] Case C-401/19 *Republic of Poland v European Parliament and Council of the European Union* EU:C:2022:297, para 67.

A similar debate can also be found in *Ligue des droits humains v Conseil des ministres* on the Passenger Name Record (PNR) Directive.[45] The case concerns a preliminary reference from the Belgian Constitutional Court, in which the Ligue des droits humains essentially claimed in their first plea that the PNR Directive is incompatible with Articles 7 and 8 of the EU Charter as it does not meet the basic standards for legality, necessity and proportionality with regard to the right to private life and the protection of personal data.[46] While the Advocate General did not follow this reasoning in his Opinion,[47] arguing that the contested Directive did not violate any fundamental rights, Christian Thönnes openly criticised this conclusion in his blog post, stating that the Directive, 'due to the severity of its effects and its inherent inefficiency in fulfilling its stated purpose, produces disproportionate interferences with Articles 7 and 8 CFR. It ought to be invalidated'.[48]

Previously, in its joined cases on *Digital Rights Ireland* and *Seitlinger and Others*,[49] the Court found that the Data Retention Directive[50] did not meet the standards of the principle of proportionality with regard to certain fundamental rights, most notably Articles 7 and 8 of the EU Charter, which thus rendered the contested Directive invalid.[51] It is important to note, however, that the Court held in Opinion 1/15 on the EU–Canada PNR Agreement that the rights enshrined in Articles 7 and 8 of the EU Charter are 'not absolute'[52] and that even severe interferences with those rights can be justified by 'an objective of general interest of the European Union'.[53] However, any such limits to the exercise of fundamental rights must be 'necessary and genuinely meet objectives of general interest recognised by the Union or the need to protect the rights and freedoms of others' according to Article 52(1) of the EU Charter. Hence, the balance struck between

[45] Directive (EU) 2016/681 of 27 April 2016 on the use of passenger name record (PNR) data for the prevention, detection, investigation and prosecution of terrorist offences and serious crime [2016] OJ L119/132.

[46] Case C-817/19 *Ligue des droits humains v Conseil des ministres*.

[47] Opinion of AG Pitruzzella in Case C-817/19 *Ligue des droits humains v Conseil des ministres*, delivered on 27 January 2022, EU:C:2022:65.

[48] C Thönnes, 'A Cautious Green Light for Technology-Driven Mass Surveillance: The Advocate General's Opinion on the PNR Directive' (VerfBlog, 2022), available at https://verfassungsblog.de/green-light. See also A Engel, 'Judicial Review in the Digital Era: Safeguarding the Rule of Law Through Added Safeguards?' (2023) *Journal of Constitutional History* 45(1), 91.

[49] Joined cases C-293/12 and C-594/12 *Digital Rights Ireland and Seitlinger and Others* EU:C:2014:238.

[50] Directive 2006/24/EC of the European Parliament and of the Council of 15 March 2006 on the retention of data generated or processed in connection with the provision of publicly available electronic communications services or of public communications networks and amending Directive 2002/58/EC [2006] OJ L105/1.

[51] See O Lynskey, 'Joined Cases C-293/12 and 594/12 Digital Rights Ireland and Seitlinger and Others: The Good, the Bad and the Ugly' (*European Law Blog*, 8 April 2014), available at https://europeanlawblog.eu/2014/04/08/joined-cases-c-29312-and-59412-digital-rights-ireland-and-seitlinger-and-others-the-good-the-bad-and-the-ugly/. See also the Court's reasoning in joined cases C-203/15 and C-698/15 *Tele2 Sverige* EU:C:2016:970.

[52] Opinion 1/15 on the EU-Canada PNR Agreement, EU:C:2017:592, para 136.

[53] ibid, para 151.

the different fundamental rights in the DSA and DMA respectively can only be approved through judicial review on a case-by-case basis, which may ultimately result in further legal challenges before the European Courts instigated by the various addressees or otherwise affected parties.

V. THE DSA/DMA PACKAGE: A HOLISTIC VIEW

The above discussion has been an attempt to showcase the inevitable conflict between fundamental rights when regulating the digital sphere. Essentially, this can be boiled down to the following. When viewed individually, both the DSA and DMA seem to protect certain interests while compromising others. On the one hand, in safeguarding the principle of digital transparency, the DSA ensures the protection of a fair and competitive EU internal market at the expense of certain fundamental rights such as data protection and privacy. The DMA, on the other, inspired by the notion of digital sovereignty, may well ensure the protection of data and privacy while at the same time interfering with the freedom to conduct a business. However, as will be suggested here, the new legislative acts for the digital sphere – the DSA and DMA – have to be considered as a package deal rather than viewed in isolation.

In general, both legislative acts come in the form of regulations with the aim of harmonising the digital market across EU Member States. While the focus for the DSA is to create a 'safe, predictable and trusted online environment',[54] the DMA seeks to ensure contestability and fair markets.[55] It could be argued that these goals set out by the Union go hand in hand. One could even go so far to claim that the DMA is simply the continuation of the DSA, ie the sixth category of service providers, five of which can be found in the DSA; or indeed *vice versa* with the DSA complementing the DMA's principle of digital sovereignty with additional layers of transparency as presented in this chapter. In addition, both Regulations are addressed to service providers irrespective of their place of establishment, as long as the recipient is based on Union territory.[56]

Aside from these generic attributes, certain spill-over effects can be identified with actual practical implications on the other respective legislative act and their addressees. It could be argued, on the one hand, that the application of the DSA to all online service providers – including gatekeepers as defined by the DMA – not only allows for the principle of transparency to be fully effective across the board, but also offers clear benefits for gatekeepers in compensation for the rather stringent obligations imposed on them by the DMA. As was argued above, gatekeepers are most likely to make effective use of market information, obtained through publishing obligations imposed on their competitors, by sheer

[54] DSA (n 6) Art 1(1).
[55] DMA (n 7) Art 1(1).
[56] DSA (n 6) Art 2(1) and DMA (n 7) Art 1(2).

virtue of their own market power. On the other hand, the exclusion or rather non-application of the DMA on online service providers which do not qualify as gatekeepers and thus their non-exposure to the obligations imposed in accordance with the notion of digital sovereignty allows for a levelling of competition in compensation for the transparency requirements under the DSA, which may indeed seem burdensome for some particularly small online service providers.

These spill-over effects or cross-benefits between the two acts go beyond pure academic relevance. As has been shown, they carry practical implications in the sense of additional constitutional safeguards, which can and should be weighed against any imposed obligations under legal scrutiny. For example, this was the case in *Poland v Parliament and Council*, where the Court held that the contested Directive contained additional safeguards, ensuring that other fundamental rights, such as the freedom of expression, were adequately observed.[57] As such, it will be crucial for future litigation to recognise the DSA and DMA Regulations as two sides of the same coin. In addition, the DSA/DMA package accomplishes legal certainty to a much greater extent, as one of the general and overarching principles of EU law, which in return contributes again – along with the principle of legitimate expectations – to the freedom to conduct a business.[58] This is lacking in *ex-post* litigation, which relies entirely on individual legal challenges, thus creating fragmentation and uncertainty which is detrimental to businesses and competition in the market as a whole.[59]

VI. SHIFTING THE BALANCE FOR THE DIGITAL SINGLE MARKET: TOWARDS REGULATORY ABSOLUTISM?

Another inherent limitation associated with the *ex-post* approach, and thus a lesson which can perhaps be learnt from it, constitutes the preferential use of some fundamental rights over others with regard to litigation as opposed to regulation. As has been observed by various scholars, the European Courts' heavy reliance on procedure (eg, Articles 41 and 47 EU Charter) rather than substance to the detriment of entire chapters of the European Charter, such as Chapter IV on solidarity (Articles 27–38), does not do justice to the true potential of all fundamental rights and their equal treatment within the EU.[60] However, in the field of digitalisation, more recent judgments of the European

[57] *Republic of Poland v European Parliament and Council of the European Union* (n 44) para 90.

[58] A Portuese, O Gough, and J Tanega, 'The Principle of Legal Certainty as a Principles of Economic Efficiency' (2017) *European Journal of Law and Economics* 44, 131–56.

[59] See, eg, M Eben, 'Fining Google: A Missed Opportunity for Legal Certainty?' (2018) *European Competition Journal* 14(1), 129–51.

[60] R Tinière and C Vial (eds), 'Les dix ans de la Charte de droits fondamentaux de l'Union européenne : Bilan et perspectives' (Bruylant, 2020). See also a review essay by X Groussot and G Thor Pétursson, 'Je t'aime … moi non plus: Ten Years of Application of the EU Charter of Fundamental Rights' (2022) *CMLR* 59(1), 239–58.

Courts seem to be foreboding a greater willingness to include those substantive values previously underused in judicial review cases.

For example, a more substantive appraisal of the EU Charter's provisions can be seen in *Poland v Parliament and Council*, where the Court scrutinised and balanced the freedom of expression and information (Article 11 EU Charter), on the one hand, and the right to the protection of intellectual property (Article 17(2) EU Charter), on the other.[61] Here, the Court observed that while 'the internet has now become one of the principal means by which individuals exercise their right to freedom of expression and information',[62] other fundamental rights have to be given due account and balanced accordingly 'with the need to reconcile the requirements of the protection of those various rights and principles at issue, striking a fair balance between them'.[63] With reference to *Promusicae*,[64] the Court found that it lies within the Member States' responsibilities to transpose and implement EU laws in such a way as to ensure consistency of their national laws with EU law and to avoid conflict with fundamental rights or other general principles of EU law.[65]

The reasoning in *Poland v Parliament and Council* with its more substantive appraisal of fundamental rights does not come as a surprise considering the wording of the contested Directive,[66] which clearly requires the application of the principle of proportionality in Article 17(5) and a balance of 'fundamental rights and of the use of exceptions and limitations' according to Article 17(10). Evidence from the wider *telos* of the internal market already suggests this recent albeit profound shift away from the de-regulatory approach, which required extensive litigation with the aim of removing obstacles to trade at the national level, towards a new wave of regulatory harmonisation in this area. In her yet unpublished work, Urska Sadl suggests that such a shift would potentially require a new set of rules and standards as a justification to regulate.[67] Indeed, for the creation of a Digital Single Market, it is clear that a greater focus will be on regulatory alignment in order to accommodate for an improved balancing of rights and principles with the inclusion of new values, such as the principle of solidarity.

Aside from the solidarity chapter in the EU Charter, the principle can also be found in Articles 2 and 3 TEU as one of the common and overarching values between Member States. It could be argued that the holistic view of reconciliation between the DSA and DMA Regulations presented above is in line

[61] See also joined cases C-682/18 and C-683/18 *Google LLC and Cyando AG* EU:C:2021:503.

[62] *Republic of Poland v European Parliament and Council of the European Union* (n 44) para 46.

[63] ibid, para 66.

[64] Case C-275/06 *Productores de Música de España (Promusicae) v Telefónica de España SAU* EU:C:2008:54, para 68.

[65] *Republic of Poland v European Parliament and Council of the European Union* (n 44) para 99.

[66] Directive (EU) 2019/790 (n 43).

[67] U Sadl et al, 'Route 66: The Mutations of the Internal Market through the Prism of Citation Networks' (unpublished, on file with the author).

with the interpretation of the judgment in *Poland v Parliament and Council* and essentially incorporates solidarity between the different stakeholders by means of the interplay between the principles of sovereignty and transparency. As such, it would establish a new level of solidarity, not only binding Member States *vis-à-vis* the EU and its institutions, but also private businesses and other economic actors on the digital market. By means of regulatory force, the shift towards a new set of digital rights receives the necessary impetus and proactive efficacy in an already fast-paced and otherwise economically motivated digital environment.

VII. BRUSSELS EFFECT 2.0: EXPORTING EUROPEAN VALUES WITH EU INTERNAL LEGISLATION

From an external perspective, it could be argued that the EU's digital agenda seems rather protectionist, particularly regarding the DSA/DMA package and the notion of digital sovereignty therein. Indeed, digital sovereignty was previously misconstrued as 'economic protectionism', but has now detached itself from this connotation often viewed as negative.[68] This is particularly due to the shift in perception about the digital market in general and a lack of enforcement under the traditional competition law regime, resulting in a 'Wild West' for the Internet as mentioned above. Thus, aside from its protectionist characteristics, digital sovereignty can contribute an element of fairness if it manages to strike the right balance between fundamental rights, which may not only remedy the current imbalances and distortions on the European market, but also go beyond its borders.

Such 'spill-over' effects are more than just a corollary; they have been very much intended by the European legislator. In fact, Article 3(5) TEU stipulates that 'the Union shall uphold and promote its values and interests' internationally with other countries around the world.[69] This forms the basis of externalising European values, also known as the 'Brussels effect'.[70] The EU pursues an 'open, but proactive international approach' as it aims to promote the European model around the world, in particular concerning the digital sphere.[71]

In a traditional sense, EU values and standards are normally introduced through international agreements which are negotiated with third countries on a

[68] See also O Andriychuk, 'Shaping the New Modality of the Digital Markets: The Impact of the DSA/DMA Proposals on Inter-Platform Competition' (2021) *World Competition* 44(3), 261–86.

[69] See also TEU, Art 21.

[70] See A Bradford, 'The Brussels Effect' (2012) *Northwestern University Law Review* 107(1), 1–67; and more recently A Bradford, '*The Brussels Effect: How the European Union Rules the World* (Oxford University Press, 2020).

[71] European Commission (n 9). See also C Kuner, 'The Internet and the Global Reach of EU Law' in M Cremona and J Scott (eds), *EU Law Beyond EU Borders: The Extraterritorial Reach of EU Law* (Oxford University Press, 2019).

bilateral or multilateral basis. They are thus exported via external legislation, ie the classic 'Brussels effect'. It could be argued that the DSA/DMA package here has to be distinguished from this classic 'Brussels effect'. It differs in so far as it constitutes EU internal legislation having a direct effect on companies operating on EU territory albeit based outside the EU. These non-EU-based companies are thus subject to EU values and standards although they are imposed on them without any negotiations that have included either the respective company or the third country concerned. As such, the export of EU values via EU internal legislation could be considered a new level of the classic 'Brussels effect'.

VIII. CONCLUSIONS

This chapter has made an attempt to shed some light on the role of fundamental rights in the EU's digital agenda and particularly the recent DSA and DMA Regulations. In general, as has been observed, the EU manages to address previous flaws derived from a severe under-regulation of digital services and a resulting lack of fundamental rights protection in this area. In addition, the EU's regulatory ambitions in the digital field now suggest a shift towards a more *ex-ante* control in certain areas, such as competition law, as well as a more regulatory approach in general. Particular attention is given to the constitutional principles of digital transparency and digital sovereignty, which promise much fairer and more trustworthy internet services for end users and businesses alike. Nevertheless, neither of these rights is absolute; they have to be weighed against other rights and principles for the most optimum outcome – either at the legislative level or otherwise at a later stage via judicial review.

As has been argued, such a balance can be achieved not only by looking at the individual legislative acts – the DSA and DMA – but perhaps even more so by perceiving them as being two sides of the same coin. The enshrined principles of digital transparency and digital sovereignty respectively create certain cross-benefits for the addressed service providers and gatekeepers which must be weighed against the obligations imposed on them and which introduces a more solidarity-based set of values. The in-built dialogue mechanism further ensures – in theory at least – ample opportunity for a balancing of benefits and obligations on a case-by-case basis. It remains to be seen whether the newly introduced regulations will deliver on the expectations in practice. After all, the balance mentioned in the beginning only constitutes a fine line between being ineffective at one end of the spectrum or arbitrary and protectionist at the other.

6

Product Liability in the Future Framework of AI (Technology) Regulation

BÉATRICE SCHÜTTE*

I. INTRODUCTION

THE 1985 PRODUCT Liability Directive[1] (1985 PLD[2]) has been one of the centrepieces of the Single Market with regard to consumer protection as it established a harmonised system of compensation for people suffering physical harm or property damage due to defective products.[3,4] The producer may be liable irrespective of negligence or fault on their part.[5] Ever since the PLD entered into force, discussions have been ongoing regarding whether the

* Postdoctoral Researcher at University of Lapland, Faculty of Law. This research has been conducted with the help of project funding granted by the Academy of Finland, decision number 330884 (2020). All online sources were last accessed on 22 April 2023. The author would like to thank the editors for the possibility of presenting and publishing her research, and for their support during the process. Special thanks also to Louise Ratford for language editing.

[1] Council Directive 85/374/EEC of 25 July 1985 on the approximation of the laws, regulations and administrative provisions of the Member States concerning liability for defective products [1985] OJ L210/29.

[2] To ensure the distinction between the two documents, the Directive from 1985 will be called 1985 PLD, whereas the proposal will be referred to as the 'new PLD'.

[3] Ecommerce Europe, 'The European Commission Proposes Revision of the Product Liability Directive' (11 October 2022), available at https://ecommerce-europe.eu/news-item/the-european-commission-proposes-revision-of-the-product-liability-directive/; European Commission, 'Proposal for a Directive of the European Parliament and of the Council on Liability for Defective Products' COM(2022) 495 final ('PLD Proposal'), Explanatory Memorandum, 1.

[4] European Commission, 'Commission Staff Working Document: Impact Assessment Accompanying the Document Proposal for a Regulation of the European Parliament and of the Council on general product safety, amending Regulation (EU) No 1025/2012 of the European Parliament and of the Council, and repealing Council Directive 87/357/EEC and Directive 2001/95/EC of the European Parliament and of the Council' SWD(2021) 169 final p 10/11 ('Impact Assessment Product Safety SWD'), available at https://eur-lex.europa.eu/LexUriServ/LexUriServ.do?uri=SWD:2021:0168:FIN:EN:PDF.

[5] See, eg, European Commission, 'Liability of Defective Products', available at https://ec.europa.eu/growth/single-market/goods/free-movement-sectors/liability-defective-products_en.

framework is fit for purpose and whether it can sufficiently accommodate new developments in line with technical progress.[6] Over the decades, the ways of producing, distributing and marketing products have undergone significant changes: digital products learn, interact with other products and receive regular updates. The development of the circular economy has led to a market for refurbished products, ie, used products that have been given a general overhaul and re-sold by a commercial operator.[7] In 2017, EU institutions started acknowledging the necessity to regulate emerging technologies such as artificial intelligence (AI). Since then, several policy papers and legislative proposals have been issued.[8] However, product liability remained untouched for some years.

In September 2022, the European Commission ('Commission') finally issued the proposal for a revised Directive (new PLD)[9] aiming at responding to the need to revisit central concepts such as product, producer or defectiveness in order to make the framework fit for the digital age. At the same time, it continues to cover 'traditional' consumer products, that is, those without implemented technological features. In March 2024, a revised version of the proposal was adopted by the European Parliament.[10] The text has since been approved by the Council of the EU. However, product liability is, where digital products are concerned, no longer an isolated matter. Instead, it will be embedded in the large body of – existing and planned – AI and technology regulations. Important legislation in this context includes, among others, the Artificial Intelligence Act (AIA),[11] the General Data Protection Regulation (GDPR),[12] the proposed AI Liability

[6] See also, eg, B Schütte, L Majewski and K Havu, 'Damages Liability for Harm Caused by Artificial Intelligence – EU Law in Flux' (*University of Helsinki Legal Studies Research Paper Series, Paper no 69*, 7, 2 August 2021), available at <https://papers.ssrn.com/sol3/papers.cfm?abstract_id=3897839.

[7] See, eg, Ecommerce Europe (n 3); European Commission, 'Questions and Answers on the Revision of the Product Liability Directive' (28 September 2022), available at https://ec.europa.eu/commission/presscorner/detail/en/QANDA_22_5791.

[8] See, eg, European Commission, 'White Paper On Artificial Intelligence – A European Approach to Excellence and Trust' COM (2020) 65 final (hereafter 'White Paper'), available at https://ec.europa.eu/info/publications/white-paper-artificial-intelligence-european-approach-excellence-and-trust_en; European Commission, 'Report on the Safety and Liability Implications of AI, the Internet of Things and Robotics' COM (2020) 64 final (hereafter 'Safety and Liability Report'), available at https://ec.europa.eu/info/publications/commission-report-safety-and-liability-implications-ai-internet-things-and-robotics-0_en; European Commission, 'Proposal for a Regulation of the European Parliament and of the Council Laying Down Harmonised Rules on Artificial Intelligence (Artificial Intelligence Act)', 2021/0106 (COD) ('AI Act').

[9] European Commission, PLD Proposal (n 3).

[10] European Parliament legislative resolution of 12 March 2024 on the proposal for a directive of the European Parliament and of the Council on liability for defective products (COM(2022)0495 – C9-0322/2022 – 2022/0302(COD)).

[11] Regulation (EU) 2024/1689 of the European Parliament and of the Council of 13 June 2024 laying down harmonised rules on artificial intelligence and amending Regulations (EC) No 300/2008, (EU) No 167/2013, (EU) No 168/2013, (EU) 2018/858, (EU) 2018/1139 and (EU) 2019/2144 and Directives 2014/90/EU, (EU) 2016/797 and (EU) 2020/1828 (Artificial Intelligence Act) [2024] OJ L2024/1689.

[12] Regulation (EU) 2016/679 of the European Parliament and of the Council of 27 April 2016 on the protection of natural persons with regard to the processing of personal data and on the free movement of such data, and repealing Directive 95/46/EC (General Data Protection Regulation or GDPR) [2016] OJ L119/1.

Directive (AILD),[13] the Sale of Goods Directive (SGD)[14] or the Digital Content Directive (DCD).[15]

This contribution will examine how product liability will be incorporated in said comprehensive framework. Due to its large scope, this analysis will focus on selected existing and planned regulations that are most relevant for questions relating to product liability.

One function of product liability legislation is to complement product safety legislation: While the latter is designed to ensure that only safe products should become available on the market, the former provides remedies in the situation where a defective, thus unsafe, product has caused damage.[16] Therefore, it is paramount that product safety and product liability legislation be properly aligned.

To this end, section II will present the new PLD and highlight the most relevant changes made to the 1985 PLD. Section III will take a look at selected pieces of legislation that are part of the bigger body of technology regulation. In section IV, there will be an analysis of the interplay of these laws in their current versions.

II. PRODUCT LIABILITY REVISITED – NOW FIT FOR PURPOSE?

With the new PLD, the Commission aims at tackling the challenges posed by both the modern digital and the circular economy as well as related issues addressed in scholarly discussions and policy papers.[17] It shall be consistent with existing provisions in the same policy area.[18] Previously, discussions on whether the 1985 PLD was fit for the digital age related to all the requirements of product liability.

[13] European Commission, 'Proposal for a Directive of the European Parliament and of the Council on Adapting Non-Contractual Civil Liability Rules to Artificial Intelligence (AI Liability Directive)' COM(2022) 496 final ('AILD Proposal').

[14] Directive (EU) 2019/771 of the European Parliament and of the Council of 20 May 2019 on certain aspects concerning contracts for the sale of goods, amending Regulation (EU) 2017/2394 and Directive 2009/22/EC, and repealing Directive 1999/44/EC [2019] OJ L136/28.

[15] Directive (EU) 2019/770 of the European Parliament and of the Council of 20 May 2019 on certain aspects concerning contracts for the supply of digital content and digital services [2019] OJ L136/1.

[16] A Bertolini, 'Artificial Intelligence and Civil Liability, (European Union, 2020) 47, 48, 50, 51, available at <www.europarl.europa.eu/thinktank/en/document/IPOL_STU(2020)621926.

[17] See, eg, European Commission, 'PLD Proposal' (n 3) Explanatory Memorandum, 1; European Commission, 'White Paper' and 'Safety and Liability Report' (n 8); European Commission, 'Report from the Commission to the European Parliament, the Council and the European Economic and Social Committee on the Application of the Council Directive on the Approximation of the Laws, Regulations, and Administrative Provisions of the Member States Concerning Liability for Defective Products (85/374/EEC)' COM(2018) 246 final, available at https://eur-lex.europa.eu/legal-content/EN/TXT/?uri=COM:2018:246:FIN; C Twigg-Flesner, 'Guiding Principles for Updating the Product Liability Directive for the Digital Age' (*Pilot ELI Innovation Paper, European Law Institute*, January 2021), available at https://ssrn.com/abstract=3770796.

[18] PLD Proposal, ibid 2.

Also the European Parliament (EP) emphasised the need for liability rules to be adapted to the digital age so that consumers suffering damage from digital products might enjoy the same level of protection as users of traditional products.[19]

A. The Notion of a Product

Whereas Article 2 of the 1985 PLD defines *products* as 'all movables, including electricity', the new PLD[20] significantly extends the scope, aiming at addressing unclarities that have also been addressed previously in scholarship and policy papers.[21] Pursuant to Article 4(1) of the new PLD, 'product' now explicitly includes software and digital manufacturing files. Only free and open-source software supplies outside a commercial activity should be excluded from the scope.[22] Developers of open-source software often work on such programs during their spare time and without remuneration. The risk of incurring liability under the PLD could discourage such important activities.[23] In addition, the provision also refers to the possible interconnectedness with other movables or immovables. Including digital manufacturing files under the scope of a product allows to conclude that not all digital data can be considered products.[24]

AI applications were always considered products under the PLD if they were movable items or incorporated in movable items. The new proposal answers the highly disputed question of whether or not software, particularly when supplied as standalone software, would be a product in the purview of the Directive. Both in its evaluation of the PLD and in the Safety and Liability Report, the Commission had proposed a further clarification of the definition of a product and to consider the complexity of emerging technologies, to ensure that damage caused by products that are defective due to digital features can be compensated.[25] Nowadays, software is often downloaded, thus an intangible good and not in the purview of the 1985 PLD. With the new PLD, it is no longer required that products be tangible. Clarification regarding the applicability of rules relating to product liability is necessary as the number of connected

[19] ibid Explanatory Memorandum, 1 2.

[20] For the purpose of this analysis, the text adopted on 12 March 2024 by the European Parliament will be used. See Position of the European Parliament adopted at first reading on 12 March 2024 with a view to the adoption of Directive (EU) 2024/ … of the European Parliament and of the Council on liability for defective products and repealing Council Directive 85/374/EEC ('PLD Proposal as of 12 March 2024').

[21] See, eg, Twigg-Flesner (n 17).

[22] See European Commission, 'PLD Proposal' (n 3), recital 13.

[23] P Hacker, 'The European AI Liability Directives – Critique of a Half-Hearted Approach and Lessons for the Future', Working Paper, 15, available at https://ssrn.com/abstract=4279796.

[24] See also S Li and B Schütte, 'The Proposal for a Revised Product Liability Directive: The Emperor's New Clothes?' (2023) *Maastricht Journal of European and Comparative Law* 30(5), 576.

[25] European Commission, 'Evaluation of Council Directive 85/374/EEC' (Working document) (2020) 23–24; European Commission, 'Safety and Liability Report' (n 8) 13.

devices is constantly increasing. In 2019, there were an estimated 14.2 billion connected devices worldwide. By 2025, it is expected that in Europe alone there will be almost five billion connected devices.[26]

B. The 'Producer'

The new PLD contains one notable change in terminology: it no longer holds solely 'the producer' liable for 'damage caused by a defect in his product', but instead, in its Article 1, 'lays down common rules on the liability of economic operators for damage suffered by natural persons and caused by defective products …'. Also, further on in Article 4(10), the new PLD defines the 'manufacturer' instead of a producer. The features of modern consumer products are often determined by software and digital services provided by parties other than the manufacturer of the finished product.[27]

The manufacturer is defined as

> any natural or legal person who develops, manufactures or produces a product or has a product designed or manufactured, or who, by putting their name, trademark or other distinguishing features on that product presents themselves as its manufacturer, or develops, manufactures or produces a product for that person's own use.[28]

The new terminology shows that the circle of potentially liable persons has been extended compared to the 1985 PLD. Already there, the scope of producers is broad and includes importers and any supplier if the actual producer cannot be identified, so that the injured party is provided with an accessible defendant.[29] The reason why the range of economic operators has been broadened is that an increasing number of products are being manufactured outside the EU.[30] The new PLD adds the fulfilment service provider, the authorised representative and the provider of a related service to the group of potentially liable persons.[31] The latter can be seen as an exception since the PLD in general applies only to products and not to services.[32]

Article 8 of the new PLD lists the economic operators that are liable for damage caused by defective products. In view of the increasing circular economy, this also includes, pursuant to Article 8(2), refurbishers, ie, any natural or legal person modifying a product that has already been placed on the market

[26] European Commission, 'Impact Assessment Product Safety SWD' (n 4), 11.

[27] European Commission, 'Commission Staff Working Document Impact Assessment Report Accompanying the Document Proposal for a Directive of the European Parliament and of the Council on Liability for Defective Products' SWD(2022) 316 final, 11 ('Impact Assessment PLD Proposal').

[28] European Parliament, PLD Proposal as of 12 March 2024 (n 20), Art 4 (10).

[29] Twigg-Flesner (n 17) 3.

[30] European Commission, 'PLD Proposal' (n 3) Explanatory Memorandum, 12.

[31] Hacker (n 23) 16.

[32] ibid.

when the modification is substantial and undertaken outside the original manufacturer's control.

In addition, the draft PLD lays down in Article 8(1)(c) that Member States shall ensure that, where the manufacturer is established outside the EU, the importer and the authorised representative can be held liable. If neither of those two operators can be identified, Article 8(3) provides the possibility of placing liability on each distributor if the injured party requires them to identify a manufacturer of the product or a component established in the EU, or the importer or authorised representative, and the distributor fails to do so within one month of the request. In the 1985 PLD, the 'distributor' was called the supplier, however, the prerequisites of holding the distributor liable have been formulated in a clearer way. Finally, also online platform providers allowing consumers to conclude distance contracts with traders can be liable, provided that the conditions set out in Article 6(3) of the Digital Services Act[33] are met. Including distributors and online intermediaries constitutes an adaptation of the liability regime to globalised value chains and reflects the EU legislator's efforts in providing the injured party with an EU-based defendant.[34] With regard to AI-enabled products, it is relevant that also AI-system providers can be manufacturers in the purview of the Directive.[35]

C. Defectiveness

In terms of the defectiveness of a product, the new PLD makes reference to the ever-growing number of digital products available on the market. Article 7 of the new PLD starts almost identically to Article 6(1) of the 1985 PLD, setting out that 'a product is defective when it does not provide the safety 'that a person is entitled to expect'. However, the new PLD adds 'or that is required under Union or national law'. Both directives request that all circumstances be taken into account. Recital 30 clarifies that Article 7 refers to the public at large and not to the safety a particular person is entitled to expect. The list of circumstances to take into account has been significantly extended in the new PLD: the presentation of the product now also includes the instructions for installation, use and maintenance. Yet, this does not mean that warnings and information can make an otherwise defective product safe.[36] Like Article 6 (1) (b) of the 1985 PLD, Article 7(2)(b) of the new PLD sets out that the reasonably foreseeable

[33] Regulation (EU) 2022/2065 of the European Parliament and of the Council of 19 October 2022 on a Single Market For Digital Services and amending Directive 2000/31/EC (Digital Services Act) [2022] OJ L277/1.

[34] See also Li and Schütte (n 24), 589, 590.

[35] European Commission, 'PLD Proposal' (n 3) Explanatory Memorandum, 3.

[36] PLD Proposal as of 12 March 2024 (n 20) recital 31.

use of a product must be considered in assessing whether it is defective or not. Recital 31 to the new PLD also suggests that this should include 'misuse that is not unreasonable under the circumstances …'. This can relate to, for instance behaviour resulting from a lack of concentration while using machinery or the foreseeable behaviour of certain user groups such as children.[37] Further relevant factors are the ability to continue to learn after deployment and its impact on the product, interaction with other products, product safety and cybersecurity requirements and interventions by regulatory authorities and economic operators mentioned in Article 8 of the new PLD. As regards the question when a product is to be regarded as defective, the 'time when the product was put into circulation'[38] has been supplemented with 'the moment in time when the product left the control of the manufacturer'.[39] Finally, the specific expectations of end-users for whom the product is intended are now also considered relevant when assessing defectiveness.[40]

Under the 1985 PLD, determining defectiveness has been particularly challenging with regard to software or algorithms, as defects and even malfunctions are not always directly obvious.[41] While the new PLD presents a longer list of circumstances to consider when assessing whether a product is defective, it does not suggest any concrete criteria. Although it is clear that it is hard or even impossible to establish criteria that can be applied to a wide array of products, clarification with regard to some points is desirable. For instance, Article 7 and Recital 34 refer to product safety and the necessity to take it into consideration. With regard to interventions by regulatory authorities such as product recalls, Recital 34 states that they do not automatically lead to a presumption of defectiveness. However, it is not explicitly stated whether a product that does not meet the requirements enshrined in general or specialised product safety legislation is automatically presumed to be defective. This has been previously suggested by academics.[42] Especially with regard to AI products, Hacker, for instance, suggests that the failure to use explainable AI could constitute defectiveness.[43] It would also make it easier for the claimant to obtain compensation as the need to prove the defect in more detail would become obsolete.

[37] ibid.
[38] 1985 PLD (n 1) Art 6(1) (c).
[39] PLD Proposal as of 12 March 2024 (n 20) Art 7(2).
[40] ibid Art 7(2)(h).
[41] See also, eg, B Schütte and L Majewski, 'Private Liability for AI-Related Harm: Towards More Predictable Rules for the Single Market' (2022) *Market and Competition Law Review* 6(1), 141, available at https://doi.org/10.34632/mclawreview.2022.10741; J-S Borghetti, 'How Can Artificial Intelligence be Defective?' in S Lohsse, R Schulze and D Staudenmayer (eds), *Liability for Artificial Intelligence and the Internet of Things* (Hart Publishing, 2019) 66.
[42] See, eg, G Howells, C Twigg-Flesner and T Wilhelmsson, *Rethinking EU Consumer Law* (Routledge, 2017) 267.
[43] Hacker (n 23) 58.

D. Damage

The new PLD provides a wider notion of damage compared to the 1985 PLD with regard to damage in Article 6. Personal injury will in the future also include medically recognised harm to psychological health.[44] While the 1985 PLD states that the provision on damage is without prejudice no national law provisions on non-material damage, the new PLD sets out that the right to compensation covers also non-material losses resulting from damage referred to in Article 6(1). Yet, pursuant to Article 6(3) and Recital 24, the new PLD does not affect the recoverability of other types of harm under other liability regimes. People suffering such harm due to a defective product may therefore resort, for instance, to the applicable national tort law if they wish to file a corresponding damages claim.

In terms of property damage, the new PLD protects any property owned by a natural person, except the defective product itself, a product damaged by a defective component of that product and property used exclusively for professional purposes. That means, property used for mixed purposes, ie private and professional, is now protected under the scope of the directive as many items, such as computers, mobile phones or cars, are increasingly used that way.[45]

Under the 1985 PLD, the question regarding whether 'property' relates to tangibles or intangibles is often raised, particularly with regard to whether damage to data is recoverable.[46] The scope of property, including the point of whether and to what extent it extends to data, is regulated in the national laws of the Member States.[47] A malfunction of a computer may cause the loss of data stored on a connected external hard drive without causing physical damage to the drive. People are storing large amounts of potentially important data on such drives or USB sticks, and the loss of or damage to these data can be detrimental for the injured party. To achieve a level playing field in this context, the recoverability of damage resulting from loss or corruption of data not exclusively used for professional purposes is now included in the new PLD.[48]

Laudably, the new PLD no longer contains the 500 Euro threshold in relation to property damage as per Article 9(b) of the 1985 PLD. Its purpose was to prevent excessive litigation.[49]

[44] PLD Proposal as of 12 March 2024 (n 20) recital 21 suggests that this could be the case if the injured party's general state of health is affected, and therapy or medical treatment are required.

[45] See ibid Art 6(1)(b).

[46] See, eg, BA Koch, 'Product Liability 2.0 – Mere Update or New Version?' in Lohsse, Schulze and Staudenmayer (n 41) 103.

[47] European Commission, 'Impact Assessment PLD Proposal' (n 27) 16.

[48] See PLD Proposal as of 12 March 2024 (n 20) recital 20 and Art 6(1)(c).

[49] European Commission, 'Impact Assessment PLD Proposal' (n 27) 22.

E. Defences

Article 11 of the new PLD addresses exemptions from liability. As in the 1985 PLD, the respective economic operators are not liable if they prove that they did not place the product on the market, put it into service or made it available.[50] The new version of this defence is slightly more differentiated compared to the 1985 PLD, taking up the increased number of economic operators that are potentially liable. The much-disputed[51] development risk defence has been kept in Article 11(1)(e) of the new PLD.

The defence in relation to the defectiveness causing the damage not existing when the product was placed on the market has been reissued in a more differentiated manner, taking into consideration that modern digital products change after being placed on the market: the economic operator cannot resort to the defence if the defect is due to a related service or software, including upgrades and updated under the manufacturer's control. The same applies in case of a lack of software updates or upgrades necessary to maintain the safety of the product or a substantial modification of the product.[52]

Article 11(1)(g) of the new PLD introduces a new defence for refurbishers: they are not liable if the defectiveness causing the damage is related to a part not affected by the modification. The defence regarding compliance with mandatory regulations and the economic operator not being the one making the product available remain basically unchanged, except for the adjustment of the different economic operators.

F. Disclosure of Evidence

The duty to disclose evidence pursuant to Article 9 of the new PLD cannot be found in the 1985 PLD. This provision relates to the complexity of modern digital products such as AI systems and the information asymmetry between the potential claimant and the defendant.[53] The duty to disclose relevant evidence at their disposal can be placed upon defendants in product liability proceedings before national courts. An injured party claiming compensation can request the court to order such disclosure if they present facts and evidence supporting the plausibility of their claim. The courts cannot order such disclosure at their own initiative.[54]

[50] See European Commission, 'PLD Proposal' (n 3) Art 10(1)(a) and (b).

[51] See, eg, Twigg-Flesner (n 17) 10; Schütte and Majewski (n 41) 144, 145 with further references.

[52] PLD Proposal as of 12 March 2024 (n 20) Art 11(2).

[53] See also Li and Schütte (n 24) 591.

[54] PLD Proposal as of 12 March 2024 (n 20) Art 9(1).

Disclosure must be limited to what is necessary and proportionate, considering all the legitimate interests of all parties, including any third parties concerned. When information that needs to be disclosed concerns trade secrets or alleged trade secrets, courts must take the necessary measures to preserve the confidentiality of that information.[55] A similar duty has been introduced in the proposal for the Directive on AI Liability in its Article 3. However, the duty to disclose evidence under the scope of the AI Liability Directive is more extensive as also 'potential claimants' may request the disclosure of such evidence before they decide whether to file a damages claim.

G. Burden of Proof

Just like under the 1985 PLD, the claimant must prove the defectiveness of the product, the damage suffered and the causal link between the two.[56] There has been an ongoing discussion for a long time relating to the practical difficulty for injured parties to actually provide the required proof. The issue was also taken up in documents issued by EU institutions such as evaluation reports concerning the PLD or the White Paper.[57]

To alleviate the injured party's burden of proof, the new PLD introduces a presumption of defectiveness and a presumption of causation in Article 10. Due to the increasing complexity of modern consumer products, injured parties can face substantial obstacles in proving their claim.[58] The presumption of defectiveness in Article 10(2) shall apply in cases where the defendant has failed to disclose evidence in accordance with Article 9, where the claimant establishes that the product does not comply with mandatory safety requirements laid down in Union law or national law designed to prevent the damage that has occurred or where the claimant establishes that the damage was caused by an obvious malfunction of the product during reasonably foreseeable use or under ordinary circumstances.

Article 10(3) establishes a presumption of causation when it has been established that the product is defective, and the damage caused is consistent with the respective defect. Article 10(4) contains a presumption for cases where it is excessively difficult for the claimant to prove anything of what is required,

[55] ibid Art 9(3) and (4).

[56] See 1985 PLD (n 1) Art 4 and PLD Proposal as of 12 March 2024 (n 20) Art 10.

[57] See, eg, Schütte, Majewski and Havu (n 6) 8, 9; European Commission, 'Evaluation of Council Directive 85/374/EEC' (n 25) 25; European Commission, 'Third Report on the Application of Council Directive on the Approximation of Laws, Regulations and Administrative Provisions of the Member States Concerning Liability for Defective Products (85/374/EEC of 25 July 1985, amended by Directive 1999/34/EC of the European Parliament and of the Council of 10 May 1999)' COM (2006) 496 final 9; European Commission 'White Paper' (n 8) 13.

[58] See also See also Li and Schütte (n 24) 592.

provided that the claimant has demonstrated, based on sufficiently relevant evidence that the product contributed to the damage and that it is likely that the product was defective or that its defectiveness was a likely cause of the damage, or both. According to Article 10(4), the defendant may contest the existence of excessive difficulties, and according to Article 10(5), they can rebut any of the presumptions.

H. Definitions

In its Article 4, the new PLD contains an extensive list of definitions of crucial terms. Besides the above mentioned 'product', 'damage' or 'manufacturer', it also defines 'component', 'making available on the market' or the 'manufacturer's control'. With this, clarification is provided and therewith legal certainty for all stakeholders involved. So component parts can be intangible, for instance, and even simply related services can constitute component parts. This avoids the need for lengthy scholarly discussions or the need to await court decisions in order to be provided with definitions. Yet, this does not mean that there will never be borderline cases giving rise to discussions or requiring clarification in court. In addition, further technological development can lead to modifications of, for instance, the scope of the manufacturer's control, types of component parts or even the scope of the notion of a product. It cannot be taken for granted that these definitions are future-proof.

III. THE INCORPORATION OF PRODUCT LIABILITY IN THE OVERALL REGULATORY FRAMEWORK

As mentioned above, with the ongoing digitalisation, product liability cannot be viewed as an isolated matter. Instead, the legislation is incorporated into the broader framework of technology regulation, which is currently undergoing amendments in order to mitigate the risks linked to digital technologies.[59] In the new PLD, several references are made to other Union legislation, both specifically related to new technologies and also to more conventional technologies. This section will address the critical points regarding a seamless integration of the multitude of applicable – existing and planned – frameworks. Relevant in this context are the General Product Safety framework, the AI Act, the AI Liability Directive, the GDPR and other frameworks. The aforementioned pieces of legislation will be analysed in more detail below.

[59] European Commission, 'PLD Proposal' (n 3) Explanatory Memorandum, 4.

A. The General Product Safety Framework

As mentioned above, product liability and product safety complement each other and shall ensure a high level of safety for consumers and good access to remedies in case they suffer damage due to a defective and thus unsafe product. The central piece of product safety legislation is the General Product Safety Directive (GPSD),[60] which applies to non-food consumer products not covered by specific legislation.[61]

Although the GPSD is significantly younger than the PLD, its applicability to new technologies, and particularly AI-related devices, is not straightforward. It does not explicitly address the fact that digital features like AI can have an impact on product safety.[62] When the legal framework on product safety first entered into force, products related to the internet of things and other sophisticated AI-driven devices neither existed nor were they anticipated.[63] Thus, the Commission acknowledged that new technologies pose challenges to the concepts and definitions used under the GPSD. New technology-based products bring new risks to consumers' health and safety, or they can change the way the existing risks might materialise. Consumer products may be affected by these new risks, such as cybersecurity threats.[64]

In response to these challenges, the Commission published in June 2021 a proposal for a General Product Safety Regulation (GPSR) (as well as a Staff-Working Document (SWD)) assessing the impact of a revision of the GPSD. The proposal aimed to strengthen the protection of safety and health for European consumers and to guarantee their right to information.[65] The new GPSR has been adopted and will be applicable from December 2024.

The new Regulation thus makes a clear reference to interconnected devices. Remarkably, it neither refers to 'movables' as in the PLD, nor does it continue to use 'any products' as under the GPSD, but instead introduces the new term

[60] Directive 2001/95/EC of the European Parliament and of the Council of 3 December 2001 on general product safety [2002] OJ L11/4.

[61] Such as medical devices or toys, see, eg, Regulation (EU) 2017/745 of the European Parliament and of the Council of 5 April 2017 on medical devices, amending Directive 2001/83/EC, Regulation (EC) No 178/2002 and Regulation (EC) No 1223/2009 and repealing Council Directives 90/385/EEC and 93/42/EEC [2017] OJ L117/1. and Directive 2009/48/EC of the European Parliament and of the Council of 18 June 2009 on the safety of toys [2009] OJ L170/1.

[62] European Commission, 'Impact Assessment Product Safety SWD' (n 4) 12.

[63] G Mazzini 'A System of Governance for Artificial Intelligence through the Lens of Emerging Intersections between AI and EU Law' (9 April 2019) 7, available at <https://papers.ssrn.com/sol3/papers.cfm?abstract_id=3369266.

[64] European Commission, 'Impact Assessment Product Safety SWD' (n 4) 12.

[65] Proposal for a Regulation of the European Parliament and of the Council on general product safety, amending Regulation (EU) No 1025/2012 of the European Parliament and of the Council, and repealing Council Directive 87/357/EEC and Directive 2001/95/EC of the European Parliament and of the Council COM(2021) 346 final (hereafter: GPSR) 14, available at https://eur-lex.europa.eu/legal-content/EN/TXT/?uri=CELEX%3A52021PC0346.

'item'. While the reference to interconnectedness acknowledges the technological development to a certain extent, the new Regulation fails to clarify whether 'item' refers to tangibles only or whether it includes intangibles such as standalone software or data. The recitals do not provide any clarification in this regard. Since the Commission has clarified in the new PLD that software is a product in the purview of the Directive, this means that the frameworks, which are meant to complement each other, provide different definitions of a product, which is the central term. This is suboptimal in view of the goal of establishing a level playing field and providing legal certainty. Therefore, the EU institutions should either change the definition of a product in the GPSR so that it is identical with the one in the draft PLD, or they should reformulate both provisions so as to provide a uniform definition of a product in both future pieces of legislation. At the very least, clarification as to whether 'items' can also be software should be provided.

B. The AI Act

In April 2021, the Commission presented a proposal for the AI Act as the first attempt worldwide at comprehensively regulating AI. After a three-year process, the AI Act entered into force in August 2024.[66] It brings up many aspects discussed in policy papers previously issued by EU institutions. The AI Act is often called a specialised product safety framework[67] and can therefore have relevance for product liability, also due to the fact that safety and liability rules complement each other. While it aims at maximum harmonisation, it does not include any private law remedies.[68]

One of the central aspects is the so-called risk-based approach. The risk classification determines certain obligations of providers and users, and procedures such as a conformity assessment. Based on a 'pyramid of criticality', there are four risk categories for AI systems: unacceptable risk, high risk, low risk and minimal risk.[69] AI systems presenting unacceptable risks, because they are incompatible

[66] European Commission, 'European Artificial Intelligence Act Comes into Force' (Press Release, 1 August 2024), available at https://ec.europa.eu/commission/presscorner/detail/en/IP_24_4123; Regulation (EU) 2024/1689 of the European Parliament and the Council of 13 June 2024 laying down harmonised rules on artificial intelligence and amending Regulations (EC) No 300/2008, (EU) No 167/2013, (EU) No 168/2013, (EU) 2018/858, (EU) 2018/1139 and (EU) 2019/2144 and Directives 2014/90/EU, (EU) 2016/797 and (EU) 2020/1828 (Artificial Intelligence Act or AI Act) [2024] OJ L2024/1689.

[67] See, eg, T de Graaf and G Veldt, 'The AI Act and Its Impact on Product Safety, Contracts and Liability' (2022) *European Review of Private Law* 5-2022, 804, 806.

[68] ibid 807.

[69] M Kop, 'EU Artificial Intelligence Act: The European Approach to AI' (2021) *Transatlantic Antitrust and IPR Developments* 2, available at https://law.stanford.edu/publications/eu-artificial-intelligence-act-the-european-approach-to-ai/.

with the core values of the EU, will be banned.[70] Minimal-risk systems will not be subject to specific regulation. Low-risk AI will be subject to certain transparency obligations. The main regulatory target under the scope of the AI Act are the high-risk AI systems. The related requirements set out in Articles 9 to 27 of the AI Act must be met. These include transparency and human oversight, risk management and accuracy, robustness and cybersecurity. Stakeholders in the value chain have obligations such as ensuring compliance with the requirements or ensuring that the systems undergo conformity assessments and are registered.[71]

There are two categories of high-risk AI systems: AI systems that are products or safety components of products covered by certain Union health and safety harmonisation legislation (eg, toys, machinery, medical devices) listed in Annex II to the AI Act and AI systems used in specific areas (eg, immigration, law enforcement, critical infrastructure) listed in Annex III to the AI Act.[72] It is currently estimated that the majority of AI systems on the market are low-risk, ie not subject to regulation or only to minor obligations.[73] For product liability, mainly AI systems falling under the scope of harmonisation legislation listed in Annex I will be relevant, such as toys.

The AI Act does not contain any provisions concerning enabling individuals to seek redress if their rights were interfered with in the course of the operation of an AI system.[74] This points towards the intention of the EU legislator to keep frameworks on safety and liability separate from each other. The new PLD does not make any clear reference to the AI Act,[75] yet, as mentioned above, questions of product safety are relevant in order to determine the defectiveness of a product. Article 7(1) of the new PLD explicitly mentions the safety required under Union law. Since the AI Act regulates the safety of AI systems, it will be relevant in this context in the future. For instance, Article 7(f) of the new PLD, which sets out that a product can be defective if it does not meet relevant cybersecurity requirements, can be linked to Article 15 of the AI Act, which regulates accuracy, robustness and cybersecurity. Measures must be adapted to the circumstances, for instance, the way an AI-enabled consumer product is used.

[70] J Chamberlain, 'The Risk-Based Approach of the European Union's Proposed Artificial Intelligence Regulation: Some Comments from a Tort Law Perspective' (2022) *European Journal of Risk Regulation* 5.

[71] See, eg, AI Act (n 66) Art 16.

[72] See also M Veale, F Zuiderveen Borgesius, 'Demystifying the Draft EU Artificial Intelligence Act' (2021) *Computer Law Review International* 4, 102.

[73] European Parliament, 'Artificial Intelligence in a Digital Age', European Parliament resolution of 3 May 2022 on artificial intelligence in a digital age (2020/2266(INI)), available at www.europarl.europa.eu/doceo/document/TA-9-2022-0140_EN.html.

[74] N Smuha, E Ahmed-Rengers et al, 'How the EU Can Achieve Legally Trustworthy AI: A Response to the European Commission's Proposal for an Artificial Intelligence Act" (2021) 45, available at https://ssrn.com/abstract=3899991.

[75] Hacker (n 23) 14.

C. The AI Liability Directive

The Commission published a proposal for an AI Liability Directive (AILD)[76] at the same time as the proposal for the new PLD. In the process leading up to the proposal, it stated that the current national rules on tort liability were ill-suited to accommodating technological developments.[77]

While the new PLD continues to introduce strict liability, the AILD applies, according to its Article 1(2), to non-contractual fault-based claims. As opposed to the new PLD, the AILD proposal does not contain any actual liability rules. Instead, it focuses on procedural aspects. As mentioned above, it introduces rules on the disclosure of evidence in Article 3, alongside a presumption of non-compliance, and a presumption of causation in Article 4. These presumptions shall alleviate the burden of proof of an injured party when an AI system is involved, due to the complexity of systems and information asymmetry. At least in relation to high-risk AI systems, the AI Act sets out the obligation to generate logs, which leads to the provider of an AI system having potential evidence at their disposal. This underlines the intention of having safety and liability legislation complementing one another.[78]

Under the scope of the AILD, also a 'potential claimant', namely a person who has not actually filed a claim yet, can request the disclosure of evidence.[79] The presumptions of non-compliance and causation are nuanced according to the risk profile of AI systems and tailored to the obligations of providers and deployers of AI systems under the AI Act.[80]

For the actual rules on liability, the AILD proposal refers to the national laws of the Member States.[81] This is in complete contrast to the proposal for a Regulation issued by the European Parliament in October 2020, which contained an actual civil liability regime with the liability of the operator of an AI system at its core.[82] The PLD and the AILD have overlapping areas of application as the provider of an AI system can also be the producer and thus liable according to both product liability and AI liability. As the AI liability refers to national laws, injured parties might even be able to recover non-material harm or pure economic loss, if the applicable national tort law rules provide for it, and if the

[76] See AILD Proposal (n 13).

[77] ibid Explanatory Memorandum, 1.

[78] See also S Li and B Schütte, 'The Proposed EU Artificial Intelligence Liability Directive Does/Will Its Content Reflect Its Ambition?' (2024) *Technology&Regulation* 146, available at https://doi.org/10.26116/techreg.2024.014.

[79] AILD Proposal (n 13), Art 3(1) AILD.

[80] AILD Proposal (n 13), Art 4 AILD.

[81] AILD Proposal (n 13), Art 1; Explanatory Memorandum, 11.

[82] European Parliament, 'Civil Liability Regime for Artificial Intelligence, European Parliament Resolution of 20 October 2020 with Recommendations to the Commission on a Civil Liability Regime for Artificial Intelligence (2020/2014(INL)), 2021/C 404/05 [2021] OJ C404/107 (European Parliament, 'Civil Liability Resolution'), available at https://eur-lex.europa.eu/legal-content/EN/TXT/?uri=CELEX:52020IP0276.

defendant was also at fault. The approaches taken in both liability directives are contrasting, ie maximum harmonisation for product liability and minimum harmonisation for AI liability.[83]

D. The Sale of Goods Directive and Digital Content Directive

The SGD and the DCD were adopted in 2019 and deal with contractual liability as opposed to non-contractual liability in the case of the PLD. Both Directives complement each other. Mapping their scope in relation to the product liability framework is relevant as in many EU Member States injured parties can claim damages based on contractual and non-contractual liability at the same time. Consumers are entitled to remedies such as replacement or reimbursement in case the goods or the digital content are not in conformity with the contract or do not work properly.[84] The SGD applies to consumer sales contracts relating to goods, including goods with digital elements. The Directive imposes liability on the seller for the lack of conformity of the goods, and it provides the buyer with a number of remedies in case the goods present a lack of conformity.

The scope of application shows certain parallels in relation to the PLD and the GPSR. A lack of conformity of the goods could, in certain cases, easily be equivalent to a product's defectiveness as under the PLD, or they might not count as 'safe products' as per Article 3(2) of the GPSR.

The notion of 'producer' in Article 2(4) of the SGD seems to have a narrower scope than that included in the PLD, as the latter also includes the producers of raw materials or the manufacturers of component parts. If both Directives are meant to have the same scope in terms of 'producers', this should be clarified. For the purpose of the SGD, it makes sense to not include the supplier under the notion of 'producer' as this is separately covered by the 'seller'.

The DCD applies to consumer contracts for the supply of digital content or digital services. Its Article 2(1) defines digital content as data which are produced and supplied in digital form. Pursuant to Recital 19, this includes computer programs, music files or e-books. As per the new PLD, these would also fall under the scope of 'products'.

The DCD does not apply to goods with digital elements as these are covered by the above-mentioned SGD.[85] It applies in Business-to-Consumer relations when digital content is supplied for a price, which can be money or digital equivalents such as cryptocurrency. In addition, the consumer also provides personal

[83] See AILD Proposal (n 13) recital 14; Bertolini (n 16) 54.

[84] European Commission, 'PLD Proposal' (n 3) Explanatory Memorandum, 2.

[85] See also, eg, H Beale, 'Digital Content Directive and Rules for Contracts on Continuous Supply' (2021) 12 *Journal of Intellectual Property, Information Technology and Electronic Commerce Law* 96.

data to the trader in exchange for the content or services.[86] Even though the Directives are contract law frameworks, the areas of application overlap with those of the PLD. Therefore, consistency, particularly with regard to certain important terms, should be ensured.

E. The General Data Protection Regulation

Relevant with regard to technical products is also the GDPR,[87] which is applicable when processing personal data. Pursuant to Article 4(1) GDPR, 'personal data' means any information relating to an identified or identifiable natural person ('data subject'). Further, Article 2(1) GDPR sets out that it applies only to 'the processing of personal data wholly or partly by automated means and to the processing other than by automated means of personal data which form part of a filing system or are intended to form part of a filing system'. Even minor personal data processing tasks may bring the entire product under the scope of the GDPR's rules. Data protection is particularly relevant with regard to interconnected devices in smart home environments where everyday devices are connected to the Internet and to each other.[88] Article 82 regulates the liability of the controller for damage caused by processing infringing the GDPR. The processor is liable for damage caused by processing only when it is not compliant with the obligations enshrined in the Regulation or where it is outside of the scope or contrary to the lawful instructions of the controller. The data controller is defined in Article 4(7) as 'the natural or legal person, public authority, agency or other body which, alone or jointly with others, determines the purposes and means of the processing of personal data'. The data processor, according to Article 4(8) GDPR, is a 'natural or legal person, public authority, agency or other body which processes personal data on behalf of the controller'. The GDPR can be relevant with regard to product liability as the manufacturer of a connected product may also be a data controller.[89]

Liability under the scope of the GDPR could complement product liability to the extent that under its scope, also non-material harm is recoverable. Thus, if the manufacturer of a defective product qualifies at the same time as a data controller or processor, they could be liable if the product in question for instance violates the consumer's privacy due to its defectiveness.

[86] ibid 97.

[87] GDPR (n 12).

[88] See, eg, V Kenyon and A Davies, 'The Connected Home: From Smart Fish Tanks to Connected Kitchen Appliances, Product Companies Must Navigate GDPR and Product Liability Directive Compliance, Cyber Risk, and Other IoT Challenges' (2019) 2 *The Journal of Robotics, Artificial Intelligence & Law* 39.

[89] ibid 42.

IV. DISCUSSION

The previous two sections give an overview of the new PLD and of other existing and prospective legal frameworks that it will be interacting with in the future. Making product liability and safety regimes – as well as other legislation – fit for the digital age is paramount if the EU does not want to lose the 'race to AI' against the US or China and if it wishes to create an 'ecosystem of excellence'.[90] Regulations and Directives dating from the pre-digital era may be ill-suited to address questions arising in relation to new technologies that either did not exist or were not anticipated at the time these pieces of legislation were enacted. The regulatory gaps and legal uncertainty jeopardise efficient consumer protection – one of the focus areas of EU law. And more importantly, they may have a chilling effect on innovation and hinder the uptake of AI and new technologies.[91]

Since the EU institutions acknowledged the need to regulate emerging technologies such as AI in 2017,[92] legislative proposals and final laws have been issued. Drafting all the relevant legislation at once is of course impossible. While links between the different regulatory frameworks can be established, the development over time also led to inconsistencies.

A seamless interplay is crucial in order to provide overall legal certainty and to achieve the envisioned level playing field.[93] However, the recent proposals might not ensure such a seamless interplay. To start with, different instruments have been chosen: Regulations for the AI Act and the new framework on General Product Safety (the same for the proposed Machinery Regulation), as well as Data Protection, and the Directives for Product Liability and AI liability. While the Regulations will be directly applicable in Member States, the Directives will need to be transposed into national laws. Along with this comes a risk of divergent interpretation by the national legislators, which might result in significantly diverging regulations across Member States. Surprisingly, this is also in contrast with previous discussions in policy papers: it has previously been suggested that AI liability should only take the form of a regulation, and that it should be considered to turn the PLD into a regulation once the regime is being overhauled.[94]

In addition, an inconsistent terminology can also lead to uncertainty with regard to the scope of application of a framework. As mentioned above, the

[90] See, eg, European Commission, 'White Paper' (n 8) 5; E Sánchez Nicolás, 'EU Falling behind in Global AI Race, MEPs Warn' (*euobserver*, 4 May 2022), available at https://euobserver.com/digital/154861.

[91] European Commission, 'White Paper' (n 8) 9, 10.

[92] European Council, European Council meeting (19 October 2017) – Conclusion EUCO 14/17, 2017, 7, available at www.consilium.europa.eu/media/21620/19-euco-final-conclusions-en.pdf.

[93] See also B Schütte, 'AI Regulation in the EU: The Future Interplay Between Frameworks' in E Gill-Pedro and A Moberg (eds), *YSEC Yearbook of Socio-Economic Constitutions* (YSEC Yearbook of Socio-Economic Constitutions, 2024) vol 2023, 40, available at https://doi.org/10.1007/16495_2023_64.

[94] European Parliament, 'Civil Liability Resolution' (n 82) paras 5, 8.

proposals on product liability and general product safety contain differing definitions of the term 'product', the central notion. If this is not remedied in the future, consumer protection will be at risk. In the AILD proposal, the terminology issue was well-solved by referring to the AI Act for important definitions.[95]

Under the scope of the PLD proposal, non-material harm will not be recoverable.[96] However, it has been acknowledged that AI-enabled products especially may pose serious risks to the immaterial interests of consumers.[97] When a producer is also a data controller in the purview of the GDPR, they could be liable for non-material damage caused by data processing that infringes the GDPR. This might prompt producers of consumer goods that also process data to outsource all activities related to data processing. That could mean an additional defendant for an injured party, making the whole process of claiming damages more onerous. In the end, injured parties could be deterred from filing a claim. In any event, non-material harm can result from wrongdoing other than the infringement of data protection rules. For instance, AI-enabled software used to create texts or picture material can create libellous or otherwise offensive content. If such content is made public, for instance on social media, it can cause damage to another person' reputation. To recover such harm, the injured party would have to resort to the applicable national tort law, where they would have to prove the defendant's fault. Therefore, it should be reconsidered to make non-material harm recoverable under the PLD.

Discussions have also been ongoing as to the compatibility of the AI Act and the GDPR. The latter has been criticised for failing to offer sufficient protection in relation to Big Data, and it has been said that the AI Act is not suitable to fill the legal void.[98] It remains to be seen whether such lack of protection has an effect on product liability.

V. CONCLUDING REMARKS

With the new PLD, the Commission is taking an important step to modernise a crucial part of the consumer protection regime. The number of digitalised consumer products has increased over the years, and will keep increasing, likely at an ever-faster pace, in the future.

To draft rules that are actually suitable in practice is challenging: consumer products are becoming more complex every day, and defects and malfunctions

[95] AILD Proposal (n 53) Art 2.

[96] European Commission, 'PLD Proposal' (n 3) Recital 18.

[97] Bertolini (n 16) 59; European Commission, 'White Paper' (n 8) 10–12; European Parliament, 'Civil Liability Resolution' (n 82), Recital 3 of the draft Regulation.

[98] H Ruschemeier, 'AI as a Challenge for Legal Regulation – the Scope of Application of the Artificial Intelligence Act Proposal' (*ERA Forum*, 2023), available at https://doi.org/10.1007/s12027-022-00725-6.

are harder to spot, the more complex these products become. Technological developments are always ahead of legal developments – and the gap is growing. As it is not always possible to anticipate technological developments, it is even more important to keep the existing laws in a shape that allows for easy adjustments to accommodate new developments, and to prevent regulatory gaps.

While the new PLD and other new pieces of legislation and pending proposals are steps in the right direction, the drafting process should be used to better align the wide array of Directives and Regulations. For central terms, uniform definitions should be drafted to be used across all relevant frameworks. If different terminology is used consciously, its purpose should be justified. This will put the EU institutions in a better position when they need to react to new developments. It will also help ensure a high level of legal certainty for stakeholders and an equally high level of consumer protection in the EU.

7

*Defining Risk and Promoting Trust in AI Systems**

JOHANNA CHAMBERLAIN** AND ANDREAS KOTSIOS***

I. INTRODUCTION

AS ARTIFICIAL INTELLIGENCE (AI) technologies continue to expand in various (perhaps most) areas of society, many new societal and legal issues are coming to light. Two concepts that will be investigated in this contribution are *risk* and *trust*. These are both broad concepts in need of delimitations, and – to complicate matters – not necessarily legal concepts; at least not in a narrow sense. Despite this they have become predominant in the AI discourse and ongoing legislative processes concerning AI, a tendency that raises questions as to what the concepts mean in the area of AI. The relationship between risk and trust in an AI context can be summed up as follows: In order to create trust with individuals for new technologies and the free flow of AI services within the EU internal market, there is a need to control the risks that AI systems pose. This is where the law enters into the equation. In this chapter we aim to nuance this new narrative, elucidating that risk and trust as emerging legal notions can be rather problematic.

In the first sections of the following text, the focus will be on the risk discourse in law and how it is evolving against the background of rapid technical developments, in particular in the EU general regulation on AI (which is compared to the data protection area). With an emphasis on the distinction between risk

* The authors would like to thank the organisers of the 2022 SNELS Conference in Uppsala 'EU Law in the Digital Age' and the participants of the panel 'Digital Data' for the opportunity to discuss this topic. We also wish to thank WASP-HS for making our research possible by funding the project 'AI and the Financial Markets'.

** Johanna Chamberlain is a Senior Lecturer at the Faculty of Law, Uppsala University, email: johanna.chamberlain@jur.uu.se, ORCID: https://orcid.org/0000-0003-0473-2076.

*** Andreas Kotsios is a Senior Lecturer at the Law and Business Unit, Department of Business Studies, Uppsala University, Researcher at the Division of Media Technology and Interaction Design, KTH and Research Fellow at the Information Society Law Center, University of Milan, email: andreas.kotsios@fek.uu.se, ORCID: https://orcid.org/0000-0002-6870-7657.

and uncertainty, the EU approach to AI will hereby be analysed critically. The discussion will then proceed to the concept of trust and its relevance in law, the connection between risk and trust in an AI setting, and the meaning of trust in relation to new technologies. We will end this chapter by laying down the problems that arise because of the uncertainties sparked by this new way of formulating regulatory goals and techniques.

II. ON RISK

A. The Concept of Risk and Research on Risk

Risk is an unruly subject that is difficult to define and does not belong to any single area of science.[1] As described by Luhmann, scientific research on risk has spread from Statistics to Computer Science and Economics, from Psychology to Political Science and Sociology.[2] Risk has thus become a very well-researched concept in the Social Sciences and also in the Humanities, including Anthropology and Philosophy.[3] In Law, too, there have been a number of important contributions on a principal level. Convincing arguments and examples have been presented concerning the challenges of determining risk in a legal context (Jarvis Thomson), the irrationality of risk perception and the costs of regulating risk (Sunstein).[4]

[1] See N Luhmann, *Risk: A Sociological Theory* (Routledge, 2005) 6–12, for a discussion on the etymology and definitions of the word risk. Luhmann notes that risk is often defined as 'measure', but that this term fails to grasp the challenges connected to the concept of risk. However, the difficulty in defining risk should not obstruct research on the topic according to the author, who concludes that it is 'generally agreed that not too much attention needs to be paid to questions of definition, for definitions serve only to delimit, not adequately describe (let alone explain) the object under investigation' (ibid 7).

[2] ibid 1–6. Some important works are F Hyneman Knight, *Risk, Uncertainty and Profit* (Houghton Mifflin Co, 1921); D MacKenzie, *Mechanizing Truth: Computing, Risk, and Trust* (MIT Press, 2004); M Power, *Organized Uncertainty: Designing a World of Risk Management* (Oxford University Press, 2008).

[3] See, eg, K Shrader-Frachette, *Risk and Rationality: Philosophical Foundations for Populist Reforms* (University of California Press, 1991). As research on risk has developed simultaneously in a number of different subjects, it makes an excellent topic for interdisciplinary research. To do the subject justice, such a study would require experts from different fields and a much broader approach than what is possible within this contribution. In this narrower context, the focus will instead be on arguments concerning risk in the legal discourse.

[4] J Jarvis Thomson, *Rights, Restitution, & Risk: Essays in Moral Theory* (Harvard University Press, 1986); see especially the essay 'Imposing Risks', where different cases of risk are tested through a variation of scenarios in connection to moral theory); C Sunstein, *Risk and Reason: Safety, Law, and the Environment* (Cambridge University Press, 2002); see especially chapter two, with a focus on human irrationality concerning risk; ie our tendency to exaggerate risks posed by dramatic events like plane crashes and to underestimate everyday risks that are actually more serious, like being overweight). See also, for a Contract Law focused discussion, Tobias Mahler's works on contractual risk management.

The legal issues related to risk are numerous.[5] The entire field of insurance law is closely connected to risk and in tort law, risk is a central element both in assessing negligence and imposing strict liability. It is interesting to observe that a dominating theme in scientific research across the disciplines appears to be the human *perception of risk*, and *how risk affects our behaviour*.[6] These are relevant points also in the legal discourse, as they correlate with the preventive function in tort law. The preventive function is complex and has traditionally often been called into question (at least in a Scandinavian context) as it is extremely hard to verify.[7] How can we confirm that the number of accidents in a certain area is lower thanks to tort law rules and potential liability? There is no way to know for sure – we can only assume. Despite this uncertainty we do assume that the prospect of liability has *some* impact on our behaviour.[8] Together with the other functions of tort law, primarily the reparative function,[9] it thus motivates regulation.[10]

B. Risk and Uncertainty in a Legal Context

Following the chronology of research on risk in different scientific areas, the concept of risk is something that is often connected to probability and calculations, and perhaps less to legal reasoning. That said, the law can be described as a safeguard against certain (often unwanted) outcomes, or it can at least regulate and thereby handle such outcomes. When something happens – be it a tort, a divorce, or bankruptcy – the possible consequences follow the legal rules we as a society have agreed upon. However, it is important to note that these outcomes are not *unknown*. We understand what a divorce, damages claim or custody battle entail, even though we wish to avoid them. In a legal sense, we understand what they entail all the more concretely by formulating the possible outcomes in the process of writing a claim, filing for divorce, etc.

[5] Concerning the definition of the concept *legal risk*, often expressed as the risk of financial or reputational loss due to legal uncertainty or other legal issues, see T Mahler, 'Defining Legal Risk' in *Proceedings of the Conference 'Commercial Contracting for Strategic Advantage – Potentials and Prospects'* (Turku University, 2007) 10–31). The author conducts an extensive discussion on existing definitions in different legal fields and presents a suggestion of a context-independent definition and classification based on norm theory.

[6] See, for instance, aforementioned H Knight (n 2); Shrader-Frachette (n 3); Sunstein (n 4).

[7] See B Askeland, 'Basic Questions of Tort Law from a Norwegian Perspective' in H Koziol (ed), *Basic Questions of Tort Law from a Comparative Perspective* (Jan Sramek Verlag, 2015) 99–161.

[8] Within Luhmann's sociological approach, prevention 'mediates between decision and risk'. See Luhmann (n 1) 29.

[9] The reparative function is often thought to be the most important function of tort law: The compensation of losses. It is a victim-oriented function compared to the preventive function, which rather focuses on the tortfeasor.

[10] See C van Dam, *European Tort Law*, 2nd edn (Oxford Academic, 2013) 349–53, on the functions of prevention and punishment and their relationship to other functions of tort law.

In contrast, risk implies an unknown element, and we do not wish the law to be unclear or to build on the unknown. This applies to the law itself, but also the legal process. Ideally, in every court case, all facts would be verifiable so that the verdict could be built on rock-solid evidence and thus so fair that no one could contest it. The judge's way of handling the risk, for example, of an innocent person being convicted of a crime is to set up legal standards. These standards need to be high enough to minimise the risk of delivering a wrongful conviction ('beyond reasonable doubt') while at the same time minimising the risk of acquitting a guilty person. This balance is always difficult to reach, but the risks have come to be accepted within the legal system.[11]

In comparison, economists seem to have more patience with and even interest in the unknown. Risk is seen as something calculable – something that can be dealt with. In economics, uncertainty appears to be even better than risk. It was the economist Frank Hyneman Knight who, in his classic work from 1921, first made the distinction between risk and uncertainty, and who illuminated the possibilities of uncertainty.[12] According to the author, while risk is something calculable (even when various outcomes are involved, as they can be considered more or less probable) and thus insurable, true uncertainty is never calculable. With the right judgment, it is therefore possible to profit from uncertain situations. For instance, with known technologies, statistics can be used to calculate the risk of certain damages, or of other complications – even if there are several alternative scenarios. With new technologies, calculations could possibly be made but will be speculative or in other words uncertain, and therefore relatively unhelpful. The relationship between risk and uncertainty has thereafter been explored further, not least by fellow economist John Maynard Keynes,[13] and different conceptions of Hyneman Knight's 'true' uncertainty have been introduced.[14]

Profit is not uninteresting in the legal system, but is typically approached at a collective and more abstract level. A good balance regarding the burden of proof in trials can be said to generate profit on the societal scale, both when it comes to making use of resources and considering the parties and their needs. At the level of the individual, you could of course also say that a person or company who has dubious dealings in order to maximise their profit is gambling with the risk to be convicted of criminal actions. However, the link between profit and uncertainty has not had a prominent position in the legal discourse, where it has so far been overshadowed by the challenges of regulating risk.

[11] See Jarvis Thomson (n 4) (especially essays 'Causation and Liability' and 'Liability and Individualized Evidence'), where the author elaborates on the burden of proof in criminal cases and in tort law, the connection to causation and the difficult-to-strike balance between the parties.

[12] Hyneman Knight (n 2), especially 19–20 and chapters 7–8.

[13] See J Maynard Keynes, *The General Theory of Employment, Interest and Money* (Macmillan, 1936), commented by J Kay and M King in *Radical Uncertainty: Decision-Making for an Unknowable Future* (The Bridge Street Press, 2013) 13.

[14] See, for instance, Kay & King, ibid, 14, building on the distinction between 'resolvable' uncertainty and 'radical' uncertainty.

In lawmaking, there are only two basic options when faced with a risky phenomenon: To regulate or not to regulate. It is very difficult, if not impossible, to (at least substantially) regulate a risk from a certain outcome, as this would require the law to be ridiculously detailed. What remains is thus to forbid the risky phenomenon as a whole, or not. If the phenomenon is allowed, which is motivated by its usefulness or other benefits to society, the pertaining risk can (hopefully) be minimised through the introduction of supervisory authorities and penalties. A common approach is to impose fines, sometimes in combination with strict liability. The aim of these safeguards is to ensure that those who are active in risky areas or enterprises are as careful as possible, in the knowledge that hefty penalties await if they cause any harm. In line with such reasoning, the concept of controlling risks has been a key part of EU regulation on, for example, product safety,[15] food chains,[16] and chemicals.[17] Furthermore, it has been the main motivation for various laws regarding strict liability that have long been part of national legal systems.[18]

C. Risk in the AI Act

The above description of the legal take on risks is generally phrased, but illustrates the development concerning the regulation of and liability for AI systems according to the new EU General Regulation.[19] This legal framework, while

[15] See Directive 2001/95/EC of the European Parliament and of the Council of 3 December 2001 on general product safety [2002] OJ L11/4. This Directive is to be replaced by a new EU General Product Safety Regulation in December 2024.

[16] See Regulation (EU) 2019/1381 of the European Parliament and of the Council of 20 June 2019 on the transparency and sustainability of the EU risk assessment in the food chain and amending Regulations (EC) No 178/2002, (EC) No 1829/2003, (EC) No 1831/2003, (EC) No 2065/2003, (EC) No 1935/2004, (EC) No 1331/2008, (EC) No 1107/2009, (EU) 2015/2283 and Directive 2001/18/EC [2019] OJ L231/1.

[17] See Regulation (EC) No 1907/2006 of the European Parliament and of the Council of 18 December 2006 concerning the Registration, Evaluation, Authorisation and Restriction of Chemicals (REACH), establishing a European Chemicals Agency, amending Directive 1999/45/EC and repealing Council Regulation (EEC) No 793/93 and Commission Regulation (EC) No 1488/94 as well as Council Directive 76/769/EEC and Commission Directives 91/155/EEC, 93/67/EEC, 93/105/EC and 2000/21/EC [2006] OJ L396/1.

[18] Examples of strict liability from Swedish law are the Law (2018:181) on Railway Traffic, the Law (1997:857) on Electricity and the Law (2007:1150) on the Supervision of Dogs and Cats. See European Commission, 'Liability for Artificial Intelligence and other Emerging Technologies' (Report from the Expert Group on Liability and New Technologies – New Technologies Formation, Luxembourg 2019) 25–27, for an overview and analysis at the European level regarding strict liability and new technologies, where it is shown that the provisions on strict liability tend to vary greatly between Member States.

[19] Regulation (EU) 2024/1689 of the European Parliament and of the Council of 13 June 2024 laying down harmonised rules on artificial intelligence and amending Regulations (EC) No 300/2008, (EU) No 167/2013, (EU) No 168/2013, (EU) 2018/858, (EU) 2018/1139 and (EU) 2019/2144 and Directives 2014/90/EU, (EU) 2016/797 and (EU) 2020/1828 (Artificial Intelligence Act) [2024] OJ L 2024/1689.

acknowledging the widespread social and economic benefits of AI,[20] also points at evolving risks that need to be addressed. Against this background, it strives to create a balance between different interests and a proportionate legislation.[21] In the AI Act, a *risk-based approach* for AI systems is established with a division of systems into four categories: Low or minimum risk, limited risk, high risk and unacceptable risk. While the latter category is in principle prohibited (see Chapter II), high risk AI may be used with a number of restrictions (Chapter III), limited risk AI with only some safeguards (Chapter IV) and low risk AI without any restrictions. High risk AI will be surrounded by rigorous safety measures and breaches will be subject to high administrative fines (Chapter XII).

With the introduction of risk as a central element of this Regulation which is generally and directly applicable throughout the European Union, lawyers will need to face issues relating to risk in an expanding area of society whether they like it or not. The structure of the Regulation raises many questions concerning risks, AI and the law. What is seen as an unacceptable versus acceptable risk in this area and why? Under what conditions can AI risks be acceptable? How are different levels of risk defined and delimited? Is it possible to handle a multitude of AI risks in the collective and systematic way suggested in the Regulation? Is it at all feasible to control risks related to AI, considering that they are largely unknown at this moment in time? In addition, regarding the relationship with uncertainty in the 'risky' areas regulated by the law, most recently expanded by the AI Act: How can the law approach uncertainty?

D. A Comparison: Risk in Data Protection

Risk has figured in EU regulations for some time. Areas mentioned above are product safety, food chains and chemicals, and more examples could be added – such as financial sector regulations[22] and legal instruments concerning cyber risk.[23] While these areas are connected to specific risks, it may be less obvious that data protection law also relies on the concept of risk.

[20] Proposal for a Regulation of the European Parliament and of the Council Laying Down Harmonised Rules on Artificial Intelligence (Artificial Intelligence Act) and Amending Certain Union Legislative Acts (COM/2021/206 final). Explanatory Memorandum, part 1.1: Reasons for and Objectives of the Proposal: 'By improving prediction, optimising operations and resource allocation, and personalising service delivery, the use of artificial intelligence can support socially and environmentally beneficial outcomes and provide key competitive advantages to companies and the European economy.'

[21] ibid.

[22] See, eg, Directive (EU) 2015/849 of the European Parliament and of the Council of 20 May 2015 on the prevention of the use of the financial system for the purposes of money laundering or terrorist financing, amending Regulation (EU) No 648/2012 of the European Parliament and of the Council, and repealing Directive 2005/60/EC of the European Parliament and of the Council and Commission Directive 2006/70/EC [2015] OJ L141/73.

[23] See the 'Cybersecurity Act', Regulation (EU) 2019/881 of the European Parliament and of the Council of 17 April 2019 on ENISA (the European Union Agency for Cybersecurity) and on

While the preamble of the General Data Protection Regulation (GDPR)[24] and the GDPR narrative in general emphasise individual rights in a 'rights-based approach', the focus of the Regulation on compliance mechanisms and risk management tools can also be said to entail a 'risk-based approach' as shown by Gellert.[25] According to Gellert, the risk-based approach has become the latest predominant regulatory model, and the similarities between the compliance mechanisms of the GDPR and the AI Act are indeed many. Again, the AI Act is centred around the notion of protecting fundamental rights, although these rights and how they might be infringed by AI technologies are not nearly as specified as the obligations to comply with risk assessment processes and the like. This is probably connected to the fact that the future impact of the new technologies is mostly unknown today.[26]

One difference in comparison to the GDPR is that the AI Act is openly risk-based (and thus innovation-based, as its starting point is the developing technology), for which it has already received much criticism. One point of controversy is that companies will be obliged to weigh operational risks against fundamental rights, which could lead to downplaying risks and negotiating rights in a way that undermines them.[27] The openness with which the risk-based approach of the AI Act has been introduced seems to have sparked more discussions regarding basic concepts such as transparency and explainability in the AI context compared to the GDPR setting and its less explicit focus on risk.[28] This is interesting, considering that broad concepts are not missing in the GDPR, as seen primarily in Article 5 (fairness, purpose limitation, accuracy and more data protection principles).

information and communications technology cybersecurity certification and repealing Regulation (EU) No 526/2013 (Cybersecurity Act) [2019] OJ L151/15.

[24] Regulation (EU) 2016/679 of the European Parliament and of the Council of 27 April 2016 on the protection of natural persons with regard to the processing of personal data and on the free movement of such data, and repealing Directive 95/46/EC (General Data Protection Regulation or GDPR) [2016] OJ L119/1.

[25] R Gellert, *The Risk-Based Approach to Data Protection* (Oxford Scholarship Online, 2020). The presentation of the GDPR as a risk-based regulation has been criticised, not least by the Article 29 Data Protection Working Party in a special statement published as early as 2014, 'Statement on the Role of a Risk-Based Approach in Data Protection Legal Frameworks', available at https://ec.europa.eu/justice/article-29/documentation/opinion-recommendation/files/2014/wp218_en.pdf. The Statement reads: '[…] rights granted to the data subject by EU law should be respected regardless of the level of the risks which the latter incur through the data processing involved'.

[26] In the 'rights and risk' context, it may be noted that the AI Act seems to be based on both Article 16 TFEU (data protection) and Article 114 TFEU (measures for the functioning of the internal market). This is reminiscent of the double goal (or 'split personality') of the GDPR. Susanna Lindroos-Hovinheimo coined the latter expression (referring to the tension between the two goals of the data protection regulation), see further S Lindroos-Hovinheimo, 'Who Controls our Personal Data? The Legal Reasoning of the European Court of Justice in Wirtschaftsakademie Schleswig-Holstein and Tietosuojavaltuutettu v Jehovan todistajat' (2019) 28 *Information & Communications Technology Law* 227.

[27] For a critical discussion, see www.accessnow.org/eu-regulation-ai-risk-based-approach/.

[28] This is a general observation, but it is generated by the rapidly growing number of scholarly contributions on basic concepts such as explainability and transparency in the field of AI.

A possible explanation for the different receptions of GDPR and AI concepts, and for their more or less open risk-based approaches, could be the fact that we know what to relate GDPR concepts to, even though they are just as broad as AI Act concepts.[29] Data protection law is not ancient, but compared to AI law it is both old and established. As individuals we know what personal data is (although not always how it is treated and used), but not necessarily what an AI system is or when it is used. Following the same line of reasoning, we understand the risks related to personal data leakage or ID theft[30] at least more than we understand risks pertaining to AI systems gone awry.[31] AI is still highly abstract and hard to grasp for most people, which is why 'black-boxing', transparency and explainability have become such important concepts in the AI discourse. The question is then if it is useful, or even realistic, to create a specific legislation for AI risks at this stage of the development?

E. Risks or Uncertainties?

> The essence of risk management lies in maximizing the areas where we have some control over the outcome while minimizing the areas where we have absolutely no control over the outcome and the linkage between effect and cause is hidden from us.[32]

In order to actually be controlled, risks must be calculable and thereby known in some way. This may have been easier in a physical world than in today's highly digitalised environment, but it still holds true. The risk categories and general risk narrative of the AI Act give the impression that we can control and mitigate AI risks, when they are in fact closer to 'unknown unknowns'[33] in the current phase of developments. Should the EU legislator not be more honest about this in the legislative process? This question leads to another more pressing concern. If we are in fact dealing with uncertainties rather than risk, going back to Hyneman Knight and the relationship between risk, uncertainty and profit,

[29] Moreover, many companies that are targeted by the AI Regulation already operate according to various risk assessments.

[30] We are now seeing cases where data leakage is seen as harm without having to prove any actual damage, due to the existence of the *risk of future harm*. See, eg, the 2017 Equifax data breach case from the US, in which the company responsible for the data agreed to fund both victim compensation and credit monitoring. This is a development that we can expect to see more of in the future.

[31] We have only just started witnessing 'AI damage', but a well-known example is the 2020 'SyRI' case from the Netherlands where AI software was used by the Dutch Government to detect cases of welfare fraud through automated surveillance. The system was halted after a court decision that stated that it violated Article 8 of the European Convention on Human Rights. See case C/09/550982 / HA ZA 18-388, NL:RBDHA:2020:865.

[32] P Bernstein, *Against the Gods – The Remarkable History of Risk* (John Wiley Sons Inc, 1998) 197.

[33] Unknown unknowns are things 'we don't know we don't know' (quoted from US Secretary of Defense Donald Rumsfeld's famous Iraq speech on 12 February 2002). This means that risks that are 'unknown unknowns' are unpredictable.

you might ask yourself: What are the effects (or side effects) of adopting a risk-based approach in a domain of uncertainties? What kind of signals are sent to individuals potentially affected by AI uncertainties? In our view, this is a matter of transparency. EU citizens should not be led to believe that they are protected from uncertainties through 'controlled risks'.

III. ON TRUST

A. Trust in AI – An Introduction

No matter the lack of clarity with regard to what risk is and what uncertain means, the AI Act clearly indicates that the idea is to regulate AI by finding or predicting risks related to applications of AI and mitigating these risks. You may ask yourself why this is so important. The obvious answer is that it is in order to protect individuals' fundamental rights when they make use of or are in general affected by the use of AI systems. This was emphasised in the proposal[34] where it was clarified that a) the use of AI has the power to affect a number of fundamental rights and b) a risk-based approach has the potential to 'facilitate the respect of […] fundamental rights'. However, this is not the only objective, since the Regulation aims at the same time to develop an 'ecosystem of trust' where 'people and other users [are given] the confidence to embrace AI-based solutions'.[35] The goal is to make people 'trust the technology' and for companies to 'promote trust among their customers'[36] by creating a 'trustworthy AI' that is also based on this risk-based approach described above.

The White Paper that led to the proposal explicitly declared *trust* as an EU policy goal.[37] The goal, according to this policy document and as in the case of the proposal, is to create an 'ecosystem of trust'. What this includes is not exactly clear, but the way to achieve this goal, at least according to the White Paper, is through legal compliance. The reason why this 'ecosystem of trust' seems to be of importance is because in this way 'citizens [will be given the] confidence to take up AI applications' while at the same time it will provide legal certainty for traders and public organisations in order to continue developments in the field. Therefore, trust among consumers and businesses in AI, generated through a 'a clear European regulatory framework' that is not fragmented, will lead to the uptake of the technology and all the positive effects this entails for the internal market.

[34] Proposed Artificial Intelligence Act (n 20) Explanatory Memorandum, part 3.5.
[35] ibid Explanatory Memorandum, part 1.1.
[36] ibid Explanatory Memorandum, part 3.4.
[37] White Paper, 'On Artificial Intelligence – A European Approach to Excellence and Trust' COM(2020) 65 final, available at https://ec.europa.eu/info/sites/default/files/commission-white-paper-artificial-intelligence-feb2020_en.pdf.

Thus, the idea behind regulating AI seems to be that AI regulation has to lead to trust and to create confidence. However, as we will point out here, these are two rather distinct notions and their confusion can be problematic.

B. The Concept of Trust in EU Law

Trust is not unknown to EU law. Especially after the economic crisis in 2008, trust started to make its appearance in a number of EU law areas, and most notably – and most relevant for our study on AI applications in the financial markets – financial law and consumer law.

An examination of EU secondary legislation in these areas reveals that when it comes to EU financial legislation, trust has been recognised as one of the main justifications for intervening in the financial markets. This was made paradigmatically apparent in Regulation 1093/2010[38] which established the European Banking Authority just after the first effects of the crisis made their appearance in the European space. As with the case of the AI Act, the discussion started with a High-Level Group making recommendations, in this case on how to better protect the citizens and 'rebuild[…] *trust* in the financial system' (emphasis added) based on supervisory arrangements at the EU level.[39] It similarly clarified the prerequisite for trust as well as the purpose of trust, namely that trust in the financial system is needed in order to 'preserve and improve the conditions for the establishment of a fully integrated and functioning internal market in the field of financial services' while it can be achieved by 'restoring and maintaining a stable and reliable financial system'.[40] In Regulation 806/2014[41] we also find that

> in order to restore *trust* and credibility in the banking sector, the European Central Bank (ECB) is currently conducting a comprehensive balance sheet assessment of all banks supervised directly. Such an assessment should assure all stakeholders that banks entering the SSM, and therefore falling within the scope of the SRM, are fundamentally sound and *trustworthy*[42] (emphasis added).

Moving to consumer law, trust is also found in EU secondary legislation. Interestingly enough, as in the case of EU financial law, trust appears almost

[38] Regulation (EU) No 1093/2010 of the European Parliament and of the Council of 24 November 2010 establishing a European Supervisory Authority (European Banking Authority), amending Decision No 716/2009/EC and repealing Commission Decision 2009/78/EC [2010] OJ L331/12.

[39] ibid Rec 3. See here also Council Regulation (EU) No 1096/2010 of 17 November 2010 conferring specific tasks upon the European Central Bank concerning the functioning of the European Systemic Risk Board defining the specific tasks of the EBA [2010] OJ L331/162.

[40] Regulation 1093/2010 (n 38) Rec 7.

[41] Regulation (EU) No 806/2014 of the European Parliament and of the Council of 15 July 2014 establishing uniform rules and a uniform procedure for the resolution of credit institutions and certain investment firms in the framework of a Single Resolution Mechanism and a Single Resolution Fund and amending Regulation (EU) No 1093/2010 [2014] OJ L225/1.

[42] ibid Rec 13.

exclusively after the crisis. To begin with, in the Directive on Consumer Alternative Dispute Resolution (ADR), it is important to gain 'Union citizens' trust'[43] with regard to ADR mechanisms since this trust 'is essential for the completion of the internal market'.[44] Similarly, and with regard to what constitutes an 'organic' product, Regulation (EU) 2018/848[45] states that it is important to 'ensure consumer trust in this production method'. However, it is mostly in the digital technologies where trust has become more apparent in consumer law. For example, in the preambles of the Sale of Goods Directive we find that there is a need to 'influence consumers' willingness to embrace and trust this type of transaction', meaning e-commerce transactions, since e-commerce is a 'key driver for growth within the internal market'.[46] This way 'legal certainty' will be promoted, something that in turn will help to 'reinforce the trust of the consumers and the seller'. The measures taken in this Directive, namely measures to strengthen market surveillance and the creation of incentives geared towards operators, have been introduced for this exact reason, to 'increase trust in the functioning of the internal market'.[47] Taking this a step further, Regulation 2019/1150, which is about regulating intermediary services in a business-to-business context, states that 'ensuring transparency of, and trust in, the online platform economy in business-to-business relations could also indirectly help to improve consumer trust in the online platform economy'.[48]

One of the earliest references to trust in consumer-related legislation, and in fact in EU law in general, can actually be found in relation to the digital environment, namely with regard to e-signatures. As many consumer services started to transform into digital services and some consumer contracts were being provided in digital form, the EU realised that security in this area was of paramount importance for the uptake of such digital services and digital transactions. It was therefore deemed important to 'ensur[e] security and trust in electronic communication'[49] by creating 'trustworthy systems' that protect and secure the processes supported by them.[50] This idea was further developed

[43] Directive 2013/11/EU of the European Parliament and of the Council of 21 May 2013 on alternative dispute resolution for consumer disputes and amending Regulation (EC) No 2006/2004 and Directive 2009/22/EC (Directive on Consumer ADR) [2013] OJ L165/63 Rec 32.

[44] ibid Rec 3.

[45] Regulation (EU) 2018/848 of the European Parliament and of the Council of 30 May 2018 on organic production and labelling of organic products and repealing Council Regulation (EC) No 834/2007 [2018] OJ L150/1.

[46] Directive (EU) 2019/771 of the European Parliament and of the Council of 20 May 2019 on certain aspects concerning contracts for the sale of goods, amending Regulation (EU) 2017/2394 and Directive 2009/22/EC, and repealing Directive 1999/44/EC [2019] OJ L136/28 Rec 4.

[47] ibid Rec 32.

[48] Regulation (EU) 2019/1150 of the European Parliament and of the Council of 20 June 2019 on promoting fairness and transparency for business users of online intermediation services [2019] OJ L186/57 Rec 3.

[49] Directive 1999/93/EC of the European Parliament and of the Council of 13 December 1999 on a Community framework for electronic signatures [2000] OJ L13/12 Rec 2.

[50] ibid Annex II.

15 years later when Regulation 910/2014[51] repealing the previous directive began by emphasising in the preamble the importance of trust in the online environment declaring that

> Building trust in the online environment is key to economic and social development. Lack of trust, in particular because of a perceived lack of legal certainty, makes consumers, businesses and public authorities hesitate to carry out transactions electronically and to adopt new services.

This trust is to be achieved through secure electronic communications which in turn will be achieved through what the Regulation calls trust services, namely encryption-related services.

Now, the relationship between trust as a policy goal and the functioning of the internal market should not strike us as an oddity since all the above-mentioned legislation is based on Article 114 of the Treaty on the Functioning of the European Union (TFEU). Therefore, trust is in a sense regarded as a general meta-goal of EU legislation since – and as long as – it goes hand in hand with the objective of the internal market. The presumption is that trust is *sine qua non* for the functioning of the internal market; thus, by achieving trust, we achieve the internal market goal.[52]

The question, however, is what trust entails in the context of Article 114.

C. Trust versus Reliance

It is important to point out here that it is not our intention to pair any normative theory of trust with the notion of trust in a legal context. However, it can be fruitful to lift some points related to the general discourse on trust in order to show what characteristics we can detect in the case of trust in EU law.

No matter which theory we use for trust, trust seems to be unanimously perceived as a triadic relationship where someone, the *trustor*, trusts someone else, the *trustee*, to do something, the entrusted *task*. However, if we take the three main paradigms of trust, namely rational, affective and normative trust, there seem to be certain differences that can help us identify the kind of trust that is envisaged in EU law.[53] Even though all three keep the same triadic relationship, they differ regarding the motivations of the trustee to perform the entrusted task. More specifically, rational trust does not bother itself with the motives of the trustee at all since it contains a rational belief concerning the possibility that

[51] Regulation (EU) No 910/2014 of the European Parliament and of the Council of 23 July 2014 on electronic identification and trust services for electronic transactions in the internal market and repealing Directive 1999/93/EC [2014] OJ L257/73.

[52] Therefore, trust has made its appearance in a number of laws based on Art 114, such as the Cybersecurity Act, where the goal is to address situations that 'undermine trust in digital service providers and in the digital single market itself'.

[53] On the three main paradigms of trust in an AI context, see M Ryan, 'In AI We Trust: Ethics, Artificial Intelligence, and Reliability' (2020) 26 *Science and Engineering Ethics* 2749.

the task will be completed by the trustee – no matter why the trustee decides to do so; affective trust is based on the belief of the trustor that the trustee's action is based on goodwill towards the trustor; while normative trust is grounded on a normative commitment by the trustee to her relationship with the trustor, in the sense that the trustor trusts the trustee because she believes that their relationship creates some kind of an imperative to complete a task.[54] Thus, two of the three types of trust are related to the capacity of the trustee to be trusted based on her presumed *motivations* and not merely her capabilities. The first account of trust, however, is disconnected from the motivations of the trustee and has, therefore, been claimed to constitute some kind of reliance and not trust.[55] In this case, the trustor is *confident* that the trustee will carry out the trusted task without any consideration related to the trustee's goodwill or normative stance.

With regard to AI, it has been argued that at least until now, AI has not had the capacity to be trusted and therefore only the first type of trust could be relevant. However, AI could also be regarded as a socio-technical system with a number of actors, such as the AI system, the developer, the provider and so on. In such a case, you could claim that as institutions (for example, the state) have the capacity to be trusted, it might also be possible to claim that AI in a socio-technical context may have the capacity to be trusted. The problem arising in this case, however, is related to the fact that law as such is used as a means to remove any subjective considerations with regard to the trustee. Law, whenever it is involved, places legal obligations on the trustee that have to be followed. In that sense, the trustee does what she does because her behaviour is sanctionable if it is not in compliance with the law. There is no possibility to prove her possible trustworthiness relying on good intentions and benevolence based on a relationship. For trust there has to be a possibility to act autonomously.[56] If the trustee does not follow the law, then she is not untrustworthy but merely non-compliant. Or alternatively, an actor believes that a task will be fulfilled by another actor, not because this other actor freely chooses to do so but because there are enforcement mechanisms in place that will be activated in case she does not act as demanded by the law. The law, therefore, is understood as a *functional equivalent of trust* – at least of the affirmative and normative kind – namely a means to minimise uncertainties, the uncertainty being the unknown behaviour of even a trustworthy trustee.

D. Trust versus Compliance

Coming back to EU consumer law and EU financial law, we saw that trust is related to the internal market: Trust is needed for the internal market to function.

[54] ibid.
[55] ibid 2750.
[56] R Hardin (ed), *Distrust* (Russell Sage Foundation, 2004) 35.

However, since these two areas of law define the obligations of a specific actor, be it the trader in general or the financial institutions, this trust is, following the line of reasoning above, neither affective nor normative trust. On the contrary, as argued by a number of scholars who have examined the relationship between trust and regulatory private law, if what is of importance is the promotion of trust based on the trustee's motivations, the law should probably be left aside.[57]

More specifically, when discussing the distinction between contracts and promises it has been argued that 'enforceability casts a thick and all-encompassing veil over parties' motives and attitudes towards each other'.[58] Therefore, in the case of contracts, for example, the law aims at the personal detachment of the parties, namely the limitation of committing to a personal relationship but nevertheless being able to do things.[59] Hardin has also illustrated this situation by stating that 'the law commonly fills in where trust would not be possible'.[60] In that sense, law is a substitute for trust in cases where there is a need for certainty or at least for minimising the risk of being betrayed or the risks when being betrayed.

Moving back to EU consumer and financial law, based on Article 114 of the TFEU, trust is related to the internal market. Since the secondary legislation in these areas of law is mostly obligatory legislation for the protection of the weaker actors in the market, it is difficult to accept that the trust provided for there is something else than the old narrative of the empowered actor who can with confidence act in the market. Interestingly enough, even the GDPR which is based on Article 16, when referring to the notion of trust, does so only in relation to the internal market,[61] where individuals will be able to have control over their data – in contrast to a notion of trust where you leave such control to others. Therefore, when the question is one of compliance, any reference to trust covers only rational accounts of trust and is therefore to be seen as confidence. This confidence is irrelevant to the motivations of the 'trustee' since both these aspects are regulated by the legal framework in place.

E. Trust versus Confidence

This distinction between trust and confidence also follows the case law of the Court of Justice of the European Union. Even though trust has appeared in the

[57] LE Ribstein, 'Law v. Trust' (2001) 81 *Boston University Law Review*; D Hult, Creating Trust by Means of Legislation – A Conceptual Analysis and Critical Discussion, The Theory and Practice of Legislation, 6:1, 1–23, DOI: 10.1080/20508840.2018.1434934; D Kimel, 'Neutrality, Autonomy, and Freedom of Contract' (2001) 21 *Oxford Journal of Legal Studies* 473, 491; A Bagchi, 'Separating Contract and Promise' (2011) 38 *Florida State University Law Review* 709.

[58] Kimel, ibid.

[59] AJ Bellia, 'Promises, Trust, and Contract Law' (2002) 47 *American Journal of Jurisprudence* 25.

[60] Hardin (n 56) 519.

[61] GDPR (n 24) Rec 7.

decisions of the Court, it normally refers to the mutual trust between Member States, for example, in relation to decisions by national courts.[62] Similarly, it has been used in relation to the trust citizens should place on democratic institutions and processes,[63] as well as the specific relationship between patients and health professionals.[64] However, we have found only one mention of the notion of trust with regard to new technology. In *StWL Städtische Werke Lauf* in a matter related to the ePrivacy Directive, the Court referred to the trust users have in their inboxes.[65] However, here, the Court did not refer to trust as a normative notion but rather as a reality relating to how users may perceive privacy related to their email accounts.

On the other hand, confidence has been more apparent in the areas of financial, consumer and data protection legislation. The Court has emphasised in a number of cases the need for confident actors, consumers as well as traders, for the functioning of the market. This confidence may originate from the information that is provided to these actors, the prohibition of specific behaviour,[66] the free movement of services,[67] and in general by creating protecting measures for those who are in a weaker position.[68] The Advocate General has also expressed this relationship between protection and confidence in the context of consumer law, by stating that EU consumer legislation is motivated by two main objectives, one being the facilitation of cross-border trade and the other being 'to provide a high level of consumer protection in order to give consumers the confidence to seek out the best deals in any Member State'.[69]

F. Trust versus Protection

Hence, what are we to take from the above with regard to trust in EU law? Firstly, when it comes to the functioning of the internal market and the protection of weaker parties in a relationship, trust is to be understood as confidence in the meaning that the motivations of the stronger party do not seem to be of importance as long as this party behaves in compliance with the rules that define her behaviour. In this case, confidence is about providing the right tools, information and rights, so that the weaker actor can be in control of her decision.

[62] See, eg, Cases C-562/21 *X and Y v Openbaar Ministerie* [2022] EU:C:2022:100; C-157/21 *Republic of Poland v European Parliament and Council of Europe* [2022] EU:C:2022:98; C-156/21 *Hungary v European Parliament of Council of the European Union* [2022] EU.C:2022:97.

[63] See C-184/20 *Vyriausioji tarnybinės etikos komisija* [2022] EU:C:2022:601; C- 896/19 *Repubblika v Il-Prim Ministru* [2021] EU:C:2021:311.

[64] Case C-649/18 *A v Daniel B and Others* [2020] EU:C:2020:764.

[65] Case C-102/20 *StWL Städtische Werke Lauf a.d. Pegnitz* [2021] EU:C:2021:954 para 55.

[66] Case C-371/20 *Peek & Cloppenburg KG v Peek & Cloppenburg KGf* [2021] EU:C:2021:674.

[67] Case C-33/20 *UK and Others v Volkswagen Bank GmbH and Others* [2021] EU:C:2021:736.

[68] Case C-639/18 *KH v Sparkasse Südholstein* [2020] EU:C:2020:477.

[69] Case C-109/17 *Bankia SA v Merino* [2018] EU:C:2018:201, Opinion of AG Wahl, para 34.

The control aspect of confidence also seems to fit in well with the contemporary data protection narrative in EU law.[70]

On the other hand, trust may also refer to the relationship between institutions and citizens, and the existence and effectiveness of enforcement mechanisms. In this case, it seems that trust is understood as affective, or better, normative trust, where citizens are by definition in a more vulnerable position and where they depend on, for example, enforcement mechanisms that can indeed work.

However, in the context of regulating AI we can detect some changes. Firstly, trust is not understood only as confidence but it also includes affective/normative aspects related, this time, to the *interpersonal* relationships between different actors in the AI chain – and therefore trust in this case is different to the institutional trust we mentioned above. Additionally, as also shown above, trust based on the motivations of others entails retaining the vulnerability of the vulnerable actor, the trustor. While until now, the main narrative in EU legislation has been about providing control to those affected by other actors' behaviour (eg, the consumer), and therefore about empowering instead of keeping the weaker actor in a vulnerable position, it is difficult to decipher whether the point with the AI Act is indeed to retain some vulnerability – and if so why. If the goal is to create some kind of affective or normative trust, vulnerability would be desirable since this would presumably promote a culture of social responsibility for the rest of the actors. This would be, however, and considering the EU legislation that we analysed above, a rather peculiar and unprecedented decision by the EU legislator, who until now has focused on confidence. Another possibility is that the legislator when talking about trust, even if indicating interpersonal trust, nevertheless means institutional trust, namely trust in a system of control and enforcement mechanisms.

IV. CONCLUSIONS

In this chapter we have demonstrated that risk and trust are establishing themselves as key concepts in EU law and have started playing important roles in today's dynamic development regarding the regulation of AI and on how AI regulation is to be understood.

AI is presumed to carry significant risks and threaten EU values and the fundamental rights of citizens. Similarly, according to this new narrative, these risks have to be controlled in order to create trust in AI, something that is seemingly a prerequisite for the uptake of AI systems. However, as indicated above, the AI risk narrative obscures a reality of uncertainties at this stage. Similarly, the new conception of trust does not exactly follow the concept of trust that has

[70] See A Furman Westin, *Privacy and Freedom* (New edition, IG Publishing, 2015) for the beginning of this narrative and GDPR (n 24) Rec 7 for the importance this idea of control still has in data protection law.

been the paradigm until now, namely trust as confidence created through the impositions of legal obligations and compliance. The law until now has been seen as a 'functional equivalent of trust' – a means of minimising uncertainties. Instead, trust in the context of the AI Act seems to fuse rational and affective/normative trust as well as interpersonal and institutional trust in a manner that creates a rather unclear intention.

We perceive the fact that risk and trust are gaining momentum in the legal discourse about AI as somewhat problematic for the following reasons: a) it sends signals that do not exactly depict reality but create expectations that are presumably difficult to meet; b) it indicates that the existing frameworks based on protection and confidence through obligatory legislation do not properly address the issues that have appeared in the AI context, but instead give the impression that it is mainly the actors that create or affect such systems that they voluntarily choose what risks to control and how; c) as new notions with a rather unclear meaning, risk and trust lead to legal confusion instead of certainty, they threaten legal certainty considering that they do not follow existing concepts in law, specifically because they signal that AI is not a matter of legal compliance but of voluntary choice.

The concepts of risk and trust may have a value but for that to be true we believe that the purpose they serve must become clear. It might be that the previous understanding of dangers related to fundamental rights or of how to create confident actors, does not suffice in the case of AI. However, at this moment in time, it is not clear why such a new approach is needed and this is why it may create more uncertainties than expected.

8

The Proposed Anti-Money Laundering Authority and the Future of FIU Collaboration in Europe

ELENI KOSTA*

I. INTRODUCTION

THE FIELD OF Anti-Money Laundering (AML) and Countering the Financing of Terrorism (CFT) is considered a complex field in European Union (EU) legislation.[1] Currently, at the EU level, the most important legal instruments in the framework on AML/CFT are Directive 2015/849 (the 4th Anti-Money Laundering Directive or 4AMLD)[2] and, introducing modifications thereto, Directive 2018/843 (the 5th Anti-Money Laundering Directive or 5AMLD).[3] Further, Directive 2019/1153[4] lays down measures to enhance access to and use of financial information and bank account information by competent law enforcement authorities by providing them with direct access to information contained in national centralised registries. It also facilitates access

* Tilburg Institute for Law, Technology, and Society (TILT), Tilburg University, email: e.kosta@tilburguniversity.edu. The research for this chapter was completed in January 2023.

[1] European Commission, 'Anti-Money Laundering and Countering the Financing of Terrorism Legislative Package' (20 July 2021), available at https://ec.europa.eu/info/publications/210720-anti-money-laundering-countering-financing-terrorism_en.

[2] Directive (EU) 2015/849 of the European Parliament and of the Council of 20 May 2015 on the prevention of the use of the financial system for the purposes of money laundering or terrorist financing, amending Regulation (EU) No 648/2012 of the European Parliament and of the Council, and repealing Directive 2005/60/EC of the European Parliament and of the Council and Commission Directive 2006/70/EC (herein referred to as '4AMLD') [2015] OJ L141/73–117.

[3] Directive (EU) 2018/843 of the European Parliament and of the Council of 30 May 2018 amending Directive (EU) 2015/849 on the prevention of the use of the financial system for the purposes of money laundering or terrorist financing, and amending Directives 2009/138/EC and 2013/36/EU [2018] OJ L156/43–74.

[4] Directive (EU) 2019/1153 of the European Parliament and of the Council laying down rules facilitating the use of financial and other information for the prevention, detection, investigation or prosecution of certain criminal offences, and repealing Council Decision 2000/642/JHA [2019] OJ L186/122–37.

to law enforcement information for Financial Intelligence Units (FIUs) and stimulates the access of investigative authorities to FIU data.[5]

In May 2020, the European Commission published a Communication on an Action Plan for a comprehensive Union policy on preventing money laundering and terrorism financing, where it expressed its intention to present new legislative proposals on AML/CFT.[6] In July 2021, aiming to clarify the existing situation and to enhance the EU's anti-money laundering rules,[7] the European Commission presented a package of legislative proposals, which aims to radically change the landscape of the European AML/CFT framework. The package consists of a proposal for the Anti-Money Laundering Regulation (AML Regulation),[8] a proposal for the 6th AML Directive (6th Anti-Money Laundering Directive or 6AMLD),[9] a proposal for a Regulation on the Anti-Money Laundering Authority (AMLA Regulation)[10] and a proposal for the Regulation on information accompanying transfers of funds and certain crypto-assets.[11] The new AML/CFT legislative package is expected to have an impact on various complex relationships between multiple actors, including the AMLA, obliged entities,[12] global organisations and governmental bodies, such as the FIUs and law enforcement authorities of the Member States.

The European Data Protection Board (EDPB) adopted a Statement on the protection of personal data processed in relation to the prevention of money

[5] ibid Art 1(1).

[6] European Commission, 'Communication of 7 May 2020 on an Action Plan for a Comprehensive Union Policy on Preventing Money Laundering and Terrorism Financing C(2020)2800 final (the 'Action Plan'), available at https://eur-lex.europa.eu/legal-content/EN/TXT/PDF/?uri=PI_COM:C(2020)2800&from=EN.

[7] European Commission, 'Beating Financial Crime: Commission Overhauls Anti-Money Laundering and Countering the Financing of Terrorism Rules' (20 July 2021), available at https://ec.europa.eu/commission/presscorner/detail/en/IP_21_3690.

[8] European Commission, 'Proposal for a Regulation of the European Parliament and of the Council on the Prevention of the Use of the Financial System for the Purposes of Money Laundering or Terrorist Financing' COM(2021) 420 final (20 July 2021).

[9] European Commission, 'Proposal for a Directive of the European Parliament and of the Council on the mechanisms to be put in place by the Member States for the prevention of the use of the financial system for the purposes of money laundering or terrorist financing and repealing Directive (EU) 2015/849' COM(2021) 423 final (20 July 2021) ('6AMLD').

[10] European Commission, 'Proposal for a Regulation of the European Parliament and of the Council establishing the Authority for Anti-Money Laundering and Countering the Financing of Terrorism and amending Regulations (EU) No 1093/2010, (EU) 1094/2010, (EU) 1095/2010' COM(2021) 421 final (20 July 2021).

[11] European Commission, 'Proposal for a Regulation of the European Parliament and of the Council on Information Accompanying Transfers of Funds and Certain Crypto-Assets' COM(2021) 422 final (20 July 2021).

[12] Obliged entities are specified in Art 3 of the 'Proposal for a Regulation on the Prevention of the Use of the Financial System for the Purposes of Money Laundering or Terrorist Financing' COM(2021) 420 final, available at https://eur-lex.europa.eu/legal-content/EN/TXT/?uri=CELEX%3A52021PC0420.

laundering and terrorist financing.[13] It also addressed a letter to the European Commission on the review of the European AML/CFT framework.[14] In both documents, the EDPB highlighted that it is of utmost importance that 'the anti-money laundering measures are compatible with the rights to privacy and data protection enshrined in Articles 7 and 8 of the Charter of Fundamental Rights of the European Union [CFR]'.[15] In the statement, the EDPB further underlined the importance of compatibility with the principles of necessity and proportionality and the jurisprudence of the Court of Justice of the European Union.[16]

Thus, the compatibility of the European privacy and data protection rules with the proposed anti-money laundering measures is not an add-on to the proposed anti-money laundering rules. The rights to privacy and data protection are fundamental rights that shall be respected, as safeguarded in the European Charter (CFR) and specified in European secondary legislation.

This chapter focuses on the proposed AMLA. Several aspects of the new landscape have been debated throughout the reform process, one of them being the procedure of data sharing among several entities,[17] which will be affected by the new regime. Data sharing unequivocally brings data protection rules to the forefront. This chapter aims at identifying areas of a potential clash between the rules of the AMLA Regulation and the EU data protection framework, especially in relation to data sharing. To this end, the role of the FIUs is pivotal as the collaboration between these institutions is enhanced in the proposed AML/CFT framework.

This chapter will first briefly outline the main EU data protection legal instruments, aiming at clarifying their scope of application and the extent to which they are relevant in the context of AML/CFT. It will then attempt to disentangle the knot of the data protection rules that apply to FIUs and to outline the implications for the AMLA. The chapter will thereafter discuss the complexities relating to the hosting of the FIU.net by the AMLA and finally, it will study the practice of joint analyses and cross-border data transfers.

[13] European Data Protection Board, 'Statement on the Protection of Personal Data Processed in Relation with the Prevention of Money Laundering and Terrorist Financing (Adopted on 15 December 2020), available at https://edpb.europa.eu/sites/default/files/files/file1/edpb_statement_20201215_aml_actionplan_en.pdf.

[14] European Data Protection Board, Letter to the European Commissioner for Financial Services, Financial Stability and Capital Markets Union and to the European Commissioner for Justice (19 May 2021), available at https://edpb.europa.eu/system/files/2021-05/letter_to_ec_on_proposals_on_aml-cft_en.pdf.

[15] European Data Protection Board Statement (n 13) 2 and European Data Protection Board Letter (n 14) 2.

[16] European Data Protection Board Statement (n 13).

[17] European Commission, 'Communication from the Commission on an Action Plan for a Comprehensive Union Policy on Preventing Money Laundering and Terrorist Financing 2020/C 164/06, available at https://eur-lex.europa.eu/legal-content/EN/TXT/?uri=CELEX%3A52020XC0513%2803%29.

II. EU SECONDARY LEGISLATION ON DATA PROTECTION

The protection of personal data in the EU is regulated through an extensive and complicated matrix of secondary legal instruments, mainly directives and regulations, with three of the most prominent pieces of legislation that are relevant for the processing of personal data in the context of AML/CFT, ie Regulation 2016/679 (General Data Protection Regulation, GDPR),[18] Directive 2016/680 (Law Enforcement Directive, LED)[19] and Regulation 2018/1725 (EU Data Protection Regulation, EUDPR).[20]

The GDPR sets high standards and strict obligations for legitimate data processing, while it leaves data processing by competent authorities for law enforcement purposes outside its scope. By virtue of it being a regulation, the GDPR is directly applicable in (European) Member States, without the need for national implementation. Nevertheless, Member States should update their existing national data protection laws in light of the Regulation. In the AML/CFT context, the GDPR is mostly applicable in the processing of personal data by obliged entities, including the sharing of data.

The LED applies when police and criminal justice authorities process the personal data of natural persons (including suspects, accomplices, victims and informants) for law enforcement purposes in a domestic context, but it also applies to cross border processing between Member States' police and judicial authorities, and to international transfers between those authorities. The provisions of the LED have been tailored to the context of law enforcement, affording law enforcement a certain degree of flexibility to enable them to carry out their tasks and duties.[21] The LED is applicable in the context of the AML/CFT framework, when data are requested or shared by law enforcement authorities (LEAs). It is debatable whether the GDPR or the LED are applicable to the processing of personal data and the problem only increases, where FIUs of a distinct nature (eg, law enforcement or hybrid) share data with FIUs that have an administrative character.[22]

[18] European Parliament and Council Regulation 2016/679 of 27 April 2016 on the protection of natural persons with regard to the processing of personal data and on the free movement of such data, and repealing Directive 95/46/EC (General Data Protection Regulation) [2016] OJ L119/1–88.

[19] Directive 2016/680 on the protection of natural persons with regard to the processing of personal data by competent authorities for the purposes of the prevention, investigation, detection or prosecution of criminal offences or the execution of criminal penalties, and on the free movement of such data (LED) [2016] OJ L119/89.

[20] Regulation (EU) 2018/1725 of the European Parliament and of the Council of 23 October 2018 on the protection of natural persons with regard to the processing of personal data by the Union institutions, bodies, offices and agencies and on the free movement of such data, and repealing Regulation (EC) No 45/2001 and Decision No 1247/2002/EC (Text with EEA relevance) ('EUDPR') [2018] OJ L295/39.

[21] European Union Agency for Fundamental Rights and Council of Europe, *Handbook on European Data Protection Law* (Luxembourg, Publications Office of the European Union, 2018) 283.

[22] M Brewczyńska, 'Financial Intelligence Units: Reflections on the Applicable Data Protection Legal Framework' (2021) *Computer Law & Security Review* 43; T Quintel, 'Follow the Money,

The EUDPR regulates the protection of natural persons with regard to the processing of personal data by the Union institutions and bodies, and introduces rules relating to the free movement of personal data between Union institutions and bodies or to other recipients established in the Union and includes the processing of personal data in the context of police and judicial cooperation for criminal matters. Chapter IX of the EUDPR is dedicated to the processing of operational personal data[23] by Union bodies, offices and agencies when carrying out activities which fall within the scope of Chapter 4 (Judicial Cooperation in Criminal Matters) or Chapter 5 (Police Cooperation) of Title V (Area of Freedom, Security and Justice) of the Treaty on the Functioning of the European Union (TFEU). It is thus a legal instrument that covers both general data processing and to a certain extent data processing in the context of police and judicial cooperation. As the AMLA is established as a Union body,[24] the EUDPR applies to the processing of personal data by the AMLA.

III. FIUs' ACCESS TO INFORMATION AND DATA SHARING UNDER THE AUSPICES OF THE AMLA

Member States have incorporated the FIUs in different ways and thus the nature of the FIUs has resulted in a patchwork of choices. Twelve European countries have indeed established FIUs that are administrative in nature,[25] nine countries have FIUs with a law enforcement/judicial nature[26] and six countries have hybrid FIUs.[27]

The European Data Protection Supervisor (EDPS) provided a short description of the differences between these FIU types: FIUs of an administrative nature are placed under the authority of Ministries of Finance, Justice, of the Interior, central banks or supervisory authorities, while FIUs that have a law enforcement nature are part of a structure with the competence to fight economic or other serious crimes. Finally, FIUs of a hybrid nature are established within national

If You Can – Possible Solutions for Enhanced FIU Cooperation Under Improved Data Protection Rules' (Europarättslig tidskrift 2019 1, March 2019 s. 35–50), available at https://lawpub.se/en/artikel/1225; F Mouzakiti, 'Cooperation between Financial Intelligence Units in the European Union: Stuck in the Middle between the General Data Protection Regulation and the Police Data Protection Directive' (2020) 11(3) *New Journal of European Criminal Law*, available at https://ieeexplore.ieee.org/document/6691683.

[23] 'Operational personal data' means all personal data processed by Union bodies, offices or agencies when carrying out activities which fall within the scope of Chapter 4 or Chapter 5 of Title V of Part Three TFEU to meet the objectives and tasks laid down in the legal acts establishing those bodies, offices or agencies (EUDPR (n 20) Art 3(2)).

[24] AMLA Regulation Proposal (n 10) Art 3.

[25] Belgium, Bulgaria, Croatia, Czechia, France, Italy, Latvia, Malta, Poland, Romania, Slovenia, Spain: EU FIUs' Platform, 'Mapping Exercise and Gap Analysis on FIUs' Powers and Obstacles for Obtaining and Exchanging Information' (15 December 2016).

[26] Austria, Estonia, Finland, Luxembourg, Ireland, Lithuania, Portugal, Slovakia, Sweden: ibid.

[27] Cyprus, Denmark, Greece, Hungary, Netherlands, Germany: ibid.

police offices or in the offices of the attorney general/prosecutor but separate from operational/judicial units and they are composed of both police officers and analysts from non-police organisations.[28] The discussion on the nature of the FIU as administrative, law enforcement/judicial or hybrid is not part of a theoretical debate as it has an impact on the applicable data protection framework on the processing of personal data by FIUs, on the type of information an FIU can get access to for the purposes of analysis and its other powers and the actual facilitation of such access.[29]

In order to clarify whether the GDPR or the LED apply when FIUs process personal data, it is first crucial to clarify the notion of competent authorities as defined in the LED.[30] As regards a competent authority in a strict sense, the LED requires it to be a 'public' body, as opposed to organisations of a private character. The second type of 'competent authority' is the authority 'entrusted' with the law enforcement task. Unlike a competent authority in a strict sense, this type of authority does not have to be public. Conversely, the definition does not preclude that a competent authority can also be a private entity if it is assigned the competence to exercise public authority and public powers for the law enforcement purposes by Member State law. Such a broad margin of manoeuvre makes it, on the one hand, easier to adjust to domestic realities, but, on the other, opens possibilities for diverging approaches and increasing differences across the EU. Thus, it is difficult to pin down which entities will in fact fall under the definition of a 'competent authority' without carrying out a detailed analysis of the national arrangements of the Member States. In addition, Mouzakiti conducted interviews with European FIUs and came to the conclusion that even FIUs that qualify as administrative ones might not necessarily fall under the GDPR's scope, and vice versa.[31]

The EDPS has repeatedly purported that FIUs are intelligence-gathering entities that act prior to any criminal investigation.[32] According to the EDPS, even if FIUs are structurally integrated within law enforcement or the judiciary, they should remain subject to the GDPR in their activities and should not be considered as competent authorities under the LED. This position can be called into question. The European Commission, in its report on the assessment on the framework for the cooperation between FIUs, recognised the lack of clarity regarding the applicable data protection framework as a known problem.

[28] EDPS Decision of 19 December 2019 relating to the technical administration of FIU.net by Europol, para 3.16.

[29] Europol letter to the Chair of the FIU.net Advisory Group, Consultation regarding the embedment of FIU.net into SIENA, 11 September 2019; EDPS Decision, ibid.

[30] LED (n 19) Art 3(7).

[31] Mouzakiti (n 22).

[32] EDPS, 'Opinion 6/2015 A Further Step towards Comprehensive EU Data Protection. EDPS Recommendations on the Directive for Data Protection in the Police and Justice Sectors' (2015) 5–6, available at https://edps.europa.eu/sites/edp/files/publication/15-10-28_directive_recommendations_en.pdf; EDPS, 'Opinion 12/2021 on the Anti-Money Laundering and Countering the Financing of Terrorism (AML/CFT) Package of Legislative Proposals (22 September 2021), available at https://edps.europa.eu/system/files/2021-09/21-09-22_edps-opinion-aml_en.pdf.

In particular, in relation to the exchange of data from FIUs to third countries, the report outlines the following:

> When Member States' FIUs exchange information with third countries, they have to comply with the relevant requirements of the applicable EU data protection regime, which in the case of FIU cooperation are determined by the General Data Protection Regulation. Despite this clear obligation, most FIUs apply the Police Data Protection Directive (Directive (EU) 2016/680) [referred to as the LED, in this report] instead or both the General Data Protection Regulation and the Police Data Protection Directive. While this issue applies to all the aspects of the work of FIUs, it is particularly relevant in relation to cooperation with the third countries, where the requirements and conditions for the exchanges are different under the Police Data Protection Directive.[33]

Based on the above, when FIUs of a law enforcement nature process personal data for law enforcement purposes, for example, when they exchange information for an AML investigation, (then) the processing can be governed by the LED. This assumes that FIUs are considered as competent authorities under the LED in the national legislation of these Member States, and hence one should look into the national laws to identify whether the FIUs are entrusted with the task of preventing crimes or not. While FIUs of a law enforcement nature would have the power to freeze transactions and to seize assets, administrative FIUs would not have similar powers.[34] Consequently, administrative FIUs would not have the competence to process data relating to seized accounts, which would become problematic in cases of exchange of information between FIUs. Further, due to their different natures, FIUs do not have access to the same type of information, nor are they able to share information with other FIUs, even if there is a legal obligation to do so.[35]

The new European legislative package on AML/CFT introduces rules that add further complexity to this issue. Article 18 6AMLD, and in particular paragraph(1)(c), envisages to give FIUs access to information which is held by competent authorities in the context of preventing, detecting, investigating or prosecuting criminal offences. FIUs in many Member States, where they are established with an administrative nature, will lack the legal basis for processing data relating to the prevention, detection, investigation or prosecution of criminal offences. In addition, the fact that FIUs can be provided access to law enforcement information will most likely not stand the scrutiny of the necessity and proportionality principles and the purpose limitation principle.

It is not clear whether FIUs sharing data under the auspices of the AMLA, will only share data regarding suspicious transactions or if they will also share

[33] European Commission, 'Report from the Commission to the European Parliament and the Council Assessing the Framework for Cooperation between Financial Intelligence Units, COM(2019) 371 (24 July 2019), 12 available at https://eur-lex.europa.eu/legal-content/EN/TXT/?uri=celex%3A52019DC0371.

[34] Quintel (n 22).

[35] Commission Staff Working Document, 'On Improving Cooperation between EU Financial Intelligence Units' SWD(2017) 275 final (Brussels, 26 June 2017).

the data types identified in Article 18 6AMLD, which qualify as law enforcement related data. In the case of the latter, administrative FIUs would obtain access to law enforcement data which may violate the legality, proportionality and purpose limitation principles. Although a solution would be for the legislator to vest the AMLA with the power to limit the access of administrative FIUs to law enforcement related data, this could become a very burdensome task for the AMLA, verifying which FIU may have access to what types of data.

IV. FIU.NET HOSTED BY THE AMLA

The AMLA Regulation further assigns the FIU.net to the AMLA, which 'shall ensure adequate and uninterrupted hosting, management, maintenance, and development of the FIU.net'.[36] The FIU.net is a decentralised computer network supporting EU FIUs in their fight against money-laundering and terrorist financing.[37] FIU.net became operational in 2007 and it was a system aimed at supporting the national authorities of the Member States in their fight against money laundering, by allowing and facilitating the exchange of information between FIUs on cross-border financial transactions.[38] As a 'decentralised' network, it did not have a central database and there was no centralised storage of data in one specific Member State where all the exchanged data were stored.[39] All the connected FIUs had their FIU.net equipment within their own premises and managed their own information. Europol was part of the network as an additional node and the AMLA is expected to play a similar role.

Upon its establishment in 2002, the FIU.net system was handled by the Dutch Ministry of Interior, with financial support from the European Commission.[40] In search for a long-term solution concerning the management of FIU.net, it was decided that FIU.net should be embedded within Europol and a Common Understanding was signed to that effect in 2013.[41] It is important that

> in order to realise the full potential of operational synergies between Europol and FIUs, the network facilitating information exchange between FIUs (FIU.net) will be

[36] AMLA Regulation (n 10) Art 37.

[37] Financial Intelligence Unit – the Netherlands, 'FIU.net', available at www.fiu-nederland.nl/en/about-the-fiu/international-cooperation/fiunet.

[38] Europol, 'Europol Joins Forces with EU FIUs to Fight Terrorist Financing and Money Laundering (28 January 2016), available at www.europol.europa.eu/media-press/newsroom/news/europol-joins-forces-eu-fius-to-fight-terrorist-financing-and-money-laundering.

[39] FIU.net (n 37).

[40] European Parliament, Parliamentary Questions, answer given by Mr Avramopoulos on behalf of the Commission, E015304/2015 (February 2016).

[41] Europol, '2014 Consolidated Annual Activity Report' (The Hague, 18 May 2015), available at www.europol.europa.eu/cms/sites/default/files/documents/consolidated_annual_activity_report_caar_2014_0.pdf.

replaced by SIENA (Europol's systems) and the services of the FIU.net Bureau will be fully embedded within Europol (including the staff of the FIU.net Bureau) ....[42]

In view of the above, FIU.net was officially integrated into Europol three years later and as of 1 January 2016, FIU.net was embedded within Europol to strengthen Europol's financial intelligence and counter terrorism capabilities. The aim of embedding FIU.net within Europol was to create more synergy between financial and criminal intelligence, ultimately boosting efforts to fighting organised crime and terrorism in the EU.[43] According to official statements, the network was set to support the work of Europol's European Counter Terrorism Centre, while FIUs would be able to request Europol to conduct searches with the Terrorist Finance Tracking Program on their behalf.[44]

The FIU.net application is explicitly referred to in a number of articles in 4AMLD[45] as the exchange mechanism for the EU FIUs. The FIU.net is mainly used for three main purposes: (1) cross-border reporting and dissemination;[46] (2) case building data exchange;[47] (3) 'anonymous' cross-match through Ma^{3}tch.[48] Ma^{3}tch (autonomous, anonymous, analysis) was a matching tool within FIU.net that made it possible for FIUs to match names in order to find potentially useful data that would be possessed by other connected FIUs.[49] Ma^{3}tch enabled each FIU to match data already in its files with data of other European FIUs in order to determine whether any of them might hold information that could be of use for their purpose. Where an FIU realised that that was the case, the other FIUs involved would be alerted and could share the actual personal data.[50] To guarantee anonymity, individual records were minimised and aggregated through technical means to ensure that any distinguishing mark could not be linked to an individual. The only characteristics that were captured in the anonymous filters were subsequently shared with selected parties, to ensure that they were able to find and attract the relevant information.[51]

[42] Europol, 'Work Programme 2013' (The Hague, 11 July 2012) 17, available at www.europol.europa.eu/cms/sites/default/files/documents/wp2013_0.pdf.

[43] Europol, 'Europol Joins Forces with EU FIUs to Fight Terrorist Financing and Money Laundering (28 January 2016), available at www.europol.europa.eu/media-press/newsroom/news/europol-joins-forces-eu-fius-to-fight-terrorist-financing-and-money-laundering.

[44] Council of the EU, 'Enhancing Counter Terrorism Capabilities at EU level: European Counter Terrorism Centre (ECTC) at Europol and Counter Terrorism Related Information Sharing' Document 14244/15 (23 November 2015).

[45] 4AMLD (n 2) Arts 51, 53 and 56.

[46] ibid Art 53.

[47] ibid Art 51.

[48] ibid Art 56(2); Mouzakiti (n 22).

[49] U Kroon, 'Ma3Tch: Privacy and Knowledge: 'Dynamic Networked Collective Intelligence'' (2013 IEEE International Conference on Big Data), available at https://ieeexplore.ieee.org/document/6691683.

[50] Mouzakiti (n 22).

[51] Kroon (n 49).

When information was sent from one FIU to another, the exchanged data were safely stored on the FIU.net databases that were located on the premises of the FIUs involved in the exchange.[52] All (at that time) 28 EU FIUs were connected to the FIU.net and in order to become a member of the FIU.net, each of those FIUs had to connect their internal database to FIU.net.[53]

In 2019, the EDPS found that the Europol Regulation did not provide a sufficient legal basis for Europol to process personal data for the purpose of performing the role of technical administrator of FIU.net. The EDPS banned all processing by Europol of data related to individuals who are not classed as 'suspects' under the applicable national criminal procedure law in the context of the technical administration of FIU.net.[54] However, considering the huge importance of FIU.net in the fight against money laundering at the Union level, the EDPS suspended the ban until 19 December 2020, in order to allow time for a smooth transition of the technical administration of FIU.net to another entity.[55] The AMLA is foreseen to take up this role as host of FIU.net.

In its Communication 'Towards Better Implementation of the EU/s Anti-Money Laundering and Countering the Financing of Terrorism Framework',[56] the Commission pointed out that there are, still today, several recurrent technical matters in the proper functioning of the FIU.net system, which have made it more cumbersome for FIUs to share information and thus, have resulted in less exchange of information and data matching between them.[57] Moreover, the Communication points at the lack of regulation on the exchange of information between Member States' FIUs and FIUs of third countries which has led to a non-harmonised approach to such exchanges, while it also indicates that the transformation of the AML/CFT Directive into a Regulation might be regarded as a potential solution towards a unified, harmonised and directly applicable Union regulatory anti-money laundering framework.[58] Apart from that, according to the EDPS, legal and practical obstacles, such as the ones mentioned above, inevitably have an impact on the accuracy and preciseness of information maintained within the FIU.net system and thus pose a risk for the protection of privacy and personal data.[59]

[52] FIU.net (n 37).

[53] ibid.

[54] European Data Protection Supervisor Decision of 19 December 2019 relating to the technical administration of FIU.net by Europol, para 5.3.

[55] ibid para 5.6.

[56] European Commission, Communication from the Commission to the European Parliament and the Council, 'Towards Better Implementation of the EU's Anti-Money Laundering and Countering the Financing of Terrorism Framework' COM/2019/360 final (24 July 2019), available at https://ec.europa.eu/info/publications/190724-anti-money-laundering-terrorism-financing-communication_en.

[57] ibid.

[58] ibid.

[59] European Data Protection Supervisor, Opinion 5/2020 on the European Commission's Action Plan for a Comprehensive Union Policy on Preventing Money Laundering and Terrorism Financing (2020) <https://edps.europa.eu/sites/edp/files/publication/20-07-23_edps_aml_opinion_en.pdf.

Even if Europol does not continue to host the FIU.net, it is envisioned as an information exchange hub in the Union. Europol receives and holds valuable information from third countries and international organisations on persons suspected of being involved in crimes that fall within Europol's objectives.[60] Recital 19 of the Europol Recast Regulation addresses the issue of the competence of Europol to process data:

> Where Member States use Europol's infrastructure for the exchange of personal data on crimes that do not fall within Europol's objectives, Europol should not have access to those data and should be considered to be a processor pursuant to Article 87 of Regulation (EU) 2018/1725. In those cases, Europol should be able to process data that do not relate to the categories of data subjects listed in Annex II. Where Member States use Europol's infrastructure for the exchange of personal data on crimes that fall within Europol's objectives and where they grant Europol access to those data, the requirements linked to the categories of data subjects listed in Annex II should apply to any other processing of those data by Europol.[61]

The Europol Recast Regulation contains concrete rules on the exchange of data with Eurojust or the European Anti-Fraud Office.

It is important to bear in mind that if Europol transfers personal data to Member States, third countries or international organisations, the responsibility for the legality of such a transfer shall remain with Europol. Europol is responsible for all data processing operations carried out by it with the exception of processing that is carried out using Europol's infrastructure between Member States, Union bodies, third countries and international organisations to which Europol has no access. The national entities in the exchange of data shall be responsible for such transfers.[62] Hence, based on Article 38 Europol Recast Regulation, it can be concluded that in the event of a transfer of data from EUROPOL to the AMLA, Europol will ensure the legality of transfer and shall take responsibility for the data processing operations carried out on data being transferred until such transfer is complete.

V. FIUs: JOINT ANALYSES OF SUSPICIOUS TRANSACTIONS AND ACTIVITIES – IMPLICATIONS FOR THE AMLA

The new legislative package on AML/CFT contains rules on the carrying out of joint analyses by FIUs both in 6AMLD[63] and in the AMLA Regulation[64] and

[60] European Parliament and the Council of the European Union, Regulation 2022/991 of 8 June 2022 amending Regulation (EU) 2016/794, as regards Europol's cooperation with private parties, the processing of personal data by Europol in support of criminal investigations, and Europol's role in research and innovation [2022] OJ L169/1 (Europol Recast Regulation), Recital 9.

[61] ibid Recital 19.

[62] Regulation (EU) 2016/794 of the European Parliament and of the Council of 11 May 2016 on the European Union Agency for Law Enforcement Cooperation (Europol), Art 38(7).

[63] 6AMLD (n 9) Art 25.

[64] AMLA Regulation (n 10) Art 33.

it foresees the set-up of a dedicated, secured channel of communication for the performance of these joint analyses.[65]

Recital 54 6AMLD explicates the rationale behind the joint analyses. Since several FIUs have reported issues which pose obstacles to the proper and ideal functioning and cooperation between the FIUs, they should be able

> to conduct joint analyses of suspicious transactions and activities and to set up and participate in joint analysis teams for specific purposes and limited period with the assistance of the AMLA. The participation of third parties may be instrumental for the successful outcome of joint analyses. Therefore, FIUs may invite third parties to take part in the joint analysis where such participation would fall within the respective mandates of those third parties.[66]

The purpose limitation and storage limitation principles are implied in Recital 54 6AMLD. Article 25(2) 6AMLD contains a reference to Article 33 AMLA Regulation, clarifying that the AMLA will assist in the setting up of a joint analysis team, instead of being responsible for coordinating it. In the Explanatory Memorandum of the AMLA Regulation, it is determined that 'The Authority will serve as a support and coordination hub assisting their work on, inter alia, joint analyses of Suspicious Transaction Reports and Suspicious Activity Reports with significant cross-border footprint, and providing stable hosting of the FIU.net platform'.[67] In order to specify whether the AMLA will be the data controller of the processing of personal data in this context, it will be important to see how the joint analyses will be organised in practice, in order to identify whether the AMLA will define the purposes and the means of the processing, as the definition of a data controller requires.

VI. CROSS-BORDER DATA TRANSFERS

One of the tasks of the AMLA is to develop appropriate methods and procedures for the FIUs to be able to conduct analyses regarding cross-border cases jointly.[68] The notion of 'cross-border' cases is not defined; however, Article 2(7) 6AMLD defines the notion of an 'entity operating on a cross-border basis' as 'an obliged entity having at least one establishment in another Member State or in a third country'. Following this definition, cases that take place in one Member State and at least one other Member State or a third country shall be considered cross-border cases. In the context of cross-border data transfers, the AMLA Regulation uses a different wording than the one used in the European data protection framework. My suggestion would be to call intra-EU data exchanges

[65] ibid Art 33(4) and 6AMLD (n 9) Art 23.
[66] 6AMLD (n 9) Recital 54.
[67] AMLA Regulation (n 10) 4.
[68] ibid Art 5(5)(c).

'transmissions' and data exchanges with third countries 'transfers', so that the term coincides with the data protection notion of 'international transfers'.

The AMLA is empowered to enter into administrative agreements with authorities in third countries that have FIU-related competences.[69] In the event of interaction between FIUs and several EU public authorities with relevant authorities of third countries that correspond to the tasks assigned to the AMLA under Article 5(5) AMLA Regulation, the AMLA shall have a leading role in facilitating such interactions.[70]

From a data protection point of view, it is important that Article 84 of the AMLA Regulation explicitly provides that the processing of personal data on the basis of the AMLA Regulation shall be considered necessary for the performance of a task carried out in the public interest or in the exercise of official authority vested in the AMLA under Article 5 EUDPR and Article 6 GDPR. The AMLA has the power to draft guidelines and recommendations to ensure the consistent application of Union law,[71] while it is required to consult the EDPS when recommendations and guidelines have a significant impact on personal data.[72] Chapter V of the EUDPR has the necessary provisions related to the transfer of data to third countries. In the absence of an adequacy decision, the EUDPR permits the transfer of data based on appropriate safeguards.[73] The transfer based on legally binding and enforceable instrument between public authorities and Union bodies[74] is particularly relevant in the context of the AMLA as the AMLA has the power to facilitate administrative agreements between the relevant authorities in the bodies of third countries and the Union.

According to Article 51 EUDPR, the EDPS, in cooperation with the Commission and the EDPB, shall take the necessary steps to develop international cooperation mechanisms to facilitate the protection of personal data in relation to third countries and international organisations. This could mean that while drafting administrative agreements between the relevant authorities of third countries and the Union bodies, the AMLA will need to ensure close cooperation with the EDPS for the exchange of personal data.

Article 35 6AMLD requires supervisors, such as the AMLA, to assess the feasibility of the implementation of policies according to Union law in third countries. In the absence of the proper implementation of the relevant policies and procedures including those related to professional secrecy and data protection, the supervisors should inform each other and take coordinated actions to pursue a solution. Member States have the power to authorise financial supervisors to conclude cooperation agreements with their counterparts in third

[69] ibid Art 81; ibid Recital 63.
[70] ibid Art 81.
[71] ibid Art 43.
[72] ibid Art 84.
[73] EUDPR (n 20) Art 48.
[74] ibid Art 48(2)(a).

countries with respect to exchanging confidential agreements.[75] These cooperation agreements must comply with the relevant data protection rules.[76] The AMLA is expected to lend assistance to determine equivalence of professional secrecy requirements of third countries for the cooperation agreements.[77]

VII. CONCLUSIONS

The AMLA is a long-awaited authority that aspires to play a central role in an integrated system composed of the AMLA and the national authorities that have a AML/CFT supervisory mandate. In this chapter, however, focus was paid to the support that the AMLA is expected to give to FIUs and the role of the AMLA in establishing and supporting a cooperation mechanism between national FIUs. Despite the lack of a pan-European FIU that could be the single point of contact for foreign FIUs, the AMLA has not been vested with such a role. This would require a different legislative and political approach towards the role of the AMLA and the structure of the European AML/CFT system.

This chapter has taken a critical look at the provisions of the AMLA from a data protection point of view. Often, AML/CFT activities have required an exchange of personal information about individuals, possibly including suspects, and the enforcement of the data protection rules has been rather lax. The newly proposed legal framework vouches to take data protection seriously and the AMLA Regulation is offered with an opportunity to take data protection rules into account in its activities from the outset. This chapter has raised a few areas of concern where the rules of the AMLA could be in conflict with the data protection rules. Most prominent in the analysis is the relationship between the AMLA and the national FIUs. The AMLA is tasked with enhancing and facilitating cooperation between FIUs, and with hosting FIU.net. In this context, the AMLA should pay close attention to the applicable data protection rules and the implications these may have both for national FIUs as well as for the joint analyses they will be carrying out. The establishment of the AMLA is a good opportunity for the AML/CFT system and its activities shall pave the way to ensure that data protection rules are not a hurdle that needs to be overcome, but are instead an essential component that ensure AML/CFT activities that are fundamentally rights-compliant.

[75] 6AMLD (n 9) Art 37.
[76] ibid.
[77] ibid.

Part III

Artificial Intelligence and Criminal Justice

9

Algorithmic Predictions, Justice and Privacy

YULIA RAZMETAEVA*

A WORLD FULL of algorithms seems more predictable, and the forecasting power of smart machines seems to be such that it can be successfully applied in the legal field and promote justice. At the same time, there are many problems, both visible and almost invisible, that call into question the credibility of algorithmic justice as such.

The understanding and application of human rights is changing under the influence of algorithms, and rights such as privacy are or should be becoming essential, designed to leave individuals with control over their lives. However, both in relation to algorithmic justice and in relation to the new meaning of privacy, the law does not always demonstrate an anticipatory ability. This is even more true in traditionally conservative areas such as criminal law, whose low volatility is based on the idea of protecting human rights, and in the digital age this feature can have unexpected vulnerabilities.

Artificial agents such as strong artificial intelligence (AI) and smart algorithms promised to be a breakthrough for humanity. They were to be one of those great achievements that can pave the way for or open the way to historical turning points, a better future and prosperity. A major role in these expectations was played by the perceived reliability, accuracy, impartiality, and strong predictive power of algorithmic tools.

The development of technologies and especially algorithms has led to a world densely populated by artificial agents invisible to the naked eye, but that significantly affect our lives. This is the world of 'ubiquitous, autonomic or pre-emptive computing'[1] in the words of Mireille Hildebrandt. The pre-emptive

* Yaroslav Mudryi National Law University / Uppsala University. Email: yulia.razmetaeva@crs.uu.se. The author expresses her gratitude to The Royal Swedish Academy of Sciences (KVA) for the opportunity to start this research and to Wallenberg Foundations for the opportunity to continue this research.

[1] M Hildebrandt, *Smart Technologies and the End(s) of Law* (Cheltenham, Edward Elgar, 2015) 8.

and predictive abilities of algorithms are often not perceived as something of a problem, given perhaps a long-standing human desire to make the world a more predictable and safer place. On the one hand, it can be difficult to deal with the unpredictability of everyday life and social practices. In this sense, algorithms, designed to deal with this uncertainty and make decisions based on rational choice and evidence, rather than on intuition, may be seen as a good response and extremely useful tools. On the other, uncertainty, the senses, and the capacity for doubt are also an important part of human nature. The 'uncertainty' that is defined as the 'unpredictability of events',[2] might be a problem, but it is not something we as humans can overcome once and for all. Algorithms, however, in addition to being aimed at certainty, seek to offer the final resolution for the cases they work with. They also seek to increase predictability to the greatest extent possible. Here we are confronted with a discrepancy between the nature of people and algorithms that cannot be bridged without answering at least two questions. The first question is: to what extent do we need predictability? The second question is: what decisions do we perceive as those that meet the requirements of justice?

To answer these questions, consider, first of all, predictive algorithmic tools in the justice system. The example of risk assessment systems that are probably the most illustrative here given their prevalence, use at various stages of the process and at the same time, doubts about transparency and non-discrimination. These systems were supposed to help partially automate justice, but the effect seems to be the opposite, since they have been introduced with a lack of safeguards and respect for human rights, without taking into account their impact on individuals and groups, and the wider impact on society, exacerbating and deepening existing biases and inequalities.[3] It seems that the deepening of biases occurs for the following reasons, together or separately: (1) algorithms are introduced without sufficient control over how they are created and tested; (2) algorithms learn from discriminatory practices without context sensitivity; (3) algorithms fail to take into account an extremely wide range of human characteristics. In the first case, risk assessment systems may repeat the biases of their creators, whether intentionally or not. In the second case, an array of data for previous years and centuries, even if this data is properly cleaned, will show those prejudices concerning race, nationality, ethnicity, etc, which today would be discriminatory from a human's point of view, but which an algorithm is likely to recognise as a pattern and repeat it. In the third case, cutting off atypical individual traits and combinations of circumstances is possible due to the limits of complexity of the algorithm. Thus, we cannot say that such algorithms are really good at making predictions, since their premises are wrong, nor can we

[2] G Merlhiot, M Mermillod, J-L Le Pennec, F Dutheil, and L Mondillon, 'Influence of Uncertainty on Framed Decision-Making with Moral Dilemma' (2018) 13(5) *PLoS ONE* e0197923.

[3] 'Automating Injustice: The Use of Artificial Intelligence & Automated Decision-Making Systems in Criminal Justice in Europe (Fair Trials, 2021 Report) 6.

say that these are exactly the kind of predictions we need, since they do not seem to contribute to fairness.

In addition, we will not be able to evaluate the fairness and accuracy of the predictions of certain algorithms due to the secrets that underlie them. AI tools are often owned by private companies and protected by trade secrets, but are used in the public sector, including in the criminal justice system. In the widely publicised case *State of Wisconsin v Loomis*, the use of the algorithmic tool Correctional Offender Management Profiling for Alternative Sanctions (COMPAS) was challenged.[4] The two reasons underlying the claim were (1) the proprietary nature of the tool, since the plaintiff could not find out exactly how a percentage estimate is created based on a number of characteristics, and therefore was not able to challenge its scientific validity, and (2) the fact that gender was one of the characteristics for forming an assessment. The Wisconsin Supreme Court refused to admit the violation of Eric Loomis' right to due process; even though the methodology used to conduct the assessment was not disclosed to either the Court or the convicted person. One of the arguments of the Court was that the assessment given by COMPAS was not the only basis for the decision, and the verdict was rather individualised, because the courts have discretionary powers and the information necessary to disagree with an assessment when necessary.[5] The dependence of the public sector on private actors who create, modify, adjust and maintain algorithms could be one of several implicit risks for justice. For example, companies may legally refuse to disclose the source code, thereby depriving users, including government organisations and institutions, of the opportunity to check potential discriminative vulnerabilities of the algorithmic tool, as well as technical errors.

Aleš Završnik wrote:

> There are competing notions of fairness and predictive accuracy, which means a simple transposition of methods from one domain (for example, earthquake prediction to sentencing) can lead to distorted views of what algorithms calculate. The current transfer of statistical modelling in the criminal justice domain neglects the balance between competing values or, at best, re-negotiates competing values without adequate social consensus.[6]

Two implications of the use of algorithms in the justice system can be particularly detrimental to justice and fairness itself. The first is the transfer of methods and models from the natural and formal sciences to the social sphere without taking into account the peculiarities of the latter. The second is the growing trust in algorithms and the habit of relying on them for decision-making. Returning to the Wisconsin Supreme Court's reasoning in the case described above, it is

[4] See *State of Wisconsin v Loomis*, 881 N.W. 2d 749 (2016).

[5] ibid para 764, 765.

[6] A Završnik, 'Algorithmic Justice: Algorithms and Big Data in Criminal Justice Settings' (2021) 18(5) *European Journal of Criminology* 630.

worth noting that while judges can still make final decisions by accepting or rejecting algorithmic scores and prompts, it is becoming increasingly difficult to ignore them. Even using these tools as an additional support for decision-making changes people's perceptions. Therefore, people may develop the habit of over-relying on algorithms in order to make decisions.

As Adam Harkens wrote: 'The "intelligence" of an algorithm is judged upon the efficiency it creates, and the economic fluidity it allows. This is justified by the rationality that an algorithm is merely objectively "crunching numbers"'.[7] The focus on efficiency leads us to a utilitarian and pure rational understanding of things. First, you have to measure and weigh the manifestations of human nature, the characteristics and individual circumstances, and deduct some of them, in order to create a working algorithm that can help make decisions. Second, perceiving algorithms as efficient and rational creates a dangerous belief that they offer better solutions than humans. After all, people are subject to fatigue, emotions, personal preferences, exposure to the work environment, and so on. Third, we might well adopt an algorithmic style of thinking, losing the flexibility, openness and originality of this.

Decision-makers, including judges, can consider all individual features and circumstances. Algorithms can only consider a limited set of them, relying on previously embedded data and codes. Some smart algorithms are capable of self-learning, however, their ability to take into account an infinite number of circumstances and individual traits is questionable, and their decision paths are even more opaque than in the case of simpler algorithms. Decision-makers are required to act within the framework outlined by the demands of justice, democracy, human rights, and specific norms and precedents. At the same time, while complying with these requirements, they may act in accordance with a sense of justice, giving proper justification for this. According to John Rawls: 'The sense of justice (as a form of moral sensibility) involves an intellectual power, since its exercise in making judgements calls upon the powers of reason, imagination and judgement.'[8] Justice based on algorithms may lead us to a world where all the results of a decision become the results of only utilitarian and rational choices. The capacity for moral judgement, empathy, intuition and imagination are revealed as unnecessary. By giving up parts of human nature, we thus lose our humanity.

Predicting the outcome of a future case may be our human desire. However, do we really need to know this exactly? The problem here may not only be that real or a perceived high level of accuracy breeds some fatalism. Problems may also include, firstly, forecasting the impact of our expectations, shaping or changing them, and, secondly, the essence of justice and the essence of law may be distorted.

[7] A Harkens, 'The Ghost in the Legal Machine: Algorithmic Governmentality, Economy, and the Practice of Law' (2018) 16(1) *Journal of Information, Communication and Ethics in Society* 20.

[8] J Rawls, *Justice as Fairness: A Restatement* (Cambridge, Massachusetts, Harvard University Press, 2001) 29.

Algorithms could help us to calculate and predict future decisions, including court decisions. It is remarkable that fairly accurate predictions can be used both to influence judges and to sell a certain outcome to interested parties. In particular, the model designed to predict the behaviour of the Supreme Court of the United States showed a 70.2 per cent accuracy at the case outcome level and 71.9 per cent at the justice vote level.[9] Decision prediction models for decisions made by the European Court of Human Rights showed that the overall test accuracy, across the 12 Articles of the European Convention on Human Rights, was 68.83 per cent, while heuristics achieved an overall test accuracy of 86.68 per cent.[10]

Some algorithmic tools are aimed at indirect forecasting, for example, to ensure that to help understand the way the justices at the Supreme Court of the United States vote, and in particular the way the justices group themselves into a majority or a minority coalition.[11] Others are aimed at a direct prediction of verdicts, for example, to predict outcomes of the courts of the Turkish legal system with a high level of accuracy using deep-learning based methods.[12] Some researches directly present the ability to apply the proposed algorithms as an advantage that assists 'lawyers and judges to verify trends of judgments' and helps 'lawyers predict the judicial outcomes for very specific situations'.[13] It is doubtful whether such predictability is beneficial to certain elements of the legal process, such as adversarial processes or legal certainty.

Indeed, the requirements of predictability are reflected in the legal certainty, which is an element of the rule of law and justice. We need to understand what the consequences of following or breaking the law will be. At the same time, compliance with or a violation of norms is a human choice. If someone has acted under duress in violation of the law, that person is not responsible for the violation. If someone's free will has been attacked in some other way, the degree of responsibility will depend on the degree of influence exerted, as well as the individual characteristics of the person and life circumstances. The law must be known and understandable to everyone. Undoubtedly, this is a simplified scheme, but its essence implies a certain balance of predictability. Roughly speaking, it cannot be zero per cent (then something is wrong in a particular case

[9] DM Katz, MJ II Bommarito and J Blackman, 'A General Approach for Predicting the Behavior of the Supreme Court of the United States' (2017) 12(4) *PLoS ONE* e0174698.

[10] C O'Sullivan and J Beel, 'Predicting the Outcome of Judicial Decisions made by the European Court of Human Rights' (27th AIAI Irish Conference on Artificial Intelligence and Cognitive Science, 2019) 101–12.

[11] N Giansiracusa and C Ricciardi, 'Computational Geometry and the US Supreme Court' (2019) 98 *Mathematical Social Sciences* 1–9.

[12] E Mumcuoğlu, CE Öztürk, HM Ozaktas and A Koç, 'Natural Language Processing in Law: Prediction of Outcomes in the Higher Courts of Turkey' (2021) 58 *Information Processing and Management* 102684.

[13] WPD Fernandes et al, 'Extracting Value from Brazilian Court Decisions' (2022) 106 *Information Systems* 10196.

or in a particular law) and it cannot be 100 per cent (then it is something other than what we now call law and justice). And the pendulum fluctuates between these two values, depending on the complexity of the case and the quality of the legal norms and precedents, without reaching these two extreme points.

Kieron O'Hara wrote:

> The regulatory function of law requires it to be broadly predictable. If it is to guide and coordinate our actions, then we must have a reasonable idea of how a new case would be interpreted in the light of past decisions.[14]

In order to determine what will be a fair decision in a particular case, judges, based on the facts, apply not only legislation and precedents, but also complex considerations based on their understanding and experience of the law. In addition, the judges must justify this decision in such a way as to convince others of its fairness. An explanation of a court decision is an important part of justice. Understanding the law, moreover, the human understanding of it, is an important part of the interpretation of the law. Algorithms, on the contrary, are distinguished by the absence of an explanation of the decisions made, both due to the complexity of the operation of certain algorithms, and due to the fact that decision-making can be completely or partially secret.

As it has rightly been pointed out:

> What counts is that legal norms are in principle made by as well as for the constituency and to have 'force of law' they must be public in the sense of being visible and legible for every person that is expected to comply with them.[15]

In most cases, algorithms are not subject to such a stage of public discussion as laws are before being introduced into the public sphere. They are also not tested for explainability in the broadest sense, and not in the sense of how a chain of code is built and data is processed so that artificial agents can issue an answer to a question or draw conclusions about a specific task.

Furthermore, the introduction and deployment of algorithms changes the models we focus on. The number of decisions that are made by algorithms or with significant reliance on them is growing exponentially and these algorithms are exercised over human decision-making and without understanding the deeper implications. Ultimately, we risk losing the desire for justice in the human sense as we understand it.

Legal responses often do not keep pace with the development of the algorithmic technologies in the digital age. This is especially evident in such conservative branches of law as criminal law and procedural law. Certainly, the strict requirements for adding a new offence to criminal law or changing the procedure for issuing a measure of restraint are due to the requirements of protecting human

[14] K O'Hara, 'Explainable AI and the Philosophy and Practice of Explanation' (2020) 39 *Computer Law & Security Review* 105474.

[15] Hildebrandt (n 1) 10.

rights. This is one of the mechanisms that helps to avoid a law treatment of the law and abuse of power. However, conservatism can lead to serious vulnerabilities in the digital age. With conservative branches of law on the one hand, and growing digitalisation on the other, this is not a very good alignment for deterring algorithmic threats. Seeing as algorithms can undermine justice, we should not open the door to algorithmic justice until we reconsider the human understanding of certain fundamental concepts and values in the digital age.

To prove this point we could consider how the concept of privacy has been affected by the implementation and deployment of algorithms, and, more importantly, how this concept will be changed and the how the right to privacy will suffer in order to algorithmise justice.

Privacy is a fundamental right, which is especially important in the digital era, and, simultaneously, is a concept that has a significant impact on the lives of individuals and societies. The changes which the concept of this right has already undergone can be expressed in the following way: it acquires the features of a collective phenomenon, the focus of communication is shifting from people to devices, trust in artificial agents is increasing, a significant part of our lives is moving to the online space and privacy is affected by the long-lasting digital footprint most people leave, and the expectations regarding private life have changed, including those that pertain to a complete control of primary, secondary, and behavioural information.[16] The very understanding of terms such as 'private and public person', 'private and public sphere', 'private and public interest' has changed.[17]

The understanding and application of human rights is changing significantly under the influence of algorithms, and rights such as privacy are or should be becoming even more essential, designed as they are to ensure that we have control over our lives. The importance of this control cannot be over-emphasised given the number of targeted, narrowly focused influences that we are already exposed to and given the fact that algorithms have settled almost imperceptibly but so powerfully into our lives. You cannot ignore the shift in the balance of power in the digital age, when the owners and beneficiaries of certain technologies become unnecessarily powerful. However, the law does not always demonstrate a leading ability in relation to algorithmic justice and the new meaning of the term privacy. The most conservative privacy doctrines cannot provide adequate and effective legal protection anymore, unless conservative approaches to privacy start to apply some changes. First of all, this is expressed in the gradual blurring of the distinction between actions performed in physical space and in cyberspace. In 2017, in the case of *Packingham v North Carolina*, the Supreme Court of the United States recognised social media websites as a modern public

[16] See R Marcinauskaitė and Y Razmetaeva, 'Privacy Protection in the Digital Age: A Criminal Law Perspective' (2021) 7(2) *International Comparative Jurisprudence* 154, 155.
[17] ibid 156.

square and protected place for the freedom of expression,[18] actually giving them the status of a public place and forum without reference to physical space.

Understanding privacy from a less conservative approach involves an increasingly complex balancing with other rights. A trend in European law that can be clearly seen in the practice of the most authoritative judicial institutions is, it seems, the maintenance of high standards of privacy protection with a dynamic and casual balance. For example, in 2019, in the case of *López Ribalda and Others v Spain*, the European Court of Human Rights did not agree with the national courts of Spain that the video surveillance used to detect the theft by the supermarket staff was proportionate and that the balance between the applicants' right to respect for their private lives and the other interests was fair.[19] In addition, the Court emphasised:

> Since there are occasions when people knowingly or intentionally involve themselves in activities which are or may be recorded or reported in a public manner, a person's reasonable expectations as to privacy may be a significant, although not necessarily conclusive, factor in this assessment.[20]

The details of the case, such as the wide coverage of the video surveillance, which was not limited in time, covered all employees at the cash registers during all their working hours and the reasonable expectations of the applicants regarding the protection of their privacy, influenced the fact that the violation of privacy was finally recognised. These reasonable expectations can be especially meaningful in the digital age, when privacy is shrinking faster and faster under the influence of ubiquitous surveillance, cyberspace interactions and pervasive algorithms.

Considering privacy violations under algorithmic detection and profiling, Bart van der Sloot wrote: 'With these types of Big Data processes, the individual interest is difficult to substantiate and it is increasingly hard to prove concrete and personal harm following from an interference.'[21] This is reflected in the protection of privacy in court, as it becomes increasingly difficult to prove violations and explain how they are made, and in its conception, since personal harm or personal data may no longer be necessary elements for such protection. The pieces of data that are tracked and interconnected by algorithms may not be personal as such private information would seriously interfere with our personal lives. Personal harm may be unclear, delayed or part of the harm done to a social group, community, or society as a whole.

The continued implementation and deployment of algorithms will require us to intervene even more in what is in the private domain. The main reason

[18] See *Packingham v North Carolina*, 582 US ___ (2017).
[19] See *López Ribalda and Others v Spain* [GC] – 1874/13 and 8567/13 (2019).
[20] ibid para 89.
[21] B van der Sloot, 'A New Approach to the Right to Privacy, or how the European Court of Human Rights Embraced the Non-Domination Principle' (2018) 34 *Computer Law & Security Review* 542.

the privacy domain will shrink is because the algorithm needs to be fed by data in order for it to survive and it needs to be well fed in order for it to evolve. In addition, the bias of algorithms, their possible discriminatory nature, and their tendency to increase unfairness require an adequate response. If the answer is to increase the diversity in the data in order to teach diversity and context sensitivity to algorithms, this will require even more sparse and sensitive data. It will also increase the risk of intrusion into the privacy of those individuals and groups who, due to their special features, small numbers, seclusion, or other characteristics, fall out of algorithmic accounting.

Roger Clarke emphasises that 'public hand-wringing about the risks inherent in AI is of no value unless it stimulates constructive action that addresses those risks'.[22] Before taking these actions, we must seriously consider them strategically and only thereafter tactically. There is a difference between trying to swim in a turbulent river if we jumped in of our own accord and had trained to do it, or if we slipped in from a steep bank unexpectedly and without being prepared. There is also a difference between each of us trying to cross a turbulent river on our own raft or in our own boat, and when we are trying to establish a crossing together.

Algorithms should appear to conform to reasonable and fair standards so that we can trust them to do part of the work. However, in their current form, algorithms are not compatible with the requirements of justice. Predictability in the algorithmic sense can undermine the foundations of justice from the sense of human understanding. As human beings we need predictability to a limited extent, that said to the extent that, firstly, it does not distort the foundations of justice and law, and, secondly, it does not make us utilitarian algorithmic fatalists, no longer capable of comprehending their essence. It is incredibly important to rethink and to save the human understanding of law and justice in the digital age.

[22] R Clarke, 'Regulatory Alternatives for AI' (2019) 35 *Computer Law & Security Review* 407.

10

Artificial Intelligence in Criminal Justice: Strengthening or Challenging the Rule of Law?

EMMANOUIL BILLIS*

I. INTRODUCTION

IN THE 'GLOBAL risk society',[1] crime is becoming more sophisticated, complex and transnational, while enforcement and judicial systems are becoming ponderous and overloaded. As a result, the practical significance of mechanisms and institutions aimed at enhancing (national and transnational) law enforcement and improving justice administration has grown. A key aspect in this regard is the revolutionary importance of artificial intelligence (AI) for many policy sectors. Numerous legal orders are currently resorting to this technology with the goal of strengthening the efficiency and effectiveness of crime control and criminal justice systems and of optimising the decision-making processes. In an era of multiple novel challenges in the fight against crime, a plethora of AI applications has emerged in parallel with traditional enforcement and judicial practices set to serve a variety of purposes: from predictive policing, crime prevention and crime detection to risk and recidivism assessment, the processing of evidence and the determination of criminal punishment.[2]

* Dr Emmanouil Billis, LLM is Research Group Leader at the Max Planck Institute for the Study of Crime, Security and Law (Freiburg/Germany).

[1] See U Sieber, 'The New Architecture of Security Law – Crime Control in the Global Risk Society' in U Sieber, V Mitsilegas, C Mylonopoulos, E Billis and N Knust (eds), *Alternative Systems of Crime Control. National, Transnational, and International Dimensions* (Berlin, Duncker & Humblot, 2018) 3ff.

[2] See, eg, in this volume the contributions by G Petri, Y Razmetaeva, K Ligeti, M Caianiello, E Bampasika, C Salvi, R Fortson and T Quintel and D Cole. See also E Billis, N Knust and JP Rui, 'Künstliche Intelligenz und der Grundsatz der Verhältnismäßigkeit' in M Engelhart, H Kudlich and B Vogel (eds), *Digitalisierung, Globalisierung und Risikoprävention – Festschrift für Ulrich Sieber zum 70. Geburtstag, Teilband II* (Berlin, Duncker & Humblot, 2021) 693, 698ff. More generally on the various possible uses of AI, *inter alia*, Organisation for Economic Cooperation and Development (OECD), 'Artificial Intelligence in Society' (Paris, OECD Publishing, 2019) 47–80; F Pereira,

As the studies in this volume so clearly demonstrate, fundamental research and legal policy are called to address not only the opportunities but also the considerable risks for the peaceful coexistence of humans that come with such an evolution mainly in two ways. On the one hand, compared to prior (conventional) technological advancements, employing new AI technology to realise ambitious anti-crime plans might result in broader, more direct and multi-layered threats to established rights and freedoms. In view of this, extensive *a priori* bans of AI uses identified as particularly dangerous for individuals or societies may be deemed necessary. On the other (hand), the debate over the 'inevitability' of the expansion of AI should not only be about getting the most out of this technology in terms of effective crime fighting. The first priority must be to develop the algorithms ('step-by-step procedure for calculation, data processing, evaluation and automated reasoning and decision-making')[3] and to program the machines in accordance with the overriding objectives of substantially protecting and securing respect for the most basic human and social values. In this context, research and policy are called to enable continuous cooperation and knowledge exchange between legal scholars, justice authorities and computer scientists from the AI field. The corresponding objectives of such a collaboration could be to promote mutual understanding about the actual operation of new technologies in the legal world and to develop strategies on how to successfully and dynamically 'translate' diachronic legal notions and protective principles into programming language.[4] Exploring particularly sensitive matters connected to broader socio-legal and legal-ethical questions about justice, legitimacy and democracy should be at the heart of any such research. In this context, issues of privacy, data protection, security, reliability, transparency and objectivity, bias and discrimination as well as the explicability and accountability parameters of the AI applications constitute significant individual subjects of discourse.[5]

P Machado, E Costa and A Cardoso (eds), *Progress in Artificial Intelligence* (Cham, Springer, 2015); M Kment and S Borchert, *Künstliche Intelligenz und Algorithmen in der Rechtsanwendung* (Munich, Beck, 2022); J Wagner, *Legal Tech und Legal Robots. Der Wandel im Rechtsmarkt durch neue Technologien und künstliche Intelligenz* (Wiesbaden, Springer, 2018).

[3] On this description of an algorithm, see the European Union Agency for Fundamental Rights (FRA) and Council of Europe, 'Handbook on European Data Protection Law' (April 2018) 351.

[4] On the problem of 'the programmability of law (i. e. whether it can be transposed in computer code instructions which a machine can follow and execute)' and 'the algorithmization of the law', see E Hilgendorf, 'Introduction: Digitization and the Law – a European Perspective' in E Hilgendorf and J Feldle (eds), *Digitization and the Law* (Baden-Baden, Nomos, 2018) 13ff. See further the studies in S Deakin and C Markou (eds), *Is Law Computable? Critical Perspectives on Law and Artificial Intelligence* (Oxford, Hart Publishing, 2020).

[5] See in general the Council of Europe, European Commission for the Efficiency of Justice (CEPEJ), 'European Ethical Charter on the Use of Artificial Intelligence in Judicial Systems and their Environment', adopted at the 31st plenary meeting of the CEPEJ (Strasbourg, 3–4 December 2018); OECD, 'Recommendation of the Council on Artificial Intelligence' (22 May 2019, OECD/LEGAL/0449). See further Artificial Intelligence in Society (n 2) 81–120. According to the EU Commission, High-Level Expert Group on Artificial Intelligence, 'Ethics Guidelines for Trustworthy AI' (8 April 2019) 2: '(…) Trustworthy AI has three components, which should be met throughout the system's entire life cycle: (1) it should be lawful, complying with all applicable laws and regulations (2) it should be

Equally important is the general discussion about whether algorithms and machines can perceive and employ fundamental legal concepts for the delivery of criminal justice, such as fairness and proportionality, and about the challenges of incorporating AI into criminal justice in a way that is consistent with core human rights standards and rule of law principles.

The design and implementation of effective and transparent policy plans and regulations in these fields require, on the one hand, a better understanding of the inner workings of the AI applications on the part of legal theory and practice. On the other (hand), AI developers need to have a firm grasp of the main ideas behind key legal concepts and their potential differentiations in different legal traditions. The joint study of the many (attempts at) definitions of AI, especially of their scope, practical significance and limitations (for example, regarding the controversial issue of autonomous or automated AI) is just one essential element.[6] In liberal democratic orders employing AI technology, the primary focus must be on the constitutive requirements of the rule of law: the principle of legality, including the consistent and impartial application of foreseeable, clear and transparent norms and institutions; the principles of equality and proportionality; the nonarbitrary use of power and the respect for fundamental rights and procedural guarantees, and the separation of state powers and the control of their exercise by independent and impartial judicial organs.[7]

ethical, ensuring adherence to ethical principles and values and (3) it should be robust, both from a technical and social perspective since, even with good intentions, AI systems can cause unintentional harm. (…) [It must be ensured] that the development, deployment and use of AI systems meets the seven key requirements for Trustworthy AI: (1) human agency and oversight, (2) technical robustness and safety, (3) privacy and data governance, (4) transparency, (5) diversity, non-discrimination and fairness, (6) environmental and societal well-being and (7) accountability.' See further the Council of Europe, Committee of Experts on Internet Intermediaries (MSI-NET), 'Algorithms and Human Rights. Study on the Human Rights Dimensions of Automated Data Processing Techniques and Possible Regulatory Implications' DGI(2017)12. On important ethical considerations in the creation of AI systems, see The IEEE Global Initiative on Ethics of Autonomous and Intelligent Systems, 'Ethically Aligned Design: A Vision for Prioritizing Human Well-being with Autonomous and Intelligent Systems' (2019). See also T Bynum, 'Computer and Information Ethics' in E Zalta (ed), *The Stanford Encyclopedia of Philosophy* (Summer 2018 Edition), available at https://plato.stanford.edu/archives/sum2018/entries/ethics-computer/.

[6] See, eg, the definitions of AI systems and techniques in: Regulation (EU) 2024/1689 of the European Parliament and of the Council of 13 June 2024 laying down harmonised rules on artificial intelligence (Artificial Intelligence Act), Art 3; Ethics Guidelines for Trustworthy AI (n 5) 36; EU Commission, High-Level Expert Group on Artificial Intelligence, 'A Definition of AI: Main Capabilities and Scientific Disciplines' (8 April 2019) 3, 7; Artificial Intelligence in Society (n 2) 15; European Ethical Charter on the Use of Artificial Intelligence in Judicial Systems and their Environment (n 5) 69–70; Council of Europe, Commissioner for Human Rights, 'Unboxing Artificial Intelligence: 10 Steps to Protect Human Rights', Recommendation, May 2019, 5; Communication from the Commission, 'Artificial Intelligence for Europe', 25.4.2018, COM(2018) 237 final, 1; Commission Staff Working Document, 'Liability for Emerging Digital Technologies', 25.4.2018, SWD(2018) 137 final; Communication from the Commission, 'Coordinated Plan on Artificial Intelligence', 7.12.2018, COM(2018) 795 final, 1.

[7] See Communication from the Commission to the European Parliament, the European Council and the Council, 'Further Strengthening the Rule of Law within the Union', 3.4.2019, COM(2019) 163 final, 1: 'The rule of law is one of the founding values of the European Union, as well as a reflec-

In terms of the relationship between AI and the rule of law specifically, the challenge is twofold: to proactively program AI tools in a way that excludes arbitrariness in decision-making processes involving such tools and to optimise the operation and learning processes of AI with the overall purpose of complementing the traditional justice sector in producing more accurate, objective and fair results. The present chapter discusses characteristic questions and problems of contemporary importance for legal theory, policy and practice associated with the key notions of human dignity, legality, proportionality, privacy, equality and procedural justice. It focuses on the meaning and significance of rule of law and human rights considerations in designing and employing AI tools for crime control and criminal justice purposes.

II. HUMAN DIGNITY, HUMAN RIGHTS AND THE RULE OF LAW: THE DEMAND FOR HUMAN-CENTRIC AND LAWFUL AI

> (…) The notion of the Rule of Law requires a system of certain and foreseeable law, where everyone has the right to be treated by all decision-makers with dignity, equality and rationality and in accordance with the laws, and to have the opportunity to challenge decisions before independent and impartial courts through fair procedures. (…) The Rule of Law and human rights are interlinked (…) The Rule of Law would just be an empty shell without permitting access to human rights. Vice-versa, the protection and promotion of human rights are realised only through respect for the Rule of Law: a strong regime of Rule of Law is vital to the protection of human rights. In addition, the Rule of Law and several human rights (such as fair trial and freedom of expression) overlap. (…) The Rule of Law is linked not only to human rights but

tion of our common identity and common constitutional traditions. It is the basis of the democratic system in all Member States, necessary to ensure the protection of fundamental rights. (…) The rule of law ensures that Member States and their citizens can work together in a spirit of mutual trust; trust in public institutions, including in the justice system, is crucial for the smooth functioning of democratic societies. The rule of law is also one of the principles guiding the EU's external action. (…) The rule of law is enshrined in Article 2 of the Treaty on European Union as one of the founding values of the Union. Under the rule of law, all public powers always act within the constraints set out by law, in accordance with the values of democracy and fundamental rights, and under the control of independent and impartial courts. The rule of law includes, among others, principles such as legality, implying a transparent, accountable, democratic and pluralistic process for enacting laws; legal certainty; prohibiting the arbitrary exercise of executive power; effective judicial protection by independent and impartial courts, effective judicial review including respect for fundamental rights; separation of powers; and equality before the law. These principles have been recognised by the European Court of Justice and the European Court of Human Rights.' See also Communication from the Commission to the European Parliament and the Council, 'A New EU Framework to Strengthen the Rule of Law', 11.3.2014, COM(2014) 158 final, 4: 'The precise content of the principles and standards stemming from the rule of law may vary at national level, depending on each Member State's constitutional system.' See, further, Rule of Law Checklist, adopted by the Council of Europe Venice Commission at its 106th Plenary Session (Venice, 11–12 March 2016) paras 9ff, 15–18, 31ff; A Perego, 'The European Commission and the EU Rule of Law Policy' in AB Engelbrekt, A Moberg and J Nergelius (eds), *Rule of Law in the EU* (Oxford, Hart Publishing, 2021) 291. See also Council of Europe Framework Convention on Artificial Intelligence and Human Rights, Democracy and the Rule of Law, Council of Europe Treaty Series – No [225], 5.9.2024, Art 5.

> also to democracy. (…) Democracy relates to the involvement of the people in the decision-making process in a society; human rights seek to protect individuals from arbitrary and excessive interferences with their freedoms and liberties and to secure human dignity; the Rule of Law focuses on limiting and independently reviewing the exercise of public powers. The Rule of Law promotes democracy by establishing accountability of those wielding public power and by safeguarding human rights, which protect minorities against arbitrary majority rules.[8]

Liberal legal orders are principally bound by the same (sometimes conflicting) obligations: to effectively prevent and suppress unlawful conduct, to aim at truthful and fair dispute resolutions, to preserve procedural economy and social peace as well as to respect the basic principles of human dignity, proportionality and leniency. At its creation, the European Union (EU) system was conceived on the basis of the ideas and fundamental values of human dignity, freedom, democracy, equality, the rule of law and human rights.[9] The notions of human dignity, human rights and the rule of law are interconnected. Mindful of this, it is first and foremost human dignity, 'the real basis of fundamental rights',[10] as enshrined in Article 1 of the EU Charter of Fundamental Rights (EU Charter) and in various national Constitutions, along with associated specific dignity rights (right to life, right to physical and mental integrity, prohibition of torture and of inhuman or degrading treatment, prohibition of slavery and forced labour), that position the individual at the centre of the states' and the EU's actions.

To acknowledge dignity as inviolable and absolute means to protect human beings from being disregarded or arbitrarily treated as mere objects by the state.[11] How to express this normative limit as an algorithmic one can be a challenge. The negative duty of rule of law systems refers not only to singling out and banning the use of applications posing direct threats to human dignity but also to programming algorithms applied in enforcement and judicial proceedings in a manner that secures respect for it. With the respect, protection and advancement of core human values being the overriding objectives of any technological evolution comes also the positive duty to direct machines towards safeguarding the individual against arbitrarily and cruelly coercive, non-lenient or disproportional actions of state organs.

Thus the necessity for a human-centric approach regarding all issues related to the operation and use of AI follows from the fundamental values of human dignity, autonomy, freedom and the rule of law. The European Commission's

[8] Rule of Law Checklist, ibid 15, 31, 33.

[9] Treaty on European Union (TEU) Preamble and Art 2.

[10] EU Charter explanations.

[11] See on this, eg, the findings of the German Constitutional Court in the cases BVerfGE 27, 1 (6) [1969] (*Mikrozensus*) and BVerfGE 30, 1 (25-26) [1970] (*Abhörurteil*); for an overview regarding the different conceptions of human dignity in German literature and jurisprudence, see R Poscher, '§ 17 Menschenwürde' in M Herdegen et al (eds), *Handbuch des Verfassungsrechts* (Munich, Beck, 2021) at 55–63 and 79–104.

Ethics Guidelines for Trustworthy AI of April 2019, stating that 'trustworthy AI' should be lawful, ethical and robust, already refer to this approach.[12] Furthermore, the AI Regulation (AI Act), which lays down harmonised rules for the EU, accepts the need to continue developing and evolving AI technology in the modern world. At the same time, it also adopts the human-first approach, *inter alia* by requiring extra checks and guarantees for specific uses of AI, especially applications with the highest potential for harming people, including with respect to systems assisting decision-making and law enforcement systems. The Regulation also identifies specific AI uses as unacceptable and prohibited, such as in the case of AI systems that provide social scoring of natural persons for the purpose of evaluating or classifying their trustworthiness. Further categorisations include applications considered 'high risk' and rather dangerous, intrusive and problematic, *inter alia* due to concerns of discrimination, bias or lack of transparency. Pertinent examples are facial recognition in public places and predictive policing systems. In these cases, the AI Act considers it necessary to restrict the use of AI based on proportionality assessments.[13]

The European Parliament's resolution on AI in criminal law of October 2021 is pointing in a similar direction.[14] According to the European Parliament, AI systems deployed for law enforcement and criminal justice purposes need to fully respect the principles of human dignity and non-discrimination, the privacy rights, the freedom of movement, the presumption of innocence and the rights of the defence (right to silence, freedom of expression and information, equality before the law, equality of arms, rights to an effective remedy and a fair trial) in accordance with the EU Charter and the European Convention on Human Rights (ECHR). The Parliament called for

[12] Ethics Guidelines for Trustworthy AI (n 5) 37: 'The human-centric approach to AI strives to ensure that human values are central to the way in which AI systems are developed, deployed, used and monitored, by ensuring respect for fundamental rights, including those set out in the Treaties of the European Union and Charter of Fundamental Rights of the European Union, all of which are united by reference to a common foundation rooted in respect for human dignity, in which the human being enjoy a unique and inalienable moral status. This also entails consideration of the natural environment and of other living beings that are part of the human ecosystem, as well as a sustainable approach enabling the flourishing of future generations to come.' See also Communication from the Commission to the European Parliament, the Council, the European Economic and Social Committee and the Committee of the Regions, 'Building Trust in Human-Centric Artificial Intelligence', 8.4.2019, COM(2019) 168 final.

[13] Artificial Intelligence Act (n 6) Arts 5ff.

[14] European Parliament's resolution on 'artificial intelligence (AI) in criminal law and its use by the police and judicial authorities in criminal matters' of 6 October 2021 (2020/2016(INI)). With respect, for example, to the scoring or persons, the resolution notes at 32: 'Supports the recommendations (…) for a ban on AI-enabled mass scale scoring of individuals; considers that any form of normative citizen scoring on a large scale by public authorities, in particular within the field of law enforcement and the judiciary, leads to the loss of autonomy, endangers the principle of non-discrimination and cannot be considered in line with fundamental rights, in particular human dignity, as codified in EU law.'

> algorithmic explainability, transparency, traceability and verification as a necessary part of oversight, in order to ensure that the development, deployment and use of AI systems for the judiciary and law enforcement comply with fundamental rights, and are trusted by citizens, as well as in order to ensure that results generated by AI algorithms can be rendered intelligible to users and to those subject to these systems, and that there is transparency on the source data and how the system arrived at a certain conclusion.[15]

The Parliament also noted the importance of human intervention with respect to all law enforcement applications of AI and stated that 'the decision giving legal or similar effect always needs to be taken by a human, who can be held accountable for the decisions made'.[16]

In this light, the human-centric approach should not be seen as a further obstacle to technological progress and especially not when technology is employed to enhance the protection of human dignity, human rights and the rule of law. However, acceptance and advancement of technological innovation do not exclude the possibility for the *a priori* imposition of oversight and intervention mechanisms, strict operating requirements, broad use restrictions and – if necessary to effectively secure dignity, autonomy and freedom – total bans on particular AI applications. At the same time, some of the protective requirements, rule of law standards and human rights guarantees prescribed in the aforementioned texts and in other contemporary soft-law and hard-law instruments may not be so easy to implement and comply with in practice, at least in the present state of technological and legal evolution. Training data sets free of errors or the risk of bias; fully explainable and transparent machine learning systems irrespective of their internal complexity or the external transparency barriers raised by intellectual property interests; objective and non-discriminating automated decisions and outputs; functioning models of accountability and responsibility: these are just some of the still unresolved issues to be urgently addressed in policy debates and interdisciplinary research.

Furthermore, the core of the human dignity concept may be subject to direct violations inflicted by (the use of) AI in the context of law enforcement and criminal justice. The normative (constitutional) importance of dignity as inviolable and absolute does not leave much room in such cases for the balancing of competing interests; nor can it be truly satisfied by the fragmentary adoption of partial restrictions and formal control measures. Hence, a more holistic approach to prohibiting certain types of algorithmic systems may be necessary, even in less obvious situations. A case in point is a voluntary social credit system that, ultimately, may also be used, directly or indirectly, for surveillance and law enforcement purposes: 'voluntariness' does not automatically equal or

[15] ibid at 17.
[16] ibid at 16.

imply respect for human dignity, autonomy and personal self-determination.[17] Similarly regarding coercive tools, which, at least for the time being, seem to have a restricted (supporting) role and more of a symbolic significance. In an otherwise human-centric world, most characteristic is the example of robots 'mimicking' human law enforcers. Judging by specific policing and investigative measures some countries imposed during the Covid pandemic, the dystopic scenario of being ordered and stopped, questioned, searched, arrested or fined with an administrative or criminal sanction by autonomous animal-shaped robots is not too distant after all.[18]

III. PROPORTIONALITY

Further drawing on control strategies and measures adopted by governments and international organisations during the outbreak of the Covid pandemic as well as on alternative and technologically advanced security,[19] prevention and enforcement practices applied in response to current global threats (international and eco terrorism, terrorist financing, cyberterrorism and other wide-scale digital attacks, novel forms of transnational organised crime and money laundering, etc.): It has become evident that the modern tools used in the war on the various kinds of 'visible' and 'invisible' enemies no longer target only traditional suspects or criminals but also more recent categories of security risks, pre-suspects and potential criminals. Enabled by the current technological progress, these tools exhibit an extensive range of intrusive and coercive characteristics potentially affecting the rights of much larger sections of populations compared to the conventional criminal justice apparatus.

[17] *cf* on Mantello's 'Ikeaveillance' and on the Chinese social credit, R Vogler, 'Big Data and Criminal Justice. Proportionality, Efficiency and Risk in a Global Context' in E Billis, N Knust and JP Rui (eds), *Proportionality in Crime Control and Criminal Justice* (Oxford, Hart Publishing, 2021) 165, 174ff.

[18] *cf* R McMorrow and G Li, 'The Robot Dogs Policing Shanghai's Strict Lockdown' *Financial Times* (14 April 2022), available at www.ft.com/content/5c437146-2d18-466b-84af-24a47b32de59. Problematic in terms of securing respect for human dignity and the rule of law may also be the 'reverse' situation where an interaction takes place between an individual and an AI system, and the individual may be led to believe that it is human or may not be able to realise that the system is non-human. To ensure *inter alia* the transparency of AI systems, the EU Commission High-Level Expert Group on Artificial Intelligence in its Policy and Investment Recommendations for Trustworthy AI of 26 June 2019 (at 12) suggested introducing the mandatory self-identification of AI systems and noted that, if there is such a likelihood, deployers of AI systems should be attributed a general responsibility to disclose that the system is actually non-human. However, especially in the context of crime control and law enforcement, where the interference with personal freedoms and rights takes its most severe form, a total ban of AI systems enabling or operating on the basis of such misleading impressions should also be considered; see, however, Artificial Intelligence Act (n 6) Art 52. On other interesting aspects of the relationship between human dignity and human-like machines and systems (from a constitutional law perspective), see C Geminn, 'Menschenwürde und menschenähnliche Maschinen und Systeme' (2020) 24 *Die Öffentliche Verwaltung* 172ff.

[19] On the 'new security architecture', see Sieber (n 1) 3–34.

Mass surveillance and the (automated) collection and analysis of personal data for the principally legitimate reasons of security and public safety have become a worldwide (national and transnational) phenomenon. The extended application of highly evolved electronic and AI technologies for the bulk registration, analytic observation and/or tracking of actual or potential hazards (and 'dangerous' or 'non-compliant' individuals) may indeed lead to broad interferences with privacy and other rights for unspecified numbers of individuals who may not even be remotely linked to criminal behaviour of any kind. Nowadays, even the most intrusive temporary and emergency legislations and the various exceptional administrative and enforcement measures restricting basic freedoms and personal rights appear to be easily justifiable as *sine qua non* for fulfilling the purpose of keeping populations safe and secure. In light of all the global, grave and imminent risks to the principal legal interests of health and life, current legal-policy agendas tend to focus more on designing the most effective security mechanisms than on the rule of law and human rights concerns surrounding their use. Further, the potential consequences in the fields of crime prevention and repression are sometimes overlooked: Exceptional monitoring measures may eventually turn into permanent and continuous (real-time) state supervision.[20] And the normalisation of pre-emptive but still massively invasive restrictions of liberty, movement and privacy rights for public security purposes may substantially transform the traditional objectives, operational methods and, most importantly, the protective limits and principles of current and future systems of crime control and criminal justice.[21]

It is therefore a positive development that – even if the absolute core of human dignity is not directly violated and the prohibition of a certain practice is not deemed *a priori* necessary – the aforementioned regulatory and soft-law instruments prescribe minimum rule of law and human rights guarantees concerning the operation of AI within the last resort sectors of law enforcement, crime control and criminal justice. It is in the framework of these particular public law branches where the most effective measures, now enhanced by current technologies, will usually turn out to be also the most intrusive and coercive, capable of widely endangering and restricting the full exercise of rights and personal freedoms. Even more so in cases where no human actor/decision-maker who can intuitively comprehend the meaning and importance of dignity and human rights is actively involved in applying the measure. In this respect, an immanent rule of law notion of crucial importance to criminal and security law in terms of its protective function against arbitrary interferences with individual rights and vested freedoms is that of proportionality.[22]

[20] *cf* YN Harari, 'The World After Coronavirus' *Financial Times* (20 March 2020), available at www.ft.com/content/19d90308-6858-11ea-a3c9-1fe6fedcca75.

[21] For further analysis with examples and references, see E Billis, N Knust and JP Rui, 'The Typology of Proportionality' in Billis, Knust and Rui (n 17) 3, 5–11.

[22] *cf* Ethics Guidelines for Trustworthy AI (n 5) 12–13; Artificial Intelligence Act (n 6) 7, 11, 21ff.; European Parliament's resolution on AI (n 14).

Proportionality shapes and limits the exercise of all state powers. It is a legal reasoning technique, a temperate method of controlling public authority and, at the same time, a rational factor for enhancing the social acceptance of actually necessary coercive and rights intrusive measures – one that can also contribute towards securing the functionality of legal systems in the long term.[23] Within the framework of proportionality assessments, the competing interests are weighted at the three different levels of public power, affecting measures and decisions of all three branches: the legislative, the executive and the judicial. At the core of such assessments is the examination of the following generally recognised elements: the existence of a legitimate aim justifying the adoption of a certain measure; the suitability of the measure for reaching this concrete aim; the necessity of this particular measure in view of the aim (requirement of the least intrusive measure); and the appropriateness of the measure in terms of its (rights-limiting) effects balanced against the benefits of the aim pursued (proportionality *stricto sensu*).[24]

In the broad context of crime control and criminal justice, the various types of proportionality have been relevant, *inter alia*, with respect to the diachronic substantive law questions of criminalisation and punishment as well as in terms of policing and criminal procedure, particularly regarding the definition and review of the applicability conditions and limits for investigations, searches and other coercive measures (communication interceptions, arrest warrants, pre-trial detentions and bails, etc).[25] In line with the above-described developments, the significance of the proportionality concept has further increased with respect to the use of the new technologies of (bulk) surveillance and AI for security and

[23] Billis, Knust and Rui (n 21) 11ff. *cf* L Zedner, 'Ends and Means: Why Effective Counter-Terrorism Requires Respect for Proportionality and Rights' in Billis, Knust and Rui (n 17) 125ff.

[24] Billis, Knust and Rui (n 21) 24. This proportionality concept is incorporated in most liberal rule of law orders, national and international, see M Kremnitzer, T Steiner and A Lang (eds), *Proportionality in Action: Comparative and Empirical Perspectives on the Judicial Practice* (Cambridge, Cambridge University Press, 2020); M Bothe and E-C Gillard, 'The Proportionality Principle in Comparative Public, European Union and International Law – "Reflections on the Proportionality Equation"' in Billis, Knust and Rui (n 17) 277ff. Within the ECHR system, the decisions and judgments of the European Court of Human Rights (ECtHR) appear to accept the applicability of all four proportionality components, see, eg, J McBride, 'Proportionality and the European Convention on Human Rights' in E Ellis (ed), *The Principle of Proportionality in the Laws of Europe* (London, Hart Publishing, 1999) 23ff; A Barak, *Proportionality. Constitutional Rights and Their Limitations* (Cambridge, Cambridge University Press, 2012) 183–84; J Gerards, 'How to Improve the Necessity Test of the European Court of Human Rights?' (2013) 11 *International Journal of Constitutional Law* 466ff; E Brems and L Lavrysen, '"Don't Use a Sledgehammer to Crack a Nut": Less Restrictive Means in the Case Law of the European Court of Human Rights' (2015) 15 *Human Rights Law Review* 139ff. The EU proportionality test, as applied by the Court of Justice of the European Union, is focusing, at least for the time being, on the elements of suitability and necessity, see V Mitsilegas and E Billis, 'Article 49 – Principles of Legality and Proportionality of Criminal Offences and Penalties' in S Peers et al (eds), *The EU Charter of Fundamental Rights. A Commentary*, 2nd edn (Oxford, Hart Publishing, 2021) 1473, 1485ff, 1498ff with further references.

[25] *cf* RA Duff, 'Proportionality and the Criminal Law: Proportionality of What to What?' in Billis, Knust and Rui (n 17) 29ff.

crime-fighting purposes.[26] Again, the problem is twofold. First, regarding the proportionate employment of AI: Legislators must be able to define clear and non-arbitrary criteria and the administrative and judicial bodies must be able to exercise self-restraint and control for ensuring the legitimate, suitable, least intrusive and appropriate utilisation of AI in the various constellations. Second, regarding the proportionate output of AI and machine learning: The main challenge here is to develop the algorithms and 'train' the machines such that they can reach decisions and take actions in conformity with the basic elements of proportionality.

In the current state of technological progress, this is easier said than done – and it may prove to be more of a challenge than a support for the entire rule of law and proportionality endeavour. Not to disregard also the opinion that calculations and decisions about the proportionality or excessiveness of a certain action cannot really result from applying a mechanical formula but (must) remain 'a value judgement' to be made by the responsible human actor/operator 'in good faith and in a reasonable manner'.[27] The field of international humanitarian (and international criminal) law, specifically concerning the use of autonomous weapon systems (AWS) in armed conflict situations, provides a characteristic example.[28] AWS processors and the algorithms set to assess the information gathered for carrying out target selections and identifying incidental harm expected from a possible military strike are not susceptible to stress and other human emotions. Free from inherent emotional weaknesses and the risk of human error that has led to criminal incidents and unjustified war escalations in the past, AWS are therefore (or, at some point, will be) able to reach more objective and proportionate decisions. However, in contrast to the *de facto* complexity of armed conflicts and the unpredicted and often spontaneous or reactive nature of military conduct, the mathematic processes and proportionality assessments conducted by AWS are rather linear. They are mostly based on technical and prefixed parameters for the collection of information by using sensors and on the rigid interpretation and application of previously defined legal rules by processors and algorithms. What AWS may still lack is the human ability to understand and adapt to constantly changing realities in a variety of ways using learned inferences that enable individuals to perceive their own actions also from the perspective of others. If military decision-making involving the choice of suitable, least intrusive and appropriate means and targets requires contextual intelligence operating, where necessary, beyond predetermined algorithms, it remains questionable whether contemporary AWS are actually capable of 'deciding', 'acting' and 'reacting' in a temperate and proportionate manner.[29]

[26] Billis, Knust and Rui (n 2).

[27] Bothe and Gillard (n 24) 295.

[28] See the analysis in Billis, Knust and Rui (n 2) 715ff.

[29] See E Billis and N Knust, 'Proportionality (Principle of)' in P Caeiro et al (eds), *Elgar Encyclopedia of Crime and Criminal Justice* (Cheltenham, Edward Elgar Publishing, 2023) with references to R Geiss, *Die völkerrechtliche Dimension autonomer Waffensysteme* (Friedrich-Ebert-Stiftung,

IV. PRIVACY

Similar considerations generally apply to the rapid technological advancements enabling the automated collection, selection and 'real-time' processing of large volumes of personal data and the highly sophisticated electronic systems assigned to (assist in) the relevant decision-making processes. The ethical and pragmatic challenges in achieving proportionate AI outputs in the fields of security, crime control and criminal justice in no way change the fact that proportionality remains an important limitation and control tool against any arbitrarily coercive and highly intrusive exercise of state powers – especially when it comes to establishing the extent of permissible use of AI. Guaranteeing legitimacy and proportionality in exercising powers has been an ever-present prerequisite, *inter alia*, for the effective protection of personal data and the safeguarding of privacy.[30] Nonetheless, in light of today's unprecedented technological dominance in (mass) surveillance and other areas of privacy intrusions,[31] proportionality is just one among many rule of law related concerns that theory, practice and policy are called to address in this context.

The personal freedoms and rights of self-determination, which are directly connected with the 'mother right'[32] to human dignity as 'the freedom to shape one's life',[33] are undisputedly crucially important in modern liberal and democratic systems. Yet, the privacy rights, which make up a significant part of them, are not absolute. However, permitted restrictions are usually subject to strict limitations: Interferences with the exercise of these rights must be provided for by law, respect their core essence and be necessary in a democratic society for protecting national security, public safety and other important public interests or the rights and freedoms of others.[34] Relevant examples in the present context are the definitions of privacy rights under Articles 7 and 8 EU Charter (respect for private life and protection of personal data) as well as the right to respect for private life under Article 8 ECHR.[35]

2015), available at https://library.fes.de/pdf-files/id/ipa/11444-20150619.pdf; M Hildebrandt, 'The Artificial Intelligence of European Union Law' (2020) 21 *German Law Journal* 74; P Scharre, 'Why Unmanned' (2011) 61 *Joint Force Quarterly* 89; and NE Sharkey, 'The Evitability of Autonomous Robot Warfare' (2012) 94 *International Review of the Red Cross* 787.

[30] See, eg, L Bachmaier Winter, 'Proportionality, Mass Surveillance and Criminal Investigation: The Strasbourg Court Facing Big Brother' in Billis, Knust and Rui (n 17) 317ff.

[31] *cf Big Brother Watch and Others v the United Kingdom* App nos 58170/13, 62322/14 and 24960/15 (ECtHR, 13 September 2018) para 316: '(…) due to recent technological developments the interception of communications now has greater potential than ever before to paint an intimate and detailed portrait of a person's private life and behaviour.'

[32] A Barak, *Human Dignity: The Constitutional Value and the Constitutional Right* (Cambridge, Cambridge University Press, 2015) 156–67.

[33] C Dupré, 'Article 1 – Human Dignity' in S Peers et al (eds), *The EU Charter of Fundamental Rights. A Commentary*, 2nd edn (Oxford, Hart Publishing, 2021) 3, 6.

[34] See EU Charter, Art 52 and ECHR, Art 8.

[35] For example, (bulk) interception, storage, processing, examination and use of communications constitute interferences with Art 8(1) ECHR rights, the permissibility of which depends on the fulfilment of the terms defined in Art 8(2), see *Big Brother Watch and Others v the United Kingdom* App

Interference with well-established privacy rights through the unrestrained and unsupervised use of AI may undermine existing protective limitations, democratic safeguards and rule of law guarantees, even if the intrusive measures and applications are programmatically aimed at keeping populations and societies safe and secure. At a practical level, novel information and interception systems consisting of advanced monitoring mechanisms and surveillance algorithms may well be significantly contributing to the preventive and suppressive efforts of intelligence and law enforcement agencies against new forms of organised and transnational crime and other types of global threat. Continuous progress in technology can be instrumental in securing wider protection for fundamental freedoms while also enhancing the effectiveness in administering criminal justice. However, a series of problematic issues involving the danger of questionable policies and strategies towards achieving greater operational benefits may arise in parallel with this process. One example pertains to the possibility of a constant, rapid, multi-layered, multi-purposed, cross-sectoral/-departmental and, hence, practically uncontrolled flow and exchange of vast amounts of massively and automatically collected and analysed personal data between cooperating agencies of different legal orders. Any opportunity for public authorities to acquire and invest in spy software developed and/or operated by private companies or third-party organisations in non-transparent terms can, in many respects, also be open to questions. The same goes for the discretion agencies enjoy in avoiding external regulatory and 'bureaucratic' obstacles by developing their own, tailor-made big data algorithms, exclusively designed and trained by internally appointed computer experts absent any prior public consultation with human rights scholars and institutions.

In any case, the stakes are already high for the rule of law and the effective protection of self-determination and privacy rights. Personal data constitute the foundational element of AI-based applications employed for the purposes of security and crime control. As we have seen, such applications are not free from the risks of manipulation, discrimination and non-transparency or from the problems of insufficient oversight and accountability.[36] Automatic processing and analysis of collected and stored data may produce new or reveal further

nos 58170/13, 62322/14 and 24960/15 (ECtHR GC, 25 May 2021) paras 324ff, 330; see also S Brinkhoff, 'Big Data Data Mining by the Dutch Police: Criteria for a Future Method of Investigation' (2017) 2 *European Journal for Security Research* 57. Private life under Art 8 regards 'personal data', which are defined as 'any information relating to an identified or identifiable individual', see *Benedik v Slovenia* App no 62357/14 (ECtHR, 24 April 2018) para 102. Personal data include 'anything from a name, photo, email address, bank details, GPS tracking data, posts on social networking websites, medical information or a computer's IP address', see Handbook on European Data Protection Law (n 3) 350.

[36] *cf*, eg, European Parliament's resolution on AI (n 14) at 1, 4, 6, 8, 9, 11, 13, 16, 17, 22, 23, 25, 28; Artificial Intelligence Act (n 6) Arts 1, 10, 13, 14, 15. See also the references in n 5 above. In the context of the tracing measures adopted during the Covid pandemic, *cf* European Institute of Innovation & Technology, 'The European Struggle with COVID-19 Contact Tracing Apps' (29 April 2020), available at eit.europa.eu/news-events/news/european-struggle-covid-19-contact-tracing-apps.

sensitive information on individuals. A main concern with respect to the use of algorithms for producing or acquiring such 'new knowledge' refers to the 'black box' problem: the public and interested parties may have knowledge of the information fed into the system and the system's concrete output, but they rarely know how the decision-making process actually works in between. Thus, unpredictable correlations and unexplainable inferences cannot be excluded. Further, it is rather unlikely for authorities or enterprises developing AI programs for purposes of security and crime control to divulge the exact functionality of their algorithms. The problem is exacerbated by the fact that today's algorithms are trained and operate mainly on the basis of statistical observations and correlations. 'No matter how sophisticated, predictive algorithms and their users can fall into the trap of equating correlation with causation.'[37] As a result, there is always the danger that the information and knowledge obtained by current algorithmic systems can be distorted, discriminatory and unreliable.[38]

It is therefore logical that the public debate focuses on both the predictability and explicability problems in AI uses and outputs as well as on questionable practices and dubious cooperation methods followed by enforcement and security agencies, national and supranational.[39] In view of the current technological developments and the legal guarantees put in place thus far, it is necessary to build more coherent and consistent models enabling transparent, predictable, accurate, proportional and non-discriminatory uses of AI technology in the personal and big data fields as well as systems designed to overcome the legal and pragmatic issues causing obstacles to independent oversight and judicial control. Again, maintaining direct communication channels and developing improved methods of collaboration between competent national and supranational authorities, computer scientists, AI developers and legal experts in the areas of privacy and data protection are essential steps in strengthening both the effectiveness of law enforcement and the rule of law.

V. EQUALITY AND PROCEDURAL JUSTICE

The problem of potential discriminatory outputs is a common topic of concern in the context of automated decision-making and AI predictions, as already noted. This issue depends mainly on such factors as the data quality, any pre-existing biases fed into the algorithmic system by its designers and trainers

[37] SK Sgaier, V Huang and G Charles, 'The Case for Causal AI' (2020) 18 *Stanford Social Innovation Review* 50.

[38] See Billis, Knust and Rui (n 2) 706–707 with detailed references and examples. See also European Parliament's resolution on AI (n 14).

[39] See, eg, for a summary of recent worrying developments in Europe, the report by A Fotiadis, L Stavinoha, G Zandonini and D Howden, 'A Data "Black Hole": Europol Ordered to Delete Vast Store of Personal Data' *The Guardian* (10 January 2022), available at www.theguardian.com/world/2022/jan/10/a-data-black-hole-europol-ordered-to-delete-vast-store-of-personal-data.

and/or the system's incapacity for true causal reasoning.[40] Thus, algorithmic decisions 'may end up reproducing historical patterns of discrimination'.[41]

The overall prohibition of discrimination derives from the principle of equality, and both equality and non-discrimination 'are part of the foundations of the rule of law'.[42] Equality rights such as those enshrined in Articles 20–26 EU Charter (equality before the law; non-discrimination; cultural, religious and linguistic diversity; equality between men and women; the rights of the child and of the elderly; integration of persons with disabilities) and the provision of Article 14 ECHR (prohibition of discrimination) also tie in with the primary demand for respecting and protecting human dignity.

In the various constellations of its use, AI may effectively promote equal treatment and fairness.[43] But it may also impair them. Relevant considerations have focused on administrative law, labour/civil law and healthcare matters. In terms of law enforcement and criminal justice, the risk of algorithmic systems generating discriminatory outputs is usually discussed in the context of identification, predictive policing and recidivism risk assessment applications.[44]

Furthermore, equality is related to procedural justice. Essential elements of procedural justice are impartiality, consistency, accuracy and truthfulness, representativeness, ethical appropriateness, transparency, the possibility to contest and review a decision and the respectful treatment of those affected by the conflict and the procedure.[45] Sometimes, these elements conflict with each other – even more so in the AI and criminal justice field.[46] In any case, in liberal rule of law orders, with respect to both conventional mechanisms and alternative means of prevention, enforcement and conflict resolution, justice and social legitimacy require the application of formal standards, adequate due-process guarantees and minimum fair-trial rights providing substantial and equal opportunities of

[40] See the European Parliament's resolution on AI (n 14) at 8, 22, 23, 24.

[41] J Ryberg and J Roberts, 'Sentencing and Artificial Intelligence – Setting the Stage' in J Ryberg and J Roberts (eds), *Sentencing and Artificial Intelligence* (Oxford, Oxford University Press, 2022) 1, 8.

[42] United Nations and the Rule of Law, 'Equality and Non-Discrimination', available at www.un.org/ruleoflaw/thematic-areas/human-rights/equality-and-non-discrimination/.

[43] See, eg, M Bagaric and D Hunter, 'Enhancing the Integrity of the Sentencing Process through the Use of Artificial Intelligence' in Ryberg and Roberts (n 41) 122ff, 131ff with further references.

[44] See, eg, the European Parliament's resolution on AI (n 14) at 9, 24, 27. On equality, discrimination and algorithmic risk assessment instruments (such as the infamous COMPAS system), see J Angwin, J Larson, S Mattu and L Kirchner, 'Machine Bias' (*ProPublica*, 23 May 2016), available at www.propublica.org/article/machine-bias-risk-assessments-in-criminal-sentencing; B Davies and T Douglas, 'Learning to Discriminate – The Perfect Proxy Problem in Artificially Intelligent Sentencing' in Ryberg and Roberts (n 41) 97; K Lippert-Rasmussen, 'Algorithm-Based Sentencing and Discrimination' in Ryberg and Roberts (n 41) 74.

[45] M Rehbinder, *Rechtsoziologie*, 6th edn (Munich, Beck, 2007) 118.

[46] See, eg, on the possibility of a negative relationship between the transparency of an algorithm and its accuracy in criminal sentencing (complicated and opaque algorithms producing more accurate predictions of future criminality *versus* algorithms which are more transparent, but produce less accurate predictions), J Ryberg and T Petersen, 'Sentencing and the Conflict between Algorithmic Accuracy and Transparency' in Ryberg and Roberts (n 41) 57.

procedural inclusion, participation and remedy.[47] Particularly significant in this regard are the provisions of Articles 5 and 6 ECHR (right to liberty and security; right to a fair trial) and Articles 47–48 EU Charter (right to an effective remedy and to a fair trial; presumption of innocence and right of defence).

In line with this, the European Parliament stressed in its resolution of 6 October 2021 that AI may only be used in law enforcement and criminal justice if it fully complies with the principles of equality before the law and equality of arms as well as the rights to an effective remedy and a fair trial. The Parliament highlighted the power asymmetry between those who employ AI technologies and those who are subject to them and noted that the use of AI must not become a factor of inequality, social fracture or exclusion.[48] It further underlined 'the impact of the use of AI tools on the defence rights of suspects, the difficulty in obtaining meaningful information on their functioning and the consequent difficulty in challenging their results in court, in particular by individuals under investigation'.[49]

Finally, the resolutions on the need to limit AI usage with rule of law safeguards and to be able to effectively contest automated decision-making[50] on the grounds of equality, non-discrimination and procedural justice are fundamentally important for a variety of criminal justice and procedure matters such as sentencing and evidence.[51] The European Parliament, having considered that 'decisions in the field of law enforcement are almost always decisions that have a legal effect on the person concerned' and that 'the use of AI may influence human decisions and have an impact on all phases of criminal procedures', *inter alia* noted that:

- in judicial and law enforcement contexts, the decision giving legal or similar effect always needs to be taken by a human, who can be held accountable for the decisions made;
- those subject to AI-powered systems must have recourse to remedy;

[47] See E Billis and N Knust, 'Alternative Types of Procedure and the Formal Limits of National Criminal Justice: Aspects of Social Legitimacy' in U Sieber, V Mitsilegas, C Mylonopoulos, E Billis and N Knust (eds), *Alternative Systems of Crime Control. National, Transnational, and International Dimensions* (Berlin, Duncker & Humblot, 2018) 39, 57, with references to J Rawls, *A Theory of Justice* (Cambridge, Massachusetts, Belknap Press of Harvard University Press, 1971) and JW Thibaut and L Walker, *Procedural Justice: A Psychological Analysis* (Hillsdale, NJ, Erlbaum, 1975). See also TR Tyler, *Why People Obey the Law* (Princeton, Princeton University Press, 2006) 163–65; TR Tyler, 'Does the American Public Accept the Rule of Law?: The Findings of Psychological Research on Deference to Authority' (2007) 56 *DePaul Law Review* 664.

[48] European Parliament's resolution on AI (n 14) at 2 and 10.

[49] ibid at 10.

[50] On the right to contest adverse decisions, which directly derives from the rule of law principle, and the challenges raised by automated decision-making systems in this context, which are associated with the 'right to a reasoned decision and the procedural equality between parties during the review', see FP Ettorre, 'The Right to Contest Automated Decisions' *The Digital Constitutionalist* (14 February 2022), available at https://digi-con.org/the-right-to-contest-automated-decisions/.

[51] AI may serve as a novel and alternative means for automatically processing/producing evidence with the purpose of enhancing effectiveness, objectivity, fairness and procedural economy in traditional criminal trials. However, mostly due to the noted asymmetry of power, this could also result in compromising the effective participation of the defendant in the process. On the merits and challenges of admitting, reviewing and assessing AI-based evidence in criminal proceedings and on the relevant risks for the defendant's rights connected with such applications, see chapter 15 by Eftychia Bampasika in this volume.

- under EU law, a person has the right not to be subjected to a decision which produces legal effects concerning them or significantly affects them and is based solely on automated data processing;
- automated individual decision-making must not be based on special categories of personal data, unless suitable measures to safeguard the data subject's rights and freedoms and legitimate interests are in place;
- EU law prohibits profiling that results in discrimination against natural persons on the basis of special categories of personal data;
- authorities making use of AI systems need to uphold extremely high legal standards and ensure human intervention, especially when analysing data deriving from such systems, and;
- the sovereign discretion of judges and decision-making on a case-by-case basis need to be upheld.[52]

VI. CONCLUDING THOUGHTS: THE CASE OF AI IN SENTENCING

In the context of security, crime control and criminal justice, the relationship between law and new technologies is a tense and multi-layered one: from the exploitation of advanced electronic tools to facilitate illegal behaviour to the employment of machine learning as an alternative means to enhance law enforcement and the administration of criminal justice. And from legal scholars and policy planners studying and adapting to the evolution of AI by re-evaluating old and designing new regulatory frameworks according to current ethics and societal values to computer scientists collaborating closely with lawyers in the interpretation and realisation of the most complex concepts and ideas. An integral part of this phenomenon is the increasing reliance of state authorities and supranational agencies on machines and automated algorithmic systems for the prevention, detection and suppression of security threats and (possible) crimes and for an improved criminal justice delivery. Such mechanisms can make the exercise of public authority more effective and efficient and legal decisions more objective and less arbitrary and noisy. At the same time, their use has the potential to radically expand the states' powers of surveillance, intrusion and coercion and entails, as we have seen, various rule of law and human rights concerns.

A characteristic example applicable to many of the considerations examined in this chapter is sentencing in criminal trials. Theory and recent practice in various legal orders have shown that the new types of AI and machine learning – praised for their presumed mathematical ability to reduce factual complexity and improve quality (especially: consistency, accuracy, objectivity) and speed in decision-making but also criticised for potentially posing risks to traditional protective principles and rule of law constraints – are already transforming the conventional criminal trial.[53] Sentencing issues have been diachronically

[52] European Parliament's resolution on AI (n 14) at 16.

[53] See, eg, with respect to the procedural stage of sentencing, the different applications and topics of concern analysed in Ryberg and Roberts (n 41).

at the core of theoretical and legal policy debates in the field of criminal law and procedure. Sentencing, which is determined by a series of concurrent (and, sometimes, conflicting) aims, consists of many layers and components (substantive and procedural) and varies from one legal tradition or system to the next in terms of structure and (division and scope of) institutional powers, has also been one of the first criminal justice sectors to be subjected to the AI experiment.[54] As Ryberg and Roberts emphasised:

> A sentencing decision involves balancing multiple objectives and many factors. (...) The use of AI at sentencing is therefore open to different interpretations and applications. At one extreme, the use of AI at sentencing may refer to the application of a simple algorithm implemented to inform a judge in the determination of a single factor [eg, offender's risk profile] that should be included in the sentencing decision. At the other extreme, it may refer to a fully automated 'Robo judge' that specifies sentences without any human involvement.[55]

Regardless, the determination of punishment is usually characterised by the application of objective indicators and a set of *a priori* defined 'measurable' criteria, even in legal orders where sentencing judges have a greater margin of appreciation in evaluating the specific circumstances of cases and offenders. A more extended use of algorithms aligned with this rather straightforward method is therefore to be expected in sentencing issues compared to other, more complex and multi-factored decision-making processes involving, for example, the systematic assessment of different types of evidence during trial and the rendering of reasoned judgments about guilt.

Notwithstanding the presumed potential of AI in minimising human error and reducing the arbitrary exercise of power, it does not mean that we have already reached the point of replacing human sentencing judges with machines, nor that we should be considering such a possibility in the first place. Even if machine-based calculations of punishment are not directly violating human dignity, the normative imperatives of the human-centric approach do not allow for the use of AI as a substitute for human decision-making but only as a supplement. In fact, we can contemplate a variety of reasons against the 'dehumanisation'[56] of sentencing, most importantly: the serious consequences of punishments for people's lives and the social necessity of maintaining clear accountability and review systems for sentencing decisions; the significance of not only objective but also subjective, moral and emotional (and, thus, not easily computable) factors, such as mercy and leniency, for effectively fulfilling

[54] ibid 1, 3ff.

[55] ibid at 5–6.

[56] See in this respect the interesting analysis by N Dagan and S Baron, 'The Compassionate Computer – Algorithms, Sentencing, and Mercy' in Ryberg and Roberts (n 41) 145, 146-47 with further references. See also M Schwarze and J Roberts, 'Reconciling Artificial Intelligence and Human Intelligence – Supplementing Not Supplanting the Sentencing Judge' in Ryberg and Roberts (n 41) 206, 208ff.

the purposes of humane punishment in contemporary rule of law states; and the legitimising effect of the human ability to comprehend and evaluate the contextual meaning of societal circumstances at the imposition of criminal penalties.

Important on similar grounds is the issue of achieving proportional results in sentencing, as prescribed, for example, in Article 49(3) EU Charter (principles of legality and proportionality of criminal offences and penalties), ie, in terms of assessing the gravity of criminal misconduct and properly determining the corresponding penalties, the severity of which must not be disproportionate to the offence.[57] Proportionality is already relevant at the legislative, regulatory and technical levels, specifically in the sense of defining *a priori* and *in abstracto*, on factors such as gravity and complexity, the types of crimes and cases to which AI-assisted or AI-based sentencing could/should be applied. Regarding proportionality assessments and proportional outputs in constellations where algorithms are used to assist/complement the responsible sentencing body in reaching the 'proper' decision, the judge and the parties need to be aware of any technical and inherent limitations of a non-human system in terms of comprehending and implementing proportionality criteria. The natural shortcomings and limitations of human sentencers cannot be ignored. Still, we must, before we entrust the electronic assistant – and, in a dystopic future, the fully automated and autonomously deciding machines replacing the human judge – with sentencing tasks, carefully consider to what extent disproportionate penalties specifically generated by an AI may further jeopardise social legitimacy of the judicial system and risk fracturing the rule of law. We also need to keep in mind that, as accepted by the European Court of Human Rights (ECtHR), a grossly disproportionate sentence could, on some occasions, even amount to *inhuman* or degrading punishment.[58]

Finally, a widely recognised goal of employing such applications in sentencing, as for other AI uses, is to secure not only swift but also more objective and impartial decisions, free from the 'restrains' of human emotions, prejudices and personal interests. However, any capabilities of new technologies in strengthening the administration of criminal justice and the rule of law must not overshadow the possible risks to equality, objectivity and impartiality caused by AI itself. Even in the case of computers used to *support* the human sentencer in his/her tasks, the question arises: to what extent can judges, consciously or unconsciously, remain independent and impartial if they, overly trusting in the technical superiority of machines or, for other reasons, overly relying on them,

[57] The EU principle of proportionality 'entails that the severity of penalties must be commensurate with the seriousness of the infringements', see Opinion of the Advocate General Bobek, Case C-384/17 *Dooel Uvoz-Izvoz Skopje Link Logistik N&N v Budapest Rendőrfőkapitánya*, EU:C:2018:494, 26 June 2018, para 32.

[58] Violating, thus, ECHR, Art 3, see *Vinter and Others v the United Kingdom* App nos 66069/09, 130/10 and 3896/10 (ECtHR GC, 9 July 2013) paras 83 and 102.

base their decisions mainly on information processed and knowledge generated by algorithms.[59]

We examined above the reasons why outputs of current algorithmic systems can be distorted, discriminatory and unreliable (systematic bias, technical difficulties in causal reasoning, etc). Designing and rigidly applying appropriate procedural safeguards to ensure, for all interested parties, equality of participation possibilities, information and resources symmetry, openness and transparency in the joint automated and human decision-making processes and, accordingly, adequate contest and review opportunities, may have a counterbalancing effect on the inherent shortcomings of AI applications in criminal justice and, at the same time, a reinforcing effect with respect to the social acceptance of the final outcome. Furthermore, it may prove fruitful to leave aside extreme and generalising positions such as the unproductive narrative about the overall inevitability of AI on the one side and the unrealistic propositions about outright AI bans on the other. Instead, focusing on how to improve the mutual understanding and cross-disciplinary collaboration between computer scientists, legal scholars and practitioners from all relevant fields and institutions could substantially contribute to the efforts to minimise the analysed systemic risks and weaknesses and to create new models of human-machine cooperation in criminal justice: models that do not challenge but strengthen the rule of law.

[59] *cf* European Parliament's resolution on AI (n 14) at 15: '(...) [If] humans only rely on the data, profiles and recommendations generated by machines, they will not be able to conduct an independent assessment; highlights the potentially grave adverse consequences, specifically in the area of law enforcement and justice, when individuals overly trust in the seemingly objective and scientific nature of AI tools and fail to consider the possibility of their results being incorrect, incomplete, irrelevant or discriminatory; emphasises that over-reliance on the results provided by AI systems should be avoided, and stresses the need for authorities to build confidence and knowledge to question or override an algorithmic recommendation'.

11

*Using AI Systems in the Promotion of EU Defence Rights: The CrossJustice Project**

MICHELE CAIANIELLO**

I. INTRODUCTION

ONE OF THE crucial challenges of our times is the ability to understand and exploit to our advantage – as individuals as well as part of a broader community – the economic and social benefits of using artificial intelligence (AI) systems.[1] The European Union (EU), (that is) well aware of this, has embarked on a digital agenda aimed at exploring all possible uses of AI while respecting the rights of citizens, as the recent establishment of the Special Committee on Artificial Intelligence in a Digital Age (AIDA) by the European Parliament confirms.[2] The ability of AI systems to interact with the

* This contribution discusses with certain adaptations and updates the chapter of a volume published a few months ago: G Lasagni, G Contissa, M Caianiello, G Sartor, *Effective Protection of the Rights of the Accused in the EU Directives. A Computable Approach to Criminal Procedure Law* (Leiden, Brill, 2022). This volume, in turn, contains the results of a research project, the CrossJustice project (Grant Agreement Number: 847346-JUST-AG-2018/JUST-JACC-AG-2018-JUST/REC MGA) funded by the European Union Justice Programme (2014–2020).

** University of Bologna.

[1] According to Contissa and Lasagni, an artificial intelligence (AI) system 'Rather than carrying out evaluations and assessments on the basis of an algorithm containing a set of rules predefined by the programmer, the system builds its own model of the domain, applying a learning algorithm to analysis of the training data. Using this model, the system generates classifications, evaluations, and predictions on new cases submitted to it. Updating and expanding the dataset automatically improves the model and the system's predictive capabilities': G Contissa and G Lasagni, 'When it is (also) Algorithms and AI that Decide on Criminal Matters: In Search of an Effective Remedy' (2020) *European Journal of Crime, Criminal Law and Criminal Justice* 280–304, 281. As Hildebrandt affirms with regard to machine learning (ML) systems (quoting Mitchell), 'A computer program is said to learn from experience E with respect to some class of tasks T and performance measure P, if its performance at task T, as measured by P, improves with experience': M Hildebrandt, *Smart Technologies and the End(s) of Law* (Edward Elgar, 2015) 35; TM Mitchell, *Machine Learning* (Burr Ridge, McGraw Hill, 1997) 2).

[2] As it is reported on the AIDA webpage, available at https://multimedia.europarl.europa.eu/it/aida-special-committee-on-artificial-intelligence-in-digital-age_16506_pk.

most diverse areas of human life has also had an impact on the thinking of legal experts, making increasing inroads into lawyers' processes of reflection. This cultural attitude towards the potentialities deriving from the interaction between AI and the law also involves criminal justice, where relevant studies have been published.[3]

The EU and the Council of Europe seem to be aware of the relevant and numerous interactions that may arise from the use of AI systems in the administration of criminal justice. This is confirmed by two well-known documents, the first issued by the European Commission for the Efficiency of Justice (CEPEJ) and the second by the European Parliament. The CEPEJ adopted the first European Ethical Charter on the use of AI in judicial systems in 2018, the ambition being to provide 'a framework of principles that can guide policy makers, legislators and justice professionals when they grapple with the rapid development of AI in national judicial processes'.[4] The LIBE Committee of the European Parliament commissioned a study, published in July 2020, on the effects on fundamental rights deriving from the use of AI systems in the area of law enforcement.[5]

There are various areas of the administration of justice where the use of AI and machine learning (ML) systems may have some relevance, and possibly a positive impact. One of them concerns the capacity of AI to improve the consistency and predictability of legal issues, and especially of potential litigations, two essential features related to the rule of law. This is specifically important for criminal law and criminal justice, where the principle of legality plays a pivotal role, as both the basis and the primary source of justification for the whole system. AI and ML systems might satisfy, in the end, that quest for certainty and predictability which constitutes the ultimate goal (and the basic philosophical justification) of criminal justice since the post-Enlightenment reforms. The goal of legal certainty could be achieved by substituting human hermeneutic ambiguity – that is, the inability of humans to reach stable interpretations of legal provisions – with computational certainty.

This contribution is dedicated to the description of a recently completed project,[6] funded by the EU Commission, on the topic of legal certainty and the protection of the rights of suspects and defendants in criminal proceedings. The aim of the research (that has been conducted) is to verify whether and to what

[3] See, among the most recent studies on the topic, S Quattrocolo, *Artificial Intelligence, Computational Modelling and Criminal Proceedings. A Framework for A European Legal Discussion* (Springer, 2020).

[4] See CEPEJ, 'CEPEJ European Ethical Charter on the Use of Artificial intelligence (AI) in Judicial Systems and their Environment', available at www.coe.int/en/web/cepej/cepej-european-ethical-charter-on-the-use-of-artificial-intelligence-ai-in-judicial-systems-and-their-environment.

[5] European Parliament, 'Artificial Intelligence and Law Enforcement – Impact on Fundamental Rights', available at www.europarl.europa.eu/RegData/etudes/STUD/2020/656295/IPOL_STU(2020)656295_EN.pdf.

[6] CrossJustice project (n *).

extent the use of AI can allow the effective protection of the individual rights of suspects and defendants to be strengthened, in a complex and multilevel system such as the one created today by the legal sources adopted by the EU.

II. THE DEVELOPMENT OF EU CRIMINAL LAW IN THE LAST TWO DECADES

European criminal law, with particular reference to criminal procedure, started to grow just over 20 years ago, following the entry into force of the Treaty of Amsterdam. With the Tampere Council in 1999, the EU laid the foundations for the development of judicial cooperation in criminal matters, while at the same time making it possible to make use of legal instruments, initially Framework Decisions (FD), which until that point had not been possible to implement in criminal matters.[7]

All in all, the path undertaken can be considered as a successful story. Within the framework of EU law, the criminal law area has developed rapidly, with a range of new legal sources regulating many different aspects. This has shed new light on the subject as a whole, contributed to the emergence of new methods of study and led to the establishment of new institutional actors, such as the European Public Prosecutor's Office (EPPO).[8] The enterprise started in Tampere has also been consolidated and developed in a crucial way after the entry into force of the Lisbon Treaty. Thanks to that Treaty, the Charter of Fundamental Rights of the European Union (CFREU) today enjoys the same value as the Treaties, thus acknowledging that it is an essential mission of the EU to ensure an adequate and effective level of protection of fundamental rights.[9]

An essential area regulated by a network of provisions adopted after Lisbon, concerns the protection of individual rights, in particular those of the victim of crimes and of the accused in criminal proceedings. With regard to the latter, the Union constructed a road map that has led to a certain harmonisation in the discipline, at the supranational level, of the essential aspects of the accused's defence. It would seem correct to say that the six procedural Directives adopted by the European legislator in accordance with the Stockholm Programme have laid down *ad hoc* rules for most of the aspects touched upon, in general terms, by Article 6 of the European Convention on Human Rights (ECHR).[10]

[7] A Klip, *European Criminal Law. An Integrative Approach* (Intersentia, 2021) 59.

[8] L Bachmaier Winter (ed), *The European Public Prosecution Office. The Challenges Ahead* (Springer, 2018) v–xii.

[9] V Mitsilegas, *EU Criminal Law after Lisbon. Rights, Trust, and the Transformation of Justice in Europe* (Hart Publishing, 2016) 9–11.

[10] Resolution of the Council of 30 November 2009 on a Roadmap for strengthening procedural rights of suspected or accused persons in criminal proceedings (2009/C 295/01) [2009] OJ C295, subsequently recognised in the Stockholm Programme – An open and secure Europe serving and protecting citizens (2010/C 115/01) [2010] OJ C 115. See A. Klip, 'Fair Trial Rights in the European

The unconcealed ambition, in this respect, has been to guarantee an EU statute of the rights of the defence, equally valid both from the horizontal perspective, that is in judicial cooperation between the different Member States, and from the vertical one, in the relationship between the EU criminal justice institutions and the national jurisdictions. In this regard, it is important not to forget that, according to Article 41 of the EPPO Regulation,[11] the Directives on the rights of the accused are the main reference also for EPPO, when its investigations interfere with defence rights.

A first conclusion we can draw, therefore, is that the Area of Freedom, Security and Justice (AFSJ), 20 years after its initial development, appears to be vital and capable of projecting its effectiveness in the different dimensions in which EU law traditionally operates. At the same time, precisely because of the abundance and diversity of new legal sources, it presents numerous aspects that need to be clarified and standardised in terms of interpretation and application.

III. A COMPLEX LEGAL FRAMEWORK

In spite of the passion in the EU for classical culture and its heritage, it is indeed difficult to adapt the image of the Greek temple, which was used to give the idea of the EU's structure before Lisbon, to describe European criminal law. This is not surprising, of course. Although certainly impetuous in terms of timing and abundant in terms of quantity, the criminal law set of normative provisions within the EU is more than ever the result of compromises and accelerations followed by sudden setbacks.

One good example concerns the issuing of a harmonised legal system in the law of evidence, and the decision to approve, at last, the European Investigation Order Directive.[12] While the original plan was to draft a directive with the ambition to establish a single regime for the mutual admission of evidence, the final legal product ended up being just an instrument to execute orders to conduct investigations more quickly. Yet, with a deeper analysis, you may discover that, among the EIO provisions, there may be hidden passages which allow, with a little hermeneutical sagacity, a fairly complete European regime of the admission of evidence to be constructed through case law.[13]

Union: Reconciling Accused and Victims' Rights' in T Rafaraci and R Belfiore (eds), *EU Criminal Justice. Fundamental Rights, Transnational Proceedings and the European Public Prosecutor's Office* (Springer, 2019) 29.

[11] Council Regulation (EU) 2017/1939 of 12 October 2017 implementing enhanced cooperation on the establishment of the European Public Prosecutor's Office ('the EPPO') [2017] OJ L283/1.

[12] Directive 2014/41/EU of the European Parliament and of the Council of 3 April 2014 regarding the European Investigation Order in criminal matters [2014] OJ L130/1.

[13] See on that point A Mangiaracina, 'A New and Controversial Scenario in the Gathering of Evidence at the European Level: The Proposal for a Directive on the European Investigation Order' (2014) 10 *Utrecht Law Review* 113.

Similar considerations apply to the rights of the accused in criminal proceedings as they have developed within the Union, which are an area of specific interest in the research at hand. Conceived as part of a unitary and coherent body of law, the 2003 Green Paper, the set of components of defence rights were segmented and approved separately following the entry into force of the Lisbon Treaty, thanks to the political solution promoted through the Stockholm Programme, in order to overcome Member States' political resistance.

Breaking down the original framework into separate sets of regulations, the EU has succeeded, in the space of about seven years, in realising its original plan by adopting legal instruments (a set of six Directives[14]) capable of providing an answer to the main problems that the defence may encounter in criminal proceedings (especially if they are transnational in nature, as those where EU law typically comes into play).

However, although the Directives certainly raise the level of protection of the right of defence within the EU AFSJ, they present quite a few problematic aspects. In some cases, they contain provisions that are not clear enough, while in others, these are not sufficiently effective: It seems undeniable, it is worth observing incidentally, that the legislator has almost always been careful to use language that would allow, with an adequate hermeneutic will, to adopt even the best possible standard of protection. Moreover, rights sometimes overlap, as in the case of the information to be given to the defendant. Finally, the use of the directives as legal sources, a condition imposed by Article 82 Treaty on the Functioning of the European Union (TFEU), always places the interpreter in front of at least two legal texts: the supranational one, and the national implementing one, which may be partially different from the former, by exploiting the margins of discretion made available by the Directive.[15] Naturally, the complexity may be far greater when the procedure is transnational and involves several legal systems. In such a case, faced with the European legal source, the interpreter may be forced to consider (and apply) as many national transposition sources as the Member States' jurisdictions involved.

[14] See the following directives: Directive 2010/64/EU of the European Parliament and of the Council of 20 October 2010 on the right to interpretation and translation in criminal proceedings [2012] OJ L280/1; Directive 2012/13/EU of the European Parliament and of the Council of 22 May 2012 on the right to information in criminal proceedings [2012] OJ L142/1; Directive 2013/48/EU of the European Parliament and of the Council of 22 October 2013 on the right of access to a lawyer in criminal proceedings and in European arrest warrant proceedings, and on the right to have a third party informed upon deprivation of liberty and to communicate with third persons and with consular authorities while deprived of liberty [2013] OJ L294/1; Directive (EU) 2016/343 of the European Parliament and of the Council of 9 March 2016 on the strengthening of certain aspects of the presumption of innocence and of the right to be present at the trial in criminal proceedings [2016] OJ L65/1; Directive (EU) 2016/800 of the European Parliament and of the Council of 11 May 2016 on procedural safeguards for children who are suspects or accused persons in criminal proceedings [2016] OJ L132/1; Directive (EU) 2016/1919 of the European Parliament and of the Council of 26 October 2016 on legal aid for suspects and accused persons in criminal proceedings and for requested persons in European arrest warrant proceedings [2016] OJ L297/1.

[15] See A Klip, 'The Substantive Criminal Law Jurisdiction of the European Public Prosecutor's Office' (2012) 20 *European Journal of Crime, Criminal Law and Criminal Justice* 367.

The same phenomenon is bound to occur in the system set up with the EPPO, which will structurally have to deal with cases with a transnational dimension. Although the legislator could choose to unify the legal discipline of rights of the accused, since Article 86 TFEU allows the adoption of a regulation in this field, it preferred referring to the directives already launched by the Stockholm Programme.[16] In this way, practitioners will necessarily have to apply, most times they come across a legal issue, two EU legal texts (the EPPO Regulation, and the Directive specifically concerned), in addition to the national legal provisions transposing the European sources.

As always, at the peak of the system is the EU Charter of Fundamental Rights, which, as if the level of complexity were not already high enough, by means of a game of cross-references carried out through Articles 52 and 53, transposes the legal precipitate of the ECHR and the common constitutional traditions as elaborated by the jurisdictions of the Member States.

IV. THE DIFFICULT APPLICATION OF THE ESTABLISHED REGULATORY SYSTEM IN PRACTICE WITH A SPECIFIC FOCUS ON THE DEFENDANT'S FAIR TRIAL RIGHTS

The observations made so far suggest that dealing with European criminal law, and in particular with the rights of defence within the framework of the EU legal system, is quite difficult. First, as we have seen, the network of rules is extremely varied. This increases combinatorial possibilities for the interpreter. The difference in legal sources also allows interpreters to make use of various interpretative methods. This aggravates the overall difficulty of making the system predictable *ex ante*. Such difficulties arise only when applying the general principles to cases, due to the complex interconnection between the two charters of rights (ECHR and CFREU).

This statement appears to be confirmed by an analysis, even if not in-depth, of the recent jurisprudence of the European Courts, including both the European Court of Human Rights (ECtHR) and the European Court of Justice (CJEU). Both courts, when confronted in recent years with a case involving both ECHR and EU law, have tried to combine the two levels, justifying the solution adopted in light of supranational law other than the one on which they formally have jurisdiction over. Thus, for example, in *Ibrahim*,[17] and in *Knox*,[18] the ECtHR arrived at its final decision after considering the relevant EU sources – the Charter and the directives specifically concerned – on the right to a lawyer and

[16] See D Brodowski, 'Article 41' in HH Herrnfeld, D Brodowsky and C Burchard, *European Public Prosecutor's Office* (Hart Publishing, 2021) 383–84.

[17] *Ibrahim and others v UK* App nos 50541/08, 50571/08, 50573/08 and 40351/09 (ECHR, 13 September 2016) §§ 203 ff.

[18] *Knox v Italy* App no 76577/13 (ECHR, 24 January 2019) §§ 106 ff.

on the right to an interpreter and the translation of documents respectively (as well as after trying to understand how these sources interact with the national rules of the State involved in the case).

The difficulty of following each step of the reasoning in the above-mentioned decisions makes it clear that the elaboration of legal solutions in the area of European criminal justice, in particular with regard to the rights of defence and to a fair trial, appears to be highly complex. This realistically implies that, very often, one and the same lawyer does not have all the necessary skills to offer an effective defence.

In order to achieve effective solutions, it is necessary to have a good knowledge of the EU legal level, and, at the same time, have a thorough knowledge of the ECtHR jurisprudence developed in this field in the second half of the last century. In addition, it is necessary to have an adequate command of the national system in which the sources are to be applied: if more than one jurisdiction is involved, as is likely when the case has a European dimension, it is also useful to have some familiarity with national systems other than one's own.

This is an unusual intellectual challenge for modern criminal jurists. It is difficult, for the reasons indicated, to find precedents to refer to, or practices to adapt to the area examined here. This is also due to the fact that, unlike other legal fields, criminal law is characterised by a claim to specificity and strictness, of clear *ex ante* predictability, which does not operate with comparable significance in areas other than that of criminal law.

V. THE USE OF AI SYSTEMS TO ADVANCE KNOWLEDGE AND IMPROVE THE EFFECTIVE PROTECTION OF FUNDAMENTAL RIGHTS IN THE EU AREA OF FREEDOM, SECURITY AND JUSTICE

To put it simply, the system is extremely complex. It requires multifarious competences, which are not easy to integrate. At the same time, it must guarantee, as an essential reason for legitimacy, high levels of a priori predictability for the citizen, in the name of the principle of legality. This is a task that is very difficult for an individual to accomplish under his/her own steam / on his/her own.

Of course, you may object that these kinds of cases will usually be handled by a group of jurists, whose background is as varied as the legal sources they have to apply. Thus, there will be justices (and defenders) capable of composing the framework of the European sources, and of the jurisprudences of the relevant supranational Courts, while there will also be other jurists who are trained specifically for the purpose of operating at the national level, in which they are experts. In other words, the solution of a European criminal case with a supra- (and trans-) national dimension will in practice always be the result of a team effort, and not of an isolated jurist.

This objection is certainly well-founded, but it does not solve all the problems. On the one hand, although you can certainly speak of teamwork, the solution to a case must ultimately be unitary (and requires an ability to develop an overall view of the legal problems involved at different levels). On the other, the very need to work in teams may produce inequalities. In particular, it may amplify the delta separating the position of the prosecution, which will hopefully be equipped with the necessary personnel resources to face the challenge posed by multilevel criminal justice, from the defence, which will rarely benefit from a comparable set of tools:[19] such as a pool of defenders able to move in a coordinated way to challenge a case built by the EPPO, across the multiple levels, national and supranational, in which it is organised.

Of course, inequalities may occur also among defendants, and between defendants and victims, depending on how many resources they can deploy to build a team of lawyers capable of dealing with a case of transnational dimensions. Such a gap between private citizens and supranational prosecution agencies, such as the EPPO, is realistically destined to never, or almost never, be closed. But this is the point: Can it be considerably reduced? From this perspective, is it possible to use technology and computational reasoning to make it easier for citizens (and at an even earlier stage for legal professionals) to become acquainted and familiar with this new area of law?

The underlying idea of the research conducted was specifically to verify if and how AI systems may improve the protection of defendants' fundamental rights, where faced with transnational criminal proceedings in the EU AFSJ area. Theoretically, it is possible to choose two different ways to test this research question. The first is to try to build AI systems in order to develop ready-made hermeneutic solutions. In this sense, the operator who has to deal with a transnational EU dimension case has only to enter the relevant data, and try to uncritically follow the solution offered by the algorithm applied by the self-learning machine. This path has recently been theorised in several studies, and is being tested in some areas (usually not including criminal law).[20] For various reasons, however, this did not seem to us to be the most appropriate direction to take.

Firstly, especially in relation to CJEU case law, there is a lack of adequate judicial decisions. In almost all the areas concerned with a defendant's rights – with the possible exception of *ne bis in idem* – interpretative guidelines seem to have been established by the CJEU jurisprudence only on a limited number of issues (incidentally, not always prominent).[21] In such a context, the possibility

[19] See in this regard the observations expressed some years ago in M Thunberg Schunke, '*Whose Responsibility? A Study of Transnational Defence Rights and Mutual Recognition of Judicial Decisions within the EU*' (Intersentia, 2013), especially at 69 ff.

[20] See A Garapon and J Lassègue, *Justice Digitale* (PUF, 2018).

[21] It could be argued that ECtHR jurisprudence on the rights of the accused is sufficient to train a ML system with an adequate amount of data for the purpose. This consideration is partially correct. It is in fact undeniable that the decisions taken in the field considered by the ECtHR are many, and cover different areas of defence rights. However, the lack of developed ECJ jurisprudence seems decisive. Only the EU system has provisions that are directly applicable within the national systems

for an AI system to come up with solutions within a reasonable timeframe that are actually helpful – ready to use, so to speak – seems somewhat illusory. In addition, the intention of the research was to improve the knowledge and familiarity of criminal law practitioners, lawyers, magistrates and scholars with this area of law, without necessarily having to provide ready-made practical solutions.

Indeed, the efficiency of the functioning of the judicial system at the EU level must be achieved through an improved knowledge of this area of law on the part of practitioners, not only by constructing algorithmic calculations that allow the latter to disregard the former. The idea is ultimately to set up a calculation platform that improves knowledge as an instrumental element for a more conscious (and more uniform) application of the law in the field of individual rights safeguards. By means of more widespread shared knowledge among the various stakeholders of criminal justice, it is possible to achieve a better uniformity and predictability of the system, as well as a more effective protection of the fundamental rights of the accused, even assuming that the written law remains with the flaws that have characterised it so far.

Beyond this, it was also felt that even if an AI system could be devised to provide a ready-made answer, it would hardly be accepted with confidence by the practitioners, since research in this area is still not sufficiently developed and known to legal practitioners. A different path has therefore been chosen, with the aim of creating a platform that would allow integrated knowledge of the different regulatory levels, meaning supranational and national ones together. For both, we tried to transpose and translate into computer language the contents of the statutory provisions and those that can be extrapolated from judicial decisions. Finally, due consideration has also been given to the hermeneutical proposals developed by scholars, which are of significant importance in the field of European criminal justice.

These results can be appreciated using the CrossJustice project's knowledge platform (the Legal Database Module and Advisory Module).[22] This database allows for an integrated set of results. Firstly, it allows the verification of the necessary information regarding the rights of the defence of each of the 11 Member States covered by the project. In particular, users of this platform can verify the level of fundamental rights through a specific functionality of the database ('transposition cross-reference' functionality). Secondly, through a different functionality of the platform (the Advisory Module[23]), it is possible for a legal professional to identify and apply relevant rules of EU and national

of the Member States (if necessary, by disapplying conflicting national legislation). This power of vertical penetration of EU sources gives ECJ case law a potentially very different role from that of the ECtHR. Training an AI system to come up with immediately applicable solutions when it still lacks a numerically significant body of ECJ judgments appeared to be an error of approach.

[22] See https://site.unibo.it/cross-justice/en/project-results/tools.

[23] See www.crossjustice.eu/en/index.html#crossjustice-platform.

legislation concerning procedural rights of persons suspected or accused of crimes, both at the domestic and the cross-border level.[24]

As a result, the practitioner, when faced with a criminal legal issue involving the safeguarding of defence rights on a transnational level, is able to visually gain an integrated picture of the different sources. The system also makes it possible to calculate the level of compliance that each legal system, of those taken into consideration, presents with respect to the normative standards required by the European sources (the directives and the CFREU). In this way, it should be easier for practitioners to decide whether to raise an interpretative prejudicial question before the Court of Justice, so as to fill gaps and lacunae that may characterise the protection of a fundamental right at the national level hermeneutically in the event of the inadequate transposition of the European source.

Actually, with a final effort, the research team also managed to create an AI system, through which a professional can obtain, by entering data and responding to questions on the platform, an initial orientation to help her find the most appropriate solution for her case. This is the closest step to obtaining an algorithmic legal opinion, a choice which, for the reasons set out above, has been deemed as one to be excluded.

The constituent elements of the AI system described so far, which has been implemented in the course of the project, should enable the following results to be achieved (as already noted at least in part in the previous considerations). Firstly, it allows a simultaneous view of the existing sources of protection of fundamental rights and fair trial rights, including case law and scholarly opinions. Secondly, it encourages an integrated view of the different levels of regulation, thanks to which it is possible to identify the areas in which a national system is not compliant (or, conversely, offers a higher level of protection) with the standards laid down at supranational level. Finally, it is able to guide the legal profession in the elaboration of solutions for a concrete case. These solutions remain, for the reasons set out above, within the interpreter's full intellectual autonomy, but are facilitated by the analysis and learning process enabled by the use of data processed by the AI system.

VI. THE BOTTOM-UP CONSTRUCTION OF A MORE UNIFORM SYSTEM THROUGH THE USE OF LEARNING MACHINES

The objective pursued was to make the legal field of fundamental rights more easily accessible and therefore more predictable in terms of a priori calculability, as a means of achieving greater harmonisation of national systems (and of this with the supranational level) by means of hermeneutics and application.

[24] The Module assesses in particular: 1) the level of compliance of national instruments with the EU acquis by highlighting potential gaps in the implementation process, and 2) the compatibility between national frameworks resulting from the implementation of EU directives.

Such an approach, if successful, could achieve some significant results. Firstly, it should be able to take into account national normative realities, including the theoretical constructs referred to therein, and better integrate them into the regulatory framework developed at the EU level. In turn, this emphasis on the legal cultures of the Member States, which are able to enter into a dialogue with EU law more quickly and in a greater number of cases, should facilitate the identification of common constitutional traditions. This element is often mentioned in EU sources, such as in Article 6(3) TFEU and Article 52 CFREU. However, thus far, this important component of the European legal edifice has rarely been used to develop new solutions.

In fact, recourse to national traditions has largely been used to stop the effectiveness and pervasiveness of EU law, rather than to expand its scope (or to strengthen its content). An emblematic case in this context is *Taricco*, where recourse to national identity justified the Italian Constitutional Court's choice to oppose the hermeneutic proposal elaborated by the Court of Justice[25] (but not to enhance a new interpretative solution that could have improved the general application of Article 325 TFEU for the whole AFSJ).

Indeed, there are signs that this is about to change soon. For example, preliminary rulings have already been submitted on the Directive concerning the interpretation of the presumption of innocence aimed at extending the fundamental rights of the accused to the area of pre-trial detention. These solicitations from purely domestic proceedings have the potential to contribute greatly to strengthening the protection of individual rights throughout the AFSJ. A relevant case in this regard is *Milev*,[26] but others have followed (see for instance the case of *RH*).[27] Some analogous indications concern the relationship between the practice of plea bargaining and compliance with the same Directive on the presumption of innocence. A relevant decision, in this regard, was adopted by the CJEU in *AH and others*.[28] In all these cases, national courts have tried to link, in proceedings with purely domestic relevance, the legal provisions of their own law with a European directive. This is in order to reinforce, or at least to verify, the respect of a fundamental right (that of the accused not to be presented as guilty before final conviction in a pre-trial detention decision, in *Milev* and *RH*, and in a guilty plea decision, in *AH and others*) by their legal system. At the same time, the referral represents an opportunity for the CJEU to promote more effective protection of defence rights.

[25] C Amalfitano and O Pollicino, 'Two Courts, Two Languages? The Taricco Saga Ends on a Worrying Note' (*Vervassungsblog*, 5 June 2018), available at https://verfassungsblog.de/two-courts-two-languages-the-taricco-saga-ends-on-a-worrying-note/; V Mitsilegas, 'Judicial Dialogue in Three Silences: Unpacking *Taricco*' (2018) 9 *New Journal of European Criminal Law* 38.

[26] See Case C310/18 PPU *Milev* (CJEU, 19 September 2018).

[27] See Order in Case C-8/19 *RH* (CJEU, 12 February 2019).

[28] See Case C-377/18 *AH and Others* (CJEU, 5 September 2019).

A case in which the search for a common constitutional tradition was evident was in *DB v Consob*,[29] concerning the presumption of innocence and the right not to be punished for choosing to remain silent in a formally administrative but criminally coloured procedure. In that case, the preliminary reference of the Italian Constitutional Court, which was followed by a decision of the Court of Justice accepting the prospect of a national referral, very effectively highlighted the search for common ground. In fact, the Italian Court strongly pointed out that the right to silence could already be considered part of the right of defence and the presumption of innocence in the light of the text of its own Constitution. However, given the transnational nature of the issue (the sanction for not responding to the administrative authority conducting the investigation had been introduced also in compliance with an EU directive), the Italian Court requested that the CJEU also express its opinion on the point, with the aim of reaching a shared view. The decision to opt for a preliminary ruling proved to be successful, since the CJEU accepted the perspective of the referring court. The overall result, if you look at the case as a whole, is that a fundamental right, that of not being punished for choosing not to answer in proceedings of a punitive nature, has now been strengthened in two different ways. First, it is protected in a clearer and more unambiguous manner by the CJEU decision. Second, it is recognised at the supranational level, by enhancing the solicitation coming from the jurisdiction of a Member State (thus enshrining that tradition as part of a common constitutional heritage). It would appear, by looking at the cases mentioned so far, that the referring national court is seeking a common ground between its own legal system and that of the EU in order to give a new, fuller meaning to the principle of the presumption of innocence.

Ultimately, it is not difficult to discern an attempt, in the references for a preliminary ruling on which the above-mentioned decisions were based, to find a common tradition, which allows the national court to interpret and develop its own system while respecting its identity – at the same time improving the protection of a certain fundamental right of the individual at the EU level.

Against this background, the use of an AI system designed to improve the knowledge of EU law, and its level of integration with individual national systems, could also be of significant help in fostering dialogue between the Courts. In turn, a clearer dialogue will be able to foster the development of the doctrine of common traditions which seems to be crucial for the harmonisation of national systems.

Ultimately, the targeted use of the platform should be able to help the creation of a legal reasoning method common to all practitioners in the area at

[29] Case C-481/19 *DB v Consob* (CJEU, 2 February 2021). See G Lasagni, 'Consob – The Court of Justice on the Right to Remain Silent in Criminal Matters (and Beyond …)' (*EU Law Live*, 3 November 2021), available at https://eulawlive.com/op-ed-consob-the-court-of-justice-on-the-right-to-remain-silent-in-criminal-matters-and-beyond-by-giulia-lasagni/.

stake, without which no vertical regulatory instrument adopted by the EU legislator will be able to produce the desired effects (a more effective and uniform protection of individual rights).

VII. LIMITATIONS OF THE RESEARCH

The research conducted has some unavoidable limitations. The first is the use of English as a *lingua franca*. The problem of languages, in relation to the objective of achieving a better harmonisation of systems, is crucial. Legal reasoning is in fact so influenced by the characteristics of the language that expresses it, that it is very often impossible to separate, in its most intimate essence, the legal question from the way in which it is conceived and presented on a linguistic level.

This problem, which has been well known to EU law scholars for a long time, also emerges clearly in the research carried out, in which, due to a practical necessity, the predominant choice was to make general use of English.[30] However, in order to balance the limitations of this decision, an attempt was made to supplement the AI system by implementing official translations of texts in the platform whenever possible (ie mainly for CJEU judicial decisions and EU normative texts).

A second limitation concerns the number of Member States involved, only 11 compared to the 27 that make up the EU. An attempt was made to select countries that would in some way represent the different geographical, legal and cultural areas of the EU, in a fair balance. However, it is clear that the work carried out, although of considerable size, represents only partially the variety of legal cultures that characterises the EU area as a whole. A system that aspired to represent all the national systems of the EU in terms of protecting the rights of the accused in criminal proceedings would require more time and resources.

VIII. CONCLUSIONS

The research carried out by the CrossJustice project leads to a number of conclusions. Among them, the first one, already known, is that the EU legal sources on defendants' rights are developing significant effects on the level of protection of the rights involved, both at the national level and within EU law itself. The process of development in this field is still in its infancy as some institutions are

[30] Actually, the need to use English as a *lingua franca* is not only a limitation, but also a strength in some respects. In this way, it is in fact possible to have access to regulations other than those of one's own reference languages.

far too recent to constitute an effective benchmark (this is a particular reference to the EPPO). There is no doubt, however, that these supranational normative sources will progressively be able to develop a relevant impact in the three dimensions that characterise the AFSJ: That of horizontal judicial cooperation in criminal matters; that of vertical cooperation, between EU institutions and national courts; that of the protection of fundamental rights at a purely or predominantly domestic level. It should also be added that a fourth relevant level concerns the extension of fair trial rights from the criminal sphere *stricto sensu* to the punitive administrative sphere. The Directives as a whole oblige the Courts, both those of the Member States and the Court of Justice, to take a position on numerous significant aspects concerning the protection of the accused in matters which lie at the crossroads of these two areas of law. This, in turn, shall be done through a constant cultural dialogue with the case law of the ECtHR.

The second result is that the use of a system of AI for gaining a more effective knowledge of this legal field appears to be significant. It provides an integrated view of the problems, meaning an understanding of the multilevel nature of legal sources and the role played by both judicial decisions and theories developed by scholars. An AI system also makes it easy to identify the level of compliance of a national system with European standards. It also makes it possible to promote issues related to the identification and transposition of common constitutional traditions faster and more effectively, which is in turn a key area for the success of the whole AFSJ.

The third result is that such an AI system helps interpreters to find their bearings in specific individual cases with a supranational and multilevel dimension, offering first rudimentary solutions (which will subsequently have to be properly developed by practitioners). This implies that the use of AI has a practical problem-solving function, although it leaves the responsibility (and the resolution of the legal issue in its entirety) to the practitioners.[31]

In other words, the assistance of an AI system is objective, in that it aids faster and more integrated knowledge of a complex and multilevel legal system. It is also subjective, in that, by proposing solutions that must then be developed and suitably adapted to the case in question, it acts as a dialectical interlocutor for the jurist. In a nutshell, the selection of the questions (the legal issues) and the final solutions remain firmly in the hands of the jurist. The AI system, however, can play an effective role in helping to identify the problem and, above all, in planning and developing the solution.

The challenge of the contemporary generation of jurists is twofold. On the one hand, they must help solve the translation problem, ie guide the transition

[31] CrossJustice outcomes will be developed in a new EU funded project, Facilex, designed to bridge gaps in the field of criminal judicial cooperation and EU mutual recognition. Facilex aims to provide a multilevel online platform based on a comprehensive comparative legal analysis on the implementation of EU mutual recognition instruments by Member States (see https://site.unibo.it/facilex/en).

of fundamental principles, conceived in a less integrated and non-automated world, into the modern world, characterised by a high level of integration between legal systems and through a constant interaction between machines and individuals. On the other, they need to ensure that the ultimate choices concerning key decisions remain in the hands of human beings, exploiting the potential offered by AI systems and ML to make legal systems more responsive to people's needs.

12

The Challenges of Deepfake Technology in the Context of Political Disinformation

CLEMENTINA SALVI*

I. INTRODUCTION

TODAY, IT IS often said that artificial intelligence (AI) is reshaping all aspects of our social existence.[1] However, seeking to understand the actual scale and impact of this transformation is a less banal response to this situation. Only recently AI has reached the point where it is capable of creating new digital content merely on the basis of initial sets of data, reproducing human language, images and sounds.[2] In this respect, among the most advanced breakthrough technologies, it is possible to mention digital media generated by AI techniques, in particular deep learning and neural networks,[3] commonly called deepfakes.[4] Such technology can both create or manipulate

* Queen Mary University of London and University of Liverpool.

[1] A Renda, *Artificial Intelligence: Ethics, Governance and Policy Challenges* (Centre for European Policy Studies, February 2019) 1.

[2] P Boucher, *Artificial Intelligence: How Does It Work, Why Does It Matter, and What We Can Do about It?* (EPRS Study Panel for the Future of Science and Technology, PE 641.547, June 2020) 12–13.

[3] Newer artificial neural networks, named Generative Adversarial Networks (GANs), considered largely responsible for increases in the ability to generate convincing artificial content, were invented in 2014 (cfr. R Chesney and DK Citron, 'Deep Fakes: A Looming Challenge for Privacy, Democracy, and National Security' (2019) 107 *California Law Review* 1753, 1760). Since then, the technology has improved constantly. According to the MIT Technology Review, synthetic data for AI is ranked nine of the 10 breakthrough technologies of 2022: see '10 Breakthrough Technologies 2022' (*MIT Technology Review*), available at www.technologyreview.com/2022/02/23/1045416/10-breakthrough-technologies-2022/. For an overall view of the state of the art digital manipulation, see C Rathgeb and others (eds), *Handbook of Digital Face Manipulation and Detection: From DeepFakes to Morphing Attacks* (Springer International Publishing, 2022) 1.

[4] The word 'deepfakes' is a combination of 'deep learning' and 'fake'; it first appeared in 2017 when an anonymous Reddit user under the nickname deepfakes posted videos of famous actresses and singers with their faces superimposed on the bodies of women in pornographic films. See S Cole, 'AI-Assisted Fake Porn Is Here and We're All Fucked' (*Vice*, 11 December 2017), available at www.vice.com/en/article/gydydm/gal-gadot-fake-ai-porn.

digital information, invent non-existent individuals (digital entities or avatars) and scenarios, or make actual individuals do things they never did.[5] The threats and risks related to the misleading and destructive potential of such technology have been emphasised by many.[6] One of the most worrying concerns is the new dimension that deepfakes bring to disinformation in the digital media landscape run by social networks, video-sharing platforms and search engines.[7] In fact, from Instagram to dating and food delivery apps, digital visuals and data are used to inform human decisions.[8] Deepfakes can distort the perception of what is real,[9] and thus impact the process of decision-making and the formation of free consent.[10] That is why the growing accessibility of such technology and its diffusion has been subject to a great deal of alarmism in news media, academia, and among policy regulators. As highlighted, deepfakes pose many potential systemic socio-political challenges such as the manipulation of civil discourse, interference with elections and national security, as well as the erosion of trust in journalism and public institutions more generally.[11] Such a development generates epistemic doubts and uncertainty concerning the veracity of each single piece of information, blurring the concepts of truth, authenticity and identity.[12] The necessity to protect the rule of law, consistency of society and democratic values, requires structural regulatory responses to those challenges.[13] However, the regulation of this technology is particularly complex,[14] especially when it

[5] M van Huijstee, P van Boheemen and others, *Tackling Deepfakes in European Policy, Think Tank, European Parliament* (EPRS Study, PE 690.039, July 2021) 7–17; R Tolosana and others, 'Future Trends in Digital Face Manipulation and Detection' in Rathgeb and others (n 3) 463ff.

[6] A Ajder, G Patrini, F Cavalli, L Cullen, 'The State of Deepfakes: Landscape, Threats, and Impact' (*Deeptrace Report*, 2019) 1–20; Chesney and Citron (n 3) 1755, 1771–85; M Caldwell, JTA Andrews, T Tanay, LD Griffin, 'AI-Enabled Future Crime' (2020) 9 *Crime Science* 14, 66; J Bateman, 'Deepfakes and Synthetic Media in the Financial System: Assessing Threat Scenarios' (Carnegie Endowment for International Peace, Cyber Policy Initiative Working Paper Series, July 2020) 6ff.

[7] Europol, 'Facing Reality?: Law Enforcement and the Challenge of Deepfakes: An Observatory Report from the Europol Innovation Lab' (Publications Office of the European Union, 2022) 5; van Huijstee, van Boheemen and others (n 5) 24; C Vaccari and A Chadwick, 'Deepfakes and Disinformation: Exploring the Impact of Synthetic Political Video on Deception, Uncertainty, and Trust in News' (2020) 6 *Social Media + Society*; R Chesney and D Citron, 'Deepfakes and the New Disinformation War: The Coming Age of Post-Truth Geopolitics' (2019) 98 *Foreign Affairs* 147.

[8] M Ibrahim, 'Commentary: Synthetic Media and Deepfakes Are Here–but Our Economy Isn't Ready' (*Fortune*, July 2022), available at https://fortune.com/2022/07/27/synthetic-media-deepfakes-economy-claims-consumers-tech-fraud-insurance-ai-mounir-ibrahim/.

[9] P Boucher, 'What If Deepfakes Made Us Doubt Everything We See and Hear?' (European Parliamentary Research Service, PE 690.046, September 2021).

[10] T Dobber and others, 'Do (Microtargeted) Deepfakes Have Real Effects on Political Attitudes?' (2021) 26 *The International Journal of Press/Politics* 69.

[11] Chesney and Citron (n 3) 1776; MA Franks and AE Waldman, 'Sex, Lies, and Videotape: Deep Fakes and Free Speech Delusions Symposium – Truth Decay: Deep Fakes and the Implications for Privacy, National Security, and Democracy' (2018) 78 *Maryland Law Review* 892.

[12] van Huijstee, van Boheemen and others (n 5) 25.

[13] ibid I.

[14] B van der Sloot and Y Wagensveld, 'Deepfakes: Regulatory Challenges for the Synthetic Society' (2022) 46 *Computer Law & Security Review*.

is used to harm political debate, and it is controversial whether criminal law should play a role in countering this phenomenon.[15]

The present contribution focuses on the role of deepfake technology in the context of political disinformation in the European Union (EU) framework.[16] There are as yet various important initiatives taking place to address issues related to the dissemination of disinformation in general as well as to deal with AI technologies, including deepfake systems. The aim is to provide a diagnostic of the state-of-the-art solutions proposed at the European level. To do so, it first contextualises deepfakes in the increasingly multifaceted and risky digital information ecosystem (section II) and explains why they are particularly impactful (section III). Then, after analysing the main challenges related to deepfakes regulation (section IV), it illustrates and further evaluates two key pieces of legislation: the Regulation on a Single Market for Digital Services (Digital Services Act)[17] and the Regulation on Artificial Intelligence (AI Act) (section V).[18]

II. POLITICAL DISINFORMATION IN THE DIGITAL ECOSYSTEM: THE DEVELOPMENT OF DEEPFAKES

Political disinformation and propaganda campaigns have always existed, but not on the scale that we are seeing now. Before going into more depth, however, it is crucial to provide some preliminary definitions regarding what disinformation is and when disinformation is political.[19] The European Democracy Action Plan crucially distinguishes between different phenomena that are commonly referred to as disinformation to allow for the design of appropriate

[15] T Kirchengast, 'Deepfakes and Image Manipulation: Criminalisation and Control' (2020) 29 *Information & Communications Technology Law* 308.

[16] Outside the scope of this research, there is a significant amount of literature in the United States focusing on deepfakes and political disinformation. See amongst others, K Manheim and L Kaplan, 'Artificial Intelligence: Risks to Privacy and Democracy' (2019) 21 *Yale Journal of Law and Technology* 106. See also, R Hasen, 'Deep Fakes, Bots, and Siloed Justices: American Election Law in a "Post-Truth" World' (2020) 64 *St. Louis University Law Journal* 535; MJ Blitz, 'Deepfakes and Other Non-Testimonial Falsehoods: When Is Belief Manipulation (Not) First Amendment Speech?' (2020) 23 *Yale Journal of Law & Technology* 160.

[17] EU Regulation 2022/2065 on a Single Market For Digital Services and amending Directive 2000/31/EC (Digital Services Act or DSA) [2022] OJ L277/1.

[18] Regulation 2024/1689 of 13 June 2024 laying down harmonised rules on artificial intelligence and amending Regulations (EC) No 300/2008, (EU) No 167/2013, (EU) No 168/2013, (EU) 2018/858, (EU) 2018/1139 and (EU) 2019/2144 and Directives 2014/90/EU, (EU) 2016/797 and (EU) 2020/1828 (Artificial Intelligence Act or AI Act) [2024] OJ L2024/1689.

[19] J Bayer and others, *Disinformation and Propaganda – Impact on the Functioning of the Rule of Law in the EU and Its Member States* (Study requested by the LIBE Committee, PE 608.864, February 2019) 22ff. In accordance with the European Commission's High-Level Expert Group on Fake News and Online Disinformation, the term 'fake news' should be avoided as inadequate as a description of the complex phenomenon of disinformation (cfr. M De Cock Buning and others, 'A Multi-Dimensional Approach to Disinformation: Report of the Independent High-Level Group on Fake News and Online Disinformation' (Publications Office of the European Union, 2018) 10).

policy responses.[20] While 'misinformation' is false or misleading content shared without harmful intent although the effects can still be harmful, 'disinformation' is false or misleading content that is spread with an 'intention' to deceive or secure economic or political gain and which may cause public harm.[21] As far as the political declination, beyond the object and the content, the strategies of disinformation, organised and repeated, designed to be credible, in order to polarise public debate, are intrinsically political, in their effects and intentions.[22] For this reason, 'political' disinformation is considered as such not only when connected to specific events such as elections and referenda, but more broadly with no time or place restrictions.

It is clear that this phenomenon has found a new field in which to operate, far from traditional media, thanks to social networks and private messaging apps. Disinformation negatively impacts democratic values, challenging the rule of law in terms of the basic norms upon which institutional legitimacy and political stability depend, through i) the alteration of electoral results and ii) the pollution of public discourse and decisions more generally.[23] Together with democracy and the rule of law, rights such as dignity, which includes decisional autonomy, and other political and voting rights are also undermined.[24] As persuasively stated, democratic processes, the rule of law and human rights are both values *per se* and also inherently and indivisibly interconnected with the idea of keeping liberal democracy alive:[25] 'they cannot be separated without inflicting profound damage to the whole and changing its essential shape and configuration'.[26] Digitalisation and technological evolutions have led to the creation of new manipulative techniques in order to influence voters and voting, such as digital micro-targeting, personalised advertising and content personalisation (resulting in 'filter bubbles') as well as data analytics.[27] The side effects of their use were first observed and debated back in 2015 with the allegations of Russian interference in the presidential elections in the United States and the Cambridge Analytica scandal.[28]

[20] EU Commission, 'Communication on European Democracy Action Plan: Making EU Democracies Stronger' COM (2020) 790 final 18.

[21] ibid.

[22] A Nicita, *Il Mercato Delle Verità: Come La Disinformazione Minaccia La Democrazia* (Il mulino, 2021) 7.

[23] For an overall view of the issues, see again the study requested by the LIBE Committee and provided by Bayer and others (n 19) 51ff.

[24] ibid 74.

[25] ibid. On 61, the study refers to S Carrera, E Guild and N Hernanz, *The Triangular Relationship between Fundamental Rights, Democracy and the Rule of Law in the EU, Towards an EU Copenhagen Mechanism* (CEPS, Study for the European Parliament, 2013).

[26] Carrera, Guild and Hernanz, ibid 49.

[27] FJ Zuiderveen Borgesius and others, 'Online Political Microtargeting: Promises and Threats for Democracy' (2018) 14 *Utrecht Law Review* 82; S Bradshaw and PN Howard, 'Challenging Truth and Trust: A Global Inventory of Organized Social Media Manipulation' (Computational Propaganda Research Project, University of Oxford, 2018).

[28] Bayer and others (n 19) 28.

The ramifications and the darker side of disinformation have been more recently seen around Covid 19 and vaccination campaigns. The pandemic has shown that disinformation strategies are often part of a single plot that does not necessarily concern political or economic topics, but every aspect that can direct the emotions and fears of citizens, or feed distrust in institutions.[29] In this scenario, the rise of AI systems plays a specific role: on the one hand, it has deeply potentiated the harmful consequences of such a phenomenon, on the other, it is also used to counter disinformation online.[30] There are multiple tools that can be used for the scope of disinformation: starting from the 'automation and alghorithmisation of the information environment'[31] and mass data on inclinations and information on personal vulnerabilities[32] to the use of updated AI trolls[33] and deepfakes.[34]

Deepfakes are particularly emblematic of the challenges AI poses for countering disinformation. In fact, in contrast to other AI tools that are used as a means of directing content to a targeted audience, when it comes to deepfakes, it is the content itself that is to be manipulated and that can be manipulative. As advances in deepfake technology gather pace, and apps and tools emerge in the market, concerns are growing about the potential for harm to both individuals and society. This technology is indeed largely accessible since it requires limited skills and training. The risks connected to the malicious use of deepfakes have been stressed in multiple studies, including reports provided by important international actors such as Europol, Interpol, and the United Nations Interregional Crime and Justice Research Institute (UNICRI).[35]

The issues are varied since deepfakes are ubiquitous. They may be used to harass or destroy the image and credibility of an individual, falsify identities, perpetrate fraud, manipulate electronic evidence for criminal justice investigations, disrupt financial markets, distribute disinformation and manipulate public opinion, political propaganda and electoral interference, incite acts of violence toward minority groups, support the narratives of extremist or even terrorist groups, and distribute and disclose pornographic images.[36] While some

[29] Nicita (n 22) 61.

[30] Bayer and others (n 19) 122.

[31] I Kalpokas and J Kalpokiene, 'Introduction' in I Kalpokas and J Kalpokiene (eds), *Deepfakes: A Realistic Assessment of Potentials, Risks, and Policy Regulation* (Springer International Publishing, 2022) 7.

[32] E Hermann, 'Artificial Intelligence and Mass Personalization of Communication Content – An Ethical and Literacy Perspective' (2022) 24 *New Media & Society* 1258.

[33] J Bayer, B Holznagel and others, *Disinformation and Propaganda: Impact on the Functioning of the Rule of Law and Democratic Processes in the EU and Its Member States – 2021 Update* (Study requested by the LIBE Committee European Parliament, PE 653.633, April 2021) 21ff.

[34] M Westerlund, 'The Emergence of Deepfake Technology: A Review' (2019) 9 *Technology Innovation Management Review* 39; Ajder and others (n 6) 9.

[35] Europol, 'Malicious Uses and Abuses of Artificial Intelligence' (Joint report Europol's European Cybercrime Centre (EC3) and UNICRI, 2021) 66.

[36] ibid; van Huijstee, van Boheemen and others (n 5) 29ff; Chesney and Citron (n 3) 1771ff.

of these harms have already occurred, especially in the case of non-consensual sexualised deepfakes,[37] others are speculative so far, and only likely to materialise in the future.[38] According to the Europol Innovation Lab report, based on interviews with over 80 law enforcement experts who identified and analysed the technologies they believed would impact their work until 2030, one of 'the most worrying technological trends is the evolution and detection of deepfakes, as well as the need to address disinformation more generally'.[39]

On the other hand, a great deal of work has been carried out so far to develop and test technical tools capable of detecting deepfakes, and major online platforms are creating internal policies to respond to these issues.[40] Between 2019 and 2020, Meta, together with other industry leaders and academic experts, created the Deepfake Detection Challenge in order to accelerate the development of new automatic ways to detect deepfake videos.[41] The results showed that none of the 2,114 participants achieved 70 per cent accuracy on hidden deepfakes in the black box data set. The most popular detection technique is to use algorithms similar to the ones that were used to build the deepfakes in question. However, once the detection methods become public, researchers developing deepfakes find new ways to overcome these results.[42]

III. THE IMPACT OF DEEPFAKES ON DEMOCRACY AND THE RULE OF LAW

As illustrated above, deepfakes can be identified as tools to influence public opinion, having an impact on the integrity and quality of public debate.[43] There are examples of deepfakes in various political contexts. One of the first dates back to early 2018, when the BuzzFeed platform published a deepfake video of Barack Obama insulting Donald Trump, made by the producer Jordan Peele with the aim of generating awareness of how easily online videos can be manipulated.[44] However, it immediately went viral and notched up five million views.[45]

[37] Ajder and others (n 6) 6.

[38] Europol (n 35) 60.

[39] Europol (n 7) 4.

[40] D Granganiello, F Marra and L Verdoliva, 'Detection of AI-Generated Synthetic Faces' in C Rathgeb and others (n 3) 191.

[41] Meta, 'Deepfake Detection Challenge Results: An Open Initiative to Advance AI' (12 June 2020), available at https://ai.facebook.com/blog/deepfake-detection-challenge-results-an-open-initiative-to-advance-ai/.

[42] P Korshunov and S Marcel, 'The Threat of Deepfakes to Computer and Human Visions' in Rathgeb and others (n 3) 113.

[43] van Huijstee, van Boheemen and others (n 5) 32; A Ray, 'Disinformation, Deepfakes and Democracies: The Need for Legislative Reform' (2021) 44 *University of New South Wales Law Journal* 983, 985; A Yamaoka-Enkerlin, 'Disrupting Disinformation: Deepfakes and the Law Comment' (2019) 22 *New York University Journal of Legislation and Public Policy* 725.

[44] Vaccari and Chadwick (n 7) 1.

[45] ibid 2.

In 2019, a manipulated video – even if not through AI – that falsely portrayed Nancy Pelosi drunk, led to a broader discussion in the United States on the issue of malicious use of video-manipulating technologies. The video went viral and was retweeted from the official Twitter account of US President Donald Trump, receiving over 6.3 million views. According to some, deepfakes are just a false alarm, a continuous threat that still has to occur. For example, before the 2020 US presidential elections, there were significant concerns about the influence deepfakes could have on electoral intercourse, but – in the end – nothing happened.[46] However, the potential scale of the problem remains unclear. Recently, there have also been concerns about the impact of digital manipulation in connection with the Ukraine conflict. For instance, media and newspapers reported in June 2022 on a deepfake of the mayor of Kyiv, Vitaly Klitschko, on a scheduled call with the Mayor of Berlin, Franziska Giffey.[47]

Of particular concern is the use of deepfake technology in election campaigns, with the first documented instance occurring in Slovakia in October 2023.[48] Similarly, in January 2024 an AI-generated robot impersonating the voice of US President Joe Biden made phone calls attempting voter suppression in New Hampshire.[49]

Deepfakes have also been described as a new threat to our society, generating a mistrust in citizens of authority and the information media. In this regard, the study conducted by Dobber, which shows the disturbing effect that deepfake videos may have on political attitudes on a large scale is particularly relevant.[50] The fact *per se* that this technology exists – and is easily accessible – can distort what is real.[51] As highlighted, 'Seeing will no longer be believing, and we will have to decide for ourselves – without reliable evidence – whom or what to believe'.[52] The other side of the coin is the so-called 'liar's dividend', meaning the cognitive bias that deepfakes cause.[53] Basically, since everything can be fake, everything can also be denied.[54] As highlighted, 'the mantra "fake news"

[46] JP Meneses, 'Deepfakes and the 2020 US Elections: What (Did Not) Happen' (*Computer Science, Cornwell University Archive*, 2021), available at https://arxiv.org/abs/2101.09092.

[47] P Oltermann, 'European Politicians Duped into Deepfake Video Calls with Mayor of Kyiv' *The Guardian* (25 June 2022), available at www.theguardian.com/world/2022/jun/25/european-leaders-deepfake-video-calls-mayor-of-kyiv-vitali-klitschko.

[48] M Meaker, 'Slovakia's Election Deepfakes Show AI Is a Danger to Democracy' (*Wired*, 3 October 2023), available at www.wired.com/story/slovakias-election-deepfakes-show-ai-is-a-danger-to-democracy/; (n) Demos 7.

[49] K Collier and S Wong, 'Fake Biden Robocall Telling Democrats Not to Vote Is Likely an AI-Generated Deepfake' (*NBC News*, 23 January 2024), available at www.nbcnews.com/tech/misinformation/joe-biden-new-hampshire-robocall-fake-voice-deep-ai-primary-rcna135120.

[50] Dobber and others (n 10) 69.

[51] Boucher (n 9).

[52] WA Galston, 'Is Seeing Still Believing? The Deepfake Challenge to Truth in Politics' (*Brookings*, 8 January 2020), available at www.brookings.edu/research/is-seeing-still-believing-the-deepfake-challenge-to-truth-in-politics/.

[53] van Huijstee, van Boheemen and others (n 5) 33.

[54] N Schick, *Deep Fakes and the Infocalypse: What You Urgently Need To Know* (Monoray, 2020) 16.

has become an instantly recognised shorthand for a host of propositions about the supposed corruption and bias of a wide array of journalists, and a useful substitute for argument when confronted with damaging factual assertions'.[55] Deepfakes represent an expression of the so-called 'post-truth era',[56] where alternative facts, personal emotions and beliefs are redesigning societies.[57] This, as explained, may in the long-term have a clear impact on democratic systems and the rule of law. It is thus, in the current information and communication environment described above, that the use and potential harms have to be evaluated and the regulatory landscape examined.

IV. REGULATORY CHALLENGES POSED BY DEEPFAKES

The rise of deepfakes poses important questions about how to deal with such technology, whether current legal frameworks suffice to address the potential harm to democracy and the rule of law,[58] and if not, which modality of regulation should be adopted: laws, private platforms' policies, technological solutions or a combination of these.[59] It is important to underline that beyond the harmful use of deepfakes, as described above, beneficial uses abound across industries ranging from marketing, advertising and entertainment to healthcare, and not forgetting satire and parody.[60] Thus, a ban on the technology *per se* is not even arguable. Nevertheless, a legal basis for mitigating the broader societal impact of deepfakes through policies and measures against disinformation is crucial.[61] In this respect, it is questionable whether criminal law should be involved as *extrema ratio*.[62] So far, the spread of deepfakes for political disinformation purposes is not illegal in most jurisdictions. However, some US states, such as Texas and Virginia, have criminalised the distribution of deepfake videos intended to injure a political candidate or influence the result of an election. Although these new inchoate offences show their limits since they do not recognise the complexity of the field, 'both technologically

[55] Chesney and Citron (n 3) 1760.

[56] Hasen (n 16) 537.

[57] J Farkas and J Schou, *Post-Truth, Fake News and Democracy: Mapping the Politics of Falsehood* (Routledge, 2019).

[58] van der Sloot and Wagensveld (n 14) 1.

[59] Kalpokas and Kalpokiene (n 31) 65; NI Brown, 'Deepfakes and the Weaponization of Information' (2020) 23 *Virginia Journal of Law and Technology* 23ff.; T Nagasako, 'Global Disinformation Campaigns and Legal Challenges' (2020) 1 *International Cybersecurity Law Review* 125, 133ff.

[60] van der Sloot and Wagensveld (n 14) 4.

[61] Brown (n 59) 33.

[62] For an overall function and purpose of criminal law see, amongst others, K Ambos, 'The Overall Function of International Criminal Law: Striking the Right Balance Between the Rechtsgut and the Harm Principles: A Second Contribution Towards a Consistent Theory of ICL' (2015) 9 *Criminal Law and Philosophy* 301; A Ashworth, *Principles of Criminal Law*, 6th edn (Oxford University Press, 2009).

and in terms of crafting the appropriate response of criminal law'.[63] In fact, it has been argued that 'the elements to be used to criminalise, whether intent to manipulate an image in addition to other elements that narrow the possible range of offending behaviours, must be critically assessed', especially considering that the technology is already integrated into everyday life and often programmed into smartphone technology that, for instance, allows filters to be applied to photographs of faces.[64]

Last, but not least, any potential legal reforms to criminally sanction disinformation in general will inevitably conflict with freedoms such as the freedom of expression, of speech and association,[65] including the freedom to lie,[66] protected at the European level by Article 11 of the European Charter on Fundamental Rights (CFREU or Charter) and Article 10 of the European Convention on Human Rights (ECHR) and relevant case law.[67] Some prohibitions on freedom of expression exist, including hatred constituting incitement to discrimination, hostility or violence, incitement to terrorism. For other forms of expression, such as in the case of political disinformation, the margin of appreciation allows a leeway for countries to determine the boundaries of acceptable expression in line with their own cultures and legal traditions. Criminal laws on defamation, the disrespect for authority and insult, for example, that apply to online expression, will face a high threshold in demonstrating that the measures are proportionate, appropriate, and the least intrusive possible. It is challenging, however, to distinguish between legitimate deception, legitimate satire, and other forms of illegitimate fakes. It is hard to say who should be allowed to draw and enforce these lines and whether political actors are able to agree on common standards of discourse in the 'post-truth' era.[68] On the other hand, there is a counterbalance to the freedom of expression in the right to information, which is also protected by Article 10 of the ECHR. In fact, the passive side of freedom of expression is freedom of information: 'if this is missing, and people lack trustworthy information, it hinders the formation of their opinion and consequently their political decision-making (voting)'.[69] As highlighted earlier, it is necessary to start from the awareness that the information ecosystem

[63] Kirchengast (n 15) 321. More broadly on issues related to inchoate offences, see J Horder, *Ashworth's Principles of Criminal Law*, 8th edn (Oxford University Press, 2016) 469.

[64] Kirchengast (n 15) 321–22.

[65] J Schroeder, 'Free Expression Rationales and the Problem of Deepfakes Within the E.U. and U.S. Legal Systems' (2019) 70 *Syracuse Law Review* 1171.

[66] Nicita (n 22) 65.

[67] CFREU, Art 11 recalls Article 10 ECHR: 'The article corresponds to Article 10 of the European Convention on Human Rights; the limitations which may be imposed on the rights defined by article 11 of the European Charter may not exceed those provided for in Article 10(2) of the Convention'. O Pollicino and E Bietti, 'Truth and Deception Across the Atlantic: A Roadmap of Disinformation in the US and Europe' (2019) 11 *Italian Journal of Public Law* 43, 55ff.

[68] van Huijstee, van Boheemen and others (n 5) 25.

[69] Bayer and others (n 19) 77.

has changed due to digitalisation and technological developments. With that in mind, it is crucial to think about rules that protect, without censoring, freedom of individuals affected by deepfakes and other falsehoods.[70]

Beyond these substantive issues, a further regulatory challenge concerns the effectiveness and enforcement of legal responses of any kind.[71] The attribution of malicious conduct can be extremely difficult, leaving accountability unclear and jurisdiction difficult to determine, also considering the ubiquitous and intrinsic cross-border nature of digital data.[72] There is a complex chain of events and a wide range of actors are involved, with different roles and positions: the deepfake creator; the user with the intent to deceive (deceiver); the deceived individual; the individual whose data is sought; individuals that share the content (with intention or mere recklessness).[73] If these are the issues related to public policies, so far, in the EU, the regulation of deepfakes has mainly been run by private platforms.[74] Content distribution platforms such as Reddit, YouTube, Facebook (now Meta) and Twitter, are 'increasingly assertive against deepfakes, with full or partial bans'.[75] For example, yet in May 2022, Google changed the terms of its service, disallowing users to create deepfakes through its collaborative machine learning platform.[76] A particular focus of discussions is the content moderation function that platforms use to control user-generated content by filtering and removing measures. This is part of a bigger trend where private companies are assuming the role of controller and the judiciary of social and societal acceptability.[77] Those platforms now use the most advanced technologies, especially algorithms, to detect illegal or allegedly harmful content and remove it.[78] AI tools used to detect deepfakes or misleading disinformation are, however, subject to false positives as well as negatives, with the risk of both over-censorship and an inadequacy to counter the phenomenon.[79]

[70] CR Sustein, 'Falshoods and the First Amendment' (2020) *Harvard Journal of Law & Technology* 33 (2) 388, 426.

[71] van der Sloot and Wagensveld (n 14) 4.

[72] Kalpokas and Kalpokiene (n 31) 70.

[73] van Huijstee, van Boheemen and others (n 5) VI, 51.

[74] Kalpokas and Kalpokiene (n 31) 68.

[75] ibid.

[76] See Google Colaboratory Frequently Asked Questions, available at https://research.google.com/colaboratory/faq.html.

[77] T Gillespie, *Custodians of the Internet: Platforms, Content Moderation, and the Hidden Decisions That Shape Social Media* (Yale University Press, 2018) 13. In general on the connection between securitisation and privatisation, see V Mitsilegas, 'Contrôle des Étrangers, des Passagers, des Citoyens: Surveillance et Anti-Terrorisme' (2005) 58 *Cultures et Conflits* 155.

[78] K Kikerpill, A Siibak and S Valli, 'Dealing with Deepfakes: Reddit, Online Content Moderation, and Situational Crime Prevention' in J Wiest (ed), *Theorizing Criminality and Policing in the Digital Media Age* (Emerald Publishing Ltd, 2021) vol 20.

[79] C Marsden and T Meyer, *Regulating Disinformation with Artificial Intelligence: Effects of Disinformation Initiatives on Freedom of Expression and Media Pluralism* (Study EPRS, PE 624.279, March 2019) 2, 17.

V. THE PATH UNDERTAKEN IN THE EU FRAMEWORK

In the EU context, there is an ongoing debate on how to deal with the possible misuse of deepfakes.[80] The next sub-paragraphs describe the two main regulatory frameworks under which political deepfakes would be tackled. The first regulates the obligations of the platforms and accountability to tackle the spread of illegal content, online disinformation and other societal risks (section V.A). This represents a key point of the Union's strategies against disinformation as designed by the 2020 European Democracy Action.[81] The second concerns the use of AI as a family of technologies that can bring both benefits and risks for internal markets (section V.B).

A. The Digital Services Act

After 22 years, the EU Digital Services Act (DSA), amended the 2000/31/EC e-Commerce Directive. Based on Article 114 of the Treaty on the Functioning of the European Union (TFEU), the DSA is enacted in order to prevent divergences from hampering the free provision of cross-border digital services and to guarantee the uniform protection of rights and uniform obligations for business and consumers across the internal market. The Regulation has been considered a critical step in providing a new legal framework for digital services aimed at mitigating the fundamental rights challenges and protecting European democratic values from threat such as the spread of disinformation.[82]

In particular, the DSA regulates the obligations for online platforms to tackle the spread of illegal or otherwise harmful online content that will apply to all digital services that connect consumers to goods, services, or content differently depending on their roles and size, within the EU, even if established outside the EU. More extensive rules apply to the so-called very large online platforms (VLOPs) and very large online search engines (VLOSEs), because of their clear significant societal and economic impact.[83] These are obliged to deal with so-called 'systemic risks' for society stemming from the design, functioning and use of their services, as well as from potential misuses by the recipients of the service.[84] Category of risks concerns the actual or foreseeable negative effects on

[80] van Huijstee, van Boheemen and others (n 5) I.

[81] Communication from the Commission to the European Parliament, the Council, the Economic and Social Committee, and the Committee of the Regions on the European Democracy Action Plan ('European Democracy Action Plan') December 2020, COM (2020) 790 final, 4.

[82] G De Gregorio and O Pollicino, 'The European Approach to Disinformation: Policy Perspectives' in IEP@BU Policy Brief June 2024, 8.

[83] Platforms with more than 45 million users in the EU (10% of the EU's population). The DSA rules apply to all platforms since February 2024, while already since the end of August 2023, they already apply to the list of VLOPs and VLOSEs.

[84] DSA (n 17) recital 79.

democratic processes, civic discourse and electoral processes, as well as public security.[85] The DSA does not offer any definition or direct mention of the term 'deepfakes', but clearly refers to the phenomenon when discussing the due diligence measures VLOPs and VLOSEs shall apply for systemic risks. These may include measures

> ensuring that an item of information, whether it constitutes a generated or manipulated image, audio or video that appreciably resembles existing persons, objects, places or other entities or events and falsely appears to a person to be authentic or truthful is distinguishable through prominent markings when presented on their online interfaces, and, in addition, providing an easy to use functionality which enables recipients of the service to indicate such information.[86]

In addition, risk mitigation measures regarding disinformation can appropriately be provided via self-and co-regulatory agreements participating and complying with given codes of conduct.[87] This leaves open the details concerning self-regulation, setting out only commitments to take specific risk mitigation measures, as well as to adopt a regular reporting framework on any measures taken and the outcome.[88]

The Codes are supposed to be 'encouraged' and 'facilitated' by the European Commission and the Board of Digital Coordinators.[89] In case of 'systematic failure to comply with the Codes of Conduct, the Commission and the Board may invite the signatories to the codes of conduct to take the necessary action'.[90]

However, the platforms still decide voluntarily to sign up to an affiliate code of conduct or not. Whether the providers do not adopt the necessary measures though, the Commission may require from them a commitment to participate in a relevant code.[91]

When there is a serious threat to public health or in the event of a security crisis, such as a pandemic or a war, the DSA will make it possible to activate a crisis response mechanism providing further urgent measures to be adopted such as adapting the terms and conditions.[92]

The above-mentioned rules on Codes of Conduct established in this Regulation serve as a basis and are complemented by a revised and strengthened version of the 2018 Code of Practice on disinformation,[93] published in

[85] ibid recital 82.
[86] ibid Art 35 1(k).
[87] ibid recital 68, Art 26, 35, recital 104.
[88] ibid Art 35.
[89] ibid Art 45(1).
[90] ibid Art 45(4).
[91] ibid Art 45(2).
[92] ibid recital 91 and Art 36.
[93] The 2018 Code of Practice on disinformation which set self-regulatory standards and best practices, presented various shortcomings and gaps, including a disparity between the measures taken by signatories, lack of consequences in case of a breach and human rights protection, lack of independent oversight mechanism. See N Bontridder and Y Poullet, 'The Role of Artificial Intelligence in Disinformation' (2021) 3 *Data & Policy* e32, e32–13.

June 2022. The new Code, signed by all major online platforms, strengthened existing measures to reduce those that are defined 'impermissible manipulative behaviours and practices', which accordingly include the malicious use of deepfakes. In this regard, the signatories should take into account transparency obligations as provided in the AI Act (see below), as well as ensuring that the algorithms used for the detection, moderation and sanctioning of impermissible conduct and content on their services are trustworthy.[94]

B. The Artificial Intelligence Act (AI Act)

In April 2021, the EU Commission released a regulatory proposal aimed at addressing the risks generated by specific uses of AI through a set of harmonised rules.[95] According to the EU Commission, among the proposal's ambitions, there was firstly the necessity to provide AI developers, deployers, importers, distributors, product manufacturers and users with clear requirements and obligations regarding specific uses of AI. This aims to implement an ecosystem of trust by proposing an adequate legal framework; and Art 114 TFEU is used as legal basis. While most existing AI systems pose limited to no risk and can contribute to solving many societal challenges, certain AI systems create risks that should be addressed in order to avoid undesirable outcomes.[96]

The use of AI with its specific characteristics (for example, opacity, dependency on data, autonomous behaviour) can adversely affect a number of fundamental rights enshrined in the EU Charter of Fundamental Rights.[97] Hence, the proposal adopts a risk-based approach to ensure a high level of protection for those fundamental rights and aims to address various sources of risks through this. After three years of intense negotiations, the AI Act came into force on the 1st of August 2024.[98]

The regulatory framework defines four levels of risk in AI systems: unacceptable risk, concerning systems that are banned; high risk systems, which are permitted in the European market subject to compliance with certain mandatory requirements and an *ex-ante* conformity assessment; limited risk systems, referring to AI tools with specific transparency obligations, and minimal or no risk (residual category). In order to ensure the effective enforcement of the designed system, the AI Act has established a new EU level regulator: the European AI Office. The AI office will monitor, coordinate, supervise and enforce the AI Act requirements in a harmonised way.

[94] See commitments 14 and 15, Strengthened Code of Practice on Disinformation.
[95] EU Commission Proposal (COM (2021) 206) for a regulation on AI 2021 (AI Act).
[96] ibid Explanatory Memorandum 1.
[97] ibid 11.
[98] AI Act (n 18).

In this context, the only safeguards expressly targeting deepfakes are transparency duties.[99] Article 3(60) describes a 'deep fake' as an AI-generated or manipulated image, audio or video content that appreciably resembles existing persons, objects, places, entities or events and would falsely appear to a person to be authentic or truthful. Chapter IV of the AI Act, titled 'Transparency Obligations for Providers and Deployers of Certain AI Systems', outlines the essential guidelines for transparency obligations. According to Article 50(4) deployers of an AI system that produces deepfakes shall disclose that the content has been artificially generated or manipulated. Recital 133 specifies further that providers of such AI systems should implement and make available reliable and effective technical solutions that allow marking in a machine readable format and detection that the output has been generated or manipulated by an AI system and not a human. These include watermarks, metadata identifications, cryptographic methods for proving provenance and authenticity of content, logging methods and fingerprints. In order to practically support the enforcement of deepfake mandatory labelling and detection requirements, the AI Office and Commission should encourage and facilitate the development of codes of practice and practical guidelines.[100]

The provisions concerning the obligations placed on providers and deployers of artificially generated or manipulated systems should be read in combination with the DSA.[101] These are particularly relevant for providers of large online platforms or search engines, as they must identify and mitigate risks associated with AI-generated content that could negatively impact democratic processes, public discourse, or elections, particularly through the spread of disinformation.

To conclude, the duty to disclose that the content is generated through automated means is subject to two exceptions for legitimate purposes.[102] The first one is when the use is authorised by law to detect, prevent, investigate or prosecute criminal offence. The second exception is where the content forms part of an evidently artistic, creative, satirical, fictional or analogous work or programme. In this latter case, the transparency obligations are limited to the disclosure of the existence of such generated or manipulated content in an appropriate manner that does not hamper the display or enjoyment of the work.

[99] It is unclear whether deepfakes can be considered as one of the prohibited AI practices, under Art 5 of the AI Act, ibid, when used as manipulative or deceptive techniques which might materially distort the behaviour of a person or a group of persons by appreciably impairing their ability to make an informed decision. See M Łabuz, 'Deep Fakes and the Artificial Intelligence Act – An Important Signal or a Missed Opportunity?' [2024] *Policy & Internet* poi3.406; F Romero Moreno, 'Generative AI and Deepfakes: A Human Rights Approach to Tackling Harmful Content' (2024) *International Review of Law Computers and Technology*; C Vanberghen, 'The AI Act vs. Deepfakes: A Step Forward, but is it Enough?' (*Eucravit*, 2024), available at www.euractiv.com/section/artificial-intelligence/opinion/the-ai-act-vs-deepfakes-a-step-forward-but-is-it-enough.

[100] AI Act (n 18) Art 50, 96(1)(d) and recital 135.

[101] DSA (n 17) recital.

[102] AI Act (n 18) Art 50(4).

VI. CONCLUSIVE CONSIDERATIONS

As shown above, the current EU approach with regard to deepfakes targets, on the one hand, AI deployers and providers, thus far providing transparency requirements (paragraph 5.2). On the other, it focuses on the responsibility of private intermediaries, specifically, on the accountability of companies that allow malicious deepfakes to be posted on their platforms (paragraph 5.1).

The DSA together with the Code of Practice is part of a broader policy aimed at addressing the challenges associated with both massive digitalisation and disinformation setting out a co-regulatory framework by enforcing diligence requirements for major providers of intermediary services (paragraph 2). Efforts to enhance the accountability of major platforms for the spread of political disinformation, shifting from self-regulation to co-regulation, are certainly appreciable. However, it remains questionable whether the path undertaken at the EU level is enough to counter the phenomenon. Even if co-regulation has the advantage of flexibility, and adaptability to changing technologies, the fact that the content of co-regulatory codes is left open and that major platforms in practice determine how to handle political disinformation are matters of concern. In fact, very large platforms will have to fulfil extremely complex duties: assessing and mitigating societal risks related to online harms and disinformation all whilst protecting fundamental rights.[103] In this regard, 'the only stakeholders with some leverage over these risk assessments are the European Board for Digital Services (composed of the national regulators) and the European Commission'.[104] Paradoxically, there is a risk that in this scenario imposing accountability with the threat of fines might increase the power of already dominant intermediaries.[105]

These considerations concern aggressive informational practices in general.[106] Deepfake technology in particular is changing the media landscape in terms of media consumption and production. Nowadays, most media accept or even foster some kind of manipulation as normal. Hence, it is necessary to elaborate a specific regulatory framework which recognises and understands the technology,[107] but at the same time is able to safeguard the rights involved from its potentially disruptive effects (paragraphs 3 and 4). It is certainly true that

[103] This issue is far from new and pertains to various areas of the law, see V Mitsilegas, 'The Security Union as a Paradigm of Preventative Justice: Challenges for Citizenship, Fundamental Rights and the Rule of Law' in S Carrera and V Mitsilegas (eds), *Constitutionalising the Security Union: Effectiveness, Rule of Law and Rights in Countering Terrorism and Crime* (CEPS Research Paperback Book, 2017) 12ff.

[104] Buri and van Hoboken (n 79) 13.

[105] ibid. See also T Gillespie, 'Content Moderation, AI, and the Question of Scale' (2020) 7 *Big Data & Society*.

[106] The topic has been extensively studied and analysed by the Occorsio Foundation project on AI and Criminal Activities and Investigation.

[107] Kirchengast (n 15) 322.

punitive populism and symbolic criminalisation without efficiency, necessity and proportionality should be avoided.[108] It is also true, however, that an over-reliance on the private sector can be dangerous. Some platforms have already banned deepfakes in their terms and conditions (paragraph 4) and the new Code of Practice on disinformation requires the signatories to adopt concrete measures to tackle deepfakes, warning users of their duty to disclose and proactively detect such content (paragraphs 5.1 and 5.2). As pointed out above, the private sector already governs the rules of public debate, with all risks being related to unlawful forms of censorship and sanctions that – even when of a private/disciplinary character – should respect a minimum set of typical criminal law guarantees and safeguards.[109]

[108] Bayer and others (n 19) 64; D Husak, 'The Criminal Law as a Last Resort' (2004) 24(2) *OJLS* 234.

[109] E Biritteri, 'Punire La Disinformazione: Il Ruolo Del Diritto Penale e Delle Misure Di Moderazione Dei Contenuti Delle Piattaforme Tra Pubblico e Privato' (2021) *Diritto Penale Contemporaneo Rivista Trimestrale* 304,12.

13

The UK's Strategy on AI – Implications for English Criminal Law

RUDI FORTSON KC*

I. THE MEANING OF 'ARTIFICIAL INTELLIGENCE' AND ITS DEPLOYMENT IN ENGLISH AND WELSH COURTS

'ARTIFICIAL INTELLIGENCE' (AI) is a vague and open-textured concept that is variously defined. The *Concise Oxford English Dictionary* defines it as 'the performance by computer systems of tasks normally requiring human intelligence, such as translation between languages'. Interestingly, the European Commission for the Efficiency of Justice (CEPEJ) has stated (correctly it is submitted) that 'AI is not a single, homogeneous object: it is actually an assemblage of sciences and techniques (mathematics, statistics and computer science) capable of processing data to design very complex computer processing tasks.'[1]

The English and Welsh judiciary and legal profession have long embraced the *concept* of AI as an aid to the preparation of cases and in the administration of criminal justice. However, *in practice*, the deployment of AI has been something of a 'slow-burn', limited by resources, awareness, training, and by tradition (such as the principle of orality). The latter may sound surprising, but in an English criminal trial, fact-finders (notably juries) rarely see statements that were written out-of-court by witnesses (still less that fact-finders retain such statements whilst deliberating on their verdicts). In *R v Lilley*,[2] the Court of Appeal (Criminal Division) dismissed a complaint on an appeal against conviction that the jury should not have received a chronology schedule (based on

* Barrister; Visiting Professor of Law at Queen Mary University of London, and Visiting Professor of Law, Law School, University of Liverpool. The author is writing in a personal capacity and not on behalf of any UK government agency, educational establishment or professional body.

[1] European Ethical Charter on the Use of Artificial Intelligence in Judicial Systems and their environment; Adopted at the 31st plenary meeting of the CEPEJ (Strasbourg, 3–4 December 2018).

[2] *R v Lilley* [2003] EWCA Crim. 1789.

police surveillance logs) that highlighted important and significant events and personalities. The appellant complained that this amounted to putting before the jury controversial evidence in written form. The Court opined that the schedule was a means of assisting the jury, which was legitimate in the circumstances of that case. These days, such schedules – often computer generated or assisted – are routinely placed before juries (typically, as 'working documents': including 'spider charts'[3] that show the connection between persons relevant to the case).

In recent years, the use of Information Technology and AI has accelerated significantly across every sector of the criminal justice process. In criminal proceedings, evidence that is to be used by the prosecution (and so-called 'unused evidence' but which has been disclosed by the prosecution) is now routinely held digitally on a web-based platform (such as the Crown Court Digital Case System). Users of the system can upload, download, view, annotate, and present case documents that may run to many thousands of pages. Those documents may be searched (eg, using keywords) and perhaps subjected to (for example) Optical Character Recognition software. Whilst this may be considered to be low-level AI (or weak AI), it is computer assistance nevertheless.

Tasks relating to the disclosure of documents and information (e-disclosure) is assisted by AI (eg, automated searching). Electronically stored information may be substantial and held on domestic and/or foreign servers.[4] English courts have taken a pragmatic approach to the questions of: (i) how much digital data should be disclosed to a party in a given case; (ii) the form in which such data should be served (eg, 'raw' data); and (iii) how it might be inspected and analysed by practitioners.[5]

In *Pyrrho Investments Ltd*[6] (a civil case), documents were being reviewed using proprietary computer software rather than reviewed by human beings. The software was designed to analyse documents and to 'score' them for their relevance to the issues in the case (a process known as 'predictive coding', 'technology assisted review', 'computer assisted review', or 'assisted review'). A representative sample of the 'included' documents was used to 'train' the software which analysed the documents for common concepts and language used. The software reviewed and categorised each individual document in the whole set as being either relevant or not. The categorisation exercises were then validated through quality assurance exercises based on statistical sampling and reviewed by a human for relevance.

[3] See, eg, *R v Kane* [2013] EWCA Crim 1487.
[4] Consider *Goodale v Ministry of Justice* [2009] EWHC B41 (QB).
[5] Consider, eg, *R v MA* [2018] 2 Costs LR 419 (a costs decision).
[6] *Pyrrho Investments Ltd* [2016] EWHC 256 (Ch).

Disclosure will necessarily require human input and oversight. As was pointed out in the case of *Veasey v MacDougall and Others*[7] (albeit a civil case), producing copies of electronic documents (or just printing out versions of them) gives less information (and sometimes different information) compared to the original native versions. The High Court remarked that mistakes occur in copying and that it was 'not unknown for electronic documents, like paper documents, to be tampered with .... It is therefore important that the rules specially formulated for electronic disclosure, in particular about disclosing electronic documents in native format, are adhered to'. In a criminal cause or matter, the failure of the prosecution to make proper disclosure can have profound adverse consequences (often for the accused, and not infrequently for a complainant or a victim when a case 'collapses' due to defective disclosure). Analysing 'raw data' may require specialist expert assistance.[8]

A. Voice Recognition

Voice recognition software has a role to play in criminal proceedings. During the 1990s and 2000s, a system known as 'Livenote' had been used in some English courts to transcribe, almost in real time, oral hearings (there are other voice transcription services). Such transcripts may have evidential or memory refreshing value,[9] and thus the accuracy and reliability of the software is of paramount importance. A service of this type is expensive and therefore it is not used in the majority of criminal cases that are tried on indictment. There is potential for such software to be used to transcribe audio files (eg, recordings made by emergency services or audio tracks recorded on Body Worn Video cameras).

B. Digital Images as Evidence in Criminal Proceedings

Digital images (including CCTV) feature regularly as evidence in criminal cases. Video images now include those recorded by way of domestic CCTV cameras, dashcams (motor vehicles) and on mobile telephones. Software (even on certain mobile telephones) has the capability of modifying digital images. So-called 'deepfakes' is a matter of obvious concern, but there may be circumstances in which it would be permissible to enhance images (eg, improve the clarity of handwriting, fonts, facial images) or to correct an image. However, this must be done in a transparent manner and be capable of independent verification.

[7] *Veasey v MacDougall and Others* [2022] EWHC 864 (Ch).
[8] Consider, for example, *R v MA* (n 5).
[9] See, eg, *R v F & B* [2009] EWCA Crim 1961; and *R v Robinson* [2002] EWCA Crim 2489.

In evidence before the House of Lords, Justice and Home Affairs Committee,[10] David Spreadborough, a Forensic Analyst, stated that 'It is now technically possible for a CCTV system to have highly advanced error correction' and that machine learning, or deep learning, 'could be used effectively to recognise known objects such as letters, logos or patterns, but they shouldn't be used to "fix" the original image to create a different version more appeasing to the eye'. He submitted that enhancement techniques which simply 'show better' what is already there, applying deterministic algorithms on the existing image data, 'should be generally considered good for evidence if based on known and validated methodologies'.[11] He remarked (correctly) that trust is at the forefront of forensic image and video analysis, warning that 'a jury could be presented a copy of CCTV from a premise [*sic.*[12]] and no one would be aware that it was not the original and that it had been converted with no forensic framework'.[13]

It is obviously important that images, including CCTV images, should be demonstrably reliable for what they depict if they are to be adduced as evidence in criminal proceedings. This is reinforced by the fact that such images usually constitute real evidence of a criminal offence having been committed and by whom. There can be cases when it is permissible for fact-finders to compare a CCTV image of a person (or a still image) with a defendant in the dock (see *R v Dodson*,[14] where photographs had been taken by an automatic security camera). This is subject to consideration being given by the court to, among other things: (i) the quality of the image;[15] (ii) its resolution; (iii) the extent and clarity of the facial features of the person photographed; (iv) evidence (or the absence of it) of a change in a defendant's appearance; and (v) the opportunity that fact-finders have to look at a defendant present in court (and over what period of time). There may be cases in which it would be desirable for fact-finders to receive guidance from the trial judge (but not invariably[16]) when he or she directs them as to how they should approach the task of evaluating such evidence.

There may also be cases when it is permissible for a witness, who knows a person, to identify them from an image (see *R v Fowden and White*[17]). Similarly, it was held in *R v Clare and Peach*,[18] that a police officer, who identified the

[10] House of Lords, Technology Committee, 'Technology Rules? The Advent of New Technologies in the Justice System', 30 March 2022, HL Paper 180.

[11] D Spreadborough, CFVA, Forensic Analyst at Amped Software – Written evidence (NTL0015).

[12] Presumably, the words 'from a premise' should read 'from premises'.

[13] Spreadborough (n 11) and see *State v Puloka, Superior Court of Washington for King County, No. 21-1-04851-2 KNT* (29 March 2024).

[14] *R v Dodson* [1984] 1 WLR 971; applied in *R v Najjar* [2014] EWCA Crim 1309.

[15] Consider *R v Ali* [2008] EWCA Crim 1522, where a conviction was unsafe.

[16] *R v Downey* [1995] 1 Cr App R 547; and see *R v Shanmugarajah* [2015] EWCA Crim 783, [2015] 2 Cr App R 14.

[17] *R v Fowden and White* [1982] Crim LR 588.

[18] *R v Clare and Peach* [1995] 2 Cr App R 333.

appellants on video film as those committing acts of violence, notwithstanding that he did not know the appellants before the day in question, but who had acquired knowledge by lengthy and studious application to the material which was itself admissible evidence.

The legal position concerning digital images is complicated (under English law) by the hearsay provisions of the Criminal Justice Act (CJA) 2003. A document that contains a representation made by a person (the purpose of which is to cause another person to believe the representation to be true) is potentially hearsay (but it may nevertheless be admitted in evidence if certain statutory conditions are fulfilled). But a document that is generated *entirely* by computer is not hearsay (as that expression is currently defined by section 115, CJA 2003).[19] Where there has been some human input in the computer generation of a document, a safeguard is afforded by section 129(1) of the 2003 Act, which provides that where a representation of any fact is made 'otherwise than by a person', but 'depends for its accuracy on information supplied (directly or indirectly) by a person, the representation is not admissible in criminal proceedings as evidence of the fact unless it is proved that the information was accurate'.[20]

In *R v Skinner*[21] (a case decided under the forerunner to the CJA 2003), the prosecution sought to prove that S accessed a website and offered the opportunity for other persons to access a large number of alleged pornographic files. The prosecution adduced screen images, taken from a computer, of a search of that website. The screen images included an overlaid window in DOS format, which revealed the internet protocol address of the offeror (who, further inquiries had revealed, was S). It was that information which prompted investigators to search S's home. At trial, the investigator said that he could not tell how the information was posted onto the website or whether one or a number of persons had been involved. The information copied was from a word document and thus he could not tell whether it had been altered or not. For the reasons given by Professor David Ormerod KC (in his commentary to *Skinner*[22]) the facts of that case would now give rise to intricate issues under the provisions of the 2003 Act, for example: (i) whether the screenshots constituted real evidence or hearsay; (ii) whether the images, even in part, included representations made by a person; and (iii) whether and to what extent the details were capable of being proved to be accurate.

[19] CJA 2003 s 115(2), (3) provides that '(2) A statement is any representation of fact or opinion made by a person by whatever means; and it includes a representation made in a sketch, photofit or other pictorial form. (3) A matter stated is one to which this Chapter applies [hearsay] if (and only if) the purpose, or one of the purposes, of the person making the statement appears to the court to have been – (a) to cause another person to believe the matter, or (b) to cause another person to act or a machine to operate on the basis that the matter is as stated.'

[20] ibid s 129(2) provides that s 129(1) 'does not affect the operation of the presumption that a mechanical device has been properly set or calibrated'.

[21] *R v Skinner (Philip)* [2005] EWCA Crim 1439, [2006] Crim LR 56.

[22] ibid.

Given the above, there is merit in paragraph 134 of the recital to Regulation (EU) 2024/1689 (the EU AI Act), which provides that (subject to the qualifications and savings provided in the AI Act):[23]

> deployers who use an AI system to generate or manipulate image, audio or video content that appreciably resembles existing persons, objects, places, entities or events and would falsely appear to a person to be authentic or truthful (deep fakes), should also clearly and distinguishably disclose that the content has been artificially created or manipulated by labelling the AI output accordingly and disclosing its artificial origin.

It may have been preferable for the words 'might mistakenly' to have been used in recital 134 rather than the words 'would falsely'. If a similar provision is thought necessary as a matter of English and Welsh law, this could be catered for under the Criminal Procedure Rules (England and Wales).

C. Facial Recognition Technology: Legality and Protections

The process and problems posed by Live Facial Recognition (LFR) software have been explained in a paper published by the UK College of Policing.[24] A camera takes digital pictures of facial images in real time, capturing images as a person moves through a zone of recognition, and using it as a live feed. The LFR software detects individual human faces and it 'automatically extracts

[23] Regulation (EU) 2024/1689 of the European Parliament and the Council of 13 June 2024 laying down harmonised rules on artificial intelligence and amending Regulations (EC) No 300/2008, (EU) No 167/2013, (EU) No 168/2013, (EU) 2018/858, (EU) 2018/1139 and (EU) 2019/2144 and Directives 2014/90/EU, (EU) 2016/797 and (EU) 2020/1828 (Artificial Intelligence Act or AI Act) [2024] OJ L2024/1689, para 134, 'Compliance with this transparency obligation should not be interpreted as indicating that the use of the AI system or its output impedes the right to freedom of expression and the right to freedom of the arts and sciences guaranteed in the Charter, in particular where the content is part of an evidently creative, satirical, artistic, fictional or analogous work or programme, subject to appropriate safeguards for the rights and freedoms of third parties. In those cases, the transparency obligation for deep fakes set out in this Regulation is limited to disclosure of the existence of such generated or manipulated content in an appropriate manner that does not hamper the display or enjoyment of the work, including its normal exploitation and use, while maintaining the utility and quality of the work.' Article 50.4 of the AI Act also provides that 'Deployers of an AI system that generates or manipulates image, audio or video content constituting a deep fake, shall disclose that the content has been artificially generated or manipulated. This obligation shall not apply where the use is authorised by law to detect, prevent, investigate or prosecute criminal offence. Where the content forms part of an evidently artistic, creative, satirical, fictional or analogous work or programme, the transparency obligations set out in this paragraph are limited to disclosure of the existence of such generated or manipulated content in an appropriate manner that does not hamper the display or enjoyment of the work.".

[24] College of Policing, 'Live Facial Recognition Authorised Professional Practice' (first published 17 March 2022; updated 22 March 2022), available at www.college.police.uk/app/live-facial-recognition/live-facial-recognition.

facial features from the image, creating the biometric template', which then 'compares the biometric template with those held on the watchlist':

> When the facial features from two images are compared, the LFR system generates a similarity score. This is a numerical value indicating the extent of similarity, with a higher score indicating greater points of similarity. A threshold value is set to determine when the LFR software will generate an alert to indicate that a possible match has occurred. Trained members of police personnel will review the alerts and make a decision as to whether any further action is required. In this way, the LFR system works to assist police personnel to make identifications, rather than the identification process being conducted solely by an algorithm.[25]

The UK Information Commissioner has identified a number of key data protection issues which can arise where LFR is used for the automatic collection of biometric data in public places:[26]

- the governance of LFR systems, including why and how they are used;
- the automatic collection of biometric data at speed and scale without clear justification, including of the necessity and proportionality of the processing;
- a lack of choice and control for individuals;
- transparency and data subjects' rights;
- the effectiveness and the statistical accuracy of LFR systems;
- the potential for bias and discrimination;
- the governance of watchlists and escalation processes;
- the processing of children's and vulnerable adults' data; and
- the potential for wider, unanticipated impacts for individuals and their communities.

There are other facial recognition technologies in existence or emerging such as Near Real-Time Face Recognition, and Retrospective Facial Recognition (RFR) – the latter being described by NEC Software Solutions UK Ltd, as identifying individuals post event from images or videos by submitting an image or a video into the system which is then matched against all subject images in the user's [police force] reference image gallery where a set of ranked candidates are returned to a person [police officer] for human adjudication.[27]

[25] ibid.

[26] 'Information Commissioner's Opinion: The Use of Live Facial Recognition Technology in Public Places' (Information Commissioner's Office, 18 June 2021)6, available at https://ico.org.uk/media/2619985/ico-opinion-the-use-of-lfr-in-public-places-20210618.pdf.

[27] NEC Software Solutions UK Ltd, available at https://bit.ly/3Q9EzLq.

The case of *Regina (Bridges) v Chief Constable of South Wales Police (Information Commissioner and others intervening)*[28] concerned Automated Facial Recognition (AFR) Locate technology which compared live camera feeds of faces against a predetermined watchlist in order to locate persons of interest. The Court of Appeal (Civil Division) and (below) the Divisional Court, were required to consider various points that included: (i) whether the AFR technology operated by the police force was compatible with the right to respect for private life under Article 8 of the Convention for the Protection of Human Rights and Fundamental Freedoms (which is one of the Convention rights set out in Schedule 1 to the UK Human Rights Act 1998[29]); (ii) the UK data protection legislation; and (iii) the public sector equality duty in section 149 of the Equality Act 2010.

Bridges was a civil liberties campaigner. The Chief Constable's police force was involved in testing and conducting trials of AFR Locate. The watchlist was created from images held on databases maintained by the police force as part of its ordinary policing activities. If the software identified a possible match between a face captured on the CCTV and an image on the watchlist, the two images were reviewed by an AFR operator. If no match (false or positive) was made (in the overwhelming majority of cases), then the AFR software did not retain the facial biometrics or image of persons whose faces were scanned but were immediately and automatically deleted. That data was not available to the system operator or to any other police officer.

On the facts of the *Bridges* case, the Court of Appeal (Civil Division) held that in determining whether an interference with the rights guaranteed under Article 8 of the Convention was 'in accordance with the law' (Article 8.2), a relativist approach was to be adopted, so that the more intrusive the act complained of, the more precise and specific the law, said to justify it, was required to be. The data concerned was 'sensitive personal data' within the meaning of the (UK) Data Protection Act 2018 and it was processed in an automated way. The scheme, as operated, involved two impermissibly wide areas of discretion falling outside the scope of the governing framework, namely (i) the selection of those individuals who would be included on watchlists when AFR Locate was being deployed, and (ii) the locations where AFR Locate might be deployed, for which no normative requirement was laid down. Accordingly, the interference with Article 8 rights occasioned by the police force's use of AFR Locate could not be justified under Article 8.2.

[28] *Regina (Bridges) v Chief Constable of South Wales Police (Information Commissioner and others intervening)* [2020] EWCA Civ 1058.

[29] Human Rights Act 1998, Sch 1, Pt I, Art 8:1: 'Everyone has the right to respect for his private and family life, his home and his correspondence. 2. There shall be no interference by a public authority with the exercise of this right except such as is in accordance with the law and is necessary in a democratic society in the interests of national security, public safety or the economic well-being of the country, for the prevention of disorder or crime, for the protection of health or morals, or for the protection of the rights and freedoms of others.'

Under section 149 of the Equality Act 2010,[30] a 'public authority'[31] has a duty to (among other matters) eliminate discrimination. In *Bridges*, the Court opined that as AFR is 'a novel and controversial technology', it would hope that all police forces would wish to satisfy themselves that the use of AFR software 'does not have a racial or gender bias'.[32]

In an informative and detailed commentary on the case of *Bridges*, Purshouse and Campbell argue[33] that the UK legal basis for police AFR surveillance 'is inadequate', that the legal framework regulating the police use of this technology is 'too imprecise to protect citizens from abuse or arbitrariness', and that the framework (as interpreted in domestic courts) 'transforms human rights protection into a tick-box exercise, foreclosing important political debate on the normative consequences of police AFR surveillance'. The commentators contend that English and Welsh police forces have been afforded 'too much discretion to 'widen the net' of biometric surveillance, without explicit democratic approval'.

There is no doubt that, what may be styled as 'residual liberty' (that is to say, 'everything is permitted except what is expressly forbidden'[34]) has been a feature of the English common law, but the limits of it have been curtailed markedly in the areas of law enforcement, surveillance and data gathering. The Court of Appeal's decision in *Bridges* that a 'relativist approach' is to be adopted (see above) requires a public body such as a local police force to critically consider whether its proposed (or current) use of facial recognition technology would be in 'accordance with the law', or not. If there were to be a judicial review of the scheme, the courts will look beyond 'ticked boxes'.

Purshouse and Campbell are concerned that the police may be able to make their AFR operations legally compliant 'through minor procedural amendments' by, for example, limiting the discretion of individual officers 'as to who can go on a watchlist and where AFR can be used' and 'making tweaks to their own internal policies'.[35] In *Bridges*, the Court of Appeal opined that it is well-established in the case law of the European Court of Human Rights (ECtHR) that local policies can be relevant to satisfy the requirement of 'in accordance with the law' and that such policies do not necessarily have to be

[30] Equality Act 2010, s 149 provides '*Public sector equality duty* – (1) A public authority must, in the exercise of its functions, have due regard to the need to – (a) eliminate discrimination, harassment, victimisation and any other conduct that is prohibited by or under this Act; (b) advance equality of opportunity between persons who share a relevant protected characteristic and persons who do not share it; (c) foster good relations between persons who share a relevant protected characteristic and persons who do not share it.'

[31] ibid s 150, and Sch 19.

[32] *Bridges* (n 28) at para 201.

[33] J Purshouse and L Campbell, 'Automated Facial Recognition and Policing: A Bridge too Far? (2022) *Legal Studies* 42, 209–27, available at https://doi.org/10.1017/lst.2021.22.

[34] Sir Robert Megarry V-C in *Malone v Metropolitan Police Comr* [1979] Ch 344, 357 who stated that 'England .... is a country where everything is permitted except what is expressly forbidden'.

[35] Purshouse and Campbell (n 33) at 218.

at a national level.[36] Minor procedural amendments may not be sufficient. In any event, local policies (eg, the policies of a local police service) are only one component of a legal framework for meeting the 'in accordance with the law' standard. Primary and secondary legislation, case law, and statutory codes of practice constitute other components. There is the potential for law enforcement agencies to think that local policies will be the primary basis (or even the decisive basis) on which an AFR operation will be judged to be in accordance with the law, or not.

As Purshouse and Campbell point out, the police commitment to use AFR has held firm. Indeed, on 12 December 2023, the then UK Minister for Crime, Policing and Fire (Mr Chris Philip) disclosed that a power in the Criminal Justice Bill [2023–24] (that was then before Parliament but which fell due to the July 2024 General Election) was designed 'to allow police and law enforcement, including the NCA, to access driving licence records to do a facial recognition search, which, anomalously, is currently quite difficult'.[37] This has led to reports that the police would be able to run facial recognition searches 'on a database containing images of Britain's 50 million driving licence holders'.[38]

Purshouse and Campbell describe the analysis in *Bridges* on the issue of proportionality as 'perfunctory'.[39] Constraints of space within this chapter limit the writer's scope for commenting on the concept of proportionality beyond merely hinting that perhaps the time has come to critically assess its value given how it has come to be interpreted and applied (at least, in England and Wales). In *Bank Mellat v HM Treasury (No 2)*,[40] Lord Reed (albeit dissenting in that case) remarked that the approach to proportionality adopted in UK domestic case law under the Human Rights Act 1998 has not generally mirrored that of the Strasbourg Court, but that 'a more clearly structured approach has generally been adopted, derived from case law under Commonwealth constitutions and Bills of Rights, including in particular the Canadian Charter of Fundamental Rights and Freedoms of 1982'.[41] In *R v Johnson*,[42] the Court of Appeal (Criminal Division) went as far as saying that a confiscation order, calculated in accordance with the provisions of Part 2 of the Proceeds of Crime Act 2002 (value-confiscation following conviction for an offence) is proportionate to it. UK courts are not empowered to strike-down legislation that has been passed by the UK Parliament.

[36] *Bridges* (n 28) at para 61.

[37] Currently, Criminal Justice Bill 2023–24, cl 21. See, transcript, Public Bill Committee, 12 December 2023, Criminal Justice Bill, available at https://publications.parliament.uk/pa/bills/cbill/58-04/0010/PBC010_Criminal_1st-th_Compilation_14_12_2023.pdf.

[38] D Boffey, 'Police to be Able to Run Face Recognition Searches on 50m Driving Licence Holders' *The Guardian* (20 December 2023), available at www.theguardian.com/technology/2023/dec/20/police-to-be-able-to-run-face-recognition-searches-on-50m-driving-licence-holders.

[39] Purshouse and Campbell (n 33) at 218 and 224.

[40] *Bank Mellat v HM Treasury (No 2)* [2013] UKSC 38, [2014] AC700 at para 72.

[41] See also, *Regina v Andrewes* [2022] UKSC 24.

[42] *R v Johnson* [2016] EWCA Crim 10, [2016] 4 WLR 57 at para 35.

D. AI Decision-Making[43]

Although much law in England and Wales is statutory, the legal system is essentially one of the common law in which case law and *stare decisis* remain key features of judicial decision-making. Case law provides distinctions (and fine distinctions) in respect of matters of legal principle even when an area of law seems to be well-trodden. AI may predict an outcome, but sound reasons may exist for departing from the prediction. The common law does not remain static and it is capable of evolving in order to meet the particular circumstances of a case, or a social need. It was judicial interpretation that decided that the infliction of mere psychological harm would not suffice to construct a manslaughter charge;[44] and that 'bodily harm' may be physical or psychiatric (*R v Ireland*[45]) but not merely psychological (*R v Dhaliwal*); and that a motorist's mistaken belief that a constable had no right in the particular circumstances of the case to require a specimen of breath, was not a 'reasonable excuse' for failing to provide the specimen (*R v Reid*[46]). Defences or elements of an offence such as 'reasonable excuse',[47] or 'good reason', are somewhat elastic and thus unlikely to lend themselves to AI determinations.

If there should come a time when AI is capable of making legally correct and just judicial decisions in criminal cases, one wonders what room would be left for appellate jurisdictions. As matters stand, the discussion appears to be focussed on AI that is designed to *predict* outcomes.

CEPEJ[48] noted that a study by University College London (UCL), which sampled 584 decisions of the ECtHR, assumed that a simple automatic learning model could predict the outcome of a case with 79 per cent accuracy for that particular court:

> The machine learning model proved to be more accurate with regard to the descriptive part of the facts of the decisions studied than with regard to the reasoning relating to the application of the Convention to the case in question.[49]

[43] See, eg, D Papp, B Krausz, and FZ Gyuranecz, 'The AI is Now in Session – The Impact of Digitalization on Courts' (2022) *Cybersecurity and Law* 7(1), 272–96, available at https://doi.org/10.35467/cal/151833; and see the European Ethical Charter (n 1); and M Dymitruk, University of Wroclaw, 'Ethical Artificial Intelligence in Judiciary' ((February 2019; Conference: 22nd International Legal Informatics Symposium IRIS 2019 at Salzburg, Austria), available at www.researchgate.net/publication/333995919.

[44] *R v Dhaliwal* [2006] EWCA Crim 1139.

[45] *R v Ireland* [1998] AC 147.

[46] *R v Reid* [1973] 1 WLR 1283.

[47] See, eg, *Attorney General's Reference on a Point of Law No. 1 of 2022* [2022] EWCA Crim 1259; the case involved questions of law arising from a prosecution in the Crown Court for allegations of criminal damage to a statue.

[48] European Ethical Charter (n 1) para81 and noting n 47.

[49] N Aletras, D Tsarapatsanis, D Preoţiuc-Pietro and V.Lampos, 'Predicting Judicial Decisions of the European Court of Human Rights: A Natural Language Processing Perspective' (*Peer J Computer Science*, 24 October 2016) available at https://peerj.com/articles/cs-93/.

AI may serve as a useful tool for researching legal principles.[50] It may usefully 'triage' cases that (for example) meet specified criteria for granting a hearing before a court. It may also give a 'steer' when formulating judgments and legal opinions. However, it is a distant prospect that, in England and Wales, 'judicial robots' would deliver e-judgments or decide outcomes. The one exception may be in respect of offences that are truly absolute (ie which involve no mental ingredient on the part of the defendant). Computer-generated penalty determinations may require a legal base (statutory) for these to be enforceable. In *Khan Properties Ltd v The Commissioners for Her Majesty's Revenue & Customs*,[51] the First-tier Tribunal (Tax Chamber) ruled that a determination of whether or not to impose a penalty under the Finance Act 1988[52] for the late filing of a tax return had (by virtue of the Taxes Management Act 1970, s 100(1)) to be made by an authorised officer of HM Revenue and Customs (ie by a human being) and not generated automatically by computer.

E. AI and the Exercise of Discretion

A further consideration is prosecutorial and judicial discretion (the writer prefers the term 'judgment') which plays an important role in the administration of justice in England and Wales even in cases where liability for an offence is absolute or strict.

It is difficult to envisage AI accommodating, in a satisfactory way, the range of circumstances and factors that would influence human decision-making when exercising discretion. The organisation Fair Trials has pointed out (albeit in the context of charging decisions) that such decisions should 'surely be based on the merits of individual cases'. It adds:

> ... it is difficult to imagine how decisions on entry into diversion programmes can be made by means other than a careful consideration of individual circumstances. These types of high impact, fact-sensitive decisions should never be delegated to automated processes, particularly those which operate by identifying correlations rather than causal links between an individual's characteristics and their likely behaviour.[53]

[50] See S Maireg Biresaw and A Umesh Saste, 'The Impacts of Artificial Intelligence on Research in the Legal Profession' (2022) *International Journal of Law and Society* 5, 1, 53–65, available at 10.11648/j.ijls.20220501.17.

[51] *Khan Properties Ltd v The Commissioners for Her Majesty's Revenue & Customs* [2017] UKFTT 0830 (TC); see also *The Commissioners for her Majesty's Revenue and Customs v Duncan Hansard* [2019] UKUT 0391 (TCC).

[52] Finance Act 1988, Sch 18, para 17.

[53] Fair Trials, 'Regulating Artificial Intelligence for Use in Criminal Justice Systems in the EU' Policy Paper, available at https://bit.ly/3WVr2cB; and see the Council of Bars and Law Societies of Europe, 'CCBE Considerations on the Legal Aspects of Artificial Intelligence' (2020), available at https://bit.ly/3vt3HDy; and a paper by the Law Society of England and Wales, 'Horizon Scanning: Artificial Intelligence and the Legal Profession', available at https://bit.ly/3X1zWWh.

Hearsay evidence that cannot be adduced under one of the standard 'gateways' under s 114(1) of the Criminal Evidence Act 2003 may be admissible if 'it is in the interests of justice for it to be admissible'.[54] But the court making that determination, 'must have regard' to the factors set out in section 114(2)(a)-(i)[55] 'and to any others it considers relevant'.[56] Determinations made under s 114(2) will be case-sensitive. An outcome that is *predicted* by AI will take the court no further forward if there are principled reasons for departing from it, especially if the court and the parties cannot readily ascertain whether the AI technology had regard to those reasons and had appropriately evaluated them.

AI decision-making will not gain traction in the UK unless users and the public have confidence in it. Concerns (real or perceived) about indirect discrimination and bias need to be addressed. In the *Bridges* case,[57] the Court of Appeal acknowledged that (as the Divisional Court found) there was no evidence before it that there was any reason to think that the particular AFR technology used in that case did in fact have any bias on racial or gender grounds. But it added that the whole purpose of the positive duty on public authorities (as opposed to the negative duties in the UK Equality Act 2010) is to ensure that a public authority 'does not inadvertently overlook information which it should take into account'. This means (it is submitted) that it will be important that AI software is similarly capable of including, and appropriately handling, all relevant information and matters that ought to be taken into account for the purposes of the process or task in question.

F. AI and the Determination of Variable Factors

There are many cases in which a criminal court is required to assess variables such as the risk of harm posed by an offender, dangerousness, or the risk of reoffending, or whether (on an application for bail) the accused poses a 'flight-risk' or that they would be likely to interfere with witnesses or otherwise obstruct the course of justice.[58] Each matter poses the potential for discrimination and bias.

[54] Criminal Justice Act 2003, s 114(1)(d).

[55] The factors set out in the Criminal Justice Act 2003, s 114(2)(a)–(i) are: '(a) how much probative value the statement has (assuming it to be true) in relation to a matter in issue in the proceedings, or how valuable it is for the understanding of other evidence in the case; (b) what other evidence has been, or can be, given on the matter or evidence mentioned in paragraph (a); (c) how important the matter or evidence mentioned in paragraph (a) is in the context of the case as a whole; (d) the circumstances in which the statement was made; (e) how reliable the maker of the statement appears to be; (f) how reliable the evidence of the making of the statement appears to be; (g) whether oral evidence of the matter stated can be given and, if not, why it cannot; (h) the amount of difficulty involved in challenging the statement; (i) the extent to which that difficulty would be likely to prejudice the party facing it.'

[56] ibid s114(2).

[57] *Bridges* (n 28).

[58] See S Greenstein, 'Preserving the Rule of Law in the Era of Artificial Intelligence (AI)' (2021) *Artificial Intelligence and Law*, available at https://doi.org/10.1007/s10506-021-09294-4.

Problems of: (i) analysis; (ii) determining the facts; and (iii) perception, have been evident in the use of (and responses to) the Durham Harm Assessment Risk Tool (HART) which was a machine learning program developed by statistical experts based at the University of Cambridge in collaboration with Durham Constabulary.[59] HART used several years of custody records and 34 pieces of individual data to predict whether someone could be classified as 'medium risk' of reoffending.[60] In January 2022, the journal *Police Professional*[61] asserted that AI 'is marginally more accurate than experienced police officers in predicting the likelihood of criminals reoffending'. But Fair Trials claimed that the system was flawed.[62] The BBC reported claims[63] made by various privacy campaigners that HART generated its assessments on reoffending by drawing on data gathered by 'Experian' (a consumer credit referencing firm). The latter responded that the information was drawn largely from surveys and public data and that it sought to avoid stereotyping in its descriptions.[64] HART has been discontinued. As the CCBE has pointed out,[65] the methodology that had been used to produce assessments was 'usually not disclosed to the defendant' and that the defendant was unable to challenge the predictions made by the algorithms. They opined that until it is possible to create AI which is free of bias, 'there is a risk that certain groups of individuals will be unfairly excluded from programmes from which they could otherwise benefit'. But, being 'free of bias' means verifying and proving the AI system to be free of bias and for there to be popular acceptance of it being so.

II. REGULATING AI

A. Positions of the EU and the UK on AI Regulation; Digital Sovereignty and Global Influence

In 2012, the European Commission published a proposal for enacting a regulatory framework comprising harmonised rules on Artificial Intelligence

[59] See M Oswald, 'Algorithmic Risk Assessment Policing Models: Lessons from the Durham HART Model and "Experimental" Proportionality' (2018) *Information & Communications Technology Law* 27, available at www.tandfonline.com/doi/full/10.1080/13600834.2018.1458455.

[60] House of Lords Justice and Home Affairs Committee, 1st Report of Session 2021–22, HL Paper 180, 'Technology Rules? The Advent of New Technologies in the Justice System' para.127.

[61] Police Professional, 'Artificial Intelligence "Marginally Better" at Predicting Reoffending' (25 January 2022), available at www.policeprofessional.com/news/artificial-intelligence-marginally-better-at-predicting-reoffending/.

[62] Fair Trials, 'FOI Reveals over 12,000 People Profiled by Flawed Durham Police Predictive AI Tool' (15 August 2022), available at www.fairtrials.org/articles/news/foi-reveals-over-12000-people-profiled-by-flawed-durham-police-predictive-ai-tool/.

[63] See BBC News, 'Durham Police Criticised Over "Crude" Profiling' (9 April 2018), available at www.bbc.co.uk/news/technology-43428266.

[64] See ibid.

[65] Council of Bars and Law Societies of Europe, 'Considerations on the Legal Aspects of Artificial Intelligence 2020', para 4.8.

(the 'AI Act')).[66] The Commission was clearly concerned at the prospect of fragmentation of the internal Union market in connection with legal requirements for AI products and services, their marketing and use, and the liability of and supervision by public authorities (and the consequential diminishment of legal certainty for both providers and users of AI systems). The AI Act (Regulation (EU) 2024/1689) is now in force (July 2024).

The stated objectives of the EU AI Act include ensuring that AI systems, which are placed on the Union market, are 'trustworthy and safe and is developed and used in accordance with fundamental rights obligations' (see recital (3)), whilst facilitating investment and innovation in the development of AI (see Art 40.3). Enhanced governance and effective enforcement of EU AI rules are key features of the AI Act.

Following the UK's withdrawal from the EU on 31 January 2020, the UK will not be bound directly by the EU AI Act and there are no indications that the current UK Government has any intention of adopting or replicating it. Nevertheless, as Oisin Tobin has pointed out,[67] AI Regulation will apply extra-territorially to providers and users of AI systems regardless of whether the provider operates in the EU or not. Indeed, the UK is now a signatory to the Council of Europe Framework Convention on Artificial Intelligence and Human Rights, Democracy and the Rule of Law (2024).[68] Tobin suggests that the Commission's strategy may be that the AI Regulation will become 'a global default' but he warns that this is a 'gamble' since 'if non-European developers form the view that the rules are too burdensome, they may simply choose to ban the use of their technology on the EU market'. The first proposition is perhaps stronger than the second, but it is evident that both the UK and the EU have ambitions to be global leaders in the development and use of AI.[69] The EU asserts that 'Only common action at Union level can also protect the Union's digital sovereignty and leverage its tools and regulatory powers to shape global rules and standards' (EU).[70] In September 2024, the UN AI Advisory Body, published its Report 'Governing AI for Humanity',[71] in which they contended that there is a need for global governance of AI.

As matters stood prior to the UK General Election in July 2024, the UK's stated aim was to be a 'global AI superpower' but that it would 'work with partners to support the international development of AI governance [such as the

[66] Proposal for a Regulation of the European Parliament and of the Council of 21.04.2021 laying down harmonised rules on Artificial Intelligence (AI Act), COM(2021) 206 final.

[67] O Tobin, 'The EU AI Regulation Proposal Journal Article' (2021) *Privacy & Data Protection* 21(6), 3–4.

[68] Council of Europe Treaty Series – No 225.

[69] The UK 'National AI Strategy' states that its strategy is to establish 'the most trusted and pro-innovation system for AI governance in the world' (UK (Gov.uk; as at December 2022). See also the 'National AI Strategy – AI Action Plan' (18 July 2022), available at www.gov.uk/government/publications/national-ai-strategy-ai-action-plan/national-ai-strategy-ai-action-plan.

[70] 2021/0106 (COD), para 2.2.

[71] See www.un.org/sites/un2.un.org/files/governing_ai_for_humanity_final_report_en.pdf.

EU AI Act] in line with our values' and that it would work 'to reflect the UK's views on international AI governance and prevent divergence and friction between partners, and guard against abuse of this critical technology'.[72]

The UK's ambitions for AI seemed to be part of a wider strategy that was foreshadowed in a paper entitled 'Taskforce on Innovation, Growth and Regulatory Reform'.[73] It states that 'Leaving the EU offers opportunities both to shed unnecessary EU-derived legislation, and to frame a UK approach to regulation with three aims in mind boosting productivity, encouraging competition and stimulating innovation'. The Taskforce complained that, in practice, the EU General Data Protection Regulation (GDPR)[74] 'overwhelms people with consent requests and complexity they cannot understand, while unnecessarily restricting the use of data for worthwhile purposes'.[75] It suggested that UK regulators should 'work with international counterparts to promote British standards, and increase cooperation in innovative areas such as AI, cybersecurity, agri-tech and fintech'.[76] It advocated that Article 22 of the GDPR 'should be removed' and that a focus should be placed

> on whether automated profiling meets a legitimate or public interest test, with guidance on how to apply these tests and the principles of fairness, accountability and an appropriate level of transparency to automated decision-making provided by the Information Commissioner's Office.[77]

Put shortly, the UK strategy appears to have been to out-compete the EU in terms of AI technology and global influence on standards. It seemed to have regarded the EU as impeding progress and innovation by imposing rules and regulation that the UK considers to be unnecessarily burdensome. The thread, which ran through UK policy and thinking, was economic growth and greater standing on the world stage, which would bring social benefits for the UK. The 2024 UK General Election resulted in a landslide victory for the current Administration, but it is too early to say whether or to what extent there will be a change of policy towards AI regulation.

B. EU versus UK Systems for Regulating AI

Unlike the EU, the UK has not expressed an intention to enact, by way of a single enactment, a comprehensive regulatory AI framework or a set of rules

[72] UK National AI Strategy (n 69).

[73] Rt Hon Sir Iain Duncan Smith MP (Chair), Rt Hon Theresa Villiers MP, George Freeman MP, 'Taskforce on Innovation, Growth and Regulatory Reform' (May 2021), available at https://bit.ly/3Q5sFCk.

[74] Regulation (EU) 2016/679 of the European Parliament and of the Council of 27 April 2016 on the protection of natural persons with regard to the processing of personal data and on the free movement of such data, and repealing Directive 95/46/EC (General Data Protection Regulation, GDPR) [2016] L119/1.

[75] Taskforce on Innovation, Growth and Regulatory Reform (n 73) para 18.

[76] ibid para 127.

[77] ibid para 225.

and practices pertaining to AI, or to create a 'national supervisory authority' that would be charged with the overall responsibility of implementing and overseeing the UK AI Strategy. However, the UK Government has expressed its intention to enact an AI Act. In September 2024, a Member of the House of Lords introduced in Parliament, for debate, the Public Authority Algorithmic and Automated Decision-Making Systems Bill (a Private Members' Bill). Its stated purpose is

> to ensure that algorithmic and automated decision-making systems are deployed in a manner that accounts for and mitigates risks to individuals, public authorities, groups and society as a whole, and leads to efficient, fair, accurate, consistent, and interpretable decisions; and to make provision for an independent dispute resolution service.

However the Bill also states that its provisions would not apply 'to any automated decision-making system used for the purpose of national security'. Experience has shown that the expression 'national security' is open to a wide construction and not limited to matters of national defence.

As matters stand, the UK has opted for a de-centralised structure by which regulators for a given sector, and various agencies (existing and emerging), would provide governance and oversight.[78] In 2018, the Government agreed with the House of Lords' view that 'blanket AI specific regulation, at this stage, would be inappropriate …. [and] that existing sector-specific regulators are best placed to consider the impact on their sector of any subsequent regulation which may be needed'.[79] The EU AI Act makes specific provision for AI practices that are prohibited (completely or which are subject to qualified exceptions)[80] as well as high-risk systems,[81] and systems in respect of which account should be taken of specific risks of manipulation that they pose.[82] It does not seem to be envisaged that a similar list should be encapsulated in a specific piece of UK legislation.

In March 2023, the UK Government published a Policy Paper[83] declaring that it is taking an 'agile and iterative approach' by a framework that is 'underpinned by 5 principles to guide and inform the responsible development and use of AI in all sectors of the economy', namely: (i) safety; security and robustness; (ii) appropriate transparency and explainability; (iii) fairness; (iv) accountability and governance; and (v) contestability and redress. It is not the intention to put those principles on a statutory footing 'initially' but will

[78] See the 'Defence Artificial Intelligence Strategy' (15 June 2022), available at www.gov.uk/government/publications/defence-artificial-intelligence-strategy/defence-artificial-intelligence-strategy.

[79] See UK National AI Strategy (n 70); and the House of Lords Select Committee Report; Session 2017–19; HL Paper 100, 'AI in the UK: Ready, Willing and Able?', available at https://publications.parliament.uk/pa/ld201719/ldselect/ldai/100/100.pdf.

[80] AI Act (n 23) Chapter II.

[81] ibid Chapter III.

[82] ibid Chapter IV.

[83] 'A Pro-Innovation Approach to AI Regulation' (updated 3 August 2023), available at www.gov.uk/government/publications/ai-regulation-a-pro-innovation-approach/white-paper.

be 'implemented by existing regulators'. The Government intends to establish 'a Central Risk Function' (CRF) to 'bring coherence to the way regulators and industry think about AI risk'.[84] This involves a 'feedback loop' by which central government decides which risks will be tackled or tolerated. The CRF identifies and prioritises new AI risks and advises whether they warrant intervention by regulators. The regulators act similarly within their respective sectors, while businesses will report new risks to regulators and CRF 'where concerned'.[85] It is conceivable that similar principles to the five mentioned above, will operate in sectors other than the economy, including the criminal justice system. In February 2024, the Department of Science, Innovation and Technology published an 'Initial Guidance for Regulators',[86] that 'sets out the considerations that regulators may wish to have when developing tools and guidance to implement the UK's approach to AI regulation', but making it clear that the guidance 'is not intended to be a prescriptive guide on implementation as the principles are voluntary and how they are considered is ultimately at regulators' discretion'.

In February 2024, the UK 'Office for Artificial Intelligence' (OAI), which had been part of the DDCMS[87] and the DBEIS,[88] became part of the Department for Science, Innovation and Technology. Although the OAI is said to be a unit 'responsible for overseeing implementation of the National AI Strategy' (and itself asserts that one of its aims is 'making sure AI works for people – ethics, governance, future of work') it remains to be seen whether its primary focus is on facilitating economic growth. However, it is encouraging that the OAI, the Government Digital Service, the Information Commissioner's Office and the Ministry of Justice, are collaborating with the Alan Turing Institute's Public Policy Programme.[89] The programme was set up in 2018 and it has provided guidance that is 'designed to outline values, principles, and guidelines to assist department and delivery leads in ensuring that they develop and deploy AI ethically, safely, and responsibly'.[90] It opines that considerations of AI ethics and safety are a 'first priority' arising 'as a response to the range of individual and societal harms that the misuse, abuse, poor design, or negative unintended consequences of AI systems may cause'. The guidance is hard-hitting, pointing out (among many other matters) that the implementation processes of AI systems 'may make it difficult to pinpoint accountable parties'. In some

[84] ibid.

[85] ibid (figure 2; 'Central Risk Function Activities').

[86] 'Implementing the UK's AI Regulatory Principles: Initial Guidance for Regulators', Department of Science, Innovation and Technology, available at https://bit.ly/47zdV7F.

[87] Department for Digital, Culture, Media and Sport.

[88] Department for Business, Energy and Industrial Strategy.

[89] See D Leslie, 'Understanding Artificial Intelligence Ethics and Safety: A Guide for the Responsible Design and Implementation of AI Systems in the Public Sector' (The Alan Turing Institute, 2019), available at https://doi.org/10.5281/zenodo.3240529.

[90] See also the 'Data Ethics Framework' (updated 16 September 2020), available at www.gov.uk/government/publications/data-ethics-framework/data-ethics-framework-2020.

applications, the processed data 'could harbour traces of discrimination, bias, inequity, or unfairness' and that 'the opaqueness of the model may be deeply problematic'. It calls for a 'deeply ingrained culture of responsibility' on the part of those who produce and operate AI systems, and that they should install 'a governance architecture that adopts ethically sound practices at every point in the innovation and implementation lifecycle'.

The UK AI regime for regulating AI is therefore likely to be a blend of piecemeal legislation, guidelines, and protocols with oversight/control being provided by various regulatory bodies and by the courts. While this may have the advantage of flexibility (in respect of which executive and judicial discretion may play a part), it may become a complex array of rules and practices that is difficult for most persons to navigate and to comprehend.

C. Safeguards and Protections: Data Protection

The EU AI Act makes provision for appropriate safeguards for the fundamental rights and freedoms of natural persons, 'technical limitations on the re-use of the personal data, and state-of-the-art security and privacy-preserving measures, including pseudonymisation'.[91] The protections include those afforded by the Charter of Fundamental Rights of the EU. By contrast, the future position of the UK is far less clear-cut. Protections concerning the handling of data exist under the UK Data Protection Act 2018. For the moment at least,[92] the UK has retained the EU GDPR,[93] but it has modified and restyled it as the 'UK GDPR'.[94] The 'UK GDPR' has to be read alongside the UK Data Protection Act 2018. Nevertheless, on 28 June 2021, the European Commission adopted two adequacy decisions for the UK. The first[95] applies in respect of the GDPR,[96] and the other[97] in respect of the Law Enforcement Directive ((EU) 2016/680). Those decisions certify (in effect) that the UK has an 'essentially equivalent' level of protection to that within the EU.

However, on 10 September 2021, the UK published a 146-page consultation document entitled 'Data: A New Direction' evincing the intention to 'create a bold new data regime .... that unleashes data's power across the economy and society for the benefit of British citizens and British businesses whilst maintaining high standards of data protection'.[98] The UK Government intends to

[91] EU AI Act (n 23) Art 10.5(b); and see Arts 13–15, 43, 50, 57, 59, 70, 73, Annex VII 4.3, 79 and 82.
[92] See the UK Retained EU Law (Revocation and Reform) Act 2023.
[93] See s 3 of the European Union (Withdrawal) Act 2018.
[94] See the Data Protection, Privacy and Electronic Communications (Amendments etc) (EU Exit) Regulations 2019 (SI 2019 No 419).
[95] C(2021) 4800 final; https://eur-lex.europa.eu/legal-content/EN/TXT/PDF/?uri=CELEX:32021D1772.
[96] GDPR (n 74).
[97] C(2021) 4801 final; https://eur-lex.europa.eu/legal-content/EN/TXT/PDF/?uri=CELEX:32021D1773.
[98] Department for Digital, Culture, Media & Sport; 'Data: A New Direction' (10 September 2021).

approach adequacy assessments 'with a focus on risk-based decision-making and outcomes'[99] which will be based

> more heavily on an assessment of the real-world outcomes of data protection regimes rather than on a largely textual comparison of another country's legislation with the UK's legislation. This approach will recognise the different legal and cultural traditions which inform how other countries achieve high standards of data protection.[100]

The document added[101] that adequacy assessments 'should continue to inspire the trust and confidence of individuals, organisations and international partners' and would 'take into account, amongst other things, the rule of law, respect for human rights and fundamental freedoms, and the existence and effective functioning of a regulator' including

> principles drawn from relevant laws, such as the European Convention on Human Rights, which has been incorporated into UK law through the Human Rights Act 1998, rather than the EU Charter of Fundamental Rights, which is not retained in UK law after exit from the European Union.[102]

In December 2023, the (then) UK Government introduced a Bill[103] in respect of which one object was to reflect aspects of policy that had been advocated by members of the Taskforce on Innovation, Growth and Regulatory Reform (May 2021)[104] and to replace Article 22 of the UK GDPR[105] with Articles 22A-D.

Had those provisions been enacted, automated decision-making, including profiling, that produced legal or similarly significant effects on data subjects could have been carried out without being restricted by the existing three conditions, namely: (i) where it necessary for entering into, or the performance of, a contract between a controller and a data subject; (ii) where such activity is required or authorised by law; or (iii) where a data subject has provided explicit consent.

Article 22B(1)-(3) was intended to prohibit the use of 'special categories of data'[106] unless *either* a data subject has provided explicit consent to being subject to such processing, *or* the activity in question is necessary for:

a) entering into, or the performance of, a contract between a data subject and controller[107] or it is required or authorised by law, which includes the reasonable use of such processing to comply with legal obligations[108] or

[99] ibid para 242.
[100] ibid para 243.
[101] ibid para 244.
[102] ibid para 246; and see s 5 of the UK European Union (Withdrawal) Act 2018 by which the UK has declared that the Charter of Fundamental Rights of the European Union is not part of its domestic law.
[103] Data Protection and Digital Information Bill (UK) 2023-2024.
[104] Taskforce on Innovation, Growth and Regulatory Reform (n 73).
[105] GDPR (n 74), subject to the UK Data Protection Act 2018.
[106] ibid.
[107] ibid Art 6(1)(b).
[108] ibid Art 6(1)(c).

where processing is necessary for the performance of a public task carried out in the public interest, or in the exercise of official authority (for example, a public body's tasks, functions, duties or powers),[109] and

b) the activity also satisfies Article 9(2)(g); that is, the activity must be in the substantial public interest.

Needless to say, concern was expressed about what this would have meant in practice. More fundamentally, there was the question of whether or not significant revision of UK data protection laws would put at risk the two EU data adequacy decisions adopted in June 2021. In the event, the Bill fell in July 2024 on the announcement of the General Election: it has not re-appeared.

D. Safeguards and Protections: Human Rights

Of equal (or greater) concern is the future of UK laws on human rights, safeguards and protections, which will have an impact within the AI sphere and on UK criminal law generally. In June 2022, the UK administration introduced into Parliament a 'Bill of Rights' Bill which, had it been enacted, would have repealed and replaced the UK Human Rights Act 1998.[110] In the event, the Bill was withdrawn on 27 June 2023 by the very Government that had introduced it.

It was not proposed then (or now) that the UK would withdraw from the European Convention on Human Rights (ECHR). However, the language of the UK Government was nuanced,[111] acknowledging that the UK had 'signed up to' the 'original' ECHR but rejecting and reversing what it sees as 'the mission creep that has meant human rights law being used for more and more purposes, and often with little regard for the rights of wider society'.

Clause 1 of the proposed Bill of Rights declared that the Bill's aim was to clarify and to re-balance 'the relationship between courts in the United Kingdom, the European Court of Human Rights and Parliament' by ensuring that it is the UK Supreme Court and not the ECtHR that determines the meaning and effect of Convention rights for the purposes of domestic law. UK courts would no longer have been required 'to read and give effect to legislation, so far as possible, in a way which is compatible with the Convention rights'. Instead, the courts would have been required to give 'the greatest possible weight to the principle that, in a Parliamentary democracy, decisions about the balance between different policy aims, different Convention rights and Convention rights of different persons are properly made by Parliament'.[112]

[109] ibid Art 6(1)(e).
[110] See https://bills.parliament.uk/bills/3227.
[111] 'Human Rights Act Reform: A Modern Bill of Rights – Consultation' (as at 12 July 2022), available at https://bit.ly/3Ge3skW.
[112] Bill of Rights Bill (2022), cl 1.

It is difficult to assess whether or to what extent case outcomes would have differed (had the Bill become law) than if the same facts were to be judged according to existing UK laws. Even now, the starting point is that UK statutory measures, enacted since the Human Rights Act 1998 came into force, are ECHR compliant. Under the (withdrawn) UK Bill of Rights, a court would have continued to have power to make a 'declaration of incompatibility' if it was satisfied that a provision is incompatible with a Convention right.[113] But this (as now) would not have affected the validity, continuing operation or enforcement of the provision in respect of which the declaration was given. The Bill differed from the Human Rights Act 1998 by obliging a court not to adopt an interpretation of a Convention right 'that expands the protection conferred by the right' *unless* the court 'has no reasonable doubt that the ECtHR would adopt that interpretation if the case were before it'. Save for that exception, a court would have been entitled to 'adopt an interpretation of the right that diverges from Strasbourg jurisprudence'.[114] It is submitted that those proposals would not sit comfortably with Article LAW.GEN.3[115] of the EU-UK Trade and Cooperation Agreement (24 December 2020) that obliges the UK to 'respect' fundamental rights as provided for in the ECHR (UK) and (in the case of EU Member States) the Charter of Fundamental Rights of the European Union. In any event, the courts of England and Wales have amassed a considerable body of domestic human rights jurisprudence which, together with elaborate rules of criminal evidence, practice and procedure, are calculated to ensure that criminal trials are fair and ECHR compliant. The prospect of the UK withdrawing from the ECHR has substantially diminished (but not completely).

III. CONCLUDING REMARKS

The UK will continue to accommodate technology as an instrument in the administration of criminal justice to the extent that it enhances and does not diminish the quality of a framework of justice that has taken centuries to develop, and which has gained broad acceptance and approval. Although some would contend that AI is a means by which justice can be expedited and the backlog of cases reduced, the reality is that justice does not lend itself to the techniques of mass-production but must be applied in a bespoke manner, case-by-case. Those who advocate de-regulation need to reflect on the reasons for the measures having been introduced and to acknowledge (what may be an inconvenient truth, post Brexit) namely, the extent to which the UK had been a proponent of a number of those measures.

[113] Currently, Human Rights Act 1998, s 4.
[114] Bill of Rights Bill (2022), cl 3.
[115] Article LAW.GEN.3; 'Protection of Human Rights and Fundamental Freedoms'.

Part IV

AI and Evidence

14

AI Evidence: Ensuring a Fair Trial in the Digital World

KATALIN LIGETI*

I. INTRODUCTION

TODAY THE DIGITAL world looms large in the daily lives of humans employing computer technology based on 'artificial intelligence' (AI). Indeed, smart phones, smart houses, and health trackers, as well as voice recognition, facial recognition, and fingerprint recognition devices or self-driving cars are ubiquitous. By working with big data solutions and machine learning technology, AI is capable not only of collecting and storing data, but of evaluating the data and drawing conclusions from its assessments. Although the workings of AI are inherently opaque ('black box') and cannot be explained by humans, AI clearly offers effective solutions in many areas of social life.

AI's promise of fast analysis and consistent, objective outcomes based on reliable science makes it attractive for use in the legal domain: it is tempting to believe that AI eliminates the human factor, which is regarded as emotional and prone to error – and thus a threat to 'correct' decision-making. To harness AI's benefits for the criminal justice system, AI developers offer their services to judicial authorities as well as to other participants[1] of criminal proceedings by developing proprietary algorithms and statistical models specifically for the prevention, repression, and adjudication of crime.

AI-driven predictive policing is used to determine when and how to deploy potentially scarce resources.[2] Programs are fed with data on the latest criminal

* Katalin Ligeti is Professor of European and International Criminal Law at the University of Luxembourg. This chapter was written in the framework of the research project supported by the Luxembourg National Research Fund, CRIM_AI.

[1] AI developer DoNotPay claimed to have created a robot lawyer powered by AI to help defendants fight traffic fines in court. So far, however, it has not yet been allowed to be used in actual court proceedings. See 'DoNotPay – Your AI Consumer Champion', available at https://donotpay.com.

[2] A Guthrie Ferguson, 'Policing Predictive Policing' (2017) 94 *Washington University Law Review* 1109, 1115.

activity in a particular jurisdiction and make predictions about when and where future criminal activity is likely to take place. Similarly, AI can inform criminal investigations, decisions to prosecute, and pretrial custody decisions. Investigators, for example, can enter details from a particular crime scene into an AI system that then searches existing, ever-growing crime databases to determine whether there are similarities to other crimes. Prosecutors may use legal analytics to decide whether or not to pursue a particular prosecution based on an analysis of past conviction rates in similar circumstances. Prosecutors and judges rely on pretrial risk assessment tools to determine, among other things, the risk that a particular individual may commit additional crimes if released pending trial.[3] And, post-conviction, judges and correctional officers and agents may rely on predictive software to make decisions regarding whether to incarcerate, where to incarcerate, and whether early release or parole is warranted for a particular convict.[4]

There is also a wide array of AI developers specialised in forensic tools ('Forensic AI') designed to enhance the efficiency of traditional tools (eg, forensic filtering tools) or to close the evidence gap by enhancing accuracy, ie by generating evidence where it is otherwise not possible using traditional methods (eg, forensic probabilistic genotyping). Courts routinely admit evidence derived from complex proprietary algorithms to establish the guilt or innocence of those accused of a crime.

AI evidence is not limited, however, to Forensic AI; it may also be derived from the AI embedded in ordinary, day-to-day commercial products, such as data collected by event data recorders (EDRs), automated telephone responses giving telephone number information, Google Earth satellite imagery and GPS coordinates, software-generated driving time estimates, Find My iPhone and similar features used to track phone theft, and Fitbit or similar health data. Law enforcement authorities use everyday, ordinary data collected and stored on mobile phones and their applications (eg, step counters), social media accounts, and connected cars to generate evidence in criminal proceedings.[5] AI embedded in those products ('Consumer Product AI') collects and stores data on their users' behaviour, discerns patterns from it, draws conclusions from the data and the patterns and, having been trained to solve specific tasks using algorithms and statistical models, acts upon its conclusions. As Gless noted '[a] modern car, furnished with AI-devices, which oversees drivers'

[3] For a description of pretrial risk-assessment tools, see, eg, 'Pretrial Release: Risk Assesment Tools' (*National Conference of State Legislatures*, 30 June 2023), available at www.ncsl.org/research/civil-and-criminal-justice/pretrial-release-risk-assessment-tools.aspx.

[4] C Slobogin, 'Assessing the Risk of Offending through Algorithms' in W Barfield (ed), *The Cambridge Handbook of the Law of Algorithms* (Cambridge University Press, 2020).

[5] On the use of Alexa voiceprints in a German case, see S Gless, 'Wenn das Haus mithört: Beweisverbote im digitalen Zeitalter' (2018) 10 *StV* 671; or on using Celbrite AI to hack the suspect's phone, see 'Wie Polizisten das Handy des Tatverdächtigen auslasen' (*Süddeutsche Zeitung*, 9 February 2018), available at www.sueddeutsche.de/digital/prozess-wegen-vergewaltigung-und-mord-wie-polizisten-das-handy-des-freiburger-mordverdaechtigen-auslasen-1.3860870.

actions, might know more about the drivers' habits and activities than their family, friends and neighbors'.[6] The data, the patterns, and the conclusions of Consumer Product AI can support a legal assessment of human behaviour potentially relevant for criminal proceedings.

The use of AI evidence can improve the accuracy and objectivity of fact-finding in the criminal process, but it also brings drawbacks and pitfalls. The key challenge relates to verifying the probative value and the admissibility (a key determination in accusatorial systems) and the reliability (a key determination for the inquisitorial systems) of AI evidence. Due to the black box nature of the technology, which cannot be explained by humans, it is questionable how a proponent of AI evidence can establish the accuracy of the data produced and its reliability (ie the degree to which a result can be expected to occur again under equal circumstances). Such opacity arguably deprives the accused of procedural and fair-trial rights and violates the principles of the rule of law.[7]

This contribution seeks to explore whether existing rules on criminal procedure, in particular evidence law and procedural guarantees, are sufficient to address the specific nature and the associated pitfalls of AI evidence. It shall examine the two foreseeable answers: the first maintains the existing provisions of evidence law and procedural safeguards in criminal proceedings offer adequate protections to all participants of the criminal justice process. In short: existing rules elaborated for the analogue world suffice, it is only their application that needs to be adapted to the digital world.[8] This stands in contrast to legal systems and scholarship that argue in favour of introducing new defence rights specifically tailored for scrutinising AI evidence. With the advent of regional and global efforts to regulate AI, the ultimate objective of this contribution is to offer solutions for supranational and national policy choices.

II. SCOPE AND OUTLINE

In this contribution, AI evidence means the use of AI's output to establish the guilt or innocence of someone accused of a crime where the AI system generated

[6] S Gless, 'Cross-Border Admissibility of AI Evidence' in J Lelieur (ed), *Artifical Intelligence and Administration of Justice* (RIDP, 2023) vol 94, issue 2, 353.

[7] Roth reasons that AI systems' veneer of objectivity is manifestly unjustified; 'black boxes' not only 'obscure how the sausage is made, they obscure that their output is sausage at all.' In truth, these processes all have hidden subjectivities and errors that often go unrecognised and unchecked, thus potentially 'facilitat[ing] the masking of illegitimate or illegal discrimination behind layers upon layers of mirrors and proxies'. A Roth, 'Trial by Machine' (2016) 104 *The Georgetown Law Journal* 1245, 1270.

[8] The discussion on the need for new rules is not only theoretical; courts are also addressing this matter. For instance, the Divisional Court in *Bridges*, a UK case that involved facial recognition technology, held that, despite being a new technology, it does not require the introduction of new laws. *R (Bridges) v Chief Constable of South Wales Police* [2019] EWHC 2341 (Admin), [2020] 1WLR 672 at para 84. The Court of Appeal disagreed with this assessment. *R (Bridges) v Chief Constable of South Wales* [2020] EWCA Civ 1058 at para 90.

the output autonomously by using some form of machine learning. The autonomous character of AI evidence corresponds to the lack of human control in the production of such evidence. It is AI itself that produces the output in accordance with its algorithm.[9]

AI evidence as used here excludes rule-based AI systems that produce their output according to fixed codes. Instead, the scope of this contribution addresses only AI systems working with machine learning. It is common to the various forms of machine learning technologies[10] that, in addition to collecting and storing data, the algorithm is capable of evaluating the data, drawing conclusions from its evaluations, and eventually acting upon those conclusions. For example, vehicle EDRs are standard parts of most vehicles travelling on roads in Europe. EDRs can record a wealth of data regarding automobile accidents, including the vehicle's speed at the time of the accident, engine revolutions per minute at the time of the accident, breaking information, airbag deployment, and more. They do not simply collect and store these data; EDRs are usually part of a vehicle's restraint system (ie the seatbelts or airbags) and help 'decide' when the restraints are deployed.[11]

The fundamental difference between traditional evidence and AI evidence lies in the functionality of machine learning that no longer clearly demarcates the generation of evidence from the assessment of evidence.[12] Hansken, a Forensic AI developed by the Dutch National Forensic Institute, provides a good example of this blurring. Hansken is designed to search large, unlabelled, and unstructured data sets combining different data sources, such as chats, images, texts, etc. As Galič et al note,

> [t]hese new tools [such as Hansken] first need to interpret the data by themselves (e.g., a tool searching for images of drugs needs to be able to determine that a particular photo indeed represents drugs). Second, they need to be able to find relevant correlations (or links) between the numerous datapoints in the dataset (e.g., resulting in a convincing time-line and scenario).[13]

By connecting datapoints that it identifies as relevant, Hansken can connect a person to a specific message, identify an image of a particular drug, identify user identity. In this second step, Hansken 'decides' which datapoints are relevant and thereby already 'decides' whether the evidence is relevant.

To describe the conflation of these two steps of the evidentiary process, generating and assessing evidence, Roth coined the term 'machine conveyances'.

[9] A Roth, 'Machine Testimony' (2017) 126 *Yale Law Journal* 1972, 1976.

[10] See generally SM Bellovin et al, 'Privacy and Synthetic Datasets' (2019) 22 *Stanford Technology Law Review* 1, for a description of machine learning.

[11] JS Daily et al, 'The Forensics Aspects of Event Data Recorders' (2008) 3 *Journal of Digital Forensics, Security and Law* 30.

[12] Gless (n 6) 359.

[13] M Galič, A Das and M Schuilenburg, 'AI and Administration of Criminal Justice. Report on the Netherlands' in Lelieur (n 6) 315–16.

In her analysis, she suggests 'machine conveyances have become so probative and powerful that an algorithm can become the primary "accuser" in a criminal trial'.[14] For example, the output from breath analyser systems used in the United States (US) to establish the blood-alcohol levels of drivers suspected of driving under the influence of alcohol *is* the evidence; some scholars suggest that if that output says the tested individual's level is over the legal limit, the accused is almost always convicted.[15] Similarly, the output from forensic probabilistic genotyping AI that generates DNA-match likelihood ratios from low-level or multi-source DNA samples *is* the inculpatory or exculpatory evidence; that output is often what ties the accused to the crime.[16]

A large variety of Consumer Product AI and Forensic AI is already commonly used today in criminal proceedings. Due to the variety of consumer products, it is difficult to offer a typology of the devices that provide output used to assess human behaviour in criminal investigations or prosecution. The following examples of AI evidence are therefore limited to Forensic AI.

A. AI Filtering Tools

AI is used to analyse large amounts of data to detect digital data, traces and anomalies. In the Netherlands, algorithms are used to analyse large amounts of data to detect indications of violence (eg, the Threat of Life tool) or to process large volumes of seized digital material in order to find relevant datapoints and the connections between them (eg, Hansken).[17] In the same vein, algorithms are used in Germany to analyse large amounts of data to detect indications of child sexual-abuse material (ie ZAC-AI Enabled Rapid Assessment, NIKI) or in the field of money laundering to flag reports as warranting particular attention/to report anti-money-laundering anomalies (FIU Analytics).[18]

[14] Roth (n 9) 2044.

[15] See, eg, C Short, 'Guilt by Machine: The Problem of Source Code Discovery in Florida DUI Prosecutions' (2009) 61 *Florida Law Review* 177; AJ Wilson, 'Discovery of Breathalyzer Source Code in DUI Prosecutions' (2011) 7 *Washington Journal of Law, Technology & Arts* 121; S Cowley and J Silver-Greenberg, 'These Machines Can Put You in Jail. Don't Trust Them' *The New York Times* (3 November 2019), available at www.nytimes.com/2019/11/03/business/drunk-driving-breathalyzer.html: 'By the side of the road or at the police station, drivers blow into a miniature science lab that estimates the concentration of alcohol in their blood. If the level is 0.08% or higher, they are all but certain to be convicted of a crime'.

[16] Scholars have questioned whether such AI-generated DNA-match evidence can be the sole source of evidence that ties the accused to the crime, particularly in the context of so-called cold hits in unsolved cold cases. See, eg, DH Kaye, 'Rounding Up the Usual Suspects: A Legal and Logical Analysis of DNA Trawling Cases' (2009) 87 *North Carolina Law Review* 425, 490–92; A Roth, 'Safety in Numbers?: Deciding When DNA Alone Is Enough to Convict' (2010) 85 *New York University Law Review* 1130, 1135; and L Meintjies-van der Walt and P Dhliwayo, 'DNA Evidence as the Basis for Conviction' (2021) 24 *Potchefstroom Electronic Law Journal* 1.

[17] Galič, Das, and Schuilenburg (n 13).

[18] D Brodowski and J Sprenger, 'Predictive Policing in Germany' in Lelieur (n 6) 117.

B. Facial Recognition Technologies

Facial recognition technologies (FRT) finds broad application in both the private (such as for unlocking mobile phones or tablets) and the law-enforcement domains. FRT's AI can identify or recognise a person by creating mathematical representations (biometric templates) of their facial features extracted from a photo or video. The algorithm compares the features captured by a camera against the existing biometric template in databases to estimate the degree of similarity between two templates. FRT is much debated in Europe because it uses vast amounts of personal data.[19]

C. Automatic Number Plate Recognition

Automatic number plate recognition (ANPR) works by having specifically adopted closed-circuit television cameras fitted with infra-red sensors that can capture the number plates of vehicles. The images are than fed into machine learning AI that 'reads' the number plates and sends the information to the police department responsible for vehicle registration information so that the vehicle and its owner can be identified.

D. Forensic Probabilistic Genotyping

Forensic probabilistic genotyping AI is commonly used in criminal cases for the interpretation of complex DNA mixtures. The two leading DNA-mixture software providers are TrueAllelle (created by a private company, Cybergenetics) and STRMix (developed by ESR and Forensic Science South Australia). Both are widely used by crime laboratories in the US and Australia to generate evidence introduced at trials.[20] Forensic probabilistic genotyping AI's algorithm does not rely purely on a statistical analysis of alleles in a DNA profile; it also uses additional (undisclosed) methods to adapt their statistics to the particular protocols of a particular crime laboratory.[21]

[19] See the compromise reached at the EU level in the recently adopted Regulation (EU) 2024/1689 of the European Parliament and of the Council of 13 June 2024 laying down harmonised rules on artificial intelligence and amending Regulations (EC) No 300/2008, (EU) No 167/2013, (EU) No 168/2013, (EU) 2018/858, (EU) 2018/1139 and (EU) 2019/2144 and Directives 2014/90/EU, (EU) 2016/797 and (EU) 2020/1828 [2024]. In particular, see recitals (33) and (43), Arts 5 and 6, Annexes II and III (1).

[20] According to the comparative research conducted by the author, forensic probabilistic genotyping is not yet used in Europe.

[21] There are a number of other probabilistic genotyping software providers around the world, including free, open software which does not involve a black box. See, eg, M Schmidt et al, 'Statistefix 4.0: A Novel Probabilistic Software Tool' (2021) 55 *Forensic Science International* 1.

To assess whether existing rules of evidence law and procedural safeguards sufficiently equip the judge and the suspect to handle AI evidence, section IV discusses the challenges related to its admissibility in criminal proceedings. Section V examines the ability of the courts and defendants to scrutinise AI evidence under the existing legal framework and presents new approaches advocating new defence rights for the digital world. First, however, section III starts with some overarching issues linked to AI evidence.

III. OVERARCHING ISSUES: BIAS, FUNCTION CREEP, TRADE SECRETS, AND PUBLIC-PRIVATE COOPERATION

The quest to scrutinise the reliability and credibility of AI evidence brings to the forefront a series of overarching issues, some of which are common to any use of AI in the legal domain, but merit specific discussion in the context of AI evidence.

One of the difficulties of using AI in the legal domain lies in its inherent opacity, which makes it difficult for humans to verify the accuracy and reliability of AI-generated output, including AI evidence. Creating AI is fraught with opportunities for misunderstandings, misinterpretations, the introduction of biases (such as mathematical biases inherent in probabilities and unintentional but potentially discriminatory biases that may derive from the chosen dataset),[22] typographical errors, and just plain human mistakes. Such mistakes and miscalculations are often unintended by those who initiate the AI-development process or those who subsequently develop the instructions and algorithms. They can occur at virtually any stage in the development of the program, via, for example, inadequate program specifications; developer or programmer misunderstandings, miscommunications; simple human errors or omissions in new human-programmed code; or a poorly conceived or improperly prepared dataset.[23] The use of historical data, unrepresentative data, data that relies on information that acts as a proxy for race and economic status (such as addresses and postal codes) or gender (such as spending habits), and even noisy data can all contribute to bias.[24] The opacity of AI is problematic because

[22] C Chessman, 'A "Source" of Error: Computer Code, Criminal Defendants and the Constitution' (2017) 105 *California Law Review* 179, 188.

[23] Andrea Roth offers an extensive overview and classification of sources of error in AI-generated proof of guilt or innocence. She distinguishes between erroneous human inputs (such as outdated, incomplete, or biased data), machine errors (ie malfunction of the machine), analytical errors stemming from oversimplification (eg, failure by the algorithm to account for important variables), analytical errors stemming from coding errors or false assumptions, machine-learning errors (eg, due to a limited training data set or non-representative data set), automation complacency. A Roth, 'The Use of Algorithms in Criminal Adjudication' in Barfield (n 4).

[24] See P Grimm et al, 'Artificial Intelligence as Evidence' (2021) 19 *Northwestern Journal of Technology and Intellectual Property* 9, 42: '[b]ecause machine-learning algorithms are trained

it conceals whether such mistakes and miscalculations are being applied. If the output generated by the erroneous AI is then introduced as evidence in criminal proceedings, it could negatively impact the individuals to whom the probabilistic AI evidence is applied.[25]

The opacity of AI has led to calls for change, and the response in several countries has been the introduction of legislation requiring that, whenever algorithmic determinations that may interfere with the rights of individuals are used, those determinations should at least be intelligible.[26] In the criminal justice field, there are two approaches to accommodate algorithmic transparency. One approach pursues 'explainable AI' (also known as XAI), ie technical solutions which can explain machine learning inferences in terms that can be understood by humans.[27] It is, however, contested whether transparency provided by explainable AI is sufficient. Some scholars agree with Grimm et al when they claim that

> [t]he problem with the requirement of transparency is that many modern AI techniques are not explainable […]. It may be inexplicable why an algorithm mistakes a 3D-printed turtle for a rifle, or a baseball for an espresso, nor is there typically a way to 'bug-fix' a way to the correct model. Developers can only improve the training data, choose different features or parameters to emphasize, and reassess the output, but otherwise, it may not be obvious why the model is performing poorly. Another challenge is that AI models are not static; they constantly adapt and update over time.

using historical data, they can serve to perpetuate the very biases they are often intended to prevent.'; see also, among many others, I Ajunwa, 'The Paradox of Automation as Anti-Bias Intervention' (2020) 41 *Cardozo Law Review* 1671 and Slobogin (n 4).

[25] Amazon, for example, tried to streamline its hiring process via AI; it stopped using it when the AI exacerbated, rather than diminished, bias in Amazon's hiring practices. The data set used to train the AI relied on the profiles of Amazon's successful hires, most of whom were male. The algorithm learned to ignore certain words and phrases that were often associated with female profiles. See, eg, J Dastin, 'Amazon Scraps Secret AI Recruiting Tool That Showed Bias Against Women' (*Reuters*, 11 October 2018), available at www.reuters.com/article/us-amazon-com-jobs-automation-insight-idUSKCN1MK08G; G Lawton, 'AI Hiring Bias: Everything You Need to Know' (*TechTarget*, 29 August 2023), available at www.techtarget.com/searchhrsoftware/tip/AI-hiring-bias-Everything-you-need-to-know.

[26] In 2016, French law created a right to request information about algorithmic decisions made by administrative bodies, including the rules and main characteristics of the algorithm. A subsequent decree elaborated that the information was to include the parameters of the algorithm as well as their weighting, and that it should be in intelligible form.

[27] There is an XAI program at the Defense Advanced Research Projects Agency in the US that aims to develop machine-learning systems that 'will have the ability to explain their rationale, characterise their strengths and weaknesses and convey an understanding of how they will behave in the future'. See D Gunning, 'Explainable Artificial Intelligence (XAI)' (Defense Advanced Research Projects Agency Project Information), available at https://sites.cc.gatech.edu/~alanwags/DLAI2016/(Gunning)%20IJCAI-16%20DLAI%20WS.pdf. The National Institute of Science and Technology has outlined four principles of XAI which include: (i) explanation – that AI systems deliver accompanying evidence or the reason(s) for all outputs; (ii) meaningful – that AI systems provide explanations that are understandable to individual users; (iii) explanation accuracy – that the explanations correctly reflect the AI system's process for generating the outputs; and (iv) knowledge limits – that the AI system only operates under the conditions for which it was designed or when the system reaches sufficient confidence in its output.

> While there has been some development of models that are more interpretable, there is typically a trade off between accuracy and explainability, so explainable algorithms have not yet achieved widespread adoption, especially when they require a decrease in predictive performance.[28]

To allow the criminal justice system to fully benefit from AI's performance without sacrificing fair-trial guarantees, a growing group of scholars argue for replacing black box AI by what they call 'glass box' AI.[29] In this approach, the algorithm is also used to describe and monitor the inputs and outputs of an AI system with the purpose of verifying the system's adherence to certain social, ethical, and legal values, therefore producing value-based explanations.[30]

The potential for inadvertently embedding biases and mistakes in the programming of AI may be compounded by function creep when applying the AI.[31] This occurs if AI is used for a purpose other than that for which it was developed. This is always the case when Consumer Product AI is used as evidence of a particular individual's whereabouts, activities, or even behaviour,[32] even though the collection and use of the data as evidence was clearly not the private AI developer's purpose when designing the AI.[33] For instance, smartphone health-tracking applications give information to the user about the distance they have moved as well as the speed of the movement. The data derived from a health app was not developed to give exact information on the user's location. AI output garnered by consumer products may not support inferences drawn that fall outside the AI's specific purpose; such function creep may therefore undermine the validity, reliability, and acceptance of AI evidence.[34]

[28] Grimm (n 24) 62.

[29] BL Garrett and C Rudin, 'The Right to a Glass Box: Rethinking the use of Artificial Intelligence in Criminal Justice' (2024) *Cornell Law Review* 34 ff.

[30] ibid 34. See also C Rudin and J Radin, 'Why Are We Using Black Box Models in AI When We Don't Need To? A Lesson From an Explainable AI Competition' (2019) 1(2) *Harvard Data Science Review*, available at https://hdsr.mitpress.mit.edu/pub/f9kuryi8/release/8.

[31] See, eg, B-J Koops, 'The Concept of Function Creep' (2021) 13 *Law, Innovation and Technology* 29.

[32] For example, 'Fitbit Data Used to Charge US Man with Murder' (*BBC News*, 4 October 2018), available at www.bbc.com/news/technology-45745366.

[33] See, eg, 'Apple's Refusal to Open Locked Phones for the FBI' (*Wikipedia*), available at https://en.wikipedia.org/wiki/FBI%E2%80%93Apple_encryption_dispute.

[34] An example of function creep was revealed in relation to the Correctional Offender Management Profiling for Alternative Sanctions (COMPAS), an AI system used in sentencing. COMPAS was initially conceived as a risk- and need-assessment tool to provide decisional support for correctional departments when making placement decisions, managing offenders, and planning treatment, and included risk score for recidivism (ie a prediction about the offender's likelihood to reoffend), which one assumes was a prediction of what was likely to happen if none of the treatment or alternative placement options suggested in the report were undertaken. Over time, it would seem, function creep saw COMPAS's initial remit shift away from its original use by correctional officers and agents toward use by judges when deciding the length of a sentence. A judge might link 'a higher likelihood of recidivism' to the need for a longer sentence, to better protect society from the offender, even though the AI was not intended for that purpose. (See, eg, *State v Loomis* 881 NW 2d 749 (Wis SCt 2016); see also T Brennan, W Dieterich and B Ehret, 'Evaluating the Predictive Validity of the COMPAS Risks and Needs Assessment System' (2009) 36 *Criminal Justice and Behavior* 21, 24).

Potential bias in an AI's programming or function creep in its use have direct (and sometimes even irreparable) consequences for the accused. Ensuring that the science behind the AI evidence is both relevant and reliable as applied in a given case might be hindered, however, by issues of trade secrecy and confidentiality raised by AI developers. Checking the credibility and reliability of AI would require access to the AI's source code, training data, and built-in efficiency enhancing priorities. The source code, machine training data, and algorithms used for designing the AI system will typically be in the possession of the AI developer, who may refuse to produce them on the basis that the relevant information constitutes its trade secrets,[35] which is particularly obvious in the case of AI embedded in commercial products but is equally applicable to Forensic AI developed specifically for law enforcement or judicial purposes. For example, Cybergenetics is a private entity that owns one of the prominent probabilistic DNA genotyping AI systems in the US, TrueAllele. Although TrueAllele is being used in the US and despite repeated defence counsels' efforts to obtain its source code and at least one US court order to disclose it,[36] to date, TrueAllele's source code has never actually been disclosed.[37] In an effort to blunt claims of confidentiality and trade secrets related to proprietary AI systems[38] such as TrueAllele, open-source-code probabilistic DNA

[35] See, generally, E Murphy, 'The New Forensics: Criminal Justice, False Certainty, and the Second Generation of Scientific Evidence' (2007) 95 *California Law Review* 721; BL Garrett, 'Big Data and Due Process' (2014) 99 *Cornell Law Review Online* 207; PW Nutter, 'Machine Learning Evidence: Admissibility and Weight' (2019) 21 *University of Pennsylvania Journal of Constitutional Law* 919; S Gless, 'AI in the Courtroom: A Comparative Analysis of Machine Evidence in Criminal Trials' (2020) 51 *Georgetown Journal of International Law* 195, 211–12; P Marshall et al, 'Recommendations for the Probity of Computer Evidence, Digital Evidence and Electronic Signature' (2021) 18 *Digital Evidence and Electronic Signature Law Review* 18; S Chesterman, 'Through a Glass, Darkly: Artificial Intelligence and the Problem of Opacity' (2021) 69 *American Journal of Comparative Law* 271.

[36] The court characterised relevant information to include not only the source code but also the 'supporting software development and related documentation pertaining to testing, design, bug reporting, change logs, and program requirements'. (*State v Pickett*, 466 NJ Super 270 (2021), rev denied 246 NJ 48 (2021) para 279).

[37] See J Jouvenal, 'A Secret Algorithm Is Transforming DNA Evidence: This Defendant Could Be the First to Scrutinize It' *The Washington Post* (13 July 2021), available at www.washingtonpost.com/local/legal-issues/trueallele-software-dna-courts/2021/07/12/66d27c44-6c9d-11eb-9f80-3d7646ce1bc0_story.htm. Jouvenal also stated that 'A state court in New Jersey also ruled this year that TrueAllele's source code had to be disclosed to the defendant in a murder case, but prosecutors have decided to withdraw the TrueAllele evidence rather than go forward with the review'.

[38] Interestingly, some scholars, including Chessman, question whether many proprietary algorithms would, on closer examination, even qualify as a trade secret, as programmers often rely on open-source code rather than attempt to reinvent the wheel to achieve the sought-after outcome. He argues that '[t]o qualify as a trade secret, information must (1) not be generally known (or knowable), (2) bring economic value to the party claiming trade secrecy, and (3) be subject to reasonable precautions to keep the information secret. If information is either already known or is even 'readily ascertainable,' trade secret protection does not apply. Many private programming companies rely heavily on publicly available, open-source code that they integrate into their private, proprietary software. Many programs also rely on segments of code, algorithms, or software organizations that

genotyping AI systems designed to perform similar DNA analysis as TrueAllele but easier to explain to the ultimate trier of fact are now available to provide much sought-after transparency.[39] It is questionable whether any trade secrets or other privilege is properly asserted regarding information concerning the operation of AI in criminal cases; some courts in the US and Europe have ordered such evidence introduced in court, under seal, to protect any commercial information.[40]

Secrecy provisions not only reinforce the explainability/interpretability problem but contribute to an opaque cooperation between AI developers and prosecutors and other judicial authorities. Some scholars rightfully worry that 'the collaborative relationship between law enforcement and the private sector is [...] growing, opaque, and insufficiently regulated'.[41] Concerns have questioned the independence of AI developers when the state is their customer. Independence might be impaired either due to the financial stakes involved[42] or because the state's agencies and bodies (as clients) may influence the AI evidence. For example, when samples or data are sent off for forensic analysis by either governmental or private analysts, information is sometimes provided that may impact the way the human in the loop perceives the sample or data and, thus, the assessment made by the analyst.[43]

The relationship between private AI developers and their judicial authority or governmental customers is even more problematic as it often extends beyond borders. Occasionally, forensic laboratories or forensic departments purchase the generic algorithm from foreign technology firms and develop them for their own needs and objectives through validation procedures. One example is Hansken, in which the AI is derived from OpenAI.

are publicly available industry standards. Programs built on a patchwork of open-source code and generally known information merit limited trade secret protection or may not merit protection at all'. Chessman (n 22) 209.

[39] See, eg M Schmidt et al, 'Statistefix 4.0: A Novel Probabilistic Software Tool' (2021) 55 *Forensic Science International*, available at www.sciencedirect.com/science/article/abs/pii/S1872497321001071.

[40] R Wexler, 'Life, Liberty, and Trade Secrets: Intellectual Property in the Criminal Justice System' (2018) 70 *Stanford Law Review* 1343, 1358–62.

[41] Oral testimony referenced in Justice and Home Affairs Committee, House of Lords, *Technology Rules? The Advent of New Technologies in the Justice System* (First Report of Session 2021/2022 HL Paper 180 2022).

[42] Deborah Won notes that 'the proprietors who contract algorithmic systems to law enforcement agencies have financial incentives to meet law enforcement expectations that the tools they pay for will help maximize the number of successful prosecutions. Thus, proprietor incentives to design overbroad tools (or to ignore errors that create overbreadth) pose the same risk to algorithms' credibility that human witnesses' incentives pose.' D Won, 'The Missing Algorithm: Safeguarding Brady Against the Rise of Trade Secrecy in Policing' (2021) *Michigan Law Review*, available at https://michiganlawreview.org/journal/the-missing-algorithm/.

[43] C Garvie, *A Forensic Without the Science: Face Recognition in U.S. Criminal Investigations* (Center on Privacy & Technology at Georgetown Law, 2022) 2.

IV. ADMISSIBILITY OF AI EVIDENCE

Criminal procedure rules grant the finder of fact (be it a judge or a jury) the freedom to determine the evidentiary value of each piece of evidence brought before it and, on that basis, determine the guilt or innocence of an accused (sometimes called *conviction intime*). Thus, judges have a duty to verify that whatever evidence is brought before the ultimate finder of fact, including AI evidence, is probative and admissible (and sufficiently reliable to be used in the pending criminal proceedings.

Several comparative law studies[44] have revealed that rules of national criminal procedure on the collection and use of evidence differ extensively from one legal system to another; this difference is not limited to the common law-civil law divide. Given the increasing relevance of European Court of Human Rights (ECtHR) case law requiring states to scrutinise evidence that might impair the overall fairness of the proceedings,[45] however, we can observe a certain convergence of legal systems, at least in the Council of Europe,[46] where a twofold approach can be observed, namely legal systems strictly filtering the information to be admitted at trial (so-called controlled systems) and legal systems leaving it to the judge to assess whether it is appropriate to disregard illegal evidence ('free-proof' systems). Beyond this general difference, the details of evidence law vary considerably. So do the rules on the collection and admissibility of the various types of evidence (witnesses, interceptions, etc).

AI evidence does not constitute a special category of evidence; it is most often considered scientific evidence and the respective rules for examining expert testimony are applied to it. AI evidence as scientific evidence enjoys a 'veneer of objectivity and certainty',[47] raising the risk that criminal courts will simply rubberstamp its validity and reliability.[48]

The importance of always testing the credibility and reliability of scientific evidence[49] is well illustrated by the emblematic Post Office case in the United Kingdom (UK). Horizon software, designed by Fujitsu and used by the UK Post Office network to handle transactions, accounting, and stocktaking, generated

[44] See G Vermeulen, W De Bondt, and Y Van Damme, *EU Cross-Border Gathering and Use of Evidence in Criminal Matters: Towards Mutual Recognition of Investigative Measures and Free Movement of Evidence?* (IRCP 37, Antwerpen Portland by Maklu, 2010); K Ligeti (ed), *Toward a Prosecutor for the European Union, Volume 1: A Comparative Analysis* (Hart Publishing, 2013); SC Thaman (ed), *Exclusionary Rules in Comparative Law* (Springer, 2013); F Giuffrida and K Ligeti (eds), *Admissibility of OLAF Final Reports as Evidence in Criminal Proceedings* (University of Luxembourg, 2019), available at http://hdl.handle.net/10993/40141.

[45] For a recent summary of the respective ECtHR case law, see Council of Europe, 'Guide on Article 6 of the European Convention on Human Rights' (updated on 31 August 2022), available at ks.echr.coe.int/documents/d/echr-ks/guide_art_6_criminal_eng.

[46] See K Ligeti et al, 'Admissibility of Evidence in Criminal Proceedings in the EU' (*Eucrim*, 2020) 201.

[47] Roth (n 9) 2044.

[48] This fear is not entirely unfounded, if we consider that so far courts regularly admit AI evidence and reject defence submissions challenging admissibility.

[49] For example, Nutter (n 35) 955; Gless (n 35) 199; Garrett (n 35).

the evidence leading to the prosecution and conviction of hundreds of Post Office branch managers between 2000 and 2014 for allegedly stealing money when they had in fact not done so. What had been asserted to be accounting discrepancies were subsequently shown to be software errors: Horizon has throughout been affected by bugs, errors and defects, and faults in the system caused it to overstate the amount of cash or stock which should be held at a particular time, thereby causing an apparent and unexplained shortfall in branch accounts. The Post Office, however, maintained for many years that Horizon was reliable. It accepted the Horizon data as establishing that money was missing: ie that there was an actual shortfall of cash held in the branch, not merely an apparent shortfall generated by Horizon.[50]

The prosecution relied upon three receipts for cash deposits (a transaction log, the branch trading statements, cash declarations) and 'variance checks' – all produced by Horizon. As the Court highlighted, 'There was no evidence to corroborate the Horizon evidence. There was no investigation into the integrity of the Horizon figures. There was no proof of an actual loss as opposed to a Horizon-generated shortfall'.[51] After multiple convictions were overturned, an independent public statutory inquiry was established to obtain a clear account of the implementation and failings of the Horizon IT system at the Post Office over its lifetime.[52]

In contrast to Horizon, which was a computer system without AI, ensuring that the science behind AI evidence is both relevant and reliable often creates practical and legal challenges. In addition to the already mentioned difficulties rooted in claims of confidentiality and trade secrecy, traditional forms of scrutiny (ie the cross examination of both direct and expert witnesses or measurement of technological evidence against established technological standards) cannot be applied to AI evidence. As Gless rightly puts it,

> [t]he fundamental differences between machine-generated evidence and more traditional types of evidence renders typical means of scrutinizing AI statements impossible. Unlike human witnesses, neither robots nor software programs can be put on the witness stand and asked to take an oath to tell the truth. They are also not deterred from lying by the threat of being prosecuted for perjury.[53]

V. THE POSSIBILITY OF THE DEFENCE TO SCRUTINISE AI EVIDENCE

In all democratic criminal justice systems, criminal procedure principles demand, inter alia, that defendants receive a fair trial. The ECtHR requires

[50] *Hamilton and Others v Post-Office Ltd* [2021] EWCA Crim 577, paras 19–20.

[51] ibid.

[52] The progress of the inquiry can be tracked at the following link: www.postofficehorizoninquiry.org.uk/.

[53] Gless (n 35) 214.

the prosecution to 'disclose to the defence all material evidence in their possession for or against the accused'.[54] Furthermore, pursuant to Article 6(3)d of the European Convention on Human Rights (ECHR), everyone charged with a criminal offence has the right to examine or have examined witnesses against him. The ECtHR has given an autonomous interpretation of the notion of 'witness' so that it includes expert witnesses,[55] to whom the confrontation clause therefore applies. Thus, the fair-trial guarantee as applied by the ECtHR obliges the prosecutor to disclose both inculpatory and exculpatory evidence to the defence and if the evidence contains forensic reports, the defence has the right to confront the forensic experts and their findings. The ECtHR has further specified that a failure of the prosecution to disclose the technical details on which an expert report is based may impede the defence's ability to challenge the expert report and thus raise an issue of equality of arms under Article 6(1).[56] The ECtHR has identified three criteria for a fair use of evidence: (i) quality of the evidence (whether the circumstances in which it was obtained cast doubt on its reliability or accuracy); (ii) contestability (opportunity of challenging the authenticity of the evidence and of opposing its use); and, if those two criteria are in question, (iii) supporting evidence (questionable evidence must be evaluated in the light of supporting evidence).[57]

A. The Right of the Defence to Confront Expert Witnesses as a Means to Challenge AI Evidence

A fair trial is only possible when prosecutors, judges, juries, defence counsel, and all other affected parties are fully informed about the use of AI evidence and the potential limitations thereof. In particular, the prosecutor, judge, jury, and affected parties must be aware that AI evidence is part of the evidence in a way that clearly indicates the weight the prosecution has given that evidence in making its case. Knowing about any AI evidence is a prerequisite for the defence to scrutinise it and potentially challenge its admissibility. In his recent testimony before the House of Lords on the topic of the use of AI in criminal proceedings, David Spreadborough, a forensic analyst, offered an illustrative example in which an algorithmic error correction protocol was built into a CCTV system through which 'parts of a vehicle, or a person, could be constructed artificially'[58] without the prosecution, judge, jury, or defence counsel ever being aware of it.

The defence may learn about the use of AI evidence via disclosure, ie when the defence receives the case file containing the evidence brought against the

[54] *Rowe and Davis v the United Kingdom* App no 28901/95 (ECtHR, 16 February 2000) para 60.

[55] *Doorson v the Netherlands* App no 20524/92 (ECtHR, 26 March 1996) paras 81–82.

[56] *Kartoyev and Others v Russia* Apps nos 9418/13 and others (ECtHR, 19 October 2021) paras 71–73.

[57] *Prade v Germany* App no 7215/10 (ECtHR, 3 March 2016) paras 34–35.

[58] Justice and Home Affairs Committee, House of Lords (n 41) 16.

accused person. Whether the use of AI evidence is specifically mentioned in the prosecutor's file depends on the national legal system. For example, criminal procedural laws in England and Wales require indication if parts of the evidence were computer-generated or assisted.[59] How evidence is obtained, and the techniques used to do so, may be the basis on which admissibility is challenged. For instance, if images have been enhanced, then this fact will/should be disclosed in witness statements that accompany the exhibiting of the image. Similarly, in the Netherlands, reports introducing complex forensic evidence must indicate whether the evidence contains original or processed data. For instance, the reports must indicate whether the law enforcement authorities have improved an image to make it easier to see what is depicted (by changing the light, sharpness, or contrast, for example, a person on a photograph can become more recognisable) and if such improvements were made by AI applications.[60]

To challenge the admissibility of AI evidence, the defence essentially needs to demonstrate that the AI output is either not valid – ie the AI system did not accurately measure or qualify what it was supposed to measure or predict – and/or not reliable because the same (or a highly correlated) result cannot be obtained under the same set of circumstances. Demonstrating that the AI evidence is not valid requires, as a first step, access to the AI's source code, its original specifications, its intended purpose, and its training data. Indeed, when probabilistic genotyping AI source code, such as for FST[61] and STRmix, was disclosed and tested in US courts, the tests revealed programming errors that could have negatively impacted defendants.[62]

Despite these past experiences, courts in the US and in Europe often deny defence requests to access the information required for an independent validation.[63] Refusal might be based on trade secrets of the proprietary AI

[59] R Fortson, V Mitsilegas and C Salvi, 'Criminal Proceedings and the Use of AI Output as Evidence: Challenges for Common Criminal Procedure Principles and the Principles of the Rule of Law, UK country report'. A copy of the report is on file with the author.

[60] P Liefrink and R Robroek, 'Criminal Proceedings and the Use of AI Output as Evidence: Challenges for Common Criminal Procedure Principles and the Principles of the Rule of Law, Dutch country report'. A copy of the report is on file with the author.

[61] Forensic Statistical Tool (FST) was a probabilistic genotyping software that had been developed and used by the New York City Office of the Chief Medical Examiner. The Court mentioned that, in 2017, a review of that software's source code 'demonstrated the software – employed in thousands of criminal prosecutions – was unreliable, did not work as intended, and had to be eliminated' *State v Pickett*, 466 NJ Super 270 (2021) rev denied 246 NJ 48 (2021) para 278.

[62] ibid.

[63] In *State v Pickett*, the appellate court ordered the disclosure of TrueAllele's source code, but the prosecution team withdrew TrueAllele's result from the evidence. In one of the cases concerning Encrochat, the defence requested the disclosure of the Hansken source code but the request was denied. The Advocate General argued that it was not necessary. However, based on the present practice related to the reliability of wiretaps in the Netherlands, it is likely that the disclosure of the source code of AI evidence will be ordered by Dutch courts. Judicial authorities have assumed that telephone wiretaps provided by telecom providers are reliable without ordering access to the taproom source code. Liefrink and Robroek (n 60).

or the court may rule that such discovery is not necessary for disposing fairly of the action or that it will incur unnecessary costs. The court therefore accepts the prosecution's (and the AI developer's) argument that existing validation by the AI's users, as well as opportunities for testing and validation offered by the AI developer without revealing the source code, are sufficient.[64] It is therefore 'relatively unusual for a judge to order the disclosure of relevant software, yet arguably it may be crucial to fully understand a report or test result generated by an automated system'.[65]

Once a court accepts the scientific reliability of AI evidence, it still needs to check whether the science or technology has been appropriately applied in the accused's particular case. That analysis requires a different, as applied analysis which may well vary for each individual. Questions about the original purpose of the AI and whether it is being used for that or different purposes (ie function creep) or whether it is appropriately applied to the particular case of the accused should all be considered. For instance, a New York court considering the admissibility of the results of a probabilistic genotyping AI, STRmix, made it clear that the New York State Police crime lab did not apply the necessary protocols to use STRmix in the proper way and found that 'the lack of internal validation by the New York State Police crime lab, as candidly admitted by [the forensic expert], precludes use of the STRmix results'.[66] To the prosecution's argument that issues with the reliability of the DNA analysis as applied were issues of weight rather than admissibility and that the evidence should still be admitted, the Court replied that '[f]orensic DNA analysis should be governed by the highest standards of scientific rigor in analysis and interpretation' and held that 'to

[64] *People v Wakefield*, 38 NY 3d 367 (2022).

[65] D Kiat Boon Seng and S Mason, (2021) 33 'Artificial Intelligence and Evidence' *Singapore Academy of Law Special Issue on Law and Technology* 241, 272–73. The Enchrochat case is a telling example of the hurdles defence lawyers face with AI evidence. 'Encrochat evidence was challenged on many reliability grounds in Dutch courts. This includes claims that the Encrochat evidence is of unknown origin, unreliable, and untestable, the ownership and use of Encro-phones, accounts and chats cannot be clearly attributed to concrete suspects or crimes; one phone might have been used by several users; the Encrochat conversations presented are incorrect, edited, incomplete, and out of context which aims at drawing an unjustifiably incriminating picture.' R Stoykova et al, 'Reliability Assessment of Digital Forensic Investigations in the Norwegian Police' (2022) 40 *Forensic Science International: Digital Investigation* 1.

[66] The Court noted, concerning the expert testimony of Dr Buckleton, the forensic expert of the New York State Police crime lab, that 'STRmix has six laboratory specific parameters to determine prior to its use. Concerning one of these parameters called stutter ratios, Dr. Buckleton testified that he received data from the New York State Police crime lab to look at "forward stutter" which "did not serve the purpose" but nonetheless was used in the April 2016 analysis. Concerning "drop-in" rates, Dr. Buckleton stated that he had entered a zero drop-in rate as the crime lab did not "have a drop-in rate because they do not do low copy number on high sensitivity methods." A "drop-in" rate greater than zero would have benefited the defendant. And in his affidavit dated August 18, 2016, Dr. Buckleton further stated that he used a "drop-in rate" that was based partly on 'our own experience.' *People v Hillary*, Decision & Order (D&O), DNA Analysis Admissibility (Hillary D&O) at 4. A copy of the Hillary D&O is on file with the author.

allow such evidence would be unduly prejudicial to the defendant'.[67] The judge subsequently rendered a not guilty verdict.[68]

Questions related both to accuracy and consistency need measuring that can only be provided by forensic experts. When the defence faces AI evidence, it needs not only the opportunity but also the means to verify its reliability. This is a particularly pressing issue in adversarial systems based on a partisan vetting of evidence where the defendant might be obliged to pay out-of-pocket costs related to forensic expertise.

B. New Approaches to Scrutinising AI Evidence

With the arrival of AI evidence in criminal trials, judges and defence lawyers are called on to apply the fair-trial guarantees laid down in Article 6 ECHR to the context of the digital world. When inspecting a prosecution case file containing AI evidence, the information in the case file alone will not allow defence lawyers to understand and independently verify the decision-making processes of the AI tool. This leads courts in the Netherlands and Germany to acknowledge new defence rights more suitable to the scrutiny of AI evidence.

In the Dutch *Ennetcom-Tandem* case, the police managed to take down an illegal server (the Ennetcom server) containing a huge amount of data related to communication by crypto phones used by criminals. The server's full data set was searched by Hansken to identify evidence, a process during which two derivative datasets were extracted. The prosecution used Hansken in a first step to narrow down the data by using search terms related to suspects' nicknames, names to describe offences or drugs, etc. The prosecution then further searched this secondary set of data for actual evidence related to suspects or crimes. The result made up the tertiary dataset that the prosecution included in the case file and made available to the defence. Although the defence was granted (upon request) access to the secondary data set by the Court, it had very limited opportunities to examine the data. As Galič reports,

> [t]he defense did receive a CD-ROM with the secondary dataset (excluding a large portion of data that the prosecution deemed irrelevant to this case but relevant to other investigations) just over a month before the judgment was delivered, they did not have an opportunity to search them with Hansken.[69]

[67] ibid.

[68] A recording of the relevant portion of Judge Catena's oral verdict can be found at 'Nick Hillary Found not Guilty of Garret Phillips' Murder' (*NCPR NEWS*, 26 September), available at www.northcountrypublicradio.org/news/story/32653/20160928/nick-hillary-found-not-guilty-of-garrettphillips-murder.

[69] M Galič, 'Defence Rights in the Context of Huge Datasets and Big Data Forensic Tools in Criminal Proceedings' (2020) *SSRN Working papers* 10, available at https://papers.ssrn.com/sol3/papers.cfm?abstract_id=3838680; B Schermer and J-J Oerlemans, 'AI, Strafrecht En Het Recht Op Een Eerlijk Proces' (2020) 1 *Computerrecht* 14.

Several scholars have argued – relying on ECtHR case law in *Sigurður Einarsson and Others v Iceland*[70] – that the defence should not only have a right to direct access to the secondary data set but also to the AI tool, Hansken, to be able to search that data.[71] Defence lawyers have since been granted access to Hansken and even use it from their own offices to carry out searches.[72] Moreover, the defence can question Netherlands Forensic Institute (NFI) forensic experts on the validation of Hansken. This development certainly helps defence lawyers; it does not allow them, however, to verify Hansken's decision-making process.

In 2020, the Federal Constitutional Court in Germany went further: in a case involving digitised radar guns, it recognised a 'right to raw data' based on Article 2 in conjunction with Article 20 of the German Basic Law[73] and emphasised the importance of being able to trace the machine's data-processing operations.[74] In contrast to this German approach, the Dutch courts have so far not ordered the disclosure of Hansken's source code, algorithms, training, or validation data. More importantly, the NFI would not be able to comply with such a disclosure obligation, since Hansken was developed using OpenAI's algorithm and only OpenAI has its source code.

The above examples reveal that even if the Court and the defendant receive access to the source code and other relevant material required for an independent validation, the ability to scrutinise reliability is not yet resolved, because

> [e]ven experts often struggle to understand what software code will do: inspecting source code is a very limited way of predicting how a computer program will behave. Machine learning […] is particularly ill-suited to source code analysis because it involves situations where the decisional rule itself emerges automatically from the specific data under analysis, sometimes in ways that no human can explain.[75]

The defence's right to confrontation was initially developed with humans in mind, allowing the defendant to confront the forensic experts at the trial. However, this standard poses significant difficulties when applied to fight the accuracy and reliability of AI evidence. Giving the defence the opportunity to put questions to an expert witness who cannot explain how the AI drew its conclusions and who is merely able to validate the AI's outcome does not satisfy

[70] *Sigurður Einarsson and Others v Iceland* App no 39757/15 (ECtHR, 4 June 2019).

[71] Galič (n 69).

[72] 'Launch of New Hansken Facility: Lawyers Can Now View Digital Traces From their Own Workplace' (*Hansken*, 20 March 2023), available at www.hansken.nl/latest/news/2023/03/20/launch-of-new-hansken-facility-lawyers-can-now-view-digital-data-from-their-own-workplace.

[73] *Grundgesetz Für Die Bunderepublik Deutschland* [GG] [Basic Law], available at www.gesetze-im-internet.de/englisch_gg: Art 2, subs 1 and Art 20, subs 3.

[74] *Bayerisches Oberstes Landesgericht* [BayObLG] [Bavarian Higher Regional Court], 9 December 2019, 202 [ObOWi] 1955/19 (Ger), available at www.gesetze-bayern.de/Content/Document/Y-300-Z-BECKRS-B-2019-N-31165?hl=true (reversing prior decisions denying an obligation to disclose such data due to the assumption that calibrated and regularly monitored devices produce valid findings).

[75] JA Kroll et al, 'Accountable Algorithms' (2017) 165 *The University of Pennsylvania Law Review* 633, 638.

the right to confrontation as laid down in Article 6 ECHR. Having access to AI source code and training data might therefore not be helpful. As Gless et al note,

> [t]he challenges are especially acute if a device draws its own conclusions from the information it has gathered without recording all conditions for its conclusion. In that instance, not all outcomes may be traceable to humans, even if the underlying raw data, measurement data, source code and algorithmic processing are available.[76]

VI. CONCLUSION

The shift from human- to machine-generated proof has, on the whole, the potential to enhance accuracy and objectivity in fact-finding. Machine evidence, like other forms of technology that came before it, has the potential to provide new sources of information and, thus, a chance for more accurate fact-finding in criminal trials. AI also has the potential to reduce certain biases and errors inherent in human judgment and, thereby, increase the efficiency of our criminal justice systems. At the same time, several important recent cases have demonstrated that AI evidence can suffer from biases or errors leading to unfairness or inaccuracy. The black box character of AI is, by definition, opaque and can render the detection of unfairness or inaccuracy in its analysis more difficult, if not impossible. Some critics go so far as to claim that AI distorts decision-making by emphasising the quantifiable aspects of reasoning and ignoring so-called human values such as dignity, equity, and mercy.[77]

In reality, AI's presence in an increasing number of applications in communication, health, finance, consultancy, research, and public administration can only lead to more AI evidence in criminal proceedings. It is unlikely that criminal justice systems can remain or, more accurately, revert to an island free of AI's impact. It is therefore paramount to ensure the validity and reliability of AI evidence. This in turn requires developing means that enable the court, the defendant, and the other participants in criminal proceedings to understand and validate the decision-making processes of the AI tool. Courts in Europe have started to acknowledge new rights for defendants derived from the fair-trial principle that would enable defendants to inspect the source code, the algorithm, and the decision-making process of the AI. Even these new rights might offer inadequate means for the defendant to scrutinise AI evidence, however, since the decision-making process of AI is not understandable to humans.

[76] S Gless, F Lederer and T Weigend, 'AI-based Evidence in Criminal Trials' (2024) *Tulsa Law Review* 1–37.

[77] Professor Michael Wooldridge, Head of the Computer Science Department at the University of Oxford, strongly believes that no technological tool, which he has described as a 'big long list of numbers', should 'ever be more than another voice in the room'. With the evolution of more sophisticated AI that can mimic human emotions, it remains to be seen whether core values of the criminal justice system can also be 'learned' by AI through its experiences.

Certification is viewed by many as a potentially adequate way to remedy the AI-testing problem (and related validity and reliability concerns). If certification is provided, the reliability of outcomes generated by such technology needs no further verification in court. Although it looks promising, no such pre-certification procedures exist today.

In the UK, the Government has pointed out that a 'lack of common and internationally agreed standards to test and benchmark against' makes certification unrealistic.[78] In 2021, the US House of Representatives considered a Justice in Forensic Algorithms Act which would ensure that any algorithms used in criminal cases be unrestricted by any claim of proprietary or trade secrets protection and be vetted by a federal scientific agency, the National Institute of Standards and Technology; the bill has, however, not been enacted into law.[79]

Regarding the scientific validity of DNA mixture interpretation the US President's Council of Advisors on Science and Technology (PCAST) reviewed in 2016 in detail the state of the research regarding probabilistic DNA genotyping and found that 'DNA analysis of complex mixtures based on CPI [Combined Probability of Inclusion]-based approaches has been an inadequately specified, subjective method that has the potential to lead to erroneous results. As such, it is not foundationally valid.'[80]

Regarding software used to conduct an analysis of DNA mixtures, PCAST found such approaches promising, but that validation work was needed for any given software. Further, PCAST noted that

> studies have established the foundational validity of some objective methods under limited circumstances (specifically, a three-person mixture in which the minor contributor constitutes at least 20 percent of the intact DNA in the mixture) but that substantially more evidence is needed to establish foundational validity across broader settings.[81]

PCAST further highlighted that given the variety of DNA software developers, some private, some open-source and some not, an

> [a]ppropriate evaluation of the proposed methods should consist of studies by multiple groups, not associated with the software developers that investigate the performance and define the limitations of programs by testing them on a wide range of mixtures with different properties.[82]

[78] Fortson, Mitsilegas and Salvi (n 59).

[79] See 'Reps. Takano and Evans Reintroduce the Justice in Forensic Algorithms Act to Protect Defendants' Due Process Rights in the Criminal Justice System' (*Tokano*, 4 August 2021), available at https://takano.house.gov/newsroom/press-releases/reps-takano-and-evans-reintroduce-the-justice-in-forensic-algorithms-act-to-protect-defendants-due-process-rights-in-the-criminal-justice-system.

[80] Executive Office of the President, President's Council of Advisors on Sci. and Tech., *REPORT TO THE PRESIDENT Forensic Science in the Criminal Courts: Ensuring Scientific Validity of Feature-Comparison Methods* (September 2016), available at https://obamawhitehouse.archives.gov/sites/default/files/microsites/ostp/PCAST/pcast_forensic_science_report_final.pdf.

[81] ibid 8.

[82] ibid 79.

Digital forensic experts seem to uphold claims made in the UK and US concerning the lack of proper standardisation. Experts in forensic science claim that '[d]igital forensic suffers from proliferation of standards, which are short-lived and insufficient to reach general acceptance in the domain'.[83] To overcome the present impasse, a group of scholars suggest developing a generic framework and standard process for reliability validation of digital forensics for criminal proceedings. Such frameworks are much needed to help participants in the criminal justice process understand the authenticity and reliability of AI evidence.

[83] R Stoykova and K Franke, 'Reliability Validation Enabling Framework (RVEF) for Digital Forensics in Criminal Investigations' (2023) 45 *Forensic Science International: Digital Investigation* 1, 2.

15

AI-Based Means of Evidence and the Defendant's Rights in the European Union

EFTYCHIA BAMPASIKA*

I. INTRODUCTION

LAW ENFORCEMENT AND judicial authorities across the world have already been making use of various artificial intelligence (AI) applications within the criminal justice context. Utilising the outcomes of the AI applications deployed in criminal investigations and at the pre-trial stage as evidentiary material to support a claim for conviction or acquittal in a traditional criminal trial setting is on a global scale the next step in the realm of criminal justice systems.

The so-called AI-based means of evidence include AI applications that either initially produce or process existing evidentiary material. The applications that fall under the first category are those that generate or recognise evidentiary material, such as the various embedded AI software types in products created by the industry for non-litigative use, smart home devices, cars,[1] or even robots, and voice or image recognition applications. The second category, however, includes applications that facilitate the extraction and processing of relevant evidence from other sources, such as knowledge extraction[2] from structured or unstructured sources.

* Eftychia-Venetia Bampasika, LL.M., Attorney at Law.

[1] On this matter, see in general the important work done by A Roth, 'Machine Testimony' (2017) 126 *The Yale Law Journal* 1972–2053 and S Gless, 'AI in the Courtroom: A Comparative Analysis of Machine Evidence in Criminal Trials' 2020 (51) *Georgetown Journal of International Law* 195–253. Last but not least, see also Katalin Ligeti in chapter 14 of this volume.

[2] See dbpedia.org/page/Knowledge_extraction. In general, for a plethora of AI applications in the criminal justice context, see the European Parliament resolution of 6 October 2021 on artificial intelligence in criminal law and its use by the police and judicial authorities in criminal matters (2020/2016(INI)) P9_TA(2021)0405 under M: eg, 'search[ing] suspect databases and identify[ig] victims of human trafficking or child sexual exploitation and abuse, automated number plate recognition, speaker identification, speech identification, lip-reading technologies, aural surveillance

All the aforementioned AI-based means of evidence could under specific requirements prove to be helpful for criminal justice officials, but they could also generate serious imbalances among the trial actors, compromising the effective participation of the defendant in a criminal trial. For the criminal justice systems based on the rule of law, the defendant's rights[3] play a crucial role in guaranteeing the fairness of the criminal procedure. Therefore, European Union (EU) legislation must provide the defendant with those procedural rights that safeguard their participatory role and counterbalance the intrusiveness of AI technology.

II. THE PROTECTION OF THE DEFENDANT'S RIGHTS UNDER EU LAW

In order for the European legislator to do that, it is useful to take a step back and examine whether the existing EU legal framework provides for some safeguards that can be implemented also in cases of AI generated evidence in criminal trials, so as to avoid regulatory fragmentation and unnecessary repetitions. This is necessary given the primarily national nature of evidence law and the consequent difficulty of reaching an agreement at an EU level on certain minimum rules and standards with regard to AI-based means of evidence in criminal trials.[4]

The EU has already acknowledged the vulnerability of the defendant's position in various statutory texts[5] and the need for uniformed regulation of the use of AI in the criminal justice sector across Member States (MS) so as to avoid a variance of standards between MS and disparate fundamental rights protection levels.[6] For example, it stresses that AI solutions for law enforcement

(i.e. gunshot detection algorithms), autonomous research and analysis of identified databases, forecasting (predictive policing and crime hotspot analytics), behaviour detection tools, advanced virtual autopsy tools to help determine cause of death, autonomous tools to identify financial fraud and terrorist financing, social media monitoring (scraping and data harvesting for mining connections), and automated surveillance systems incorporating different detection capabilities (such as heartbeat detection and thermal cameras)'.

[3] In the present chapter, I only deal with the procedural rights of the defendant in the context of a traditional criminal trial, specifically with regards to AI technology used in evidentiary proceedings, leaving out of the scope of this chapter the rights of the person of interest, the suspect and the accused at the pre-trial stage and the difficult implications for the data protection rights of these subjects. I begin my examination taking as a given that the data of the defendant was collected in a lawful way.

[4] See, eg, K Ligeti, B Garamvölgyi, A Ondrejová and M von Galen, 'Admissibility of Evidence in Criminal Proceedings in the EU' (3) 2020 *Eucrim* 201–208.

[5] Eg, in the ABC Directives that refer to the legislative agenda for strengthening the procedural rights of suspected or accused persons in criminal proceedings, adopted in the respective Roadmap, the so-called Stockholm Programme by the Council [2009] OJ C295/01.

[6] See the Regulation (EU) 2024/1689 of the European Parliament and of the Council of 13 June 2024 laying down harmonised rules on artificial intelligence (AI Act) [2024] OJ L 2024/1689; under 7. of the European Parliament Resolution (n 2). A comprehensive guide of the important milestones

and the judiciary need to fully respect the principles of human dignity, non-discrimination, the presumption of innocence and right of defence, including the right to silence, equality before the law, the principle of equality of arms and the right to an effective remedy and a fair trial, in accordance with the Charter and the European Convention on Human Rights (ECHR), while the use of AI applications must be prohibited when incompatible with fundamental rights.[7] Further, the Council of Europe's (CoE) regulatory activity in this field is in line with the EU's course of action, promoting human rights by design, and there is an open dialogue between the two.[8]

In the EU, the close judicial cooperation, mutual assistance and recognition between the MS further justifies the need for an equal level of protection with regards to procedural rights of persons accused in criminal proceedings across the EU.[9] Differences in the way national law enforcement and judicial authorities deal with and deploy information conveyed by AI should not result in creating uneven levels of protection in the EU when it comes to AI-based evidence and the defendant's rights.[10] Against this backdrop, I examine the challenges concerning the defendant's rights and possible regulatory solutions at the level of the EU, using the ECHR and the Charter of Fundamental Rights of the European Union (CFR) as the main reference points to reflect upon the reconceptualisation of the traditional procedural rights of the defendant and the conception of new defence rights at the trial stage.

concerning AI in the EU can be found here: digital-strategy.ec.europa.eu/en/policies/european-approach-artificial-intelligence. See, further, V Mitsilegas, 'Legislating for Human Rights: The EU Legal Framework on the Rights of Individuals in Criminal Proceedings' in V Mitsilegas (ed), *EU Criminal Law* (Hart Publishing, 2022) 254–95.

[7] Under 2. of the European Parliament Resolution (n 2).

[8] See the European Ethical Charter on the Use of Artificial Intelligence in Judicial Systems and their Environment by the European Commission for the Efficiency of Justice (CEPEJ) of the Council of Europe in 2018. On the various practical ways in which AI applications could enforce human rights by design, see the Feasibility Study of the CEPEJ of the CoE on the possible introduction of a mechanism for certifying AI tools and services in the sphere of justice and the judiciary, CEPEJ(2020)15Rev, available at rm.coe.int/feasability-study-en-cepej-2020-15/1680a0adf4, eg, the checking of the existence of explanatory information and the auditing of research results, inclusion of reports presenting decision trees, and training data and methods explaining how fundamental rights and freedoms are taken into account, the use of open source code or transmission of the source code on a confidential basis and clear information for the defendant on the use of AI in their case. All initiatives of the CoE with regards to AI can be found here: www.coe.int/en/web/artificial-intelligence/work-in-progress#01EN.

[9] See, eg, Directive 2014/41/EU of the European Parliament and of the Council of 3 April 2014 regarding the European investigation order in criminal matters [2014] OJ L130/1; Council Framework Decision 2002/584/JHA of 13 June 2002 on the European arrest warrant and the surrender procedures between Member States [2002] OJL190/1; Regulation (EU) 2018/1805 of the European Parliament and of the Council of 14 November 2018 on the mutual recognition of freezing orders and confiscation orders [2018] OJ L303/1.

[10] See, eg, for a comparative analysis on device evidence between the US and Germany, S Gless, F Lederer and T Weigend, 'AI-Based Evidence in Criminal Trials' (2024) 59 *Tulsa Law Review* 1, 1–35.

Article 6 ECHR and Article 47 CFR enshrine the right to a fair trial,[11] which is a basic principle of the rule of law in a democratic society[12] and must be recognised as a 'structured right, comprising several separate subjective fundamental rights'.[13] In accordance with Article 52(3) CFR, Article 47 of the Charter has the same meaning and scope as Article 6 of the ECHR, which in general provides an absolute floor below which the EU must not fall and must be used as an interpretative tool. In addition, fundamental rights as guaranteed by the ECHR and as they result from the constitutional traditions common to the MS constitute general principles of EU law according to Article 6 of the Treaty on European Union, and are therefore binding for the EU.

Moreover, due to the nature of the ECHR as a 'living instrument',[14] certain rights that constitute sub-parts of the 'mother-right' to a fair trial can and must be interpreted under the conditions generated by the use of AI in law enforcement and the judiciary, strengthening the safeguards that the defendant needs in this new judicial environment. Therefore, the ECHR forms the basis of the following analysis. The list of the rights examined is not exhaustive, but rather focuses on the most important aspects with regards to AI-driven evidentiary proceedings.

A. The Principle of Equality of Arms and Adversary Proceedings

Procedural equality of arms is designed to

> treat the accused as a thinking and feeling human being worthy of respect, who is entitled to be given the opportunity to play an active part in procedures with a direct and possibly catastrophic impact on their life, rather than as object of state control to be manipulated for the greater good.[15]

Even though it is not a defendant's right *stricto sensu*, the principle of equality of arms has been one of the cornerstones of the criminal justice systems that are based on the rule of law under Article 6, section 1 of the ECHR. It requires that a fair balance of procedural rights is struck between the interests of the prosecution and the defence.[16]

[11] The right to a fair trial is also explicitly mentioned in Art 10 of the Universal Declaration of Human Rights proclaimed by the General Assembly of the United Nations on 10 December 1948, in Art 14 of the International Covenant on Civil and Political Rights, and among many other international conventions and national legislations.

[12] P Leanza and O Pridal, *The Right to a Fair Trial – Article 6 of the European Convention on Human Rights* (Kluwer Law International BV, 2014) 6.

[13] ibid 9.

[14] On the Convention as a 'living instrument', see *Tyrer v the United Kingdom* App no 5856/72 (ECtHR, 25 April 1978) para 31; *Soering v the United Kingdom*, App no14038/88 (ECtHR, 7 July 1989) para 102.

[15] P Roberts and A Zuckerman, *Criminal Evidence*, 2nd edn (Oxford University Press, 2010) 21.

[16] J Jackson and S Summers, *The Internationalisation of Criminal Evidence: Beyond the Common Law and Civil Law Traditions* (Cambridge University Press, 2012) 95–97. See *Faig Mammadov v Azerbaijan*, App no 60802/09 (ECtHR, 26 January 2017) para 19.

The use of AI in the criminal justice sector threatens to jeopardise this 'equal' relationship between the trial actors by giving rise to manifold power asymmetries and inequalities. According to the CoE, the traditional asymmetry of power and information between state structures and individuals is shifting towards an asymmetry of power and information between operators of algorithms, who may be public or private, and those who are acted upon and governed.[17] In the context of a criminal trial, these asymmetries concern the interaction of the defendant with the state mechanism, but also the relationship between the state and the private AI company which has developed and owns the proprietary source code used by the law enforcement and judicial authorities of the given state.

Since the use of AI is a state privilege, at least in this phase of the digital judicial transformation, the defendant needs to be equipped with such procedural rights that will preserve the equality of arms between them and the state, and the overall fairness of the trial.[18] The defendant must not be degraded to a mere spectator in the court handling their case, but rather they must be encouraged to play an active role in the process.[19] To ensure the equality of arms in this context and the right to an adversarial trial, both the prosecution and the defence must be given the opportunity to gain knowledge of and comment on the observations filed and the evidence adduced by the other party.[20] Linked to this is the need for full disclosure of all relevant evidence adduced before the court.[21] If it is legitimate to withhold some evidence, the court must ensure that other parts of the proceedings compensate for this curtailment of defence rights.[22]

[17] 'Algorithms and Human Rights – Study on the Human Rights Dimensions of Automated Data Processing Techniques and Possible Regulatory Implications' (Strasbourg, Council of Europe, 2018) 33.

[18] E Bampasika, 'Artificial Intelligence as Evidence in Criminal Trial' in G Giannakopoulos, E Galiotou and N Vassilas (eds), *Workshops of the 11th EETN Conference on Artificial Intelligence 2020*, (2020) 2844 *CEUR Workshop Proceedings* 133–38, 135, available at ceur-ws.org/Vol-2844/. See also the *Borgers v Belgium* (1999) Series A no 214-B, para 24 and the *Bulut v Austria*, Judgment of 22 February 1996, Reports 1996-II, para 47.

[19] See *Kuopila v Finland* App no 27752/95 (ECtHR, 27 July 2000) para 38, where the defence was not given an opportunity to assess the relevance and weight of the supplementary police report and to formulate any such comment as she deemed appropriate, which weighed in favour of the ECtHR's finding that the principle of equality of arms had been breached. For an extensive list about AI systems that have been or are still deployed by law enforcement and judicial authorities across the EU at the stage of prediction, prosecution, sentencing and probation, see the Fair Trials' Report 'Automating Injustice', published in September 2021, available at www.fairtrials.org/articles/publications/automating-injustice/.

[20] *Krčmář and others v the Czech Republic* App no 35376/97 (ECtHR, 3 June 2000) para 42; *Brandstetter v Austria* App nos 11170/84, 12876/87 and 13468/87 (ECtHR, 28 August 1991) para 67.

[21] *Reinhardt and Slimane Kaid v France* App nos 21/1997/805/1008 and 22/1997/806/1009 (ECHR, 31 March 1998) paras 105–107; *Rowe and Davis v United Kingdom* App no 28901/95 (ECtHR, GC, 16 February 2000) para 60. For a detailed overview of the legal implications of AI evidence to the foundations of criminal trial in general, see K Quezada-Tavárez, P Vogiatzoglou and Dr S Royer, 'Legal Challenges in Bringing AI Evidence to the Criminal Courtroom' (2021) 12 *New Journal of European Criminal Law* 4, 531–51.

[22] *Van Mechelen and Others v the Netherlands* App nos 21363/93, 21364/93, 21427/93 and 22056/93 (ECtHR, 23 April 1997) paras 54, 58, 60; *Rook v Germany* App no 1586/15 (ECtHR, 25 October 2019)

The importance of the adversarial principle in this context has also been highlighted by the CJEU, which stated that

> [i]f a court takes the view that a party is not in a position to comment effectively on evidence pertaining to a field of which the judges have no knowledge and that is likely to have a preponderant influence on the findings of fact, it must find an infringement of the right to a fair trial and exclude that evidence in order to avoid such an infringement.[23]

With regard to AI-based means of evidence, the denial of any kind of access to the source code of the AI applications used would be a breach of the principle of equality of arms[24] if no other effective safeguards can outweigh its negative effects on the defendant's position. Nevertheless, the reinforcement of other procedural rights could return the balance to the criminal trial.[25]

B. The Right to Confrontation

One major due process right that AI-based evidence may compromise is the right to confrontation. According to Article 6, section 3(d) of the ECHR, everyone charged with a criminal offence has the right to examine or have witnesses against him examined and to obtain the attendance and examination of witnesses on his behalf under the same conditions as witnesses who testify against him. Although the provision explicitly mentions only witnesses, the right to challenge evidence applies equally to all types of evidence, including expert opinions[26] and thus also AI-based means of evidence. According to the relevant ECtHR case law, every piece of evidence the conviction is based upon

para 70; *Sigurður Einarsson and others v Iceland* App no 39757/15 (ECtHR, 4 November 2019) paras 91–92.

[23] C-746/18 *HK v Prokuratuur* [2021] EU:C:2021:152, para 44.

[24] *Kartoyev and Others v Russia* App nos 9418/13, 9421/13 and 49007/13 (ECtHR, 19 October 2021) paras 71–73, where the ECtHR ruled that a failure of the prosecution to disclose the technical details on which an expert report is based may impede the possibility for the defence to challenge the expert report and thus raise an issue of equality of arms under Art 6 § 1.

[25] *Ibrahim and Others v the United Kingdom* App nos 50541/08, 50571/08, 50573/08 and 40351/09 (ECtHR, GC, 13 September 2016) para 251.

[26] *Mantovanelli v France*, App no 21497/93 (ECHR, 18 March 1997) paras 35–36. In *Matytsina v Russia* App no 58428/10 (ECtHR, 27 March 2014) para 169, the ECtHR stated especially with regard to expert opinions that under Art 6 it is normally not the Court's role to determine whether a particular expert report available to the domestic judge was reliable or not. Subject to some exceptions, the general rule is that the domestic judge has a wide discretion in choosing from conflicting expert opinions and picking one which he or she deems consistent and credible. However, the rules on admissibility of evidence may sometimes run counter to the principles of equality of arms and adversarial proceedings, or otherwise affect the fairness of the proceedings. In the context of expert evidence, the rules on its admissibility must not deprive the defence of the opportunity to challenge it effectively, in particular by introducing or obtaining alternative opinions and reports. In certain circumstances the refusal to allow an alternative expert examination of material evidence may be regarded as a breach of Art 6 § 1.

must be produced in court with the defendant present and with the view to an 'adversarial argument'.[27]

The underlying principle is that the defendant in a criminal trial should have an effective opportunity to challenge the evidence against them. Exceptions to this principle are possible for public security and witness protection reasons but must not infringe the rights of the defence, which, as a rule, require not merely that a defendant should know the identity of their accusers so that they are in a position to challenge their probity and credibility but that they should be able to test the truthfulness and reliability of their evidence, by having them orally examined in their presence, either when the witness makes the statement or at some later stage of the proceedings.[28] The same rationale should be applied in cases with robot witnesses or AI applications, where only proprietary issues are at stake.

Just like in the case of witnesses against the defendant, the latter has a right to know who is testifying against them, the 'know the identity' principle applies also in the context of AI-based means of evidence. Arguably, the source code of an AI application or robot constitutes its identity and, therefore, the defendant has a right to be given access to it, in order to be able to exercise their right to confrontation. But even if the witness (or source code) remains anonymous, there must be other safeguards in place that counterbalance the resulting disadvantages for the defence.[29] Further, the ECtHR has stated that a conviction based solely or to a decisive degree on depositions of a person whom the accused had no opportunity to examine or have examined, either during the investigation or at trial, restricts the rights of the defence to an extent that is incompatible with Article 6 ECHR.[30]

The importance of this right is further underlined when reflecting upon the dangers and challenges for the law arising from the use of deepfake technology.[31] Securing the authenticity of the AI-based means of evidence and protecting them against malicious attacks is going to be a herculean task. Just as there are

[27] *Matytsina v Russia*, ibid para 152 with further case law references.

[28] *Sievert v Germany* App no 29881/07 (ECtHR, 19 July 2012) para 58; see *Lucà v Italy* App no 33354/96 (ECtHR, 27 February 2001) para 39 and *Solakov v "the former Yugoslav Republic of Macedonia"* App no 47023/99 (ECtHR, 25 January 2001) para 57.

[29] *Windisch v Austria* App no 12489/86 (ECtHR, 27 September 1990) para 30.

[30] The ECtHR has defined the term 'decisive' in *Al-Khawaja and Tahery v the United Kingdom* App nos 26766/05 and 22228/06 (ECtHR, GC, 15 December 2011) para 131 as follows: '"Decisive" (or "déterminante") in this context means more than "probative". It further means more than that, without the evidence, the chances of a conviction would recede and the chances of an acquittal advance. […] [T]he word "decisive" should be narrowly understood as indicating evidence of such significance or importance as is likely to be determinative of the outcome of the case. Where the untested evidence of a witness is supported by other corroborative evidence, the assessment of whether it is decisive will depend on the strength of the supportive evidence; the stronger the corroborative evidence, the less likely that the evidence of the absent witness will be treated as decisive'. See also, *Schatschaschwili v Germany* App no 9154/10 (ECtHR, GC, 15 December 2015) paras 123–24.

[31] For a detailed analysis on deepfakes, see Clementina Salvi in chapter 12 of this volume.

AI systems for the generation or processing of evidence for law enforcement reasons, there are also AI systems for tampering with evidentiary material or the creation of fake evidence from scratch. Thus, finding authenticity verification methods to confront the present dangers of deepfake technology and training judicial staff, professional and lay judges with regard to deepfakes is key for the development of a minimum level of cybersecurity.

C. The Right of Access to Evidence

When it comes to an effective participation of the defendant in a criminal trial, their access to the incriminating evidence against them is an indispensable condition. It is only logical that if the defendant is not aware of the evidence collected against them, they are not in a position to defend themselves and exercise their right to confrontation. Furthermore, any difficulties encountered by the defence through the limitations of its rights must be sufficiently counterbalanced by the procedures before the national judicial authorities.[32] According to the case law of the ECtHR, all parties must be given the opportunity to gain knowledge of and comment on the evidence introduced by the other party.[33]

With regard to AI-based means of evidence, this right requires that the proprietary nature of the source code cannot act as a veil of ignorance in the sense that states are denied access to the inner workings of that source code. Otherwise, the use of proprietary AI tools by law enforcement and judicial authorities will become a factor of inequality, social fracture and exclusion, given the existing impact of the use of AI tools on the defence rights of the defendant, the difficulty in obtaining meaningful information on their functioning and the consequent difficulty in challenging their results in court.[34]

One solution according to the European Commission for the Efficiency of Justice (CEPEJ) could be the possible introduction of a certification mechanism for AI tools and services in the sphere of justice and the judiciary.[35] However, plain access to the means of evidence is of little or any significance when it comes to AI applications. What is needed is meaningful access. The latter requires an IT expert explaining the workings of the AI application, so that defence can contest the data and exercise their right to confrontation.

[32] *Jasper v the United Kingdom* App no 27052/95 (ECtHR, GC, 16 February 2000) para 52. See also *Doorson v the Netherlands* App no 20524/92 (ECtHR, 26 March 1996) para 72; *Van Mechelen and Others v the Netherlands* (n 22) paras 54, 58.

[33] See *Brandstetter v Austria* (n 19) para 67; *Jasper v the United Kingdom*, ibid para 51; *Öcalan v Turkey* App no 46221/99 (ECtHR, GC, 12 May 2005) para 146; *Matytsina v Russia* App no 58428/10 (ECtHR, 27 March 2014) para 151.

[34] CoE Study on Algorithms and Human Rights (n 17) 35.

[35] CEPEJ feasibility study (n 8).

The General Data Protection Regulation, for example, regulates the right to access to knowledge of the logic involved in any automatic processing of data concerning the subject of the personal data collected.[36] The forensic experts could play the role of the intermediary between the two sides of the trial, the adjudicators and the defendant.

Nevertheless, the danger remains that human experts will act 'as scriveners on the witness stand, regurgitating the conveyances of machines. The human testimony might create a veneer of scrutiny when in fact the actual source of information, the machine, remains largely unscrutinized'.[37]

D. The Right to the Free Assistance of an Interpreter

Closely connected to the right examined above is the right of the defendant to the free assistance of an interpreter if they cannot understand or speak the language used in the court proceedings. Article 6, section 3(e) of the ECHR stipulates that such interpretation is to be free of charge. This right is meant to support the defendant's ability to participate effectively in the proceedings, serving the equality of arms.[38]

A teleological interpretation of this right that supports the free provision of AI experts in aid of the defendant in the case of AI-driven criminal trials is in line with the Convention and the relevant EU Directive[39] and must be granted, in order for the defendant who does not speak or understand the language of the criminal proceedings to fully exercise their right of defence. Defendants must be provided with an AI expert that will serve as an interpreter for them, since it must always be possible to reduce the computations of an AI system to a form that is comprehensible to humans.[40]

Especially in cases where the court does simply employ AI-based means of evidence to demystify just one specific aspect of the trial case, while there is

[36] Art 15, Right of access by the data subject of the Regulation (EU) 2016/679 of the European Parliament and of the Council of 27 April 2016 on the protection of natural persons with regard to the processing of personal data and on the free movement of such data, and repealing Directive 95/46/EC (General Data Protection Regulation).

[37] Roth (n 1) 1979.

[38] B Weisser, 'The European Convention on Human Rights and the European Court of Human Rights as Guardians of Fair Criminal Proceedings in Europe' in DK Brown, J Iontcheva Turner and B Weisser (eds), *The Oxford Handbook of Criminal Process* (Oxford University Press, 2019) 108.

[39] Arts 2 and 3 of Directive 2010/64/EU of the European Parliament and of the Council of 20 October 2010 on the right to interpretation and translation in criminal proceedings [2010] OJ L280/1. See, also, recital (47) of the Preamble of the AI Act: To address the opacity that may make certain AI systems incomprehensible to or too complex for natural persons, a certain degree of transparency should be required for high risk AI systems. Users should be able to interpret the system output and use it appropriately. High risk AI systems should therefore be accompanied by relevant documentation and instructions of use and include concise and clear information, including in relation to possible risks to fundamental rights and discrimination, where appropriate.

[40] European Parliament Resolution (n 2).

corroborating evidence for the case facts, but where it bases the whole criminal trial on the outcome of an AI application, the right to the free assistance of an AI expert functioning as an interpreter for the defendant must be afforded. Otherwise, in the latter case, the defendant will be a mere spectator in their own trial, since they will probably not be able to understand the 'language' of the proceedings in the same way as the other human actors of the trial (judges and jury).

E. The Rules of Evidence

As already mentioned, evidence in the EU is primarily a nationally regulated matter. The difficulties in reaching an agreement as regards certain common rules on the admissibility of evidence are already familiar to the EU MS.[41] Even though according to the case law of the ECtHR, the rules of evidence do not fall explicitly under the scope of the ECHR, the Court assesses the applicant's trial as a whole in order to conclude with regards to its fairness.[42] Part of this assessment forms the rules of evidence. Nevertheless, the ECtHR is rather careful in its judgments regarding evidentiary issues, due to the numerous differences in the national rules of evidence among the Contracting States and the overarching dichotomy of the criminal justice systems as either adversarial and inquisitorial.[43] The adoption of this 'overall examination method' with regard to procedural and evidentiary questions in individual cases makes the identification of the 'common structural elements that need to be uniformly applied in the evidentiary proceedings of the Member States' based on the interpretation of the ECtHR harder.[44]

In *Van Mechelen and Others v The Netherlands*, the ECtHR reiterated that the admissibility of evidence is primarily a matter to be regulated in national law and as a general rule it is for the national courts to assess the evidence before them. The Court's task under the Convention is not to issue a ruling regarding whether statements of witnesses have been properly admitted as evidence, but rather to ascertain whether the proceedings as a whole, including the way in which evidence has been taken, were fair.[45] Some scholars and practitioners do not welcome the application of a wide margin of appreciation in criminal matters by the ECtHR, since at least for the EU, it translates

[41] On this matter, see Ligeti et al (n 4) 201–208.

[42] *Van Mechelen and Others v the Netherlands* (n 22) para 50; *Garcia Ruiz v Spain* [GC] App no 30544/96 (ECtHR, 21 January 1999) para 28.

[43] Leanza and Pridal (n 12) 182.

[44] E Billis, 'The Structure of Evidentiary Proceedings as Reflected in the Case-Law of the ECtHR on Article 6 (3) ECHR' in CD Spinellis, N Theodorakis, E Billis and G Papadimitrakopoulos (eds), *Europe in Crisis: Crime, Criminal Justice, and the Way Forward. Essays in honour of Nestor Courakis* (Ant. N. Sakkoulas Publications, 2017) Vol II, 957–78, 972.

[45] *Van Mechelen and Others v The Netherlands* (n 22) para 50; *Mantovanelli v France* (n 26) para 34.

into an increase in legislative interventions at the EU level in order to ensure a level playing field for the fairness of trials.[46]

Nevertheless, especially within the EU, where the establishment of an area of freedom, security and justice by means of the different cooperation and assistance channels requires and permits among other things the circulation of evidence without a review of procedures conducted in another MS, common safeguards in order to reduce the legal fragmentation and systemic gaps for the rights of the defence arising from this 'free movement of evidence, persons and decisions' in the criminal justice area are of extreme importance.[47] The so-called de-territorialisation of evidence as a general phenomenon due to its electronic nature calls for ensuring that the EU has broad minimum common rules at least concerning AI-based means of evidence and their admissibility.

F. The Right to a Reasoned Judgment

The final concrete aspect of the right to a fair trial to be addressed in this chapter is the right to a reasoned judgment; that is a judgment that 'adequately outlines the legal and factual basis of the decision'.[48] According to the case law of the ECtHR, it suffices if the trial court provides a sufficient reply to the foundational elements of the factual or legal claim,[49] in order to avoid arbitrary decisions.

Due to the highly complex technological nature of AI and its use as a black box, there is grave concern among legal scholars that judges will practically delegate the administration of justice to AI. If adjudicators, whether professional or lay, do not understand how AI works, but ultimately trust its outcomes with regard to fact finding, it will be impossible for them to form a reasoned judgment. This could *de facto* happen with the use of AI-based means of evidence.

Human-computer interaction research on the biases involved in all algorithmic decision-making systems has further shown that it is extremely difficult for a human decision- maker to refute a 'recommendation made by a high-tech tool'.[50] Consequently, if humans only rely on the data, profiles and

[46] V Costa Ramos, M Luchtman and G Munteanu, 'Improving Defence Rights Including Available Remedies in and (or as a Consequence of) Cross-Border Criminal Proceedings' (3) 2020 *Eucrim* 230–48, 230.

[47] ibid 240.

[48] Leanza and Pridal (n 12) 151.

[49] See *Suominen v Finland* App no 37801/97 (ECtHR, 1 July 2003) para 34; *Ruiz Torija v Spain* App no 18390/91 (ECtHR, 9 December 1994), Series A no 303-A, para 29.

[50] A Završnik, 'Criminal Justice, Artificial Intelligence Systems, and Human Rights' (2020) *ERA Forum* 20 567–83, 574. Research on the field has shown that when an AI system has anthropomorphic characteristics, then the disregard of an AI conclusion becomes even harder for the human actors. On this matter, see E Hilgendorf, 'Vom Werkzeug zum Partner? Zum Einfluss intelligenter Artefakte auf unsere sozialen Normen und die Aufgaben des Rechts' in M Engelhart,

recommendations generated by machines, they will not be able to conduct an independent assessment. This over-reliance of judicial officials on the seemingly objective and scientific nature of AI tools and possible failure to consider the possibility of their results being incorrect, incomplete, irrelevant or discriminatory, could entail adverse consequences for the delivery of justice and the way a criminal justice system based on the rule of law operates in general.

However, the European Parliament keeps underlining the fact that many algorithmically driven identification technologies currently in use disproportionately misidentify and misclassify and therefore cause harm to racialised people, individuals belonging to certain ethnic communities, LGBTI people, children and the elderly, as well as women.[51] The false aura of infallibility around AI technology could further potentially lead criminal justice systems to the actual delegation of cases to the AI. AI-based means of evidence would then function as a *de facto* form of prohibited automated individual decision-making.[52] If AI applications used as a means of evidence could affect the reasoning of the adjudicators of a case so gravely that the latter would unreflectively adopt whatever the AI evidentiary outcome, then the criminal justice systems need to be aware of this possible judgmental 'atrophy' of the adjudicators and safeguard the judges' leading role in criminal proceedings.

Therefore, the justification of a court's decisions[53] and the imposition of strict requirements on verdicts based on AI-based means of evidence that will have to explain how machine-generated data was evaluated against human statements in order to justify an acquittal or conviction could serve as safety valves against the aforementioned dangers. After all, that is exactly the function of judicial reasoning; to explain and justify against further control how the court reached its decision based on the evidence available. To put it simply, to prove is to explain, which in reverse means that without an explanation, that is a reasoned judgment, there is no proof.[54] Given the intersubjective nature of the

H Kudlich und B Vogel, *Digitalisierung, Globalisierung und Risikoprävention Festschrift für Ulrich Sieber zum 70. Geburtstag* (Duncker & Humblot, 2021) 767–78.

[51] Under 9. of the European Parliament Resolution (n 2).

[52] At least according to the *prima facie* wording of Art 11 of the Law Enforcement Directive (Dir (EU) 2016/680 of the European Parliament and of the Council of 27 April 2016 on the protection of natural persons with regard to the processing of personal data by competent authorities for the purposes of the prevention, investigation, detection or prosecution of criminal offences or the execution of criminal penalties, and on the free movement of such data, and repealing Council Framework Decision 2008/977/JHA) [2016] OJ L119/89.

[53] According to the European Court of Justice in *Heylens*, the principle of effective judicial protection requires that national authorities give reasons for their decisions so that the persons concerned are able to defend their rights under the best possible circumstances; Judgment of 15 October 1987, C-222/86 *Heylens* EU:C:1987:442 para 15. In general, on Art 47 of the Charter, see A Ward 'Article 47 – Right to an Effective Remedy and to a Fair Trial' in S Peers, T Hervey, J Kenner and A Ward (eds), *The EU Charter of Fundamental Rights* 2nd edn (C.H.BECK, Hart Publishing, Oxford & Nomos Publishing House, 2021) 1245–383.

[54] N Androulakis, 'I poiniki apodeixi os aitiologia kai i oloklirosi tis' (5) 2014 *NOMIKO VIMA* 1089–103 (in Greek) 1090.

proof, the latter exists only when its recipient, in our case the defendant, understands the reasoning of the trial judge.[55] Therefore, a judicial decision merely echoing the outcome of AI-driven evidentiary proceedings would violate the right to a reasoned judgment.

G. The AI Act

Recently, the long-awaited AI Act[56] that constitutes a major milestone towards the direction of developing AI that respects fundamental rights was adopted. It presents a good example of harmonisation in a very technical and complicated domain, setting the first boundaries and safeguards of AI-systems within the context of criminal justice. However, it should be noted that it leaves the door open to some – otherwise deemed by its very text as prohibited – AI systems when deployed for law enforcement or criminal justice purposes,[57] exposing the defendants to possible dangers for their procedural rights. For example, the general prohibition of risk assessment AI systems to assess or predict the risk of a natural person committing a criminal offence, based solely on their profiling or on assessing their personality traits and characteristics, does not apply to AI systems used to support the human assessment of the involvement of a person in a criminal activity, if that assessment is already based on objective and verifiable facts directly linked to a criminal activity (Article 5, para 1(d)). Another example is the only prima facie prohibition of the 'real-time' remote biometric identification systems in publicly accessible spaces for the purposes of law enforcement (Article 5, para 1(h) of the AI Act) that is followed by a list of exceptions where it could actually be used. Further, Annex III of the Regulation contains an amendable and non-exhaustive list of high-risk AI systems[58] that need to comply with stricter legal and technical requirements,[59] among which

[55] ibid 1093 ff. Due to the limited space, a further analysis on this matter and the differences between the inquisitorial and adversarial legal systems with regard to the justification of the judicial decisions cannot be included.

[56] AI Act (n 6).

[57] ibid Art 5.

[58] Already listed as high risk in Annex III, under point 6. are AI-systems '- in so far as their use is permitted under relevant Union or national law – intended to be used by or on behalf of law enforcement authorities, or by Union institutions, bodies, offices or agencies in support of law enforcement authorities or on their behalf (a) to assess the risk of a natural person becoming the victim of criminal offences; (b) as polygraphs or similar tools; (c) to evaluate the reliability of evidence in the course of the investigation or prosecution of criminal offences; (d) for assessing the risk of a natural person offending or re-offending not solely on the basis of the profiling of natural persons as referred to in Article 3(4) of Directive (EU) 2016/680, or to assess personality traits and characteristics or past criminal behaviour of natural persons or groups; (e) for the profiling of natural persons as referred to in Article 3(4) of Directive (EU) 2016/680 in the course of the detection, investigation or prosecution of criminal offences.'

[59] Eg AI Act (n 6) Art 9 (risk management system), Art 10 (data and data governance), Art 11 (technical documentation), Art 12 (record keeping), Art 13 (transparency and provision of information to deployers), Art 14 (human oversight), and Art 15 (accuracy, robustness and cybersecurity).

also AI systems for the evaluation of the reliability of evidence in the course of the investigation or prosecution of criminal offences. Article 27(1) regulates though the obligation for deployers that are bodies governed by public law, or private entities providing public services of performing a fundamental rights impact assessment for high-risk AI systems prior to deploying a system referred to in Article 6(2). Thus, while the AI Act marks a critical step forward, it is clear that when it comes to criminal justice and law enforcement, the conversation among legislators, policymakers and stakeholders is only just beginning, and the real challenge lies in ensuring that the current and future AI regulatory choices will uphold the same level of protection for the defendant's rights.

III. CONCLUSION

One underlying conclusion can be drawn from the analysis above. Even though rules regarding evidence are primarily a matter of national regulation, the use of AI technology in evidentiary proceedings has such an effect on the fairness of the criminal trial as a whole that EU-coordinated regulatory action is required. A possible creation of AI-driven criminal justice 'paradises', patterned after the tax havens or money-laundering hubs, where the lack of regulation and oversight could affect the level of protection of the defendant's rights in criminal justice systems across the world and lead to grave injustices in general must be avoided.[60]

Therefore, a set of international guiding governance principles on AI as a means of evidence in criminal trials could be a first step in this direction. After all, the ECHR and the EU show that international cooperation among states[61] with differing procedural systems is possible albeit not perfect. Furthermore, the legal analysis and processing on AI matters is not in its infancy anymore. The AI Act showed that it is possible for a fully-fledged piece of legislation to be adopted, even though regulators and policymakers around the world are still getting acquainted with AI technology, its advantages and disadvantages.

However, using the existing regulatory texts in order to build on them, either by reinterpreting them or by introducing piecemeal legislation when

[60] See, also, Ramos et al (n 46) 236, who underline the danger of forum shopping by the prosecuting authorities depending on which rights of the accused are granted in a given case.

[61] The latest example is the Council of Europe Framework Convention on Artificial Intelligence and Human Rights, Democracy, and the Rule of Law (CETS No 225), which constitutes the first legally binding international agreement on AI and was signed by the European Commission for the EU, Andorra, Georgia, Iceland, Norway, the Republic of Moldova, San Marino, the UK as well as Israel, and the USA, available at www.coe.int/en/web/conventions/full-list?module=treaty-detail&treatynum=225.

actually needed,[62] while letting the AI evolve, could be a solution. This is also the path to follow as regards AI-based means of evidence and the defendant's rights. The ECHR and consequently the CFR can already provide minimum protection when it comes to AI evidence, if interpreted, as did the Court of Strasbourg already many years ago, 'as a living instrument in the light of present-day conditions',[63] paving the way for more clear-headed, targeted legislative interventions at the EU and international levels.

[62] See CEPEJ European Ethical Charter on the use of artificial intelligence (AI) in judicial systems and their environment, Council of Europe Convention on the Protection of Personal Data; The European Committee on Legal Co-operation (CDCJ) is preparing guidelines to ensure the compatibility of these mechanisms with Articles 6 and 13 of the Convention on Human Rights; The European Committee on Crime Problems (CDPC) is currently studying the topic of AI and criminal law and may propose the creation of a new specialised legal instrument. Relevant for the analysis are also the Council of Europe Convention for the Protection of Individuals with regard to Automatic Processing of Personal Data (ETS 108), and its amending protocol (Convention 108+).

[63] *Tyrer* (n 14); Ramos et al (n 46) 243, express the opinion that the ECHR system may not be sufficient in order to achieve a common European justice era when it comes to defence rights, calling for EU multilevel legislative action.

16

Transborder Access to e-Evidence – Data Protection Concerns under the e-Evidence Regulation

TERESA QUINTEL* AND MARK D COLE**

I. INTRODUCTION

AS COMMUNICATION NOWADAYS commonly takes place via electronic means and online, the use of electronic evidence (e-evidence) has become a crucial element in criminal investigations. Due to the borderless nature of the Internet, a substantial number of criminal investigations that take place in the 'offline world' include a cross-border dimension and commonly require access to electronic data and evidence that is stored outside the territorial jurisdiction of the investigating authority.

Since these data are typically held by private companies that are often located in a different country than the investigator, law enforcement authorities (LEAs) are either dependent on the willingness of these service providers to cooperate on a voluntary basis in order to have the data available for investigations, or resort to existing legal procedures. The relevant procedures to access data stored outside the European Union (EU) under the framework applicable so far is based on so-called Mutual Legal Assistance Treaties (MLATs), whereas judicial cooperation within the EU is governed by the Directive on the European Investigation Order (EIO)[1] in the form of the national transposition acts. The latter aimed to render cross-border investigations across the EU faster and more efficient by

* Dr Teresa Quintel is an Administrator for the European Parliament Committee on Civil Liberties, Justice and Home Affairs. This chapter expresses only the personal opinion of the author and not of the European Parliament.

** Mark D Cole is Professor for Media and Telecommunication Law at the Faculty of Law, Economics and Finance of the University of Luxembourg and Director for Academic Affairs at the Institute of European Media Law (EMR) in Saarbrücken.

[1] Directive 2014/41/EU of the European Parliament and of the Council of 3 April 2014 regarding the European Investigation Order ('EIO Directive') [2014] OJ L130/1.

using several investigative measures with a view to gathering evidence on the basis of mutual recognition.[2] MLATs, on the other hand, provide for domestic judicial review in both the requesting and the receiving state. This is one of the reasons why the MLAT procedure is said to imply practical challenges, which have to do with a bemoaned slowness owed to the mandatory involvement of different judicial authorities, an alleged systemic inefficiency and legal uncertainty within the prevailing MLAT regime. Although the procedure under the EIO within the framework of mutual recognition is significantly faster, similar criticism exists with regard to the duration to gather e-evidence.

Since e-evidence is, due to its volatile nature, prone to modification and deletion, a timely acquisition of the data stored by private actors is vital for LEAs. Therefore, informal cooperation between LEAs and relevant private companies became a common method to obtain e-evidence, thereby bypassing the Mutual Legal Assistance (MLA) mechanisms. Thus, whereas under MLATs a request for access to data would be sent by a judicial authority in the requesting state to a judicial authority in the receiving state to be then dealt with vis-à-vis the concerned service provider, direct cooperation often entails the issuing of a domestic investigative measure by a LEA directly to a (foreign) service provider. Such informal cooperation between LEAs and foreign service providers has progressively become an important channel to obtain (primarily) non-content[3] data.[4]

The tendency of state authorities to more proactively assert jurisdiction beyond their national borders in cyberspace, thereby bypassing the more time-consuming MLA procedures, implied that particularly service providers were increasingly confronted with conflict of laws concerns when they were required to decide whether or not to comply with requests.[5] From the service provider's perspective, the orientation away from the legal framework of the country with traditional jurisdiction – typically the state of the provider's establishment – and data protection concerns under that legal regime led to an understandable hesitation to comply with such requests on an informal level. Nevertheless, direct cooperation between law enforcement and private companies, which is commonly carried out on a unilateral basis, has led to a fragmented framework,

[2] It replaced the system of letters rogatory, where companies would provide user information in response to domestic legal processes, requested by foreign judicial authorities on behalf of foreign law enforcement authorities.

[3] Such as access data, subscriber data or types of metadata.

[4] G Robinson, 'Report: The European Commission's e-Evidence Proposal' (European Data Protection Law Review (EDPL), May 2018) 4, 3, 347–52; V Franssen, 'The European Commission's E-Evidence Proposal: Towards an EU-Wide Obligation for Service Providers to Cooperate with Law Enforcement?' (*European Law Blog*, 12 October 2018), available at https://www.europeanlawblog.eu/pub/the-european-commissions-e-evidence-proposal-toward-an-eu-wide-obligation-for-service-providers-to-cooperate-with-law-enforcement/release/1.

[5] C Bartolini, C Santos and C Ullrich, 'Property and the Cloud' (2017) *Computer Law & Security Review: The International Journal of Technology Law and Practice* 23, available at doi: 10.1016/j.clsr.2017.10.005.

inter alia, due to differences in the types of data requested, divergent procedures for submitting requests, unreliable outcomes and unpredictable response times.[6]

Against this background, the European Commission (Commission), on 17 April 2018, proposed new rules on access to e-evidence,[7] to secure and obtain e-evidence more quickly and effectively and to ensure that all providers that offer services in the Union are subject to the same obligations.[8] The proposal included a Regulation[9] and a Directive[10] to develop a common framework for cooperation with service providers for the purposes of obtaining specific categories of data and to improve legal certainty and clarity. In December 2022, the Council and the European Parliament agreed on a final compromise text on the so-called e-Evidence proposals and on 25 January 2023, the Council confirmed the agreement on the e-Evidence Regulation[11] and accompanying Directive,[12,13] with an entry into force date of 17 August 2023, applicability as of August 2026 and transposition requirement as of February 2026.[14]

[6] European Commission, 'Non-Paper: Progress Report following the Conclusions of the Council of the European Union on Improving Criminal Justice in Cyberspace' ('Commission Non-Paper 1'), available via Council of the European Union, doc 15072/1/16 REV (7 December 2016), para 1.2.1, available at https://data.consilium.europa.eu/doc/document/ST-15072-2016-REV-1/en/pdf.

[7] Proposal for a Regulation of the European Parliament and of the Council on European Production and Preservation Orders for electronic evidence in criminal matters COM(2018) 225 final (Strasbourg, 17 April 2018) ('e-Evidence Proposal'). The proposal defines e-evidence as evidence stored in electronic form by or on behalf of a service provider at the time of receipt of a production or preservation order certificate, consisting in stored subscriber data, access data, transactional data and content data.

[8] European Commission, 'Migration and Home Affairs', available at https://home-affairs.ec.europa.eu/policies/internal-security/cybercrime/e-evidence_en#:~:text=The%20European%20Production%20Order%20will,representative%2C%20in%20another%20EU%20country. See for an overview Robinson (n 4).

[9] e-Evidence Proposal (n 7).

[10] Proposal for a Directive of the European Parliament and of the Council laying down harmonised rules on the appointment of legal representatives for the purpose of gathering evidence in criminal proceedings, COM(2018) 226 final (Strasbourg, 17 April 2018).

[11] Regulation (EU) 2023/1543 of the European Parliament and of the Council of 12 July 2023 on European Production Orders and European Preservation Orders for electronic evidence in criminal proceedings and for the execution of custodial sentences following criminal proceedings [2023] OJ L191/118 ('e-Evidence Regulation').

[12] Directive (EU) 2023/1544 of the European Parliament and of the Council of 12 July 2023 laying down harmonised rules on the designation of designated establishments and the appointment of legal representatives for the purpose of gathering electronic evidence in criminal proceedings [2023] OJ L191/181 ('e-Evidence Directive').

[13] Council of the EU, 'Electronic Evidence: Council Confirms Agreement with the European Parliament on New Rules to Improve Cross-Border Access to e-Evidence' (25 January 2023), available at www.consilium.europa.eu/en/press/press-releases/2023/01/25/electronic-evidence-council-confirms-agreement-with-the-european-parliament-on-new-rules-to-improve-cross-border-access-to-e-evidence/. The respective votes on the final compromise text were at first reading in Parliament on 13 June 2023 and by the Council on 27 June 2023. For an overview of both instruments, see S Tosza, 'The E-Evidence Package is Adopted: End of a Saga or Beginning of a New One?' (2023) 9(4) *European Data Protection Law Review* 163–72.

[14] Transposition date of 18 February for the Directive (Art 7 (1)) and applicability from 18 August 2026 for the Regulation (Art 34 (2)), see also: European Commission, 'E-evidence – Cross-Border Access to Electronic Evidence Improving Cross-Border Access to Electronic

Meanwhile, similar developments concerning the adoption of legislative acts or other instruments regarding law enforcement access to data stored by private companies took place elsewhere. Exemplary for the area of Europe (and also beyond), the developments within the Council of Europe (CoE) should be mentioned and, because of the high relevance as far as IT companies are concerned, on an international level especially the United States of America (US). While in the US, the so-called Clarifying Lawful Overseas Use of Data Act (CLOUD Act) already entered into force in 2018 to enable US authorities to directly access data held by US IT companies. At CoE level, an additional Protocol to the Cybercrime Convention to improve cross-border access to e-evidence to be used in criminal proceedings[15] was opened for signature in May 2022.[16] These legislative measures will be assessed by this contribution concurrently with the e-Evidence Regulation, as all of them cover the same matter and exist in parallel. Hence, it is no longer possible to evaluate one of the measures in isolation, since individuals could be subject to orders under each of them at once.

This contribution will address concerns regarding the role of private companies as the 'extended arm' of LEAs and discuss the impact of the updated framework on access to e-evidence with regard to EU data protection standards.

Section II will briefly describe the traditional procedures for cross-border access to e-evidence while, section III will illustrate the main data protection concerns related to the solutions that were found at the level of the CoE (section III.A) as well as across the Atlantic in the US. (section III.B). Section IV will present the e-Evidence Regulation and accompanying Directive that were adopted at the EU level in order to ensure improved access to electronic evidence. While the Regulation touches upon additional fundamental rights, the discussion in this contribution will specifically focus on data protection concerns (section V). The Conclusion will provide a summary concerning the three different frameworks.

II. THE EU SYSTEM: FROM MUTUAL LEGAL ASSISTANCE TO MUTUAL RECOGNITION

Traditionally, MLA refers to a mechanism that facilitates cooperation between states for the purposes of gathering and exchanging information when investigating crimes. Such cooperation commonly serves to assist in the investigation

Evidence', available at https://commission.europa.eu/law/cross-border-cases/judicial-cooperation/types-judicial-cooperation/e-evidence-cross-border-access-electronic-evidence_en.

[15] Second Additional Protocol to the Convention on Cybercrime on enhanced co-operation and disclosure of electronic evidence, CETS No 224, Strasbourg, 12 May 2022 (Treaty open for signature by the States Parties to Treaty ETS 185).

[16] See: Council of Europe: 'Second Additional Protocol to the Cybercrime Convention on Enhanced Co-Operation and Disclosure of Electronic Evidence (CETS No 224)', available at www.coe.int/en/web/cybercrime/second-additional-protocol.

or prosecution of criminal offences with a cross-border dimension. Under MLA procedures, competent state authorities may request from another competent (foreign) state authority legal assistance by submitting a judicial decision that may be verified by the receiving authority, which will then decide whether or not to comply with the request.[17]

In the EU, cooperation in criminal matters was mainly developed with the introduction of the Schengen Area, but progressively replaced by mutual recognition instruments.[18] The principle of mutual legal assistance and, in the EU, the principle of mutual recognition goes hand in hand with mutual trust between the Member States. Moreover, mutual recognition requires a minimum harmonisation of national laws, meaning that a criminal offence in one Member State must also constitute a criminal offence in the other Member States.[19] Likewise, for MLA, the approximation of national criminal procedural laws is a prerequisite in order to prevent conflicts regarding minimum standards.

The first European treaty on mutual legal assistance was the CoE's European Convention on Mutual Assistance in Criminal Matters, which was concluded on 20 April 1959.[20] This Convention was supplemented with a Protocol of 17 March 1978[21] and a second Protocol of 8 November 2001.[22] The CoE is a separate international organisation from the EU and has 46 Member States, but allows for some of its Conventions – which are open for signature to states and sometimes international organisations – to be signed and ratified by non-Member States. This permits the reach of CoE instruments to go well beyond the geographical limits of Europe. Yet, it needs to be noted that the CoE works purely on the basis of public international law treaties, which do not enable it to implement 'law' by supranational force directly on the states bound by its treaties.

The most relevant CoE Convention is the European Convention on Human Rights (ECHR), which, in its Article 8, enshrines the rights to respect for private and family life. While for the ECHR, individuals may take complaints against states based on violations of Convention provisions to the European Court of

[17] See, for instance: RJ Currie, 'Human Rights and International Mutual Legal Assistance: Resolving the Tension' (2000) 11 *Criminal Law Forum* 143.

[18] European Commission, 'Mutual Legal Assistance and Extradition', available at https://commission.europa.eu/law/cross-border-cases/judicial-cooperation/types-judicial-cooperation/mutual-legal-assistance-and-extradition_en.

[19] K Lenaerts, 'The Principle of Mutual Recognition in the Area of Freedom, Security and Justice' (2015) Il *Diritto dell'Unione Europea* (3)2015.

[20] European Convention on Mutual Assistance in Criminal Matters, ETS No 030, Strasbourg, 20 April 1959.

[21] Additional Protocol to the European Convention on Mutual Assistance in Criminal Matters, ETS No 099, Strasbourg, 17 March 1978, available at www.conventions.coe.int/Treaty/Commun/ChercheSig.asp?NT=099&CM=8&DF=24/08/2014&CL=ENG).

[22] Second Additional Protocol to the European Convention on Mutual Assistance in Criminal Matters, ETS No 182, Strasbourg 8 November 2001, available at www.conventions.coe.int/Treaty/Commun/ChercheSig.asp?NT=182&CM=8&DF=24/08/2014&CL=ENG) (hereafter 'ETS No 182').

Human Rights (ECtHR) in Strasbourg, the jurisdiction of that Court is limited to the ECHR and does not cover any of the CoE instruments mentioned in this contribution.

For the EU (respectively the previous European Community, EC), the establishment of the internal market in 1992 and the abolishment of the national borders within the Schengen Area in 1995[23] marked the beginning of closer cooperation in criminal matters among the EU Member States. In that context, the Maastricht Treaty had led to the creation of the so-called 'Third Pillar', giving the EU limited competences to legislate in the area of certain criminal matters.[24] This pillar was in those days of an intergovernmental nature and had to rely on full support by all Member States. Eventually, with the entry into force of the Treaty of Lisbon in 2009, the Third Pillar was fully integrated into the only remaining pillar of the EU, now being part of the supranational fields of action.[25]

The EU Convention on Mutual Assistance in Criminal Matters between the Member States of the European Union,[26] established by Council Act of 29 May 2000 in accordance with Article 34 of the Treaty on European Union (TEU) was the first MLA instrument at the EU level. Supplementing the provisions of the CoE and its 1978 Additional Protocol, the EU MLA Convention's aim was to facilitate the application of those legal instruments, without affecting more favourable provisions in bilateral or multilateral agreements between the Member States.[27] Unlike previous international MLA agreements, the EU MLA Convention contains explicit provisions on the interception of telecommunications.[28]

Council Framework Decision 2008/978/JHA[29] of 18 December 2008 established the European Evidence Warrant (EEW) for the purposes of obtaining objects, documents and data to be used in proceedings in criminal matters to

[23] European Commission, 'Schengen Area', available at https://ec.europa.eu/home-affairs/what-we-do/policies/borders-and-visas/schengen_en.

[24] S Glaser, A Motz and F Zimmermann, 'Mutual Recognition and its Implications for the Gathering of Evidence in Criminal Proceedings: A Critical Analysis of the Initiative for a European Investigation Order' (THEMIS, 2010).

[25] European Parliament, 'The Treaty of Lisbon', available at www.europarl.europa.eu/factsheets/en/sheet/5/the-treaty-of-lisbon#:~:text=The%20Treaty%20of%20Lisbon%20completes,matters%2C%20into%20the%20first%20pillar.

[26] Council Act of 29 May 2000 establishing in accordance with Article 34 of the Treaty on European Union the Convention on Mutual Assistance in Criminal Matters between the Member States of the European Union [2000] OJ C197/1 ('EU MLA Convention'). This Convention was supplemented with a Protocol on 16 October 2001: (2001) OJ 326/2.

[27] ibid Art 1. The EU MLA Convention also supplements and repeals certain provisions on mutual assistance in criminal matters of the Convention of 19 June 1990 implementing the Schengen Agreement of 14 June 1985 (Arts 1 and 2(2) of the EU MLA Convention).

[28] ibid Arts 17 to 22 of the EU MLA Convention.

[29] Council Framework Decision 2008/978/JHA of 18 December 2008 on the European evidence warrant for the purpose of obtaining objects, documents and data for use in proceedings in criminal matters [2008] OJ L350/72 ('Framework Decision on the EEW').

further enhance mutual assistance in the field of gathering evidence. The EEW supplemented a Framework Decision from 2003 on the execution of orders freezing property or evidence in the EU,[30] which had been the first instrument that implemented the principle of mutual recognition in the field of obtaining evidence.[31]

As mentioned above, the principle of mutual recognition builds on mutual trust between the Member States, meaning that judicial decisions from one Member State shall be recognised in another Member State. Thus, under those instruments, legality, necessity and proportionality of a request are verified by the authorities in the requesting Member State and do not have to pass additional procedures of recognition in the receiving Member State.[32] In 2009, the Lisbon Treaty codified the principle of mutual recognition under Articles 67 (3) and 82 Treaty on the Functioning of the European Union (TFEU), the latter granting the European Parliament (EP) and the Council of the European Union (Council) the power to adopt legislative acts to facilitate mutual recognition of judgments and judicial decisions under paragraph 2.

Based on Article 82(1)(a) TFEU, Directive 2014/41/EU of 3 April 2014 regarding the European Investigation Order in criminal matters (EIO Directive)[33] implemented the principle of mutual recognition, aiming to facilitate the gathering and transmission of evidence in criminal matters between the EU Member States. The EIO replaced the EEW by adding certain provisions and expanding its scope while maintaining some of the rules of the Framework Decision. Covering the entire process from the freezing of evidence to the transfer of existing data, the EIO's main objective is to reduce the level of fragmentation for the gathering of evidence and to establish a more coherent instrument that is applicable to additional types of evidence.[34] Moreover, it set stricter deadlines to accept and answer requests, it limited grounds for refusal of requests, and introduced a standard format to submit requests to overcome language barriers.[35] Being technology neutral, the EIO Directive does not specifically refer to 'electronic' or 'digital' evidence. Hence, e-evidence is included within the scope of the EIO. Thereby, the EIO marked a further step away from the MLA mechanism towards cooperation based on mutual recognition in obtaining evidence. Yet, the arguably most important Member State when it comes to access to e-evidence

[30] Council Framework Decision 2003/577/JHA of 22 July 2003 on the execution in the European Union of orders freezing property or evidence [2003] OJ L196/45.

[31] Glaser, Motz and Zimmermann (n 24) 7.

[32] Lenaerts (n 19).

[33] EIO Directive (n 1).

[34] L Bachmaier Winter, 'European Investigation Order for Obtaining Evidence in the Criminal Proceedings. Study of the Proposal for a European Directive' (2010) *Zeitschrift für Internationale Strafrechtsdogmatik*9, 581.

[35] European Commission Press Release, 'As of Today the "European Investigation Order" Will Help Authorities to Fight Crime and Terrorism' (22 May 2017), available at https://ec.europa.eu/commission/presscorner/detail/en/IP_17_1388.

held by private service providers, Ireland, where most non-EU IT companies are established – chose to opt out of the EIO.

III. CROSS-BORDER ACCESS TO DATA AT THE INTERNATIONAL LEVEL

The concept of authorising access to data across borders has been discussed and developed not only within the EU but also elsewhere at the international level. An early form of cooperation concerning 'internet-enabled crime', then so-called 'cybercrime', was the still highly relevant 'Budapest Convention' (or Cybercrime Convention) of the CoE: The Convention on Cybercrime of 23 November 2001 and its Additional Protocol[36] concerning specific forms of online crimes such as the dissemination of incitement to hatred. Discussions at the level of the CoE to supplement the Convention with a Second Additional Protocol concerning cross-border access to electronic evidence started before the e-evidence proposal of the Commission was published. Contrary to the predictions of many, these discussions were finalised before the agreement on the final version of the proposed EU Regulation and accompanying Directive was reached and the Second Additional Protocol[37] was opened for signature already in May 2022.

Below, the main elements of the Cybercrime Convention and its Second Additional Protocol will be assessed in terms of data protection concerns. In addition, the legislative measures that took place in the US already prior to those in Europe will be discussed, as they are relevant not only because major US IT companies storing data concerning (European) customers on EU territory have been requested to hand over such data to US LEAs, but also because the developments at different levels are interwoven and need to be assessed jointly.

A. The Situation in Europe Apart from the European Union: Council of Europe

i. The CoE Cybercrime Convention

The CoE's Budapest Convention on Cybercrime has been open for signature since 2001 and entered into force in July 2004.[38] By March 2023, 91 states had

[36] Convention on Cybercrime, ETS No 185, Budapest, 23 November 2001; Additional Protocol to the Convention on Cybercrime, concerning the criminalisation of acts of a racist and xenophobic nature committed through computer systems, ETS No 189, Strasbourg, 28 January 2003.

[37] Second Additional Protocol to the Convention on Cybercrime on enhanced co-operation and disclosure of electronic evidence, CETS No 224, Strasbourg, 12 May 2022.

[38] See: P de Hert, C Parlar and J Sajfert, 'The Cybercrime Convention Committee's 2017 Guidance Note on Production Orders: Unilateralist Transborder Access to Electronic Evidence Promoted via Soft Law' (2018) *Computer Law & Security Review* 2. For current ratification overview, see www.coe.int/en/web/conventions/full-list?module=signatures-by-treaty&treatynum=185.

signed it or were invited to accede, out of which 69 had become parties to the Convention.[39] With the exception of Ireland,[40] the Cybercrime Convention has been ratified by all EU Member States.

Dealing with internet-enabled crimes, the Convention establishes international mechanisms for cooperation against cybercrime[41] and obliges its members to set up procedures to acquire e-evidence within an MLA framework.[42] In that context, parties to the Convention are required to introduce production orders and preservation orders, the former in order to either obtain data from service providers in their territory or subscriber data from service providers offering services in their territory, the latter in cases where there are grounds to believe that data is particularly prone to modification or deletion.[43] Due to the challenges to enforce national production orders outside the territorial reach of parties to the Convention, additional measures regarding cross-border access to e-evidence were negotiated in the framework of the Second Additional Protocol, which will be discussed below.[44]

ii. The Second Additional Protocol, New Safeguards and Related Data Protection Concerns

The Second Additional Protocol to the Cybercrime Convention was adopted in November 2021 and opened for signature on 12 May 2022. It introduced new

[39] A total of 22 countries have observer status. See: 'Parties/Observers to the Budapest Convention and Observer Organisations to the T-CY' (Council of Europe, 2023), available at www.coe.int/en/web/cybercrime/parties-observers.

[40] Ireland is one of the observer countries to the Budapest Convention.

[41] In the 2013 Cybersecurity Strategy of the European Union, the Budapest Convention was recognised as the main multilateral framework for the fight against cybercrime – Joint Communication of the Commission and the High Representative of the European Union for Foreign Affairs and Security Policy on a Cybersecurity Strategy of the European Union: An Open, Safe and Secure Cyberspace, JOIN(2013) 1 final. e-Evidence Proposal (n 7) 4.

[42] Article 32 of the Convention addresses international cooperation, in particular mutual assistance regarding investigative powers. The Article deals with unilateral trans-border searches where data are publicly available (Article 32.a. on trans-border access to publicly available (open source) stored computer data) or where data are disclosed on a voluntary basis (Article 32.b. on trans-border access with consent), see: de Hert, Parlar and Sajfert (n 38) 3.

[43] Article 18 of the Cybercrime Convention stipulates that parties to the Convention shall adopt measures to empower their competent authorities to issue production orders either against a person (Article 18.1.a.) or against a service provider offering its services in the territory of the party (Article 18.1.b.). With regard to a person in the territory of the party, the Explanatory Report states that a person would have to provide 'specified computer data' stored in a computer system, or data storage medium that is in that person's possession or control. According to the Explanatory Report, Article 18.1.b. requires a service provider offering services in the territory of the issuing Party to 'submit subscriber information in the service provider's possession or control'. The subscriber information must be related to the services offered in the territory of the Party and may either be in the service provider's physical possession, or remotely stored, but under the provider's control.

[44] See also Cybercrime Convention Committee (T-CY), 'Preparation of a 2nd Additional Protocol to the Budapest Convention on Cybercrime, Discussion Guide for Consultations with Civil Society, Data Protection Authorities and Industry', T-CY (2018)16, Strasbourg, 21 May 2018, 3.

provisions on the expedited production of subscriber information[45] and traffic data,[46] disclosure of stored computer data in an emergency based on a concept similar to that of mutual recognition,[47] emergency MLA mechanisms,[48] the possibility to permit testimony and statements to be taken from a witness or expert by video conference[49] and an option to set up international joint investigation teams.[50]

Most importantly for the discussion of this contribution, in its Chapter 2, the Additional Protocol introduces new tools for direct cooperation between the competent authorities in one party to the Convention/Second Additional Protocol and a service provider established in the territory of another party. Article 7 of the Protocol allows for the disclosure of subscriber information by a service provider directly to a LEA requesting the disclosure of specified, stored subscriber information in that service provider's possession or control. In a nutshell, the LEA of one party to the Convention and its Additional Protocol may issue an order for the disclosure of subscriber data to a service provider in another state party to the Convention, while the person whose data are requested does not need to be on the territory of either of the parties. Parties to the Convention may decide whether requests may only be sent after obtaining prior authorisation by prosecutors, judges or other independent authorities.[51]

While for orders under Article 7 of the Additional Protocol, the state authority issuing an order will not have to use the mutual legal assistance process when requesting subscriber data from a service provider in another party to the Convention, requests for other types of data such as traffic data or content data still require government-to-government cooperation. In addition, the Protocol only allows the disclosure of *specified* and *stored* subscriber data where the information is needed for *specific* criminal proceedings and investigations.

[45] For the purpose of Production Orders under Article 18 of the Cybercrime Convention, paragraph 3 of that Article defines the term 'subscriber information' as 'any information contained in the form of computer data or any other form that is held by a service provider, relating to subscribers of its services other than traffic or content data and by which can be established: a the type of communication service used, the technical provisions taken thereto and the period of service; b the subscriber's identity, postal or geographic address, telephone and other access number, billing and payment information, available on the basis of the service agreement or arrangement; c any other information on the site of the installation of communication equipment, available on the basis of the service agreement or arrangement'.

[46] Article 8 Second Additional Protocol to the Convention on Cybercrime on enhanced co-operation and disclosure of electronic evidence, CETS No 224, Strasbourg, 12 May 2022. Under Article 1 of the Cybercrime Convention, 'traffic data' means any computer data relating to a communication by means of a computer system, generated by a computer system that formed a part in the chain of communication, indicating the communication's origin, destination, route, time, date, size, duration, or type of underlying service.

[47] CETS 224, ibid, Art 9.

[48] ibid Art 10.

[49] ibid Art 11.

[50] ibid Art 12.

[51] ibid Art 7.2.b.

Under its Article 14, the Second Additional Protocol introduces new provisions on data protection safeguards. Those measures include limitations on the use of the data to purposes described in the Protocol, safeguards for sensitive data, data retention requirements, restrictions on automated decisions, requirements for data security measures, access and rectification, limitations on onwards transfers, and requirements to have in place judicial and non-judicial remedies to provide redress for violations of that provision.

An additional safeguard is the possibility for a party to the Protocol to suspend transfers of personal data to another party.[52] However, the suspension of transfers is to be used only as a final measure. This means that such suspension is permitted only if there is a systematic or material breach of data protection obligations, and where the party suspending the transfer can provide substantial evidence of such systematic and material breach that poses a significant and imminent risk to life or safety of a person.[53] In such a case, the party suspending the transfer must engage in a consultation process with the other party while the personal data transferred before the suspension shall continue to be processed in accordance with the Convention. The Explanatory Report specifies that a systematic breach could mean, for example, 'frequently recurring violations of the data protection safeguards', while a failure to apply certain safeguards in relation to the processing of personal data in an individual case would not provide a sufficient ground for suspension.[54] In such individual cases, the individual concerned would have to address alleged violations through non-judicial and judicial remedies in the country where the breach takes place.

On the one hand, this means that it will be up to the party that wishes to suspend a transfer to provide credible and factual evidence that a material or systematic breach takes place. In addition, prior to suspending the transfer, the party must notify the other party and engage in consultation during a reasonable period without finding a solution, while the data already transferred would continue to be processed. Consequently, where data have already been transferred to the authority that systematically violated the provisions on safeguards, these would nevertheless be used in accordance with the Convention and potentially shared with other partners. In addition, the party intending to suspend the transfer would have to demonstrate the wrongdoing of the other party, which is an opposite logic to data protection law, where the party committing a data breach would have to demonstrate that no harm is caused to the fundamental rights of the person concerned.[55]

[52] ibid Art 14, s 15.

[53] Or substantial reputational or monetary harm to a natural person.

[54] Explanatory Report to the Second Additional Protocol to the Convention on Cybercrime on enhanced co-operation and disclosure of electronic evidence, CETS 224, Strasbourg, 12 May 2022, no 282.

[55] See, for instance, Articles 24, 32 and 33 on the obligations of controllers of Regulation (EU) 2016/679 of the European Parliament and of the Council of 27 April 2016 on the protection of

On the other hand, individuals who suffered a violation of their data protection rights should seek non-judicial and judicial remedies in the country requesting the data, meaning that that person might have to seek remedies before a court or non-judicial authority in a country with a questionable human rights record.

Evidently, it is very important to always bear in mind that although the Protocol includes provisions on data protection, its aim is not to create an international data protection instrument but rather a practical criminal justice cooperation framework. However, although the new provisions on data protection contained in the Second Additional Protocol might mean a substantial improvement for some members to the Convention, in comparison to the EU framework the rules remain at best very basic.

In addition, the Second Additional Protocol will need to be assessed in relation to other mechanisms that were adopted in recent years and that will be discussed in the subsequent sections. Only where those other mechanisms on direct access to e-evidence are taken into account can one evaluate the complexity that the different layers of cooperation will bring, and estimate their potential impact on fundamental rights.

B. The Situation in the US

In the US, the *Microsoft Ireland*[56] case played a pivotal role in shaping the legal landscape surrounding access to data held by service providers and laid the groundwork for the enactment of the Clarifying Lawful Overseas Use of Data Act (CLOUD Act).[57] *Microsoft v Ireland* addressed the issue of whether a US warrant, issued under the Stored Communications Act (SCA) of 1986,[58] could compel a US-based company to turn over emails and other communication content stored on servers located outside the US. The case originated from a dispute between Microsoft and the US Government over access to customer emails stored in a data centre in Ireland.[59]

In 2013, Microsoft challenged a search warrant seeking the emails of a customer involved in a drug trafficking investigation. Microsoft argued that the warrant, issued under the SCA, did not have extraterritorial reach and therefore

natural persons with regard to the processing of personal data and on the free movement of such data, and repealing Directive 95/46/EC (General Data Protection Regulation or GDPR) [2016] OJ L119/1.

[56] *United States v Microsoft Corp* (*Microsoft Ireland*), No 17-2, slip op at 3 (17 April 2018).

[57] Clarifying Lawful Overseas Use of Data (CLOUD) Act, H.R. 1625, 115th Cong div V (2018) (enacted) (to be codified in scattered sections of 18 USC).

[58] Stored Communications Act, Pub L 99–508, tit II, 100 Stat 1848, 1860–68 (1986) (codified as amended at 18 USC §§ 2701–12).

[59] J Daskal, 'Microsoft Ireland, the CLOUD Act, and International Lawmaking 2.0' (2018) *Stanford Law Review* 71, available at www.stanfordlawreview.org/online/microsoft-ireland-cloud-act-international-lawmaking-2-0/.

could not compel the company to produce emails stored in a foreign country. The legal question revolved around the interpretation of the SCA and whether it applied to data stored internationally. Microsoft contended that the law was outdated and did not contemplate the global nature of modern data storage and communication technologies. The US Government, on the other hand, argued that the focus should be on the control and possession of the data by a US company, regardless of its physical location. The case gained significant attention due to its potential implications for privacy, data protection, and the global reach of US law enforcement.[60]

On 23 March 2018, before the *Microsoft v Ireland* case was heard, US Congress passed and former President Trump signed the CLOUD Act, which amended the SCA.[61] According to the US Government, the CLOUD Act resolved the question presented in the *Microsoft v Ireland* case by specifying that a service provider responding to an SCA order must produce information within its 'possession, custody, or control, regardless of whether such information is located within or outside of the United States'.[62] Under the CLOUD Act, the US Government obtained a new warrant, declaring that Microsoft's objection that the warrant was impermissibly extraterritorial, no longer applied.[63] With the entry into force of the US CLOUD Act, the *Microsoft* case was dismissed as moot by the US Supreme Court on 17 April 2018.[64]

The US CLOUD Act essentially creates alternative mechanisms to obtain data outside the scope of traditional MLA procedures based on the unilateral assertion of jurisdiction. The Act consists of two parts, one that authorises US LEAs to require US service providers to preserve, backup or disclose communications data of US users that are stored outside US territory without the involvement of an authority in the country where the data are located.[65] Under the second part of the CLOUD Act, the US may enter into executive agreements with so-called 'qualifying foreign governments'.[66] Essentially, these agreements enable non-US

[60] ibid.

[61] As part of the Consolidated Appropriations Act, 2018, HR 1625, Div V, 115th Cong, 2d Sess (2018).

[62] Motion to vacate the judgment of the Court of Appeals and remand the case with Directions to dismiss as moot. On writ of certiorari to the United States of Appeals for the Second Circuit Motion. No 17-2, March 2018, 2.

[63] ibid.

[64] Supreme Court of the United States, 'Motion to Vacate the Judgment of the Court of Appeals and Remand the Case with Directions to Dismiss as Moot', 4 April 2018. On 17 April 2018, the judgment was vacated and the case remanded and on 21 May 2018, the judgment was issued; www.scotusblog.com/case-files/cases/united-states-v-microsoft-corp/.

[65] Amendment to Chapter 121 of title 18 of the United States Code (USC) §2713.

[66] So far, the US has signed Agreements with the UK and Australia and is negotiating with Canada and the EU, see: US Department of Justice, 'CLOUD Act Resources', available at www.justice.gov/criminal/cloud-act-resources. See also, 'CLOUD Act: Civil Society Urges US Congress to Consider Global Implications' (*EDRi* (blog), 19 March 2018), available at https://edri.org/cloud-act-letter-uscongress-global-implications/. See also M Rojszczak, 'CLOUD Act Agreements from an EU Perspective' (2020) 38 *Computer Law & Security Review* 105442, 1–14.

authorities to directly request data of non-US individuals if they comply with the requirements under the executive agreement.[67] Those 'qualifying' states that concluded executive agreements must conversely afford reciprocal rights of access to data for US LEAs to data stored by service providers in their jurisdiction, including providers subject to US jurisdiction.[68] US law has been amended insofar as it is no longer unlawful for service providers to intercept or disclose the content of wire or electronic communications in response to an order from an authority in another state that is subject to an executive agreement.[69] In addition, the provisions include a liability exemption for service providers when acting in 'good faith' for orders from foreign authorities that are subject to an executive agreement.

Executive agreements are concluded by way of certification issued by the US Attorney General and shall enter into force 180 days after the date on which notice was provided,[70] unless Congress disapproves by resolution.[71] In order to enter into an executive agreement, a state must satisfy a list of conditions regarding the confidentiality of data and requirements regarding the rights and obligations of each party. These requirements include, *inter alia*, that the domestic law of the party to the executive agreement affords robust substantive and procedural protections for privacy and civil liberties, has clear legal mandates and procedures governing the seizure of data and has sufficient mechanisms to provide accountability and appropriate transparency regarding the collection and use of the data sought.[72] The CLOUD Act names adherence to the Cybercrime Convention or consistency to the definitions and requirements[73] of the Convention as the determining factor to demonstrate compliance with these requirements.[74]

All orders issued by states under an executive agreement shall be for the purpose of obtaining information relating to the prevention, detection, investigation, or prosecution of serious crime, including terrorism, and must identify a specific person, account, address, or personal device, or any other specific identifier.[75] The orders shall be based on requirements for a reasonable

[67] Meaning that if the other state requests data of a US person, such request would have to be sent via MLA procedures.

[68] CLOUD Act (n 57) § 105 (codified at 18 USC §§ 2523 (b)(I)); J Daskal and P Swire, 'A Possible US-EU Agreement on Law Enforcement Access to Data?' (*Just Security*, 21 May 2018), available at www.justsecurity.org/56527/eu-agreement-law-enforcement-access-data/.

[69] CLOUD Act, ibid, s 104, Additional Amendments to Current Communications Laws.

[70] Not later than seven days after the date on which the Attorney General certifies an executive agreement under subsection; 18 US Code § 2523(d)(1) – Executive agreements on access to data by foreign governments.

[71] 18 US Code § 2523(d)(2). See also, K Rodriguez, 'The U.S. CLOUD Act and the EU: A Privacy Protection Race to the Bottom (9 April 2018), available at www.eff.org/deeplinks/2018/04/us-cloud-act-and-eu-privacy-protection-race-bottom.

[72] CLOUD ACT (n 57) § 2523(b)(1)(B).

[73] Demonstration of respect for the rule of law and the principles of non-discrimination and adherence to applicable international human rights obligations and commitments.

[74] CLOUD Act (n 57) § 2523(b)(1)(B)(i).

[75] ibid § 2523(b)(3)(D)(ii).

justification based on articulable and credible facts, in particular, legality and severity regarding the conduct under investigation.[76] Moreover, orders shall be subject to review[77] prior to, or in proceedings regarding, enforcement of the order. Where an order concerns the interception of wire or electronic communications, such an order shall be for a fixed and limited duration, last no longer than is reasonably necessary to accomplish the approved purposes of the order and shall be issued only if the same information could not reasonably be obtained by another less intrusive method.[78]

In addition, material collected shall promptly be reviewed, only be processed in accordance with minimisation procedures[79] and may not be used to infringe freedom of speech.[80] Further, states subject to executive agreements shall afford reciprocal rights of data access, thus, remove restrictions on service providers (not only providers subject to US jurisdiction) to enable them to respond to valid requests from US authorities.[81]

Finally, the state party to an executive agreement must agree to a periodic review[82] of compliance with the conditions under the executive agreement and the US Government reserves the right to render the agreement inapplicable regarding any order for which the agreement was not properly invoked.[83] Executive agreements with certified countries under the CLOUD Act shall be renewed on a five-year basis.[84] If the renewal of an executive agreement is rejected, the agreement shall no longer be considered to satisfy the requirements of the relevant provisions under the CLOUD Act.[85] Alternatively, agreements may be revised and shall then be treated as a new agreement.

This means that the procedure for renewal is relatively strict. However, the period of five years seems rather long considering that the political situation in certain countries may change rapidly and lead to a lowering of human rights standards. Moreover, besides the publication of certifications, renewals or termination of executive agreements, the Act does not further clarify how transparency concerning the implementation of executive agreements shall be achieved and whether the content of executive agreements will be included in the publication. However, as the negotiations between the EU and the US on an agreement to access e-evidence were only resumed after the e-Evidence Regulation was adopted, it is currently not possible to assess the potential agreement between these two parties.[86]

[76] ibid § 2523(b)(3)(D)(iv).
[77] ibid § 2523(b)(3)(D)(v).
[78] ibid § 2523(b)(3)(D)(vi)(III).
[79] ibid § 2523(b)(3)(G).
[80] ibid § 2523(b)(3)(E).
[81] ibid § 2523(b)(3)(I).
[82] ibid § 2523(b)(3)(J).
[83] ibid § 2523(b)(3)(K).
[84] ibid § 2523(e)(1).
[85] ibid § 2523(e)(3).
[86] See on this E Kyriakides, 'The CLOUD Act, E-Evidence, and Individual Rights' (2019) 5(1) *European Data Protection Law Review* 99–106.

IV. EUROPEAN PRESERVATION / PRODUCTION ORDERS

As has been shown above, there is a general trend towards extending jurisdiction extraterritorially when it comes to accessing e-evidence. States increasingly seek to transcend the boundaries of the offline world and create new conditions for the establishment of unilateral jurisdiction in the online world.

As previously mentioned, within the EU, the use of MLA mechanisms that traditionally governed transnational cooperation, gradually shifted towards the mutual recognition of judicial decisions, a procedure which was eventually codified in the EIO Directive. An EIO is a judicial decision which has been issued or validated by one Member State to have one or several specific investigative measure(s) carried out in another Member State to obtain (electronic) evidence.[87] The EIO entered into force on 22 May 2017,[88] but was already at that time transcended by new motions on how to improve the means for law enforcement to obtain access to e-evidence.

In June 2016, three months after the terrorist attacks in Brussels, the Council had adopted conclusions on improving criminal justice in cyberspace, requesting the Commission to deliver reports on the progress made with regard to improving cooperation with service providers, streamlining MLA and mutual recognition proceedings and reviewing the rules on enforcement of jurisdiction in cyberspace.[89] With regard to enhancing the cooperation with service providers, the Council requested the Commission to 'develop a common framework for cooperation with service providers for the purpose of obtaining specific categories of data, in particular subscriber data, when allowed by third countries' legislation, or any other 'comparable solution that allows for a quick lawful disclosure of such data'.[90] To that end, the Commission was tasked to explore possibilities to use aligned tools to ensure swift procedures and to increase transparency and accountability of the process of securing and obtaining e-evidence.[91]

In a non-paper of December 2016, the Commission acknowledged that Member States and their judicial and law enforcement authorities had taken diverging approaches regarding investigatory measures granting access to e-evidence.[92] According to the Commission, the systematic use of MLA for all

[87] EIO Directive (n 1) Art 1(1). See, on the further development in comparison to European Production Orders, S Tosza, 'All Evidence is Equal, but Electronic Evidence is more Equal than any Other: The Relationship between the European Investigation Order and the European Production Order' (2020) 11 *New Journal of European Criminal Law* 161–83.

[88] See European Commission Press Release, 'As of Today the "European Investigation Order" Will Help Authorities to Fight Crime and Terrorism' (Brussels, 22 May 2017), available at http://europa.eu/rapid/press-release_IP-17-1388_en.htm-.

[89] Council of the European Union, 'Council Conclusions on Improving Criminal Justice in Cyberspace' (9 June 2016), available at www.consilium.europa.eu/media/24300/cyberspace-en.pdf.

[90] ibid 3.

[91] ibid.

[92] Non-paper: Progress Report following the Conclusions of the Council of the European Union on Improving Criminal Justice in Cyberspace, 15072/1/16 REV 1, Brussels, 7 December 2016, 4.

types of access requests for e-evidence was increasingly viewed as problematic and time-consuming.[93] Consequently, and despite the efforts to achieve enhanced cooperation through mutual recognition, there had been a further shift away from applying MLA mechanisms towards the use of informal channels between LEAs and (foreign) service providers to directly obtain e-evidence.[94]

After an additional non-paper,[95] during public consultations[96] and the issuing of an Inception Impact Assessment, the Commission proposed, on 17 April 2018, new rules to facilitate access to e-evidence by police and criminal justice authorities. The proposal comprised a Regulation for the launch of European Production Orders and European Preservation Orders and a Directive to oblige service providers offering services in the EU to designate a legal representative in the Union who would receive such orders from LEAs.[97]

The following section will briefly describe the rationale of the adopted provisions and thereafter address some of the concerns relating to the fundamental right to the protection of personal data.

A. The e-Evidence Regulation and Accompanying Directive

The e-Evidence Regulation lays down the rules under which competent authorities in the EU may order a service provider offering services in the Union to produce or preserve e-evidence.[98] The legal basis of the proposed Regulation is Article 82(1) TFEU, which relates to measures on judicial cooperation that may be adopted to lay down rules and procedures for ensuring recognition of all forms of judgments and judicial decisions throughout the Union and to facilitate cooperation between judicial or equivalent authorities.[99] The service providers

[93] ibid 5.

[94] K Ligeti and G Robinson, 'Transnational Enforcement of Production Order for Electronic Evidence: Beyond Mutual Recognition?' in R Kert and A Lehner (eds), *Vielfalt des Strafrechts im internationalen Kontext – Festschrift für Frank Höpfel zum 65. Geburtstag* (Verlag Österreich, 2018) 626.

[95] Non-Paper of the EU Commission services of June 2017, Improving Cross-border Access to Electronic Evidence: Findings from the Expert Process and Suggested Way Forward ('Commission non-paper 2').

[96] Public consultation on improving cross-border access to electronic evidence, available at https://ec.europa.eu/info/consultations/public-consultation-improving-cross-border-access-electronic-evidence-criminalmatters_en.

[97] European Commission, 'E-Evidence-Cross-Border Access to Electronic Evidence. Improving Cross-Border Access to Electronic Evidence', available at https://ec.europa.eu/info/policies/justice-and-fundamental-rights/criminal-justice/e-evidence-cross-border-access-electronic-evidence_en.

[98] e-Evidence Regulation (n 11) Recital (15). See also Tosza (n 13) 166 et seq.

[99] In relation to proceedings in criminal matters and the enforcement of decisions. According to the Commission proposal, that Article also applies where a judicial authority in the issuing State addresses a legal person in another Member State, for instance when imposing obligations on it, regardless of whether a judicial authority in the other Member State is involved in the process, see: e-Evidence Proposal (n 7) 5. On the discussion around the appropriateness of the chosen legal basis, see Tosza (n 13) 169.

covered by the Regulation are required to comply with production or preservation orders for e-evidence, regardless of the location where the requested data are stored.[100]

The accompanying Directive obliges those service providers covered by the Regulation to designate at least one legal representative for the receipt of, compliance with and enforcement of decisions and orders issued for the purposes of gathering e-evidence in criminal proceedings.[101]

Under the Regulation, e-evidence in the shape of both content and non-content data shall either be produced via so-called European Production Orders or retained after the receipt of a European Preservation Order. While European Production Orders for subscriber data or data requested for the sole purpose of identifying a user may be issued for all criminal offences,[102] orders for traffic and content data may only be issued for criminal offences punishable by a custodial sentence of a maximum of at least three years or for particular crimes that are exhaustively listed in the e-Evidence Regulation.[103]

The Issuing authorities competent to send Production or Preservation Orders vary from Member State to Member State and could be a court, judge, investigating judge, prosecutor, or any other competent authority as defined by the issuing state if the orders are validated by a judge, a court, an investigating judge or a public prosecutor in the issuing state.[104] In emergency cases, orders for subscriber data and data requested for the sole purpose of identifying a user may be issued without prior validation, in which case ex-post validation would be required.[105]

Issuing authorities in one Member State must submit Production or Preservation Orders through a European Production Order Certificate or a European Preservation Order Certificate respectively to the designated establishment or to the legal representative designated by the service provider.[106] The addressees would have to comply with those orders within a specified timeframe and in any event with the deadlines stipulated in the Regulation.[107] With regard to European Production Orders, the competent authorities in the requested Member State would have to be notified of such orders and would be granted an

[100] e-Evidence Regulation (n 11) Art 1(1).

[101] e-Evidence Directive (n 12) Art 3(1).

[102] And for the execution of a custodial sentence or a detention order of at least four months. In addition, the principle of double criminality must be satisfied, see e-Evidence Regulation (n 11) Arts 5(3) and 6(2).

[103] ibid Art 5(4)(b).

[104] ibid Art 4.

[105] ibid Art 4(5).

[106] ibid Art 7(1) in conjunction with the e-Evidence Directive (n 12) and e-Evidence Regulation (n 11) Art 8(1).

[107] e-Evidence Regulation (n 11) Art 10 concerning European Production Order Certificates (EPOCs) and Art 11 of the e-Evidence Regulation with regard to European Preservation Order Certificates (EPOC-PR).

opportunity to refuse them.[108] A service provider would be able raise concerns if it considers that the execution of the Order could interfere with immunities or privileges or the double criminality requirement, in which case it would have to inform both the issuing and the executing authorities.[109] In addition, service providers may object to an order where they consider that complying with the order would be in conflict with applicable laws of a third country, in which case a review procedure would be triggered.[110]

On the one hand, the Regulation foresees high sanctions for non-compliance with Production and Preservation Orders. On the other, service providers shall not be held liable if they acted in good faith when complying with requests to produce or preserve data.[111] Pursuant to Article 9 of the e-Evidence Regulation, the addressee of the order, the service provider's legal representative, shall ensure that the requested data are transmitted directly to the issuing authority. The deadline for transmission is in regular cases 10 days and in the case of an emergency eight hours.[112]

i. Adequate Novelty? The Notification Requirement

While under the e-Evidence proposals, the authorities in the enforcing state were only to be involved in specific situations such as in cases of non-compliance with a European Production Order, the adopted e-Evidence Regulation now foresees a notification of the competent authority of the enforcing state at the time the order is sent to the service provider.[113] Where appropriate, such notification shall include any information that may be necessary to allow the enforcing state to raise grounds for refusal.[114] In addition, a notification will have a suspensive effect on the addressee's obligation to enforce the European Production Order. However, in emergency cases, the suspensive effect will not apply.[115] Furthermore, the second paragraph of Article 8 of the e-Evidence Regulation foresees two derogations from the obligation to notify the authority of the enforcing state: Where there are reasonable grounds to believe that the offence for which the European Production Order shall be issued, has been, is being or is likely to be committed in the issuing state, or where the person whose data are sought resides in the issuing state, notification may be omitted.

After being notified, the enforcing state is granted a maximum of 10 days to raise any grounds for refusing the order.[116] Orders may be refused if the data

[108] ibid Art 8.
[109] ibid Art 10(5).
[110] ibid Art 17.
[111] ibid Art 15(2).
[112] ibid Art 10.
[113] ibid Art 8.
[114] ibid Art 8(3).
[115] ibid Art 8(4).
[116] ibid Art 10(2).

requested is protected by immunities and privileges granted under the law of the enforcing state, where there are substantial grounds to believe that the execution of the order would entail a manifest breach of a relevant fundamental right as set out in Article 6 TEU and the Charter of Fundamental Rights of the EU, if it does not comply with the *ne bis in idem* principle, or if the order would be contrary to the requirement of double criminality.[117] Prior to raising the ground(s) for refusal, the notified authority must contact the issuing authority to discuss appropriate measures to be taken and to allow the issuing authority to adapt the order.[118] Instead of refusing the order in its entirety, the enforcing authority may allow only certain parts of the order to be transmitted or may attach conditions for the use of the transmitted data.[119]

In cases of emergency, the deadline for the enforcing authority to raise grounds for refusal is reduced to 96 hours following notification, while the service provider will have to transmit the requested data at the latest within eight hours upon receipt of the European Production Order Certificate. Hence, there could be situations in which the service provider transmitted the data before the authority in the enforcing state was able to raise grounds of objection. In such cases, the transmitted data have to be deleted, processing restricted and any conditions imposed by the enforcing authority have to be complied with.[120]

Arguably, the derogations from the mandatory notification requirement are rather broad and may be interpreted extensively. For instance, the issuing authority would merely have to indicate that there are grounds to believe that the offence regarding which the data are requested is *likely to be committed* in the issuing state.[121] Compared to the *substantial grounds* to believe, on *the basis of specific and objective evidence* that would have to be demonstrated in *exceptional situations* in order to refuse an order based on a *manifest breach* of fundamental rights, proving such likeliness of a criminal offence to be committed in the issuing state seems relatively simple.

Furthermore, it remains doubtful whether notification under Article 8 of the e-Evidence Regulation will be effective and indeed lead to refusals of orders by the enforcing state. On the one hand, it might be that the enforcing state will simply rubber stamp the notified European Production Order Certificates (EPOCs), in particular, where the orders concern individuals who are not nationals of the enforcing state. On the other hand, it is not clear which authorities will be the issuing and enforcing authorities in each respective case. It might very well be the case that the competent authority of the enforcing state pursues the same

[117] Unless it concerns an offence listed within the categories of offences set out in Annex IV as indicated by the issuing authority in the EPOC, if it is punishable in the issuing state by a custodial sentence or a detention order for a maximum period of at least three years. See ibid Art 12(1)(a) to (d).

[118] ibid Art 12(3).

[119] ibid Art 12(4).

[120] ibid Art 10(4).

[121] In accordance with ibid Art 8(2)(a).

interests as the issuing authority and might not put an emphasis on the assessment of individual rights. Finally, the time limits are rather tight, in particular for emergency situations. In certain cases, the enforcing authority might simply have to prioritise and eventually decide that it can trust the issuing authority without assessing the European Production Order in detail.

Ultimately, the added-value of the notification requirement under the adopted e-Evidence Regulation as compared to the previously existing mechanisms seems to be lacking. In addition, and although there are fewer grounds for refusing an order,[122] the added benefit of the e-Evidence Regulation as compared to the system under the EIO cannot be entirely achieved. It might have been a more favourable option to improve the effectiveness of the EIO by, *inter alia*, reducing time limits to reply to requests and by granting more flexibility to issuing authorities. Instead, the EU legislator opted for a solution that puts in place two parallel systems without having established the ineffectiveness of the previous system established on an evidence-based assessment, and without proving the necessity of establishing an additional layer of cooperation at the EU level. Evidently, it could be argued that Ireland neither participates in the Cybercrime Convention nor in the EIO, whereas it will take part in the e-Evidence Regulation. Whether this argument is sufficient to prove the necessity and proportionality of the latter, however, is questionable.

ii. Grounds for Refusal of Orders by Service Providers

Whether notification of the issuing state authority is required or not, the service provider must preserve the requested data and transmit those data within 10 days directly to the issuing authority or the LEA in the issuing state. Where the enforcing authority has notified both issuing authority and addressee prior to the 10 days that it will not raise grounds of refusal, the data must be sent as soon as possible.[123]

The Regulation provides for several grounds for non-compliance with orders: Where the addressee is of the opinion that the execution of the European Production Order could interfere with immunities or privileges, or with rules on the determination or limitation of criminal liability that relate to the freedom of the press or the freedom of expression in other media in the enforcing state, it shall inform both the issuing and the enforcing authority.[124] The issuing authority will then decide on whether to withdraw, adapt or maintain the order, possibly taking into consideration the view of the enforcing authority.[125]

[122] As compared to the grounds for non-recognition or non-execution under the EIO Directive (n 1) Art 11(1).

[123] e-Evidence Regulation (n 11) Art 10(2).

[124] ibid Art 10(5).

[125] ibid.

In addition, where the Production Order is incomplete, contains manifest errors, does not contain sufficient information to execute the EPOCs or cannot be executed due to de facto impossibility, the addressee shall inform the issuing authority without undue delay and ask for clarification.[126] In such cases, the requested data shall be preserved until production is possible, whether on the basis of a clarified Production Order or through other channels such as MLA, or until the order is withdrawn.[127]

Where the service provider fails to comply with an order, the issuing authority may request the competent authority in the executing Member State to enforce the order.[128] In such cases, the executing authority shall 'without further formalities' recognise and take necessary measures for the enforcement of the respective Production or Preservation Order transmitted to it within five days.[129] By setting a deadline for compliance with the order, the enforcing authority must require the addressees to comply with the relevant obligation and inform the addressee of the possibility to impose sanctions in case of non-compliance.[130] In accordance with Article 16(4)(a) of the e-Evidence Regulation, enforcement of the Production Order may be denied where the initial order has not been issued or validated by an issuing authority, was not issued for an offence listed under the Regulation,[131] because the addressee was unable to comply due to circumstances not attributable to the addressee,[132] or because the European Production Order Certificate contains manifest errors.[133] Moreover, enforcement may be refused based on additional grounds.[134]

Depending on the type of data and whether notification is required, no judicial authority in the issuing Member State would be required to intervene, as would be the case for traditional MLA procedures or executing requests for judicial cooperation within the mutual recognition framework. Only where the initial addressee of a European Production Order fails to comply with the orders, where notification is required or where the service provider refuses to

[126] ibid Art 10(6).
[127] ibid Art 10(9).
[128] ibid Art 16(1).
[129] ibid Art 16(2).
[130] ibid Art 16(3).
[131] ibid Art 16(4)(b).
[132] ibid Art 16(4)(c).
[133] ibid.
[134] In accordance with ibid Art 16(4), where (f) the data requested is protected by immunities and privileges granted under the law of the enforcing State, or the data requested is covered by rules on the determination or limitation of criminal liability that relate to the freedom of press or the freedom of expression in other media, which prevent execution or enforcement of the Order or where (g) based on the sole information contained in the EPOC-PR, it is apparent that it in exceptional situations, there are substantial grounds to believe, on the basis of specific and objective evidence, that the execution of the order would, in the particular circumstances of the case, entail a manifest breach of a relevant fundamental right as set out in Article 6 TEU and the Charter. Under Art 14(5), enforcement of preservation orders may be denied on the same ground, with the exception of orders not issued for an offence listed under the Regulation, since this requirement does not apply for preservation orders.

comply with the European Production Order based on the grounds listed in the Regulation, the competent authority of the enforcing state would be involved.

Compared to the initial proposal, the opportunities for the addressee to object to an order have been further limited and no longer allow refusals where orders manifestly violate the Charter or when they are manifestly abusive. Although it was often argued that this previous ground for refusal would grant too much power to service providers to decide on the assessment of fundamental rights,[135] it nevertheless represented an additional safeguard, which has now been removed in the adopted Regulation. Hence, even if the criticism to bestow service providers or their legal representative with the assessment of fundamental rights is valid, this option as well as the one to refuse manifestly abusive requests should have remained in the text.

In addition, the e-Evidence Regulation, just like the proposal, does not provide for data retention periods, and only specifies in its Recitals that the rules under the Regulation should neither stipulate a general data retention obligation for service providers nor should it have the effect of resulting in any general and indiscriminate retention of data.[136] Whether this will indeed be sufficient to comply with the conditions required by the Court of Justice of the European Union (CJEU) in the data retention case law may be questionable.

iii. Disregarding Data Subject Rights?

The adopted e-Evidence Regulation contains certain provisions that either seem to disregard data protection rules, or to impose broad limitations on the exercise of the rights of those individuals whose personal data are processed (data subjects), potentially going beyond the necessity and proportionality requirements. Below, three provisions that could lead to situations in which important data protection principles might not be complied with will be addressed. The focus on these particular provisions shall not signify that those are the only provisions under the adopted e-Evidence Regulation that are in non-compliance with or at least problematic in view of data protection rules and obligations.

Under EU data protection law, the entity determining the purposes and means of the processing of personal data is the so-called controller, which is ultimately held accountable for non-compliance with the rules. Under both the General Data Protection Regulation (GDPR) and the so-called Law Enforcement Directive (LED),[137] the controller is primarily responsible for responding to data

[135] See, ie, V Mitsilegas, 'The Privatisation of Mutual Trust in Europe's Area of Criminal Justice: The Case of e-Evidence' (2018) 25(3) *Maastricht Journal of European and Comparative Law* 263–65.

[136] e-Evidence Regulation (n 11) Recital 19.

[137] GDPR (n 55); Directive (EU) 2016/680 of the European Parliament and of the Council of 27 April 2016 on the protection of natural persons with regard to the processing of personal data by competent authorities for the purposes of the prevention, investigation, detection or prosecution of criminal offences or the execution of criminal penalties, and on the free movement of such data, and

subject requests.[138] However, in some cases, the processor may be required to assist in responding to data subject requests. While processors may only act on instructions received from the controller and are not directly responsible for complying with data subject requests, they are required to assist the controllers in fulfilling their obligations under the GDPR.[139] This means that processors may need to provide information or support to the controller in responding to data subject requests.

While European Production Orders generally have to be addressed to service providers that act as controllers, Article 5(6) of the e-Evidence Regulation contains a possibility for issuing authorities to address orders directly to service providers processing personal data on behalf of a controller. Such an exception is deemed to be justified where the controller cannot be identified despite reasonable efforts, or where addressing the controller could be *detrimental* to the investigation. Hence, while, according to EU data protection law, the processor must inform the controller that it has been requested to comply with a production order, the new provisions foresee a possibility for the issuing authority to request the processor to refrain from informing the controller about the Production Order. In such cases, the issuing authority is supposed to add a justification in the certificate to the addressee.[140] The processor may be requested to withhold the information for as long as necessary and proportionate, in order not to obstruct the relevant criminal proceedings.

It remains unclear whether there will be a review of the proportionality and necessity assessment of the issuing authority, whether and when such a review will take place and at what point the processor may inform the controller. Presumably, the addressee of the EPO may only inform the controller once the issuing authority has lifted the restriction. This means that during that time, the controller will neither be fully aware of the processing that takes place with the data under its responsibility, nor will it be possible to adequately respond to data subject access requests. Arguably, data subject rights may be restricted under EU data protection law where these are based on a legislative measure and in order not to obstruct official or legal inquiries.[141] However, the provision under the e-Evidence Regulation disregards the architecture of EU data protection law in relation to controller-processor relationships, sets aside the conditions for the restriction of data subject rights and ignores the transparency principle under the GDPR.

As mentioned above, ultimately, it is the responsibility of the controller to ensure that data subject requests are handled in accordance with data protection

repealing Council Framework Decision 2008/977/JHA (Law Enforcement Directive, LED) [2016] OJ L119/89. On the LED, see E Kosta and F Boehm, '*The EU Law Enforcement Directive (LED)*' (Oxford University Press, 2024).

[138] On Access to personal data pursuant to the LED, see T Quintel, '*Data Protection, Migration and Border Control. The GDPR, the Law Enforcement Directive and Beyond*' (Hart Publishing, 2022).

[139] GPDR (n 55) Art 28(3)(e).

[140] e-Evidence Regulation (n 11) Art 5(7) and recital 43.

[141] In accordance with GDPR (n 55) Art 23.

law. However, processors may have a role to play in fulfilling these obligations and must make available to the controller all information necessary to demonstrate compliance with the rules under the GDPR.[142] Where the processor fails to provide the required assistance to the controller, the latter may not be able to fully comply with those obligations. For instance, where a data subject submits an access request[143] to a controller and the processor does not provide the required assistance, the controller may not be able to adequately respond to the data subject's request. This could result in a delay or a failure to provide the data subject with the necessary information or reply to access requests they submitted and, eventually obstruct them from exercising their additional data subject rights.[144]

Therefore, it is important for both controllers and processors to be able to comply with their respective roles and obligations under the GDPR. Since generally, the controller-processor relationship is governed by contractual arrangements to facilitate compliance with their respective obligations and specifications as to the responsibilities of each party with respect to data subject requests, prohibiting a processor to inform the controller of production orders would lead to a breach of that contract. In addition, questions arise as to whether a processor, responding to a European Production Order without involving the controller, would ultimately become a separate controller for the specific processing operation of submitting the data pursuant to the Production Order Certificate.

Furthermore, a paragraph in Article 5 of the e-Evidence Regulation newly added during the legislative negotiations allows issuing authorities to request the production of traffic and content data protected by a professional privilege, where addressing the privileged professional might be detrimental to the investigation, where the privileged professional resides in the issuing state, or where the privileges were waived.[145] This could be the case where data are stored or processed by a service provider as part of an infrastructure provided to professionals protected by professional privilege. Professional privilege helps to preserve the integrity of the relationship between professionals and their clients. This relationship is built on trust, and the principle of professional privilege ensures that this trust between the parties is not undermined. By keeping their communications confidential, clients can avoid the risk of their confidential information being used against them in legal or other proceedings. This helps to ensure that legal proceedings are fair and just by preventing the use of

[142] GDPR (n 55) Art 28(3)(h).

[143] Under ibid Art 15, a data subject shall have the right to obtain from the controller confirmation as to whether or not personal data concerning him or her are being processed, and, where that is the case, access to the personal data, including additional information on the processing, the personal data processed, and the entities processing the personal data.

[144] Such as the right to rectification, right to erasure or right to the restriction of processing under ibid Art 16, 17 and 18 respectively.

[145] e-Evidence Regulation (n 11) Art 5(9).

confidential information that has been obtained improperly. Thus, the purpose of professional privilege is to ensure that clients can communicate freely and openly with their professionals, without fear that their confidential information will be disclosed to others.

Finally, Article 11 of the e-Evidence Regulation on user information and confidentiality underwent certain changes compared to the initial proposal in that it now no longer refers to the addressee that may be requested from refraining to inform the person concerned. Instead of obliging the service provider that is requested to respond to a European Production Order, it will be the issuing authority that will be responsible for notifying the individual that his or her personal data have been processed. This constitutes a gap in the provision as the issuing authority and the service provider are covered by different data protection rules. While the issuing authority will apply the LED to its processing activities, the service provider falls within the scope of the GDPR. The latter foresees stronger transparency obligations whereas the former allows for more flexibility when restricting data subject rights, including the right to information.[146]

Article 11 of the e-Evidence Regulation obliges the issuing authority to inform the person whose data were requested without undue delay about the production of his or her personal data. Since the Article solely refers to the data being sought, it may be assumed that individuals will not have to be informed where their data was preserved. The second paragraph of the provision foresees an option for the issuing authority to restrict the right to information in accordance with the rules under the LED. The latter allows for the restriction of the right to information by way of legislative measures in order to protect public or national security, or to avoid jeopardising ongoing investigations for as long as it is necessary and proportionate, as well as taking into account the fundamental rights and legitimate interests of the person concerned.[147] Importantly, a restriction should not simply refer to the grounds that are laid down in the LED, but specify by way of national law, the specific purpose of the restriction as well as the categories of processing that would be covered by the restriction.[148] Consequently, the restriction of data subject rights by simple reference to the ground under the Directive would allow for excessively broad restrictions. In addition, restrictions are to be duly documented and made available to the data protection authority in order to allow for effective review and ultimately the right to an effective remedy where processing was unlawful or rights were restricted in an unjustified manner.

Where a restriction can no longer be justified, the data subject must be notified that his or her data have been processed. This means that the controller will have to lift the restrictions as soon as the circumstances that justified them no

[146] GDPR (n 55) Art 13R. On the topic of the right of access under the LED, see Eleni Kosta and Franziska Boehm, 'The EU Law Enforcement Directive (LED) – a commentary' (Oxford University Press, Part III: Rights of the Data Subjects (Articles 12–18).

[147] LED (n 137) Art 13(3).

[148] ibid Art 13(4).

longer apply, will have to proactively contact the data subject and inform him or her about the processing and any related information about that processing. Yet, the e-Evidence Regulation merely provides for the issuing authority to 'indicate in the case file the reasons for the delay, restriction or omission'. Moreover, Section H of Annex I of the Regulation seems to adopt an approach to allow for broad restrictions as it requires the issuing authority to indicate solely one of the grounds under the LED to allow for the delay, restriction or omission of information to be given to the person whose data are sought.

Under its Article 17, the LED creates an obligation for Member States to provide for the indirect exercise of data subject rights through the intermediary of a supervisory data protection authority (DPA) where the rights under the LED have been restricted by a competent authority. After having exercised the right, the supervisory authority must inform the data subject at least that all necessary verifications or a review of the lawfulness of the processing by the authority has taken place. This is an additional safeguard for the data subject in order to compensate for broad limitation possibilities to restrict data subject rights under the LED. This two-level approach has significantly improved the situation of data subjects whose data are processed by LEAs, as it introduces another line of checks by an independent supervisory authority.[149]

Where the data subject cannot, either via a direct access request with the controller (the service provider) or an indirect access request via the DPA, ascertain whether or not his or her personal data are processed in a lawful manner and in compliance with all data protection principles, the processing of inaccurate data could potentially lead to wrong conclusions about the data subject.

This could have a negative impact on the data subject's right to a fair trial including the principle of equality of arms within the meaning of Article 47 of the Charter.[150] If the equality of arms is not guaranteed, the data subject cannot defend him-/herself against wrongful accusations and cannot adequately contest a decision that was taken about him/her. It will be interesting to see what the CJEU will decide in its upcoming judgment regarding a case referred by an Austrian court, where a defendant's mobile phone was seized and searched by the police whereas the defendant himself only became aware of that measure after testimony was given by a police officer under oath.[151]

Ultimately, it will be essential that data subjects will be able to effectively exercise their data subject rights under both the GDPR and the LED. On the one hand, they should be able to address service providers in order to exercise their right of access and any subsequent rights such as the right of rectification,

[149] J Sajfert and T Quintel, 'Data Protection Directive (EU) 2016/680 for Police and Criminal Justice Authorities' (10 December 2018), available at https://papers.ssrn.com/sol3/papers.cfm?abstract_id=3285873. Also see CJEU, Case C-333/22 *Ligue des droits humains ASB*, 16 November 2023, EU:C:2023:874 on that matter.

[150] CJEU, Case C-548/21, Summary of the request for a preliminary ruling pursuant to Article 98(1) of the Rules of Procedure of the Court of Justice, *C.G. v Bezirkshauptmannschaft Landeck*, 7; see also Opinion of Advocate GEneral Sánchez-Bordona of 20 April 2023.

[151] ibid.

erasure and restriction of processing. For that purpose, service providers should be notified at the moment the issuing authority must inform the data subject that his or her data have been processed within the framework of a production order, as soon as notification no longer jeopardises ongoing investigations. The data subject will then be able to exercise his or her rights against both the service provider and the issuing authority.

The system of safeguards available under both the GDPR and the LED should be respected in order to lay a foundation for the equality of arms principle. This means that the notification requirement should be carried out consistently in order to enable the data subject to know that his or her personal data were requested by an issuing authority. In addition, the data subject should be able to exercise his or her right of indirect access under Article 17 of the LED. Where the supervisory authority that was approached by the data subject is not the competent DPA, Article 50 LED on mutual assistance between the supervisory authority would come into play so as to enable the DPA that is competent to supervise the issuing authority to carry out all necessary checks regarding the lawfulness of the processing, the accuracy of the data and the compliance with the other rules and obligations under the LED. Ultimately, the supervisory authority should also verify whether the Production Order was based on reasonable grounds and whether the restriction of the right to be informed was justified.

V. CONCLUSION AND OUTLOOK

In a world where criminals are using modern communication techniques, timely access to electronic evidence is necessary, as stored data are prone to deletion or modification. Moreover, most investigations include a cross-border dimension and MLAT agreements are often outdated and too slow. Effective mechanisms to secure and obtain digital evidence are crucial for investigations that involve volatile data. These circumstances progressively led to a paradigm shift, away from classical MLA towards mutual recognition in the EU, and, more recently, direct cooperation between (foreign) service providers and LEAs.

While the involvement of two or more judicial authorities was inherent in existing MLA or mutual recognition mechanisms, the frameworks described above go beyond traditional MLA procedures, as the involvement of the authority of the country where the service provider is established will often no longer be required. This approach removes important safeguards and, by streamlining the preservation and acquisition of e-evidence, renders the entire process more effortless. Like the CLOUD Act, the e-Evidence Regulation extends enforcement jurisdiction to service providers outside the EU. While the Second Additional Protocol to the Cybercrime Convention only includes subscriber data in direct LEA to service provider cooperation, the potential membership to the Protocol includes countries that might not have a robust system of fundamental rights protection. In addition, the data protection rules in the Second Additional

Protocol are by far more basic than the ones under the EU data protection framework. Whether the EU data protection rules will be upheld in the future agreement on the exchange of e-evidence between the EU and the US remains to be seen.

The e-Evidence Regulation is (for the time being)[152] the final piece in the puzzle. Like the US CLOUD Act and the provisions under the Second Additional Protocol to the Cybercrime Convention, the e-Evidence Regulation allows the substitution of traditional MLA procedures for international cooperation on criminal law enforcement access to data, requiring service providers to comply with Production Orders regardless of where the data are stored.

With regard to the exercise of individual rights, the extraterritorial effect of domestic Production Orders may lead to complex issues if the relationships between the different instruments are not sufficiently well defined to prevent overlap or contradiction. Thus, the initiatives on different levels that are each applicable in their own corners may result in a situation where individuals will neither be aware that their data have been sought nor against whom to exercise their rights and in which jurisdiction.

While the e-Evidence Regulation is not sufficiently clear on the restriction of the right to information and the requirement to notify the concerned person in the Second Additional Protocol not even any form of mandatory notification is foreseen. For many of the states that will potentially join the Additional Protocol, the rules under its Article 14 will be the only data protection rules they will have to comply with and the enforcement of those rules will not be a priority under the Protocol.

Further questions remain with regard to handing what were previously judicial tasks of receiving orders to preserve or produce evidence over into the hands of private companies.[153] Although the initiatives are to create a more harmonised framework for a rapid gathering of electronic data (evidence), it should not per se be *easy* for LEAs to access and gather e-evidence, as there is a risk that data may become subject to abuse.

[152] Negotiations on a United Nations Cybercrime Convention are still ongoing, see Ad Hoc Committee to Elaborate a Comprehensive International Convention on Countering the Use of Information and Communications Technologies for Criminal Purposes, available at www.unodc.org/unodc/en/cybercrime/ad_hoc_committee/home. After submission of the final manuscript the agreement was found, see press release of 9 August 2024, available at www.unodc.org/unodc/frontpage/2024/August/united-nations_-member-states-finalize-a-new-cybercrime-convention.html, the final agreed version of the text is available at https://daccess-ods.un.org/access.nsf/Get?OpenAgent&DS=A/AC.291/L.15&Lang=E, however it still needs to be approved by the General Assembly of the UN, which is planned for late 2024.

[153] S Tosza, 'Internet Service Providers as Law Enforcers and Adjudicators. A Public Role of Private Actors' (2021) 43 *Computer Law & Security Review* 1–17. Also G Robinson, 'Like Oil and Water? Effective Data Protection and Direct Cooperation on Digital Evidence' (15 May 2023), in V Franssen and S Tosza (eds), *The Cambridge Handbook of Digital Evidence in Criminal Investigations* (forthcoming, 2025), available at https://ssrn.com/abstract=4541609. Also see: S Tosza, 'Gathering Electronic Evidence for Administrative Investigations Exploring an Under-the-Radar Area' (2023) 2 *eucrim*, available at https://eucrim.eu/articles/gathering-electronic-evidence-for-administrative-investigations/.

Part V

AI and Migration, Databases and Mobility

17

The Traveller and the Digital Border

ELSPETH GUILD*

I. INTRODUCTION

IN THIS CHAPTER I will examine the privacy rights of travellers from the perspective of the international human rights legal framework. My focus is on how the crossing of international borders by individuals intersects with states' concerns regarding the identity and intentions of travellers resulting in friction as regards privacy as a human right. The international border is a place of particular interest in this context as it is where the performance of state sovereignty regarding migration takes place most visibly. Except in border control free areas (such as the Schengen area in the EU), everyone is subject to a border control check on entering a state.[1] In the context of border control (or preparation for it, for instance, complying with visa or travel authorisation requirements), personal data is the tool on the basis of which admission or rejection takes place. As Global North states, in particular, have established sophisticated databases containing an increasingly wide range of information on individuals, they have sought to capitalise on access to this data for the purpose of security in the form of border control. Thus, visa information,[2] travel authorisation data,[3] Advanced Passenger Information (API)[4] and Passenger

* University of Liverpool.

[1] At least in theory.

[2] The requirements of information for the processing of visa applications varies widely across the world. It also differs depending on the kind of visa for which the individual is applying; see S Mau et al, 'The Global Mobility Divide: How Visa Policies Have Evolved Over Time' (2015) *Journal of Ethnic and Migration Studies* 41.8, 1192–1213.

[3] The best known example of this type of authorisation is the United States' (US) Electronic System for Travel Authorization (ESTA) system where all non US (or privileged other nationals) must obtain an authorisation before travelling which must be applied for online providing ever increasing amounts of information about the individual, see: T Spijkerboer, 'The Global Mobility Infrastructure: Reconceptualising the Externalisation of Migration Control' (2018) *European Journal of Migration and Law* 20.4, 452–69.

[4] This is standard personal information contained in passports combined with travel information regarding flights: R Koslowski, 'International Cooperation on Electronic Advanced Passenger Information Transfer and Passport Biometrics' (Montreal, International Studies Association, 2004); see also IATA, 'Guidelines on Advance Passenger Information (API)' (2014), available at www.iata.org/contentassets/18a5fdb2dc144d619a8c10dc1472ae80/api-guidelines-main-text_2014.pdf.

Name Records (PNR),[5] all forms of personal data about travellers, are not only added to these databases but are also subject to various forms of search and use. These searches use algorithmic tools (artificial intelligence[6] enhanced by machine learning[7] (AI/ML)) to 'match' terms within and across databases to find out more about travellers through the aggregation of their data. A task which would have been impossible for humans to carry out manually because of the size of the data, becomes possible with the use of AI/ML tools. Thus the interest in having ever increasing amounts of personal data becomes an end in itself, and within some interior ministries, parts of border guard institutions and security bodies, the view is taken that the state will be ever more secure if it has as much personal data about travellers as possible. But in using databases to determine who might be a security risk, the privacy of travellers is at stake. The right to privacy protects many other rights and the choice of terms to use is critical. For instance, searches based on nationality, place of birth, age, gender, and meal preference on a flight are all potentially discriminatory on prohibited grounds. Nationality linked with place of birth will potentially discriminate against persons who have acquired a citizenship otherwise than by birth.[8] Age and gender[9] are both grounds of prohibited discrimination in international law.

[5] These are records created by the private sector, travel companies, mainly for their commercial purposes. However, since the 1990s some countries (starting with the US) have required airlines (in particular but not limited to them) to transfer to their authorities PNR data on travellers planning to come to their country. See International Civil Aviation Organization, 'Guidelines on Passenger Name Record (PNR) Data' (First Edition 2010), available at www.iata.org/contentassets/18a5fdb2dc144d619a8c10dc1472ae80/new_doc_9944_1st_edition_pnr.pdf and E Fahey, 'Law and Governance as Checks and Balances in Transatlantic Security: Rights, Redress, and Remedies in EU-US Passenger Name Records and the Terrorist Finance Tracking Program' (2013) *Yearbook of European Law 32.1*, 368–88.

[6] E Rich, *Artificial Intelligence* (McGraw-Hill, Inc, 1983). Artificial intelligence is a disputed term among scientists. However, a generally accepted core is that it consists of computer programmes or machines capable of behaviour which would be regarded as intelligence by humans; J Kaplan, *Artificial Intelligence: What Everyone Needs to Know* (Oxford University Press, 2016). The European Commission defines it as: 'Artificial intelligence (AI) refers to systems that display intelligent behaviour by analysing their environment and taking actions – with some degree of autonomy – to achieve specific goals. AI-based systems can be purely software-based, acting in the virtual world (e.g. voice assistants, image analysis software, search engines, speech and face recognition systems) or AI can be embedded in hardware devices (e.g. advanced robots, autonomous cars, drones or Internet of Things applications)': Communication from the Commission to the European Parliament, the European Council, the Council, the European Economic and Social Committee and the Committee of the Regions on Artificial Intelligence for Europe, Brussels, 25.4.2018 COM(2018) 237 final.

[7] N Kühl et al, 'Machine Learning in Artificial Intelligence: Towards a Common Understanding' (arXiv preprint arXiv:2004.04686, 2020). The European Commission considers that ML is a type of AI, which works by identifying patterns in available data and then applying the knowledge to new data, COM(2018) 237, ibid. Not all scientists consider ML to be a form of AI but an element which may be used to enhance AI.

[8] Such discrimination was found unlawful in 2016 by the European Court of Human Rights: *Biao v Denmark* App no 38590/10 (ECtHR, 24 May 2016).

[9] See, ie, Convention on the Elimination of all Forms of Discrimination Against Women 1979, MA Freeman, C Chinkin and B Rudolf (eds), *The UN Convention on the Elimination of all Forms of Discrimination Against Women: A Commentary* (Oxford University Press, 2012);

Meal preference (an element of PNR data sets) may imply characteristics which are protected, such as religion.[10]

The four types of data I refer to above fall into two groups: first, data which is exclusively about aliens (visa and travel authorisation) and secondly, data sets which mix together information about aliens and citizens (API and PNR). These groups do not necessarily have the same legal rights in respect of their personal data. There are plethora of international legal issues which are raised by states' use of travellers' personal data. Thus in this chapter I have chosen three main questions to examine:

1. The legal status of the individual at the border and the transformation of personal data into currency (*The Traveller at the Border)*;
2. Travellers and their data: obtaining, accessing and sharing for AI/ML uses (*Travellers' Data or Travellers' Privacy?*);
3. What justifications do European states provide to the courts to justify privacy interferences (*The Grounds for Interference)*?

Through these three questions, my objective is to understand the data-privacy relationship of the border and the traveller and to apply international legal standards to that intersection.

II. THE TRAVELLER AT THE BORDER

International borders are places which create anxiety for states and travellers. States seek to protect their territory and people from the presence of unwanted travellers and travellers seek to avoid being categorised as unwanted by states they are seeking to enter. The key to this sorting of the goats from the sheep lies in the examination of the traveller and his or her documents: the border check. This check may be undertaken by a border guard visually checking documents and individuals or by a glass box within which a computer reads personal material and data and with very little manual assessment, either opens the gates or not. Where the individual is a citizen returning to his or her home state, usually he or she has a sense of entitlement to enter and is fairly casual about the border check. Though this insouciance can be very quickly destroyed by a border guard questioning whether the passport is not being used fraudulently suggesting that the individual is not in fact a citizen entering his or her own state but an 'unwanted traveller' trying to slip in. For aliens (people who are not nationals of the state they are seeking to enter) the border is usually a restless place where a sense of uncertainty is everywhere. Frequently, there are long queues of people

or Convention on the Rights of the Child 1990, J Tobin (ed), *The UN Convention on the Rights of the Child: A Commentary* (Oxford University Press, 2019).

[10] Art 24 International Covenant on Civil and Political Rights, see WA Schabas, *UN International Covenant on Civil and Political Rights: Nowak's CCPR Commentary* (NP Engel Verlag, 2019).

waiting to be checked. People in these queues have already been subject to an initial sorting into citizens coming home (with the right passport) and everyone else (does this mean they have the wrong passport?). While waiting, it is impossible not to watch what is happening at the gate, whether manned by a human being or a machine.

In front of the human, every time someone is delayed, asks additional questions, or worse, is taken away to some other place hidden from the rest of the queue, presumably for further additional checks, the stress level among those left in the queue goes up. When faced with a glass box, the problem is slightly different as the box does not ask questions. Rather, it may refuse to open its doors to let the traveller in. Or, it may admit the traveller into the box but then reject the passport which it is reading and refuse to open the doors on the other side. In the worst scenario, the machine not only blocks the person in the box but also sets off an alarm which draws everyone's attention to the person caught. The alarm does not stop until a border guard turns it off and collects the unfortunate person stuck in the box. Anything but a smooth and rapid passage either through a check by a border guard or by a machine creates anxiety for the traveller.

What I am highlighting here are the elements of the performance of state sovereignty which take place at international border crossing points. They may be more or less intrusive, but they are omnipresent. The longer the delay in crossing a border, the more precarious the traveller feels. Even citizens begin to feel uncomfortable about their entitlement to enter their state of citizenship. This precariousness transforms the traveller from a rights holder in law to a suppliant who needs to justify his or her entry into the state to the guard or the machine. The longer the experience goes on, the more the individual wishes it to end and to be through to the other side. The traveller knows that the essential element to getting to the other side is providing the guard or the machine with the information which he/she/it wants and considers to be sufficient for the purposes of the crossing. Thus, the traveller is already prepared to hand over personal data to achieve the objective. These conditions are perfect for preparing people to provide as much personal data, no matter how intrusive, to the guard, or to the machine with the follow up of the guard. Indeed, by the time the traveller gets to the guard or the machine, he or she is usually already prepared to hand over whatever it takes to get through this unpleasant experience. The traveller knows, though, that offering the usual currency of exchange, that is money, to the guard is likely to result in him or her ending up in jail so it is another currency which is at issue to get the traveller to where he or she wants to go. This is personal data. But like any currency, once offered, personal data tends to go into circulation. EU law has developed strong protections in the form of purpose limitations, a duty to delete data and the principle of data subject consent against such circulation but even there exceptions have been made for the field of borders and migration. Elsewhere, protections are frequently scarce on the ground.

Personal data also travels without its owner's specific knowledge when that owner becomes a traveller. The often cited sources of international law for this data exchange is the Convention on International Civil Aviation adopted in 1944 (the Chicago Convention).[11] It is under the auspices of the International Air Transport Association (IATA), the International Civil Aviation Organization (ICAO) and the World Customs Organization (WCO) which organisations are primarily concerned with ensuring the smooth operation of transport and work closely with governments. Annex 9 of the Convention is entitled 'Facilitation' and provides for Standards and Recommended Practices to assist landside formalities for clearance of aircraft and passengers, goods and mail, with respect to the requirements of customs, immigration, public health and agriculture authorities. Under this capture-all heading, specific standards have been designed to comply with state demands that airlines transfer API information to their border authorities before the travel commences. This API data transfer was pushed by the US on grounds of increasing national security in air transport and was incorporated in the Annex 9 standards.[12] The first API standards were developed in 1993 and have been refined on numerous occasions thereafter.[13] In that decade, API transfers were required by all states in North America, most of Europe,[14] Australia, Japan, Korea, New Zealand and South Africa. Twenty years on, with the exception of the Middle East, Africa (except South Africa) and about half of South American states, most other countries require API.

The travellers' consent to the transfer of API is implied or expressed in the travel contract as a requirement of transport. PNR also travels without the travellers' specific knowledge but there are still only a minority of countries which require PNR data. The IATA Annex 9 guidelines on PNR data were only developed in 2006.[15] This is much more intrusive as it includes all the data which the airline has collected on the traveller such as phone numbers, addresses, bank and credit card details, as well as information ancillary to travel like hotel bookings or car hire. In the cases of API and PNR, it is the private sector which is required to transfer personal data to state authorities irrespective of the relationship of the citizenship of the individual with the requesting state. Through API and PNR requirements, states obtain substantial amounts of information about their own citizens which they would otherwise not be able to gather.

[11] See www.icao.int/publications/Pages/doc7300. The Convention has 193 state parties.

[12] See https://www.iata.org/contentassets/18a5fdb2dc144d619a8c10dc1472ae80/passenger_data_exchange.pdf.

[13] See K Mikuriya,'API and PNR: Two Key Words on the Global Security Agenda' (*WCO News*, 10 June 2015), available at https://mag.wcoomd.org/magazine/wco-news-77/api-and-pnr-two-key-words-on-the-global-security-agenda/https://mag.wcoomd.org/magazine/wco-news-77/api-and-pnr-two-key-words-on-the-global-security-agenda/.

[14] Except Iceland, Ireland, Portugal, Switzerland and some Western Balkan states.

[15] See Mikuriya (n 13). https://mag.wcoomd.org/magazine/wco-news-77/api-and-pnr-two-key-words-on-the-global-security-agenda/.

I have chosen the term traveller rather than alien or any other term related to the citizenship of the person travelling. The reason for this is because national exceptions to personal data protection are very frequently made on the basis of the citizenship status of the individual. Aliens (the term preferred in international law, but also referred to as migrants, asylum seekers, foreigners, the list is virtually endless) are often defined out of national data protection laws[16] or constitutional protections which apply to citizens of the state.[17] But the traveller is the person who is between his or her own state, in which he or she is a national and another country where he or she will be an alien. The reverse of course also applies, the alien returning to his or her country of nationality ceases to be an alien on arrival and becomes a citizen again with citizens' data protection rights. In the following discussion, I will examine the legal challenges attendant on these transfers.

III. TRAVELLERS' DATA OR TRAVELLERS' PRIVACY?

There are effectively three main ways in which states capture the data of travellers. The first is through pre-travel authorisations where the traveller him or herself provides information to obtain a visa or other form of travel authorisation. This means applies only to aliens who are travelling. The second is at the border where a machine or an individual collects and corelates data contained in the travel document with the travellers' own description of his or her travel and other documents which the authorities may require of the traveller. This source is mainly applicable to aliens though citizens may also be questioned about their bona fides. The third is through requirements on the private sector (the travel industry) to provide information on their customers to state authorities (API and PNR). The data collected through these techniques covers all travellers irrespective of their citizenship. The result is the acquisition of or access to enormous amounts of personal data from simple elements of identity contained in passports (an essential element of all the means) to extensive information about past travel (frequently a question in visa applications, travel authorisation applications and possibly available from PNR data), family relationships (again visa applications and travel authorisations) and work histories (mainly from visa applications). Some countries also require information of bank accounts

[16] In the UK, for instance, the Data Protection Act 2018, sch 2, part 1, para 4 and has been amended by the Data Protection Act 2018 (Amendment of Schedule 2 Exemptions) Regulation 2022 sets out an immigration exemption for aliens' data: https://ico.org.uk/for-organisations/guide-to-data-protection/guide-to-the-general-data-protection-regulation-gdpr/exemptions/immigration-exemption/#exemption1.

[17] V Mitsilegas, 'Immigration Control in an Era of Globalization: Deflecting Foreigners, Weakening Citizens, Strengthening the State' (2012) *Indiana Journal of Global Legal Studies* 19, 3.

and tax returns for some kinds of visa applications.[18] A frequent question on visa and travel authorisation applications relates to criminal convictions.[19]

Increasingly, this information must be delivered in electronic form to the authorities. This is exclusively the case for travel authorisations, API and PNR data. State authorities' possession of or access to massive amounts of personal data of travellers in electronic form creates the possibility (and temptation) to use AI/ML tools on it to carry out a range of activities from simple cross referencing to verifying the information provided, to the design of profiles of travellers who might be suspect and the search through the data of all travellers to find those whose identities seem to match a profile. State authorities seeking to verify data provided to them by potential travellers (but also aliens within the state) increasingly seek access to other intra-state databases to run checks about individuals.[20] As regards profiles, there is substantial evidence that state authorities are using these to facilitate decision-making in visit visa applications[21] as well as in much more complex areas of border, migration and asylum law.[22] There is a substantial problem as regards the accuracy of this data. Data collection standards and checks on accuracy are not shared across government departments let alone states. The private sector, in particular as regards PNR data, is notorious for poor quality data which depends on customers entering their own data (for instance, address and phone numbers) into forms online to purchase goods and services where the interest of the private sector is primarily on the quality of the payment data only.[23]

Some states also obtain travellers' data through data sharing agreements with other states. Thus, personal data which one state has gleaned in border, migration or related activities, is made available to another state on the basis of

[18] See, ie, the UK: www.gov.uk/student-visa/money.

[19] See, ie, https://travel-visa-info.com/get-us-visa-with-criminal-record/.

[20] See, ie, Independent Chief Inspector of Borders and Immigration, 'An Inspection of Home Office (Borders, Immigration and Citizenship System) Collaborative Working with other Departments and Agencies' (31 January 2019), available at www.gov.uk/government/publications/an-inspection-of-home-office-borders-immigration-and-citizenship-system-collaborative-working-with-other-government-departments-and-agencies; V Papageorgiou et al, 'Patient Data-Sharing for Immigration Enforcement: A Qualitative Study of Healthcare Providers in England' (2020) *British Medical Journal*.

[21] Independent Chief Inspector of Borders and Immigration, 'An Inspection of the Home Office's Network Consolidation Programme and the "Onshoring" of Visa Processing and Decision Making to the UK (September 2018–August 2019), available at https://assets.publishing.service.gov.uk/government/uploads/system/uploads/attachment_data/file/863627/ICIBI_An_inspection_of_the_Home_Office_s_Network_Consolidation_Programme.pdf.

[22] See, ie, P Molnar and L Gill, 'Bots at the Gate: A Human Rights Analysis of Automated Decision-Making in Canada's Immigration and Refugee System' (The Citizen Lab, University of Toronto, 2018).

[23] The accuracy of PNR data is not necessarily the responsibility of travel companies which collect it. They have no way of verifying whether the information their customers have provided is accurate. E Brouwer, 'The EU Passenger Name Record (PNR) System and Human Rights: Transferring Passenger Data or Passenger Freedom?' (*CEPS Working Document* 320, 2009).

an agreement (but also on more casual bases).[24] For example, a 2013 agreement between the UK and the US exemplifies the formal arrangements.[25] In the agreement, information to be shared is defined as

> data on Nationals of a Third Country seeking authorization to transit through, travel to, work in, live in, or take citizenship of, the United Kingdom (UK) or the United States (U.S.), and other immigration and nationality-related data about Nationals of a Third Country, including data from admissibility, immigration or nationality compliance actions and/or decisions rendered in accordance with the immigration and nationality laws of the respective Parties. Information may consist of personal data, statistical data, or both.[26]

The only reference to consent is that of the parties specifically as regards further transfer to another state (not the data subject) and the scope of use of the personal data is extremely wide.

In the face of these state data collection, use and sharing challenges, it is now time to examine what the traveller's right to privacy and data protection is and where it is to be found. The core right which is at stake is the right to privacy, though this is also a gateway right. Once the right to privacy has been breached, there may be many knock-on breaches of human rights such as the right to opinion, non-discrimination on prohibited grounds, etc. The right of travellers to privacy has multiple sources. While privacy rights in national law may distinguish between citizens and aliens[27] this is not the case in international and regional human rights law. Nor is it the case in EU privacy and data protection rules. The international starting place for the right to privacy is the Universal Declaration of Human Rights 1948 (UDHR), Article 12.[28] This Declaration which was made after the Second World War is the first legal document to set out the fundamental human rights to be universally protected.[29] Two Covenants, adopted in 1966, gave treaty form to the rights contained in the UDHR.[30] Privacy was included in the International Covenant on Civil and Political Rights 1966 (ICCPR) in Article 17: '1. No one shall be subjected to arbitrary or unlawful interference

[24] See, ie, www.gov.uk/government/publications/personal-information-use-in-borders-immigration-and-citizenship/borders-immigration-and-citizenship-privacy-information-notice.

[25] Agreement between the Government of the United Kingdom of Great Britain and Northern Ireland and the Government of the United States of America for the Sharing of Visa, Immigration, and Nationality Information Treaty Series No 6 (2014).

[26] ibid Art 1(a). E Guild, 'Data Protection, Privacy and the Foreigner' in *Research Handbook on EU Law and Human Rights* (Edward Elgar Publishing, 2017).

[27] R Aldana, 'Of Katz and Aliens: Privacy Expectations and the Immigration Raids' (2007) *University of California Davis Law Review* 41, 1081.

[28] Universal Declaration of Human Rights 1948 (UDHR), Art 12: 'No one shall be subjected to arbitrary interference with his privacy, family, home or correspondence, nor to attacks upon his honour and reputation. Everyone has the right to the protection of the law against such interference or attacks.'

[29] See www.ohchr.org/en/what-are-human-rights.

[30] The International Covenant on Civil and Political Rights and the International Covenant of Economic, Social and Cultural Rights, both of 1966.

with his privacy, family, home or correspondence, nor to unlawful attacks on his honour and reputation; 2. Everyone has the right to the protection of the law against such interference or attacks.'[31] The Human Rights Committee, which is responsible for monitoring the national implementation of the ICCPR and assists states to do so correctly, issued General Comment 16 in 1988 regarding the correct implementation of Article 17.[32]

The 2013 Snowden revelations of US mass surveillance programmes, shone a spotlight on the right to privacy.[33] General disapprobation of states around the world to the USA's mass collection and use of personal data was expressed in the forum of the UN Human Rights Council. There was a sense of urgency to update Article 17 ICCPR in light of technological changes in the late twentieth and twenty-first centuries. The result was a Human Rights Council Report (and resolution), the Right to Privacy in the Digital Age (2018).[34] It was proposed by the Brazilian and German governments and supported by 57 other states in the Human Rights Council and then adopted by the UN General Assembly. Its starting place is the universality of the right to privacy which is not reserved to citizens but applies equally to all. It expressed the deep concern of the international community regarding the enhanced capacities of governments to use new information and communication technologies to undertake surveillance, interception and data collection possibly in violation of Article 17 ICCPR. It further acknowledges the importance of the right to privacy for the realisation that the right of freedom of expression, and thus interference with it, can be a threat to one of the foundations of a democratic society.

The resolution condemns unlawful or arbitrary surveillance and/or interception of communications, as well as the unlawful or arbitrary collection of personal data. These acts are characterised as highly intrusive and violations of the right to privacy. As regards the possible justifications for interferences with privacy, the report acknowledges that public security concerns may justify the gathering and protection of certain sensitive information but states must ensure full compliance with the human rights obligations. It states that state authorities must ensure that any measures taken to combat terrorism (the prime justification of states) are in compliance with their obligations in international law and particularly human rights. The report concluded that there is a clear and universal framework for the promotion and protection of the right to privacy in international human rights law. This framework is universal and binding on all state parties to the ICCPR and prohibits arbitrary interference with everyone's right to privacy.

[31] Schabas (n 10).

[32] UN Human Rights Committee (HRC), 'CCPR General Comment No. 16: Article 17 (Right to Privacy), The Right to Respect of Privacy, Family, Home and Correspondence, and Protection of Honour and Reputation' (8 April 1988), available at www.refworld.org/docid/453883f922.html.

[33] Z Bauman et al, 'After Snowden: Rethinking the Impact of Surveillance' (2014) *International Political Sociology* 8.2, 121–44.

[34] A/HRC/39/29.

The European regional sources of privacy protection are multiple but I will focus on the human rights framework of the European Convention on Human Rights (ECHR)[35] and the EU Charter of Fundamental Rights (the EU Charter).[36] The ECHR is a founding convention of the Council of Europe which is composed of 46 states. The purpose of the Council of Europe is standards setting in human rights. Article 8 ECHR provides that everyone has the right to respect for his private and family life, his home and his correspondence. Any interference must be justified on the grounds set out in Article 8 itself.[37] It is a cornerstone right though a qualified one. The European Court of Human Rights (ECtHR) has interpreted widely both the scope of the right and the meaning of privacy and has required states to adopt clear and transparent laws in respect of its protection. In the context of interpreting the scope of the right to privacy, the ECtHR has had regard to another Council of Europe instrument: the Convention for the Protection of Individuals with Regard to Automatic Processing of Personal Data 1981 (Convention 108).[38] This Convention is open to signature and ratification by non-Council of Europe countries, a number of which have availed themselves of the opportunity. This Convention has recently been updated and, its successor, 108+, is awaiting sufficient ratifications to come into force.[39]

The primary purpose of the Convention 108 is to protect the processing of personal data of every individual regardless of their nationality or residence (Article 1). The Convention outlines that personal data must be obtained and processed fairly and lawfully which engages the right of the data subject to consent or not, used and stored for a legitimate purpose (the purpose limitation principle), must be adequate, and where necessary, kept up to date and preserved in a form which permits identification of the subject for no longer than is required (Article 5(a)-(e)). Article 9 reinforces the purpose limitation principle imposing strict limitations upon any exceptions or derogations. The data controllers (including state bodies) are accountable where they obtain and process personal data outside the scope of the legitimate purpose. The Convention also includes special categories of data which may not be processed without specific safeguards. The categories are those which reveal racial origin, political opinions or religious or other beliefs, as well as personal data concerning health and sexual life. Further, as its title indicates, the Convention prohibits automated decision-making where this may result in human rights breaches. The ECtHR has found

[35] ETS 005.

[36] S Peers, et al (eds). *The EU Charter of Fundamental Rights: A Commentary* (Bloomsbury Publishing, 2021).

[37] ECHR, Art 8(2): 'There shall be no interference by a public authority with the exercise of this right except such as is in accordance with the law and is necessary in a democratic society in the interests of national security, public safety or the economic wellbeing of the country, for the prevention of disorder or crime, for the protection of health or morals, or for the protection of the rights and freedoms of others.'

[38] ETS 108.

[39] It will come into force either when all the Parties to Convention 108 ratify it or on or after 10 October 2023 when it has 38 parties. By September 2024, 31 countries had ratified the Convention.

the standards of Convention 108 relevant to the interpretation of the right to respect for privacy.[40]

The European Union (EU) is composed of 27 Member States with a complex and rich constitutional structure. In EU law, the starting place is the Charter, Article 7 of which protects the right to respect for private and family life, including home and communication. Article 8 entitles everyone to data protection of information concerning him or her. It requires that data processing must be fair and for specific purposes on the basis of the person's consent or some other legitimate basis laid down in law. It also includes the right to access and rectification by the data subject. The relationship between Articles 7 and 8 of the Charter has been the subject of some academic discussion but the Court of Justice of the European Union (CJEU) has held that the right to privacy is the individual's right and the right to data protection is the individual's right and that the state should implement the right to privacy. The Charter rights are now central to the interpretation of EU data protection law. The General Data Protection Regulation (GDPR)[41] goes further than Convention 108 specifically in the breadth of the definition of personal data and the limitations on its use. The GDPR defines personal data as any information that relates to an individual who can be directly or indirectly identified.[42] Processing is any action performed on data, whether automated or manual.[43] Consent of the data subject is defined as any freely given, specific, informed and unambiguous indication of the data subject's wishes by which he or she, by a statement or by a clear affirmative action, signifies agreement to the processing of personal data relating to him or her.[44] While consent is the primary ground for personal data use there are other grounds which are carefully set out in Article 6.[45] Article 5 requires that

[40] See, ie, *Benedik v Slovenia* App no 62357/14 (ECtHR, 24 April 2018) para 46.

[41] Regulation (EU) 2016/679 of the European Parliament and of the Council of 27 April 2016 on the protection of natural persons with regard to the processing of personal data and on the free movement of such data, and repealing Directive 95/46/EC (General Data Protection Regulation or GDPR) [2016] OJ L119/1; EU, Directive 95/46/EC of the European Parliament and of the Council of the Protection of Individuals with Regard to the Processing of Personal Data and on the Free Movement of Such data [1995] OJ L281/31-0050.

[42] GDPR Art 4(1).

[43] ibid Art 4(2).

[44] ibid Art 4(11).

[45] ibid Art 6(1): 'Processing shall be lawful only if and to the extent that at least one of the following applies:

(a) the data subject has given consent to the processing of his or her personal data for one or more specific purposes;
(b) processing is necessary for the performance of a contract to which the data subject is party or in order to take steps at the request of the data subject prior to entering into a contract;
(c) processing is necessary for compliance with a legal obligation to which the controller is subject;
(d) processing is necessary in order to protect the vital interests of the data subject or of another natural person;
(e) processing is necessary for the performance of a task carried out in the public interest or in the exercise of official authority vested in the controller;

personal data be collected for specified, explicit and legitimate purposes and not further processed in a manner that is incompatible with those purposes ('purpose limitation').[46] This includes the data minimisation principle (the collection is adequate, relevant and limited to what is necessary in relation to the purposes for which it is processed). There is a duty on the data controller (for instance, interior ministries in respect of aliens' data) to ensure that they comply with the accuracy duty (data must be accurate and, where necessary, kept up to date; every reasonable step must be taken to ensure that personal data that are inaccurate, having regard to the purposes for which they are processed, are erased or rectified without delay).[47] The storage limitation principle requires that personal data is kept no longer than is necessary for the purposes for which the personal data are processed.[48] Discrimination is prohibited in Article 9 which states that the

> processing of personal data revealing racial or ethnic origin, political opinions, religious or philosophical beliefs, or trade union membership, and the processing of genetic data, biometric data for the purpose of uniquely identifying a natural person, data concerning health or data concerning a natural person's sex life or sexual orientation shall be prohibited.[49]

As can be seen, there is a thick web of international and regional standards regarding privacy and data protection which are applicable either universally or in Europe. The application of these standards to travellers' data is highly questionable. In particular, the principles of data subject consent and purpose limitation are virtually invisible. But none of the data rights are absolute, so there is always the possibility for a state authority to seek to justify interferences with privacy on grounds contained therein. This is where the current legal challenges are the most ferocious.

IV. THE GROUNDS FOR INTERFERENCE

The claim of states to interfere with the right to privacy must always be justified, whether under the ICCPR, ECHR or EU law. In the ICCPR this is contained in

(f) processing is necessary for the purposes of the legitimate interests pursued by the controller or by a third party, except where such interests are overridden by the interests or fundamental rights and freedoms of the data subject which require protection of personal data, in particular where the data subject is a child.'

[46] There is an exception for public interest, scientific or historical research purposes or statistical purposes. We will consider the public interest exception further below.

[47] GDPR (n 41), Art 5(d).

[48] 'In Article 5(e) there is an exception: personal data may be stored for longer periods insofar as the personal data will be processed solely for archiving purposes in the public interest, scientific or historical research purposes or statistical purposes … subject to implementation of the appropriate GDPR approved technical and organisational measures in order to safeguard the rights and freedoms of the data subject.

[49] There are 10 exceptions to this limitation on processing which are carefully circumscribed to apply only in justified situations such as with the data subject's consent or for scientific purposes, though here again the term 'public interest' is used three times in respect of specific exceptions.

the requirement that interferences must be in accordance with the law and may not be arbitrary. The Human Rights Committee in its General Comment 16 on this provision stated that

> in the Committee's view the expression 'arbitrary interference' can also extend to interference provided for under the law. The introduction of the concept of arbitrariness is intended to guarantee that even interference provided for by law should be in accordance with the provisions, aims and objectives of the Covenant and should be, in any event, reasonable in the particular circumstances.[50]

Many of the practices in visa processing, travel authorisations, API and PNR collection and use by state authorities raise serious concerns about their compatibility with this requirement.

In the ECHR, the justification is more extensively developed, like the ICCPR, the legality requirement is foremost, but the ECHR goes on to require necessity in a democratic society (a proportionality test which is the reserve of the ECtHR), and must meet at least one of the requirements of national security, public safety or the economic wellbeing of the country, for the prevention of disorder or crime, for the protection of health or morals, or for the protection of the rights and freedoms of others. There is very extensive case law from the ECtHR on what interferences can be justified and in which circumstances, the detail of which is set out in various Council of Europe documents but, in general, as regards the personal data of travellers two grounds are used: the fight against serious crime and terrorism.[51] Once again, the data practices at borders raise serious questions about compliance.

In the GDPR, Article 23 sets out the restrictions which states can lawfully place on the right to privacy.[52] While the grounds are wide, they are carefully

[50] HRC General Comment 16 (n 32), para 4.

[51] See https://rm.coe.int/t-pd-2018-15-case-law-on-data-protection-may2018-en/16808b2d36.

[52] GDPR (n 41): '1. Union or Member State law to which the data controller or processor is subject may restrict by way of a legislative measure the scope of the obligations and rights provided for in Articles 12 to 22 and Article 34, as well as Article 5 in so far as its provisions correspond to the rights and obligations provided for in Articles 12 to 22, when such a restriction respects the essence of the fundamental rights and freedoms and is a necessary and proportionate measure in a democratic society to safeguard:

(a) national security;
(b) defence;
(c) public security;
(d) the prevention, investigation, detection or prosecution of criminal offences or the execution of criminal penalties, including the safeguarding against and the prevention of threats to public security;
(e) other important objectives of general public interest of the Union or of a Member State, in particular an important economic or financial interest of the Union or of a Member State, including monetary, budgetary and taxation a matters, public health and social security;
(f) the protection of judicial independence and judicial proceedings;
(g) the prevention, investigation, detection and prosecution of breaches of ethics for regulated professions;
(h) a monitoring, inspection or regulatory function connected, even occasionally, to the exercise of official authority in the cases referred to in points (a) to (e) and (g);

drafted to be specific in order to limit states' margin of manoeuvre. The use of justifications by EU states as regards travellers' data and privacy is twofold. On the one hand, states claim that it is valuable in the fight against terrorism.[53] The argument is that advanced knowledge of who is trying to come to a country permits states to check (electronically using AI/ML tools) whether the traveller is a threat. In the absence of specific information about the individual in other databases against which the traveller's information may be checked, AI/ML tools have been designed to identify profiles of persons likely to be a terrorist risk.[54] On the other hand, states claim that it helps to prevent or prosecute serious transnational crime. Again, AI/ML tools are used to check whether individuals are on criminal justice databases (or whatever databases are available to the authorities doing the checking) and as in the case of terrorism, to establish profiles of travellers whose characteristics resemble the profile which has been designed.

These claims have not been particularly well served when interrogated by courts. In the case which came before the CJEU regarding the legality of the EU-Canada PNR Agreement, the best evidence which was put before the Court was that

> … the Canadian authorities have provided information showing that PNR data has made a decisive contribution to the ability to identify potential suspects involved in terrorist acts or serious crime. Thus, whereas 28 million air passengers flew between the European Union and Canada between April 2014 and March 2015, that data made it possible to arrest 178, and to carry out drugs seizures in 71 cases and seizures

(i) the protection of the data subject or the rights and freedoms of others;
(j) the enforcement of civil law claims.

2. In particular, any legislative measure referred to in paragraph 1 shall contain specific provisions at least, where relevant, as to:

(a) the purposes of the processing or categories of processing;
(b) the categories of personal data;
(c) the scope of the restrictions introduced;
(d) the safeguards to prevent abuse or unlawful access or transfer;
(e) the specification of the controller or categories of controllers;
(f) the storage periods and the applicable safeguards taking into account the nature, scope and purposes of the processing or categories of processing;
(g) the risks to the rights and freedoms of data subjects; and
(h) the right of data subjects to be informed about the restriction, unless that may be prejudicial to the purpose of the restriction.'

[53] N Vavoula, 'Artificial Intelligence (AI) at Schengen Borders: Automated Processing, Algorithmic Profiling and Facial Recognition in the Era of Techno-Solutionism' (2021) *European Journal of Migration and Law* 23.4, 457–84; CR Han, R McGauran and H Nelen, 'API and PNR Data in Use for Border Control Authorities (2017) *Security Journal* 30, 1045–63, available at https://doi.org/10.1057/sj.2016.4.

[54] Vavoula, ibid; MC Horowitz et al, 'Artificial Intelligence and International Security' (Center for a New American Security, 2018); D Broeders, and J Hampshire, 'Dreaming of Seamless Borders: ICTs and the Pre-Emptive Governance of Mobility in Europe' (2013) *Journal of Ethnic and Migration Studies* 39.8, 1201–18.

> of child pornography material in two cases. That data also made it possible to initiate or further pursue investigations in relation to terrorism in 169 cases.[55]

In June 2022, the CJEU once again had to determine the legality of interferences with the privacy of travellers on the basis of serious crime. It was particularly concerned about states' use of the claim to combatting serious crime as a ground to interfere with two fundamental rights of everyone within the jurisdiction of the EU: Articles 7 and 8 of the EU Charter.

The CJEU held:

> Lastly, it is important also to bear in mind that, although, in accordance with the principle of proportionality, the objective of combating serious crime is capable of justifying the serious interference with the fundamental rights guaranteed in Articles 7 and 8 of the Charter which the PNR Directive entails, the same is not true of the objective of combating criminality in general, since the latter objective may justify solely non-serious interferences … Thus, that directive must ensure, by means of clear and precise rules, that the application of the system established by the said directive is limited to offences amounting to serious crime and thereby excludes those amounting to ordinary crime.[56]

This judgment is, of course, limited to the EU (though it may also affect data sharing between the EU and third countries).[57]

Clearly, the CJEU sought to ensure that states could not use a general claim that collecting and processing personal data of travellers was useful for law enforcement and combatting crime to justify uses of PNR data. Instead, the CJEU insisted that only serious crime as defined in the measure itself could justify such an interference with personal data. Further, the CJEU went on to limit the use of PNR data to combat serious crime or terrorism to a specific collection of the data:

> Consequently, PNR data collected and provided in accordance with Annex I to the PNR Directive must relate directly to the flight operated and the passenger concerned and must be limited in such a way as to, on the one hand, meet solely the legitimate requirements of public authorities to prevent, detect, investigate and prosecute terrorist offences or serious crime and, on the other, exclude sensitive data.[58]

In making this finding, the Court limited very substantially the possibility for states to use AI/ML tools based on profiles of people whom they considered to be possible risks. There must be a passenger concerned for the interference to be lawful.

For the moment, the most extensive judicial consideration of travellers' right to privacy and data protection has taken place in the EU. While not all

[55] Opinion 1/15, ECLI : EU:C:2017:592.

[56] ibid.

[57] E Guild, and EM Kuskonmaz, 'EU Exclusive Jurisdiction on Surveillance Related to Terrorism and Serious Transnational Crime: Case Review on Opinion 1/15' (2018) *European Law Review*.

[58] C-817/19 *Ligue des droits humains v Conseil des ministres* ECLI:EU:C:2022:491.

commentators are satisfied with the CJEU's approach, it is nonetheless generally privacy protective in the face of state practices.[59]

V. CONCLUSIONS

At the outset, I aimed to address three questions regarding the traveller and his/her data. The first is the way in which the ambition, intention or practice of seeking to cross an international border has transformed personal data into the currency which must be paid by the traveller to succeed. That data then goes into circulation beyond the control of the traveller defying both the international and regional privacy principles of consent and purpose limitation. The second question relates to what state authorities do with the personal data they acquire from the traveller. Here it is apparent that technological tools of AI/ML enhance the value of that personal data as they make it possible to apply a wide range of applications to it. Some of those applications are related to criminal justice, others to counter-terrorism, but the intersection with other databases makes many other kinds of uses possible, such as work records, health status, tax payments, etc. Arguments can and are made that these other kinds of uses are directly relevant to criminal justice enforcement and counter-terrorism but they become weaker and weaker and the purposes become more diffuse as the outcomes regarding uses become less predictable (at least for the traveller). As has been stated elsewhere, personal data is the new gold.[60] For state authorities, nowhere is this more evident than as regards the traveller. As a new currency, data is traded among ministries, in return for access to a database some other benefit can be required of the requesting authority. As regards international agreements, reciprocity between the parties relies on each hoping to benefit as much (if not more) than the other from data access, the driving force. Travellers' data is easily acquired and weakly protected making it a low lying fruit for collection of the new currency. Finally, examining the justifications permissible in international and European regional law which states have put forward for this personal data collection on travellers, they are rapidly wearing thin. In the EU at least, the CJEU is increasingly reluctant to take such justifications presented by states as fulfilling the requirements of the right to privacy.

[59] A Vedaschi and G Marino Noberasco, 'From DRD to PNR: Looking for a New Balance Between Privacy and Security' in D Cole (ed), *Surveillance, Privacy and Trans-Atlantic Relations* (Hart Publishing, 2017) 67–90; CA Kuner, 'Court of Justice International Agreements, Data Protection, and EU Fundamental Rights on the International Stage: Opinion 1/15, EU-Canada PNR' (2018) *CMLR* 55.3.

[60] J Angwin, 'The Web's New Gold Mine: Your Secrets' (2010) *Wall Street Journal* 30.07, 2010.

18

Towards Artificially Intelligent EU Migration, Asylum and Border Management? The AI Act, Interoperable Large-Scale IT Systems and the Role of Agencies

AI for EU Migration, Asylum and Border Control

NIOVI VAVOULA*

I. INTRODUCTION

IN RECENT YEARS, there has been a heightened interest in artificial intelligence (AI), understood as a set of techniques used to train machines to approximate some aspects of human or animal cognition. In the field of migration, broadly encompassing migration, asylum and border management, AI has the potential to revolutionise the way states manage mobility, decision-making and community integration. AI systems, such as facial, dialect or emotion recognition and risk assessment tools, promise modernised identity checks and border controls, as well as expedited, consistent and more efficient decision-making, for example, in relation to visas, residence permits or asylum applications.[1] Other AI tools, such as predictive analytics, may also be used for more evidence-based policy-making, and even for predicting increased numbers of refugee and migrant arrivals[2] or for enhanced situational awareness around borders by

* University of Luxembourg.

[1] P Molnar, 'Technology on the Margins: AI and Global Migration Management from a Human Rights Perspective' (2019) 8(2) *Cambridge International Law Journal* 305.

[2] A Beduschi, 'International Migration Management in the Age of Artificial Intelligence' (2021) 9(3) *Migration Studies* 576.

analysing surveillance footage collected by various sensors deployed at states' frontiers and transforming it into actionable information and alerts for border and coast guard authorities.

To an extent, this highly technologised model of migration management is already a reality in some countries. For example, in Canada, the use of algorithmic decision-making in immigration and refugee status determination has been promoted since 2014,[3] whereas at the US-Mexico border, the assessment as to whether an irregular migrant must be placed in pre-deportation detention is determined on the basis of an algorithm.[4] In the United Kingdom (UK), in August 2020, the Home Secretary withdrew an algorithm used to stream visa applications into three channels, including a so-called 'fast lane' facilitating 'speedy boarding for white people' from highly developed countries, when challenged by an non-governmental organisation on the basis of racial discrimination, among other things.[5] A number of European countries, such as Germany and the Netherlands, are testing the waters of AI in migration, asylum and border management by developing algorithms that predict migration flows and assist in the determination of applications for international protection or residence permits (through dialect recognition or extraction and the analysis of mobile phone data).[6]

The AI Act aims to regulate the use of AI across different fields, including migration,[7] but the interest in AI in this domain dates back to some years before. The large-scale IT systems for third-country nationals that will become interoperable by 2027 have the potential to employ AI tools to process facial images for biometric identification at the borders and on national territory, and to profile applicants for Schengen visas and travel authorisation. This is notwithstanding the fact that EU documentation and legal instruments do not explicitly refer to AI, but rather to algorithms. Furthermore, EU agencies with a migration-related mandate, namely the EU Asylum Agency (EUAA), European Border and

[3] P Molnár and L Gill, 'Bots at the Gate: A Human Rights Analysis of Automated Decision Making in Canada's Immigration and Refugee System' (International Human Rights Program-Faculty of Law, University of Toronto and the Citizen Lab-Munk School of Global Affairs and Public Policy, University of Toronto 2018) Research Report No 114 14–15.

[4] R Koulish, 'Immigration Detention in the Risk Classification Assessment Era' (2017) 16 *Conecticut Public Interest Law Journal* 3.

[5] 'Home Office to Scrap "Racist Algorithm" for UK Visa Applicants' *The Guardian* (4 August 2020), available at www.theguardian.com/uk-news/2020/aug/04/home-office-to-scrap-racist-algorithm-for-uk-visa-applicants. For an analysis, see C Barclay and E Guild, 'Brexit, Personal Data and Aliens' (2023) 37(3) *Immigration, Asylum and Nationality Law* 271.

[6] For an overview see D Ozkul, 'Automating Immigration and Asylum: Mapping the Landscape of New Technologies in Europe' (Working Paper AFAR 1/2022).

[7] Regulation (EU) 2024/1689 of the European Parliament and of the Council of 13 June 2024 laying down harmonised rules on artificial intelligence and amending Regulations (EC) No 300/2008, (EU) No 167/2013, (EU) No 168/2013, (EU) 2018/858, (EU) 2018/1139 and (EU) 2019/2144 and Directives 2014/90/EU, (EU) 2016/797 and (EU) 2020/1828 (Artificial Intelligence Act or AI Act) (Text with EEA relevance) [2024] OJ L 2024/1689. For the proposal see Commission, 'Proposal for a Regulation of the European Parliament and of the Council laying down harmonised rules on Artificial Intelligence (AI Act) and amending certain Union legislative acts' COM(2021) 206 final.

Coast Guard Agency (EBCG Agency), and eu-LISA, have taken an interest in AI paving the way for the increase in their tasks and foreshadowing the high-tech future of migration, asylum and border management in the EU. These initiatives are coupled with various research projects funded by the EU and a 2020 Commission report announcing a portfolio with initiatives to be implemented within a 'roadmap' by 2025.[8]

Against this backdrop, this contribution aims to provide a broad overview of the use of AI in this domain and provide an anthology of the fundamental rights challenges particularly relating to the rights to non-discrimination and privacy and data protection, as enshrined in Articles 21, 7 and 8 of the EU Charter of Fundamental Rights respectively. This overview entails the examination of three related developments at the EU level; the regulation of AI systems employed at the EU and national levels in the field of migration, asylum and border management following the adoption of the AI Act, the implementation of AI tools in the operationalisation of interoperable large-scale IT systems and the role of EU agencies in developing and promoting the use of AI in this field.

Although research on these topics is growing,[9] there are numerous legislative and jurisprudential developments that herald revisiting these issues to provide additional and complementary remarks. To that end, the chapter is organised as follows: section II provides a concise synopsis of the use of AI (operational or under development) in EU Member States, both developed at national level or through various EU-funded projects. Section III places these initiatives within the context of the AI Act to demonstrate the extent to which the classification of AI systems under EU legislation falls short of the existing developments. Sections IV and V investigate whether and to what extent interoperable large-scale IT systems will rely on AI tools. Facial recognition technology (FRT) in the IT systems and automated risk assessments in the context of examining applications for travel authorisations (ETIAS) and Schengen visas (VIS) are analysed, viewed through the lens of the case law of the EU Court of Justice (CJEU) on the automated processing of personal data. Section VI then looks into the temporary exclusion of IT systems from the scope of the AI Act analysing its rationale and implications. Section VII examines the role of EU agencies in the

[8] Commission, 'Opportunities and Challenges for the Use of Artificial Intelligence in Border Control, Migration and Security' (2020). However, with the delays in the implementation of interoperability, the timeline for implementation of new AI tools will be delayed.

[9] N Vavoula, 'Artificial Intelligence (AI) at EU Borders: From Automated Processing to Algorithmic Profiling and Facial Recognition in the Era of Techno-Solutionism' (2021) 31(4) *European Journal of Migration and Law* 457; Ch Derave, N Genicot and N Hetmanska, 'The Risks of Trustworthy Artificial Intelligence: The Case of the European Travel Information and Authorisation System' (2022) 13 *European Journal of Risk Regulation* 389; T Zandstra and E Brouwer: 'Fundamental Rights at the Digital Border: ETIAS, the Right to Data Protection, and the CJEU's PNR judgment' (*Verfassungsblog*, 2022), available at https://verfassungsblog.de/digital-border; A Musco Eklund, 'Rule of Law Challenges of 'Algorithmic Discretion' & Automation in EU Border Control: A Case Study of ETIAS Through the Lens of Legality' (2023) 25 *European Journal of Migration and Law* 249.

field of migration, asylum and border management, with a focus on EUAA, the EBCG Agency and eu-LISA. Europol's role, though significant in the field of human smuggling, is not analysed as the agency is treated primarily as a law enforcement organisation. The Conclusion summarises the main findings of the research.

II. THE MANIFOLD EXPERIMENTATION WITH ALGORITHMS IN EU/SCHENGEN STATES

In 2022, Ozkul mapped out the existing uses of new technologies at the national level, taking a temporal approach to these practices, by dividing them into those employed prior to the arrival of third-country nationals, at the border; and on national territory.[10] The report examined various tools enabling the automation of processes that were previously performed by humans, using simple closed-rule algorithms, as well as more complex AI systems. In particular, certain Member States have relied on their own means to develop and test new tools, with an emphasis placed on various forecasting tools predicting future immigration and displacement towards Europe (Germany,[11] Sweden[12] and Denmark).[13] In 2023, it was made known that the Dutch authorities implemented an algorithm to assess short-stay (Schengen) visa applications, which was criticised as discriminatory as it labelled all young men from Suriname for intensive assessment.[14] In Norway[15] and Sweden,[16] tools have been developed to automate the processing of short- and long-term residence and citizenship applications, but in both cases where the systems are less advanced and do not entail machine learning.

Another popular AI-based software enables the checking of whether travellers' or applicants' identities and other supporting documents are genuine and thus the detection of possible identity fraud. This is the case in the Netherlands[17] but similar tools are under development in Belgium and France. Speech recognition is also on the rise; for example, in Latvia it constitutes part of the process

[10] Ozkul (n 6).

[11] The PREVIEW project monitors ongoing conflicts, and its long-term aim is to develop a forecasting tool for future events. Commission, 'Feasibility Study on a Forecasting and Early Warning Tool for Migration based on Artificial Intelligence Technology (2020) 36.

[12] The PREDICT project has used supervised machine learning techniques to predict migration flows to Sweden, the processing times of different types of cases (such as asylum, residency permit, work permit), and settlement of migrants across Sweden in different months of the year.

[13] The forecasting tool can predict forced displacement around the world.

[14] 'Dutch Foreign Ministry Using Discriminatory Algorithm for Visa Applications' (*NL Times*, 2 May 2023), available at https://nltimes.nl/2023/05/02/dutch-foreign-ministry-using-discriminatory-algorithm-visa-applications.

[15] Two robots can register documents, 'filter and mark applications and send out confirmations of legal residence'. See Ozkul (n 6) 22–23.

[16] This concerns a rule-based system to verify the age of the applicant or in the case of applications for a work permit, verifying the presence of sponsorship and checking the eligibility of the applicant.

[17] This software uses pattern recognition and augmented intelligence and classifies documents according to their risks based on features of the presented document. See Ozkul (n 6) 25.

of citizenship applications. In Germany, name transliteration, that is converting asylum applicants' names into the Latin alphabet, aims to prevent spelling errors and standardise the spelling of names, but can also assist in identifying the country of origin,[18] although this function has a low accuracy rate in respect of applicants from Maghreb countries.[19] Furthermore, reliability issues exist in relation to dialect recognition for the identification of asylum seekers' country of origin implemented in Germany, as the recognition of dialects relies on the training of dialects of a language from numerous regions.[20]

Mobile phone data extraction is another tool employed in the Netherlands, Germany, Norway and to some extent Denmark. In Germany, mobile phone data extraction based on the asylum seeker's consent has raised concerns regarding the violation of privacy, lack of meaningful consent, lack of necessity and proportionality, and lack of transparency as to the opaque nature of the software and algorithms.[21] These concerns have been confirmed by the German Federal Administrative Court (BVerwG) which in February 2023 ruled that the practice of regularly analysing data carriers, including mobile phones, by the Federal Office for Migration and Refugees (BAMF) when registering asylum applicants was illegal.[22]

These initiatives at the national level are coupled with a wide range of research projects funded by the Commission, some of which are pursued taking stock of the findings of previous research in a continuum of ever-growing techno-solutionism.[23] In particular, lie detection technologies, entailing emotion recognition, although not employed at EU borders, were tested in Hungary, Latvia and Greece in the context of the iBorderCtrl research project. The latter combined several technologies, including biometric verification, deception detection, document authentication and risk assessment, in one system and attracted heavy criticism for its lack of accuracy and thus reliability.[24]

[18] H Hohn, 'Digital Identification Systems and the Right to Privacy in the Asylum Context: An Analysis of Implementations in Germany' (Master's Thesis, Leuphana Universität Lüneburg, 2020) 40.

[19] Ozkul (n 6) 40.

[20] ibid 43–48.

[21] Gesellschaft für Freiheitsrechte e.V, 'Invading Refugees' Phones: Digital Forms of Migration Control in Germany and Europe' (2020).

[22] BVerwG 1 C 19.21. For an analysis see F Palmiotto and D Ozkul, 'Like Handing My Whole Life Over' – The German Federal Administrative Court's Landmark Ruling on Mobile Phone Data Extraction in Asylum Procedures' (*Verfassungsblog*, 28 February 2023), available at https://verfassungsblog.de/like-handing-my-whole-life-over/.

[23] The projects relating to the use of AI are as follows: FLYSEC, BODEGA, PROTECT, iBorderCtrl RANGER SafeShore, E2mC, ROBORDER MARISA, CAMELOT, SMILE Smart-Trust, FOLDOUT, MIRROR, COMPASS2020, BorderSens, ARESIBO< D4FLY, PERCEPTIONS, ANDROMEDA, ITFLOWS, BorderUAS, EFFECTOR, iMPARS, EURMARS, REACTION, Silent-Border, CRITERIA, PROMENADE, AI-ARC, SECTRONIC AMASS TALOS WIMAAS EFFISEC SCIIMS ARGUS 3D SEABILLA OPARUS I2C PERSEUS SMART, FIDELITY, BEAT, FASTPASS, CLOSEEYE, INGRESS, ABC4U, SNOOPY, SUNNY, MOBILEPASS, EWISA, EU CISE 2020.

[24] D Van Den Meerssche, 'Virtual Borders: International Law and the Elusive Inequalities of Algorithmic Association' (2022) 33(1) *European Journal of International Law* 171.

The lack of transparency has also been notable leading the General Court of the CJEU to opine that the public can partially access the project documentation where it generally discusses the reliability, ethics and legality of such technology. However, the Court considered that commercial interests rule out public access to information on the specific iBorderCtrl technology, including its legality, its reliability (false positives), the risk of discrimination and mitigation measures.[25] The next stage of iBorderCtrl, under the title TRESSPASS, also explored the feasibility and usefulness of behaviour analysis, including emotion recognition of individuals being interviewed by border guards and customs officers.[26] Another important initiative is the ROBORDER project (autonomous swarm of heterogeneous RObots for BORDER surveillance) aimed to develop and demonstrate a fully-functional autonomous border surveillance system with unmanned mobile robots including aerial, water surface, underwater and ground vehicles.[27] Predictive analytical tools are also under development through multi-stakeholder cooperation; ITFLOWS has developed the EUMigraTool (EMT) to predict the number of migrants coming to a specific European country, provide an analysis on drivers, patterns and choices of migration, as well as public sentiment towards migration and identify the risks of tensions between migrants and EU citizens.[28]

Countries in the periphery of the EU, have been testing grounds for these projects, particularly Greece, where the REACTION project (Real-Time Artificial Intelligence for Border Surveillance), currently implemented, combines the findings from ROBORDER and AIDERS – another EU-funded project aimed at processing data from drones, sensors and cameras to improve emergency responses in case of a fire, flood or shipwreck.[29] Through AI, the purported aim is to conduct surveillance, identify and monitor targets of interest, and deploy the necessary resources.[30]

III. THE AI ACT: OMISSIONS AND MISCLASSIFICATIONS OF AI SYSTEMS

The aforementioned initiatives demonstrate the multiplicity of AI tools that are currently being developed, piloted and tested in individual Member States or under research consortia without a corresponding supranational regulatory

[25] Case T-158/19 *Patrick Breyer v European Research Executive Agency (REA)* EU:T:2021:902. An appeal was rejected in September 2023. Case C-135/22 P *Patrick Breyer v European Research Executive Agency (REA)* EU:C:2023:640.

[26] See www.trespass-etn.eu/.

[27] See https://roborder.eu/.

[28] See www.itflows.eu/.

[29] See https://ydeap.gr/reaction/.

[30] For criticism see J Lulamae, 'Greece Plans Automated Drones to Spot People Crossing Border' (*Algorithm Watch*, 23 September 2023), available at https://algorithmwatch.org/en/greece-plans-automated-drones/.

framework and without proper scrutiny, transparency or an understanding of their fundamental rights implications. The latter differ as regards the nature and degree of seriousness depending on the AI tool employed, thus ranging from algorithmic biases to the risk of a violation of the principle of non-refoulement and the right to seek asylum.

This brings to the fore the question of whether the AI Act that includes different levels of risk corresponding to certain AI systems and leads to regulation of varying levels of density, captures the multitude of AI tools in this field and their corresponding risks for fundamental rights. Based on a central assessment of their fundamental rights implications,[31] AI systems may be divided into four discrete risk categories: an *unacceptable* risk that results in absolute prohibition; this is the case with AI systems that deploy subliminal techniques, exploit vulnerabilities, social scoring systems, and 'real-time' biometric identification systems in law enforcement;[32] a *high* risk[33] that leads to a series of legal obligations imposed on the providers, users, and third parties[34] of AI systems intended to be used as a safety component of a product or that are products themselves (Annex II) and – as such – are required to undergo a third-party conformity assessment with a view to a market placement or being put into service pursuant to the Union harmonisation legislation *as well as* stand-alone AI systems employed for the purposes listed in Annex III; a *limited* risk that gives rise to transparency requirements;[35] or a *minimal* risk that may be addressed through codes of conduct intended to foster voluntary application to AI systems.[36]

Although Recital 39 of the proposed AI Act recognised that AI systems used in migration, asylum and border management 'affect people who are often in particularly vulnerable positions and who are dependent on the outcome of the actions of the competent public authorities', no AI system in this field is prohibited. Instead, in Annex III, the Commission opted to classify as high-risk four AI systems intended to be used by the competent public authorities charged with tasks in the fields of immigration control: polygraphs and similar tools to detect the emotional state of a natural person; AI systems to assess the security, irregular immigration, or health risk posed by individuals intending to enter or that have entered the territory of a Member State (eg, applying for a visa or asylum); AI systems to verify the authenticity of the relevant documents of natural persons; and AI systems to assist in the examination of applications for asylum, visas, or residence permits and associated complaints to establish the eligibility of a natural person applying for either.

[31] AI Act (n 7) recitals 13, 27–28.
[32] ibid, Art 5.
[33] ibid, Art 6.
[34] ibid, Arts 8–51.
[35] ibid, Art 52.
[36] ibid, Art 69.

The proposed classification was problematic as not only were certain AI systems wrongly classified, but, in addition, the list of high-risk AI systems was incomplete. A paradigmatic example of incorrect classification is emotion recognition based on scientific theories of dubious validity.[37] Lie detectors are considered to be a pseudo-scientific technology that infers emotions based on biometric data, while behavioural analytics detects 'suspicious' individuals based on how they look. Their use reinforces a process of racialised suspicion towards people on the move and can automate discriminatory assumptions.[38] Automated risk assessments of third-country nationals to determine whether they present a security, irregular migration or public health risk could also be prohibited considering that, as explained in section V, such systems may lead to indirect discrimination of groups of third-country nationals when the algorithms used for risk assessment rely on proxies of protected characteristics drawing discriminatory inferences.

Furthermore, there were significant gaps in the list of high-risk AI systems. In particular, predictive analytics systems did not feature in Annex III at all. By predicting the arrival of migrants and refugees in any given state, these systems can help ensure that states are sufficiently prepared for an increase in the number of people arriving (eg, assessing and allocating resources for reception needs). Moreover, predictive analytics may be used to facilitate preventive responses to halt movement, for example, through pushbacks or by recruiting third countries to act as the gatekeepers of EU borders and thus reinforce non-entrée policies and unlawful non-refoulement practices and prevent people from seeking international protection.[39] As such, they risk intensifying global or regional asymmetries, and curtailing fundamental rights. Another important omission concerned the lack of reference to AI systems for border monitoring and surveillance. These include: the establishment of autonomous surveillance towers fielded in border regions, with surveillance capabilities to detect irregular border crossings; Automatic Identification Systems (AIS) used for maritime awareness and surveillance; and unmanned robotic and aerial systems, essentially systems tested in the ROBORDER and REACTION projects.

The impact of these systems on individuals who resort to an irregular border crossing in the absence of legal pathways to EU territory can be significant, exacerbating border violence and facilitating collective expulsions and pushbacks. Moreover, biometric identification at the borders and on national territory, such as in detention facilities, including FRT, is not subject to tailor-made rules in this field and the deployment of AI systems that would scan border areas to deter and prevent migrants and refugees from entering and seeking asylum is

[37] F Cabitza, A Campagner and M Mattioli, 'The Unbearable (Technical) Unreliability of Automated Facial Emotion Recognition' (2022) 9(2) *Big Data & Society*.

[38] Access Now and Others, 'The EU AI Act Must Protect People on the Move' (2022).

[39] A Beduschi, 'International Migration Management in the Age of Artificial Intelligence' (2021) 9(3) *Migration Studies* 576; C Blasi Casagran and others, 'The Role of Emerging Predictive IT Tools in Effective Migration Governance' (2021) 9(4) *Politics and Governance* 133.

not banned.[40] Although real-time remote biometric identification was prohibited to an extent by the proposed AI Act, such a prohibition did not concern migration, asylum and border management, but only law enforcement. In turn, Annex III separately classified *e-post* recognition – where the biometric data have already been captured, and where a comparison and identification do not occur instantaneously – as high risk.

The aforementioned points were not addressed by the Council, which instead removed AI-based document verification from high-risk systems.[41] However, the Parliament's position reflected the aforementioned concerns better.[42] First, it opted for a ban of AI systems that infer the emotions of a natural person in the area of border management.[43] Second, it classified as high risk AI systems intended to be used to monitor, survey or process data in the context of border management activities, for the purpose of detecting, recognising or identifying natural persons.[44] The reference to surveillance is crucial in this respect, as this category of AI systems focuses on the impact rather than on the tools used and thus can encompass a wider range of systems. A third category of AI systems classified as high-risk consisted of those intended to be used 'for the forecasting or prediction of trends related to migration movement and border crossing' irrespective of their use to reallocate resources or to curtail migration.[45] Nevertheless, the Parliament's position had important shortcomings, particularly regarding AI systems based on individual risk assessment and profiling systems. Whereas this particular point was not picked up by the Parliament, as explained above, its position contained another ban on AI systems for making risk assessments in law enforcement settings.[46] Considering that risk assessment in the field of immigration control entails an assessment of the security risk, which incorporates the commission of a crime, this ban could have spillover consequences beyond the law enforcement remit. The Parliament's position was slightly disappointing for another reason; it lacked ambition which meant that the Parliament had limited room for manoeuvre in the negotiations with the Council.

The co-legislators agreed on the AI Act on 8 December 2023 and the AI Act entered into force in August 2024 and by mid-2026 it will be fully enforceable. It appears that the Council position has prevailed on most fronts; a ban on emotion recognition will not cover the field of migration, asylum and border management, solely work and educational settings, with a clause for medical treatments. From the Parliament, additions to the list of high-risk systems

[40] Access Now and Others (n 38).

[41] Council, Document 14954/22 (25 November 2022).

[42] Parliament, 'Artificial Intelligence Act Amendments adopted by the European Parliament on 14 June 2023 on the proposal for a regulation of the European Parliament and of the Council on laying down harmonised rules on artificial intelligence (Artificial Intelligence Act) and amending certain Union legislative acts (COM(2021)0206 – C9-0146/2021 – 2021/0106(COD))' (P9_TA(2023)0236).

[43] ibid, Art 5(1.dc).

[44] ibid, Annex III: point 7(da).

[45] ibid, Annex III: 7(db).

[46] ibid, Art 5(1.da.).

predictive analytics have not made the final cut and document verification has been reclassified as low risk. This means that a series of AI systems will be equated with AI systems such as chatbots and be merely subject to information and transparency obligations.

IV. SEARCHING FOR AI IN INTEROPERABLE LARGE-SCALE IT SYSTEMS: THE CASE OF FRT

There is no other domain in the EU Area of Freedom, Security and Justice (AFSJ) that has undergone such massive transformation in recent years through legislative activity than the field of large-scale IT systems processing personal data of third-country nationals taking into account the evolution of modern technologies. Next to the currently operational Schengen Information System (SIS),[47] Eurodac[48] and the Visa Information System (VIS),[49] which are being

[47] Regulation (EU) 2018/1860 of the European Parliament and of the Council of 28 November 2018 on the use of the Schengen Information System for the return of illegally staying third-country nationals [2018] OJ L312/1; Regulation (EU) 2018/1861 of the European Parliament and of the Council of 28 November 2018 on the establishment, operation and use of the Schengen Information System (SIS) in the field of border checks, and amending the Convention implementing the Schengen Agreement, and amending and repealing Regulation (EC) No 1987/2006 [2018] OJ L132/14; Regulation (EU) 2018/1862 of the European Parliament and of the Council of 28 November 2018 on the establishment, operation and use of the Schengen Information System (SIS) in the field of police cooperation and judicial cooperation in criminal matters, amending and repealing Council Decision 2007/533/JHA, and repealing Regulation (EC) No 1986/2006 of the European Parliament and of the Council and Commission Decision 2010/261/EU [2018] OJ L312/56.

[48] Regulation (EU) No 603/2013 of the European Parliament and of the Council of 26 June 2013 on the establishment of 'Eurodac' for the comparison of fingerprints for the effective application of Regulation (EU) No 604/2013 establishing the criteria and mechanisms for determining the Member State responsible for examining an application for international protection lodged in one of the Member States by a third-country national or a stateless person and on requests for the comparison with Eurodac data by Member States' law enforcement authorities and Europol for law enforcement purposes, and amending Regulation (EU) No 1077/2011 establishing a European Agency for the operational management of large-scale IT systems in the area of freedom, security and justice (recast) [2013] OJ L180/1. See Commission, 'Proposal for a Regulation of the European Parliament and of the Council on the establishment of 'Eurodac' for the comparison of fingerprints for the effective application of [Regulation (EU) No 604/2013 establishing the criteria and mechanisms for determining the Member State responsible for examining an application for international protection lodged in one of the Member States by a third-country national or a stateless persons], for identifying an illegally staying third-country national or stateless person and on requests for the comparison with Eurodac data by Member States' law enforcement authorities and Europol for law enforcement purposes (recast)' COM(2016) 272 final (2016 Eurodac proposal); Commission, 'Amended proposal for a Regulation of the European Parliament and of the Council on the establishment of "Eurodac" for the comparison of biometric data for the effective application of Regulation (EU) XXX/XXX [Regulation on Asylum and Migration Management] and of Regulation (EU) XXX/XXX [Resettlement Regulation], for identifying an illegally staying third-country national or stateless person and on requests for the comparison with Eurodac data by Member States' law enforcement authorities and Europol for law enforcement purposes and amending Regulations (EU) 2018/1240 and (EU) 2019/818' COM(2020) 614 final.

[49] Regulation (EC) No 767/2008 of the European Parliament and of the Council of 9 July 2008 concerning the Visa Information System (VIS) and the exchange of data between Member States on short-stay visas (VIS Regulation) (VIS Regulation) [2008] OJ L218/60, as amended by

refurbished, the Entry/Exit System (EES),[50] the European Travel Information and Authorisation System (ETIAS)[51] and the European Criminal Record Information System for Third-country Nationals (ECRIS-TCN)[52] are currently being developed.[53] Furthermore, IT systems are bound to be interconnected in different ways under the umbrella concept of interoperability.[54] The large volume of personal data (to be) contained in the various IT systems has justified the use of algorithms for making sense and making the most out of the stored data. But is there AI, and if so, where exactly?

A. Preparing the IT Systems for FRT

With the exception of ETIAS, IT systems are designed to process different types of biometric identifiers, with an emphasis in the past few years on verification and identification first through fingerprints and increasingly via facial images. The preference for digitally tagging individuals using their biological characteristics is attributed to a number of qualities that they carry, such as their universality, distinctiveness and permanence.[55] Biometrics create an 'anchor' for

Regulation (EU) 2021/1134 of the European Parliament and of the Council of 7 July 2021 amending Regulations (EC) No 767/2008, (EC) No 810/2009, (EU) 2016/399, (EU) 2017/2226, (EU) 2018/1240, (EU) 2018/1860, (EU) 2018/1861, (EU) 2019/817 and (EU) 2019/1896 of the European Parliament and of the Council and repealing Council Decisions 2004/512/EC and 2008/633/JHA, for the purpose of reforming the Visa Information System (2021 VIS Regulation) [2021] OJ L248/11.

[50] Regulation (EU) 2017/2226 of the European Parliament and of the Council of 30 November 2017 establishing an Entry/Exit System (EES) to register entry and exit data and refusal of entry data of third-country nationals crossing the external borders of the Member States and determining the conditions for access to the EES for law enforcement purposes, and amending the Convention implementing the Schengen Agreement and Regulations (EC) No 767/2008 and (EU) No 1077/2011 (EES Regulation) [2017] OJ L327/20.

[51] Regulation (EU) 2018/1240 of the European Parliament and of the Council of 12 September 2018 establishing a European Travel Information and Authorisation System (ETIAS) and amending Regulations (EU) No 1077/2011, (EU) No 515/2014, (EU) 2016/399, (EU) 2016/1624 and (EU) 2017/2226 (ETIAS Regulation) [2018] OJ L236/1.

[52] Regulation (EU) 2019/816 of the European Parliament and of the Council of 17 April 2019 establishing a centralised system for the identification of Member States holding conviction information on third-country nationals and stateless persons (ECRIS-TCN) to supplement the European Criminal Records Information System and amending Regulation (EU) 2018/1726 [2019] OJ L135/1.

[53] For an overview see N Vavoula, *Immigration and Privacy in the Law of the EU: The Case of Information Systems* (Brill Nijhoff, 2022).

[54] Regulation (EU) 2019/817 of the European Parliament and of the Council of 20 May 2019 on establishing a framework for interoperability between EU information systems in the field of borders and visa and amending Regulations (EC) No 767/2008, (EU) 2016/399, (EU) 2017/2226, (EU) 2018/1240, (EU) 2018/1726 and (EU) 2018/1861 of the European Parliament and of the Council and Council Decisions 2004/512/EC and 2008/633/JHA [2019] OJ L135/27; Regulation (EU) 2019/818 of the European Parliament and of the Council of 20 May 2019 on establishing a framework for interoperability between EU information systems in the field of police and judicial cooperation, asylum and migration and amending Regulations (EU) 2018/1726, (EU) 2018/1862 and (EU) 2019/816 [2019] OJ L135/85 (collectively Interoperability Regulations).

[55] A Jain, R Bolle and S Pankanti, *Personal Identification in Networked Society* (Kluwer, 1999). For an analysis on implementing biometrics at the borders see Commission, 'Biometrics at the Frontiers: Assessing the Impact on Society' (2005).

identity in the human body, to which information can be fixed,[56] resulting in its 'informatisation'.[57] Under EU data protection law, biometric data constitute a special category of personal data[58] and are defined as 'personal data resulting from specific technical processing relating to the physical, physiological or behavioural characteristics of a natural person, which allow or confirm the unique identification of that natural person'.[59] Furthermore, facial images fall within the remit of Article 8 of the European Convention on Human Rights (ECHR).[60] Facial images constitute biometric data: they are largely unique, they cannot be changed by individuals (eg, destroyed) and in comparison to fingerprints they can easily be captured; individuals are unable to prevent the capture of their facial images.[61]

At the time of writing, FRT is not applied by any operational IT system. By 2027, the processing of facial images for the purpose of verification and/or identification will be facilitated by two interoperability components: the shared Biometric Matching Service (sBMS) that will store the biometric templates of all biometric data collected,[62] and the Common Identity Repository (CIS) that will store certain biographic data and the biometric data of the systems.[63] The first step towards the insertion of facial images in information systems took place in the setting up of the EES. The EES Regulation requires the collection of four fingerprints and a facial image and prescribes the use of facial recognition technology for verification purposes at the border[64] and on national territory.[65] EES will rely on machine learning techniques for biometric matching.[66] Facial images may also be used *in combination with fingerprints* to identify individuals, and border authorities or immigration authorities shall have authorisation to search using the fingerprint data or the fingerprint data combined with the

[56] Surveillance Studies Network, 'A Report on the Surveillance Society' (2006) 23.

[57] I van der Ploeg, 'Biometric Identification Technologies: Ethical Implications of the Informatization of the Body' (No 1, Biometric Technology & Ethics, 2005).

[58] Regulation (EU) 2016/679 of the European Parliament and of the Council of 27 April 2016 on the protection of natural persons with regard to the processing of personal data and on the free movement of such data, and repealing Directive 95/46/EC (General Data Protection Regulation or GDPR) [2016] OJ L119/1, Art 9. See Directive (EU) 2016/680 of the European Parliament and of the Council of 27 April 2016 on the protection of natural persons with regard to the processing of personal data by competent authorities for the purposes of the prevention, investigation, detection or prosecution of criminal offences or the execution of criminal penalties, and on the free movement of such data, and repealing Council Framework Decision 2008/977/JHA [2016] OJ L119/89, Art 10.

[59] GDPR, ibid, Art 3(13).

[60] See *Peck v UK* (2003) 36 EHRR 41; *Gaughran v UK* App no 45245/15 (ECtHR, 13 February 2020).

[61] GDPR (n 58) Art 4(14).

[62] Interoperability Regulations (n 54), Arts 12–16.

[63] ibid, Arts 17–24.

[64] EES Regulation (n 50) Art 23(2).

[65] ibid, Art 26. Also according to Articles 24 and 25, facial images may be used as search keys to conduct searches in EES for the purposes of examining a visa application or having access to facilitation programmes.

[66] eu-LISA, 'Artificial Intelligence in the Operational Management of Large-scale IT Systems' (2020).

facial image, for the sole purpose of identifying any third-country national who may have been registered previously in EES under a different identity or who does not fulfil or no longer fulfils the conditions for entry to, or for stay on, the territory of the Member States.

Furthermore, Articles 22–23 of the 2018 SIS framework regulate the processing of photographs, facial images and dactyloscopic data that fulfil minimum data quality standards and technical specifications, and must be processed following a data quality check.[67] Facial images will not only be used to confirm the identity of a person, but also facial images may be used to identify a person in the context of regular border crossing points 'as soon as it becomes technically possible, and while ensuring a high degree of reliability of identification'.[68]

Before the implementation of this functionality, the Commission shall present a report on the availability, readiness and reliability of the required technology. The Parliament shall be consulted on the report. In delegated acts, the Commission will also determine 'other circumstances in which photographs and facial images may be used to identify persons'.[69] The wording of these provisions is vague, particularly the last part which leaves the door open to the Commission to enable live FRT at the borders without the knowledge of the persons affected. The Parliament's limited role in ensuring democratic scrutiny is problematic, and even more so since the introduction of facial images – and generally the adoption of the revised SIS framework – was not accompanied by an impact assessment evaluating the necessity and proportionality of this new functionality.

The impetus towards the incorporation of facial images in SIS is high. The Joint Research Centre of the Commission conducted a study in this respect noting that 30 per cent of alerts in SIS already contain facial images (out of the 965,000 alerts on persons stored in SIS)[70] and concluding that FRT could be integrated in SIS, listing 19 recommendations for the rollout of the technology, including different measures to ensure the highest possible quality of the stored data.[71] Furthermore, the possibility to use 'computer vision to detect SIS alerts using cameras' deployed at border points has been included in the 2020 Commission roadmap.[72] As stated above, this essentially involves 'plugging CCTV cameras into an AI-enabled, EU-wide police database so that wanted or suspected individuals can be tracked down via their faces or vehicle number plates'.[73] Although it is recognised that inaccurate technology may lead to

[67] The Commission will adopt those standards and specifications. See Regulation 2018/1861 (n 47), Art 32(4). Also see Regulation 2018/1860 (n 47), Art 4.

[68] Regulation 2018/1861 (n 47), Art 33(4).

[69] ibid.

[70] eu-LISA, 'SIS II – 2020 statistics' (March 2021).

[71] J Galbally Herrerro et al, 'Study on Face Identification Technology for its Implementation in the Schengen Information System' (Publications Office of the European Union, 2019) 9.

[72] Commission, 'Opportunities and Challenges' (n 8) 63.

[73] EuroMed Rights, 'Europe's Techno Borders' (2023) 31.

unjustified police checks of individuals, it is included in the roadmap with the note that 'it would most likely be easier to begin with detecting vehicles and expand to people and other objects'.[74]

Similarly, with respect to ECRIS-TCN, which will also be used for border management purposes, Article 6 of the ECRIS-TCN Regulation foresees that in the first phase, facial images may only be used to confirm the identity of a third-country national who has been identified as a result of an alphanumeric search or a search using fingerprint data. In the second phase, and following a Commission delegated act, facial images will be used for the purpose of identifying third-country nationals to determine which Member States hold information on previous convictions concerning such persons.

As regards Eurodac, the 2016 proposal foresaw the inclusion of additional alphanumeric data and facial images to 'prime the system for searches to be made with facial recognition software in the future'.[75] The rules on facial images were agreed by the co-legislators in 2018 according to which facial images will be included to enable comparisons on that basis.[76]

Finally, in the revised VIS Regulation, the collection of live facial images is foreseen during the application process to enable biometric matching using facial recognition technology.[77] Furthermore, in rules mirroring the EES Regulation, facial images will be used to verify the identity of a visa holder at a border[78] or to identify them in combination with their fingerprints.[79] However, it is explicitly stated that facial images shall not be the only search criterion.[80]

B. The Reliability and Accuracy of Facial Images, Algorithmic Bias and Lurking Surveillance

FRT has the potential to identify individuals at a distance, in real-time or ex post, even without the knowledge and with limited interaction and inconvenience of the individual involved. Although FRT has progressed in the past few years, it 'remains far more prone to errors than other biometrics'.[81]

The fundamental rights challenges of facial images are directly associated with their future use for facial recognition purposes. In particular, the degree of accuracy in facial recognition technology is vital to minimise the risk of false positive matches, namely results that may be unrelated to the individual, or

[74] Commission, 'Opportunities and Challenges' (n 8) 64.
[75] Commission, '2016 Eurodac proposal' (n 48) 13.
[76] ibid Art 2(1).
[77] 2021 VIS Regulation (n 49), Art 22a(1)(j).
[78] ibid Art 18.
[79] ibid Art 20.
[80] ibid.
[81] T Israel, 'Facial Recognition at a Crossroads: Transformation at our Borders and Beyond' (Samuelson-Glushko Canadian Internet Policy & Public Interest Clinic, 2020).

false negative results, when the facial recognition algorithm fails to identify a correct match. Therefore, depending on the task, purpose and context of the use of facial images (verification or identification), the errors as well as the consequences may differ significantly for the individuals affected. When applying this technology in public spaces for identification purposes in particular, even a relatively small proportion of errors (for example, 0.01 per cent) still signifies that hundreds of people may be wrongly flagged. This is crucial, as FRT will be used for identification purposes, and thus searches will be made on the basis of a facial image (a portrait type picture or a probe retrieved from a camera from video surveillance) against the full content of IT systems in the sBMS. False positive matches in particular may have important consequences for individuals, who may be flagged for secondary checks because of incorrect matching, or identified as potential security risks based on SIS alerts and even be subject to discriminatory practices by national authorities.

Accuracy will be dependent on the quality of facial images in accordance with the underlying requirements of each IT system on data quality.[82] However, data quality remains a fundamental issue. In the case of VIS, it has been found that biometrics were attached to the wrong application file, resulting in false matches.[83] As a result, the move towards FRT will be affected. In the case of EES, users are allowed to exceptionally extract facial images from the chip of the electronic machine-readable travel document, provided that the image has 'sufficient image resolution and quality to be used in automated biometric matching'.[84] This is notwithstanding the fact that the Joint Research Council study on the introduction of FRT in relation to SIS recommended to always use a live picture of the traveller and avoid using the face image stored in the passport chip because its low resolution reduces accuracy.[85] The obligations imposed on Member States concerning data quality may be insufficient, particularly in the near future with six, massive, interoperable information systems that are already experiencing data quality issues and whose records will grow exponentially. As a result, enabling eu-LISA to conduct automated quality checks to highlight potential data quality issues is not sufficient,[86] unless it is coupled to specific obligations for the Member States to follow-up, by rectifying or deleting the flagged data within specific and tight deadlines and notifying eu-LISA about their actions. Penalties for persistent violations are another option to consider.

[82] See Regulation 2018/1861 (n 47), Art 44; 2021 VIS Regulation (n 49) Art 29; EES Regulation (n 50) Art 39. Also see GDPR (n 58) Art 5(1)(d).

[83] FRA, 'Under Watchful Eyes: Biometrics, EU IT-Systems and Fundamental Rights' (2018) 16.

[84] EES Regulation (n 50) Art 15.

[85] Galbally Herrerro et al (n 71).

[86] As is currently the case. See Regulation (EU) 2018/1726 of the European Parliament and of the Council of 14 November 2018 on the European Union Agency for the Operational Management of Large-Scale IT Systems in the Area of Freedom, Security and Justice (eu-LISA), and amending Regulation (EC) No 1987/2006 and Council Decision 2007/533/JHA and repealing Regulation (EU) No 1077/2011 [2018] OJ L295/99, Art 12.

Another relevant factor is the age of the facial image. There is a gradual increase in the possibility of a false match as the years go by. This will be particularly relevant in the case of children whose physical appearance and facial shape is subject to change. A 'considerable degradation in performance' for face recognition algorithms on children has been found in comparison to the performance obtained on adults.[87] With the revised Eurodac and VIS rules, lowering the threshold for capturing biometric identifiers to the age of six, these concerns are significantly heightened. Besides, as regards SIS, EES and ECRIS-TCN, such a threshold for capturing facial images does not exist. Finally, the fact that there are different ways to calculate and interpret error rates, which must be defined in advance, must also be taken into account.[88] In its Implementing Decision specifying data quality standards as regards EES, the maximum false positive identification rate is 0.1 per cent and a false negative identification rate is one per cent.[89] These rates may seem quite low, but considering the aforementioned factors, particularly the size of the system that is expected to process more than 50 million records, the false positive rate will result in a large number of third-country nationals being affected.[90]

Even if reliable FRT could be designed, the potential for public surveillance through 'covert, remote and mass capture and identification of images'[91] must also be addressed, as it may lead to a transformation in the way people understand and experience public spaces. It has been eloquently argued that 'facial recognition technologies are transforming ports of entry and exit into true panopticons, tracking and identifying travellers at numerous points throughout their border control journey and linking identification points that were previously distinct'.[92] Indeed, FRT employed *en masse* will further deepen and systematise the cloak of suspicion with which third-country nationals and generally people on the move are viewed.[93] The potential of extending the technologies adopted at the borders to other contexts, resulting in surveillance creep, cannot be overruled. As mentioned earlier, the Joint Research Centre study on SIS mentioned the potential of collecting additional facial images for further additional and future uses.

[87] N Srinivas et al, 'Face Recognition Algorithm Bias: Performance Differences on Images of Children and Adults' (Proceedings of the IEEE/CVF Conference on Computer Vision and Patter Recognition Workshops, 2019).

[88] On evaluation metrics, see Galbally Herrerro et al (n 71).

[89] Commission Implementing Decision (EU) 2019/329 of 25 February 2019 laying down the specifications for the quality, resolution and use of fingerprints and facial image for biometric verification and identification in the Entry/Exit System (EES) [2019] OJ L57/18.

[90] European Parliamentary Research Service (EPRS), 'Artificial Intelligence at EU Borders' (2021) 25.

[91] J Lynch, 'Face Off Report – Law Enforcement Use of Facial Recognition Technology' (Electronic Frontier Foundation, 2020) 7.

[92] Israel (n 81).

[93] See Statewatch, 'Automated Suspicion: The EU's New Travel Surveillance Initiatives' (2020).

Finally, the inherent limitations of FRT should be underlined. As research by NIST demonstrates,[94] the algorithms embedded in facial recognition systems produce higher false positive matches in cases of black people and women, particularly of black women. In that regard, NIST tested 189 facial recognition algorithms and found that most of them displayed bias. This finding is corroborated by another study that concluded that demographic factors may significantly influence various biometric algorithms and that current technology shows some degree of bias towards certain demographic groups.[95] Translated in the context of IT systems, it may be the case that people of colour may find themselves wrongly flagged by the systems in far more cases than white people, due to algorithmic bias. The consequences could range from secondary checks at the borders and to discriminatory practices on national territory, such as refusals of entry or degrading treatment. Such bias may be attributed to the training of the algorithms, which could be based on insufficient or flawed data or because algorithms replicate and reflect the biases and prejudices of those developing them.

In order to address this challenge, eu-LISA has proposed either the use of representative datasets for training algorithms or the creation of synthetic datasets with the characteristics that are representative of that population.[96] However, neither solution is satisfactory; the former could pose data protection risks, particularly regarding purpose limitation and potentially data minimisation depending on how large the datasets used for training the algorithms are. The latter solution could entail higher error rates associated with the use of synthetic data.[97] Therefore, not only must human intervention in establishing a hit be ensured at all times, but also no automated exchange of data based on image matching should be allowed. Importantly, the maturity of facial recognition technology must be carefully monitored prior to and after its implementation so that these challenges are prevented as much as possible.

V. SEARCHING FOR AI IN INTEROPERABLE LARGE-SCALE IT SYSTEMS: THE CASE OF ALGORITHMIC PROFILING OF VISA AND TRAVEL AUTHORISATION APPLICANTS

Algorithmic profiling is defined in Article 4(4) of the GDPR as

> any form of automated processing of personal data consisting of the use of personal data to evaluate certain personal aspects relating to a natural person, in particular

[94] National Institute for Standards and Technology (NIST), 'Face Recognition Vendor Test (FRVT) Part 3: Demographic Effects' (2019).

[95] P Drozdowski et al, 'Demographc Bias in Biometrics: A Survey on an Emerging Challenge' (2020) 1(2) *IEEE Transactions on Technology and Society* 89, 98.

[96] eu-LISA, 'Artificial Intelligence' (n 66).

[97] EPRS (n 90) 27.

to analyse or predict aspects concerning that natural person's performance at work, economic situation, health, personal preferences, interests, reliability, behaviour, location or movements.

Therefore, the automated processing of the data of third-country nationals enables their classification as high risk or high priority individuals whose applications thus merit increased attention and review.[98] In the case of IT systems, algorithmic profiling is embedded in the operationalisation of the forthcoming ETIAS to enable an assessment of the applications for travel authorisations by visa-free applicants and the revised VIS for the assessment of applications for short-stay (Schengen) visas.

A. A Synopsis of the ETIAS and VIS Rules on Algorithmic Profiling

Regulation (EU) 2018/1240 – the founding legal instrument of ETIAS – requires visa-free travellers to apply online for travel authorisation prior to travelling to the Schengen area and disclosing a series of personal data including biographical data, travel arrangements, home and email address, phone number, level of education and current occupation.[99] Based on that information, ETIAS will operate as a pre-emptive control mechanism: travellers will be pre-vetted on the basis of background checks against three elements: (a) the other IT systems, Europol data and the Interpol databases Stolen and Lost Travel Document database (SLTD) and the Interpol Documents Associated with Notices databases (TDAWN) – this cross-checking will be facilitated by one of the interoperability components, the European Search Portal (ESP);[100] (b) screening rules, enabling profiling on the basis of risk indicators;[101] and (c) a dedicated watchlist of persons suspected of terrorism or a serious crime.[102] The aim of the automated processing is to determine whether the presence of the ETIAS applicant in the territory of the Member States would pose a security, irregular migration or high epidemic risk.[103]

Visa-free travellers will thus be subjected to an automated risk assessment to identify whether the applicant's data are listed in any of these IT systems, watchlist or correspond to the screening rules for a reason that merits further attention and may justify the refusal of the travel authorisation. Whereas automated

[98] Molnár and Gill (n 3).

[99] ETIAS Regulation (n 51) Art 17.

[100] In addition to ibid rt 20, see Regulation (EU) 2021/1152 of the European Parliament and of the Council of 7 July 2021 amending Regulations (EC) No 767/2008, (EU) 2017/2226, (EU) 2018/1240, (EU) 2018/1860, (EU) 2018/1861 and (EU) 2019/817 as regards the establishment of the conditions for accessing other EU information systems for the purposes of the European Travel Information and Authorisation System [2021] OJ L249/15.

[101] ETIAS Regulation (n 51) Arts 20(5) and 33.

[102] ibid Art 34.

[103] ibid Art 20.

processing of ETIAS applications against databases and the watchlist will assist in identifying known individuals, the ETIAS screening rules, which will be developed by the ETIAS Central Unit, established in the EBCG Agency, are meant to identify persons who are otherwise unknown to the competent national authorities. Flagging an applicant as a potential risk will take place not because of any specific actions they have engaged in but because they display particular category traits in a probabilistic logic devoid of concrete evidence.[104] The screening rules will be created after the determination of risk profiles based on statistical data from ETIAS itself and EES, on overstayers or refusals of entry or refusals of travel authorisations (see below) and information provided by Member States. The statistical data are to be compiled in a tailor-made way through another interoperability component, the Common Repository for Reporting and Statistics (CRRS).

If automated processing reveals a hit, then Articles 21 and 22 of the ETIAS Regulation provide that the ETIAS Central Unit shall be consulted to verify the hit. If the hit is verified, then the application will be processed manually (a human in the loop) by an ETIAS National Unit.[105] Otherwise, if no hit is reported, the travel authorisation will be automatically granted.[106] Ultimately, automated processing will allow the reallocation of screening resources to 'risky' individuals prior to their departure, while facilitating travel for low-risk profiles.[107]

In the case of VIS, the system was originally set up for the processing of personal data (both biographical and biometric) of applicants for short-stay (Schengen) visas. Under the revised rules, laid down in Regulation (EU) 2021/1134, VIS will not only extend its personal scope to applicants for long-term visas and residence permits, but will also enable the automated processing of the application data. The approach is similar to the ETIAS rules. However, there are some noticeable differences: first, even if automated processing does not reveal any hits with other information systems, databases or algorithms (which in the case of VIS are called specific risk indicators and not screening rules), the visa application will be processed manually at the national level and there is no automated positive decision-making.

The purpose of automated processing of VIS data is thus to assist human decision-making by flagging potentially risky individuals, the application of whom merits specific attention by the national authorities and thus conduct automated social sorting of potentially risky visa applicants. Second, the verification of a hit (or hits) will be performed by national authorities, with the

[104] S Alegre, J Jeandesboz and N Vavoula, 'European Travel Information and Authorisation System (ETIAS): Border Management, Fundamental Rights and Data Protection' (Study for the European Parliament, 2017) 23–26.

[105] ETIAS Regulation (n 51) Arts 25–32.

[106] ibid Art 21.

[107] M Leese, 'The New Profiling: Algorithms, Black Boxes, and the Failure of Anti-Discriminatory Safeguards in the European Union' (2014) 45(5) *Security Dialogue* 494.

VIS Regulation prescribing specific follow-up actions depending on the database or information system to which/where there was a match with the data from the visa application matched.[108] Third, the risk indicators are devised separately and will not be used in respect of long-stay visa and residence permits applicants (as the examination of these applications remains a national competence). Thus, there is no algorithmic profiling in those cases, only a cross-check against EU and international databases as well as the watchlist. Fourth, as for the devising of the algorithms, similar rules are envisaged in the VIS Regulation,[109] with a few tweaks. Thus, for example, instead of using ETIAS statistics, the screening rules will take VIS statistics into consideration.[110]

B. Does Algorithmic Profiling Entail the Use of AI?

Neither legal instruments nor implementing and delegated acts mention the term AI and reference is only made to algorithms, thus leaving open the question of whether the algorithms that are implemented will be classified as AI or not. This may be seen as a means of avoiding this loaded term to avoid additional complications in terms of supervision or political scrutiny or to leave this issue open for introducing AI in the future. Even the term algorithm has been contested; as mentioned by Zandstra and Brouwer, when a group of researchers at the Université Libre de Bruxelles reached out to the EBCG Agency to request details concerning ETIAS' risk assessment algorithm, Frontex insisted that it would actually be more appropriate to refer to filtering queries than algorithms, and that no sophisticated analysis methods or any form of AI is involved in the risk assessment.[111] This is notwithstanding the fact that it is actually eu-LISA that is involved in the development of the databases from a technical perspective.

It is also notable that neither the ETIAS nor the VIS rules were subject to an *ex ante* Impact Assessment prior to the adoption of the Commission proposals. While ETIAS was only subjected to a feasibility study,[112] and no Impact Assessment was conducted, including when consequential amendments to the legal instruments of other IT systems were adopted, the VIS revision focused predominantly on the expansion of its scope to holders of long-stay visas, residence permits and residence cards.[113]

The potential of using AI in the implementation of the screening rules and the specific risk indicators may be deduced by various other sources and may be

[108] ETIAS Regulation (n 51) Arts 9c–9g.

[109] 2021 VIS Regulation (n 49) Arts 9a–9l and 22a–22b.

[110] ibid Art 9j(2).

[111] Zandstra and Brouwer (n 9).

[112] PwC, 'Feasibility Study for a European Travel Information and Authorisation System (ETIAS)' (2016).

[113] Commission, 'Legal Analysis on the Necessity and Proportionality of Extending the Scope of the Visa Information System (VIS) to Include Data on Long Stay Visas and Residence Documents' (2018).

hidden in one of the interoperability components, the CRRS, aimed to 'support the objectives' of the systems and to 'provide cross-system statistical data and analytical reporting for policy, operational and data quality purposes'.[114] A (non-public) report by eu-LISA states that the CRRS that will collect and store (among other things/for instance) statistical data from VIS, EES and ETIAS of over-stayers and information regarding refusals of entry of third-country nationals, can use AI tools to enhance the identification of risks for specific groups of travellers by identifying patterns or a set of common characteristics from the analysis of historical data in the CRRS related to security, irregular migration and high epidemic risks.[115] Furthermore, in the Report of the Future Group on Travel Intelligence and Border Management by Europol and the EBCG Agency, it is stated that in cooperation with eu-LISA and other partner agencies, the joint analysis capability could leverage the full potential of the CRRS as a data source for analytical purposes and develop appropriate analytical tools for risk assessment with the support of AI.[116] The possibility that CRRS could use AI tools to assist in the design of risk profiles for ETIAS and VIS demonstrates the true potential of interoperability, which is not exhausted in aggregating data from the underlying systems, but entails putting them to novel uses beyond the contours of their operation.

Furthermore, AI tools could enhance the automated processing of textual information by detecting common textual characteristics in manually uploaded data and will facilitate the identification of specific groups of risky travellers. Aside the CRRS, according to eu-LISA, ETIAS itself can employ AI tools in four different ways: first, to review and validate the *ex ante* assessment process of screening rules assisting officers in the examination of an application by using stored and historical data and generating an indicator for normal and suspicious outcomes for a specific set of travellers. Second, AI technology could be embedded in ETIAS in the identification and analysis of correlations amongst the risk profiles from its own historic data to allow more precision in the definition of the risk profiles. The AI technology will analyse and detect deviations, and propose further review of the risk indicators during the *ex post* assessment process. Finally, AI technology could support the verification of a hit using ETIAS historical data by implementing model training of the corresponding risk profiles. The extent to which this is embedded remains unclear, but the mere existence of the eu-LISA report indicates that all options are open.[117]

Another reason why AI may be embedded in algorithmic profiling comes directly from the AI Act. Article 83 of the Commission Proposal for an AI Act *ab initio* excluded 'AI systems which are components of the large-scale IT systems',

[114] Interoperability Regulations (n 54) Art 39(1).
[115] eu-LISA, 'AI in CSSR in the Context of ETIAS and the Revised VIS Final Report' (2022).
[116] European and EBCG Agency, 'Future Group on Travel Intelligence and Border Management – Final Report' (2021) 65.
[117] eu-LISA, 'AI in CSSR' (n 115).

or EU large-scale IT systems, from its scope, in contrast to national AI applications for migration and law enforcement purposes. Whilst section 6 will examine the implication of this provision in more detail, it is worth stressing already at this stage that the exclusion – even a temporary one – of large-scale IT systems from the scope of the AI Act points in the direction of IT systems being reliant on AI tools. Maybe the exclusion concerns FRT only, but in light of the eu-LISA report it is likely that Article 83 concerned algorithmic profiling as well.

C. The Fundamental Rights Challenges of Algorithmic Profiling: The CJEU Benchmark

Guidance on the use of algorithms, albeit in the context of processing Passenger Name Records (PNR) and telecommunications metadata, has been provided by the CJEU on various occasions. In Opinion 1/15 on the draft agreement between the EU and Canada on the transfer of PNR data to Canadian authorities, the CJEU considered the legality of the automated processing of passengers' data in the context of Canada's border control pre-screening programme, which involves automated cross-checking against various Canadian databases and analysis of information on the basis of pre-determined criteria about everyone who buys a flight ticket to Canada.[118] The CJEU found that the proportionality of the automated processing of PNR data 'depends on the pre-established models and criteria' (on which the algorithms are based) as well as on the databases on which that type of data processing is based.[119] The Court held that the pre-established models and criteria should be 'specific and reliable' and should be non-discriminatory. Any hit following the automated processing of that data must be subject to an individual re-examination by non-automated means and ensuring that the pre-established models and criteria as well as the databases used are not discriminatory and are limited to that which is strictly necessary. Finally, the reliability and topicality of those pre-established models and criteria as well as the use of databases should be subject to review, taking account of statistical data and results of international research.[120]

These considerations were echoed in *Quadrature du Net and Others*.[121] There the CJEU clarified that such automated analysis is in itself a limitation to the rights of privacy, personal data protection and confidentiality of communications and thus, must be subject to a strict proportionality test. Adding to the requirements laid down in Opinion 1/15, the CJEU opined that the models or criteria used to conduct an automated analysis cannot be based on sensitive

[118] Opinion 1/15, EU:C:2017:592.

[119] ibid para 172.

[120] ibid paras 172–73.

[121] Joined Cases C-511/18, C-512/18 and C-520/18 *La Quadrature du Net and Others v Premier Ministre and Others* EU:C:2020:791.

data *in isolation* (emphasis added).[122] Furthermore, the Court acknowledged the need to regularly re-examine the algorithms and the databases used to ensure that they are reliable, up-to-date and in practice non-discriminatory and limited to what is strictly necessary to achieve the intended purpose.[123] Last, the CJEU held that because of the margin of error that may result from the automated analysis, there has to be an individual non-automated re-examination of a positive result before adopting a measure that may have an adverse effect on the person concerned.[124]

In *Ligue des Droits Humains*, the CJEU reiterated a number of these points and elaborated further on the use of algorithms to automatically process PNR data and filter out risky air travellers. First, the judgment restricted the 'use of artificial intelligence technology in self-learning systems ("machine learning")', by prohibiting systems that are 'capable of modifying without human intervention or review the assessment process and, in particular, the assessment criteria on which the result of the application of that process is based as well as the weighting of those criteria'.[125] Although not all AI systems were prohibited, central to its assessments was the 'opacity which characterises the way in which artificial intelligence technology works', which may deprive individuals of their right to an effective judicial remedy.[126]

The Court further highlighted the risk of discrimination, which covers both direct and indirect discrimination.[127] Algorithms must be 'targeted, proportionate and specific'[128] and not rely on protected characteristics.[129] The technologies used will have to incorporate incriminating as well as exonerating circumstances,[130] thus bolstering their reliability and reducing false positive rates. In addition, the Court underscored that the Data Protection Officer and national supervisory authorities must be equipped with robust rights of access to the content of pre-determined criteria.[131]

Whilst acknowledging the fairly substantial number of false positives, the CJEU stressed that the appropriateness of the system essentially depends on the proper functioning of the subsequent verification of the results by non-automated means.[132] For that purpose, the Court determined that Member States must 'lay down clear and precise rules capable of providing guidance' for the review,[133] which is meant to prevent both discriminatory results and

[122] ibid para 181.
[123] ibid para 182.
[124] ibid.
[125] Case C-817/19 *Ligue des droits humains ASBL v Conseil des ministers* EU:C:2022:491, para 194.
[126] ibid para 195.
[127] ibid para 197.
[128] ibid para 198.
[129] ibid para 199.
[130] ibid para 200.
[131] ibid para 212.
[132] ibid para 124.
[133] ibid para 205.

false matches to be transferred to the competent authorities, thus subjecting passengers to false suspicions of being involved in terrorist offences or serious crimes. It also aimed at reliable documentation and self-monitoring,[134] as well as guaranteeing uniform administrative practices in different Member States that observe the principle of non-discrimination. The results of individual human reviews must take preference over those of automated processing.[135]

Finally, the judgment bolstered the right to an effective judicial remedy:

> The competent authorities must ensure that the person concerned [...] is able to understand how those criteria and those programs work, so that they can decide with full knowledge of the relevant facts whether or not to exercise [their] right to the judicial redress.[136]

The Court also established that the competent court and the person concerned, except in the case of a threat to state security, must have the opportunity to examine all the grounds and evidence on the basis on which the decision was made.[137]

D. The Many Faces of Algorithmic Bias

The aforementioned pronouncements were elaborated in the law enforcement domain, where Member States' authorities enjoy a wide degree of discretion, should be transplantable to algorithmic profiling in the cases of ETIAS and VIS. Profiling in this context entails the use of the same tools – algorithms, including potentially self-learning algorithms. ETIAS should also be considered as a spiritual successor to the PNR legal framework; it entails the automated processing of previously unknown material or persons in large data pools to protect public security. To the Commission, AI seems like a natural fit for that task. Finally, decision-making in the field of migration is also highly discretionary.

In assessing the extent to which the CJEU standards are reflected in the ETIAS and VIS legislation and the fundamental rights challenges posed by algorithmic profiling, there are four issues that this contribution will examine; biases in the development of the algorithms, biases in manual processing, inadequate judicial remedies and the exclusion of the systems from the scope of the proposed AI Act.

i. Biases in the Development of the Algorithms

A series of issues may arise in the development of the algorithms. The first aspect concerns the statistical data and information based on which the risks will be

[134] ibid para 207.
[135] ibid para 208.
[136] ibid para 210.
[137] ibid para 211.

determined. In particular, Article 33 of the ETIAS Regulation and Article 9j of the VIS Regulation prescribe that specific ETIAS screening rules, or, in the case of VIS, risk indicators, will be built in an algorithm, enabling profiling, to sift unknown third-country nationals that fit pre-defined risk profiles and may constitute immigration, security or public health risks. It is the Commission that must further define, via a delegated act,[138] what must be regarded as such risks, taking into account various factors, in particular:

a) EES statistics indicating abnormal rates of overstaying and refusals of entry;
b) ETIAS or VIS statistics on abnormal rates of refusal of travel authorisations;
c) ETIAS or VIS statistics on correlations between data and overstaying by travellers or refusals of entry;
d) 'information substantiated by factual and evidence-based elements' provided by Member States on specific security risk indicators or threats;
e) information substantiated by factual and evidence-based elements provided by Member States concerning abnormal rates of overstaying and refusals of entry; and
f) information concerning specific high epidemic risks provided by Member States as well as epidemiological surveillance information and risk assessments by the European Centre for Disease Control and disease outbreaks reported by the World Health Organization.[139]

There are reasons to question the reliability of those statistical data. With respect to EES, the reliability of its statistics on overstayers may be called into question, as the system will automatically detect individuals who may not have been entered.[140] Arguably, statistical data will be based on large amounts of records and therefore even though it will have a margin of error, the risks drawn could still remain correct. Furthermore, it is premature to employ statistical data from IT systems, such as EES and ETIAS that have not even started their operations yet and will thus be evaluated in terms of data quality and possible malfunctions in the future for supporting the operation of other systems. This disregards the mounting and unresolved data quality issues that operational systems experience. The experience of the existing operational information systems shows that such issues regularly arise and, more importantly, have spillover effects when combined with data from other systems.[141]

[138] Commission Delegated Decision on further defining security, illegal immigration or high epidemic risks [2021] C(2021)4981.

[139] ETIAS Regulation (n 51) Art 33(2).

[140] For criticism on the reliability of EES entry/exit records, see Vavoula (n 53) 444–48; Standing Committee of Experts on International Immigration, Refugee and Criminal Law (Meijers Committee), 'Note on the Smart Borders Proposals (COM(2013) 95 final, COM(2013) 96 final and COM (2013) 97 final' (CM1307, 2013).

[141] Vavoula (n 53) 184–86, 278–79, 281–82, 357–60. See FRA (n 83) 81–98; European Court of Auditors, 'EU Information Systems Supporting Border Control – a Strong Tool, but more Focus Needed on Timely and Complete Data' (2019).

Another possible source of concern revolves around the reliability of the information provided by the Member States. Both Regulations require that the information provided be based on facts and evidence-based elements, but the extent to which this can be checked and validated remains to be seen. As with the registration of SIS and Interpol alerts,[142] Member States may have a very different understanding of security risks and may abuse this possibility to promote highly securitised agendas. Regrettably, the implementing act detailing those risks on which the specific risk indicators will be based does not provide much clarity in that respect.[143] The ETIAS risk indicators shall consist of a combination of data including one or several of these categories of data:

a) age range, sex, nationality;
b) country and city of residence;
c) level of education;
d) current occupation.[144]

In the case of VIS, the measures for screening under a), b) and d) will be used for developing the VIS risk indicators along with data on the Member States of destinations, the Member State of first entry and the purpose of travel.[145]

Aside the reliability issues, bias in the development of the algorithms is an important challenge because algorithmic tools are trained on pre-existing data and past decision-making, and hence, they run the risk of replicating implicit and inherent biases of those earlier decisions. Thus, the danger that the algorithms are discriminatory by design cannot be excluded. For example, the UK Home Secretary decided to withdraw an algorithm used to filter visa applications similar to that prescribed by the revised VIS Regulation after being called out as racially discriminatory.[146]

In recognition of the fact that the list of risk indicators contains a series of grounds of prohibited discrimination under the 1965 UN Convention for the elimination of all forms of racial discrimination[147] and the Charter, both Regulations note that the risk indicators shall be 'targeted and proportionate' and specific, all of which are referred to by the CJEU. Going beyond the requirements of the CJEU, the risk indicators are not to be used 'based solely on a

[142] See S Meacham, 'Weaponizing the Police: Interpol as a Tool of Authoritarianism' (*Harvard International Review*, 11 April 2022), available at https://hir.harvard.edu/weaponizing-the-police-authoritarian-abuse-of-interpol/.

[143] Commission Implementing Decision of 23 November 2021 on specifying risks related to security, illegal immigration or high epidemic risk as defined in Regulation (EU) 2018/1240 of the European Parliament and of the Council C(2021) 4980.

[144] ETIAS Regulation (n 51) Art 33(4).

[145] 2021 VIS Regulation (n 49) Art 9j(4).

[146] See n 5.

[147] International Convention on the Elimination of All Forms of Racial Discrimination of 21 December 1965.

person's sex or age',[148] which leaves it open as to whether permissible risk factors could be based on a combination of gender and age (eg, 'women below the age of x').[149] Furthermore, in line with these judgments, the ETIAS and VIS Regulations also state that the risk indicators should under no circumstances be based on information revealing a person's colour, race, ethnic or social origin, genetic features, language, political or any other opinion, religion or philosophical belief, trade union membership, membership of a national minority, property, birth, disability, or sexual orientation.[150]

Here, however, there are significant issues that need to be pointed out. Designating sex may often indicate sexual orientation, city of residence will often reveal ethnicity and colour, level of education – in the case of ETIAS only – and current occupation will often be an indicator of property and trade union membership.[151] Nationality may be a proxy for race, ethnic origin, or religion; differences of treatment on grounds of nationality can turn into discrimination on prohibited grounds. Furthermore, algorithms based on the level of education or job group have the potential to lead to undue and unlawful discriminatory profiling.[152] For example, the combination of data on occupation, level of education along with previous criminal convictions could 'weave in' people from a specific trade union group, due to the specific policy of a single state on demonstrations or on access to occupation and education. Overall, the ETIAS and VIS algorithms may still lead to indirect discrimination, prohibited by the CJEU pursuant to *Ligue des Droits Humains*, where it may not be done by reference to a protected characteristic, but where it nonetheless has a discriminatory effect on a group of people sharing the same protected characteristics if it puts them at a particular disadvantage.[153]

The establishment of the ETIAS and VIS Fundamental Rights Guidance Boards[154] to enable checks and balances in the configuration of algorithms are

[148] ETIAS Regulation (n 51) Art 33(5); revised VIS Regulation (n 49) Art 9j(5). González Fuster correctly notes that gender is not covered as sensitive data by Art 9(1) of the GDPR, therefore this addition is particularly welcome. See G González Fuster, 'Artificial Intelligence and Law Enforcement – Impact on Fundamental Rights' (Study for the LIBE Committee of the European Parliament, 2020) 42.

[149] González Fuster, ibid 34.

[150] ETIAS Regulation (n 51) Art 33(5); 2021 VIS Regulation (n 49) Art 9j(5).

[151] E Guild and N Vavoula, 'Travel Authorization in the EU: Automated Processing and Profiling' (*openDemocracy*, 12 October 2020), available at www.opendemocracy.net/en/can-europe-make-it/travel-authorization-eu-automated-processing-and-profiling/.

[152] Fondazione Giacomo Brodolini, 'Fundamental Rights Review of EU Data Collection Instruments and Programmes' (2019) 39.

[153] A Romei and S Ruggieri, 'Discrimination Data Analysis: A Multi-disciplinary Bibliography' in B Custers et al (eds), *Discrimination and Privacy in the Information Society – Data Mining and Profiling in Large Databases* (Springer, 2013) 109. *La Quadrature du Net and Others* (n 121) blurs this issue of indirect discrimination. For a critical analysis, see E Guild, E Mendos Kuşkonmaz, V Mitsilegas and N Vavoula, 'Data Retention and the Future of Large-Scale Surveillance: The Evolution and Contestation of Judicial Benchmarks' (2023) 29(1–2) *European Law Journal* 176.

[154] ETIAS Regulation (n 51) Art 10; 2021 VIS Regulation (n 49) Art 9l.

particularly important. The Boards will have an advisory and appraisal function to the ETIAS and VIS Screening Boards that will be consulted on the definition, establishment, assessment *ex ante*, implementation, evaluation *ex post*, revision and deletion of the specific risk indicators. Judging from its tasks (access to the audits) and composition (the EDPS is part of it), it will partly have an oversight role, but will also perform regular appraisals and issue recommendations. Yet, the extent to which any recommendations will be taken on board by the (ETIAS and VIS) Screening Boards is unclear as there is no such requirement. Presumably, the Fundamental Rights Guidance Boards could have important insights into the potential discriminatory use of algorithms in the systems; this could be useful for the EDPS in its supervision of the EBCG Agency and in its cooperation with national supervisory authorities in the context of the Coordinated Supervision Committee.

ii. Manual Processing: Additional Personal Data and the Potentially Biased 'Human in the Loop'

The second aspect involves the importance of the 'human in the loop' and the opacity in the decision-making process. A referral for manual processing with a flag that the individual constitutes a security, irregular migration or public health risk itself entails consequences for the affected individual, particularly in the case of ETIAS such as the provision of additional information and documentation, or less commonly, the requirement to attend an interview. Indeed, according to Article 27 of the ETIAS Regulation, if the ETIAS National Unit manually examining the application for travel authorisation deems the information provided by the applicant in the application form to be insufficient to enable it to decide whether to issue or refuse a travel authorisation, it may request additional information or documentation from a predetermined list of options laid down in a Commission delegated act.[155] The latter contains no less than 44 categories of data and information that may be requested by the applicant, which can range from information on criminal records to more controversially proof of family connections and prior visits to family and friends in the EU, including the personal details of these individuals. As a result, the manual processing of a travel authorisation application will become quite close to that envisaged for Schengen visas.

The ETIAS National Units, the visa authorities or the immigration authorities that will conduct the manual examination may also not be in a position to ensure meaningful human intervention. In the case of ETIAS, given that the screening rules are drawn up under the responsibility of the ETIAS Central Unit

[155] Commission Delegated Decision (EU) 2022/1612 of 16 February 2022 specifying the content and format of the predetermined list of options to be used to request additional information or documentation pursuant to Article 27(3) of Regulation (EU) 2018/1240 of the European Parliament and of the Council [2022] OJ L241/7.

(Art 33 (4)), National Units may not have the necessary expertise on the inner workings of the ETIAS screening rules. While National Units will be supported by the ETIAS Screening Board, there is no independent supervisory entity, except the Fundamental Rights Guidance Board, which does not have solely clear-cut supervisory functions. In addition, a Practical Handbook, envisaged in Article 93 of the ETIAS Regulation, must be devised, although its content remains underspecified in the Regulation. In the case of VIS, the Visa Code Handbook will remain the primary source of guidance for visa authorities for the examination of a visa application and there does not seem to be any additional guidelines even though the process has been substantially changed.[156] Leaving national decision-making authorities completely in charge without clear guidelines and independent oversight may not only lead to false suspicions, but could also perpetuate discrimination through automation bias or selective adherence bias.[157] The former concept refers to situations where there is a propensity to favour suggestions from automated decision-making tools. Rather pessimistically, Leese notes that 'the human reviewers lose true agency, as they can only enact what algorithmic categorizations indicate'.[158] Selective adherence or confirmation bias refers to situations where the human in the loop may have their own, culturally – and historically – grown biases against certain groups of individuals and therefore they may have a greater or lesser incentive to manually examine an application if the algorithmic result confirms or is at odds with their own prejudices and biases. This creates an additional layer of potential indirect discrimination, which may be particularly difficult to detect due to the inherent opacity of decision-making. However, not only must faith in modern technologies be taken into account, also the inherent distrust towards third-country nationals, particularly visa applicants who originate from 'blacklisted' countries, must be considered. Thus, it is highly probable that individuals singled out during the automated processing of their applications will be at a disadvantage.

VI. THE APPLICATION OF THE AI ACT TO INTEROPERABLE LARGE-SCALE IT SYSTEMS: WHAT IS AT STAKE?

As mentioned above, the proposed AI Act excluded AI systems already placed on the market or put in place, including large-scale IT systems 'unless the replacement or amendment of those legal acts leads to a significant change in the design

[156] ANNEX to the Commission Implementing Decision amending Commission Decision C(2010) 1620 final as regards the replacement of the Handbook for the processing of visa applications and the modification of issued visas (Visa Code Handbook I) C(2020) 395 final.

[157] S Alon-Barkat and M Busuioc, 'Human-AI Interactions in Public Sector Decision-Making: "Automation Bias" and "Selective Adherence" to Algorithmic Advice' (2023) 33(1) *Journal of Public Administration Research and Theory* 153.

[158] Leese (n 107) 505.

or intended purpose of the AI system or AI systems concerned'.[159] However, its requirements would be taken into account, *where applicable*, in the evaluation of each database. The exclusion created an unjustified divide between AI systems deployed at the national level and those deployed at the EU level, which is beyond reproach. This is because AI systems entailing an assessment of a risk, including a security risk, a risk of irregular immigration, or a health risk, posed by a natural person who intends to enter or has entered into the territory of a Member State, in accordance with ETIAS and VIS, have been classified as 'high-risk' AI systems. Furthermore, what amounts to a 'significant change' in the design or intended purpose of an AI system(s) was utterly unclear. Recital 66 of the proposal specifies a lower threshold for conformity re-assessment 'whenever a change occurs which may affect the compliance' and it has been rightly argued by the EDPS and the European Data Protection Board (EDPB) that a similar threshold would have been appropriate for Article 83 as well, at least for high-risk AI systems.[160]

The rationale behind the exclusion was that this was only temporary to ensure legal certainty, bearing in mind that the IT systems and the interoperability components are under development or refurbishment, and that waiting for the requirements of the AI Act would slow down the process. It could also change the procedures for testing the algorithms that are to be used. This argument could be interpreted as encompassing two significant admissions; first, that the deployment of algorithms in the case of ETIAS and VIS may not have been in line with the requirements of the AI Act and that therefore, subjecting the systems to its requirements would require going back to the legislative procedure. For example, the deployment of high-risk AI systems requires a prior risk assessment.

The lack of prior Impact Assessments in relation to both systems is a very significant oversight in that respect. Similarly, no Impact Assessments were conducted when the revised legal bases for Eurodac and SIS, which encompass the use of facial recognition technology, were adopted. Second, the die has already been cast for IT systems subjected to further reforms in the future. The 2020 Commission report on opportunities and challenges for the use of AI in border control, migration and security provides an indication concerning the future direction of IT systems; chatbots and intelligent agents; risk assessment tools; knowledge management tools; policy insight and analytics tools; and computer vision tools.[161] Besides, while the proposal also provides that the

[159] Commission, 'Proposal for AI Act' (n 7) Art 83(1).

[160] EDPS and EDPB, 'Joint Opinion 5/2021 on the proposal for a Regulation of the European Parliament and of the Council laying down harmonised rules on artificial intelligence (Artificial Intelligence Act)'.

[161] Commission, 'Opportunities and Challenges' (n 8). Different AI systems could be used to assess visa and travel authorisation applications, such as chatbots during the online application process to answer applicants' queries or check data quality, and to 'triage' applications and determine which

requirements of the AI Act shall be taken into account when evaluating each database, it must be noted that in the past, the legal bases of the systems have been amended before an evaluation has been conducted and therefore it is possible that the AI Act prescriptions will not be taken into account.

The Parliament amended Article 83 putting IT systems within the scope of the AI Act and requiring the systems to be brought in line with its requirements within four years of its implementation.[162] On the one hand, this approach is helpful because the application of the AI Act was not dependent upon any further revisions to the legal instruments of the large-scale IT systems or interoperability. On the other hand, the four-year breathing space, coupled with the expected timeline that the AI Act will become applicable in 2026 means that essentially large-scale IT systems will be outside the scope of the AI Act until 2030. This reference to 2030 has been made explicit in Article 111 of the AI Act and it is important because the implementation of interoperable large-scale IT systems is expected to be completed in 2027. This means that the implementation of the initiatives mentioned in this chapter can continue without significant hiccups.

The delay in applying the AI Act in the context of interoperable IT systems is highly problematic for an additional reason: as mentioned earlier, the CRRS is likely to use AI tools in the compilation of tailor-made, cross-system statistical data and analytical reporting for policy, operational and data quality purposes. Statistical data are anonymised data that will be drawn from the individual systems and stored in the CRRS pursuant to Article 39 of the Interoperability Regulations. Because they are anonymised, they do not qualify as personal data and therefore are not subject to EU data protection law, including the rules on supervision by national supervisory authorities and the EDPS. Halting the application of the AI Act signifies that the supervision of AI tools at the national level, as envisaged in the AI Act aimed at ensuring accountability, is also delayed. The result will be that the CRRS will not be subject to any supervision, either from the perspective of EU data protection law or from the AI Act until 2030. This accountability gap is particularly significant; it means that, for a number of years, the operation of this interoperability component will essentially become

require a more thorough risk analysis, as in the case of the UK. AI could be used to detect irregular travelling patterns, which would require extensive data collection. At EU level, this can take place through the CRRS, but any additional data needed from airlines or Member States would require legislative intervention at the national level. Similarly, for long-term stays or migration in the Schengen area, chatbots for the application process and the 'triaging' of applications to speed up risk assessments and background checks could be developed. In the asylum procedure, AI systems could be used for 'sensory analysis of an individual', to determine whether they should be further checked by a human social worker or granted special procedural guarantees and to assess the likelihood of absconding (for detention), to allocate refugees to geographical regions where they are more likely to find work and integrate smoothly, and assist with the risk assessment of returns to country of origin. Triaging of border crossers to improve swift border crossings could also be promoted as a means of enhancing consistency in the selection of travellers being called for the second line border check.

[162] Parliament, 'Artificial Intelligence Act Amendments' (n 42).

a black site. From 2030 onwards, the supervision of AI systems will include the systems as well and will probably encounter additional difficulties through *ex post* audits of the CRRS.

VII. THE ENHANCED ROLE OF EU AGENCIES IN THE ERA OF AI

EU agencies in the EU Areas of Freedom, Security and Justice (AFSJ), namely eu-LISA, Frontex, and the EU Asylum Agency (EUAA) are also heavily invested in AI-related research, although their powers with AI relevance have been off the radar. These agencies along with other EU agencies within the AFSJ, particularly Europol, cooperate within the latter's EU Innovation Hub for Internal Security, a joint EU platform to support the delivery of innovative cutting-edge products for the security of citizens in the EU, with a view to better assessing the risks and fostering the use and development of advanced and emerging technologies.[163] This section aims to analyse how these agencies have utilised their existing powers and how they envisage their future role in migration, asylum and border management in the AI era.

A. The EUAA

The EUAA, formerly the European Asylum Support Office (EASO), was set up to facilitate, coordinate, and strengthen practical cooperation among EU Member States. This includes the gathering and exchange of country of origin information (COI), as well as the provision of training for asylum officials. The involvement of the EUAA in implementing AI tools is quite interesting. During the so-called refugee crisis, the EUAA developed a tool to match asylum seekers with countries of relocation – the transfer of a person in need of international protection from one EU Member State to another – in line with the respective Council Decisions.[164] The tool was expected to benefit both Greece and Italy which were under pressure at the time and countries of relocation by minimising the chances for further onward movement post relocation, as well as individuals whose integration would be facilitated.

More controversially, since 2017, the Agency has developed its Early Warning and Preparedness System to monitor the situation in third countries

[163] Council Document 5757/20 (21 February 2020). See Council Document 5905/21 (17 February 2021) which details various initiatives proposed by EU agencies. This cooperation has led to the adoption of 'Accountability Principles for Artificial Intelligence (AP4AI) in the Internal Security Domain' (2022).

[164] Council Decision (EU) 2015/1523 of 14 September 2015 establishing provisional measures in the area of international protection for the benefit of Italy and of Greece [2015] OJ L239/146; Council Decision (EU) 2015/1601 of 22 September 2015 establishing provisional measures in the area of international protection for the benefit of Italy and Greece [2015] OJ L247/80.

and to forecast the number of asylum applications expected by Member States. The agency used machine learning to analyse big data on conflict and disruptive events in countries of origin and transit in order to clarify the root causes of individual displacement events.[165] Due to a lack of legal basis and various data protection issues related to purpose limitation, a lack of transparency, the absence of an appointed Data Protection Officer and no Impact Assessments, the EDPS issued a temporary ban on the production of monitoring reports based on analysing posts on social media.[166]

Following the adoption of Regulation (EU) 2021/2303 that upgraded the Agency's mandate,[167] the lack of legal basis remains an obstacle; according to Article 5(2), the EUAA must gather and analyse information on the situation of asylum in the EU and in third countries insofar as it might have an impact on the EU. The basis of its analysis must be information provided,

> *in particular*, by Member States, relevant Union institutions, bodies, offices and agencies, the European External Action Service (EEAS) and the UNHCR, in particular the UNHCR Global Resettlement Needs reports. The Agency may also take into account information available from relevant organisations on the basis of their expertise (emphasis added).

The wording of Article 5(2) may create confusion as to whether the list of sources is exhaustive or not and whether social media monitoring could also be included within the scope of the provision. However, the fact that the list refers to Member States or international and EU entities indicates that the sources of information cannot be social media.

The role of the EUAA does not end here. The EUAA has already engaged in significant research within its remit by participating in the development of a new model for forecasting asylum claims lodged in the EU, known as DynENet, which is based on machine learning and big data. The model is aimed at increasing the preparedness of EU Member States for sudden increases in asylum applications in order to process them quickly and fairly; while also foreseeing proper reception conditions.[168] It has been created by integrating traditional migration and asylum administrative data, such as the detection of irregular border-crossing and recognition rates in countries of destination, with big data on negative and conflict events, as well as internet searches in countries of origin. It can forecast asylum applications lodged in the EU up to four weeks in advance.

[165] EASO, 'EASO Asylum Report' (2020) 57.

[166] EDPS, 'Formal Consultation on EASO's Social Media Monitoring Reports (case 2018-1083)' (14 November 2019).

[167] Regulation (EU) 2021/2303 of the European Parliament and of the Council of 15 December 2021 on the European Union Agency for Asylum and repealing Regulation (EU) No 439/2010 [2021] OJ L468/1.

[168] M Caramnia, S Maria Iacus and T Wilkin, 'Forecasting Asylum-related Migration Flows with Machine Learning and Data at Scale' (2022) *Scientific Reports* 1457.

In addition, in the EUAA's Strategy on Digital Innovation in Asylum Procedures, the Agency states that it will co-lead to develop and apply state-of-the-art technologies, including tools using AI.[169] The first one involves the establishment of a Common European platform to identify the country of origin of applicants through language assessment, in other words, language/dialect recognition, which as mentioned earlier is already being tested in Member States.[170] Whereas language assessment for the determination of origin has traditionally relied on human expertise solely, the development of a large-scale tool[171] accessible to all Member States and complemented by a common pool of language analysts would eliminate an unnecessary duplication of investments and result in considerable savings. The challenges of language/dialect recognition are varied, but the coverage of more than 7,000 languages spoken in the world, with an uncountable number of accents and dialects remains the most important one. This issue can only be overcome through an expanded dataset to achieve optimal training for the AI mode; in other words, the more countries/regions an AI solution has to cover, the more diverse the dataset needs to be.

Another tool contemplated by the EUAA, based on its strategic position overlooking the implementation of the Common European Asylum System, is the development of an AI-reliant asylum case worker assistant. Such an assistant could be entrusted with numerous tasks: filtering big data, tracing the digital presence of applicants, identifying people (through pictures/videos uploaded online), and conducting semi-automated text-mining of records (including registration or personal interview records).[172] An assistant could extract case-relevant country of origin information and case law from large amounts of data, support a risk analysis, filter open source intelligence or applicants' mobile devices. An assistant could benefit by identifying persons of concern as early as possible or tackling cases of abuse of the asylum system. However, the various roles that an assistant can play pose different challenges concerning fundamental rights; for example, mobile phone data extraction has been criticised for violating individuals' privacy. Importantly, automation bias or selective adherence cannot be discounted; in fact, the greater the number of tasks that are entrusted to AI systems, the easier it is for a case worker to rely on the input provided by the tool and the more difficult it is for individuals to contest an outcome concerning their application and to identify where the assisted decision-making has gone wrong.

[169] EUAA, 'Strategy on Digital Innovation in Asylum Procedures and Reception Systems' (2023).
[170] ibid 28.
[171] A similar tool was developed in 2015–2017 by the Federal Office for Migration and Refugees of Germany that developed a machine learning tool able to provide fast and reliable assessments indicating geographical area(s) of origin based on recorded voice samples.
[172] EUAA (n 169) 30.

B. The EBCG Agency

Since its establishment in 2004, the EBCG Agency has seen a gradual increase in its mandate and has become a powerful information hub next to Europol, with the processing of personal data becoming central to its activities.[173] The Agency has integrated EUROSUR and has numerous tasks relating to the processing of personal data; it may deploy operational staff and technical equipment to provide assistance in screening, debriefing, identification and fingerprinting; provide assistance at all stages of the return process, which involves information exchanges, cooperate with other EU Agencies, such as Europol, to facilitate the exchange of information and process so-called operational personal data; develop technical standards for information exchange, provide the necessary assistance for the development of a common information-sharing environment, including interoperability of systems, as appropriate and manage the False and Authentic Documents Online system (FADO).

Its AI-related tasks are perhaps less known and relate to the operationalisation of large-scale IT systems, namely ETIAS and VIS. The EBCG Agency is responsible for defining, establishing, assessing *ex ante*, implementing, evaluating *ex post*, revising and deleting the screening rules (for ETIAS) and specific risk indicators (for VIS) that will be used for assessing the risk posed by applicants for ETIAS authorisations and visas.[174] The Agency has already set up an ETIAS Central Unit in this respect. Furthermore, representatives of the agency participate in the ETIAS and VIS Screening Board and the ETIAS and VIS Fundamental Rights Boards.[175] Importantly, the increased powers of the Agency in this respect raise the bar regarding the need for close supervision by the EDPS. The participation of the latter in the ETIAS and VIS Fundamental Rights Guidance Boards is important to gain insights into the correct implementation of the IT systems. However, the mandate of the EDPS centring on personal data protection may delimit its ability to conduct in-depth supervision. Besides, it is neither sustainable nor correct to cram AI-related issues under the auspices of data protection law, as these two fields though related are not one and the same.

Beyond the operation of IT systems, the EBCG Agency also heavily lobbies in favour of further use of AI-based systems in the context of border management. This is in line with its mandate to support research and innovation and

[173] See Regulation (EU) 2019/1896 of the European Parliament and of the Council of 13 November 2019 on the European Border and Coast Guard and repealing Regulations (EU) No 1052/2013 and (EU) 2016/1624 (EBCG Regulation) [2019] OJ L295/1, Art 3(1)(d) and (j), according to which integrated border management consists of, for instance, information exchange and cooperation between Member States and the Agency, including the support coordinated by the Agency and the use of state-of-the-art technology including large-scale information systems that form part of integrated border management.

[174] ETIAS Regulation (n 51) Art 7; 2021 VIS Regulation (n 49) Art 9j.

[175] ETIAS Regulation (n 51) Arts 9–10; 2021 VIS Regulation (n 49) Arts 9k and 9l.

contribute to the development of the EU's Integrated Border Management.[176] It has participated in the Horizon 2020 Promenade (ImPROved Maritime awarENess by means of AI and BD mEthods) project, aimed at optimising vessel tracking, behaviour analysis and automatic anomaly detection in relation to maritime surveillance.[177] Furthermore, Frontex also collaborated with the US National Center for Border Security and Immigration (BORDERS) for the project AVATAR (Automated Virtual Agent for Truth Assessments in Real-Time), which developed a deception detection system on the basis of an analysis of facial expressions, voice, body and eye signals.[178]

Moreover, various studies have been published identifying synergies with ongoing AI studies and initiatives in the EU and contributing to a Europe-wide AI landscape, with the approach spanning from automated border control (e-gates, document scanning and verification, facial recognition and other biometric verification) to maritime domain awareness, surveillance towers and autonomous unmanned aerial systems.[179] A Commission study has been developed with the precise aim of assisting the Agency by identifying and monitoring existing and emerging technological solutions relevant in this context, many of which can rely on AI systems, such as video surveillance systems and learning to identify objects, people, activities, emotions – in real time or *ex post*, or in Unmanned Aerial Vehicles (UAV).[180]

The interest in AI has increased the appetite for the Agency to reconsider its role in shaping the future landscape of AI-based capabilities in European border security. Previous research has identified a number of potential roles in this context: ranging from mapping future requirements and opportunities associated with AI and AI-based systems in border security (an exercise which Frontex is already engaged in), strengthening the knowledge and evidence base, such as conducting impact assessments (arguably the existing report barely touches upon the relevant challenges), facilitating information and knowledge exchange, gathering and sharing lessons learned or developing training and education materials/programmes for end users in Member States.[181] As such, Frontex could take a role in developing or facilitating public awareness campaigns or education policy. The agency could even facilitate the coordination between different stakeholder groups (agencies, institutions etc), although here competition with

[176] EBCG Regulation (n 173) Art 10(1)(x).

[177] See www.promenade-project.eu/.

[178] University of Arizona, 'Automated Virtual Agent for Truth Assessments in Real-Time', available at https://eller.arizona.edu/departments-research/centers-labs/border-security-immigration.

[179] EBCG Agency, 'Artificial Intelligence-based Capabilities for the European Border and Coast Guard – Final Report' (2020); Another study on biometrics and the future of travel highlighted the potential of integrating AI in biometric systems (feature extraction and matching) and in detecting biometric data manipulation. See the EBCG Agency, 'Technology Foresight on Biometrics for the Future of Travel' (2021).

[180] Commission, 'Weak Signals in Border Management and Surveillance Technologies' (2022).

[181] K Cox et al, 'From Lab to Field: Challenges and Opportunities for Operationalising Border Security Research' (Frontext, 2017).

Europol may become an issue, or it may support the development of national capabilities or multi-national/EU projects by sponsoring or hosting technology demonstrators. In light of the above, it is likely that the EBCG Agency will request additional powers relating to AI in the future, for example, by testing AI systems using data to which it has access, mirroring the new Europol tasks on research and innovation.[182] However, the Agency's interest in AI capabilities comes amidst criticisms regarding its severely underdeveloped data protection culture.[183]

Besides research, the Agency has, along with Europol, set up the Future Group on Travel Intelligence and Border Management to draw up proposals to strengthen checks at external and internal borders, including a European system for traveller screening (ESTS), a decentralised, yet EU-wide, screening function for travellers. Among the recommendations, it is stated that

> Border management should also rely on automated targeting or screening systems for performing risk management on the travellers with advance information. It would be beneficial, from an operational perspective and for the purpose of assessing the risk of the individual traveller, if the targeting system were to include not only API, PNR, and Visa or ETIAS application data, and if the risk management were to include combinations of these data. The experiences of border authorities outside the EU have demonstrated the operational added value of this. This would require legislative changes and most likely the use of AI to combine those sources effectively.[184]

Furthermore, the ESTS functionality could include AI technology

> to implement self- learning processes from previous case handling, including actions or decisions taken without the need to store additional personal data. These tools can assist the officers and help them spend less time on repetitive tasks, but can never be a substitute for their individual assessment.[185]

C. eu-LISA

eu-LISA has been kept relatively off the radar, even though the proliferation of large-scale IT systems and their interoperability have substantially increased its powers. The potential of IT systems and the interoperability components

[182] Regulation (EU) 2016/794 of the European Parliament and of the Council of 11 May 2016 on the European Union Agency for Law Enforcement Cooperation (Europol) and replacing and repealing Council Decisions 2009/371/JHA, 2009/934/JHA, 2009/935/JHA, 2009/936/JHA and 2009/968/JHA [2016] OJ 135/53 (as amended), Art 33a.

[183] S Tas, 'Frontex and Data Protection' (*Verfassungsblog*, 9 September 2022), available at https://verfassungsblog.de/frontex-and-data-protection/; L Stavinoha Apostolis Fotiadis and G Zandolini, 'EU's Frontex Tripped in Its Plan for Intrusive Surveillance of Migrants' (*Balkan Insight*, 7 July 2022), available at https://balkaninsight.com/2022/07/07/eus-frontex-tripped-in-plan-for-intrusive-surveillance-of-migrants/.

[184] European and EBCG Agency (n 116) 50.

[185] ibid 67.

making use of AI systems has led eu-LISA to study the potential uses of AI in the operational management of large-scale IT systems, thus essentially to reflect on how to exploit the AI momentum to increase its own role.[186] The ultimate goal is for eu-LISA to become 'the EU's Centre of Excellence in Artificial Intelligence in the area of internal security, migration and justice'.[187] A non-public 'Roadmap for AI initiatives at eu-LISA' has been developed[188] and a Working Group on Artificial Intelligence (WGAI) was set up in September 2022, comprising experts from the European Commission, EU Agencies and Member State authorities to support the implementation of the roadmap.

The WGAI discusses priorities for the application of AI in the area of internal security. The fusion of migration and criminal justice under the term 'internal security' is notable, setting the undertone of the Working Group. Its aim is to identify use cases for the implementation of AI solutions within the large-scale IT systems entrusted to the management of eu-LISA, to maximise the added value of the services the Agency provides to its stakeholders, and to facilitate the development of a common approach for the use of AI-based solutions.

In this regard, the agency has already adopted the 2020 roadmap and has prioritised various AI tools. For example, the identification of irregular travelling patterns (eg, a Libyan travelling to Belgium via Japan) as an additional piece of risk analysis and the identification of so-called *mala fide* travellers. In this respect, AI could monitor, search and combine data from different sources such as ETIAS and EES (but also PNR data) to detect possible irregular travelling patterns. The AI could detect irregularity either at the 'node' level of a sequence of stops (is it uncommon to travel from point A to point B?) or at the aggregate travel pattern level (does the overall length and shape of this travel pattern appear to be different to usual behaviour?). The output of this analysis could either prompt a human to investigate further, or require asking the applicant for further information/documentation. The triaging of applications for long-stay visa and residence permits identifies automatically and swiftly standard applications and the classification of more complex ones for human review is also a priority.

Classification is understood as the grouping of similar applications (eg, from a certain country or with a similar reason for travel) for review by an expert experienced in dealing with a certain type of application. By grouping the applicants, the officers in question would save time regarding 'basic' applications, and would spend more time working on those classified as complex. With regard to asylum, the focus is on conducting a 'vulnerability check' to determine whether a person is in immediate danger or has special needs, and this requires expertise and experience. Here, AI could perform a real-time analysis of an applicant's

[186] eu-LISA, 'Artificial Intelligence in the Operational Management of Large-scale IT Systems' (July 2020).

[187] eu-LISA, 'Single Programming Document 2023–2025' (2023).

[188] eu-LISA Working Group on Artificial Intelligence, 'Workshop – Prioritisation of AI Use-cases'.

facial movements, spoken language and body language (plus any other potential aspects) to detect signals which might better inform decision-making by a human social worker/specialised expert (eg, if the person should be granted special procedural guarantees). Techniques would aim to identify and assess the emotional cues implied by both what the applicant says/does and the way that they do it to detect changing or unusual behaviour (rather than detecting vulnerability).

In addition, eu-LISA examines the possibilities, benefits and limitations of the use of AI in sBMS, ETIAS, or the CRRS with an emphasis on AI tools, such as computer vision, encompassing FRT, analysed above, and natural language processing technology. Second, the Agency wishes to benefit from the deployment of AI solutions in the context of the operational management of large-scale IT systems, in particular, focusing on the improvement of performance, stability and the overall quality of the services. This interest in promoting AI tools has gone hand in hand with the Agency's new role in digitalising cross-border criminal justice cooperation, with eu-LISA and Eurojust mapping out possible AI-based solutions also in this field, such as natural language processing and facial recognition.[189]

The technical nature of the work of the agency, evidenced by the fact that its staff is primarily composed of technicians and where lawyers only represent a small portion, affects the ability and interest in conducting meaningful fundamental rights assessments of the impact of these technologies on different groups of third-country nationals. As a result, far-reaching solutions are in the pipeline and are expected to be piloted in the next few years without proper scrutiny, as a legal culture beyond certain data protection matters, such as data security, is missing from the Agency. Furthermore, eu-LISA is lagging behind in terms of accountability mechanisms, be it political accountability, supervision by the EDPS, whose resources are primarily concentrated on supervising the EBCG Agency and Europol, or even internal accountability mechanisms, such as an equivalent to the Frontex Fundamental Rights Officer. This means that with the burst of interest in AI solutions, there is a danger that these developments are viewed as technical additions to the IT systems and not as distinct legal developments with renewed fundamental rights implications.

VIII. CONCLUDING REMARKS

This chapter has aimed to provide a bird's eye view of the future outlook of AI-reliant migration, asylum and border management by examining three main issues; the regulation of AI tools employed both at the national and EU levels

[189] eu-LISA, Artificial Intelligence Supporting Cross-border Cooperation in Criminal Justice (Joint report prepared by eu-LISA and Eurojust, 2022).

through the AI Act, the embedding of AI tools in the operationalisation of interoperable large-scale IT systems for third-country nationals and the interest of EU agencies to further technologise this domain and accordingly increase their powers.

With regard to the regulation of AI, the contribution demonstrates that the AI Act contains several protection gaps and has not adequately taken into account the significant fundamental rights implications and the limitations of the underlying technologies in the classification of AI systems. In particular, the fact that no AI system is prohibited is telling regarding the perception of migration as a threat which justifies the use of even the most contested tools subject to certain requirements. It is also indicative of the particularly weak position of migrants, refugees and other people on the move, whose political participation in the legislative process and contestation of technological fixes is extremely limited.

The operationalisation of interoperable large-scale IT systems by 2027 provides a particularly fruitful ground to examine the potential embedment of AI systems. The chapter has looked into FRT and algorithmic profiling, highlighting the existing rules in the underlying legal instruments and in view of the lack of explicit reference to AI has sought to identify whether and where AI tools could be incorporated. To bring more clarity to this area, the chapter stresses the role of one of the interoperability components, the CRRS, and demonstrates that the deliberate omission to refer to AI and the use of the more neutral term 'algorithms' (which may or may not be AI) enables the embedment of various AI systems in the functioning of the IT systems not only in the current form, but also in the future through additional reforms.

The chapter has also aimed at highlighting the fundamental rights risks of FRT and algorithmic profiling in the context of ETIAS and VIS, focusing on the rights to privacy, data protection and non-discrimination. The reliability of these tools and the potential biases both in the design of the algorithms and during human review have been at the forefront of the analysis. Of course, the reinforcement of effective remedies for third-country nationals who are affected and raising awareness about their existence are equally central.[190]

Finally, the chapter maps out the AI-related initiatives of three key players in the AFSJ, the EUAA, the EBCG Agency and eu-LISA, all of which have an increased appetite for harvesting the potential of AI, as shown by the various initiatives and research projects in which they are involved. These initiatives are not always in line with their mandate, for example, in the case of the EUAA, and importantly have come from agencies whose fundamental rights culture has either been particularly limited, such as in the case of eu-LISA, or heavily criticised, as in the case of the EBCG Agency, risking that the understanding of

[190] See N Vavoula and A Karaiskou, 'Algorithmic Risk Assessments and (Inadequate) Access to Remedies: The Cases of ETIAS and VIS' (forthcoming 2025).

AI-based solutions is downgraded to merely technical issues losing sight of their fundamental rights implications. Instead, this chapter purports that accountability, transparency and close monitoring in the development and application of AI is central, both for EU agencies and in the development of interoperable IT systems.

The potential of AI tools in this domain is endless. In immigration systems suffering from backlogs, lengthy delays and uncertain outcomes, the deployment of AI technology appears as a panacea for treating pathogenic practices and promoting superficial neutrality in the decision-making of applications for travel authorisations, visas or asylum. Furthermore, AI could also, more broadly, improve adaptation to a fast-paced geopolitical and security environment. It could even work to the benefit of individuals, for example, to aid the human trafficking mitigation efforts, by maintaining the anonymity of victims during human trafficking investigation interviews through AI-based avatars. As such, an ecosystem of artificially intelligent migration, asylum and border management ecosystem emerges. However, these developments come at a high cost for the fundamental rights of third-country nationals and must first be understood, mapped out and carefully scrutinised. This chapter has (hopefully) chipped into this heated debate, however, as the development of AI is fast-paced, research on these matters is inevitably evolving too.

19

The Digital Border and the Rule of Law. Lessons from the Establishment of the European Travel Information and Authorisation System

VALSAMIS MITSILEGAS*

I. INTRODUCTION

THE EVOLUTION OF EU immigration policy in the Area of Freedom, Security and Justice (AFSJ) has been marked by a growing reliance on the digitalisation of border controls. The EU digital border consists primarily of a growing number of EU immigration databases.[1] The list of the 'first generation' EU databases – namely the Schengen Information System (SIS), the Visa Information System (VIS) and Eurodac – has been expanded recently with the addition of databases and systems including the Entry/Exit System (EES), the European Travel Information and Authorisation System (ETIAS) and the European Criminal Records Information System for Third Country Nationals (ECRIS-TCN).[2] The first generation databases have evolved and the second generation databases have been established to reflect a marked move from immigration control to border security – whereby the digital border does not only fulfil border control purposes, but is also clearly a border security tool.[3] The proliferation and evolution of EU databases has been accompanied by EU law to ensure that these databases are interconnected and interoperable. Moreover,

* University of Liverpool.

[1] E Brouwer, *Digital Borders and Real Rights* (Brill, 2008); N Vavoula, *Immigration and Privacy in the Law of the European Union. The Case of Information Systems* (Brill, 2022).

[2] For a thorough analysis, see Vavoula, ibid.

[3] V Mitsilegas, 'Border Security in the European Union. Towards Centralised Controls and Maximum Surveillance' in E Guild, H Toner and A Baldaccini (eds), *Whose Freedom, Security and Justice? EU Immigration and Asylum Law and Policy* (Hart Publishing, 2007) 359–94; V Mitsilegas, *The Criminalisation of Migration in Europe. Challenges for Human Rights and the Rule of Law* (Springer, 2015).

recent initiatives have demonstrated a shift towards automated digital border controls, through the use of risk assessment and algorithms.

The transformation of digital borders in these terms poses significant challenges for the protection of fundamental rights and the rule of law. This chapter aims to focus specifically on the impact of the digitalisation of EU border controls on the rule of law, by analysing the evolution, design and consequences of the establishment of ETIAS. ETIAS constitutes a prime example of the new paradigm of a securitised, pre-emptive, algorithmic digital border in EU law. The chapter will evaluate critically the impact of the establishment of ETIAS on the rule of law by analysing in turn: the legislative history of and justification for the ETIAS Regulation; the main functions and components of ETIAS; the impact of the model of pre-emptive risk assessment introduced by the ETIAS Regulation; and the multi-actor design and architecture of ETIAS. The chapter will conclude with an analysis of the rule of law implications of interoperability, which lies at the heart of the ETIAS design and operation.

II. THE CONTESTED EVOLUTION OF ETIAS

The introduction of ETIAS has not been straightforward. It was originally framed as an electronic travel authorisation system following the United States' Electronic System for Travel Authorisation (ESTA) model, and as part of a new EU approach to smart borders.[4] In its 2008 Communication on 'Preparing the Next Steps for Border Management in the European Union'[5] the Commission put forward a number of ideas reflecting an interlinking between free movement, migration management and border security objectives. The Commission claimed that the preventive effect of VIS was limited as Advance Passenger Information (API) data could not be used for the purpose of preventing a person from arriving at the border crossing point of the Member State of destination.[6] Developing its position on the SIS, the Commission stated that if the EU wanted to reach the objective of a truly integrated border management, with the aim of meeting the two objectives of enhancing security and facilitating travel for third-country nationals, further steps could be considered.[7] It was noted that from a security angle, third-country nationals not requiring a visa were currently not subject to any systematic check for border control purposes before arriving at the border itself.[8] The Commission thus floated the idea of the introduction

[4] On the US influence on EU border security, see V Mitsilegas 'Immigration Control in an Era of Globalisation: Deflecting Foreigners, Weakening Citizens, Strengthening the State' (2012) 19 *Indiana Journal of Global Legal Studies* 1, 3–60.

[5] Commission, 'Preparing the Next Steps in Border Management in the European Union' COM(2008) 69 final, Brussels, 13.2.2008.

[6] ibid 3.

[7] ibid 4.

[8] ibid 5.

at EU level of tools including the facilitation of border crossing for bona fide travellers, the possible introduction of a registration of entry/exit; and examining the introduction of an ESTA.[9] The ESTA would apply to third-country nationals not subject to the visa requirement who would be requested to make an electronic application supplying, in advance of travelling, data identifying the traveller and specifying the passport and travel details. The data could be used for verifying that a person fulfils the entry conditions before travelling to the EU, while using a lighter and simpler procedure compared to a visa.[10] The Commission undertook to launch a study in 2008 to analyse the feasibility, the practical implications and the impacts of such a system.[11]

The proposal for the establishment of an EU-ESTA system was eventually discarded by the Commission. In its 2011 Communication on smart borders,[12] the Commission stated that it considered that the establishment of an ESTA for visa-exempted third country nationals 'should be discarded at this stage as the potential contribution to enhancing the security of the Member States would neither justify the collection of personal data at such a scale nor the financial cost and the impact on international relations' (emphasis added).[13] The Commission added that, as for the gradual substitution of the visa requirement by an EU ESTA, it seemed unfeasible for the foreseeable future, given the difficulty to assess the migratory risk and the problems linked to internet access and the use of electronic identification. In addition, for establishing an ESTA, a fully functioning EES would be a prerequisite. The Commission added that it was clear that any EU ESTA was not an alternative for an entry/exit system as it could not be used to monitor actual border crossings – neither was ESTA relevant for facilitating such border crossings, as the use of biometrics would make a system of electronic applications impractical. The Commission stated that it would not proceed further with preparations for the development of an EU ESTA at this stage.[14]

Yet calls for an ESTA-type system resurfaced after the Paris attacks. The 2016 Commission Communication on 'Stronger and Smarter Information Systems for Borders and Security' reflects the centrality of border security in the EU approach post-Paris in its very title.[15] From the outset the Commission expressly linked external border controls with internal security, using the Paris

[9] For an analysis, see V Mitsilegas, 'The Borders Paradox. The Surveillance of Movement in a Union without Internal Frontiers' in H Lindahl (ed), *A Right to Inclusion and Exclusion? Normative Faultlines of the EU's Area of Freedom, Security and Justice* (Hart Publishing, 2009).

[10] Commission, 'Preparing the Next Steps' (n 5) 9.

[11] ibid.

[12] Commission, 'Smart Borders – Options and the Way Ahead' COM(2011) 680 final, Brussels, 25.10.2011.

[13] ibid 7.

[14] ibid.

[15] Commission, 'Stronger and Smarter Information Systems for Borders and Security' COM(2016) 205 final, Brussels, 6.4.2016.

and Brussels attacks to claim that migration flows constitute a threat to internal security.[16] The Commission argued that action was needed to address gaps in existing EU information systems and to improve their interoperability.[17] The Commission argued in particular that there was an information gap prior to arrival at the borders as concerns third-country nationals who are exempt from holding a visa.[18] The Commission noted that while law enforcement authorities could obtain information on visa-holders from the VIS if necessary for the combating of serious crime and terrorism, no comparable data was available on visa-exempt persons, with the Commission arguing that this lack of information was particularly relevant for the management of the land borders of the EU, in a situation where substantial numbers of visa-exempt travellers arrive by car, bus or train.[19] In view of this statement, the Commission undertook to assess the feasibility of the establishment of an EU ETIAS, where visa-exempt travellers would register relevant information regarding their intended journey. It was envisaged that the *automatic* processing of this information could help border guards in their assessment of third-country visitors arriving for a short stay (emphasis added).[20] The Commission noted that countries such as the USA, Canada and Australia have already put similar systems in place, including for EU citizens, and claimed that in addition to its security benefits, such a system would also serve as a travel facilitation tool.[21]

The Commission published its proposal for a Regulation on the establishment of ETIAS only a few months after the publication of its Communication on information systems and border security.[22] The proposal was not accompanied by an *ex ante* impact assessment, only a feasibility study was conducted.[23] The proposal clearly reflected a logic of preventive border security. From the outset the Commission stated that, in comparison to visa-required third country nationals, the competent border and law enforcement authorities had little information on visa-exempt third country nationals as regards risks they may pose *before* their arrival at the Schengen border, and argued that adding this

[16] ibid 2. The document states that: 'Beyond these regular travel flows, in 2015 alone, conflict in Syria and crises elsewhere triggered 1.8 million irregular border crossings at Europe's external borders. EU citizens expect external border controls on persons to be effective, to allow effective management of migration and to contribute to internal security. The terrorist attacks in Paris in 2015and in Brussels in March 2016 bitterly demonstrated the ongoing threat to Europe's internal security.'

[17] ibid 2.

[18] ibid 3.

[19] ibid 13. Several neighbouring countries of the EU are already visa-free, and visa liberalisation dialogues between the EU and other neighbouring countries are proceeding. This is likely to lead to a considerable increase of visa-exempt travellers in the near future.

[20] ibid.

[21] ibid.

[22] Proposal for a Regulation of the European Parliament and of the Council establishing a European Travel Information and Authorisation System (ETIAS) and amending Regulations (EU) No 515/2014, (EU) 2016/399, (EU) 2016/794 and (EU) 2016/1624 COM (2016) 731 final, 16.11.2006.

[23] Vavoula (n 1) 475.

missing layer of information and risk assessment on visa-free visitors would bring significant added value to existing measures to maintain and strengthen the security of the Schengen area and would allow visa-free visitors to fully enjoy their visa-free status.[24] ETIAS would aim to ensure interoperability with other EU information systems and for that reason would be developed in parallel with the EU EES.[25] The main aim of ETIAS would be preventive risk assessment. ETIAS would be an automated system created to identify any risks associated with a visa-exempt visitor travelling to the Schengen Area, gathering information on these travellers prior to the start of their travel, to allow for advance processing.[26] The examination of information provided by visa-exempt third country nationals ahead of their arrival at the EU external border would allow to determine that there are no factual indications or reasonable grounds to prevent a travel authorisation being issued.[27] According to the Commission, the system would facilitate travel but also reinforce internal security in two ways: first, through the identification of persons that pose a security risk before they arrive at the Schengen external border; and second, by making information available to national law enforcement authorities and Europol, where this is necessary.[28]

The ETIAS Regulation was eventually published in the Official Journal in September 2018.[29] The Regulation is clearly a preventive border security measure. It was adopted under the dual immigration/policing legal basis of Articles 77(2)(b) and (d) and Article 87(2) of Treaty on the Functioning of the European Union (TFEU). Its Preamble states that ETIAS should contribute to a high level of security, to the prevention of illegal immigration and to the protection of public health by providing an assessment of visitors prior to their arrival at the external border crossing points.[30] Its opening Article states that ETIAS will enable consideration of whether the presence of those third-country nationals in the territory of the Member States would pose a security, illegal immigration or high epidemic risk.[31] The aims of the Regulation include: to contribute to a high level of security by providing for a thorough security risk assessment of applicants, prior to their arrival at external border crossing points, in order to determine whether there are factual indications or reasonable grounds based on factual indications to conclude that the presence of the person on the territory

[24] Proposal for ETIAS Regulation (n 22) 2.
[25] ibid 3.
[26] ibid.
[27] ibid 4.
[28] ibid.
[29] Regulation (EU) 2018/1240 of the European Parliament and of the Council of 12 September 2018 establishing a European Travel Information and Authorisation System (ETIAS) and amending Regulations (EU) No 1077/2011, (EU) No 515/2014, (EU) 2016/399, (EU) 2016/1624 and (EU) 2017/2226 (ETIAS Regulation) [2018] OJ L236/1.
[30] ibid recital 10.
[31] ibid Art 1(1).

of the Member States poses a security risk;[32] to contribute to the prevention of illegal immigration by providing for an illegal immigration risk assessment of applicants prior to their arrival at external border crossing points;[33] to contribute to the protection of public health by providing for an assessment of whether the applicant poses a high epidemic risk within the meaning of point 8 of Article 3(1) prior to his or her arrival at external border crossing points;[34] and to contribute to the prevention, detection and investigation of terrorist offences or of other serious criminal offences.[35]

The ETIAS Regulation thus embraces a broad concept of preventive border security ranging from addressing terrorism and irregular migration to addressing threats to public health. The scope of the objectives is very broad, blurring the boundaries between the different purposes and constituting another example of the (in)security continuum in the EU.[36] It is questionable whether the legal bases to the Regulation are appropriate to cover its public health preventive objective.

III. ETIAS: THE KEY ELEMENTS

The ETIAS Regulation establishes a system of securitised, preventive risk assessment of all third country nationals not requiring a visa prior to their arrival at the EU external border. Applicants are obliged to submit in advance a wide range of personal data, including information on their education and current occupation.[37] Upon the submission of such information, applications are assessed through a multi-layered risk assessment and profiling process. Applications are assessed in the light of information contained in three sets of data sources: information contained in various EU and international databases on immigration control and security; information contained in the screening rules developed for ETIAS; and information contained within the ETIAS watchlists. In terms of the use of EU and international databases, it is provided that the ETIAS Central System will compare the relevant data to data registered in the ETIAS Central System, the SIS, the EES, the VIS, Eurodac, Europol land Interpol data.[38] A subsequent legislative initiative has added

[32] ibid Art 4(a).

[33] ibid Art 4(b).

[34] ibid Art 4(c). High epidemic risk is defined in this context as any disease with epidemic potential as defined by the International Health Regulations of the World Health Organization (WHO) or the European Centre for Disease Prevention and Control (ECDC) and other infectious diseases or contagious parasitic diseases if they are the subject of protection provisions applying to nationals of the Member States.

[35] ibid Art 4(f).

[36] On the securitisation of migration in this context, see D Bigo, 'Security and Immigration: Toward a Critique of the Governmentality of Unease' (2002) *Alternatives* 27, Special Issue, 63–69; see also D Bigo, *Polices en réseaux: l'expérience européenne* (Presses de Sciences Po, 1996).

[37] ETIAS Regulation (n 29) Art 17, in particular Art 17(2)(h) and (j).

[38] ibid Art 20(2).

the ECRIS-TCN[39] to the list in order to enhance the security objectives of ETIAS.[40] Thus, not only are applications assessed in comparison to EU immigration databases, but also in comparison to databases by law enforcement agencies whose input in the process is not subject to meaningful scrutiny and accountability standards. This is the case in terms of Europol but in particular regarding Interpol, a non-EU, global organisation whose databases depend on unilateral input from a variety of states and the compatibility of whose operations with EU law is challenging to assess. ETIAS applicants who submit applications to conduct the everyday activity of visa-free travel to the EU, are thus assessed on the basis of unaccountable security databases whose input is opaque and hardily challengeable.

The challenges of such unaccountable securitised risk assessments are compounded by the two further processes of ETIAS comparison. Firstly, the ETIAS Central System will compare the relevant data to the risk indicators developed by the ETIAS screening rules[41] and to the data included in the ETIAS watchlist.[42] The ETIAS screening rules are an algorithm enabling profiling through the data recorded in an application file in the ETIAS Central System with specific risk indicators established by the ETIAS Central Unit pointing to security, illegal immigration or high epidemic risks.[43] The definition of these risks is entrusted to the Commission through the adoption of a delegated act.[44] The Commission will further specify these risks in which specific risk indicators established by the ETIAS Central Unit[45] will be based by means of a reviewable implementing act.[46] Secondly, the ETIAS watchlist will form a part of the ETIAS Central System and will consist of data related to persons who are suspected of having committed or taken part in a terrorist offence or other serious criminal offence or persons regarding whom there are factual indications or reasonable grounds, based on an overall assessment of the person, to believe that they will commit a terrorist offence or other serious criminal offence.[47] The watchlist will be established on the basis of information related to terrorist offences or other serious criminal offences[48] which will be entered into the system by Member States or by Europol.[49]

[39] Regulation (EU) 2021/1151 of the European Parliament and of the Council of 7 July 2021 amending Regulations (EU) 2019/816 and (EU) 2019/818 as regards the establishment of the conditions for accessing other EU information systems for the purposes of the European Travel Information and Authorisation System [2021] OJ L249/7, Art 7b.

[40] ibid recital 9.

[41] ETIAS Regulation (n 29) Arts 20(5) and 33 (hereinafter provisions refer to the ETIAS Regulation unless stated otherwise).

[42] ibid Arts 20(4) and 34.

[43] ibid Art 33(1).

[44] ibid Arts 33(2) and 89.

[45] ibid Art 33(4)-(6).

[46] ibid Arts 33(3) and 90(2).

[47] ibid Art 34(1).

[48] ibid Art 34(2).

[49] ibid Art 34(3).

Both under the Screening Rules and under the watchlist, ETIAS introduces a system of risk assessment targeting perceived dangerousness and underlined by limited transparency and accountability mechanisms. The development of what constitutes a risk under the Screening Rules is entrusted to the Commission via delegation and not to the legislators via an open and transparent process. As it has been pointed out, the screening rules will result in individuals being flagged as a risk not because of any specific actions they have engaged in but because they display particular category traits in a probabilistic logic devoid of concrete evidence.[50] The introduction of a watchlist system, on the other hand, represents a contamination of EU border management with a 'war on terror' securitised logic which has proven problematic in terms of the rule of law and fundamental rights protection in litigation involving watchlists generated by the UN Security Council after 9/11.[51] Application files will be processed automatically by the ETIAS Central Unit[52] and the comparison with information contained in the EU and international databases, the ETIAS screening rules and the ETIAS watchlist will take place by automated means.[53] Where the automated processing of the applications reports one or several hits, the ETIAS Central System will automatically consult the ETIAS Central Unit for verification purposes.[54] The application will be further processed manually by the ETIAS National Unit of the Member State in question.[55] The ETIAS National Unit will proceed to a risk assessment in view of the information contained in the relevant databases, in the ETIAS screening rules and in the ETIAS watchlist in order to reach a decision on the ETIAS application in question.[56] The general profiling feature of ETIAS has been summarised eloquently by the European Data Protection Supervisor (EDPS) as follows:

> the EDPS notes that the ETIAS will collect and process a huge volume of personal data (including on criminal offences) about millions of individuals and will cross-check these data with data stored in several other largescale IT systems including central databases for law enforcement cooperation. These data will be used to support decisions that may adversely affect individuals. In addition, a set of screening rules will be used to profile data subjects and to determine automatically the potentially risky individuals for whom a manual processing of their applications will be required.[57]

[50] N Vavoula, 'Artificial Intelligence (AI) at Schengen Borders: Automated Processing, Algorithmic Profiling and Facial Recognition in the Era of Techno-Solutionism' in (2021) *European Journal of Migration and Law* 23 457–84.

[51] On the development of watchlists by the UN Security Council, see G Sullivan, *The Law of the List* (Cambridge University Press, 2020).

[52] ETIAS Regulation (n 29) Art 20(1).

[53] ibid Preamble, recital 24.

[54] ibid Art 22.

[55] ibid Art 26(1). Preamble, recital 24.

[56] ibid Art 26(2)-(6). Preamble, recital 24.

[57] EDPS Opinion on the ETIAS DPIA (Case 2021-0640) 4.

IV. ETIAS RISK ASSESSMENT AND THE RULE OF LAW

The process and parameters of risk assessment leave many questions in terms of the compliance of the ETIAS assessment of the perceived risk posed by a third-country national with the rule of law. Research conducted by Derave, Genicot and Hermanska demonstrates the lack of transparency and the difficulties of obtaining clarity as to the operation of the ETIAS screening rules by the key bodies and institutions involved in its architecture – eu-LISA, Frontex and the Commission.[58] They further point out that the Commission Delegated Decision refers to a continuous, dynamic process of risk assessment, requiring data used to determine risk profiles to be collected 'in a manner that makes it possible to continuously identify sets of characteristics of specific groups of travellers who exhibit a perceived irregular migration risk,[59] namely overstaying, refusal of entry or refusal of travel authorisation'.[60] They also point out that Articles 4 and 5 of the Delegated Decision contain extremely broad definitions as to what Member States can report as irregular migration risks.[61] They rightly note that the ever-changing nature of ETIAS screening rules may well conflict with the nature of a 'rule' itself[62] – thus failing to meet the legality, legal certainty and foreseeability requirements of the rule of law. The opacity in the development of risk assessment criteria which have the potential to have a considerable negative effect on the everyday lives of individuals, coupled with the wide discretion that EU institutions and agencies have in this context, leaves much to be desired in terms of both legality and transparency.[63]

Further concerns have been expressed regarding the way in which the ETIAS Regulation maps out the processes of what has been characterised as an automated decision-making system on the basis of algorithmic profiling.[64] The ETIAS Regulation provides for a first stage of automated assessment which will lead to a hit/no hit result, with a hit leading to a subsequent individualised assessment by the competent ETIAS National Unit. Doubts have been expressed concerning whether this system is compatible with the requirements for algorithmic data assessment set out by the CJEU in its ruling

[58] C Derave, N Genicot and N Hetmanska, 'The Risks of Trustworthy Artificial Intelligence: The Case of the European Travel Information and Authorisation System' (2022) *European Journal of Risk Regulation* 13, 389–420, 404–406.

[59] ibid 407.

[60] Commission Delegated Decision on further defining security, illegal immigration or high epidemic risks, C(2021) 4981 final, Brussels, 23.11.2021, Art 3(2) and recital 4, available at https://ec.europa.eu/transparency/documents-register/detail?ref=C(2021)4981&lang=en.

[61] Derave et al (n 58) 406. They further point out that Member States will transmit their periodic reports to Frontex via the established risk analysis channels.

[62] ibid 407.

[63] On algorithmic discretion and the principle of legality, see https://verfassungsblog.de/frontex-and-algorithmic-discretion-part-i/.

[64] See Vavoula (n 50).

on *Ligue des Droits Humains*, concerning the compatibility of the EU PNR Directive,[65] and its preventive and pre-emptive system of passenger data transfer and processing, with EU law.[66] It has been argued that while the manual processing of hits envisaged by the National Unit under Article 26 of the ETIAS Regulation appears to require human intervention, it is unclear to what extent such human intervention will be meaningful in practice as in ETIAS, the human is 'looped in' at the end of the decision-making chain, where their judgment is already mediated by the 'risk score'.[67]

It has further been argued that it is unclear whether ETIAS complies with the Court's standards regarding 'clear and precise' criteria ensuring meaningful human review at the earlier stage of verification of hits by the ETIAS Central Unit before these are transferred to the National Unit for manual processing. It has been argued that the Regulation does not contain such criteria, only stating that the ETIAS Central Unit should conduct an initial verification of any hit(s) (Art 22(3)). Hereupon, the ETIAS Central Unit forwards verified hits to the responsible ETIAS National Unit, which should then assess the risks in question.[68] It remains to be seen how the ETIAS system will operate in practice and the extent to which meaningful criteria meeting the CJEU benchmarks will be developed. A key question in this context is whether the development of such criteria behind closed doors through technical input and delegation meets the requirements of deliberation and transparency which are essential for the development of standards which may have a significantly averse effect on the everyday life and the rights of individuals.

Concerns have also been expressed regarding the compatibility of the system established by the ETIAS Regulation with the right to an effective remedy. It has been pointed out that it is unclear whether the grounds for refusal provided to the unsuccessful applicant enable that applicant to adequately contest the decision. Article 38(2)(c) of the ETIAS Regulation provides that the applicant is only entitled to the category of grounds for refusal (as listed under Article 37(1)).[69] These refusal decisions will not include substantiated or individualised information.[70] It has been argued validly that this system fails to meet

[65] Directive (EU) 2016/681 of the European Parliament and of the Council of 27 April 2016 on the use of passenger name record (PNR) data for the prevention, detection, investigation and prosecution of terrorist offences and serious crime [2016] OJ L119/132–49.

[66] Case C-817/19 *Ligue des Droits Humains* EU:C:2022:491. For an analysis, see E Mendos Kuskonmaz, 'The Grand Gala of PNR Litigations, Case C-817/19, *Ligue des Droits Humains v Conseil de Ministres* (2023) *European Constitutional Law Review*; V Mitsilegas, 'The Criminalisation of Travel as a Global Paradigm of Preventive (In)Justice. Lessons from the EU Response to 'Foreign Terrorist Fighters' (2023) 14 *New Journal of European Criminal Law* 183–205.

[67] See https://verfassungsblog.de/digital-border/.

[68] See https://verfassungsblog.de/pnr-threat-detection-ii/.

[69] See n 66.

[70] E Brouwer, 'Schengen and the Administration of Exclusion: Legal Remedies Caught in between Entry Bans, Risk Assessment and Artificial Intelligence' (2021) *European Journal of Migration and Law* 23, 485–507.

the requirement imposed by the CJEU in the *Ligue des Droits Humains* case.[71] The Court held there that the competent authorities must ensure that the person concerned – without necessarily allowing that person, during the administrative procedure, to become aware of the pre-determined assessment criteria and programmes applying those criteria – is able to understand how those criteria and those programmes work, so that it is possible for that person to decide with full knowledge of the relevant facts whether or not to exercise his or her right to judicial redress in order to call into question, as the case may be, the unlawful and, inter alia, discriminatory nature of the said criteria.[72]

It has been further argued that the CJEU case law on refusal of entry, a visa or a travel authorisation to the Schengen area should be applicable also to ETIAS refusals: the Court held that individuals who have been denied entry, a visa, or travel authorisation for the Schengen area should always be informed about the information system in which the record exists, and that subsequently resulted in a refusal.[73] Brouwer has pertinently made a broader point, which is that the complexity of the legal instruments at stake (in combination with the further use of personal information via the interoperability scheme) hamper the effective use of individual data protection rights and judicial remedies as protected in Article 47 of the EU Charter.[74]

V. THE ARCHITECTURE OF ETIAS: A PARADIGM OF SECURITISED, MULTI-ACTOR GOVERNANCE

In order to further evaluate the rule of law challenges posed by the digitalisation of the border through ETIAS, it is necessary to cast light on the complex, multi-layered governance of this information system – consisting, to use an expression coined by Curtin and de Goede, of a complex constellation of actors.[75] The multiplicity of actors involved in ETIAS is reflected at various levels: at the level of input to the ETIAS database; at the level of architecture and governance of ETIAS; and at the level of output, as regards the question of who has access to ETIAS data. To begin with the latter point, a wide range of national authorities has access to information contained in the ETIAS Central System including border authorities for the purpose of data verification at the external border,[76]

[71] See n 66.

[72] *Ligue des droits humains* (n 66) para 210.

[73] Brouwer (n 70). Joined Cases R.N.N.S and K.A. C-225/19 and C-226/19 *R.N.N.S and K.A. v Minister van Buitenlandse Zaken* EU:C:2020:951. The CJEU required the disclosure of *the specific ground for refusal of a visa, accompanied, where appropriate, by the essence of the reasons for that objection*, para 56.

[74] Brouwer (n 70).

[75] D Curtin and M de Goede, 'Buts, Bytes, Searches and Hits: Logging in Accountability for EU Data-led Security' in D Curtin and MV Catanzariti (eds), *Data at the Boundaries of EU Law* (Oxford University Press, 2023) 175–217.

[76] ETIAS Regulation (n 29) Art 47–48.

immigration authorities[77] and law enforcement authorities.[78] In a further extension of the system of preventive border control introduced by ETIAS, its system can also be queried by private actors – by air, sea and coach carriers in order to verify whether or not third-country nationals subject to the travel authorisation requirement are in possession of a valid travel authorisation.[79] The ETIAS Regulation provides for the establishment of a 'carrier gateway' to ensure the linkage between carriers and ETIAS.[80] Carrying passengers who do not comply with ETIAS requirements triggers sanctions and return obligations under the EU carriers' liability regime.[81] Thus, the ETIAS system is used as a further means of control of the obligations of carriers, but presents an additional rule of law challenge: as a passenger who is not allowed to board a carrier will have to challenge not only the decision of the carrier but also the underlying ETIAS rejection leading to the carriers' refusal to carry. There is a risk of automaticity in refusal to carry on the basis of the results of the consultation of ETIAS.

Rule of law challenges also emerge in terms of the securitised and technocratic multi-agency architecture of ETIAS, with its central role, together with the role played by national authorities, by three EU agencies (EU-LISA, Frontex and Europol), while account must also be taken of the role of the Commission in the development of the system. eu-LISA has a key role in the development and architecture of ETIAS. eu-LISA will develop the ETIAS Information System, ensure its technical management[82] and develop further technically the ETIAS watchlist, which it will host.[83] In addition, eu-LISA will host the ETIAS Central System.[84] It will define the design of the physical architecture of the system, develop and implement it.[85] It will be responsible for the technical development of the ETIAS Information System, for any technical development required for establishing interoperability between the ETIAS Central System and the EU information systems and for enabling the querying of Interpol databases.[86] Following the entry into operation of ETIAS, eu-LISA will be responsible for the technical management of the ETIAS Central System and the national units.[87] eu-LISA will also have a role in the implementation of the carriers' liability regime or for the purpose of resolving any potential dispute arising from its application by keeping logs of all data processing operations carried out within the carrier gateway by carriers.[88] eu-LISA will also have a leading role in the

[77] ibid Art 49.
[78] ibid Art 50–52.
[79] ibid Art 45(1).
[80] ibid Art 6(2)(k).
[81] ibid Art 45(5) and 8).
[82] ibid Art 6(1).
[83] ibid Art 35(7).
[84] ibid Art 73(1).
[85] ibid Art 73(3).
[86] ibid.
[87] ibid Art 74(1).
[88] ibid Art 45(7).

monitoring and evaluation of ETIAS, and will report regularly to the European Parliament and to the Council on the development of the system.[89]

Frontex will host the ETIAS Central Unit.[90] The Agency will be responsible for setting up the Unit, for the automated processing of applications and for the ETIAS screening rules.[91] The ETIAS Screening Board with an advisory function is established within Frontex and is composed of a representative of each ETIAS National Unit, of the European Border and Coast Guard Agency and of Europol.[92] The Fundamental Rights Officer of Frontex will be a member of the ETIAS Fundamental Rights Guidance Board, together with a representative of the Frontex consultative forum on fundamental rights, a representative of the EDPS, a representative of the European Data Protection Board and a representative of the European Union Agency for Fundamental Rights.[93] Europol has considerable input powers to the ETIAS system. It contributes data for the purpose of the initial automated processing of applications in ETIAS[94] and enters data into the ETIAS watchlist.[95] The Commission has, as seen above, a key role in defining the risk indicators informing the ETIAS screening rules through the adoption of a delegated act.[96] The Commission will further specify these risks on which specific risk indicators established by the ETIAS Central Unit[97] will be based by means of a reviewable implementing act.[98]

Thus, the architecture of ETIAS reveals a highly securitised and technocratic paradigm of governance. A central role is entrusted to eu-LISA, which, as will be seen in the interoperability discussion below, is a single-agenda depoliticising agency which is framed as having a technical, and not a legal, competence. The other two key EU agencies involved, Frontex and Europol, both have a strong security mandate[99] and face serious concerns regarding accountability and compliance with fundamental rights.[100] Accountability and transparency concerns in the operations of these agencies within ETIAS are compounded by

[89] ibid Art 92(1) and (2).
[90] ibid Art 7(1).
[91] ibid Art 75(1).
[92] ibid Art 9(1).
[93] ibid Art 10(1).
[94] ibid Arts 20(2) and 77.
[95] ibid Arts 34 and 35 and 77.
[96] ibid Arts 33(2) and 89.
[97] ibid Art 33(4)-(6).
[98] ibid Arts 33(3) and 90(2).
[99] On the transformation of Frontex into a border security agency where risk assessment is ever more prominent, see Mitsilegas (n 4) and V Mitsilegas, 'Cartografía de la Externalización del Control Migratorio: Ideas a Partir del Régimen de la UE sobre Tráfico Ilícito de Migrantes' (2020) 73–74 *Revista Española de Derecho Europeo*, 23–64.
[100] On Frontex, see E Guild (ed), *Monitoring Border Violence in the EU. Frontex in Focus* (Routledge, 2023); V Mitsilegas, 'The EU External Border as a Site of Preventive (In)justice' (2022) 28 *European Law Journal* 263–80. On Europol, see N Vavoula and V Mitsilegas, '*Strengthening Europol's Mandate. A Legal Assessment of the Commission's Proposal to Amend the Europol Regulation* (Study commissioned by the Civil Liberties Committee, Study PE 694.200, May 2021).

the key role entrusted to the Commission in developing risk assessment criteria through delegation with limited external scrutiny and deliberation. The ETIAS Regulation aims to address fundamental rights concerns through the set-up of the Fundamental Rights Board and supervision arrangements by national authorities[101] and by the EDPS, which is responsible for monitoring the personal data processing activities of eu-LISA, Europol and Frontex.[102] Yet the scrutiny of the development of risk assessment criteria, of the input to ETIAS leading to automated risk assessment, and of decisions on risk and dangerousness remains limited. These concerns become more acute with the involvement in the ETIAS input of even less accountable third parties such as Interpol.

VI. ETIAS AND INTEROPERABILITY: EXACERBATING THE RULE OF LAW CHALLENGES

These rule of law concerns are exacerbated by the fact that ETIAS is part of the system of interoperability of EU databases, confirming the linkages between ETIAS and the other EU information systems in the field of border management[103] as well as with Europol. The ETIAS Regulation itself states that interoperability between ETIAS, other EU information systems and Europol will be established.[104] While the amending Regulation to include ETIAS consultation of ECRIS-TCN states that it is necessary to establish interoperability between the ETIAS Information System, on the one hand, and the EES, the VIS, the SIS, Eurodac and the ECRIS-TCN and Europol data, on the other, in order to enable the ETIAS Central System to process application files and for the purpose of automatically identifying hits.[105]

Calls for the introduction of interoperability in relation to the EU databases are not new. The Commission presented its Communication a year later, in November 2005.[106] The purpose of the Communication was to highlight how, beyond their present purposes, databases 'can more effectively support the policies linked to the free movement of persons and serve the objective of combating terrorism and serious crime'.[107] On the basis of this approach, the Commission argued strongly in favour of access of authorities responsible for internal security to immigration databases such as SIS, VIS and Eurodac.[108] The Communication provided a definition of 'interoperability', which is the

[101] ETIAS Regulation (n 29) Art 46.
[102] ibid Art 47(1).
[103] According to ibid Art 23, ETIAS supports the objectives of SIS.
[104] ibid Art 11(1).
[105] Regulation 2021/1151 (n 39) recitals 3 and 4.
[106] Commission, Communication on Improved Effectiveness, Enhanced Interoperability and Synergies among European Databases in the Area of Justice and Home Affairs COM(2005) 597 final, Brussels, 24.11.2005.
[107] ibid 2.
[108] ibid 8.

'ability of IT systems and of the business processes they support to exchange data and to enable the sharing of information and knowledge'.[109] What was striking was that the Commission presented interoperability as a technical rather than a legal/political concept,[110] in a clear attempt to de-politicise the issue and to shield it from legal and democratic scrutiny, notwithstanding its considerable potential consequences for the protection of human rights.[111]

Legislation was adopted in 2019, in the form of two Regulations on establishing a framework for interoperability between EU information systems in the field of police and judicial cooperation, asylum and migration.[112] The Regulations aim to establish interoperability between a number of EU databases including the EES, the VIS, ETIAS, Eurodac, SIS and ECRIS-TCN.[113] They also establish procedures and conditions for designated authorities and for Europol to access EES, VIS, ETIAS and Eurodac.[114] Blurring the boundaries between immigration control and security purposes is thus clear, and it is also confirmed by the objectives of the Regulations, which include a contribution to a high level of security within the AFSJ[115] and a contribution to the prevention, detection and investigation of terrorist offences and of other serious crime.[116] The Regulations envisage a central role for eu-LISA in developing key elements of interoperability including the European search portal,[117] creating profiles within the system[118] and establishing an interface control document;[119] developing shared biometric matching services[120] and ensuring its technical management; and developing the common identity repository and an interface control document.[121] eu-LISA will host the various interoperability components and ensure that their central infrastructures are operated in accordance with the Regulations.[122]

[109] ibid 3.
[110] ibid.
[111] On interoperability as de-politicisation at the time, see Mitsilegas (n 4).
[112] Regulation (EU) 2019/817 of the European Parliament and of the Council of 20 May 2019 on establishing a framework for interoperability between EU information systems in the field of borders and visa and amending Regulations (EC) No 767/2008, (EU) 2016/399, (EU) 2017/2226, (EU) 2018/1240, (EU) 2018/1726 and (EU) 2018/1861 of the European Parliament and of the Council and Council Decisions 2004/512/EC and 2008/633/JHA [2019] OJ L135/27–84; Regulation (EU) 2019/818 of the European Parliament and of the Council of 20 May 2019 on establishing a framework for interoperability between EU information systems in the field of police and judicial cooperation, asylum and migration and amending Regulations (EU) 2018/1726, (EU) 2018/1862 and (EU) 2019/816 [2019] OJ L135/85–135 (referred to hereafter as the Interoperability Regulations).
[113] Interoperability Regulations, ibid, Art 1(1).
[114] ibid Art 1(4).
[115] ibid Art 2(1)(c).
[116] ibid Art 2(1)(f).
[117] ibid Art 6(3).
[118] ibid Art 8(1).
[119] ibid Art 9(3).
[120] ibid Art 12(3).
[121] ibid Art 17(3) and (5).
[122] ibid Art 54.

Interoperability serves further to exacerbate the rule of law challenges underpinning this 'maximum' securitisation approach by creating a platform enabling activity with significant human rights consequences (maximum, large-scale access to personal data) on a perceived 'technical' basis and under the supervision of 'technical' agencies.[123] A key example of the supervision of a 'technical' interoperability system by a 'technical' agency is eu-LISA: an EU agency established to 'run' the proliferating EU databases, and to advance interoperability (emphasis added).[124] The establishment of a technical, single-agenda institution in this context poses further challenges to the rule of law requirements of transparency and accountability in the access and processing of personal data in the European Union. As Bigo has noted, what is at stake is an incremental logic where the language, knowledge of technology imposes itself in security matters, not as a solution, but as a way of reasoning, reframing what counts as security and danger and adding that eu-LISA becomes a central node of power, delegitimising the legal arguments of purpose limitation and favouring speed in politics, as well as narratives of prevention and prediction.[125]

The rule of law challenges concerning a lack of transparency and accountability on the one hand, and the lack of an effective remedy on the other, are exacerbated by the combination of opacity and data maximisation that interoperability seeks to offer.[126] The interoperability Regulations have introduced a multi-layered system of elements aiming to ensure maximum access to and exchange of personal data located in a number of EU databases set up for different purposes. In addition to the attempt to shield sensitive data processing and pre-emptive large scale surveillance from legal and fundamental rights scrutiny through its 'technical' framing, interoperability – also in the context of the operation of ETIAS – forms a challenge to the rule of law by constituting a clear attack on the purpose limitation principle, as data collected for distinct and specific migration management purposes can be shared and transformed

[123] D Bigo and L Bonelli, 'Digital Data and the Transnational Intelligence Space' in D Bigo, E Isin and E Ruppoert (eds), *Data Politics. Worlds, Subjects, Rights* (Routledge, 2019) 119, point out that interoperability imposes certain characteristics and criteria on the formatting of data, which is helpful if they are to be exchanged on a regular basis and in large quantities and highlight the supervision of this exercise by new technical actors.

[124] See European Council Press Release 285/18, eu-LISA: Agreement between the Council Presidency and the European Parliament (24 May 2018), according to which new legislation has been agreed to entrust the agency with developing and operating new EU systems and for eu-LISA to contribute to the development of technical solutions to achieve interoperability. The repeated emphasis on the technical is noteworthy.

[125] D Bigo, 'Interoperability: A Political Technology for the Datafication of the Field of EU Internal Security?' in D Bigo et al, *The Routledge Handbook of Critical European Studies* (Routledge, 2021) 408.

[126] On the challenges of opacity and lack of an effective remedy, see also Curtin who notes that it becomes hard to pinpoint at exactly what level of administration mistakes are made: D Curtin, 'Second Order Secrecy and Europe's Legality Mosaics' (2018) 41 *West European Politics* 4, 846–68 at 856.

by a variety of different actors and for different purposes, including security purposes. Various technical components are layered one after the other, and, as the EDPS has noted, the measures add another layer of complexity to the existing systems, as well as those that are still in the pipeline, and with interoperability implemented in this way, it leads to more complexity rather than simplification, both in terms of data protection and in terms of governance and supervision.[127] The complexity of the system presents a rule of law challenge in itself.

VII. CONCLUSION

This chapter examined the evolution of the digitalisation of the border in EU law by focusing on the pre-emptive, future-looking, securitised, multi-purpose, algorithmic, interoperable profiling system established by ETIAS. ETIAS is a key development in the digitalisation of the border as it is the first database which combines all of the above elements and it requires the risk assessment of *all* third country nationals who do not require a visa before their arrival at the EU border. ETIAS thus introduces, as with the public/private partnerships established in EU law involving the transfer of PNR and communications data by private actors to state authorities, a system of generalised pre-emptive surveillance of ordinary everyday activities.[128] ETIAS is thus instrumental in creating what Bigo has deemed a 'digital pre-border regime'.[129] As Musco Ekliund and Brewcynska have eloquently pointed out, together with the PNR requirements, ETIAS represents a new logic of what can justify a fundamental rights interference:

> it is not a person's behavior, or any reasonable suspicion that subjects you to the first interference, but simply being a passenger, or in the case of the ETIAS regime, being a third-country national from a visa-exempt country. 'Reasonable suspicion', in this risk-based approach, is replaced by other triggers for interferences: who you are, in the case of ETIAS, which base risk indicators on data such as education level, age and occupation (Arts. 17(2), 20(5)), or how you travel, in the case of the PNR directive (Annex 1).[130]

The rule of law challenges in the establishment and design of ETIAS are multiple. In the first place, there is a rule of law deficit in the justification and adoption of the ETIAS Regulation. The need for the adoption of the Regulation was not always accepted by EU institutions, with its adoption rejected initially

[127] EDPS Opinion 4/2018, paras 23–24.
[128] V Mitsilegas, 'The Privatisation of Surveillance in the Digital Age' in V Mitsilegas and N Vavoula (eds), *Surveillance and Privacy in the Digital Age. European, Transatlantic and Global Perspectives* (Hart Publishing, 2021) 101–58.
[129] See Didier Bigo in chapter 20 of this volume.
[130] See https://verfassungsblog.de/foreseeability-pnr/.

and resurfacing within a renewed security framing after the Paris terrorist attacks. In a climate of the 're-emergence of emergency',[131] a measure which was not deemed to be of added value was suddenly repackaged as essential for security purposes and as a way to make the most of the new imperative of interoperability in EU databases. But the design and operation of the Regulation present significant rule of law challenges as well. A fundamental rule of law deficit lies with the process of risk assessment of third country nationals in terms of the development of the risk assessment criteria, which remains opaque; in terms of the scrutiny of the input of information which forms the basis of automated decision-making, which relies on the largely unchallenged and secretive risk assessment of a number of national, EU and non-EU law enforcement agencies; and in terms of the foreseeability and explainability of an ETIAS decision and the limited, if any, availability of an effective remedy against that decision.

Further rule of law challenges arise from the securitised, technocratic and complex architecture of ETIAS. ETIAS is multi-purpose, blurring the boundaries between immigration control, security and the protection of public health. A number of technocratic (eu-LISA) and security (Frontex and Europol) agencies are heavily involved in its design and operations, agencies with serious underlying fundamental rights and accountability issues themselves. These issues are exacerbated by the very complexity of the multi-actor architecture of ETIAS, and, of course, by the insertion of ETIAS into the web of interoperability of EU databases. The multiple rule of law challenges surrounding the EU interoperability framework – in terms of transparency, accountability and judicial protection – are applicable to the work of ETIAS and are particularly acute in terms of its clear profiling capacity. In a world where individuals are constantly being risk assessed and treated not as trusted travellers (a discourse which has largely been abandoned by the EU)[132] but as suspects, vigilance and scrutiny of the day-to-day operations of ETIAS within its interoperable setting are essential to safeguard the rule of law.

[131] V Mitsilegas, 'Counter-terrorism and the Rule of Law in an Evolving European Union: *Plus Ça Change?*' (2021) 12 *New Journal of European Criminal Law* 36–52.

[132] On the EU discourse on Registered Travellers and Trusted Travellers, see Mitsilegas (n 9) 33–64.

20

Digital Controls, Mobility and Surveillance; the Social Universe of 'Reasonable Suspicion' and its Different Guilds

DIDIER BIGO*

I. INTRODUCTION

IN THIS CHAPTER, I will examine how mobility and border controls have been strongly affected by digitisation and the practice of exchanging the data of travellers in advance for security reasons. The attempt to justify by a 'reasonable suspicion' will be questioned. The terminology of reasonable or even legitimate suspicion is now included in policy documents, legal doctrines, court judgments, even if nobody agrees on the tension arc of a suspicion, which has to be checked against all travellers, in order to be certain that not one single dangerous individual is able to travel, and the reasonable dimension which is to check travellers only if they have already been identified as a danger by previous actions and not by algorithms which calculate the correlation and proximity of patterns via statistical correlations, without any direct or indirect effective links. As we will see, digitisation has allowed the possibility to check all travellers before they land, a task which was impossible before the development of the high-speed exchange of data. But the technical possibility has been used to justify a philosophy of preventive security coming from the ideology of counter-terrorism set up after the declaration of the war on terror and which has been perpetuated in the different services in charge of elaborating risk profiles, from 2002 to the present, even if the development in Europe of norms of privacy and data retention, with court decisions and sanctions against data controllers (private and public), are changing the rules of the game, not only in Europe but worldwide. I argue in this chapter that the conflation of the two logics via the

* University of Liverpool.

colonisation of this temporal digital mechanism of pre-border registration by border security authorities in search for an all-encompassing form of surveillance needs to be disentangled first and analysed as a specific measure which can be changed if the doxa it has generated is challenged; a challenge that lawyers and courts have to take up.

II. WHAT DIGITIZATION HAS DONE TO BORDER CONTROLS: THE PRE-BORDER VIRTUAL SPACE, SPEED AND TIME AS A 'SPACE' FOR CONTROL

Digitisation has allowed an acceleration in the speed of the exchange of data between private multi-modal (air, sea and even land) travel companies to the point that the exchange of digital data takes place before the physical passage of the person, at least in theory.[1] Private companies have used this advantage to customise their services and ask about preferences in advance for a long time, but digitisation has multiplied the number of people benefiting from this 'personalisation' and the criteria for the consumers' 'choices'.[2] For border guards, customs officers, and immigration authorities, it has also changed the essence of their professions.[3] The examination of documents can be spread over a certain period of time and does not have to be concentrated to the arrival of the individual. The exchange of information between the bureaucracies of the countries of departure, transit and arrival is not (or at least is less) dependent on communication with the holder of the document, the individual. Administrations can exchange documents between themselves and verify whether a person (reduced to being a body and the bearer of documents) is the one (s)he claims to be.

The traditional story of that one moment of sovereignty when the border guard asks for a 'passport' and investigates the truth is now only a short moment

[1] In the case of short air travel, you can often see planes waiting to land even if slots are available at the airport because of a 'data traffic jam', as one of our interviewees put it.

[2] See the literature on the invention of privilege cards by air companies, the birth of advanced passengers information. D Lyon, 'Airport Screening, Surveillance, and Social Sorting: Canadian Responses to 9/11 in Context' (2006) 48 *Canadian Journal of Criminology and Criminal Justice* 3, 397–411; JP Carvajal-González, J Valencia-Aguirre and G Castellanos-Domínguez, 'Silhouette Classification by Using Manifold Learning for Automated Threat Detection' in *Proceedings – International Carnahan Conference on Security Technology* (2013 47th International Carnahan Conference on Security Technology, ICCST 2013, Institute of Electrical and Electronics Engineers Inc., 2014), available at https://doi.org/10.1109/CCST.2013.6922080.

[3] On the evolution of the professions linked to control, border guards and military polices, immigration and border polices, asylum officers at the borders, customs authorities, and their interactions as public authorities of control with private organisations, see the works of K Côté-Boucher, *Border Frictions: Gender, Generation and Technology on the Frontline* (Routledge, 2020). K Côté-Boucher, 'Smart Borders? Customs, Risk Targeting, and Internal Politics in a Border Agency1' (2019) *Security and Risk Technologies in Criminal Justice: Critical Perspectives* 225; A Crosby and A Rea, 'La Fabrique Des Indésirables. Pratiques de Contrôle Aux Frontières Dans Un Aéroport Européen' (2016) *Cultures & Conflits* 103–104, 63–90.

in a continuum of practices of surveillance largely beginning before and continuing after the person has crossed the border.[4]

A digital pre-border regime has been created to extend the space and time of the operations of control.[5] The 'space' is not the place of the 'check' at the border anymore, the time is not just a question of checking a person at a certain moment in time, but these are instead a question of the collection of personal and non-personal data, of a relational analysis of a person within a group of travellers in the same vehicle, the validity of their authorisations, their past travel, and so on.[6] This set of information, now digitalised, is collected, stored, organised by sorting mechanisms, and retained for a certain period of time in order to examine in advance, in a preventive way, who is travelling. The political economy of power at the borders has therefore been changed, first, by the existence of this new 'space' and second, by its instrumentalisation as a tool in a strategy of preventive security which began with the decision of a war on terror, the 'patriot' act and the externalisation of homeland security abroad; a United States' (US) hegemonic strategy which has been both transformed but also partly duplicated by European countries in 2004 and 2015, exacerbating the tensions between the controls of all travellers, digital surveillance, privacy and freedom of movement. These tensions have generated multi-scalar struggles between international and regional organisations, governments, executives and courts, non-governmental organisations (NGOs) and activists.

[4] A long tradition of political science has equated the notions of territory and border controls through the metaphor of the body of the politics of the state, and the borders as the envelope, the skin of this body. Everything coming in is therefore a danger, a 'virus', and the state has the right to have special powers of investigations at the border, stripping away some, but not all, basic rights of individuals. Borders are considered 'loci' of 'exception', justified by sovereignty. However, international political sociology has shown that controls are not, on the contrary, always linked with borders, that the economy of power is complex and that the right to declare an exception is not a legitimate claim. Post-colonial studies have arrived at the same conclusions. See D Bigo and E Guild, *Controling Frontiers. Free Movement into and within Europe* (Ashgate, 2005). MB Salter (ed), *Mapping Transatlantic Security Relations: The EU, Canada, and the War on Terror* (Routledge Studies in Liberty and Security, 2010). M Leese, and S Wittendorp, *Security/Mobility: Politics of Movement* (Oxford University Press, 2017).

[5] For a detailed history of the pre-border regime in the EU, see E Brouwer, 'Data Surveillance and Border Control in the EU: Balancing Efficiency and Legal Protection' in T Balzacq and S Carrera (eds) *Security Versus Freedom?* (Routledge, 2016) 151–68. See also Maria Nagore-Casas showing both the passive and active players of this field of action and the difficulties created for asylum seekers in the enforcement of these sets of rules. Paix & Sec. Int'l -1-2019.

[6] See V Mitsilegas, 'Before Entry: Criminalisation as Prevention' in V Mitsilegas, *The Criminalisation of Migration in Europe* (Springer, 2015) 5–45; V Mitsilegas, 'The Transformation of Privacy in an Era of Pre-emptive Surveillance' (2015 *Tilburg Law Review* 20.1, 35–57. S Carrera, G Fuster, E Guild and V Mitsilegas, *Access to Electronic Data by Third-Country Law Enforcement Authorities. Challenges to EU Rule of Law and Fundamental Rights* (CEPS, 2015); N Vavoula, 'Interoperability of EU Information Systems: The Deathblow to the Rights to Privacy and Personal Data Protection of Third-Country Nationals?' (2020) *European Public Law* 26.1; N Vavoula, 'The "Puzzle" of EU Large-Scale Information Systems for Third-Country Nationals: Surveillance of Movement and Its Challenges for Privacy and Personal Data Protection' (2020) *European Law Review* 3, 348–72; E Kuskonmaz, Research Handbook on EU Criminal Law (Bergstrom, Mitsilegas).

The multiplication of legal texts and courts' interpretations are the result of these tensions and judges have been reluctantly involved in this small maelstrom of disputes regarding the ways in which to control people who want to travel using digital surveillance is based on 'reasonable suspicions'.

III. BORDER CHECKS AND THE DIGITISATION OF CONTROL

An important literature has described the movement of borderisation and territorialisation of the national state projects. The tyranny of the national, the invention of passports and visas have regulated the nineteenth and twentieth centuries.[7] More recent works emanating from critical European Union (EU) studies and border studies have pointed out the impact of both the creation of regional areas of internal free movement, and the use of digital tools to manage these enlarged areas. Taking stock of this literature, I would like to highlight the impact this digitisation of the operations of control has had on the transformation of the professions required to implement this control. In a nutshell, the documents given to an individual for travel by the sending country still have their strength (albeit depending on the 'strength' or 'weakness' attributed to the state in question by the receiving states), but faith in their validity is not absolute, far from it. If any information gleaned by the state of destination, when comparing the traveller's documents with its own records, contradicts the information in the documents presented by the traveller, this will lead to a higher rate of suspicion. Receiving states, which have the means and money to collect billions of data on foreigners, will always prefer their own data over the data sent to them. International agreements are less and less seen as a way to manage travel by the richest states which only want to trust their own databases, even if recent initiatives such as the Global Compact try to reverse the trend.

As Elspeth Guild explains, the traveller is a citizen who becomes a foreigner when he leaves his own country, but he is protected by multiple agreements. He is nevertheless in his weakest position when he crosses the border, and the weakness depends on whether he is protected by a regional free movement regime, a visa facilitation agreement, a no visa reciprocity rule, or whether he is obliged to have a visa.[8] The balance of power between the administration and the traveller has changed, the administration has more and more time to suspect more and

[7] G Noiriel, *La Tyrannie Du National: Le Droit d'asile En Europe, 1793-1993* (Calmann-Lévy, 1991) 355. JC Torpey, *The Invention of the Passport: Surveillance, Citizenship and the State* (Cambridge University Press, 2018).

[8] See Elspeth Guild in chapter 17 of this volume. See also E Guild and A Baldacinni, *In Search of Europe's Borders* (Brill, n.d); E Guild, *Security and Migration in the 21st Century* (Polity Press, 2009); E Guild, 'Borders on the Move: Where Does Security Go When Sovereignty Migrates?' (2017) *REMHU: Revista Interdisciplinar Da Mobilidade Humana* 25, 51, 109–28, available at https://doi.org/10.1590/1980-85852503880005108; E Guild, 'Moving the Borders of Europe' *Repository.Ubn.Ru.Nl*, 2001.

more people for more and more reasons. The traveller is rather the object of a decision instead of an actor of it. He is no longer in an asymmetrical dialogue where he has a say, instead he is inside a triangulation where the truth of both the documents of the sending and receiving states have a greater value than his own words. He has the passive support of his documents via the identification made by his body biometrical identifiers, which is why the more difficult it is to alter these biometric identifiers, the better they are considered by the receiving administration. The narrative of the individual is no longer the core mediation of the relationship and, as we shall see, is not used to give him a chance to declare his identity, but as a test against fraud. The interaction with the border guard when he asks questions of the traveller is itself stereotyped and a process of verification instead of an inquiry, for better or worse.[9] Border guards mostly follow the list of items exchanged using electronic forms and shared via different databases they are connected to, and rarely come back to perform a (secondary) investigation. They just have time to verify data and they often already know the signals regarding who, on the list, may be a potential danger, a suspect of a certain kind of activity involving fraud, crime, terrorism, illegal entry ….

As regards those who perform controls, border guards certainly continue to play a visible role as being at the end of the line, there to 'protect' the country, but their powers have been strongly diminished; in contrast the people who design the criteria for each suspicion and elaborate the correlations, who are mostly invisible as they are often reduced to the technical object they elaborate (the algorithms), are by far much more important for the fate of the traveller. This is also the case for the staff managing the online databases, who allow differential access to the databases for anyone asking for data, according to juridical but also technical rules of interoperability.[10]

The first group, rightly called the 'algocrats', are the ones who elaborate specific algorithms for a specific objective and they are often mathematicians, although even more often designers specifying a generic algorithm for a specific purpose. While the second group consists of data engineers who call themselves 'plumbers' of the net, and they work to manage the interoperability of databases.[11] These two new groups have specific tasks, and they are creating

[9] Boucher, *Border Frictions* (n 3); see also B Hayes and M Vermeulen, 'The EU's New Border Surveillance Initiatives' (Heinrich Böll Foundation, 2012).

[10] On interoperability, see Vavoula, 'Interoperability of EU Information Systems' (n 6); B Oliveira Martins, K Lidén and M Gabrielsen Jumbert, 'Border Security and the Digitalisation of Sovereignty: Insights from EU Borderwork' (2022) *European Security* 31.3, 475–94. P Šarf, 'Automating Freedom, Security and Justice: Interoperability of AFSJ Databases as a Move Towards the Indiscriminate Mass Surveillance of Third-Country Nationals' in A Završnik and V Badalič (eds), *Automating Crime Prevention, Surveillance, and Military Operations* (Springer, 2021) 85–108. D Bigo, L Ewert and E Mendos Kuşkonmaz, 'The Interoperability Controversy or How to Fail Successfully: Lessons from Europe' (2020) *International Journal of Migration and Border Studies* 6.1-2, 93–114. K Luyten and S Voronova, 'Interoperability between EU Border and Security Information Systems' (2019) *EPRS*.

[11] J Danaher, 'The Threat of Algocracy: Reality, Resistance and Accommodation' (2016) *Philosophy & Technology* 29.3, 245–68. D Bigo, 'Interoperability: A Political Technology for the

what I have called a different guild of managers of suspicious travellers. These two groups working in the digital realm, have interests, organisations, rules and socialisation skills that differ from those of the traditional border and immigration authorities rooted in the arguments of territorial borders, sovereign decisions and national security exceptions. As we shall see, they reject and block fewer people than the latter but they extend the scope of electronic surveillance and validate *a priori* suspicion as a legitimate way of thinking, thus transforming what is at stake when you cross a border. It is these relationships and tensions between different logics of security and their actors which are important to understand in order to see how freedom and privacy are put at risk by different and sometimes contradictory logics. Unfortunately, all too often, the history of the emergence of these digitalised practices of surveillance is conflated with the politics of some security actors and the policy of some governments. If the latter is certainly true and very well known, I would nevertheless like to describe in greater detail the articulation between the effects of digitisation, the emergence of new 'crafts' and professions, and the impact of a policy of preventive security through predictive tools.

IV. THE PROFESSIONAL GUILDS OF DIGITAL MANAGEMENT OF PRE-BORDER AND BORDERS CONTROLS

The move towards digitisation has its own autonomy and like in many professions, digitisation has redistributed the lines of power, often in favour of those operating at a distance from the 'product', the 'object', the subject or the consumers, they are theoretically 'managers'.[12] The so-called digital revolution of artificial intelligence (AI) automatising many repetitive actions and affecting even social relationships by mimicking conversations has reinforced the sense that the individual is alone in front of a system without a personal embodiment. It has reinforced the Kafkaesque experience of life under bureaucratic rules, where it is impossible to complain. This is happening in many shops, either online or not, in public services, but more importantly for the subject at hand, this is affecting relations with coercive authorities in the situation of a border crossing, where being allowed to enter a country or not may be a question of life or death.[13]

Therefore, what may look like 'progress', like genuine and technical comfort for speedy movement, with fewer physical stops at checkpoints, where you in

Datafication of the Field of EU Internal Security?' in Didier et al (eds) *The Routledge Handbook of Critical European Studies* (Routledge, 2020). 400–17.

[12] D Bigo, 'The Transnational Field of Computerised Exchange of Information in Police Matters and Its European Guilds' in N Kauppi and M Rask Madsen (eds), *Transnational Power Elites: The New Professionals of Governance, Law and Security* (Routledge, 2013) 155.

[13] J-G Ganascia, *Servitudes virtuelles* (Seuil, 2022). D Bigo, 'Sociology of Transnational Guilds' (2016) 10 *International Political Sociology* 4, 398–416; T Monahan, *Crisis Vision* (de gruyter, 2022).

exchange deliver a great deal of data in advance about many areas of your private life, is in actual fact by far much more disputable than the image of 'smart borders' may suggest.[14] Digitization as such depersonalises relations. The different 'smart borders' initiatives in North America, Europe or Latin America are facilitating travel for certain privileged people but they *de facto* multiply the number of digital records for each person, as all the actors involved, both private and public, are repeatedly asking for the very same data. In addition, this leads to the impression for the person who wishes to travel that he/she has no choice but to comply. For example, most of the 'freedom passes' at the borders, proposed by companies, airports, or governments, often including the charging of fees, are *de facto* the extraction of data that are not destroyed afterwards. They sell speedy passes for the rich in the name of freedom; freedom equated with less time spent waiting for physical checks.[15] Wealthy people therefore believe that they are freer than others, and the poorest people in the queues are envious of them, but they are in fact both experiencing different forms of surveillance.[16] The only difference, the digital aspect, is perhaps less visible or feels less coercive, and this may explain the indifference or lack of loud complaints against this digitisation of borders. This is why this belief in the fact that 'there is no alternative' to surveillance in the digital world has led some authors to despair about resistance and juridical litigation without social mobilisation supporting privacy and rights. Zygmunt Bauman speaks of a 'do it yourself surveillance' and a form of desire to be under surveillance. Bernard Harcourt evokes limited disobedience in the digital age and the role of the desire to be a consumer immediately and for everything.[17] Others are less pessimistic and insist on the capacity of the digital Lilliputians to resist the Gullivers of platforms and professional security.

To resume, in the neoliberal economy, digitisation is in itself a way to reinforce speed and to expand surveillance, but the technology is not the only factor

[14] R Koslowski, 'International Cooperation to Create Smart Borders' (Ottawa at the Conference on North American Integration: Migration, Trade and Security, 2004); J Jeandesboz et al, 'Justice and Home Affairs Databases and a Smart Borders System at EU External Borders' (Centre for European Policy Studies, 2012); M Leese, 'Exploring the Security/Facilitation Nexus: Foucault at the "Smart Border"' (2016) *Global Society* 30.3, 412–29; L Everuss, 'AI, Smart Borders and Migration' in A Elliott (ed), *The Routledge Social Science Handbook of AI* (Routledge, 2021) 178.

[15] K Rygiel, 'Governing Borderzones of Mobility through e-borders' in V Squire (ed), *The Contested Politics of Mobility: Borderzones and Irregularity* (Routledge,2011) 143–68. S Sontowski, 'Speed, Timing and Duration: Contested Temporalities, Techno-Political Controversies and the Emergence of the EU's Smart Border' (2017) *Journal of Ethnic and Migration Studies* 1–17. P Trauttmansdorff, 'The Politics of Digital Borders' in C Gűnay and N Witjes (eds) *Border Politics* (Springer, 2017) 107–26.

[16] See the thesis of Zygmunt Bauman on liquid modernity, liquid surveillance. Z Bauman and D Lyon, *Liquid Surveillance a Conversation* (CPolity Press, 2013); Z Bauman, *Le cout humain de la mondialisation* (Hachette Littérature, 1999); Z Bauman, 'Europe: An Unfinished Adventure' (*Polity Press*, 2004).

[17] BE Harcourt, *Exposed: Desire and Disobedience in the Digital Age* (Harvard University Press, 2015); D Bigo, 'Diagonal Mass Surveillance: Gulliver versus the Lilliputians' (*Open Democracy*, 2014).

in the change, it has an engrained capacity to facilitate any form of surveillance via the process of speedy and easy extraction of data. This is why it also contributes to the preventive logic security which also needs more and more data to operate full-scale surveillance in order to detect suspicious behaviour or individuals, and even if the two logics are not the same, they are intertwined.

V. UNLIMITED SECURITY, COLONISATION OF THE FUTURE AND GENERALISATION OF SURVEILLANCE: THE ARGUMENT OF 'PREVENTIVE' SECURITY VIA PREDICTIVE TECHNOLOGIES

The ambition to solve the problem of violence and bring political order through coercive actions and the generalised surveillance of people beyond travellers is not new. The examples of the Stasi and other secret services in repressive regimes show that their ambition was large-scale surveillance, but they did not have the digital technology. The ratio of four to one was necessary in order to ensure a sufficient record of a person under surveillance and the human labour within the intelligence services was time consuming, taking weeks if not months. This changed after the 2000s, with the spread of the Internet, emails and smartphones. The ease of capturing data and intercepting communication changed dramatically, and now everyone has potentially left sufficient traces in the digital realm so that an operator of surveillance can mobilise within a couple of hours if the person is directly targeted. Nevertheless, without the decision to employ the military and intelligence forces in the fight against Al Qaeda and the massive reorganisation of the security forces with the US Department of Homeland Security, the fusion of forces at the borders and their interconnections with policing and intelligence services, via different Fusion Centers working with different levels of different actors but whose information circulates asymmetrically, the situation today would be very different. The view that these practices of capturing the maximum of data were the best way to fight terrorism was strongly opposed by human rights lawyers, privacy organisations, but also police intelligence services and their supervisory authorities. They considered that this ideology of Total Information Awareness was irrational, and certainly not a 'necessity'.[18] But if during the Clinton administration the fight was still in favour of the latter, the arrival of George W Bush and Dick Cheney changed the political situation worldwide.

[18] SR Anderson, 'Total Information Awareness and Beyond, Bill of Rights Defense Committee; White Paper', *The Dangers of Using Data Mining Technology to Prevent Terrorism*, 2004. N Murray, 'Profiling in the Age of Total Information Awareness' (2010) *Race and Class* 52, 2, 3–24, available at https://doi.org/10.1177/0306396810377002. D Bigo, 'Sécurité maximale et prévention? La matrice du futur antérieur et ses grilles' in B Cassin (eds), *Derrière les grilles: sortir du tout évaluation* (Fayard, 2013).

The so-called war on terror has mobilised the technology of digitisation for the objective of suspicion instead of the presumption of innocence and has created a narrative about the predictive capacities of technology which is far removed from what they can do effectively, thus the 'reinvention' of lie detectors/polygraphs, of 'facial' recognition, in the name of 'new' criminology (despite its racialist past), of algorithmic calculations of correlations and associations of 'groups' whose predictive actions can supposedly be detected. Even now, 20 years later, and after the dramatic failure to combat terrorism and crime using this approach, not many people and institutions dare to challenge the block of institutions, legal bodies, proliferations of networks that have been set up and organised to circulate and spread these ideas, that are maintaining their own interests and profits.[19] Certainly, the 2020s have seen more and more debates partially debunking the value, efficiency and legitimacy of this regime of suspicion and digital surveillance, but centrally, the argument about the ineluctability of behaviours once engaged in a trend (against the possibility of changing one's mind which was the root of liberal thought) is still accepted by most parliamentarians, judges and even critical academics.

It is this transformation of the general philosophy of the role of justice and rehabilitation, of the nature of freedom as a core principle under which security is only a tool to achieve some positive freedom, which has modified the political economy of borders and used digitisation for the objective of a preventive form of control anticipating the actions of an individual or of a group, supposedly predicted via algorithms of danger. This pretence about knowing the future truth (in singular), and reading the future as if it was already the past and detecting a 'path' through weak signals has unfortunately for its targets more in common with astrology and sacrificial logic than with science.[20]

The idea of total information awareness, and a one per cent doctrine justifying the detention of innocent people if it makes it possible to stop a future terrorist, has led to narratives of alternative truths, of a universe in permanent uncertainty and the dangers we need to be protected against at any cost by the knowledgeable authorities foreseeing the best way, or at least the least dangerous way.

This has not been restricted to the US, it has been a temptation worldwide, and some international organisations as well as certain governments, fascinated by the possibilities of declaring exceptional measures, have helped the dissemination of this security 'logic' conflating in their structure the administrative-penal logic of punishment with the preventive coercive logic of intelligence.

[19] F De Londras, 'The Transnational Counter-Terrorism Order: A Problématique' (2019) 72(1) *Current Legal Problems* 203–251.

[20] M Bosworth, C Hoyle and L Zedner (eds), *Changing Contours of Criminal Justice* (Oxford University Press, 2016). M Delmas-Marty, 'The Limits of Human Rights in a Moving World – Elements of a Dynamic Approach' in B Fassbender and K Traisbach (eds), *The Limits of Human Rights* (Oxford Academic Press, 2019) 331; V Mitsilegas, 'The Law of the Border and the Borders of Law: Rethinking Border Control from the Perspective of the Individual' in *Rethinking Border Control for a Globalizing World* (Routledge, 2015) 37–53. L Zedner, 'Against Prediction: Profiling, Policing, and Punishing in an Actuarial Age' (Oxford Academic Press, 2008) 359–62.

Nevertheless, in many countries, and especially in Europe, as well as in many institutions that defend that criminal justice should be based on evidence, the rule of law and human rights, resistance has appeared, as well as alternatives, so that we can rethink the digital world outside the 'box' of preventive security logic. The role of national and European courts in limiting the excess of unlimited security desired by many executive powers in a world that opposes privacy and data protection because they wish to retain data for a long period of time and to extract more and more data, has been central.[21] But it has not been through a debate on ideas and principles, it has been through very specific cases and specific constraints, leading to diverse initiatives. Nevertheless, one can see that the locus of borders has been the node, the point of concentration of the most difficult problems and tensions concerning travel, freedom, the rights of minorities, the powers of law enforcement and border authorities and the need for supervision in democratic regimes.

VI. THE INTRODUCTION OF PREVENTIVE SECURITY LOGIC IN THE EU FIELD OF INTERNAL SECURITY

This doxa about a maximum security logic and an absolute necessity to establish an order in the midst of uncertainties using tools that are said to be predictive explains the depolitisation of the question of political violence and crime, and the tactical moves of some politicians to allow the European Commission and experts to take more initiative in the domain of internal affairs, by letting them be in charge instead of the respective governments. This game has generated an acceptance that security is a 'technical' matter and not a political and diplomatic one. It is through this argument of management that the EU has borrowed its preventive reasoning from the US, while distancing itself from the excess of the practices of the intelligence-led coalitions of secret services (the Central Intelligence Agency extraordinary rendition programme, the National Security Agency large scale surveillance programme). It has created a belief that the 'solutions' are to be found in new technologies, that it is an economic and technological matter and not a societal one, and that the interest of the EU is to close the gap with the US in terms of digital surveillance, whatever the cost in terms of privacy. But the context of the freedom of movement, the less clear sense of panic after terrorist attacks, and the strength of privacy and human rights lawyers have allowed a different configuration to emerge with, on the one hand, the promotors of an internal field of security building an equivalent to the US Homeland Security complex, and, on the other, a rise in the concerns for the freedom of movement, privacy, dignity supported by some of the EU institutions and some national bureaucracies working in networks, who are

[21] See GDPR, ECJ and ECHR judgements discussed in the conclusion and in other chapters of this book.

finally challenging the idea of 'reasonable' suspicion applied to all travellers at the borders.

The different fights and alliances of all these players are neither random nor the grand strategy of some hegemonic actors, instead they are the result of effects on fields, speaking as a sociologist inspired by Pierre Bourdieu. Without this framework of analysis, the logics of distinction and mimetic competitions are ignored. This is why it is important to introduce the overall field of internal security into the EU before speaking to the part of it dealing with border and digital controls, as the latter do not have a real specificity or an autonomous logic.

Of course the existence of an EU internal security domain called Justice and Home Affairs largely predates the war on terror narrative and is neither a follow up of US doctrines nor an autonomous domain that security studies can isolate as an object as such.[22] The question of EU internal security is derivative of the practices of the freedom of movement in the EU, of who is entitled to cross borders, to stay, to work and to live with his family.[23] What is occurring in what has been called the field of EU internal security is therefore the product of the history of policing, border controls and intelligence in each country of Europe over the centuries, the legal creation of a common market and a EU changed by its enlargements and its specialisations, including the third pillar of 'home affairs', and the history of socio-technical mechanisms affecting all the actors of this field. This area, or rather, this social space, is constructed as a field because many social actors who work with policing, border controls, migration management, or the reception of refugees have been interested in and pushed for lively discussions on the idea of a European internal security system and have fought to ensure that their reasoning and tools prevail over those of others, in order to also guarantee their funding and mission. The notion of a field is used to avoid a situation whereby a vision of the multiple different practices of the actors that gather and compete to define security and insecurity, is reduced to a discussion on the progress or not of the institutions of the EU and an analysis of the success or failure of a spillover in matters of sovereignty. The socio-genesis of the field of EU internal security is correlated with the transformation of the practices of the freedom of movement for people and the ways this management of their travel has been correlated with the traditional tasks of coercion regarding crime and violence normally performed by the police, as well as the way they treat their citizens and foreigners in these cases.

The field of internal security is therefore a field of power, where different professionals engage transnationally regarding the best and worst practices that the other national traditions consider as legitimate options for coercing individuals in a specific state. Far from opposing homogeneous cultural

[22] K Groenendijk, 'The Genesis of Free Movement of Persons in the EU: Why and for Whom? in Didier et al (n 11) 283–306.

[23] E Guild, 'The EU's So-Called Mediterranean Refugee Crisis: A Governmentality of Unease in a Teacup' in Didier et al (n 11) 307–24.

entities of nations represented by their governments and their representatives (commissioners, and permanent representation), a study of the last 40 years shows that alliances and battles are often about the way actors do their jobs, the similarities or dissimilarities of their procedures, their habitus and trajectories.[24]

Being a policeman, a gendarme, a border guard, regardless of the country, is more important than nationality, and frames how people act, beyond the diplomatic negotiations that take place in Brussels. This is what I have called transnational guilds. These guilds are structured by the specific skills necessary to do a job, and the form of recognition about who is an expert in this domain, sometimes not in accordance with the formal hierarchies at work within institutions. As it has been explained many times, such research entails combining different disciplines, which all have their own narratives about the history of EU internal security.[25] We insist here that the professionals of security who were in charge for centuries (policemen; gendarmes, border guards, judges and the agencies of the EU in which they have congregated, ie Europol, Frontex, Eurojust) have now to take into account the emergence of a new guild with a different background consisting of engineers, data analysts, experts on IT systems, that we can call a guild of 'digital technologies' which has emerged due to the tendency of all the actors in the field of reducing security problems to an issue of governmentality of unease which has thus to be resolved by technical experts. They were not initially interested in border controls or security matters but they have been used for work in these domains and after becoming specialised, they have taken more and more of their own logic of work, forms of knowledge and interests into the field.

This is illustrated by the creation of a specific EU agency, not very well-known to the public, but very central in terms of power politics, called eu-LISA, an acronym for the full long title: the European Agency for the Operational Management of Large-Scale IT Systems in the area of freedom, security and justice. This EU agency is *de facto* the embodiment of the entanglement of the digitisation of controls and the will to continue with surveillance on all travellers.[26]

[24] R Adler-Nissen and V Pouliot, 'Power in Practice: Negotiating the International Intervention in Libya' (2014) *European Journal of International Relations*; R Adler-Nissen, 'Bourdieu in International Relations Rethinking Key Concepts in IR' (2013) 249; D *Bigo*, *Thinking Tools for Analysing the Transnational Guilds of Professionals of Management of Unease* (n.d.).

[25] R Bossong and M Rhinard, *Theorizing Internal Security in the European Union* (Oxford University Press, 2016).

[26] M Illamola Dausa, 'EU-LISA, the New Model of Operational Management of the Various EU Databases' (2015) *Revista CIDOB d'afers Internacionals* 111, 105–26; H Pötzsch, 'The Emergence of iBorder: Bordering Bodies, Networks, and Machines' (2015) *Environment and Planning D: Society and Space* 33.1, 101–18. Trauttmansdorff (n 15) 107–26; G Glouftsios, *Engineering Digitised Borders: Designing and Managing the Visa Information System* (Springer Nature, n.d.).

VII. EU-LISA: THE LOCUS OF THE ENTANGLEMENT OF DIGITAL TECHNOLOGY AND PREVENTIVE SECURITY

eu-LISA presents itself as having a role of support for the implementation of the EU's justice and home affairs policies by managing large-scale IT systems. Established in 2011 and operational only from the 1 December 2012, the staff seems moderate with only 137 people (in 2019), which are in addition split between three sites; the headquarters in Tallin (Estonia), the operational site in Strasbourg (France), and a back-up site in Sankt Johann in Pangau (Austria). However, the strong association between eu-LISA and private firms (their tenderers) strongly boosts the number of people involved in the network of the agency and shows the specific public-private characteristic of the technologies at stake.

The agency officially has the task of managing the three databases which have been central in the EU to address the questions of justice and home affairs (Schengen Information System (SIS), Eurodac, and Visa Information System (VIS)), eu-LISA has also more recently been put in charge of developing new projects of large-scale IT systems with different databases: first, the EU Entry/Exit System (EES), second, the European Travel Information and Authorisation System (ETIAS), and third, the European Criminal Records Information System for third-country nationals (ECRIS-TCN). So, in total there are therefore six EU information systems which are concerned with the interoperability mechanisms connecting them, and which relate to Justice and Home Affairs-security only in part, while JHA wants access to almost all of the databases.[27]

Even if privacy and purpose limitations have been addressed by courts and scholars, most comments made on interoperability take for granted the presentation that these six systems are coherently necessary for JHA and therefore 'belong' to policing and border guards first and foremost as well as of course to eu-LISA, which is a way of denying the validity of the previous separation of tasks, or more exactly the compartmentalisation, distinguishing for good reasons, crime-terrorism and judicial requests, on the one hand, and border crossings, visas and travel, on the other, in the way the EU has done for more than 20 years (from the Amsterdam Treaty and as a customary practice after Lisbon).

As long as they were not interoperable, were allocated to different tasks and had different access to authorities designated expressly for their main activities, there were problems concerning function creep, but the difficulties were limited. Now the implementation of the project of interoperability has deeply changed the global architecture and what a single search can bring as a result. Even if the

[27] N Vavoula, *Immigration and Privacy in the Law of the European Union: The Case of Information Systems* (Brill, 2022).

principle for the police and intelligence services is still not 'nice to know' and is still driven by the 'need to know', requiring justification in order to have access and the possibility to have information on screen quickly, allow the different authorities to try to use these tools to the maximum of their possibilities, to relax their own self-discipline especially when what they want to find is just a click of the mouse away but with forbidden access. The tools of interoperability between the six databases when they are finally implemented, will finally bring a huge amount of data and will unravel the legal purpose limitations set up in the previous pieces of legislation in the name of avoiding silos in computation logic. The form of mentality and knowledge of security is therefore changed by this inclusion of data analysts' approach. This has been presented by the actors themselves as a move from integrated borders management (IBM) to integrated data management (IDM).

VIII. IBM AND IDM: WHY ACTORS ARE RESISTING PRIVACY AND LEGAL OBLIGATIONS

If we want to understand the current configuration of IDM at the world, regional and national levels, and its multiple deviations, we have to first see what has been the effect of this way of thinking concerning borders and to manage it, while continuing to operate simultaneously with the territorial and sovereign imperatives. As we shall see, the struggle between the logic of security and border controls, and the logic coming from the area of the primacy of freedom and ownership of personal data is intense, but this struggle is not completely random or disjointed, it is oriented by a sort of magnetic field, of a convergence towards the question of defiance regarding foreigners or their assimilated categories.

I am using here the terminology of defiance and not of the one of 'trust' for at least two reasons. Using the terminology of trust is often a way of organising the conversation in terms of a practice of giving rights to someone on the condition that he is trustworthy and obeys the rules. It is therefore an almost univocal stance of the 'respect' of the values and practices of the 'welcoming' country. Some narratives have certainly insisted that a reciprocal move on both sides was necessary to create truth, but they have rarely been put into practice. On the contrary, these ideas have been on the decline, some argue about the failure of multiculturalism, the melting pot, convergence and the value of diversity. They have instead insisted on the advantages of ultra-patriotism, unilateral border sovereignty, and loose cooperation between states. The trust vis-à-vis a person travelling has been changed into a 'test' based on distrust. If there still is some trust, it is more between some bureaucracies of control with the same goals and tasks and operating to control the individual. Even there it is sociologically meaningful to see that the explosion of the discourse on trust is correlated with the decline in the practice of trust (which goes without saying) and the emergence of a permanent questioning of the truth of a person's narrative, even of their own identity. Defiance captures what is at stake better. This is the initial move, and the minimisation of face-to-face meetings reinforces doubts about the other's word.

IX. HOW MANY PEOPLE DO YOU PLACE UNDER SURVEILLANCE: ALL OR A FEW? INTERNAL DEBATE

As mentioned in the introduction, the idea of validity by default of documents delivered by third countries has diminished and has been replaced by an *a priori* test of the person who wants to travel against the presumption that they may be a danger for the country of arrival. Suspicion is the rationale for identification and surveillance via the interoperability of the different databases and the differential access to the services in charge of managing different forms of risks and dangers. But, can we avoid becoming 'unreasonable', ending up in a paranoid world? What is reasonable?[28] The number of people affected by the operation, the criteria used for each of them, the existence of a link between a flag in the results of an algorithm and the person as such, or any unknown individual bearing the same characteristics? Is it possible to be guilty, just by association? Clearly there is now a debate within each professional group coming up with different answers, often led more by political opinion than evidence. The external intelligence services continue to be willing to use data under secret agreements, but police and border guards show more constraint, and the notion of law enforcement means that they feel more obliged to listen to judges even when they disagree with their opinion.

In the different enquiries about the social universe of border guards, be they land border guards or airport staff, in North American or in Europe, the ethnographic studies have shown that despite differences, a strong belief in the need for extensive information on everyone to stop a few, is central, and it is difficult to know whether it is the effect of the preventive security discourse and/or the effect of digitisation itself.[29] The institutional memory of authorities and the

[28] The Miriam Webster definition of suspicion gives two connotations of the word explaining the problem of 'reasonable suspicion': The first is: the act or an instance of suspecting something wrong without proof or on slight evidence: mistrust as well as a state of mental uneasiness and uncertainty: doubt. The second is: a barely detectable amount: trace. The strategy of authors using preventive security has been to conflate the two meanings and to try to say that a trace is sufficient, even without proof, to justify a reasonable suspicion. The practices we are analysing show that *de facto*, it is the first meaning, mistrust, doubt, prejudices which are at the core of the data suspicion. An attempt to justify suspicion as legitimate suspicion is F Defferad, *la suspicion légitime*, (LGDJ, 2000). Most of the doctrine of Human Rights has refuted these arguments. We follow the latter.

[29] D Bigo, 'The Socio-Genesis of a Guild of "Digital Technologies" Justifying Transnational Interoperable Databases in the Name of Security and Border Purposes: A Reframing of the Field of Security Professionals?' (2020) *International Journal of Migration and Border Studies* 6, 1–2, 74–92; B Didier, 'Adjusting a Bourdieusian Approach to the Study of Transnational Fields' in

behaviour of their agents (be they Frontex, Europol, eu-LISA, border agencies of EU Member States, or of neighbouring countries) have almost forgotten what freedom of circulation means in terms of travel (especially sea and air travel) and the idea of European citizenship for all is long gone in their imagination. When they describe the implicit norms that they have in mind, they refer to the norms and rules imposed by the International Air Transport Association (IATA), after strong lobbying on the part of the US authorities in 2002. For them, the rules concerning Advance Passenger Information (API), Passenger Name Records (PNRs), no fly lists, data retention, trump the idea of individual freedom. They certainly believe that the Patriot Act in the US may have taken it all a step too far, but they nevertheless consider that they have a 'duty to suspect in order to detect irregularities'. All travellers need to be identified and tested to detect whether one of them is dangerous. This is the 'essence' of their job as one interviewee put it. The mindset diverges if they believe that human forces at the borders are the most efficient tools or if they are part of a newer generation and a new profile of job where their work is mainly performed online, managing passenger lists together with their private counterparts.

In contrast with some North American colleagues, they know that the EU, due to the principle of freedom of circulation inside the Single Market of 1992 and the implementation of the Schengen agreements in 1995, has a different logic. In addition, they know that an area where border controls have been lifted for the benefit of internal circulation within the area, is regarded as something positive by the general public, while all these authorities in charge of travel (border guards or border police or airport authorities and ministries of the interior) consider the Schengen Area, not as an advanced form of cooperation leading the way forward, but as an exception, as something almost irrational. They dare not to complain *viva voce*, but they insist that their work is rendered more difficult compared to the work of their colleagues, and at international conferences, they often insist that intra-Schengen travel with free movement is a form of exception, and not a model. They have been active pushing for national PNRs and a system of pre-border authorisation inside the zone. One of their 'mottos' has been to develop smart data for smart borders where people are not stopped and can travel easily, but on the condition that they agree to provide all the 'necessary' information concerning their reason for travelling. Where they are more open to change it is on the conditions of drawing up a list of suspicious behaviour, and they consider that algorithms, even with machine learning incremental processes, creates too many false positives. They ask for a 'limitation' of the scope of what 'all' means. More targeted lists of suspects, ie shorter but smarter lists, are not a problem for them but are instead an advantage.

C Schmidt-Wellenburg and S Bernhard (eds) *Charting Transnational Fields: Methodology for a Political Sociology of Knowledge* (Routledge, 2020).

Their main opposition to new privacy regulations comes from the fact that they consider the legal obligation to delete data after a check as an 'aberration', forcing them to begin again from scratch. In that way, they try to oppose the opinions of the courts that say that this deletion is necessary to respect freedom and privacy. They are not at all happy with the de-listing of their databases and they often transfer the previous lists to private databases or other countries less 'constrained' by their laws and judges (interview).

In order to justify this lack of implementation of new EU regulations, they add that the more data they have, the better the results of the algorithms, insofar as these results are more 'fine-grained' and avoid sorting the wrong people, the false positives. Therefore, for them, the 'real' freedom of these individuals is the acceptance to provide their data and to be transparent vis-à-vis them regarding their state of origin and destination, in order to be truly 'protected'. They refuse to bend their desire to ever more data and continue to believe that progress in AI will technically solve the value of their predictions, that science and progress are with them and that lawyers and judges are technophobic. This is why this question of machine learning and AI has been marketed as the main justification for the acceleration of the move from IBM to IDM, and they say that they will not stop.

In the last few years, with Covid related exceptions, the idea, not of a complementarity role, but of a move from border management towards IDM beyond questions of internal security and justice, integrating health data and interconnected international data highways linking Europe and North America, has become more accepted.

Even traditional border guards who despised the pre-border checks and the automation of their jobs now accept the argument of machine learning detection as long as they continue to master their agenda and their choices. In sum, for them, the data revolution's need for efficient and speedy work trumps the argument of privacy which is *de facto* obsolete.

Two types of arguments concerning need are combined: the need for digital progress and the need to detect dangers in order to devalue the legal argument regarding the need for their operation. They refuse to speak of surveillance but speak now of protection.

X. THE ROLE OF EUROPEAN COURTS: HOW FAR CAN THEY GO?

All contributors to this issue insist on the underpinning logic which the Courts have progressively taken seriously regarding their role for data protection, privacy, freedom of movement, access to territory, statistical and algorithmic discrimination, even when there have been breaches by public authorities using the national security argument. They have been certainly more prone to limiting and controlling the private providers first, the firms working for the public authorities than the latter and the acceptance of the 'need' to fight against terrorism and serious crime has often limited the extent to which general directives concerning privacy (GDPR) apply. Courts have been compliant with the idea that if actual risks relevant for the internal security of the EU exist, it is not their role to challenge the actions of a government in deciding the shape of the dangers entering into the specific regulations that governments use when national security is at stake. They have considered that politicians and governments have to assume their political responsibility. Nevertheless, in their reasoning, they have focused on the margins of appreciation of a government and even more so the authorities in charge of digital controls and their supervision of the authorities. Recently, with the PNR decision, they have requested more precise detail concerning the modalities of algorithmic decisions and have forbidden the curtailment of human responsibility. They have accepted the idea of threat assessments on terrorism and serious crime but believe that they need to be based on a direct or indirect link between the danger of an individual already listed as dangerous and individuals unknown to the services but they forbid to list those who emerge only due to the correlations of the algorithms. They have asked about the temporality of the assessments and their topicality, considering that annual reports, such as Europol's EU Terrorism Situation and Trend Report (TE-SAT) and the Serious and Organised Crime Threat Assessment (SOCTA) may be too general or outdated for actual risks. They have questioned the granularity of risk assessments, and the fact that searching for one person may not be a sufficiently 'reasonable' suspicion to control a full flight for a long period of time, or a systematic route between a country of origin and a country of destination. The conflation between systematicity and necessity has been raised. The exchange of alerts and their acceptance at face value between European authorities and third countries may also be a problem in terms of a 'link' between a person and a threat, especially when the sources target political opponents, journalists, and NGOs. This is an incremental process, not a philosophy of stark opposition, which may be the best way of disentangling suspicion from preventive logic and the digital practice of control, by understanding how to limit both, in order to resolve the oxymoron of reasonable surveillance, which cannot continue to be a Pandora's box to avoid human rights.

Index